Ritual to Realism

Collected Lectures and Fragments of Theatre History

3rd Revised Edition

by

John Franceschina

BearManor Media

Orlando, Florida

Ritual to Realism: Collected Lectures and Fragments of Theatre History
© 2021 John Franceschina. All Rights Reserved.

No portion of this publication may be reproduced, stored, and/or copied electronically (except for academic use as a source), nor transmitted in any form or by any means without the prior written permission of the publisher and/or author.

Published in the USA by
BearManor Media
1317 Edgewater Dr. #110
Orlando, FL 32804
www.BearManorMedia.com

Softcover Edition
ISBN: 978-1-62933-639-8

Printed in the United States of America

Table of Contents

Introduction by David Boynton   ix

RITUAL
1. Classical Beginnings   1
2. Theatre in Rome   29
3. Theatre in the Middle Ages   51

NEOCLASSICISM
4. Theatre in the Italian Renaissance   89
5. Drama in the English Renaissance   119
6. Spanish Drama to the 18th Century   185
7. The Theatrical Renaissance in France   203

THE ENLIGHTENMENT
8. Theatre in England during the Restoration and 18th Century   227
9. Theatre in Italy during the 18th Century   283
10. French Theatre in the 18th Century   299
11. German Theatre in the 18th Century   331
12. Theatre in Russia through the 18th Century   355

ROMANTICISM
13. The Romantic Movement throughout Europe during the 19th Century   369

REALISM
14. The Development of Realism in the 19th Century   401
15. Realism and Naturalism   435

POST-REALISM
16. Reactions to Theatrical Realism in the 19th and 20th Centuries   473

Index   509

For all my long-suffering students

and

In memory of

John Degen

and

Lowell Manfull

Introduction

There has never been a time, in the history of the theater, when a lack of education in theatrical history has prevented someone from having a long, successful career as a theatre professional. And today, the situation is no different. An actor needs little else besides ambition and luck to begin a career in the business. With or without theater history, a stage manager may never go unemployed. In fact, a college education, much less theater history, is unnecessary to win a Tony Award. Theater has always been a profession where most of the learning happens at the workplace, on or around the stage. You learn from those who are more experienced, you immediately put that knowledge into practice, and someday you eventually pass on what you know to the next generation. A liberal education, which theater history is a part of, has always run tangentially to the working education one inevitably gets in the theater business. So why then should a student of the theater study the subject of theater history?

Perhaps a better question is: how can a soon-to-be practitioner of the theater use theater history? Theater history gives the student important ideas, or tools, by which a theater professional can develop him or herself as an artisan. I use the word artisan rather than artist because tools imply the construction of a crafted object, like a blacksmith using a hammer to make a horseshoe. All theater professionals are, to one degree or another, artisans fashioning a role, on or behind the stage to create a whole object, the performance. How one uses the tools, and the array and utility of the tools themselves, determines whether or not the craftsperson is an artist or just a layman.

Think about how you, the theater student, use theater classes. In an acting class, the professor will employ a variety of exercises to strengthen an actor's commitment to the character. For instance, acting games involving a simple objective between two people, or scene work to discover the character's paths through conflict. Through these exercises, the professor equips the student with ideas, or tools, that an actor includes in his process of developing a character. Similarly, a costume design class provides a student with ideas about color and shape and line in order to create the best textile representation for the play's inhabitants. The function of theater classes is to give the students workable tools, ones that have been tested throughout history, through trial and error, and continue to be refined to best create a theatrical production.

So, what is the tool that theater history provides? To work on a show written by Sophocles, or Molière, or Chekhov or any playwright for that matter, one must have an historical context in order to best serve the play. It is said that the style of the any given production is where the play is set. Where would the play be without history? How would one perform Shakespeare without any knowledge of his original meanings? Can a Brecht play be successfully performed without an understanding of his theory of alienation in the theater? These questions and their answers are not what will turn your performance or direction into a critical and public success, necessarily, they are what will make productions work, period.

Next to the resource for historical context, one finds hundreds of examples of pure innovation in history which can play as large a part today as they once did. Knowing that Herbert Beerbohm Tree infamously used live animals in his productions of Shakespeare is useful for an exam, perhaps, but can knowing how he did it and why help a director or stage manager who's working on a production today? As arbitrary an example as this is, its potential for use could be obvious given the right show. Remember, stealing ideas from those that came before you is one of the greatest traditions the theater has. With the fruitful information that history can provide, one can never run out of ways to craft a role, a scene, a production run into an eminently functional, thrilling piece of theatre.

Besides the veritable goldmine that theater history presents itself as for a theater artisan, the subject is part of a liberal education, and you, the student, are taking the class for that reason, too. But, as I have previously shown, history's function to a student as a timeline is evident. Theater classes provide tools that have been developed throughout history and as you participate in theater classes, you unconsciously share in over 2000 years of dramatic creativity, you actually find historical context within what you are doing. Search through *Ritual to Realism* however you like, line by line, back and forth through the chapters that interest you, or strictly as you need to through the index. No matter how you do it, every page, every paragraph will give you pieces of information and ideas that remain as fresh, subversive and radical today as they were in Ancient Greece or Restoration England. Plays, like all artistic creations, have never really changed, holding steadfast in opposition to conventional ideas and commonplaces, striking against the grain, so to speak, as untouchable, blinding entities that have mesmerized the minds of people for millennia.

It is easy to find such a notion as historical context to be too abstract, not personal enough to do a student any good in the theater right now. It is through the evolving process by which one develops as an artisan throughout life that one inevitably feels tied ever closer to the historical long-view of the theater. This class, and all theater classes for that matter, are small steps along that process. This book is designed to fill your arsenal with tools. Let it be a step that will influence the way you create dramatic art for the rest of your career.

1. Classical Beginnings

Whereas all ancient religions have rituals and liturgies performing the same story year after year, only the Greek worshippers of the god Dionysus developed myths out of which true drama could emerge. There are certain peculiarities of the Dionysian religion that may account for its being the source of ancient Greek theatre. First of all, belief in Dionysus was accepted in Greece later than that of Zeus, Hera, Athena, Demeter, and Apollo, at a time when both the epic and lyric were fairly mature forms of poetry. It is accepted that cults of Dionysus came to Greece from Asia Minor as early as the thirteenth century B.C. but actually flourished in the eighth or ninth centuries, after Homer composed the *Iliad*, since he devotes only some dozen lines to Dionysus in Book Six. The *Iliad* (as everyone now knows because of Brad Pitt and the 2004 film, *Troy*), was a poetic account of the destruction of the city of Troy (or Ilium as it was then called) by the Mycenean Greeks between 1184 and 1174 B.C. Homer extemporized his verse around 850 B.C. and somewhere between then and 800 B.C. when the city-state (*Polis*) became the major political unit of Greece, Dionysus developed a substantial following.

The worship of the god involved supreme exultation (as well as repulsion) as it commemorated the suffering of Dionysus at the hands of the Titans when, like the Egyptian Osiris, his body was torn to pieces by his enemies. Legend ascribes the persecution of the god to Hera, Zeus's wife, who was jealous of the child her husband begat during one of his famous trysts, this time with the mortal woman, Semele. Athena was said to have collected the body parts of her step-brother and, with the help of Apollo, buried Dionysus on Parnassus, retaining his heart which she gave to Zeus who recreated the god (through a variety of means—the legends are numerous). One version of the myth also suggests that a vine sprung from the earth where a drop of the god's blood fell after his murder. This may account for the so-called triple-birth of Dionysus: born of woman (Semele); born of man (Zeus); and born of the earth. Because of the death and resurrection of the god, Dionysian worship became associated with the concept of Zoë—the principal of eternal life—as well as the human responses of pity and fear. Typically, a goat (one of many animals associated with Dionysus) was sacrificed during the religious rituals. The animal represented both the enemies of the god (who had to be punished for their sin) and the god himself. Participants in the service felt pity for the creature—the goat had to bear responsibility for sins he did not commit (our idea of scapegoat)—and fear of what would happen if they did not fulfill the requirements of the ritual.

In addition to blood sacrifice, Dionysian worship involved wine drinking and song and dance: all of the participants were expected to share in an ecstatic (almost out-of-body) experience where each individual loses him-or-herself and becomes one with the god. The elements of loss of personal identity—becoming someone else, the victim being both god and the god's enemy, as well as the emotional responses of pity and fear will all have important effects on the development of Greek tragedy as it has come down to us. The wine, song, and dance ritual became codified in the celebration of a dithyramb—a song performed in chorus by the worshippers (usually while under the influence of the god). As early as 680 B.C. there is an account of one man, Archilochus, leading the dithyramb while inebriated so the connection between wine drinking and worship seems fairly sound.

Fifty years later, in 630 B.C. Arion is credited with giving the singers of the dithyramb a unique costume to consecrate the association between Dionysus and satyrs, the forest creatures who helped him escape his persecutors in one or another of his mythical adventures. The satyr costume involved the wearing of masks with equine ears, tails, and garlands of leaves in the hair (and other strategic places). In some vase paintings, the satyr costume includes an erect phallus (to honor the life-giving, fertility aspect of Dionysian worship) but, at least at the start, that does not seem to have been a necessary requirement for all participants who were generically called *komoi* (plural) or *komast* (singular). These are singers of the drunken song and procession called the *komos* (from which we derive our word comedy). Please note that while most images on the early vases are of men, there are pictures of women as early as 630 B.C. participating in the rituals—though not dressed as satyrs. The women wear long dresses or tunics and are clearly differentiated from the inebriated men. Because of the role playing involved in Dionysian worship, it is difficult to know definitely whether the women portrayed are really women and not simply men in drag. However, Dionysian cults of women did exist throughout Greece and Asia Minor so female participation in the ritual seemed to be fairly common.

The Development of Tragedy
Possibly the first type of drama in Greece emerged from this *komos* by singers wearing satyr costumes—something we call the *satyr play*, a form Pratinas is credited with creating some time before 534 B.C. (though as a genre, it will come to fruition in the 440s B.C. with *The Trackers* by Sophocles and *Cyclops* by Euripides). Early vase paintings showing satyrs entertaining themselves help show a clear progression toward what we might call legitimate drama:

  1) There is evidence that the first choral leader of the satyr chorus was one of the satyrs in disguise. He wore the satyr mask, but in addition to the other requirements of the costume, he added some other element of representation to suggest the impersonation of a god or hero.

  2) A second step occurred when the satyr mask was replaced by the mask of the god or hero.

3) The third step involved the actual separation of the choral leader from the chorus of satyrs—the origin of the first actor. At this point, the character of Silenus stepped into place as the choral leader and acted as a kind of intermediary between the chorus (typically of fifty singers) and the actor, now impersonating a god or hero of mythology.

The third step occurred sometime around 534 B.C., and **Thespis** is credited with this development.

The most important event in the life of Dionysus (at least according to the religious ritual) was the god's visit to Icarius in Icaria, a town north of Athens, during which he caused a grapevine to spring out of the ground. Iconography celebrating the event shows Icarius grasping a vine branch with his left hand (as a sign of ownership), and leading a goat to be slaughtered in honor of the god with his right hand. The Greek word for goat, *tragos*, plus the word for song, *oide*, was conflated into what became our word *tragedy*, and with Thespis who was born in Icaria, a new art form was created. Thespis invented the interplay between actor (*hypokrites*—an answer and response giver) and chorus leader (*exarchos*). The dialogue between them was developed as interpolations between choral songs and was called an episode (*epeisodion*). An aulos (a double-reed instrument) accompanied the chorus when it performed while the kithara or lyre (stringed instruments) accompanied the individual actor. The subject matter of tragedy was taken from heroic saga already familiar to the audience. The chorus maintained its lyrical function although the choral singers were now changed, according to the requirements of the story, into male or female figures of myth. This new form of artistic expression was brought into Athens in 534 B.C. when Thespis appeared at the City Dionysia, a festival devoted to the god that had been established as early as 560 B.C.

Thespis is said to have treated the face of his actors, first with white lead, then subsequently covered it with cinnabar (mercuric sulfide), or rubbed it with wine lees. Finally, he settled on a mask made of unpainted linen. In any case, these devices all had a grotesque effect and were not designed to be representational. Thespis's successor, Choerilus (who flourished c. 523-

520 B.C.), experimented further with masks to attempt a more realistic portrayal of human features. Phrynicus (c. 511-476 B.C.), a pupil of Thespis, introduced women masks and was probably the first to allow the chorus to appear as women. It is believed that his women's masks were uniformly light to contrast with the men's masks which were typically dark. Phrynicus was also the first playwright to bring historical events into tragedy. His *Capture of Miletus* was presented soon after the destruction of Miletus by the Persians in 494 B.C., an event that led to the Persian invasion of Greece in 490 B.C. He also dramatized the defeat of the Persians at Salamis in 480 B.C. in the *Phoenician Women*, performed in 476/475 B.C. In these historical plays which were set in Persia, the usual temporal remoteness of myth is replaced by a remoteness of place. Phrynicus also boasted that he had "invented more figures in dancing than there are waves in a stormy sea." During this period, the chorus was choreographed by the playwright who also composed the music for the production and typically was the leading actor. Later choruses were instructed by a chorus teacher, rod in hand, like a ballet master, who also kept attendance records.

Dramatic Festivals

Before we move on to the three great tragedians of ancient Greece, we should talk about the dramatic festivals that occasioned theatrical performances throughout the Greek year. The first festival in the Athenian calendar was the least organized and possibly the least significant. The Rural Dionysia, traditionally held during the month of Poseidon (December), was a local, "countrified" version of the Great Dionysia held in the spring. Because the month of Poseidon was the wettest month of the year, the date was often changed for this particular festival. Greek comic playwright Aristophanes's first surviving play, *The Acharnians*, provides a sense of what went on during this celebration. A procession, symbolizing Dionysus's entrance into Athens, is peopled by one basket-bearer, two phallus carriers, and a man leading a goat. A cake is ritually ladled with soup, and off-color songs are sung. Pitchers of wine and baskets of raisins are passed around to the crowd and a goat is sacrificed in honor of the god. Because of the lack of organization of the Rural Dionysia, it is believed that it was a kind of theatrical fringe where novice performers could develop their craft in a kind of out-of-town tryout. Acting was often over the top, as a troupe called "The Heavy Groaners" might suggest, and talent was not often in high relief.

The month after Poseidon was Gamelion (January), a time for two festivals on the calendar. Gamelion, a festival relating to marriage, had only tangential reference to theatrical activity, but the Lenaea, named for *lenos* (wine vat) and devoted to the worship of Dionysus, featured some kind of dramatic activity as early as 630 B.C. before tragedy was instituted formally at the City Dionysia and long before comedy was formalized at the Lenaea in 442 B.C. This early activity is thought to have had an element of satire, personal invective, and licentiousness—all of which combine to create the necessity of wearing animal masks to protect the satirists from the objects of their satire. Because the Lenaea was a domestic festival attended only by Athenians, it was the perfect locus for social and political satire. Playwrights writing specifically for the Lenaea could count on their audience's awareness of the topical allusions present in their plays.

By the time comedy was formalized at the festival (c. 442 B.C.), the celebrations occupied four or five days. The processions, sacrifices, and rituals that had been a part of the festivities since the beginning were maintained and it is believed that women were permitted to participate in them as well as attend the dramatic performances. Most of the celebrations before the fifth century took place in a special rectangular area called the Lenaeon. Five comic poets participated in the contest for best comedy and two tragic playwrights competed for the tragic prize (once tragedy was officially recognized at the festival in 432 B.C.). Unlike the City Dionysia, there were no satyr plays or dithyrambic contests at the Lenaea. Prizes were awarded not only to playwrights but also to the leading actors in comedy and tragedy.

After the Lenaea came the City Dionysia, a mere eight weeks later during the month of Elaphebolion (March/April). While the plays scheduled for competition at the festival had been chosen a year ahead of time, it is commonly believed that the eight weeks between festivals were spent rehearsing and polishing the plays. The City Dionysia had been instituted by the demagogue Pisastratus in honor of Dionysus Eleuthereus, when a wooden image of the god had been brought from Eleutherea to Athens in the sixth century B.C. More than any other Greek festival, the City Dionysia had great significance and purpose. It was the occasion when honors were presented for services to the state, and memorials were celebrated for the children of fallen heroes. All business and legal proceedings were suspended, and prisoners were released on bail during the course of the festival. Athenian citizens who sponsored the dramatic activity joined prominent public figures and athletes, and the spectacle was not unlike the entrance of celebrities to the Academy Awards or Tonys. Non-Athenian citizens who attended the event (this was a global festival) were supposed to be overwhelmed by the splendor and power of the Athenian state and, clearly, the City Dionysia was designed to be one huge commercial for the artistic, intellectual, social, political, and military power of Athens.

On the eighth day of Elaphebolion the *proagon* occurred—which, in the latter part of the fifth century was held in the Odeion, a square-roofed addition to the Theatre of Dionysus erected by Pericles between 446-442 B.C. During the *proagon*, competing playwrights gathered with their casts to give a preview of the plays to be performed. It is unknown whether this was intended as a teaser of coming attractions, or a kind of reverse curtain call, showing the actors without costumes or masks to the spectators, but it was, in any case, a popular portion of the festival. On the ninth day were scheduled processions, sacrifices to the god, and dithyrambic contests with ten competing choruses (one from each of the ten tribes of Greece). The tenth of Elaphebolion began the dramatic contests officially, and the next four days were given over to the tragic competition with three competing playwrights each presenting a tragic trilogy plus a satyr play, and a comic competition with five playwrights each presenting a single comedy. On the fourteenth day of the month, the competitors and audience assembled for the awarding of prizes to playwrights and actors, and the chastisement of unseemly activity during the festival.

To be allowed to compete in a festival, a playwright applied to an *archon*, a government official, for a chorus. To compete at the Lenaea, one went to the *archon basileus* (the king archon); for the City Dionysia, the *archon eponymous* (head of the state) was in charge. Choices for the coming season were made based on an audition about a month after each festival (of the previous season) was finished. After 501 B.C. the cost of hiring, clothing, and training actors and chorus was borne by the *choregoi*, citizens who performed this duty as part of their civic responsibility. The office of the *choregia* was abolished between 318-307 B.C. and replaced by the function of the *agonosthesia* (a city office set up to produce plays). Before each festival, a list of potential judges from each of the ten tribes was drawn up and sealed in ten urns. In the theatre, before the crowd, the archon drew a name from each of the urns, creating the panel of judges for the festival. After the competition, each judge then placed his vote into another urn, from which the archon drew five ballots. The winners of the contests were based on the outcome of these five votes.

Tragic Playwrights

The three Greek tragedians we know most about (because their plays survive intact) are Aeschylus, Sophocles, and Euripides. **Aeschylus** (c. 525-456 B.C.) was the son of Euphorion, an Athenian noble, and spent his childhood at Eleusis, home of the Eleusian Mysteries (rites celebrating the abduction and return of Persephone as well as Zagreus, Persephone's child by Zeus, an early variant of Dionysus). In 499 B.C. Aeschylus competed for the first time at the City Dionysia and lost first prize to Thespis. In order to be able to compete again, he offerered to reduce the size of the chorus from fifty to twelve, creating an important innovation in the structure of tragedy. In 490 B.C. he fought as an infantryman against the Persians at the Battle of Marathon. Around the same time, he was charged with impiety for revealing (while inebriated) certain parts of the Eleusian Mysteries and escaped the fury of the crowd by holding on to the altar of Dionysus in the theatre. At his subsequent trial, he was acquitted by the Court of the Areopagus because he fought bravely at Marathon.

Finally, in 484 B.C., at the age of 41, Aeschylus won his initial first prize at the City Dionysia and introduced the second actor into tragic structure. Four years later, he was in the navy, fighting the Persians at the Battle of Salamis, which he would celebrate in his first extant tragedy, *The Persians*, which won first prize in 472 B.C. It is the only existing Greek tragedy based on a historical subject and was so popular that Aeschylus was invited to restage it in Syracuse by the Sicilian demagogue, Hieron. Back in Athens after touring with his play, Aeschylus was beaten at the City Dionysia in 468 B.C. by Sophocles who was competing for the first time. The following year, however, Aeschylus was back in form and won first prize with the tetralogy containing *Seven Against Thebes*, and a few years later, his tragedy *The Suppliants* took first over Sophocles. In 458 he produced his most famous tetralogy, the *Oresteia*, the only tragic trilogy that exists intact today: *Agamemnon*, *Choephoroe*, and *Eumenides* (the ending satyr play, *Proteus*, is lost). Winning first prize, *Oresteia* also exhibits another innovation: the inclusion of a third speaking actor. In 456 B.C. while wandering along the seashore composing a new play, Aeschylus was killed by an eagle looking for a stone on which to crack the shell of a tortoise it held in its beak. Aeschylus's celebrated bald head was evidently mistaken by the eagle for a rock and the bird slammed the turtle down on the poet's head, cracking his skull. He was buried in Sicily with this self-inscribed epitaph: "This memorial stone covers Aeschylus, the Athenian Euphorion's son, who died in wheat-bearing Gela. His famed valor the precinct of Marathon could tell, and the long-haired Mede, who knows it well." Oddly, Aeschylus mentions nothing about his theatrical endeavors.

Shortly after his death, Athens passed a decree that Aeschylus's plays should be exhibited at public expense, and that whoever wanted to produce one of them would be granted a chorus. His tomb became a place of pilgrimage and, at the suggestion of the orator Lycurgus, in the fourth century B.C., his statue was erected in the Theatre of Dionysus at Athens. Aeschylus's family continued to produce tragic poets for more than two centuries: his nephew Philocles, for example, took first prize over Sophocles's *Oedipus Rex*. Aeschylus composed some 90 plays (authorities insist that he wrote only while under the influence of wine) of which only seven still exist. Between 484-458 B.C., he won twelve first prizes. Aeschylus was also a significant contributor to the satyr-play genre (recent discoveries of fragments demonstrate his expertise in that format), and he often explored human behavior in his plays in ways that were often contrary to conventions in tragedy: in his *Myrmidons*, for example, the relationship between Achilles and Patroclus is frankly depicted as homosexual, and in *Kabeiroi*, Jason and the Argonauts appear drunk onstage.

In addition to the innovations mentioned above, Aeschylus is credited with introducing more imposing costumes and footwear for the performers: he added an *onkos*, a high headdress imitating archaic hairdressing to the mask; he gave the actors a *chiton*, a long-sleeved robe that covered them from shoulder to foot; he added to the actor's height with *cothurni*, thick-soled boots (a kind of elevator shoe). He developed some kind of painted scenery and employed more elaborate stage machinery than his predecessors. He preferred tetralogies that are connected plot-wise, and developed a kind of tragic diction that is different from that of colloquial speech. Aeschylus wanted plays to be a sacred and elevated experience that explored the relationship between universal laws and society. In all of his extant plays, the fates of communities are as directly involved in the dramatic action as the fate of any single individual. As a result, with few exceptions, 45% of all the lines in his plays go to the chorus which subsequently takes a very active part in the action of the play. Typical of the playwright of the period, Aeschylus functioned as his own composer and choreographer, and he invariably played the leading role in each of his plays.

Sophocles (496-406 B.C.) was the son of a munitions' maker named Sophillus. According to the Roman historian, Pliny, Sophocles was born into the upper class. As a school boy, he was celebrated for his beauty and won many prizes in athletics and literature. He was educated in musical arts by Lamprus (praised by Plutarch as the most sober of educators), and when he was 15 or 16, he was chosen to lead the boys' chorus that celebrated with music and song the Greek victory over the Persians at Salamis. In 468 B.C. at the age of 28, Sophocles competed for the first time and won first prize over Aeschylus with *Triptolemus*. By the time he died in 406 B.C. and some 120 plays later, he never took third place in any contest. He was always first or second (96 plays (grouped into 24 tetralogies) earned 1st prize, 24 (grouped into 6 tetralogies) won 2nd prize. At some point before 443 B.C. he began to use a third actor in his plays and enlarged the chorus to 15 participants. In 443 B.C., he was elected president of the Imperial Treasury and given charge of collecting tribute from Greece's allies (tax collector). In 442/441 B.C., he wrote *Antigone*, considered by many to be the ideal model of Greek tragic form, and in 440 B.C. he was elected a general and served with Pericles in the Samian War. In 430/429 B.C. he composed *Oedipus Rex* (second prize), and in 428 B.C. he served as a general in the Anaean War. In 415 B.C. he composed his version of the Electra myth, and in 412 B.C., he was chosen one of the ten elders to guide Athenian policy. In 409 B.C., he produced *Philoctetes* and won yet another first prize.

Although he was an adversary of Euripides in the tragic contests, he had much respect for his abilities as a playwright, and when Euripides died in 406 B.C., Sophocles mourned him by marching his chorus dressed in mourning during the proagon of the City Dionysia. Finally, in 401 B.C. five years after Sophocles died, his last play, *Oedipus at Colonus*—with 1,779 lines, the longest extant Greek tragedy—was produced posthumously and won first prize! Before his death, Sophocles was brought to court by his son, Iophon, who alleged that his father was senile and incompetent to govern his finances (a jealous and selfish reaction on the son's part because Sophocles had adopted his bastard son, Ariston). To defend himself against the charge of senility, from memory, Sophocles recited an entire chorus from *Oedipus at Colonus* at his trial and won the case. When he died in 406 B.C., Sophocles was made a demigod by the people of Athens and worshipped under the name of Dexion. Excavations under the west face of the Acropolis have uncovered a shrine to Dexion and his brother-god Asclepius, of whose rites Sophocles was a priest during his lifetime.

Like Aeschylus, Sophocles originally acted in his own plays, being particularly effective in women's roles such as the title role in *Nausikaa*, a play that seems to abound with realistic detail but unfortunately does not survive. Early in his career, however, he decided to give up acting and focus on playwriting and composing the music for his plays. Because of his popularity, Sophocles initiated a trend for playwrights to separate themselves from acting and hastened the movement toward the awarding of an actor's prize (in addition to the playwright's prize) at the competitions. In addition, he is credited with a further development of scene painting: he is considered the first to put a definite background behind his actors (precisely how representational this background is no one knows for sure). Sophocles also abandoned the practice of connected tetralogies, preferring to present four individual plays with little or no thematic interrelationship. In his hands, each play had to deal with an entire myth, and as a result, Sophocles was less interested in global issues than Aeschyus. Instead, he chose to narrow the dramatic focus to a single critical moment in the life of an individual in an attempt to communicate the idea that it is only time, pain, and death that bring humankind into contact with the truth of existence.

Euripides (485/484-406 B.C.) was the son of Mnesarchus, a merchant, and Cleito, an upper class "debutante." The ancient story (now believed apocryphal) was that Euripides's mother was a greengrocer who sold rotten lettuce. But despite the gibes of the comic playwrights of the period, it appears that he was neither poor nor of humble origin. As a boy, he poured wine for dancers and carried the torch in religious festivals—both things impossible for a boy of inferior social position. He was called upon for his public duty to equip a warship and to act as a consul for the province of Magnesia, so Euripides must have had some independent means of support. In addition, he possessed a large library which was rare in Greece, especially for a private citizen.

In accordance with a prophecy that suggested that the boy would "win victories," Euripides's father had him trained as a professional boxer. The playwright had little stomach for fighting actually—he was far more inclined to the arts and, initially, painting seemed to be his chosen career (a number of highly original and well-crafted paintings were attributed to him and displayed at Megara after his death). A student of the new science and philosophy that had developed late in the fifth century in an Athens weakened by almost a century of wars, Euripides was a good friend of the philosopher Protagoras ("Man is the measure of all things"), and a pupil of Anaxagoras who had a direct influence on the poet's way of thinking. It was Anaxagoras, for example, who audaciously asserted that the sun was not a god but a burning stone, and who sought to explain natural phenomenon in terms of physics rather than myth or religion. The philosopher Socrates was also a particular fan of Euripides and it was said that he never went to the theatre unless a play of Euripides was in the competition.

The young poet began to write formally at the age of eighteen but he was thirty by the time he was first permitted to compete in a competition (455 B.C.). He did not win first prize until 442 B.C. with a play called *Rhesus*. In all he wrote about 90 plays and only won first prize five times, one of which was awarded after he had died. He was consistently the butt of satires, and often he was defeated by substantially inferior playwrights, but long before he died, he had managed to acquire a significant reputation throughout the Greek world. In his *Life of Nicias*, Plutarch reported that Athenian prisoners in Syracuse could escape the death sentence, and even have their convictions overturned, if they could recite passages from the works of Euripides. In spite of what he thought of the playwright's disregard for dramatic structure, Aristotle called Euripides, "the most tragic of poets," and he was more quoted by Plato and Aristotle and translated into more languages than Aeschylus and Sophocles combined.

Unlike the older playwrights, Euripides appeared to have taken no part in politics or war, except for the consulship in Magnesia. The ancients thought of him as a gloomy recluse who never laughed. Stories suggested that he wore a long, shaggy beard, lived alone—he married twice, both unhappily—and hated society at large. He evidently lived at Salamis in a cave with two openings and a beautiful view of the sea, where he spent all of his time communing with nature and composing plays. Near the end of his life, Euripides was invited to the court of King Archelaus in Macedonia where he received many honors and distinctions. One night in 406 B.C., however, a little drunk after dinner, Euripides was said to have made the mistake of seducing the king's favorite. On his way home after the tryst, Euripides was torn to pieces by the Mollosian Dogs, huge and fierce animals that served as watchdogs of the palace. Whether by accident or revenge, the dogs had not been secured in their kennel that night and the poet was their easy victim. History reports that the king cut off his hair at the news of the playwright's death as a public gesture of grief. Emissaries from Athens were sent to retrieve the body but King Archelaus refused to give it up. As a result, a monument to the memory of Euripides was erected on the road between Athens and Peiraeus. Later the poet's lyre, stylus, and tablets were bought by Dionysius of Syracuse who enshrined them in the Temple of the Muses.

Euripides's innovations were far more extensive than those of either Aeschylus or Sophocles. He created a kind of tragic realism, portraying men as they are rather than what they ought to be. For example, his play *Telephus* (438) depicts a hero in rags, and the chorus in *Andromeda* wears Negroid masks. Unlike his predecessors, he used lower-class environments in tragedy and mixed the comic with the tragic to produce a kind of romantic melodrama. He was fond of anachronisms and portrayed the gods in his plays with great ambivalence (they must be worshipped but do not appear to deserve it). Frequently gods were used to provide exposition in his tragedies and as often were called upon to unravel the complications of the plot in a device called "deus ex machina." He sought to lessen the function of the chorus in most of his plays, focusing primarily on the scenes (episodes) between the characters. Most of Euripides's principal characters are women, and fourteen of his nineteen surviving plays have choruses of women. In addition, he used children as significant central motifs in ten of his plays. Because of his keen interest in abnormal psychology, he excelled in his portrayals of passion and madness. Clearly, he could understand and depict weakness that was not wickedness. Of his plays, the most famous are probably *Hippolytus* depicting mother-son incest, *Medea*, and *Bacchae*, both depicting a child-murderess.

Theatre Architecture

The classical theatre building has four main periods: 560-500 B.C., during which time Pisistratus and his sons built a rectilinear orchestra in the Agora (Market Place); 499-432 B.C., the time of Aeschylus and early Sophocles, when a circular orchestra, wooden seats, and temporary decorations were erected in the sacred precinct of Dionysus, and when Pericles built the Odeion and a sustaining wall around the auditorium; 421-415 B.C., the time of the Peace of Nicias during the Peloponnesian War, when a stone *skenotheke* and provisions for a wooden *paraskenion* theatre were erected; and, 338-326 B.C., when Lycurgus built a stone *theatron* and stone *paraskenion* in Athens and Polycleitus built the same in Epidaurus.

It is generally accepted that the first performance space in Greek theatre was constructed as wooden stadium-like seating in the Agora. Because wood has the tendency to rot when left out in the rain for long periods of time, and because of the weight of great numbers of spectators on wooden bleachers, the seats collapsed around 500 B.C. and the performance area was moved to the hillside adjacent to the Temple of Dionysus. There the natural curvature of the hill assisted in the creation of the *theatron* (viewing place). A circular *orchestra* (dancing place) about 66 feet in diameter, with a *thymele* (an altar to Dionysus) close to the center, was the primary playing area for the chorus, while a *logeion* (acting platform) of varying heights was the typical playing area for the actors. At least by 458 B.C. a *skene* (scene building) was in use as a background for the action of the play as well as a functional dressing area for the actors. It is commonly believed that after 458 B.C., all plays used the *skene* as a scene background and that scene changes could be effected by the use of *pinakes* (painted panels similar to contemporary flats that could be attached to the *skene* when needed), *katablemata* (painted cloths or screens), and *periaktoi* (triangular units with a different scene painted on each of three sides).

In the fifth century B.C. there were several important theatrical effects employed in the Greek theatre:

1) The *eccyclema*, a device for revealing offstage tableaux, was a platform that could be rolled out from the central door of a *skene*. Some scholars

suggest that it was a revolving platform, while others argue that it was on an upper level of the *skene*.

2) The *mechane*, a crane, was used to show characters in flight or suspended above the ground. Often characters are said to be in chariots or on the backs of birds, though most frequently, the actor is simply in a harness.

3) The *charonian steps* was a tunnel underneath the orchestra that extended from the *skene* to just behind the altar. It was used for ghostly apparitions and resurrection scenes.

4) The *theologeion* was a high platform made of wood where gods could be discovered.

5) The *distegia* was an upper story in the *skene* to represent the upper floors of a building.

6) There were thunder machines, prop rocks and cliffs to create a sense of realism.

7) Certain *loci* (locations) were specified to accent a sense of realism for the audience as well: audience right (stage left) was a western entrance, leading to city or harbor; audience left (stage right) was the eastern entrance, coming from the country.

Later, during the Hellenistic Period (323-146 B.C.) inaugurated by the reign of Alexander the Great, theatre architecture underwent considerable changes, the most important of which was the development of a raised stage, varying between eight to thirteen feet off the ground and often as long as 140 feet, though seldom more than fourteen feet deep. This acting platform was open at both ends, thereby eliminating the side wings of the earlier theatres. A *proskenion* (the façade of the lower story of the skene building) supported the front edge of the acting platform while the *episkenion* (the façade of the second floor) was fitted with one to three doors. Typically, the upper and lower facades were of equal heights. In the early Hellenistic theatres, the *proskenion* was composed of pillars spaced several feet apart and notched to enable the use of *pinakes*. In later theatres, the pillars are not notched, suggesting that the lower story became a less important playing area as time went on and the action switched to the raised stage. The façade of the upper story also underwent changes in time: through the second century B.C. the *episkenion* was converted into a series of large openings (usually one to seven of them) called *thyromata*. These openings were ten to twelve feet wide and usually as high as the façade itself. The *thyromata* were separated from one another by narrow upright supports and were used to supply greater illusion in scenery behind the acting area.

Theatre Criticism

Both **Plato** (428-348/347 B.C.) and **Aristotle** (384-322 B.C.) had a lot to say about the theatre in Greece. Plato was the only one of the classical philosophers who was alive to see plays by Sophocles and Euripides in their original productions and he found the theatre to be dangerously subversive to society. In his *Republic* (380 B.C.) he argued that plays encourage the spectator to indulge in feelings which ought to be kept in check in public life: "empathizing with the distress of characters on the stage interferes with our own self-restraint." He warned that laughing at folly in a comedy, a spectator may run the risk of becoming a real fool at home, and experiencing the passions of sex and anger in the theatre makes it difficult for people to control them in real life.

Aristotle felt differently and believed that the theatre offered the audience a way to learn that was both pleasurable and natural (since he believed that *mimesis* was characteristic of animals). In his famous and often quoted *Poetics* (335-323 B.C.) he provided the first definitions and analyses of the new art form called tragedy:

The three differences which distinguish artistic imitation are—the medium, the objects, and the manner.

Since the objects of imitation are men in action ... it follows that we must represent men either as better than in real life, or as worse, or as they are.

Tragedy . . .is an imitation of an action that is serious, complete, and of a certain magnitude; in language embellished with each kind of artistic ornament . . . in the form of action, not of narrative; through pity and fear effecting the proper purgation of these emotions.

Every tragedy... must have six parts... namely. Plot, Character, Thought, Diction, Song, Spectacle... But most important of all is the structure of the incidents. For Tragedy is an imitation, not of men, but of an action, and life consists in action, and its end is a mode of action, not a quality... Without action there cannot be a tragedy... besides which, the most powerful elements of emotional interest in Tragedy—*Peripeteia or reversal of the situation*, and *Recognition scenes*—are parts of the plot.

Proper Magnitude is comprised within such limits that the sequence of events, according to the law of probability or necessity, will admit of a change from bad fortune to good, or from good fortune to bad... Of all plots and actions the episodic are the worst. These are plots in which the episodes or acts succeed one another without probable or necessary sequence.

Plots are either Simple or Complex. An action which is one and continuous is simple when the change of fortune takes place without reversal of the situation and without recognition. A complex action is one in which the change is accompanied by such Reversal, or by Recognition, or by both.

Reversal of the Situation is a change by which the action veers round to its opposite... Recognition, as the name indicates, is a change from ignorance to knowledge, producing love or hate between the persons destined by the poet for good or bad fortune.

Pity and fear may be aroused by spectacular means; but they may also result from the inner structure of the piece, which is the better way, and indicates a superior poet.

The perfect plot... must have a single action; the change in the hero's fortune must be not from misery to happiness, but on the contrary from happiness to misery; and the cause of it must lie not in any depravity, but in some great error on his part, the man himself being either as we have described [the intermediate kind of personage, a man not preeminently virtuous and just], or better, not worse than that.

In respect to character there are four things to be aimed at: First, and most important, it must be good... the character will be good if the purpose is good. [Even a woman may be good, and also a slave; though the woman may be said to be an inferior being, and the slave quite worthless.] The second thing to aim at is propriety. There is a type of manly valor; but valor in a woman or unscrupulous cleverness is inappropriate. Thirdly, character must be true to life ... The fourth point is consistency...

In constructing the plot and working it out with the proper diction, the poet should place the scene, as far as possible, before his eyes... [he] should work out his play ... with appropriate gestures; for those who feel emotion are most convincing through natural sympathy with the characters they represent; and one who is agitated storms, one who is angry rages, with the most lifelike reality.

Every tragedy falls into two parts—Complication and Unraveling or Denouement. By the Complication I mean all that extends from the beginning of the action to the part which marks the turning point to good or bad fortune. The Unraveling is that which extends from the beginning of the change to the end.

There are four kinds of Tragedy: the Complex, depending entirely on Reversal and Recognition; the Pathetic, where the motive is passion; the Ethical, where the motives are ethical. The fourth kind is the Simple (without the Reversal and/or Recognition).

The Chorus too should be regarded as one of the actors; it should be an integral part of the whole, and share in the action, in the manner not of Euripides but of Sophocles.

... Under Thought is included every effect which has to be produced by speech, the subdivisions being—proof and refutation; the excitation of the feelings, such as pity, fear, anger, and the like; the suggestion of importance or its opposite.

Greek Old Comedy (487-400 B.C.)

According to Aristotle, Comedy developed from improvisations created by the leaders of phallic ceremonies and the reciters of phallic songs. The *Komos*, or comedy song, was supposed to have been quite licentious as well as abusive to unpopular people in town. The *Komast*, not wanting to be recognized, wore masks of which the animal mask was by far the most popular. Looking at ancient vase paintings of the sixth century B.C., we see choruses of men dressed as animals, dancing and singing to the sound of a flute, played by a musician in normal attire: a long *chiton* and freely draped mantle. The earliest element of comedy involved the *Komasts* stepping forward to the audience and issuing a direct address that included personal invective and satire. This would eventually earn the name, *parabasis*, from the Greek verb "to step across," or "come forward."

Just as neither satyr plays nor tragic plays could evolve from the chorus until a real actor had been added, so were dialogue parts necessary additions to the *Komos* of comedy. The first fragments of dialogue were probably a series of loose farcical scenes in which the hero is brought into contact with a variety of odd characters who challenge him, but who are also easily defeated. These farcical scenes were first developed not in Athens but in Megara, a nearby Doric state. Vase and jar paintings suggest the scenarios for these early farces:

1) Dionysus and others are bringing Hephaestus home drunk. All are wearing short tunics that reveal gigantic phalluses that are thickly padded. Everyone's face is grotesque, with bulging eyes and bristly beards.

2) The capture and punishment of wine thieves by locking them in the stocks in a wine cellar.

3) The capture of fruit thieves wearing short tunics and brandishing huge padded phalluses and bulging eyes.

Epicharmus of Syracuse (530-440 B.C.) is credited with giving the improvised farces some literary merit and because of this, he is considered the father of Greek Old Comedy (his plays, however, cannot be formally called comedies because they do not have a chorus). His most important contribution was the development of the *agon*, a scene of conflict between two parties (typically protagonist and antagonist). His chief themes were travesties of heroic sagas and the ridicule of contemporary life. In his plays, and in Doric farce in general, the most popular characters were Heracles and Odysseus who are depicted as a gourmand and a coward, though the parasite, the *miles gloriosus* (boastful soldier), and the cook were also hearty stock characters.

When all of these Doric elements migrated to Attica, they were united with the *Komos*, under the influence of tragic structure: the first part of Old Comedy is little more than an imitation of the first half of a tragedy. While the first comedies were only a few hundred lines long, they became longer as they became a staple of the City Dionysia in 486 B.C. Doric farce brought with it stock costumes and situations: all comic performers wore *somatia*, flesh-colored tights that were stuffed with huge cushions front and back to represent the naked body. Young women are depicted with a large paunch (a reminder of the Dionysian demons) and old women have masks painted yellow (to suggest withering skin). All women followed the sacred tradition of the padded bodice (large breasts not only were a prayer for fertility, anything oversized in the Greek world was funny). Just as the horsetail was a requirement for the satyr play, the padded, fat body was necessary for comedy. Even though all actors were male, transvestitism was a popular motif in comedy. In some plays there is even double cross-dressing: in Aristophanes's *Women in Assembly*, the woman (male actors in drag) take the clothes from their sleeping husbands and cross-dress as men, forcing their husbands to dress as women when they get up!

Cithara and *aulos* were employed in comedy as well as tragedy. In addition, clappers and *tympana* were used as rhythm instruments. The typical dance of the comedy was the *Kordax*, highly licentious when compared to the solemn *emmeleia* of tragedy and the merely off-color *sikinnis* of the satyr play. The *Kordax* was a kind of jig or tarantella performed by men (as men and as women) that suggested copulation and various kinds of sexual foreplay. To properly understand the comedy of Aristophanes that spans the years 425-388 B.C., it is important to remember that the dialogue scenes originated in highly inartistic Doric farce and the chorus came from the light-hearted improvisatory revelry of the Rural Dionysia. This helps explain what some consider the faults of Old Comedy: its uncouth character, the indecency of much of the humor, and the loose construction of the plots. Before Aristophanes, **Cratinus** (who flourished between 450-422 B.C.) was regarded as the first outstanding comic writer, and **Crates** (flourishing between 449-425 B.C.) was credited with downplaying personal satire in favor of more general topics in comedy.

Aristophanes (c. 448-380 B.C.) was the son of Philippus and Zenodora, members of the wealthy, conservative, upper class. It is believed that he spent much of his youth in the country since his family had property on the Island of Aegina. Like his father, Aristophanes appeared to be conservative and supportive of the "ancestral democracy" of the land-owning class. In 427 B.C. he won his first second prize for a play, *The Banqueters*, a satire on contemporary educational methods. Because the author was too young to compete in the contest, it was presented by Callistratus who staged the play. In 426 B.C. Aristophanes produced *Babylonians*, a satire about the demagogue Cleon, who responded by subjecting the playwright to persecution and accusations that he had falsely claimed the privilege of citizenship. Undaunted, the following year, Aristophanes wrote *Acharnians*, his first extant play, which continues his attack on Cleon (and provides details of Cleon's personal persecution of the author). Produced under the aegis of Callistratus, the play ultimately won first prize.

In 424 B.C. Aristophanes presented *Knights*, in which Cleon competed with a sausage seller for the right to rule Athens. Even though popular confidence in Cleon's political activities was at its highest level, Aristophanes's satire managed to secure the poet first prize in the competition. The following year saw *Clouds*, a vindictive satire of Socrates (who was actually in the audience) and Sophists, charlatan educators whose claims of competence were only slightly more inflated than their tuition fees. Evidently the gods appreciated satires of demagogues but not of academics and the play only came in third place at the contest. Aristophanes subsequently rewrote the piece, chastising the audience for not appreciating it the first time, criticizing his rivals for using cheap tricks to get laughs, and playing upon the audience's sympathies and guilt. In spite of his efforts, *Clouds* never won first prize. However, in 422 B.C. Aristophanes was in the winner's circle again with *Wasps*, a satire of the Athenian judicial system, and the playwright's final attack on Cleon. Evidently the sting of defeat was still felt by the playwright who employed the *parabasis* in *Wasps* to review his professional career and rebuke the audience again for not supporting *Clouds*! 421 B.C. brought *Peace* which took second place in the competition, and was significant if only because it is believed that Peace's two attendants, Harvest and Festival, were performed by women, not men in drag.

In 414 B.C. Aristophanes produced the longest extant Greek Old Comedy, *The Birds* (1765 lines), a second-place winning satire of the Athenian lifestyle in the creation of a city in the sky called Cloud Cuckooland! 411 B.C. saw *Women at the Thesmophoria*, produced at the Lenaea, mocking Euripides and the women of Athens with parodies of Euripides's tragedies, *Helen* and *Andromeda*. The same year saw *Lysistrata* at the City Dionysia, Aristophanes's most famous play about the women of Athens going on a sex strike until their husbands and lovers agree to stop fighting in the war against Sparta. The *Frogs*, another satire against Euripides, appeared in 405 B.C. and won first prize at the Lenaea Festival. The last two extant plays by Aristophanes, *The Women in Assembly* (392 B.C.) and *Plutus, the God of Wealth* (388 B.C.) belong to the genre of Middle Comedy and do not share the characteristics of the other plays listed above.

Using music, dance, personal lampoon, luxuriant wordplay, political satire, and surrealistic fantasy, Aristophanes created comic portraits of contemporary Athenian life. His characteristic structure was as follows:

1) Prologue, in which an intolerable situation is identified and an unusual solution (the "happy idea") is suggested;

2) Agon, in which the solution is debated and finally accepted;

3) Parabasis, in which the chorus of twenty-four members addresses the audience directly. Note that the chorus in comedy is twice the number of Aeschylus's chorus in tragedy. This is because twelve members of the chorus support the "happy idea," and twelve are against it;

4) Episodes, or short dialogue scenes, in which the solution is tested;

5) Exodus and Epilogue, in which a new order is established and the comedy ends in a wedding and/or a dance.

Greek Middle Comedy (400-320 B.C.)

Greek Middle Comedy moved away from the strong political and personal satire that marked Old Comedy by having a less episodic structure and by toning down the obscenity and ribald nature of the earlier form. In addition, the Chorus is practically eliminated from the action of the play. The themes of Middle Comedy are more representatively domestic, and the characters tend to be more home-spun and realistic, much less extreme than their old Comedy counterparts. Typical themes included food, greed, money, thievery, and the ridicule of physical imperfections (rather than social or political activities); characters included courtesans and young prodigals. An important character development in this period was the introduction of the clever servant, a stock character type that would have a great impact on New Comedy (as well as practically all other comic drama written to this day).

While Middle Comedy was in transition, farce (which lampooned heroic characters and depicted trivial scenes from daily life) continued to flourish. Greek audiences laughed at Cadmus, Heracles, Dionysus, in a juxtaposition of solemn tragedy and uncouth comedy. Private festivals also thrived with acrobats (typically women) performing naked on the dinner table. Performances included dances (sword dances, war dances) in which naked women would carry shields and wear helmets, and bearded men dressed as women, carrying umbrellas to the accompaniment of female *aulos* players. Around 350 B.C. professional singers and dancers began to replace the amateurs in theatrical activities and professional trainers took over the education of choruses for the performance of plays. By 341 B.C. old tragedies have begun to be "revived" at the City Dionysia, and the satyr plays declined significantly in popularity. From this point on, only one satyr play would be produced annually at the City Dionysia. During this period, actors began to modify the texts of old tragedies in order to create for themselves more effective and elaborate roles. To put an end to such abuse, the statesman **Lycurgus** deposited state copies of classical tragedies in the Archives. Failure to conform to these texts was punished severely with heavy fines. It is believed that Alexander the Great was so enamored of the actor **Lycon** that, having requested him to rewrite a role to demonstrate his abilities to play various passions, the young conqueror happily paid all the fines. Finally, around 330 B.C. performers (called *technitai* in Greek) began to bond together in a union, the **Artists of Dionysus**, which was formalized in 288 B.C. and given official sanction eleven years later.

Greek New Comedy (320 B.C.)
New Comedy as a form began to appear in the second half of the fourth century B.C. and was subsequently adopted by Roman comic writers. Characteristic of this new form include: a coherent and well-constructed plot written in verse; a background of contemporary life (borrowed from Euripidean tragedy) in which myth is replaced by folk tales; the use of type characters, such as the young wastrel (usually the most important character in the play), the recalcitrant father, the courtesan, the parasite, the clever slave, the braggart warrior, the cook, and the slave dealer; the action of the play typically centers on a love affair and the opposition of the older generation; complications are resolved by a discovery of some kind (typically a long-lost child is recovered), and obstacles to marriage are removed; the chorus is reduced to the performance of entr'acte entertainment; the action of the play moves indoors necessitating an interior scene and realistic detail; bawdiness is long gone; and, the sense of fate present in tragedies and Old Comedy is replaced by luck accompanied by a reasoned acceptance of the ironies of life.

The Greek New Comedy playwright whose plays have survived (in varying degrees, from whole texts to substantial fragments) is **Menander** (c. 342-c. 292 B.C.), who was a pupil of **Theophrastus**, educator and author of a book entitled *Character Types* (from which the playwright borrowed many of his stock characters), and a friend of the military governor of Athens, Demetrius of Phaleron. Menander was also a friend of **Epicurus** who developed the philosophy of Epicureanism preaching ideal freedom from pain and tranquility in suffering, and of **Zeno** who promoted the concept of Stoicism, advocating the primacy of right reason and adherence to duty. Borrowing from Theophrastus's book and his friends' philosophies, Menander produced 130 comedies over a period of about 33 years. In 321 B.C., it is believed that Menander produced his first play, *Anger*, at the Lenaea Festival and won first prize. In 316 B.C. he wins first prize again at the Lenaea with the *Grouch*, an "Archie Bunker" type of misanthrope who refuses to allow his daughter to marry the boy next door, until the lad saves the Grouch from falling down a well (television sitcom plots owe much to Menander). In 315 B.C. he won first prize at the City Dionysia with a play that is lost (we do not even know the title, we know simply that Menander won). In 307 B.C. the political climate of Athens changed and his friend, Demetrius was exiled. Finding himself in political hot water, Menander was saved from exile through the efforts of his influential friends and he continued to write and produce plays until 292 B.C. when he died while swimming at Piraeus.

Little is known of Menander's private life except for contemporary gossip that whispered about his squinting eyes and untraditional work habits. Plutarch, for example, wrote that when asked, a few days before the festival, why his play was not yet complete, the playwright answered: "Yes, it is. I've written the plot, now all I have to do is write the dialogue."

Plots of Menander's plays that cannot be dated with certainty offer a good insight into the nature of Greek New Comedy. In *The Girl with Her Hair Cut Short*, for example, Glycera, the mistress of Poleman, a soldier, is discovered by her lover kissing a young man named Moschion. In retribution, the soldier cuts her hair off. The scandal is resolved when Poleman discovers that the young man and mistress were twins left to die by their indigent father. Coincidentally, the boy ends up being raised by a widow who unknowingly married his real father, and Glycera serendipitously moves next door to them (and critics groan at coincidences in television and film today). In *The Girl from Samos*, Chrysis (the eponymous character) is loved by an old man who cannot marry her because she is not an Athenian citizen. This same man has an adopted son, Moschion (Menander exhibits little originality in his repetition of character names in his plays) who is in love with the girl next door. While the old man is away on a business trip, Chrysis gives birth to the old man's baby, and the girl next door bears a child by Moschion. When

Chrysis's baby dies soon after birth, she offers to care for Moschion's child until the couple can tie the knot officially. When the old man returns home, confusion reigns as his servants report that Moschion is the father of the baby Chrysis is nursing. After some clever explanations, the young lovers run off to the altar.

Perhaps even less politically correct is Menander's comedy, *Arbitrators*. Returning home from a festival, Pamphile is raped by a drunk but succeeds in pulling an identifying ring from his hand. A few months later, pregnant from the incident, she marries her fiancé, Charisius. When he goes away on a business trip, his wife has the baby and leaves it to die on a mountaintop, along with the ring of her seducer. When her husband returns, he learns about the baby and abandons his wife, believing her to be nothing more than a courtesan. Ultimately it is discovered that Charisius was the rapist (he recognizes the ring pulled from his finger); he saves his baby, and returns to his wife. Politically correct or not today, most often Menander makes use of plot devices that have become the stock in trade of comedies around the globe: a child (or, more often, twins) is unaware of his true parents; a brother mistakenly attempts to make love to his sister; a slave turns out to be freeborn; a husband falsely accuses his wife of infidelity. In every case, the tie-up always shows a family reunited and emphasis is placed on the power of money in society. In Menander, happy endings depend on coincidence and money not the power of destiny!

Mime

After 300 B.C., while New Comedy was in development, mime performers began to regularly appear at theatrical festivals. Though certainly not a new genre (mime was related to the farces in Megara in the sixth century B.C. that later developed into Old Comedy), between the years 300-250 B.C., a school of "literary mime" developed in Alexandria and Southern Italy (**Theocritus** is credited with giving mimes a literary form). Several playlets by **Herondas**, a third-century B.C. Alexandrian playwright, still survive and seem to be divided into masculine and feminine subject matter: male mimes were about peasants and tuna fishermen while female mimes dealt with sewing and sorcery. In Southern Italy, these mimes are called *phylakes* and the genre was formalized by **Rhinthon of Tarentum** between 300-250 B.C. Most of Rhinthon's 38 plays are burlesques (or satires) of tragedies and called *Hilarotragoediai*.

Like the actors in the *commedia dell'arte* that would develop from the *phylakes*, the performers in mimes were divided into normal types (young men and women) and ugly, deformed character types who wore padded tights, a short chiton, and a huge, padded phallus. Both men and women performers participated in mime performances and, as far as we know, no masks were worn. Character actors were hired on the basis of their physical deformities and ugliness.

2. Theatre in Rome

Roman dramatic literature traditionally began in the year 240 B.C. when **Livius Andronicus** adapted both a Greek tragedy and a Greek comedy for production at the Ludi Romani, a festival established by **Tarquin the Elder** between 616-579 B.C. Various rudimentary forms of theatre had existed in Rome since 364 B.C. when, in the midst of a deadly plague, Etruscan dancers first appeared at the Ludi Romani and performed to appease the wrath of the gods. Serendipitously, the end of the plague was attributed to the magic of the Etruscan dancers and dancing became a staple of the Ludi Romani from then on. Over time, the Romans added gesticulation and rough dialogue to the dance. The historian Livy associates the dialogue passages with the *Fescennine Verses*, coarse, improvised jokes and personal satire popularized at harvest festivals. Not unlike Greek Old Comedy, the personal invective and bawdiness got so out of hand that these early dialogue dances had to be kept within bounds by law. Typically, the dances alternated with athletic contests that included boxing, wrestling, and chariot races; the dancer was called *ister*, from which the Latin word *histrio* (actor) is derived. Another development, something called *Satura*, a medley of song, dance, and dialogue without any real plot, was relatively short lived and replaced by the copies from Greek plays introduced by Livius Andronicus (more about him below).

Accompanying the plays with actual plots were *exodia* (afterpieces) called the *Fabula Atellana*, a kind of farce comedy that developed in the Campania District as a Roman version of the Greek *phylakes* mimes. They introduced the various stock characters of the mimes (*senex*, the *miles gloriosus*, the glutton, the school-master, the courtesan, et al.) and the traditional stage business of the *phylakes* to Roman audiences, and brought to Rome an important kind of temporary stage—actually, simply a rough wooden platform supported by three or four rectangular posts. As time progressed, the height and depth of the platform would be modified, but typically the stage had a short flight of steps in the center leading from the audience to the platform, and a curtained back wall from which actors could make entrances and exits. Some vase paintings also show stages that have a portico over the acting area, though it is unknown whether this was a standard feature of all temporary stages. Typically, the settings used in these farces were simple and spare: trees, altars, chairs, thrones, a dining table, a money chest, a ladder, a basin—just enough to satisfy the basic requirements of the plot.

It is believed that whatever the plot of an Atellan farce, the actors played the same stock character roles with an identifying mask. Dialogue was improvised from a scenario (decided upon ahead of time) and the actor at a loss for words typically resorted to slapstick (literally and figuratively, since hitting another actor with a stick that made a slapping sound was a popular comic gag). Comedians freely drew upon daily life for their material, poking fun at the customs and frailties of all classes of people. Some critics argue that performers acted in close proximity to their audience without heavy soled shoes and masks but, instead, were costumed with colors that were indigenous to the roles they were playing. All free characters, for example, wore white; slaves wore short tunics colored gray, red wigs, and padded bodies; courtesans always wore yellow garments and blond wigs.

Plays were performed by troupes of professional actors—slaves, headed by a producer-director who may have been their owner (hence the clichéd association between producers, directors, and slave-masters). During the Republic (509-27 B.C.) when Roman ideals emphasized discipline, economy, endurance, military precision, and loyalty to family and state, Roman citizens were forbidden by law from appearing on the stage. As in Greece, women were permitted to appear as acrobats and mimes, and it is believed that during the time of Julius Caesar (100-44 B.C.) they were even allowed to perform on stage in plays. The custom of permitting women to participate in theatrical activities came to Rome via Sicily. Not surprisingly, before women acted in plays, their roles were played by boys.

Livius Andronicus (d. 204 B.C.) was born in the wealthy and theatre-loving Greek city of Tarentum which became a Roman possession in 272 B.C. At an early age, Livius was taken to Rome as a slave and, as an adult (able to speak and write both Greek and Latin), he become the tutor in the house of a wealthy citizen named Livius. Out of gratitude for his service, Livius not only gave the slave his freedom but also his name. In 240 B.C. Livius Andronicus began a series of translations of the tragedies of Sophocles and Euripides and of Greek New Comedy that would occupy him until 207 B.C. The first performance of a real tragedy and comedy in Rome occurred in 240 B.C. at the *Ludi Romani* with Andronicus acting in both plays. In addition to his theatrical endeavors, Livius also translated Homer's *Odyssey* into Latin for use in the Roman schools.

A younger contemporary of Livius Andronicus, **Naevius** was a Roman citizen who wrote original plays based on Greek tragedies and comedies. Between 235 B.C. and 204 B.C., he produced nine tragedies (all based on plays by Euripides) and a series of comedies based on Greek New Comedy. However, in addition to writing comedies based on Greek life, Naevius used Roman motifs, names, and locations, and blended them with the Greek models. As a result, comedies that were copies of Greek plays using Greek names, places, and themes were called *Fabula Palliata*; those using Roman names, places, and themes were called *Fabula Togata*. Naevius found that he could use Roman subjects for tragedy as well as for comedy and, as a result, he is considered the creator of a Roman national drama, or Latin tragedy. This was called *Fabula Praetexta* and had native Roman subjects taken from either older history or legend (i.e., Romulus founding the city of Rome), or contemporary events (i.e., his play *Clastidium*, in which the victory of Claudius Marcellus over the Gauls in 222 B.C. is described). Roman tragedies that were based on Greek myth, or simply adaptations of Sophocles or Euripides were called *Fabula Crepidata*.

Among other tragedians during the Republic was **Quintus Ennius** (239-169 B.C.) who wrote twenty plays (of which we have titles and about 400 lines) borrowed from Euripides. Tending toward rhetorical effect in his tragedies, Ennius also composed two Roman historical dramas, *Sabine Women* and *Ambracia*. His nephew, **Marcus Pacuvius** (220-130 B.C.), also wrote twelve tragedies based on Euripides and a historical play, *Paullus*, in honor of a military victory in 168 B.C. The most important tragic dramatist during the Roman Republic was **Lucius Accius** (170-86 B.C.) who wrote *Fabula Crepidata* based on Aeschylus, Sophocles, and Euripides, of which his adaptation of Euripides's *Medea* was especially noteworthy. Still popular in the Empire, Accius anticipated Seneca in using horrific and melodramatic themes, majestic rhetoric, and flamboyant characters.

Of the comic writers, Naevius stood out as the third best comic playwright of the Republic (after Plautus and Terence who are discussed below). **Caecilius Statius** (c.219-168 B.C.) wrote 42 comedies (of which we know titles and have about 300 lines). His titles suggest that he was a disciple of Greek New Comedy, especially Menander, and the few hundred lines extant from his work suggest a Hellenistic style that lies somewhere between that of Plautus and Terence.

Plautus and Terence
Titus Maccius Plautus (c.251-184 B.C.) was born in Sarsina, Umbria. As a young man, he went to Rome where he found work as an actor in the Atellan farces. Some historians believe that he got the name Maccius from his having performed the role of Maccius, the Clown. The story goes that he made a fortune as an actor, spent it all, and ended up becoming a mill worker. Tired of that position, and ill-equipped to work in any other capacity, Plautus decided to write plays for a living. Of the more than 100 plays attributed to Plautus,

possibly as many as 45 were actually written by him though the Roman scholar, Terentius Varro only lists 21 plays that are irrefutably by Plautus. These are the twenty extant plays and a fragment called *Vidularia*, all of which are of the *Fabula Palliata* genre, based on originals in Greek New Comedy. Only two of the existing plays can be dated with certainty: *Stichus* (200 B.C.), based on Menander's *Adelphoe*, and *Pseudolus* (192 B.C.). The others are *Amphitruo*, *Asinaria* (based on *Onagos* by Demophilus), *Aulularia* (based on a play by Menander), *Bacchides* (based on *Dis Expaton* by Menander), *Captivi* (based on *Clerumenoe* by Diphilus), *Casina*, *Cistellaria* (based on *Synaristosae* by Menander), *Curculio*, *Epidicus*, *Menaechmi*, *Mercator* (based on *Emperos* of Philemon), *Miles Gloriosus* (based on *Alazon* by an unknown author), *Mostellaria*, *Persa*, *Poenulus* (based on a play by Menander), *Rudens*, *Trinummus* (based on *Thesauros* by Philemon), and *Truculentus*.

Plautus uses the following theatrical devices with regularity:

1) A prologue that establishes the given circumstances of the plot;

2) Plots with improbable situations and unexpected and ludicrous developments;

3) Humorous monologues by slaves and parasites;

4) Violation of dramatic illusion by direct address to the audience, and informational asides;

5) A language rich in alliteration, assonance, puns, and plays on words;

6) Jokes (sometimes obscene) and monstrous name formations (in *Persa*, for example, a character is called Vaniloquidorus Virginesvendonides Nugiepiloquides Argentumextenebronides Tediginiloquides Nugides Palponides Quodsemelarripides Numquameripides);

7) Non sequiturs, hyperbole, and social satire;

8) Dialogue alternates between *diverba* (straight dialogue written in six-foot iambic verse) and *cantica* (an elaborate recitative accompanied by flute, lyre, and tympanum and written in a variety of iambic, trochaic, and dactylic meters);

9) *Contaminatio*—the practice of borrowing plots from two or more plays and combining them to form the plot of a single, new play.

Typical of Plautus's plots is *Menaechmi* in which one twin (from Syracuse) travels to Epidamnus in search of his brother and is subsequently mistaken for his brother by his brother's wife and household. *Miles Gloriosus* turns on Pyrgopolynices (the braggart warrior of the title) who carries off a young courtesan, separating her from her young lover. The young man's slave saves the day by digging a tunnel between their houses so that the lovers can meet in secret. *Pseudolus*, about a slave who tries to unite his master with the courtesan he loves so that he can earn his freedom, became the source material for the successful Broadway musical, *A Funny Thing Happened on the Way to the Forum*.

Publius Terentius Afer (c. 195-159 B.C.) was born in Carthage and brought to Rome as a slave. He was educated and manumitted by his master, the senator Terentius Lucanus, who, typically, bestowed his name upon the freed slave. Terence soon won the friendship of Scipio Aemilianus and became a member of the literary and philosophical group known as the Scipionic Circle (an organization that included among its members, the Roman satirist Lucilius, and the Greek historian Polybius). Terence is said to have submitted his first comedy, *Andria*, to the comic playwright **Caecilius Statius**, at whose home it was read with great applause after a dinner party. The story is suspect because Caecilius died two years before Terence had his first play produced. It is possible, however, that the reading was of an early draft of the play. Terence produced six comedies, all produced by the actor-director **Ambivius Turpio**, and all based on Greek New Comedy no longer in existence. Around 160 B.C. the playwright traveled to Greece to research the plays of Menander. During his stay, he is reported to have written a large number of new plays. Unfortunately, on the return trip from Greece, a shipwreck caused his bundle of manuscripts to be lost at sea. Terence is reported to have died of heartbreak soon after.

The accepted order of Terence's plays is:

1) *The Woman of Andros* (taken from Menander's *Andria*), produced at the Ludi Megalenses in 166 B.C. Forced to marry Philumena (Chremes's daughter) who in turn is in love with Charinus, Pamphilus seduces Glycerium

to get out of the wedding. Glycerium turns out to be Chremes's daughter as well, so she ends up marrying Pamphilus.

2) *The Mother-in-Law* (based on *Hekyra* by Apollodorus), produced at the Ludi Megalenses in 165 B.C. This performance was a failure because the audience was distracted by a rope-dancer performing in a nearby sideshow. Here Pamphilus marries Philumena against his will and refuses to consummate the marriage. While he is off on a business trip, his wife gives birth to a child. He discovers that, before the marriage, he had raped and impregnated his wife in a drunken stupor, and that the baby is his own, so all is well.

3) *The Self-Tormentor* (based on Menander's play of the same title), produced at the Ludi Megalenses in 163 B.C. Here Menedemus is tormented by guilt over having alienated his son because of his dislike for his son's girlfriend. He comes to like the girl (who ingratiates herself to him disguised as the maid next door) and reconciles with his son.

4) *The Eunuch* (based on Menander's *Eunuchus*), produced at the Ludi Megalenses in 161 B.C. with great success. Terence's most popular play involves the love of two brothers for two courtesans: Phaedria, the elder brother, is involved with Thais (who also has a braggart soldier on a string), and Chaerea is infatuated with Pamphila. To get access to her, Chaerea masquerades as the eunuch his brother had planned to send as a gift to Thais. Inside the brothel, Chaerea's libido gets the better of him and he rapes Pamphila. She turns out to be a free-born citizen and not really a courtesan, so Chaerea gets to marry her with his father's blessing. Phaedria ends up accepting the triangular relationship with Thais since the soldier has more money than he has.

5) *Phormio* (from *Epidikazomenos*—the *Lawsuit*—by Apollodorus), produced at the Ludi Romani in 161 B.C. In this play, Phormio, a poor adventurer, engineers a love affair between Phaedria and Pamphila (copying the practice of Greek New Comedy playwrights, Terence uses the same character names again and again in his plays).

6) *The Brothers* (based on the *Adelphoe* of Menander), produced at the funeral games for Aemilius Paullus in 160 B.C. At this same event, *The*

Mother-in-Law was presented again without success, being unable to compete with the gladiatorial combat next door. Later in 160 B.C. at the Ludi Romani, *The Mother-in-Law* had its third production and was finally a hit. In Terence's new play, two brothers raise their sons in entirely different ways: one too harshly and the other too permissively. Both sons get in trouble because of their rearing and the parents learn moderation.

Terence's achievements as a comic playwright include:

1) He is the master of conversational, cultured Latin;

2) He uses subtle humor, avoiding the improbably farcical situations that characterize Plautus;

3) He revises theatrical conventions: begins scenes in the middle of a line and uses asides to express inner thought rather than simple information;

4) The slave character is no longer only a trickster, he is also a bungler, and vulnerable;

5) The prologue no longer sets up the given circumstances. Instead, it is used as a mouthpiece for the playwright to defend himself against critics and jealous competitors;

6) He uses double plots in which two young men are involved in closely interwoven and interdependent love affairs;

7) The plays are formally close to perfection: entrances and exits are properly motivated, plots conclude logically, every scene is functional, every speech contributes to the development of the story, and characters are well developed (if not completely three dimensional);

8) He uses a *distegia* (an upper floor) in his sets and calls for props that are significant to the development of the plot;

9) He has great interest in psychological problems, particularly those involving father-son relationships.

Roman Ludi

In the text above we have stumbled across several *ludi* at which the plays of Plautus and Terence have been performed. The Roman *ludi* were festivals, not unlike the City Dionysia in Athens, though the Roman festivals where plays would be produced were dedicated to a variety of gods (not a single deity as in Greece). Below is a chronological list of the various festivals on the Roman calendar.

Ludi Romani (4-19 September) originated as a one-day festival (13 September, though some give November) celebrated sporadically between 616 and 579 B.C. After 366 B.C., the festival was extended to 15 days and became an annual event. Chariot races and military displays were joined by dances in 364 B.C. and traditional dramatic performances (called the *Ludi Scaenici)* were added in 240 B.C.

Ludi Saeculares (Ludi Tarentini) (May-June) founded in 509 B.C., included games (to insure protection against pestilence) and eventually harbored three nights of theatrical performances.

Ludi Florales (28 April-3 May) was instituted between 240 and 238 B.C., with theatrical performances as a major part of the festival. Animal baiting was added in 173 B.C. when the games became an annual event. This festival featured women performing in mimes.

Ludi Flebeii (4-17 November) was created in 214 B.C. to strengthen the morale of the Roman people during the Punic Wars. The first reference to theatrical activity dates from 200 B.C.

LudiApollinares (6-13 July) was established in 212 as a one-day festival to appease an epidemic. It began to include plays in 179 B.C. when it was extended to a week-long celebration. Two days were spent watching chariot races and two days were devoted to producing plays.

Ludi Megalenses (April) was created in 204 B.C. to honor Cybele with games celebrated in the Circus Maximus. Theatre began in 194 B.C.

Ludi Cereales (April) was instituted in 202 BC to honor Ceres with more games in the Circus. Plays arrived after 27 B.C.

By 190 B.C., between seven and seventeen days were devoted to theatrical performances yearly.

In 186 B.C., *Venationes* ("animal hunts," contests between men and beasts) were established at the Circus Maximus.

By 150 B.C., twenty-five days were devoted to theatrical performances annually.

In 105 B.C., Gladiatorial contests become part of the festivals.

Ludi Victoriae Caesaris (20-30 July) was established to celebrate the battle of Pharsalus in 48 B.C. (originally held in September, but transferred to July in 45 B.C.). Plays, chariot races, gladiatorial contests, and animal baiting all had a part in this celebration.

Roman Theatres

For a long time, chariot races, athletic contests, and gladiatorial combat were the main entertainments in Rome. As a result, the first permanent building that was used for spectacle was the Circus Maximus built in 600 B.C. When the Etruscan dancers appeared in 364 B.C., they brought temporary wooden stands that could be erected anywhere in the Circus or Forum. These temporary scaffolds developed into the Roman theatres, built as free-standing buildings rather than along hillsides as was the case with the Greek *theatron*. When the first tragedies and comedies were performed in Rome, they were presented on wooden platforms that were adapted to the needs of individual plays (Plautus's *Amphitruo*, for example, required a second story and windows, and typically Terence's plays called for three openings to represent different houses).

Although the stage was temporary, the audience's wooden seats were often permanent since they were sued for the games that followed the theatrical event. Special seats near the stage were assigned to Roman Senators as early as 195 B.C. Because of the fire hazards caused by wooden temporary buildings, stone *auditoria* began to spring up in Syracuse and Pompeii. While the development of a *scaenae frons* (a highly ornamented permanent background to the action with columns and doors creating the illusion of the exterior of a Roman building) was of great significance to the look and design of the Roman stage, the auditorium itself was significantly altered by the Romans from the Greek model. Seating, like in Greek times, was in a semicircle, but entrance to the seats was by way of *vomitoria* rather than the *parados* in the Greek theatre. A corridor divided the various galleries of seats, and the orchestra, now only a semicircle (as opposed to the Greek's full circle), was reserved for places of honor and not used by the actors or the chorus. Around 133 B.C. the *auleum* (front curtain) was introduced in the Roman theatre: typically, the curtain rested within a hole in the floor and was raised only before the play began.

In 99 B.C. **Claudius Pulcher** is said to have constructed a theatre with realistic painted details on the *scaenae frons*, but until about 80 B.C., all Roman theatres were considered to be simply conversions of the Greek model. In 75 B.C., however, we have the first example of a pure Roman theatre—the Small Theatre at Pompeii. Having a capacity of only about 1500 spectators, it has a roofed auditorium with a semicircular orchestra filled with broad steps to enable the use of moveable seats provided for members of the city council and other political dignitaries. The stage is low and deep, no more than five feet off the ground, and the *scaenae frons* is painted. The roof is supported by the upper part of the *scaenae frons* (at an angle to help project sound into the auditorium) and the side walls of the auditorium. In c. 70 B.C. a *velum* (awning) was erected in a larger open-air theatre to keep the sun out of the eyes of the spectators. *Siparia* (drop curtains) were also hung from the *scaenae frons* and used to mask or reveal scenery.

In 58 B.C. **Marcus Aemilius Scaurus** supposedly built a theatre to accommodate 80,000 spectators and three years later, the first permanent stone theatre in Rome was built by **Pompey** with a straight *scaenae frons* and a covered colonnaded gallery, level with the back wall of the stage, to be used by spectators in case of rain and during intermissions. In 50 B.C. **Gaius Scribonius Curio** built two wooden theatres back to back and connected by a pivot. They could function as two separate theatres or, when joined together, a single arena for athletic events. In 13 B.C. **Balbus** built a second stone theatre in Rome, and two years later, Augustus completed a theatre dedicated to the memory of his nephew and son-in-law Marcellus.

Roman Drama in Decline

The passion of the Romans for plays of every kind increased during the Republic. By the time Augustus was crowned emperor, the Roman calendar (*fasti*) indicated over 60 days on which public spectacles were given in connection with old religious festivals. The festivals invariably began with plays followed by circus performances. As a result of the 60 days of *ludi*, about 40 of them were devoted specifically to theatrical events. During the Empire, however, interest in plays declined and the popularity of athletic spectacles grew steadily. By the year 354 (A.D.), 175 days were set aside for festivals and only 100 of those days were devoted to theatrical activities. Even though the number of play days had doubled, the days devoted to games and athletic events had increased almost four times.

The forms of plays created during the Republic lived on through the Empire, but the emphasis was shifted from more serious to lower classes of plays. During the Empire the popular *Fabula Crepidata* (tragedy) was eclipsed by *Fabula Saltica* (Pantomime), with a chorus, musicians, and a single mute dancer acting out the story narrated by the chorus. The heir of *Fabula Palliata* (comedy) was *Fabula Riciniata* (Mime), with large casts (without masks), elaborate spectacle, and a satiric—often lascivious—point of view in its depiction of daily life. Finally, the popular Atellan farce was replaced by the Latin farce with its coarse and low-class plots and characters. In order to compete with the circus and gladiatorial entertainments, theatre plays had to become steadily more sensational.

Lucius Annaeus Seneca (4 B.C.-65 A.D.)

The only tragedies in Latin from this period that still exist were written by Lucius Annaeus Seneca who was born in Cordova, Spain. A renowned orator, politician, and Nero's speech-writer, Seneca was a stoic who saw in theatre an opportunity to project his philosophical beliefs. For him stoic philosophy was essentially a moral rather than a metaphysical pursuit designed not only to demonstrate a way to live life, but to help insulate humans from the disturbances of the outside world (and the dark forces within themselves), and to enable them to accept (and even welcome) their inevitable death.

The central issues of Seneca's moral philosophy involved the control of the passions and the attainment of inner peace through rational conformity with nature. Not surprisingly, his plays depict characters who fall substantially short of attaining inner peace and brilliantly portray human neuroses, especially the crippling effects of desire, fear, and anger which he considered to be the most destructive of the passions. Tragedy permitted Seneca the opportunity of depicting human beings under extreme emotional pressure. Although Seneca's tragic formula—a struggle between reason and passion—was not entirely foreign to the Greek tragedians, Seneca manages to provide a much more aggressive depiction of the destructive nature of passion. Like the Greek tragedians, Seneca focuses on characters who are divided: more or less virtuous people who have to deal with the temptations of the world or their own uncontrollable emotions. Whereas the tragic flaw in Greek tragedy lies in some error in judgment, the tragic flaw in Seneca is caused by some overwhelming passion.

Ten plays are attributed to Seneca. Because there is no specific connection between any of the plays and a specific festival, scholars continue to debate whether or not these works were written to be performed or simply read. Between 45-55 A.D., while Seneca was in exile at Corsica, he is believed to have written *Medea, Phaedra*—both based on the tragedies of Euripides—*Oedipus*, based on Sophocles's *Oedipus Rex*, *Troades*, based on Euripides's play of the same name, *Agamemnon*, based on the play by Aeschylus, and *Hercules Oetaeus*, the longest ancient classical drama (1996 lines) portraying the apotheosis of Hercules, the patron-hero of the Stoics, on a funeral pyre on Mount Oeta. Between 60 and 62 A.D., Seneca is thought to have composed *Phoenissae*, based on the play by Euripides with a nod to Sophocles's *Oedipus at Colonus*, and *Thyestes*, based on Euripides and Sophocles (as well as *Atreus* by Accius, *Thyestes* by Ennius, and *Thyestes* by Rufus, a closet tragedy). *Hippolytus*, and *Hercules Furens*, both based on plays by Euripides, were also composed by Seneca at some point in his career. Another play, *Octavia*, the only surviving example of *Fabula Praetexta* in which real-life people appear as characters (Nero, his wife Octavia, the ghost of his mother, Agrippina, and even Seneca himself appear in the play), has also been attributed to Seneca.

All of Seneca's tragedies ascribe to the following formal structure:

1) Act one serves as a kind of prologue in which a god (as in *Hercules Furens*), a ghost (*Agamemnon, Thyestes*) or a major human character speak a long monologue evoking the oppressive atmosphere out of which evil is about to burst;

2) In act two, the principal character meditates on a crime or passion. He is typically talked out of it by a subordinate character, but ultimately succumbs to it.

3) Acts three to five develop the catastrophic effects that arise from the performance of the crime or the unleashing of the passion.

4) Choral odes separate each of the acts with the following themes: a plea to the gods for assistance, a recollection of past history, and an imagined contemplation of the present.

In act one of *Thyestes*, for example, the ghost of Tantalus appears and a fury orders him to infect the palace of Argos with incorrigible evil. In act two, Atreus (Thyestes's brother) discusses his revenge with an unnamed servant. The servant is not only unable to change his master's mind, he finds himself helping his master commit the crime (thus providing the play with one of its chief themes: evil victorious over feeble resistance). In act three we find Thyestes attracted to a life of wealth and power committing an error in judgment by accepting his brother's offer to share in the rule of the kingdom. Act four is devoted to a messenger's account of the murder and dismemberment of Thyestes's sons by Atreus. As a travesty of a ritual feast, Thyestes ultimately eats his children as they are served up to him. In act five, Atreus reveals the reasons for the murders and finds that his only sorrow lies in the fact that neither the father nor the sons were conscious of what was happening when dinner was served and eaten. Grief stricken, Thyestes curses the House of Atreus, and the tragedy ends without a final chorus.

Seneca's contributions to the development of tragedy include:

1) The division of plays into five acts;

2) The use of forensically constructed speeches;

3) The presence of *sententiae* (quotable moral speeches);

4) Highly violent actions described, and sometimes depicted on stage;

5) A preoccupation with magic and death;

6) Characters dominated by a single motivation—usually a central moral evil that demonstrates the crippling effects of fear, desire, or anger;

7) The presence of theatrical devices such as the aside, the soliloquy, and the confidant;

8) The use of iambic hexameter;

9) Typically, no more than three speaking actors on stage at a time.

Drama during the Roman Empire (27-476 B.C.)

Seneca may also have inspired his pupil Nero to give tragic recitations on the stage. Nero appeared as a god, hero, or heroine; he sang the parts of the blinded Oedipus, the insane Heracles, and Orestes. He even took the role of Canace in the mime drama, *Macaris and Canace* and mimicked the cries of a woman in labor, (it should be noted here that during the empire, the official sanctions against citizens acting in plays was relaxed and there are records of many free-men becoming actors). The last appearance of Nero onstage was that of Oedipus in exile, a role presented in Greek. When performing, the emperor wore the traditional tragic costume which had been grotesquely exaggerated. Lucian reports: "What a repulsive and frightful spectacle is a man tricked out to disproportionate stature, mounted upon high clogs, wearing a mask that reaches up above his head, with a mouth that is set in a wide yawn, as if he meant to swallow the spectators. I forbear to speak of the pads for the breast and for the paunches wherewith he puts on an artificial and counterfeit corpulence so that the disproportion in height may not betray itself the more in a slender figure." Philostratus goes on to say: "When the actor was silent walking on high stilts which made him over life-size, and with a wide-open mouth, they were already fearful. But when he lifted his voice, the spectators fled from the theatre as if persecuted by a demon."

During the time of Nero, pantomime became increasingly popular, and good writers such as **Lucanus** (39-65), Seneca's nephew, and **Statius** (45-96) began to write these *Fabulae Salticae*. The music for these works was undignified, frivolous and sensual, with loud yet enervating tunes. Double pipes, lyre, trumpets, and foot clappers (rattles beaten by the feet for rhythm) were used. Sometimes "abnormal" musicians such as dwarfs were used. The pantomime dancers themselves were well-built men and women with supple bodies who wore masks with closed mouths. Most of the pantomimes were Greek and highly prized by the Emperors. Ballet is related to Pantomime, when a solo dance, and to Mime when a group dance. In Greece, it was called *Pyrrhiche* when danced by armed men who presented sham battles. In Rome, this dance was given a dramatic content. Male and female dancers fought with each other, or represented satyrs, or maenads. They were dressed in tunics embroidered with gold, wore purple mantles, and had golden wreaths. Luxurious scenery represented Mount Ida with animals, plants, and springs on it. The settings and costumes were sophisticated and rich. Venus appeared naked save for a transparent silken skirt around her hips. Water ballets and aquatic plays were given in small water basins which were built into the theatres. A mosaic designed about 297 shows ten female athletes and ballerinas in skimpy bathing suits looking rather like contemporary bikinis.

In the second century and beyond, plays were brought to the Roman Empire by the guilds that had developed from the Roman troupes of actors and the Hellenistic *technitae*. These guilds had their headquarters in Rome and had become a world organization, a professional body no longer under the patronage of Dionysus. They traveled not only to public festivals for all gods, but also to private festival celebrations including important funeral games. They were obliged to give plays as varied as possible in order to satisfy the restless and novelty-loving public of the Empire.

Mime enjoyed the greatest popularity because of its lack of masks, its depiction of ordinary life, and its frequent use of current themes and political satire. In later centuries, it reigned over the stage almost exclusively. The mockery of the gods taken over from comedy and farce was exaggerated to absurdity. Luna appeared as a man, Diana was whipped, and Jupiter made his last will and testament. Love and adultery were also popular themes for civic mimes and low-class comedy. In other mimes, the play catered to popular morals—the rich were persecuted, the poor became rich, and lovers were discovered and driven off. Animals were even permitted to take part: during the rule of Vespasian, a dog—anticipating Rin Tin Tin and Lassie—had the chief role in a mime at the theatre of Marcellus in Rome. In Corinth, after the ballet, the character of Lucius changed into a donkey (anticipated Bottom in *A Midsummer Night's Dream*) and was supposed to take part in a sordid mime. Instead, the donkey ran away.

Attempts were also made to compete with the cruel games of the amphitheatre. On the day when Caligula was murdered (41 A.D.), the robber Laureolus took part in a mime and was actually nailed to a cross and died before the eyes of the spectators. The boy emperor, Heliogabalus (ruled 218-222) introduced live sex acts into plays and advertised rewards for actors who had substantial "talents." He also was reported to have appeared naked on stage in the role of Venus in *The Judgment of Paris*. Heliogabalus had a desperate need to be female and attempted to castrate himself a number of times. Evidently appearing in women's roles in the theatre was an acceptable alternative to castration. Women who were allowed to appear in mimes and pantomimes often were naked or semi-naked in performance; as a result, female performers managed to develop very bad reputations. The Christian writers began to preach that the theatre was degenerate and rightly so. Not only had the mimes become totally lascivious, they even started to ridicule the rites of Christian worship.

The mime performers did not wear masks; actors with grotesque faces were employed instead. Typical of a low-class mime actor were a stupid, yet cunning expression, thick lips, a large nose and ears, beady eyes, and a distorted, long, bony, bald head. Some mimes wore only a cap and a loincloth while others were dressed in a kind of cloak with a hood. The most characteristic costume of the mime was the *centunuculus*, an outfit patched together with many swatches of different colored cloth. Mimes also associated themselves with jugglers, rope-dancers, acrobats, and animal acts, giving farce-like entertainments outside the theatre and delving deeply into the seamier side of life. This motley crew lived on through the Middle Ages!

Higher class entertainments still persisted through the Empire (actual tragedy and comedy lasted until the third century) but most plays degenerated into sensational amusements for the common crowd. During the reign of Nero (54-68 A.D.) a *fabula togata* by **Afranius** called *House on Fire* was performed. In it, a house was realistically burned down and the actors were directed to plunder the rich furnishings from the burning building. The actors who managed to survive the smoke and the flames were permitted to keep whatever they stole from the house. Coarse Latin versions of the Atellan Farces were particularly popular with the audiences, and since the actors wore masks, they could dare to criticize public affairs as well as the emperor himself. Such audacity, however, often became dangerous: one actor who pointedly criticized Caligula was burned to the death in the amphitheatre; another actor who ridiculed the poisoning of the Emperor Claudius was banished. Actors of the Latin farces were people with abnormally ugly bodies, extremely lean and small, or excessively tall or fat for comic effect. An actor named Manducus, for example, was famous for his enormous chattering teeth. A woman called Lamia appeared as a spook to frighten children, since if they were naughty, they would be eaten by her and subsequently pulled live from her body (much to the fiendish delight of their parents).

Animal bouts in the amphitheatres were also very popular theatrical spectacles. Gladiators no longer fought one another, they struggled against wild beasts, such as lions, panthers, bears, and elephants. When amphitheatres were unavailable for such high-brow entertainment, the wild games fought their way into the theatre buildings. The large theatre at Pompeii, for example, built barracks for the gladiators behind the theatre in 63 A.D. Not surprisingly, most Roman theatres had access for wild animals into the orchestra area which was also often filled with water for performances of water ballets or for fighting beasts like crocodiles and hippopotami. Historian believe that special buildings were constructed for the occasional mock naval battle since the arena space in a regular theatre would have been too small to support two fully rigged naval vessels.

As years passed, the games in Roman theatres and amphitheatres became continually wilder and bloodier. During the reign of Trajan (98-117), 10,000 pairs of gladiators, as well as 11,000 animals were presented in the Flavian amphitheatre at Rome within a period of four months. During one of these spectacles, a musician dressed as Orpheus was actually torn to pieces by wild beasts. Gradually, slaves, prisoners of war, and criminals, who had to fight for their lives or be defenselessly slaughtered before a cheering audience, were replaced by Christians whose martyrdoms often shared the bill with pantomimes, farces, and mimes.

Although all spectacles ended in Rome in 568 after the coming of the Lombards, theatre continued in the Byzantine Empire as late as 692 (remember that Emperor Constantine moved the capital of the Roman Empire to Constantinople in 330, thereby creating an Eastern and Western Empire).

Roman Theatre Criticism

Horace (65-8 B.C.) was a popular poet and satirist writing during the reign of Augustus (27 B.C.-14 A.D.), the first Roman Emperor. His commentary on theatre, *Ars Poetica; or, Epistle to the Pisos*, was composed about 12 B.C. and designed to be a source of advice to a budding playwright. He suggests that a poet should limit himself to "subjects within his power," and be careful in his choice of words (since words can change their meanings or become obsolete). He also notes that a play must appeal to the emotions of the audience and the language used must be appropriate to whoever is speaking. The plot of the play should be developed in action and narrative, though the latter is best used to describe horrifying and improbable incidents that are better kept off stage. Every play should be in five acts with never more than three speaking characters onstage at any one time; the chorus should be intrinsically involved in the action of the play and function as the voice of morality in its sung odes, which should never be irrelevant to the story. In the denouement, the *deus ex machina* should be employed in the rare instance when the plot can be unraveled only by divine intervention. Horace argues that the purpose of drama (and poetry in general) is to teach and entertain and that a popular book or play is produced by a careful combination of the *utile* (usefulness) with the *dulce* (entertainment).

Two centuries after Horace, **Lucian of Samosata** wrote a famous treatise *On Dance*, shedding light on the various forms of dance and movement prevalent in the theatre of the ancient world. He ridicules the excesses of actors with their platform shoes, grotesque masks and body padding, screeching away at the top of their lungs to be heard in the audience. In comparison, the dancer is lean and artistic, with a body and limbs supple enough to communicate a variety of different characterizations: "the dancer sets out manners and feelings, the lover, the angry man, madman, or grief-stricken, but all in suitable form. The most remarkable thing is that he can, on the same day, display raving Athmas, terror-stricken Ino, and a little later Thyestes, Aegisthus, or Aerope. All in one man." Emphasizing the appeal of dance to both the eye and the ear, Lucian concludes that "Dance works its magic so that a lover can go into the theatre and come to his senses by watching the dreadful consequences of love. Someone overwhelmed with grief can emerge more cheerful, as if he had taken some potion to forget."

A contemporary of Lucian, the Egyptian **Athenaeus of Naucratis** wrote a fifteen-volume gossip column called *Deipnosophists* (*After-Dinner Philosophers*) containing a wealth of inside information about what was going on behind the scenes in the theatre of Greece and Rome. For example, he notes that "Thespis, Pratinas, Cratinas, and Phrynichus used to be called *dancers* from not only relying on choral dance in their own performance but teaching it for other people's productions. Aeschylus wrote his tragedies when he was drunk, according to Chamaeleon. Sophocles reproved him by saying that even if what he achieved was all right, he did it unconsciously."

Vitruvius dates from the first century B.C. and was a contemporary of Horace. Vitruvius wrote ten books of architectural notes called *On Architecture* and they will be the books that are often referred to in the Italian Renaissance when questions are asked about how classical theatres were built and what made them work. Vitruvius also gives us the information about the size of the stage in Rome, the size of the stage in what we believe were Greek theatres, and so forth. Much of our data about theatre technology in the ancient world stems from Vitruvius and a man named **Pollux**, a second century scholar who wrote a book called *Onomasticon*, an encyclopedia of things theatrical. In it, he tells us that when an audience didn't like a play in Greece or Rome, they would beat their heels on the benches in front of them, very much like the practice at a football stadium. Also, audiences would boo or hiss to drive an actor off the stage. Pollux also tells us that the audience right entrance, stage left entrance would always be coming from the outside (i.e., the harbor, or the city). It's interesting because he then says anyone else coming on foot comes in from the other entrance. In other words, if you're a foreigner you probably enter from stage left because you're coming from the city or harbor. If you're a native, you come in stage right, audience left.

He also talks about significant aspects of the Greek and Roman theatres, including: a wheeled platform, the eccyclema, which apparently was the same thing as the eccyclema of the Greek theatre, except that the reveal could be rather like a revolving door, instead of something that was just wheeled in; a lookout post which was a separate unit that was constructed; walls; towers; a lighthouse, a tower where there would be torches burning to suggest that we are now in the middle of the sea or some kind of shore; a second story; a lightning machine which was supposedly a *periaktoi* which was spun around very quickly; a thunder machine (to create thunder he says that they rolled a bag of pebbles into copper pots); a god platform; a lift; trap doors; a crane; and swings where an actor would literally sit on a swing and be suspended above the action. This wasn't a lift because ultimately the focus of the lift was to take the actor up and out. What is significant about Pollux is that he tells us that the Greek and Roman theatre was a spectacular theatre. Other than the machinery that we use to create our effects, there is really very little in contemporary theatre that is different from all of what was used in the theatre of Greece and Rome.

3. Theatre in the Middle Ages

There are several reasons why following Rome we go into a period of relative silence for the theatre. One of the most significant reasons why the theatre was pushed underground is the emergence of Christianity, which became lawful under Constantine somewhere around 324–327 A.D., and, under the Emperor Theodosius, all other religions were made unlawful in the year 393 A.D. Due to Christianity, gladiatorial contests were abolished the year 404, and animal fighting was banished in 523. During this period the church discouraged Christians from attending plays and, in 398, the Council of Carthage excommunicated every Christian who went to the theatre instead of church on Sundays. This is significant because in Greece and Rome the theatrical event was a religious celebration. Now all of a sudden, if you go to the theatre instead of going to worship you are excommunicated—so clearly, we are now separating the theatre from the established religion. Actors (and all theatre people) were also forbidden to receive the sacraments unless they gave up the theatre. Plainly, the development of Christianity is one reason the theatre went underground.

Another reason is the decay of the Roman Empire. In 330 Constantine moved the capital to Constantinople and that divided the empire into "east" and "west"—a division that was firmly established by 395, when we had an emperor of the west and an emperor of the east. In 410, the Visigoths attacked and destroyed Rome. In 476 the Roman Empire was sacked again and the last emperor was deposed. It is interesting, however, that between 493 and 526, the barbarian leader Theodoric restored the Theatre of Pompey in Rome because the barbarians saw that the theatre was useful in restoring order (i.e., get all the people in the theatre and preach what you want to them). In 533 A.D. there was the last definite record of a theatrical performance in Rome—the last time a specific theatrical performance is mentioned. Subsequently, in 568, the Lombards attacked Rome and the theatre virtually disappeared in the west.

Another reason why the theatre began to go into a dark period is the rise of Islam, a religion which discouraged the theatre and all representational acts in general. Although Islam forbade drama professionally, crude forms of folk drama managed to persist. We find records of shadow-puppet dramas in the Eastern Empire , around Turkey which were called *karagoz*, and some remnants of theatrical activity of the Roman variety persisted in Constantinople; but in the Islam empire only the folk-like *karagoz* was permitted to exist. In the western empire theatrical activity continued informally through the ever-present mimes that would travel as itinerant performers, dressed with animal heads, enacting various crude and licentious acts.

As we move into the Middle Ages, therefore, theatre is kept alive through (1) mimes; (2) German minstrelsy, the *scop* tradition, in which a German minstrel would deliver the news and gossip from one place to another (i.e., the "look who's having an affair with whom" sort of thing); (3) popular festivals and pagan rites (maypole celebrations for example); (4) Christian ceremonies like the mass, the feast of the boy bishop, the feast of fools (which took place on the 1st of January); and, (5) popular farces. You will notice that the farce tradition, a group of people who liked to satirize local officials, problems in government, etc., (and often dealing with cuckolding, and priests who seduced parishioners) managed to sustain a place in theatrical culture from the Greeks on through the Middle Ages (and even up to *Saturday Night Live*). People just enjoy to ridicule their higher ups.

In the German territory that is now Switzerland, at the monastery of St. Gall, two monks whose names are **Notker Balbulus** (c.840-912) and **Tuotillo** began to develop a series of tropes in the service of the Catholic mass which gradually developed into the Judeo-Christian drama which emerged in the Middle Ages. Now, Balbulus, so named because he stuttered, was a poet who got together with a monk named Tuotillo, who was essentially a painter. They were concerned about clarifying to parishioners the Christian message sung at certain parts of the mass. Their first successful attempt at doing this was the Easter *Quem Queritis* trope (a version dating from 925 still exists). What began to develop at the Monastery of St. Gall was a "troping" of particular responses of the mass. Tropes are essentially elongations of phrases and sometimes even additions to a particular phrase or message in the Bible that was sung during the mass. Musically, a trope would be all of the long "Amens" that you hear in any kind of gospel or liturgical singing. All of those musical additions are added to the original sense of a phrase and embellishing it. In the Lord's Prayer, for example, "For thine is the kingdom and the power and the glory" is often considered a trope because scholars believe it was an addition to the original text.

The *Quem Queritis* trope embellished the story of the three virgins at the tomb of the risen Christ. Rather than saying that the three virgins went to the tomb and they saw that Jesus was gone, and then ran back to tell everybody (which is essentially the story), the trope version has the angel at the tomb say to the virgins, "Whom do you seek?" They say "Christ." And the angel answers, "But he has risen." And they go, "'Hallelujah.' We've got to go run back and tell everybody." It seems basic, but that necessitated dividing the chorus in half: one half of the chorus representing the angel, the other part of the chorus representing the Marys. One group speaks to the other—a kind of question and answer, reminiscent of the chorus leader and chorus in Greece—and gradually, like the early plays that developed out of choral songs in Greece, the divided chorus further split into individuals who subsequently acted the roles (i.e., "I am now going to play the angel. I am now going to sing the three Marys").

Gradually the text was embellished even further. To the initial trope was added an apostles' scene with Peter and John running to the empty tomb, adding a kind of physical action to the event. This was subsequently enhanced by the addition of a contest to determine which apostle could get to the tomb faster. With the enacting of a race came spectacle. Then was added Christ appearing to Mary Magdalene, and even a contemporary scene of a spice merchant selling his wares to the virgins, so that they could anoint Christ in the tomb. Consequently, there was a short scene between the Marys haggling with the spice merchant over the cost of the wares. With this came the development of specific types of characters. For example, the merchants in medieval society were expected to haggle so that archetype was adopted in the theatre. In addition, parishioners expected the apostles to run a race, and Christ to be noble, so he was also presented with wounds in his hands (from being nailed to the cross), and a kind of halo around his head.

As tropes became popular, the church began to employ them at other times of the year. The Easter trope was the first one mostly because Easter is a very important holy day for the Christian Church. The next highly celebratory event was Christmas. Another trope, the *Officium Pastorum*, was developed at Christmas and included the visit of the Magi, the massacre of the innocents, and Herod's anger. This developed the archetype that Herod was supposed to run around and yell like a madman (note Hamlet's line about over-the-top actors: "he out-Herods Herod"). Between the twelfth and sixteenth centuries, playwrights began to develop troping by adding topical references and local detail, so that at one point they may emphasize the sacred text, and at the next they would emphasize the local event. By such means they would make the Bible as clear as possible—and as immediate as possible—to the parishioners in church. They had one huge problem, however: the liturgy was in Latin and not all the people understood Latin. To solve this problem, playwrights had to (1) become more physical/visual; and (2) experiment with writing in the vernacular.

Between 965 and 975, a monastic agreement was compiled by **Ethelwold**, the Bishop of Winchester, called in Latin, the *Regularis Concordia*. In this document, Ethelwold used dramatic devices to educate and entertain his monks, and it is believed that the first extant playlet of the Middle Ages comes from this work. This is significant because the playlet is complete with directions for performance. Ethelwold indicated where people were supposed to stand, when they spoke, and so forth.

The next significant developer in terms of the drama was **Hrosvitha** (c.935-1001), a woman of high class and stature who, deciding early in her life to become a nun, entered the Convent of Gandersheim in northern Germany. Gandersheim was a convent that was very high up in the monastic order particularly since the Emperor Otto's niece founded it and another Emperor's daughter became one of the nuns there. As a result, it was very highly polished, and had a fair amount of property and control over the surrounding districts. Hrosvitha was a poet whose most famous work other than her six plays is *The Fall and Conversion of Theophilus*, about a priest who sells his soul to the devil to obtain worldly advancement. It was turned into a play during the medieval period by a man named **Ruteboeuf** and later by **Goethe** as *Faust* (this nun was the inspiration for one of the great masterpieces of dramatic literature). Hrosvitha wrote six Christian moral comedies to replace the six frivolous comedies of Terence that all the nuns happened to be reading to learn Latin. Her Latin is pretty basic but the plays were good enough to teach the nuns Latin grammar and sufficiently entertaining to be performed to visiting dignitaries.

I should say perhaps early on that her plays are divided into two groups: one discussing the sins of the flesh against the spirit, and the other dealing with Christian martyrdom. *Abraham* is clearly one of the sins of the flesh plays since it depicts a hermit, Abraham, who rescues his niece Mary from a brothel. *Calamachus* is an early version of *Romeo and Juliet*. *Dulcitius* is her one honest comedy, dealing with the follies of a young husband and governor who wants to rape three virgins, Agape, Chionia, and Irene. As he is about to rape them, he is driven mad by the power of God, and he ends up making love to pots and pans in the kitchen, and reemerges full of soot and grease all over. The three virgins make fun of him. Many scholars refuse to believe that Hrosvitha was a nun because of some of her plots, but ultimately, it is the power of God that prevents the rape. *Paphnutius* is a play in which Thais, a very famous whore, renounces worldly pleasures for eternal joys. It happened that a hermit visited Thais and told her, "Give all of this up and come live with me in a cave and believe in Christ." And so she did. In *Gallicanus*, Constantia, daughter to the Emperor Constantine, agrees to marry Gallicanus just before he goes off to war, even though she had taken a vow of chastity. Upon his return, he decides to take a vow of chastity as well (having been converted in the heat of battle) and dies a Christian martyr.

Sapientia, her masterpiece, is another of the "martyrdom" plays in which Faith, Hope and Charity are tortured. What is interesting about the play is that it prefigures the delight that the Middle Ages took in witnessing physical torture. There are extended passages in the play graphically explaining how the virgins are being tortured, how their breasts are being slashed, and how fire is consuming them. It really gets grisly. But what is important is that through all of these tortures, the virgins don't die. They ultimately have to be slashed to death. Their mother, Sapientia, buries them and is then taken to heaven. The first part of the play deals with a mathematical exercise which some scholars think Hrosvitha wrote to entertain the spectators with how much her nuns really knew about mathematics and physics.

The next significant development was the creation of a vernacular drama and the changing of the position of the trope in the religious service. Both of these elements come from a writer named **Hilarius** in the twelfth century. What is significant about Hilarius's work, especially in a play called *Daniel*, is that he says, "if this play is performed at Christmas, sing the following songs. If this play is performed at Easter, sing the following songs." All of a sudden, the trope which is supposed to embellish a particular liturgical idea is no longer just limited to the needs of a single service but can be transferred from one service to another. This gives the trope a kind of autonomy. Also, in two of his plays, Hilarius introduces vernacular lyrics among the Latin words so that all the parishioners can understand what is being said (or sung). This vernacular urge was developed in an anonymous play called *The Bridegroom* written around 1100 where half the play is in the vernacular (French). Now, that's not saying too terribly much because the play is only 105 lines so you'll get 50 lines in the original Latin, and 50 lines in the language of the people. Ecclesia opens the play by announcing the coming of Christ and warning the virgins to be watchful. The foolish virgins ask the wise ones for oil; they've slept too long and have no more. They are sent to merchants who cannot help them. Christ appears, chastises the foolish virgins, and the foolish virgins are led to hell by demons. That's the play in 105 lines! This identifies the typical formula for liturgical drama:

1) Warning: If you do this, you're going to be in trouble.

2) Hope is kindled: Let's go to the merchants, they surely will have some oil; and

3) Despair. Hope is crushed.

Now why do you suppose the emphasis would be on a warning: if you're bad you're going to hell, but if you're good you won't—but you've been bad so to hell you go. Why do you suppose this is popular? How did the Church keep the people in line? It did not keep the people in line by showing them how wonderful things are in heaven. It kept them in line by showing them how bad things are in hell. Again, there is an emphasis on the delight in descriptions torture that existed in the period, as well as a delight in depictions of physical deformity and pain.

A significant point about these early liturgical dramas is that they were all performed inside the church which meant that they made use of what we call a *mansion setting*. Anyone who's ever been inside of a Gothic cathedral or any cathedral of a traditional plan, you notice that there are side altars that are placed at various locations in the cathedral. In the medieval period, the side altars would generally form the various mansions or settings for scenes in the various plays. This is significant because there were two ways of viewing plays. The audience can move from mansion to mansion very much like the way parishioners perform the stations of the cross (14 depictions of Christ's suffering on the day of the crucifixion). Another way of viewing would have the audience sit in a particular place in the church and watch the participants (actors) go from place to place.

One play that was not performed inside the church was called *The Play of Adam*, written at some point between 1140 and 1174, and entirely in French. This was also a development in the medieval form because it was meant to be acted, not sung. Remember the early *Quem Queritis* tropes and some of the early liturgical dramas were sung by one choir to the other and various participants would sing the roles. Now priests and deacons are beginning to act (speak) them. *The Play of Adam* is actually a trilogy comprised of the story of Adam and Eve, the slaying of Abel, and, tacked onto the end of that, the procession of prophets. In it you get the Warning, God's insistence on obedience; the Hope, Adam's refusal to be tempted; and Despair, Satan's temptation of Eve. In the play, Eve is tempted by a devil who is apparently well versed in feminine psychology. Here we have an early example of psychological motivation. The devil preys on her phobias and her subconscious mind. And Eve is a wife who knows how to get what she wants from a husband since she is well versed in the male psychology a well. Once again, this is still done with all the traditional requirements: priests and acolytes perform the roles, under the auspices of the church; the church produces (pays for) it; and the play is done to provide people with a religious message.

Another play, the *Play of St. Nicholas* written around 1200 develops the medieval aim of liturgical drama which was to educate and to entertain. If you can keep the faithful awake, you can actually teach them something. In *St. Nicholas*, we have mansion scenes representing various locales, particularly taverns, and in the play the audience is treated to the miraculous restoration of a stolen treasure, long tavern scenes, and a climactic battle scene between the Christians and the Saracens. The play would have a great influence on future drama, specifically the cycle plays and morality plays that would follow. Now remember Ruteboeuf who was mentioned in the discussion about Hrosvitha? He wrote a play called *The Miracle of Theophile* in 1261, portraying an angered ecclesiastic who makes a pact with the devil only to repent and be saved by the intercession of the Blessed Virgin Mary. What is significant here is that we have an emphasis now on the power of the Blessed Virgin to lead a soul to Christ. This was a new doctrine that was being taught by the Church. And in addition to teaching the latest Christian dogma, the play was an important step in the development of lyric poetry in drama. The play has less in terms of action and more in terms of the lyric self-consciousness or stream of consciousness that is going on in the characters' minds. In actuality, *The Miracle of Theophile* is a very primitive stream of conscious play.

The last play I want to talk about before we get into the cycle plays is called *The Play of the Canopy*, written in 1276, a rambling comedy about a group of men talking about women as they watch them go off to a religious festival. Half the play is male chauvinist dialogue about the commodification of women, and about 1 percent of the play is, "Oh by the way they're going to this religious festival, and they'll probably get religion and become very holy." Most of the play is about sex although it ultimately presents a religious lesson. Once again, we find playwrights going more to the comic and non-religious themes so that the audience will stay attentive to the religious message of the play. After many years of telling the audience, "If you're bad you go to hell. If you're good you go to heaven," playwrights felt the need to spice plays up in some way to keep people interested.

Cycle Plays

The development of cycle plays comes from three separate movements:

1) The Church began to feel it was inappropriate for their priests and acolytes to be dressing up as women, playing roles in plays. Even though they were supposed to be liturgical and religiously focused, there was a real concern about the appropriateness of priests acting, specifically acting as women, but generally acting at all.

2) The *Corpus Christi* feast day was established outdoors in 1311 by Pope Clement V. Occurring early in summer two months after Easter, and the second Sunday after Pentecost, it became a day of popular celebration to get a whole body of people together to celebrate the religious phenomenon of the body of Christ. Nearly all the cycle plays were destined for presentation

on either the Corpus Christi day itself or during the previous week. Corpus Christi occurred only two weeks after Pentecost, so any time between the feast days could have been used to put on plays.

3) Rise of the trade guilds. The trade guilds were self-governing corporations of artisans. They were very much like workers' unions today except that from the various guilds of artisans, a lord mayor and town officials would be elected.

Between the fourteenth and sixteenth centuries, in England there were cycle plays in the cities of Chester, York, Townley or Wakefield, Coventry, Norwich, and Newcastle. Cycle plays went on in France and in the Low Countries as well. The Chester cycle, comprising twenty-four plays appears to be the oldest in date of composition and we have evidence that performances began as early as 1328. That year, a text was prepared by a writer named **Ranulph Higden** whose other claim to fame was a book he wrote called *Polychronicon* which was supposed to be history of the universe from creation to modern times, in seven books modeled after the seven days of creation in the Bible. It was a kind of universal encyclopedia. Higden is both the first and the last literary personality who can be credited with the composition of the cycle plays. Every other cycle was written by someone anonymously. The Coventry Cycle began somewhere around 1468 and comprises 42 plays, and the Townley or Wakefield plays belong to somewhere at the beginning of the fifteenth century.

A little earlier than Coventry is the York cycle which is first mentioned in 1378. It is referred to in an off-handed way. The Bakers' Guild is fined by the city of York and they are told to give half of the fine in support of the creation of a cycle play at Corpus Christi time. As a result, we know at least, at that point, they were performing plays. The ripest city for cycle plays was York because not only did it produce cycles, it produced a famous *Lord's Prayer Play* which began in 1389 and was such a hit that a guild of men and women (the *Pater Noster* Guild) was founded just to keep the play in performance. By 1399, the *Pater Noster* Guild numbered 100 men and their wives. Among the duties of this guild, the members had to ride or walk with the players through the city streets to ensure the safety of the audience. They literally functioned as bouncers.

In 1408, a Corpus Christi Guild was founded to develop the Corpus Christi procession that went along with the cycle plays. As the cycle plays became more spectacular in production, the Church formed the Corpus Christi Guild to make the procession a big show as well. In 1446, the guild began producing the *Creed Play*, which grew out of the procession and subsequently became so popular that it served as competition to the cycle plays. The *Creed Play* is significant as the direct antecedent of the morality play. Incidentally, the Corpus Christi Guild also produced a play about *St. George*, patron saint of England.

At York and Coventry, the word "pageant" was used for both the traveling scaffold (the actual wagon) and for the presentation itself. In other words, they called the cycle plays pageants. There are many differences of opinions about how the cycle plays were produced:

Some historians feel that there was a pageant wagon in which there were two floors, an upper open platform where the play was acted and a lower, enclosed dressing room where the actors could change. Others feel that the pageant wagon itself was like a float in a parade that moved to a platform on which the actors would then perform in front of the parade float. In this way, the parade float only functioned as a background for the action, and might have some space underneath for special effects, trap doors, costume storage, and the like. The actual size of the city streets, at that time in England, tells us that the pageant wagons could not have been terribly wide, and so the idea of the pageant wagon coming to an enclosed area with a free-standing platform seems more likely than to have actors play these plays on top of a very narrow pageant wagon. The fixed platform stages could be anywhere from 120 ft. to 200 ft. wide and 60-80 feet deep, much more suitable for a theatrical performance.

Often in these pageant wagons, two scenes were represented on the same stage, which began to establish in the minds of the British theatre-goer the idea of simultaneous staging. Each of the cycle plays had a prompter's book which recorded the action, where characters are supposed to stand, who they would address, and even the motivation they would have when delivering a line. There is only one extant prompter's book and it comes from a Scrivener's play called *The Incredulity of Thomas*—play number 42, at York. In 1394, a proclamation at York decreed that the players and pageants should assemble at 4:30 a.m. Of the 48 plays at York, whose total length is 13,121 lines, the playing time of each play would be about 15 minutes so that if you allow 5 minutes for the time taken between the end of one pageant and the beginning of the other, the entire series of plays would last 15 hours. Which means it would start at 4:30 in the morning and last until 7:30 that night. It must also be considered that if only three stations can be done in an hour (15 minutes per play plus a 5-minute turnaround equals 20 minutes), and there are 12 stations in the city, the first play of the cycle gets to the twelfth station four hours after the series began, around at 8:30 in the morning. The actors in play number 1 can change their costumes and become part of play number 37 and go around again. It would always be the worst job if your lot was to be in the first and last play. You'd have to be there at the very beginning and you stay there until the very end. It was a grueling experience. You also have to remember that the audience at any particular station would see the entire cycle at once, though, like in continental time zones, spectators at the first stations saw the performance four hours earlier than those who gathered at the twelfth station.

A four-man committee was chosen from the guilds to examine all the players in the city and determine which of them should represent the town in the cycle plays. Since York was considered the seat of Catholicism in England, actors from London and other surrounding areas would go to York to audition. The four-man committee cast the entire cycle plays, and it was determined that no player would be allowed to take two roles in an individual play. In other words, all the roles in a single play had to be played by different actors—but they could, of course, come around again in a different play. Whether actors performed on the wagon or on the platform, they used a rear curtain which was half black and half white to depict and night. They used strips of red fabric as Moses crossed the red sea, and painted backdrops which hid the flying equipment that literally flew people in, and whatever other machinery they needed to create the special effects which were called *secrets*. As in Hollywood films, the secrets grew to such significance, that a Master of Effects was finally chosen who would design all of the secrets for a particular play. They used trap doors for appearances; water effects for floods, fishing, and for walking upon; elaborate schemes of torture and execution suggested the Spanish Inquisition; and in an early version of *smell-a-vision*, when an actor was burned at the stake, the odor of burning animal bones and entrails wafted across the noses of the audience.

Every guild had its own Master of Effects. Needless to say, they competed with one another over who could create the best Hell's mouth. Soft animal bladders were employed to depict the scourging of Christ. Also, highly realistic decapitations and crucifixions were simulated when necessary. In a French pageant play, for example, Peter's severed head bounces three times and leaves a pool of blood each time that it bounces. Also, there was a statue of the Virgin Mary with a moveable head, arms, and hands, and eyes. The eyes of the Virgin would appear to be watching the audience and her head would turn for dramatic effect. King Herod killed himself with a blade-retracting sword and also lions, tigers, leopards, and snakes were used in performance. Because these were associated with the Christian liturgy, it was believed that the lions and various animals would not harm the actor because the actor was operating for God. If the actor—remember women in England were never allowed to perform in these plays—if the actor was mauled by a lion, the Church would argue that he had sin in his heart and shouldn't be doing the play anyway. Moreover, in use were thunder machines, flame-blowing dragons, fountains that spouted water, and sailing ships that appeared on the pageant wagons in pools of water. The Master of Effects even managed to create the effect of a staff turning into snake, a wife turning into a pillar of salt and then evaporating, and turning water into wine. Clearly, the point is that the Master of Effects for these plays was a miracle worker and the star of these events.

In the area of costuming, the actors supplied their own clothes. Inside their clothing they wore pots or leather body suits to protect them from stage beatings and attacks. Costume generally followed the trend for contemporary realism which means that historical figures were actually dressed in the analogue of the time. Roman soldiers wore medieval armor. Shepherds wore alpine peasant garb. Pilate was dressed as a medieval lord or city official. Jewish high officials wore the clothes of Christian priests but Jews in general wore the mandated clothes for medieval Jewry which was long robes and pointed hats. Devils were dressed as Jews only with the exaggerated characteristics of claws and tails, with scales and horns added. God was dressed as the emperor or the pope. In addition to costuming, various characters had identifiable characteristics. The Archangel Michael had a flaming sword. Judas wore a red wig and a yellow robe. St. Peter had keys to the kingdom. St. Catherine was identified by her spinning wheel. Wearing white meant your soul was saved. Wearing black, it was damned. Swords and scales meant justice. A mirror meant prudence. A snake represented envy. An owl or spider meant Satan. A scorpion represented the Jew. A lily was the Blessed Virgin, and a clover represented the blessed trinity.

300 actors were generally employed for use in cycle plays. These were local merchants, nobles, and professional players. Sometimes companies of fools supplied the comic actors. There were professional jesters and jongleurs, the idiots who would play for the kings or lords. Most actors were men and boys, though France occasionally let women participate. In 1468 we have a record of a glazier's daughter playing St. Catherine and, in the sixteenth century, a woman actually played Mary in the plays at the French city of Valenciennes.

A large hall served as the rehearsal space and the script was usually divided into 12 parts for rehearsals. Typically, each cycle would have 48 rehearsals. The favorite role was generally Herod because actors could improvise as Herod—he was supposed to go mad and rage a lot. He would go through the audience and beat people. Actors did not like playing Judas or Jesus because, in 1437, an actor playing Jesus almost died during the crucifixion. During the same year a Judas nearly died when he hanged himself. As a result, the actors playing those roles felt one shouldn't play Christ because it was too close to God, and one shouldn't play Judas because of what he did. Actors were allowed two weeks to decline or accept a role once cast. If one decided to drop out after that grace period, his soul was damned. All actors were subject to a schedule of fines, mostly for tardiness or drunkenness. Actors simply performed character actions without becoming the characters. Music rather than histrionics set the mood of the event since people in the medieval period believed that music was heaven's intervention into earthly affairs (their version of the Greek belief that moral and ethical instincts arose from various musical sounds).

One of the ways that the various guilds could compete with one another, in addition to the contest of spectacle, was that of buffoonery. To keep the audience interested, the guilds began to develop a variety of comic scenes in their cycle plays. A number of plays or characters allowed a great opportunity for comedy. Cain, for example, has a boy servant who is very wasteful and lazy, and the boy allows his cart to fall into a ditch. Cain has to get a horse to try to get the cart out of the ditch so that he can plow the fields (with a lazy boy and a lazy horse). Half of the *Cain and Abel* play is spent with Cain wrestling with his boy and his horse. After a fair amount of comic business, Cain kills his brother, and suddenly the play turns grotesquely serious. Noah is also a source of humor, mostly because of his wife who becomes the quintessential shrew, with lines, such as: "I will not get in the boat, nothing you can do will make me get into that pile of wood, nothing... oh my God, the water's up to my ankles... did you really want to decorate [the boat] like this, Noah?" Even though such stereotyping might be problematic with audiences today, in the chauvinistic middle ages, Noah's Wife was a comic masterpiece. Pilate was another source of comedy because he is unable to wash his hands in his big scene: he keeps spilling the water. King Herod, yet another comic figure, was expected to rave and go crazy.

Also offering comic opportunity were minor characters such as Augustus Caesar, usually played as a dolt, and the shepherds of the nativity in the *Second Shepherd's Play*. They have stolen a neighbor's sheep and, to hide the theft, they put the sheep in bed and pretend it's a child. In addition, the torturers of the crucifixion were comical figures because they would make fun of dividing Christ's clothes with a lot of physical business. The Chester *Crucifixion Play* is one of the most grotesquely funny plays of the entire cycle. Lucifer was oftentimes a funny character many of whose characteristics would transfer to the Vice character in the morality play which would gradually merge in the Renaissance with the clever servant character of Plautus, Terence, and Menander. Remember the clever servant who always works out all the events of the play? The vice character and the clever servant would gradually join together to create characters like Mosca in *Volpone* and some of Shakespeare's more clever servants (and villains). Also, the demons of the Final Judgment were usually laugh-riots. The least comic was the Cycle at York because York was the Episcopal seat of Catholicism in England. Perhaps the most comic was the Wakefield or Townley Cycle.

Along with the Wakefield cycle's use of comedy arises a new theory of how the cycle plays might have been done. It is thought that the Wakefield plays were produced in three parts and for that reason we have two shepherds' plays: the first part ends with the *First Shepherds' Play* and the second part begins with the *Second Shepherds' Play*. It is believed that these plays were produced in the round with the wagons located as individual stations around the circle, not unlike medieval illustration of the *Castle of Perseverance*, with the audience standing inside the circle. At each individual station or mansion, a pageant wagon would drive up with the actors on it and the scenery that would create the background for the play. In this way the audience doesn't have to move at all except to change their focus, and the pageant wagons do not have to travel through city streets. We tend to believe that not all of the cycle plays were produced like this because we do have records of little stations through towns as we've discussed before. However, for some of the cycles, we know that there could be no way a pageant wagon of the size necessary to carry the stage machinery could have traveled through a city street. Such a wagon was probably designed to function in a circular "mansion" venue, such as the one described above.

Morality Plays

The next significant theatrical development was the morality play, which was first mentioned under the title of *Pater Noster* or *Creed* play, beginning about 1378. This is significant because in the *Creed* plays, the seven deadly sins (lust, gluttony, greed, sloth, wrath, envy, pride) fought the seven cardinal virtues (chastity, temperance, charity, diligence, patience, gratitude, humility) for possession of Mankind's soul. Mankind's soul was always saved, though, in some of these plays, Mankind dies before he embraces salvation, and a host of angels come and take his soul to heaven through the generosity of Christ's mercy. Morality plays are didactic drama concerned with proper and improper conduct. Usually the subject is generalized so the whole play is an allegory and the protagonist a symbolic character: i.e., Everyman, Mankind. There were two kinds of moralities: the morality play which deals with conduct in relation to a religious doctrine—either salvation or damnation; and the moral interlude which deals with conduct in relation to secular doctrine—rather like letters to Miss Manners or Dear Abby. Plays such as *Wit and Science* and *Youth* are moral interludes, whereas *Everyman*, *Mankind*, and *Castle of Perseverance* are morality plays, dealing with the issue of salvation.

There are five extant morality plays written before 1500. The earliest is *The Pride of Life*, of which we only have about half a play. It was written in 1400. The first morality play of which we have a complete text is the *Castle of Perseverance* (1425), which was pronounced "Per-**sev**-er-ance" (emphasis on "sev") in the Middle Ages. This was followed by *Wisdom* in 1460, *Mankind* in 1466 of which we have about two-thirds of the play, and *Everyman*, dating from 1490, or thereabouts. The *Castle of Perseverance* deals with the ages of man in a life cycle. In over 3,500 lines, the morality play deals with the birth, youth, maturity, and death of Mankind. It begins with a debate between good angel and bad angel over the soul of man, after which man follows bad angel to the World, the Flesh, and the Devil where he has a lascivious scene with Lechery. He is subsequently overthrown by Death so that Mankind dies without repentance. But the daughters of God debate with the Almighty over whether or not Mankind should be saved. Ultimately, they win, and

Mankind's soul is brought to Heaven. *Castle of Perseverance* is the first complete play that uses the personification of psychological states or ideas. All of the characters are symbolic or allegorical (World, Salvation, Covetousness), which recalls the fifth-century book called *Psychomachia*, written by **Prudentius**. Thus, morality play can be regarded as a dramatized sermon showing the warfare between good and bad, the seven cardinal virtues, the seven deadly sins. In *Castle of Perseverance*, there is a huge pitched battle between the sins and the virtues where the seven cardinal virtues pelt the sins with red roses. Why red roses? Red for the blood of Christ shed on the cross. That's how it is explained in the play.

For performances of the *Castle of Perseverance*, it is believed that the audience sat inside a circle, beyond which there was a ditch filled with water with bridges from the outside into the circle (so that whoever did not pay for admittance could not come in). The actual castle was located in the middle of the circle with a note asking that nobody stand around the castle because the sightlines would be bad for everyone else. Mankind's soul lives under the castle and hides there until it's time for him to come out late in the play. In the 5-hour production, it became extremely difficult to keep the soul awake, never mind alive throughout the entire piece. Various other scaffolds or platform areas were located on the outside of the circle: God's scaffold or Heaven, for example, faced the east. Stage directions abounded in the play, especially when concerning the comic devil: "He that shall play Belyal, look that he have gunpowder burning in pipes in his hands, and in his ears, and in his arse, when he goes to battle." You can see now what the joke of Belyal was: he farts and he explodes. These people were obviously not as interested in performance-safety as we are. The text also indicated that "the four daughters [of God] shall be clad in mantles, Mercy is clad in white, Righteousness in red, Truth in sad green, and Peace is dressed in black." Peace is in black because she's mourning for Mankind. We believe that the play was performed by a traveling company of professional (or, at least, paid) actors.

Wisdom dates somewhere around 1460 and employs 36 roles to be played by 6 men and 7 boys. The boys play the women's parts, of course. *Wisdom* dramatizes the struggle between Christ and Lucifer to win Man's soul. The play begins and ends as a sermon and this ultimately emphasizes the feeling that the play is just an extended homily. Not surprisingly, Wisdom who is dressed as Christ speaks to the Soul giving it good advice. Lucifer, however, enters and disguises himself as a proud gallant and persuades Man (the Soul) to devote himself to Pride. He also persuades him to turn to Covetousness, and Lechery. The Lechery scenes are really quite effective. They portray the sins of the flesh as very attractive. Actually, what happens is that each of these, Pride, Covetousness, and Lechery call in six followers, and they engage in a very merry dance. This is actually a prefiguring of what becomes the masque in English drama where you invite someone into your household and they then perform various kinds of dances in disguise. Ultimately Wisdom makes the Soul repent by showing how badly it has become disfigured by following Lechery, Covetousness, and Pride. Ultimately, the Soul is contrite and confesses her sins (the Soul is a female character in this particular case. In Latin, the Soul is *anima* which is a feminine noun). After the Soul confesses, she returns with Five Wits and Three Mights in order to fight Pride, Covetousness, and Lechery. So, what Might would fight Pride? Humility. Covetousness? Charity. And Lechery? Chastity. After the battle, the Five Wits and the Three Mights dance and the Soul is taken up to heaven.

More significant perhaps is the play of *Mankind* which was written somewhere around 1466 and treats the subject of Mankind in maturity. It was acted by professional traveling players, and it is the first English play to mention the gathering of money from the audience. Within its text, it actually talks about going out and passing the hat among the audience—and it has some of the comic villains go out and shame the audience (or threaten them) into giving them money (i.e., "if you don't pay, we'll stay around, so you've got to pay to get rid of us"). There are only seven roles in this play. And what is significant here is that there is only one virtuous character: of seven roles, one is devoted to Mankind, one is devoted to Mercy, and the rest of the characters are vices. What does that tell you about the direction that the morality play is going into? Show us the evil. It is more interesting to see the evil being done. Also, what is unusual is that Mercy appears in this play not as the feminine character which it had been up to this point, but in a masculine role—the father confessor of Mankind. The vice character in this play is a merry devil, Titivillus, who tricks mankind into giving up Labor and Prayer for New Guise, Nowadays, and Nought. New Guise dresses Mankind in apparel which is unseemly to a Christian man. Nowadays brings Man to drink, and Nought leads Man to sloth. What is also interesting in this play is that Titivillus keeps appearing from trap doors underneath the stage. There are a great many fire pots so that you get the sense of flashing appearances (there's a lot of flash in this play). New Guise, Nowadays, and Nought help Mankind steal a group of horses which were really on stage, and a character called Mischief summons Mankind to a mock court where he swears to steal, rob, and kill. Mischief, by the way, enters with blood on his hands, having just killed half the population of a particular town with great joy. Finally, despairing of Mercy, Mankind is about to hang himself when Mercy rescues him, shows him the way to confession, and all is forgiven.

All these plays were professional productions performed by traveling players. However, to be allowed to perform in the play, actors had to have the blessing of the Church. What we see, however, is that, as the plays progress through the fifteenth century, there is less time spent on the religious lesson, and more time spent on mankind being tempted. In *Mankind*, we get four-fifths of the play with Mankind drinking, debauching, and murdering, and only at the very end, Mercy arrives and saves Mankind. In that way, the play could have the fun, the comic aspect, but still keep the traditional elements of the morality.

Everyman, which dates from about 1495, is a translation of a Dutch play called *Elckerlijg*. It is regarded as the masterpiece of the morality tradition in English and unifies elements of all the plays we have discussed so far. *Everyman* is the journey of the Soul in preparation for Death. Death visits Mankind and Mankind attempts to take his worldly possessions with him to the grave. However, the only things that do him any good whatsoever are his good deeds. On his way to the grave, Mankind goes to his friends, the Five Wits, the senses. Do they go with him? No. He goes to everyone, and it is finally his Good Deeds, a character who begins in the play as rather limited and weak. By the end of the play, through Faith and through the Mercy of God, Mankind's Good Deeds become stronger and they help him into the grave. This is believed to be a version of a Buddhist parable which was brought into Europe during the Middle Ages. More than any other of the morality plays, *Everyman* is serious, almost tragic in tone, and this was perhaps the most significant of the Church's message plays because it proved that mankind could not take his earthly goods with him in death. We will see later in the sixteenth century, that the moral interlude will start to involve a more academic sense of knowledge where the instruction of the soul would not be dependent on purely moral attitudes, but upon the world as a scientific sphere or the world as a commercial domain, and so we find plays called *Wyt (Wit) and Science*, written by John Redford (c.1500–1547) for the boys' choir of St. Paul's Cathedral.

Farce

Farce actually emerged in France around 1266 with one of the earliest comic plays still in existence called *The Boy and the Blind Man*. This particular plot will become archetypical to the French farce of the 14th, 15th, and 16th centuries. A blind man seeking to hire a boy to lead him around, to help him beg, and to get entrance into rich households, puts up a sign saying, "boy for hire." A young man looking for work enters and thinks that money can be made from the situation. They haggle and finally the boy is hired by the blind man. Time passes. The blind man gives the boy lessons in how to beg, how to get money from passersby, tearing at the-heartstrings, and so forth. The boy learns his lessons well. After a time, he gets the idea to bilk the blind man. He tells him, "I've got to go take a piss." And so, the boy goes off stage, then runs back, and using a strange voice, he attacks the blind man and steals some of his loot. When the boy returns saying (in his own voice), "Gee, I really needed that," the blind man tells him all about the attack. The boy, pretending to be concerned for the blind man, tells him, "Well, golly, if somebody robbed you of your money here, what you really ought to do is give me your chest of money, because, since you can't see, I should be the person to protect the cash." So, the old blind man, who has taught the boy how to connive, gives the boy the box. Of course, the boy runs off with the money and the blind man is left lamenting his stupidity in trusting the boy. This is the origin of the "duper-duped" kind of plot which will become the stock in trade of French farce straight through Molière.

One other important work is called *The Tale of the Herbs* which is late 13th century. This is a kind of dramatic monologue in which the speaker details various herbs in his garden and suggests the medicinal cures to be gotten from them. We're talking the kind of medicine man shows in the great old American West. *The Tale of the Herbs* inspires the tradition of fast-witted, fast-talking con men that are going to people Molière's plays, such as *The Doctor in Spite of Himself*

The word farce as a dramatic genre first appeared in France in 1398 in a document forbidding the inhabitants of Paris to give farces without permission. The earliest surviving example of a conventional French farce appeared around 1420 where, in the middle of a manuscript in the St. Genevieve Abbey, emerged the words, "Here is placed a farce," in the middle of a longer morality play (the word "farce" originally meant "stuffing"). Farces were characterized by swift repartee, brevity, and the use of contemporary persons and local satire. The most significant *dramatis personae* of farce were philandering priests (inevitably, in a farce, the priest was the person who was going to cuckold the husband), unfaithful wives or husbands, inept doctors and soldiers; and the effects included beatings, disguises, and role reversals. The playing and writing of these farces in the 15th and 16th centuries, was largely in the hands of societies devoted to writing comic plays. And the two most significant were the *Enfants-sans-souci* (Children without care) and the *Basochiens* (a fraternity of law students). The *Enfants-sans-souci* were *sots* (fools) who performed in the *sotties* (fools' plays) and the *basochiens* were law clerks. Both societies were writing farces and performing in them. In the middle of the 15th century, both of these groups joined the *Confrèrie de la passion* (the Society of the

Passion), a group performing liturgical plays that couldn't make ends meet by writing serious liturgical plays, and from that point on, the *Enfants-sans-souci* and the *Basochiens* played comedies in conjunction with religious plays of the *Confrèrie*. In other words, we would see part of a morality play, and then we would see a very lewd comedy, and then we would see the rest of the morality play. In some of the French moralities, dating from the middle of the 15th century, the result of this union caused the moralities themselves to include a number of comic scenes.

The most significant of these moralities is called *Les Enfants des Maintenants (The Children of Now)* which is one of the most fascinating plays of-the period. The moral of this story is that parents must not spoil their children by indulging them but must insist upon discipline and a good education. Maintenant (Now) and his silly wife ask Good Advice what to do with their boys. They're told to take them to Instruction where they might be taught a trade or profession. The wife is afraid of the destructive effects of education. She's frightened that a little learning will ruin her boys. Nonetheless, she finally consents and tells Instruction that she wants her boys to learn everything in the skills and sciences—if he can teach it to them over a weekend. And if he can't teach them everything, she wants him, at least, to teach them how they can live without working. The two boys are called Sly Rogue and Ill-Bred. They refuse to learn, they run away from school, they blackmail their father into giving them money and fine clothes, and they go off to seek an easy life in the service of some great lord. They like the looks of a female character named Discipline, but when she gives them her sound advice (and she carries heavy whips), they decide that she turns out to be as bad as Instruction. Finally, they meet up with a character named Ne'er Do Well who promises to make them masters of dice, cards, and other tricks if they will disavow God, practice vice, and force themselves on women. The brothers prove to be apt pupils and are especially taken with Ne'er Do Well's beautiful daughter whose name is Luxury. The young men play various games with Luxury and, in a particularly unpleasant roll of the dice, they lose everything they have including their clothes (hence the expression, everything including the shirt off their backs). Ill-Bred repents of his evil life and wants to give up the teachings of Ne'er Do Well, but Sly Rogue continues to sin and goes from bad to worse. He's dragged before Shame, beaten, tortured, taken before Despair, and condemned to be hanged. Ill-Bred, now penitent, reappears and goes back to Discipline and Instruction. Learning his lessons from them, he returns home to seek his father's forgiveness, and the play ends with the homecoming and the forgiveness of the prodigal son. One of the children is hanged after being tortured with grotesque, bloody whips, and the other is saved in accordance with the story of the prodigal son. The play is extremely funny in the inner scenes when dealing with Luxury and the games that Ne'er Do Well tries to teach the boys, and the whole idea of the boys blackmailing their father into giving them money and rich clothes is, in a real way, extremely modern. Yet, the play does have a very significant, if somewhat dangerous, moral at the end of it: If you don't tow the mark, you really do get killed.

Master Pierre Pathelin

The farcical masterpiece of the period is *Master Pierre Pathelin*. The date when it was written is unknown but we know that it was before 1470 because in 1470 the word *patheliner* appears in a legal document when a lawyer is outdone by his client. Since the word appears and it has a direct reference to the action of the play, we know that the farce must have existed before then. The popularity of the piece is attested because from about 1489 on, the play went into a number of renewed editions, and was translated into many foreign languages. In it, there are two dupings. In the first part, Pathelin dupes Guillaume the cloth merchant out of paying for his wares. In the second part, Pathelin is out-witted by a shepherd whom he takes as a client over the loss of sheep. Here we have a kind of unification of the farce tradition and the sot tradition in the comic play. It uses the contemporary characters that farce employed. There is a middle-class lawyer and his wife, cloth merchants, both middle class workers. However, there is also Pathelin speaking in tongues in one part of the play, speaking gibberish which comes entirely out of the *sottie* tradition. The second part of the play deals with a great number of double-entendres with the use of sheep. The cloth merchant is complaining about the loss of his sheep which of course would drive up the cost of his materials. The shepherd accused of stealing the sheep hires Pathelin, the lawyer, to defend him against Guillaume, the cloth merchant who was duped by Pathelin in the first part of the play. This is Pathelin's opportunity to dupe him twice, which he does by convincing the Shepherd not to say anything but "Baa." However, when the lawyer then asks the shepherd for his pay, the shepherd just answers him, "Baa." By talking the shepherd into behaving in a particular fashion so he can win the case, the lawyer has duped himself. This goes back to *The Blind Man and the Boy*, in which the blind man, having taught the boy how to behave, now has to deal with being duped.

These plays were essentially performed by professional fools, law clerks, students, and churchmen. We know that churchmen took part both in the performance and writing of them because there are lots of writs from the period saying that churchmen should not do this sort of thing. They were performed both in and out of doors in private halls or public squares and in conjunction with religious plays and (what is even more significant), at town festivals or weddings. So now these kinds of plays which began as stuffing in between the morality plays are beginning to take on a life of their own. Just as we said early on in the development of liturgical drama when the trope can go from one part of the Church service to another, these comic plays are beginning to be treated on their own terms, rather than being considered simply stuffing between longer plays.

Interludes

The interlude is a short play in dialogue produced by a small company of actors, sometimes schoolboys, sometimes adult professionals, on small stages backed by a screen or booth in a banquet hall or in an open-air pavilion (i.e., tents that you'd see in a fair). The word "interlude" dates back to 1418 and is often coupled with singing, wrestling, and summer games. The idea of interlude is kind of variety type entertainment. With the interlude we see the rise of the professional itinerant player, and, simultaneously with the development of the player, we see the change of interlude from a moral to a secular play.

It was King Henry VII in 1485 who developed a group of four players who would perform at court for a fee and then travel around the countryside with their hands and hearts open to the community saying "Please pay us and we will play for you." In addition to the company that Henry developed, various small itinerant players began to be employed by the Dukes of Buckingham, Gloucester, and York. Interludes, as a result, were not tied to any particular feast days but would be produced at the behest of the lord or agency which was paying the bill. The interlude company maintained by Henry VII constituted four men led by a man named John English. From the King they received a retaining fee of five marks plus their room and board, and they received a gratuity every time they performed at court. When not at court they traveled, performing before other nobility in dining halls and performing for mayors in guild halls and city merchants in their assembly rooms. Gradually they began to use outdoor spaces for one very obvious reason: larger spaces equal more gratuity. In the late 15th century—the end of the 1400s and into the 1500s—more and more, the players began to set up tent-like structures in the open air with an opening that would require the people who came within the barrier to pay a particular fee.

Interludes were also performed by amateur groups such as schoolboys, and oftentimes since the schoolboys were performing them as part of their curriculum or in the guild hall of their patron, they were not concerned with raising money. Schoolboys generally performed indoors and in smaller surroundings, and this becomes the antecedent of the private theaters of the Elizabethan period where schoolboys would play inside converted chapels or converted banquet houses. The staging of interludes by these companies, professional or amateur, almost always involved a backdrop of some sort; and given the existence of a banquet hall where interludes were often produced, we assume that the master and his entourage was in one part of the room, on the dais, and at the other end of the hall, usually in front of the tapestry that was opposite the dais, would a small stage be erected where the interludes would be performed. This becomes really significant because we know that some interludes required artificial ships and various other kinds of castle turrets to be built, so a fair amount of spectacle was packed into a small amount of space.

What is also significant is that actors were required to play more than one role. Since the companies were 4 to 6 people and oftentimes the interlude could have up to twice or three times as many characters in them, actors would have to double. Therefore, costumes were very simple, allowing maybe just the change of a piece—a hat or some kind of prop that would indicate the difference of character. The style of costume was of contemporary fashion, making it possible for the actors to sit among the audience and actually to look like guests in the banquet hall. Because they were performed before a lord or some sort of sponsoring organization, interludes typically had prologues or epilogues which would be apologetic or sycophantic. This becomes the true antecedent of all the epilogues and prologues that would characterize the drama during the Renaissance. In addition, interludes were rife with ad-libs because the actors were about as close to their audience as a teacher is to a classroom. They literally would be talking to somebody, and that person, full of food and drink, would often talk back, so the actor might have to ad-lib. This is true dinner theatre with the exception that in this kind of theatre, if the spectators didn't like the performance, they would actually throw the food at the actor. The player of the interludes therefore had to be quick-witted—ready to come back with a repartee, and also a singer, dancer, and acrobat. The fact that he was a member of some lord's household required him to behave with dignity but, at the same time, he was supposed to be able to mimic and satirize all of the abuses of the time. The subjects of their parodies were most often grasping merchants, pretentious lawyers, corrupt churchmen, and teachers. It is interesting that when Henry VIII came to the throne, he decided to double the number of professional players that he had under his employ from 4 to 8—he so enjoyed the idea of lampooning the clergy, the lawyers, and other political figures in his kingdom.

Now, about the interlude itself. Once again Henry VII is significant because during his reign, 1485-1509, the interludes shifted their attention from moral to intellectual abstractions. The first play to do this was called *Nature* by Henry Medwall. *Nature*, written before 1500 and performed by choir boys, pretends to deal with man's passage through the world from infancy through old age, and talks about various lapses into sin and ultimate repentance. While this sounds like a morality play, the supreme power of the play is Nature, and Nature exhorts man to study Aristotle, not the Bible. This is a major change in focus, with the substitution of a semi-pagan Renaissance ethic for the religion of the morality play. Another play called *A New Interlude and a Merry of the Nature of the Four Elements Declaring Many Proper Points of Philosophy Natural and of Diverse Strange Lands and of Diverse Strange Effects and Causes*, commonly referred to as *The Four Elements* was written by John Rastell between 1509 and 1518. In this play (and see how different this is from the kind of morality plays we've been discussing), Nature, Studious Desire, and Experience all take turns in teaching Humanity the secrets of the earth and the visible universe. Notice that we don't have Truth, Love, Charity, or Justice, but Nature, Studious Desire (the desire to learn), and Experience. They also make use of a globe which is an important prop in the play. For a time, the pupil behaves as a typical student and goes off with Sensual Appetite, Ignorance, and a Taverner. Sensual Appetite is not called Lust, as in the morality plays, because lust is a sin. Instead, Sensual Appetite comes from a different point of view, because man's sensual appetite is not looked upon as a sin, but as something that is inherently human. Humanity quickly discovers that the Taverner does not give him a whole lot of joy because of hangovers; Sensual Appetite is also short-lived, and Humanity discovers that Ignorance doesn't go very far. Since he is easily won back to the pursuit of knowledge, this play becomes the archetype of a series of educational interludes.

Here is a list of some others: *Wyt (Wit) and Science* in which a foolish young Wit sets out to woo and marry his natural complement, Science. During his wandering attempts to do just that, he is mauled by a giant named Tediousness. In the end, he conquers Tediousness through the help of his servants, Instruction, Diligence, and Study. In *The Marriage of Wit and Wisdom*, there are six characters which have nothing to do with the allegorical issues of the story at all, but are just in there for local color. This is an attempt for the interlude playwright to interest the audience through kind of topical satire, but the characters have no allegorical significance whatsoever. The six characters are named Catch, Snatch, Mother Bee, Lob, Doll, and Search.

The influence of the burgeoning Italian Renaissance on the English drama is illustrated in a play called *The World and the Child* which was published in 1522. Once again, the play treats man's life from childhood to old age through sin and repentance but only five characters appear, and man's entire career is dealt with in 900 lines. Most significantly, the world is no longer portrayed as a vale of sorrow; instead, it is a place of variety with experiences to be savored. Moreover, in this play the spectator is presented, perhaps for the first time, with a comprehensive view of the actual life in London. This is a further development of the topicality in *The Marriage of Wit and Wisdom*, where the characters actually do deal with the allegorical action of the play, but are also portrayed as real people in London at the time. This was followed by a very funny interlude called *Hickscorner* which is set in London, very much like *The World and the Child*, with only six characters, three of which are vices: Hickscorner, Free Will, and Imagination. It's interesting that Imagination and Free Will are vices. And three virtues: Pity, Contemplation, and Perseverance. There is a significant character absent—Mankind. Having been the dullest character in all of these interludes, Mankind has finally been jettisoned from the play. Basically, *Hickscorner* is about three virtues and three vices fighting over the soul of a man we never see.

Another possibility of dealing with the character of Mankind (rather than getting rid of him entirely) was to select a particular part of man's history and to devote the entire focus of a play to that. Which part of man's life do you think was most popular to deal with? Youth. Yes, playwrights enjoyed the opportunity of writing about puberty and all those wonderful temptations, but more importantly, youth is the point in life where a man can actually change. If you're dealing with a person at the end of his life, what's the big deal? He says he's sorry and he goes to heaven. But when you're young there's the possibility of a great number of things that can happen to you. Two of the interludes that are devoted to youth are *The Interlude of Youth*, which is, frankly, a bore, and *Lusty Juventus* which deals with the seduction of the young hero by temptations proper to his state in life. Sex and money are his greatest temptations, but he is finally converted through a character called Good Sense. *Lusty Juventus* also introduces two other elements to the interlude: argument and polemics. Suddenly, plays were becoming highly political, dealing with societal issues, not simply social satire, and the most significant issue both politically and religiously of this period in England was the Reformation.

The first important political allegory in the form of an interlude was called *Magnificence*, written in 1516, in which the protagonist is not frail and sinful Mankind, but a magnificent worldly prince. This worldly prince is surrounded by counselors, some who are good and some who are evil. He is drawn into extravagance and misgovernment by the advice of self-seekers and rescued, at last, from the ensuing problems by his true and trusted advisors. The characters are reminiscent of the old religious plays, but instead of having purely allegorical names, they are called True Advisor, False Advisor, Good Counselor, Bad Counselor. Among the first of the interludes dealing with the tumultuous state of religion and politics at the time was *Lord Governance and Lady Public-Weal* which was acted between 1526 and 1527 and dealt specifically with the reformation of the English Church. This was followed by the very famous *A Comedy Concerning the Three Laws of Nature, Moses, and Christ Corrupted by the Sodomites, Pharisees, and Papists*, written by John Bale in 1547 to promote the Reformation. *Lord Governance* was more of an informational interlude simply depicting the situation; it was not quite as slanted as Bale's "comedy."

Bale was a very interesting character. He was the first author to have domesticated in English drama the terms "comedy" and "tragedy." Remember in the Middle Ages we did not have comedy and tragedy, we had interludes, moralities, farces, cycle plays. Even though Christ was portrayed dying on the cross, certainly a tragic event, playwrights didn't refer to it as tragedy. Bale, who was a bishop of the Anglican Church, was also one of the earliest, if not *the* earliest writer in English, to reintroduce the Latin division of plays into five acts. In addition, he wrote a play called *King John* in the 1540s which was actually the first English historical play.

Bale's comedy—commonly referred to as *The Three Laws*—has a Senecan five-act structure: In Act 1, God the Father introduces three laws and assigns each a period of guardianship over mankind: the first law which has guardianship over nature is about Adam and Eve; the second law deals with Moses leading the Jews out of Egypt; and the third deals with Christ saving humankind through the sacrifice on the cross. Acts 2–4 deal with the subversion of each of these laws by the embodiment of evil which, for Bale, was characterized by the sodomites, Pharisees, and Papists. In Act 5, after these three groups attempted to destroy the three laws, God reappears as a kind of *deus ex machina*, to banish the evils and rehabilitate the laws.

The most famous of all the interlude writers was **John Heywood** (1497 – 1580) who broke from the established tradition of interludes to produce a style of drama that was satiric and amusing rather than being didactic. He was not interested in teaching but in entertaining an audience. He was employed as a singer and musician by Henry VIII, Edward VI, and Queen Mary. Significantly, he was a Catholic and managed to maintain a career in England during the Protestant Reformation. He married the daughter of a printer who just happened to have a theatre on his estate. All of Heywood's interludes were performed there and, subsequently, published by his brother in law. It is believed that after his plays were produced at the home of his father-in-law, they were presented at court by the King's Men, the eight professional players that Henry VIII had hired, who would become the direct antecedents of the professional companies of players that developed during the reigns of Elizabeth and James.

The simplest of Heywood's plays is called *Witty and Witless*, an 800-line rhyming couplet play dealing with the academic question of who is happier: he who has wit or he who is without? Ultimately the play determines that King Solomon was better off than the king's fool, and so it is decided that to have wit is better than being stupid! Another play called *The Play of Love*, published in 1533, depicts the Court of Love through the interrelationship between four characters: The Woman Beloved Not Loving, The Lover Not Beloved, The Lover Beloved, and the vice character—Neither Loved nor Lover. In this play, it is significant that the characters behave as individuals while maintaining remnants of the ticket names of old allegories. Also, in 1533, was published *The New and Very Merry Interlude of All Manner Weathers* (known as *The Interlude of the Weather*). This is unique in that it involves ten characters all of whom are on stage at the same time at the end of the play. Among the cast are Jupiter, a merchant, a forest ranger, and a laundress. This strange group of people is assembled by Jupiter who, seeking to settle the problem of meteorology, asks what kind of weather these different people would prefer so that he can ultimately provide it. Of course, no one is in agreement over the weather. The forest ranger wants rain for the trees to grow; the laundress wants sun for the clothes to dry; the merchant wants the weather to make the Thames flow properly so he can get his ships up and down on schedule. In the end, Jupiter decides to let the weather do as it pleases and function purely serendipitously—obviously an attempt on the playwright's part to explain why weather is so changeable.

Two of Heywood's most significant interludes are *The Play Called the Four Ps*, and *A Merry Play; Johann, Johann and Tyb His Wife*. The *Four Ps* is so called because the characters are The Palmer, the Pardoner, the Peddlar, and the 'Pothecary who meet and decide to combine their knavish talents and elect the leader among them. The choice of leadership is to be determined by which of the four can tell the biggest lie. After several reasonable attempts, the Palmer speaks and tells the biggest lie of all: "I have seen women—500,000 wives and widows, maids and married, and oft with them have long time tarried. But of all places I have been, of all the women that I have seen, I never saw nor knew in my conscience, any one woman out of patience." To which the apothecary replies, "By the mass that's a great lie." And that's the end of the patently chauvinistic play.

Heywood's interlude called *A Merry Play; Johann, Johann and Tyb His Wife* is based on a French comedy called *The Farce of Pernet Who Goes to the*

Wine and signals a significant departure from the abstractions of the morality plays and the moral interludes. In *Johann, Johann* we no longer have allegorical characters who represent ideologies, abstractions, or scientific concepts. Here, Johann is a husband. He doesn't represent Good Faith, Chastity or Justice, he is just himself. Tyb, his wife, is nothing but a shrewish wife, and, similarly, Johann is nothing but the cuckolding parish priest. The three characters may be standard types of the period, but they are, at least, flesh and blood.

At the beginning of the play, Husband Johann spends three pages talking about beating his wife, but when his wife walks in, he immediately becomes a coward. This situation becomes the source for another duper-duped plot. Johann starts the play saying "I'm going to show my wife who's the boss," but, by the end of the play, she is cuckolding him right before his eyes. This is the quintessential interlude—brief, few characters, dealing with a domestic situation (usually cuckolding), and full of obscenity or double-entendres. This is not the kind of play that would be performed for a large number of people outside a church. This is the kind of play performed in a lord's house or the *burghermeister's* dining room before an audience of select people. For this reason, we get the sense that the interludes by nature are a much more open-minded, cosmopolitan entertainment than the cycle plays or even the morality plays. This particular interlude has nothing to teach other than how a clever wife can cuckold her husband.

Despite its brevity, the play presents basic character types that emerge as individual people, and we get a kind of change in venue from the sly servant or vice character who is the person causing all the trouble in the play, since in *A Merry Play*, every one of the characters is the vice character. The husband causes trouble because he wants to teach his wife a lesson; the priest causes trouble because he's seducing the wife; the wife causes trouble because she enjoys seeing her husband become a cuckold. No longer are we reduced to a single idea in a play (i.e. there are good characters and then there's a bad character that foments the trouble). Now there is good and bad in everybody. Ultimately, we rejoice when the wife manages to dupe the husband because of his threats to beat her. Not only is he a threatening bully, he cannot even follow through on his threats. He's both a threatening bully and a fool and the audience enjoys seeing him get what he deserves.

Fastnachtsspiel

From the *mardi gras* entertainment held in the German provinces, we get an interlude-like species of comedy called the *fastnachtsspiel*. It is a carnival play closely aligned to the farce and interlude, dealing with everyday situations, family scenes (domestic comedy), peasant settings (lower classes), and courtroom trials. Usually in one act, about 400 lines, and written in a verse form that is called *knittelvers* (four beat lines of doggerel verse), these plays are spoken in declamatory fashion by three to six type characters: the shrewish wife (the wife who wants to cuckold her husband), the woebegone husband (husband to be cuckolded), and the cuckolding agent, usually a lawyer or priest which tells us how the playwrights of Middle Ages viewed lawyers and priests. Changes of scene in these plays were announced rather than presented (very much in the Shakespearean sense of "Now we are in the Forest of Arden"). The theme of these plays was the exposure of human folly, particularly of the lower classes, and the advancement of the good moral burghers (being the mayor and administration of the city). To perform the *fastnachtsspiel* required the permission of the local burghers, therefore it made good sense for playwrights to say that the local burghers are the good guys in the plays.

Among the most famous of these plays are *The Play of Rumpold and Maret*, and *Neidhart*, which broke the usual rule because it was 2000 lines long, depicting the exploits of Neidhart the prankster. In addition, there was a very popular play called *The Play of William Tell* produced in 1511. What is interesting is that the *fastnachtsspiel* went from being short and farce-like to adopting serious and tragic overtones as the play of *William Tell* demonstrated. It has farce-like sections with cuckolding wives and the like, but there is also the very serious story of the burgher telling William Tell to shoot an arrow off his son's head. Like *commedia dell'arte* scenarios, the *fastnachtsspiel* did not always have to be funny.

There are four great writers of the *fastnachtsspiel*. 1) Hans Rosenplut, the earliest of the *fastnachtsspiel* writers, who wrote plays that were moral and expressed a political point of view. The next is Hans Folz (1450-1515) who introduced a strong realistic quality to the form, adding specific details and a heavy dose of satire to his plays. **Hans Sachs** (1494-1576) in turn wrote four plays which are regarded as masterpieces of the genre. The first is called *The Calf Hatching* in which a farmer is shown sitting on a basket full of cheeses hoping to hatch out a cow. Needless to say, it is a futile exploit, but he sits there for quite some time, while everyone else in the play tries to remove him from the cheese. *The Wandering Scholar from Paradise* is a cuckolding play not unlike *A Merry Play*, in which a priest who is seducing a wife dresses up as the devil to escape the wrath of the husband who comes home unexpectedly. In this play the wife argues that the priest has to come to exorcise a devil in the bedroom, so the priest plays both the devil and himself. *The Pregnant Farmer* is a miser trying to hoard his money in a substantially inflated money belt, so he declares himself pregnant. His neighbors discover his secret and force him to give birth to gold at the end of the play. If not the most famous, the most grotesque of his plays is *The Hot Iron*, in which a husband carries home a hot iron in order to force his wife into a confession of her infidelities. Sachs is followed by a man named Jacob Ayrer (1540-1605) who is significant because he introduced the character of Hans Wurst into German drama. Ayrer also managed to borrow from English Elizabethan comedies and began a consolidation of folk elements and classical elements within the *fastnachtsspiel*.

Other Forms of Medieval Theatre
Important other forms of theatrical production during the Middle Ages included **Minstrelsy**, the practice of minstrels going around to the houses or castles of lords and ladies, singing songs and acting them out. We know that minstrels traveled through the medieval period singing dramatic monologues, sometimes singing antiphonal songs which were very much like the early tropes. Various types of **Folk Drama** were also popular. Sword dances required a fiddler or piper, a singer to tell the story, and dancers equipped with swords. Characters that emerged were called the *bessy* (a man dressed as a

woman), the *tommy* (a fool—in the Middle Ages a fool was always known by the name of Tom), and a hobby horse which would be dragged out on stage and swing back and forth. Another important element was a collection box that accompanied all the folk plays—performers always passed the hat. The sword dance developed out of the sacrificial rites signifying the end of winter, and always ended up with the lopping off of some kind of a head. It survives in two distinct forms: children's games and fairy tales (of which we know that *Sleeping Beauty* is an example). The sword dance itself can be traced back to a German ritual during Roman times. Tacitus tells us that "the game is invariably played in every assembly, the object of which is for naked youths to jump over and between sharp swords and threatening spear points. The purpose of this feat is to execute it gracefully. The reward lies in the fun of the risks taken and the pleasure of the spectator." The basic ritual always takes the form of a linked circular dance around a sacrificial victim and usually the sacrificial victim is either the *bessy* or the *tommy*, the drag queen or the fool. Because these were essentially celebrations of fertility, what happened at the end of the killing was the resurrection of the victim. Gradually plays emerged to provide the explanation for the sacrificial ritual. *Sleeping Beauty*, for example, depicts the prick of the spinning wheel, the victim going to sleep, and her subsequent resurrection. *Snow White* is another example where the victim dies and is also resurrected.

The *Maying* celebrations were the festivals of spring and early summer that were generally licentious and full of sex and debauchery. Because of the licentious quality of the festival the Church sought to control it, and by 1445, the May plays had become the responsibility of the Guild of the Holy Cross. Needless to say, the ribald quality of the plays was taken away and replaced by the stories of Robin and Marian, which makes sense because the May plays always had to do with a lord and lady romping in the forest. The first example of a Robin Hood play comes out of France and is called *The Play of Robin and Marian* by Adam de La Halle. The play presents Marian as a shepherdess and Robin as her rustic lover. Their romance is challenged by a traveling knight who outwits Robin but who is later outwitted by Marian herself. This kind of Robin Hood play is later developed into the Sheriff of Nottingham plays on the one hand, and the wild or green man of the forest plays on the other (following in the tradition of *Sir Gawain and the Green Knight*).

Mummers Plays are perhaps more significant than the two previous traditions. *Mumming* developed from the custom of people disguising themselves during celebrations, most properly during New Year's Day and Mardi Gras. Mummers disguised themselves not only to lose their individuality and personality so they could pretend to be someone else, they disguised themselves because they wanted to loot, pillage, and debauch. Gradually, the Church began to exert its authority over the mummers causing them to become less debauched and more socially acceptable, with their behavior controlled within strict guidelines. Mummers Plays always had a specific structure. There was always a presenter, usually Father Christmas, but occasionally a devil or an old woman (played by a man). The presenter then called out a champion, whose name was frequently St. George, or Prince George (here is the origin of the St. George and the Dragon plays). The champion was always followed by an antagonist—sometimes a Turkish knight, sometimes the king of Morocco, and sometimes a character called the Slasher. They fight, and the champion kills the antagonist. A doctor is then summoned to affect the resurrection of the dead body; characters enter with collection boxes, pass them amongst the audience, and perform a dance. These plays oftentimes are extended to include rivalry over a woman, over territory, or over a particular cause. Interestingly enough, during this period, Mummers Plays were often used to raise money.

Civic Pageantry

In addition to all of the plays mentioned above, actors in the Middle Ages did *industrials*. As you know, an industrial is a long, live-performance commercial for a product, and, during this period, civic pageants served as commercials for local and national history during events, such as the installation of a new mayor, or the arrival of visiting dignitaries. Along the parade route for the arrival of the mayor or visiting dignitary, various stations would be built depicting scenes of past accomplishments or some other kind of historical relationship to either of the people involved. The dramatization of historical subjects would demonstrate the theatrical potential of historical subjects and ultimately assist in the development of the History Play, during the English Renaissance. We have already seen how vice characters and the allegorical characters of the cycle and morality plays became realistic types in the interludes and farces. The use of historical subjects to support civic events would soon mature into full-length dramas designed to support the political predisposition of the reigning monarchs.

Another very significant form of civic pageantry during the Middle Ages was the public execution, a highly theatrical event, with the scaffold for the execution, the hang man or masked headsman with an axe, and the convicted felon, who, in front of an audience of onlookers, was always expected to give a farewell address. The head would actually roll off the scaffold and onto the spectators who would throw the head from one to another and splatter themselves with blood. Felons actually vied to be executed in public because they felt they would have a better chance of being remembered by posterity if they gave the audience a good show.

4. Theatre in the Italian Renaissance

The most obvious association of the Italian Renaissance was with the concept of humanism which demonstrated a reemphasis on the worth of earthly existence as opposed to the expectation of a heavenly reward. In addition, the Renaissance marked a revival of interest in classical antiquity. These two things, humanism and interest in antiquity, gave birth to a great curiosity and a spirit of adventure. God was still the master of all things, but blind faith was given over to experimentation and investigation. There are several reasons why Italy was the cradle of the Renaissance:

1) Location. Sticking out like a boot in the Mediterranean, Italy was well-suited for trade, and in a good position to absorb the cultures from the Eastern Empire ;

2) Trade produced wealth, and wealth usually permitted art to expand through patronage;

3) Skepticism surrounding the Church as a guide for daily life led to the search for alternatives. Up to this point, the papacy was the guide to morality. Once the papacy had been removed from Rome to Avignon, however, with two popes and various conspiracies—one pope trying to knock off the other—people started to make up their own minds about moral issues. If there are suddenly two papal arbiters of morality, each one claiming, "No, I'm

right. And I speak infallibly," people began to question, "Come on now. How can there be two infallible people who disagree?" So, the whole idea of organized religion began to be suspect. Many of the great Renaissance artists and sculptors, of course, would continue to create wonderful paintings of God and saints and other religious subjects, but they were all done on commission. The devotion of the medieval period had given way to patronage;

4) Since the Church argued that the pope was the legitimate successor of the Roman emperors, it wasn't a great leap to re-establish interest in the Roman Empire and its secular accomplishments. When trust in the papacy began to crumble in the present, people became interested in the achievements of the past;

5) With the disintegration of the supremacy of the papacy, various lords in the small city states of Italy began to vie for power and prestige. This is when the famous families emerge—the Estes, the Borgias, the Medicis—all vying with one another over who had the greatest wealth, the strongest army, and the best art;

6) Gradually, an appreciation of the individual and his accomplishments grew, so that the anonymous medieval craftsman gave way to the Renaissance writer who was highly touted and highly paid;

7) Bible stories and morality plays gave way to classical myths, historical stories, and then original ideas. With the exception of the interlude and farce during the medieval period (which was supposed to have been an evocation of what was going on in the town in that particular time, since everyone knew that somebody was being cuckolded somewhere), there wasn't an original play done in the entire medieval period. Everything was based on the Bible or catechism, preaching some kind of moral lesson.

Technically speaking, the Renaissance is said to have begun with **Dante** (1265-1321). His famous poem, *The Divine Comedy* (which comprises the *Inferno, Paradiso* and *Purgatorio*) was based on the work of the celebrated Latin poet Virgil. The Renaissance also began with **Giotto** (1266-1337), the painter who broke away from the stiff decorative style of medieval painting. Other seminal figures of the Renaissance included **Petrarch** (1304-1374) who patterned his writing after Cicero, Seneca, and Horace, and **Boccaccio** (1313-1375) who produced a collection of irreligious and lusty tales called the *Decameron*. Renaissance theatre developed out of the love and admiration for the classics, and, between the late fourteenth and early sixteenth centuries, several events occurred to emphasize this appreciation of Greek and Latin drama:

1) In 1429, twelve of Plautus's plays were rediscovered. They had been considered lost up to this point, though they were probably stored in the Eastern Empire and had never had been heard of in the West;

2) In 1453, Constantinople fell, which brought scholars and Greek manuscripts into Italy;

3) In 1465, the printing press was introduced to Italy. Why is this significant? Classical texts could be published and disseminated;

4) Between 1472 and 1518, all the known Greek and Roman plays were published;

5) From about 1485, Italian rulers began to patronize the drama. At first, they supported performances of plays in Latin, and then to reach more people, they sought to translate the Latin plays into Italian. This led to new plays based on the Latin models, very much like Roman playwrights writing plays on the Greek models.

Renaissance Comedy

The vernacular drama in Italy began with the production of *The Casket* in 1508, written by **Lodovico Ariosto** (1474–1533). It was produced at the Court of Ferrara where the Este family lived. The Este family had a passion for festivals and the theatre. As a result, early in the sixteenth century, Ferrara becomes the theatrical capital of Italy. When Ariosto joined the service of the Este family, a theatre was built in the ducal palace. He wrote five comedies, of which the most significant are: *The Casket* (1508), and *The Bawd* (1528). *The Bawd* is really quite a funny play. It is about a young man who has a passion for a young woman whose guardian doesn't want him to have anything to do with her. So, with the help of the madam of a whorehouse he devises a plan to see the lady: the master of the house, the guardian, is having a law dispute over barrels of wine. So that people will not steal his wine, every day he takes a barrel of wine and brings it to his house for safekeeping. Each day it's a different barrel. So, the young man hides in a barrel of wine every day and is taken to the house. He and the young lady meet then he departs. The next day another barrel goes in, and they meet and have fun. What's interesting about the play is we never see the young lady. We never see the love interest. The action of the play is more dependent on the machinations of getting the lover in and out of the house than the actual love-making. Ariosto had a great admiration for the Latin playwrights. He sought to imitate a classic elegance of style and form, and produced plots that are the stuff of Roman theatre: frustrated lovers, misunderstandings, injuries inflicted on covetous old men, and recognitions at the last moment. Lots of "Aha!" in Ariosto's plays. Unlike the typical classical imitations, however, Ariosto always set his plays in Italy, not in Rome. They were set in Ferrara or some other Italian city. What he tried to do was *vernacularize* them, not only in their locales but through a growing attention to characters and dialogue drawn from contemporary life.

Another important play in the development of vernacular comedy is called *La Calandria* written in 1513 by **Cardinal Bernardo Dovizi da Bibbiena** (1470–1520). Based on *Menaechmi* by Plautus, *La Calandria* involves twins of different sexes who get involved with one another in complicated intrigue and finally are set right at the end of the play. This play was followed by perhaps the early masterpiece of the period, *The Mandrake Root,* written between 1513 and 1520 by **Niccolo Machiavelli** (1469–1527). This is another cuckolding play involving an old husband and a young wife who is unfruitful and cold to him. Her lover appears as a doctor saying, "I know the cure for her sterility. She has to take the mandrake root potion." But here's the problem: the first person to sleep with her after she takes the potion will die. The husband, obviously, doesn't want to sleep with her immediately after the potion is taken, so, the doctor suggests that the old husband simply pick up the first man he sees on the street and have him sleep with the wife. He'll be sure to die and then she'll be cured. Of course, the doctor arranges to be the first man to be seen on the street. The husband takes him in and forces him to sleep with his wife, but the doctor doesn't die. The doctor argues that the root didn't take, so the process has to be repeated, and repeated, and repeated. It really was a very popular play.

The high-water mark in vernacular comedy appeared with **Pietro Aretino** (1492-1556) who was one of the great literary figures of the Renaissance. He was one of the richest men in Italy because he blackmailed popes and princes, wrote nasty articles about them and promulgated them. People would pay him money so that he would keep them out of the press. Aretino was an exceptionally resourceful man, and his writing was divided into three periods: Roman, Mantuan, and Venetian.

The Roman period extended from 1517 to 1525, when he moved in papal circles and developed a talent for political and clerical gossip which he published in acrimonious, violent satires called *Pasquinate*. The *Pasquinate* were pieces of parchment which he would attach to a statue in the city square; the statue was devoted to a war hero named Pasquin, so the diatribes written on the parchment were called *Pasquinate*. These were very scurrilous documents. In other words, in the morning, everybody would be gathered around the town square reading the latest gossip, such as: "Yes the cardinal so and so was seen seducing a nun last night," or "Two priests were seen *doing it* in the catacombs." Needless to say, these led to violent polemics and persecution, and Aretino left Rome after being stabbed by the henchmen of one of the people he wrote about. He didn't put his name on the *Pasquinate* but everyone knew they were his doing.

In Mantua, where he just spent one year—1526-1527—he wrote *The Stable Master* and continued to write personal satires as broad-sheet newspapers called *Avisi*. These were *The Star* and *The Enquirer* of the Renaissance. In addition, he started to predict the future, much in the manner of a modern astrologer. Among the things that he foretold was the sack of Rome by the Spanish in 1527, and it actually happened. After that, everything he said was taken very seriously because his predictions really came true. However, the Duke of Mantua felt uneasy about having Aretino in his household and urged him to leave.

In 1527, Aretino left for Venice where he stayed for the rest of his life. In Venice he began writing letters to political figures telling them that he knew everything that they had done, and he published the letters. It would be like our writing a letter to a congressman who, say, had seduced us or performed any kind of graft. And we're writing a letter saying, "I know you did this," and rather than just sending him the letter, we publish it in the *New York Times*.

Early in his career, Aretino was a nonjuring priest. He had taken holy orders but he didn't say mass. He was *in the know* among all classes of people. While he was in Venice, he also produced a series of dialogues which he developed from spying on convents and monasteries. For example, this is a dialogue between two nuns:

When they had pushed and squirmed and twisted for half an hour, the general suddenly cried "Now all at the same time and you, my dear boys, kiss me, and you too my dove." And the finale—the nuns on the bed with the two young men, the general and the sister he was mounted on together with the fellow at his behind and last of all the nun with her *murano* prodder, all agreed to do it together as choristers singing unison or more to the point, as blacksmiths hammer in time. So, each attended to his task. Some were whimpering, others were moaning loudly and listening to them you would have thought they were running the scales, their eyes popping out of their heads, their gasps and groans, their twistings and turnings, making the chests, wooden beds, chairs and chamber pots shake and rattle as if the house had been hit by earthquake.

This was the style of Aretino. Needless to say, this was a very popular book, particularly since everything else that he wrote about was fact-based, everyone assumed that this too was based on fact. In any event, there is little in contemporary literature that outdoes the sexual frankness of Aretino who earned enough from his writing—his blackmail—to become one of, if not the richest man in the town. As a result, he became a patron of artists and his house became a celebrated artist colony where young artists could go, be subsidized, and create. Aretino and his best friend, a painter named Titian controlled the artistic and literary life of Venice.

In his comic masterpiece, *The Marescalco* or *The Stable Master*, Aretino portrayed the whole gamut of social experience. The cast of characters evoked the typical Renaissance town on all levels of society. At the top was the Duke, and at the bottom was the stable boy, who, when you read the play, is on the bottom in more than one way. Aretino satirized the merchant class, especially the Italian view of the Duke. He satirized the school master or pedant, which would quickly become the *dottore* figure in the *commedia dell'arte*. What is significant about the drama of the Renaissance is that, since the power in the universe was that of the Duke or King, there is always a sense in these plays that they are playing up to some civic official. Even in *The Stable Master* one gets the sense that the lord of the particular city-state, even though he is a practical joker, is still the arbiter of goodness and badness in the play.

Moving away from Aretino, we come to a Venetian playwright named **Andrea Calmo** (1510–1571). He is significant because he experimented with the use of dialect in plays. He is often coupled with the playwright **Giovanni Alione** (1460–1521), who wrote rough and tumble farces without any classical influences. In terms of his vocabulary, Alione was kind of the David Mamet of his day. Very rough dialogue. No classical influences whatsoever. The person who blended the popular vernacular dialogue with classical form was a Paduan named **Angelo Beolco** (c.1496–1542), who was called "Il ruzzante." Ruzzante (from his rural comedy, *La Pastoral*), who spoke in vulgarities and obscenities, was the character that really put him on the map. Beolco completely abandoned the use of cultivated language—literate, sophisticated, well-turned phrases. Rather, he substituted dialect and elliptical language. Think Mamet as opposed to Shakespeare. In addition, he attempted to portray the society of common folk and peasants, dramatizing the fundamental feelings of love, jealousy, hunger, and the fear of war.

Along the lines of dialect comedy with classical influences come two anonymous plays. The first is called *The Deceived Ones* written in 1531 by a group called the *Intronati*. Lelia, the protagonist, to regain the love of Flaminio dresses as a man and enters his service. Flaminio, however, is in love with Isobella and uses Lelia as a messenger to his love. Suddenly Lelia's twin brother Caprisio appears and Caprisio and Lelia then get constantly sent to the wrong person. It's very evocative of Shakespeare's *Twelfth Night*. Another anonymous comedy written in 1540 called *The Venexiana* has a very unusual use of language. The protagonist, Julio, speaks in a high, learned Italian which means phrases which are highly articulate and possess a very well-cultivated structure. The women speak in a Venetian dialect, and the servants speak in a Bergamasque dialect. This is the first time when there were several different dialects in a play. Up to this point if there was the use of a dialect, it was always of one particular region: Bergamo, where the Harlequin figure in the *commedia dell'arte* usually comes from—a kind of "country" dialect. The Venetian patois, in contrast, was one that had a great many foreign words in it because Venice was a merchant city.

The Venexiana is a very chauvinist play. Julio, a youth, newly arrived in Venice, falls in love with a young married woman named Valeria. Simultaneously, he inspires a passion in Angela, described in the play as an elderly but *vigorous* widow. Angela takes him to her house and presents him with a golden chain after a vigorous night of love. Julio subsequently goes to meet Valeria but she, recognizing the golden chain of her rival, dismisses him. She says, "Now that you've been seducing the old lady, I don't want to have anything to do with you." Julio, spurned by the young lover, goes back to Angela but Valeria repents, and just as he's about to bed Angela again, Valeria's servant comes in and says, "Valeria wants you." He leaves Angela cold in bed and goes to the house of the younger married woman. The play ends with her taking him to her room and telling her maid not to let anyone disturb her, especially her husband. There is no moral sense in the play, no resolution about what happens to poor Angela, and no one saying what an unpleasant character Julio is for playing these women off one another. It just happens, rather like Mamet's *Sexual Perversity in Chicago*.

Literary comedy during the first half of the 16th century prompted a kind of cynical laughter at the Renaissance civilization without making any kind of moral judgment. The second half of the century was dominated by the Council of Trent (1545–1563). This was the influential council that solidified the rule of clerical celibacy, and intolerance toward other religions. This began to usher in a new spiritual climate with a heavy sense of morality. The last Renaissance comedy was written during this period by Dominican Friar, mathematician, philosopher, cosmologist, occultist, and poet **Giordano Bruno** (1548–1600), and called *The Candle Maker*.

Written in 1582, *The Candle Maker* is a euphemism in Italian for sodomist. The title character likes women but likes to sodomize boys as well. The play is in five acts with no fewer than three prologues that discuss the moral importance of the play. The plot revolves around a trick played by a sorcerer on Bonifacio, an elderly miser who takes pleasure from both women and young boys. Bonifacio had trusted the sorcerer to help him win the affection of a courtesan named Vittoria. Believing he's going to bed with Vittoria (the sorcerer told Bonifacio that if he takes a special potion, he will be invisible), he ends up lying in bed with his own wife. And of course, that's a sin worse than death itself when a husband is expecting someone new, and he ends up with his wife. The wife then takes her own revenge by running off with a lover. Imagine this scene: he runs into a bedroom, calls his wife by the name of Vittoria, and says how much he's been waiting for her. His wife lights a candle and says "How dare you speak that way to me." He says, "Oh my God. I didn't mean it, I was sleep walking, I was in a dream." She runs off with the first person she sees on the street corner. Ultimately, he gets his come-uppance, and the moral lesson of the play is that artifice is wrong: "thou shalt not lie with anyone other than your wife, and thou shalt not lie"—tell a falsehood. The play is essentially cynical, sarcastically dealing with a distasteful world. Bruno's cynicism and heretic philosophies (such as the transmigration of souls) did not make him popular with the Catholic Church. On Ash Wednesday, 17 February 1600, he was stripped naked, hung upside down, and burned at the stake. Thus ends our discussion of Renaissance Comedy.

Renaissance Tragedy

The first important vernacular tragedy during the Italian Renaissance was called *Sofonisba*, written in 1513 by **Gian Giorgio Trissino** (1478–1550).

This was an imitation of Euripides, which means he used a chorus of fifteen members and no act division. Trissino was deliberately trying to diffuse the Senecan influence in Renaissance tragedy. Why would Seneca be more influential than Euripides? He was writing in Latin, the language that ultimately turned into Italian, so the Italians felt much more of an association with him. In his attempt to go back to the Greeks rather than to Latin writers, Trissino began a controversy that was going to last for several years, one camp saying let's base our plays on the Greeks, the other saying let's base our plays on the Latins.

The most influential proponent of the other school, the Senecan/Latin school, was **Giovanni Battista Giraldi Cinthio** (1504-1573). He was the first to enunciate the neoclassical principle of the unities of action and of time, a concept he had developed in his book called *Concerning the Writing of Tragedies and Comedies*. It would be Julius Caesar Scaliger and Lodovico Castelvetro who would insist on the unity of place (which, in addition to Aristotle's insistence on a unity of action would comprise the "three neoclassical unities"). Cinthio's tragedies are *Orbecche* (1541) a revenge tragedy based on Seneca and the first tragedy in Italian to be produced. His plays show a rigorous adherence to what he called the Aristotelian unities—time and action (Aristotle didn't concern himself with location since many Greek tragedies do not have the unity of place. It was the Neoclassical critics trying to develop an idea of verisimilitude and truth who developed the concept of unity of place). Cinthio also wrote about the horrible and the monstrous in his plays. He loved blood and the depiction of severe torture. Interestingly, he wrote happy endings to his tragedies, creating the neoclassical notion that tragedy can end happily. He did this because he believed that audiences preferred a happy-ending. For example, he wrote a play called *Cleopatra* where Cleopatra changes her mind before the asp actually bites her. She loses her love but she keeps her life.

Another playwright closely allied to Cinthio was **Torquato Tasso** (1544-1595). Tasso was a diplomat, a poet, a lover, and considered by all his biographers to be certifiably insane (he spent seven years in an insane asylum).

His great tragedy called *King Torrismondo* written in 1587 shows a clearly abnormal mind. It deals with sadistic torture, murder, horror, decapitations, incest, and rape. In a way, *Torrismondo* makes Shakespeare's *Titus Andronicus* seem like a nursery rhyme. This one is truly filled with buckets of blood. The problem with the early Renaissance tragedies is that they are generally an arid imitation of the classics. By and large they are not as fun and lively as the comedies. The one exception, I believe, is *King Torrismondo*, written in exquisitely poetic phrases that both juxtapose and heighten the malicious brutality of the plot.

Pastoral Plays
Another genre of play emerged in the Italian Renaissance, and this was called the pastoral play, which was infinitely more popular than tragedy to Italian audiences. The pastoral drama draew its subject from classic bucolic poetry. Do you know what bucolic poetry is? Virgil, the classical poet, who wrote *The Aeneid*, also wrote a series of *eclogues*, which were pastoral poems dealing with shepherds and nymphs running about in the fields. The episode in Walt Disney's *Fantasia*, with the shepherds and the unicorns in the fields, and the thunderstorm and satyrs is what bucolic poetry is on the page. It's a highly escapist, anti-city, and "let's go lie in the fields and go back to the simple basics of life" kind of poetry. The characters portrayed in pastoral plays are mythological. The first pastoral drama was called *Orpheus* written in 1480. It established the format of the pastoral play:

   1) Five acts written in verse;

   2) Usually rhymed (one of these pastoral plays is over 4,000 lines long and has rhymed couplets throughout);

   3) It presents a mythical golden age—time when life was perceived as better;

   4) Love is highly idealized (no one ever actually has sex in the pastoral plays);

   5) Plays are set in well-manicured woods and streams;

6) Cast is always comprised of nymphs, shepherds, satyrs, and mythological beasts. Satyrs were horny woodland folk who generally scared the nymphs.

There were two significant examples of the pastoral play. Perhaps the most important was *Aminta* written in 1573 by Torquato Tasso. It is set in Arcadia in a mythical golden age, and deals with the love of a shepherd named Aminta for the girl who is called the "reluctant Sylvia." Aminta's friend counsels him to meet Sylvia while she is at the spring admiring herself, but before he can get there, a satyr appears and surprises Sylvia, causing her to run away, even though Aminta had arrived in time to prevent the satyr from raping her. Remember this is idealized love; we don't have any real sex in these plays. After Sylvia flees, her veil is found covered with blood near a group of wolves who are tearing apart a shapeless mass of meat. Having discovered her veil near the wolves, Aminta thinks they have eaten his girlfriend. Believing she's dead he decides to take his own life by jumping off a cliff. After he jumps, however, Sylvia reappears and laments the fate of her lover who has killed himself for nothing. However, like in *Indiana Jones*, the shepherd is saved by the branch of a bush growing on the side of the cliff. He climbs over the cliff, the two are reunited, and the play ends with a wedding.

The next most popular or significant pastoral was called *The Faithful Shepherd*. Composed by Giambattista Guarini, it was published in 1590 and produced eight years later in 1598. *The Faithful Shepherd* is also in five acts and, like *Aminta*, takes place in Arcadia. Amarilis, a nymph, is engaged to the youth Sylvio, but Amarilis loves (and is loved by) Mertillo (A is engaged to B but she loves C and C loves her back). However, Mertillo is loved by Corisca (A is engaged to B who loves C, but D loves C too). So, we have two triangles already in place. Corisca is envious. She connives to have Amarilis and Mertillo surprised in a grotto where they are meeting in secret. According to the laws of Arcadia, if two unmarried nymphs and shepherds are found together in a grotto, they have to die. Amarilis is condemned to death and Mertillo wants to die beside her. However, Marcano, Sylvio's father (remember the youth that Amarilis is supposed to marry) discovers, as he is about to condemn the two people to death, that Mertillo is his own son whom he had conceived on the wrong side of the sheets. Once Mertillo and Sylvio are discovered to be brothers, an oracle comes in saying that the god doesn't want the sacrifice of death. Mertillo and Amarilis marry and Sylvio finds love with a character named Dorinda who had only appeared to see the execution. Even though Dorinda does not appear in the play except at the execution, Sylvio looks at her and says, "I love you," and she replies, "Let's get married." Corisca, who caused all the trouble in the first place, decides to change her evil ways and becomes a nun at the end of the play. The play is in blank verse, not rhymed, and is 7000 lines long.

Renaissance Theatre Criticism
With its interest in classical antiquity, the Italian Renaissance emerges as the starting point of modern dramatic criticism. During the Roman Empire through the Middle Ages when Aristotle was virtually unknown, it was Horace's *Ars Poetica* that influenced dramatic construction and theory. But with the rebirth of interest in Greek antiquity and the assimilation of the Eastern Empire into the West, Aristotle's *Poetics* once again became the focus for dramatic criticism. The *Poetics* had been preserved in the Eastern Empire after the fall of the Western Roman Empire. It was first translated into Arabic in 935 A.D. by Abu-Baschar and abridged by Averröes in the 12th Century. This version was translated into Latin by a German monk named Hermann in the 13th Century, while the original was translated into Latin by a Spaniard, Mantinus of Tortosa, in the 14th Century. Giorgio Valla published yet another Latin translation in Venice in 1498, ten years before the original Greek text was reedited in 1508. Nearly thirty years later, in 1536, Allessandro di Pazzi published the Greek text with a simultaneous Latin translation. Robortello published the first Renaissance commentary of the *Poetics*, issued with a Latin translation in 1548, and Bernardo Segni published the first translation of Aristotle's work into Italian in 1549.

Among the earliest treatises on poetry in the Italian Renaissance were Vida's *De Arte Poetica* (1527) which, contrary to nearly every other work of a similar title, contained only tangential references to the drama. Daniello's

Poetica (1536), written in Italian, includes the first references to tragedy and comedy in the vernacular. Daniello's ideas are clearly derived from Horace and Aristotle. He argues that a play should not exceed five acts, nor comprise less; that four characters must not speak at once, but only two or three at most, while the others stand to one side, quietly listening. He advises against the introduction of the *deus ex machina* unless man cannot unravel the problem himself, and argues in favor of a chorus in Tragedy, and against it in Comedy, substituting music and dancing in its place. Most importantly, Daniello promotes *decorum* suggesting that certain acts should not be portrayed on the stage: the things that cannot be done are "the cruel deeds, the impossible, and the unseemly," such as Medea's murder of her children, the impossible premise of *The Birds*, or lascivious acts in comedies.

Explicationes (1550) by Maggi and Lombardi appeared as a commentary on the *Poetics* and emerged as pedantically diffuse, overly detailed, and more confusing than helpful. This work served to inculcate the misinterpretations and misconceptions of Aristotle's work that were to thrive throughout the Renaissance.

Giraldi Cinthio's *Discourse on Comedy and Tragedy* (1554) continued the tradition begun by Daniello and dealt specifically with the concept of theatrical "unities." **Minturno's** two books, *De Poeta* (1559) in Latin, and *Arte Poetica* (1564) in Italian, were the fullest discussions of dramatic theory to appear in the Renaissance up to that point. Although the influences of Horace and Aristotle are evident, Minturno does offer a great deal of original insight. He divides drama into three camps:

1) Serious and grave happenings dealing with members of high rank—Tragedy;

2) Middle strata of society, the common folk of the city or country, the farmer, the common soldier, the petty merchant—Comedy;

3) Humble persons, low-class and ludicrous, with all those who seem most fitted to provoke merriment—Satirical or Satyric Drama.

He suggests that plays should take between three and four hours in performance since the dramatic time should take place within a single day, and never beyond two.

Minturno also divides drama into six constituent parts:

1) Plot;

2) The manners or customs;

3) The sentiments expressed;

4) The words;

5) The singing;

6) The stage apparatus.

He divides the structure of Drama into four parts:

1) Prologues;

2) Discourses (speeches or scenes);

3) Choruses;

4) Exits.

He emphasizes Aristotle's theory of *catharsis* noting that "the memory of the grave misfortunes of others not only renders us more ready and willing to support our own, it makes us more ware in avoiding like ills... The physician who... extinguishes the poisonous spark of the malady that infects the body is no more powerful than the tragic poet who purges the mind through emotions aroused by his charming verses." Minturno notes that the function of Comedy is to teach and to entertain and that the comic poet awakes pleasant and human feelings in the spectator.

The Commentarii of Vettori, published in 1560, was yet another Latin treatment of this view, but **Julius Caesar Scaliger**'s *Seven Books of the Poetics*, published in 1561, was much more important. In this book, Scaliger, one of the most influential critics in the Renaissance, tried to reconcile Aristotle's *Poetics* not only with the teachings of Horace and the definitions of the Latin grammarians, but with the entire practice of Latin Tragedy, Comedy, and Epic Poetry. Scaliger argued that tragic language is serious (grave), polished, and removed from colloquial expression. In Tragedy, there is a pervading sense of doom, exiles, and deaths involving the fates of kings and princes whose affairs are global and dynastic (i.e., of the city, fortress, and military camp). Comedy, on the other hand, presents a confused state of affairs which is happily resolved at the end. The language of Comedy is that of everyday life.

Scaliger defines Tragedy as the imitation of the adversity of a distinguished man. It employs the form of action, presents a disastrous denouement, and is expressed in impressive metrical language. He notes that the events in a play "should be made to have such sequence and arrangement as to approach as near as possible the truth, for the play is not acted solely to strike the spectator with admiration or consternation—a fault of which Aeschylus was often guilty—but should also teach, move, and please." He argued for unity of place, cuts down the length of dramatic time to six or eight hours and suggests an artificial plot structure so that a multiplicity of incidents can be included within a sense of verisimilitude.

In 1570, **Castelvetro** produced his *Poetica*, a work of great significance as it developed the concept of unity of place suggested by Scaliger, leading to an endless discussion among Neoclassicists of Aristotle's "three unities." Castelvetro was the first to consider a play as limited and directly affected by stage representation. In his view, Tragedy could not realize its proper function without staging and acting. He argued that the time of the representation (performance) and the time of the dramatic action must be exactly coincidental, that the scene of the action must be constant, "not merely restricted to one city or house but indeed to that one place alone which could be visible to one person." In addition, Tragedy should have for its subject, an action that occurred within a very limited extent of place and time, not to exceed twelve hours.

Castelvetro promotes a unity of action based on unity of time and place and concludes, in agreement with Aristotle, that the plot of a play should necessarily comprise one action of one person, or two, interdependent upon one another. He suggests that both Tragedy and Comedy may have either a happy or unhappy ending, and that the solution of the plot ought to be brought about by the plot itself, following the nature of the situation (the rules of probability and verisimilitude). He also notes that the greatest source of the comic in drama is deception, either through folly, drunkenness, a dream, or delirium; or through ignorance of the arts, the sciences, and one's own powers; or through the novelty of the good being turned in a wrong direction or of the duper duped, or through deceits fashioned by man or by fortune. This is Castelvetro's analysis or definition of tragedy: "Tragedy ought to have for subject an action which happened in a very limited extent of place and in a very limited extent of time." For him the time of action is not to exceed the limit of twelve hours. This becomes a little complicated when you understand that Castelvetro also said that the time of representation and the time of dramatic action should be coincident. So, if the tragic action takes twelve hours, you're expected to sit in the theatre for twelve hours.

He also suggests that tragedy can have either a happy or unhappy ending: the joyful denouement of tragedy is formed by the cessation of impending death, sorrowful life, or loss of kingship to the hero or one dear to him. In other words, if the hero doesn't die, doesn't lose his kingdom, and doesn't experience any more unhappiness in life, that's the happy denouement of tragedy. He goes through the entire play expecting sorrow and then at the last moment it doesn't happen. The sad ending of tragedy, of course, is death, or the kingdom is destroyed or the protagonist doesn't get what he/she wants. Castelvetro also says that comedy can have a happy or unhappy ending. In other words, the long-lost children in comedy do not necessarily have to be found at the end of the play. He suggests that the solutions of the plot ought to be brought about by the plot itself based on probability and verisimilitude (this is trying to get away from the *deus ex machine*, an attempt to make the endings of plays as logical as possible). Finally, Castelvetro argues that the greatest source of the comic is deception, and the deception can be accomplished through a variety of ways: folly, drunkenness, and misunderstanding.

Other important works of dramatic criticism published during the Italian Renaissance are *De Arte Poetica* (1579) by Viperano, *Discorsi dell'Arte Poetica* (1587) by Tasso, *Poetica* (1588) by Denores, and *Discorsi Poetiei* (1600) by Summo. In addition, playwrights often wrote prefaces and prologues to their various plays advocating one or another of these critical ideas.

Renaissance Production

Though there was a rebirth of interest in classical drama in the 14th century, actual production of ancient works began in 1486, because in that year Vitruvius' *Treatise on Roman Architecture*, which was rediscovered in 1414, was published. Fourteen years later, by 1500, the *Treatise on Roman Architecture* had achieved the position of authority in all matters relating to theatrical staging. It became the *Poetics* for theatre practitioners. Because Vitruvius had not indicated any illustrations in his book but actually just wrote all the instructions down, he was as misunderstood as much as Aristotle. And what we have with Vitruvius, is the same kind of bowdlerizing that we get of Aristotle. The first two theorists to mistranslate, misinterpret, and misunderstand Vitruvius were Jocundus and Philander.

In 1486, when the Roman Academy wanted to stage a play, they looked to Vitruvius. What they found in his work was an attempt to create a stage and what they came up with was a platform stage backed up by a continuous facade, a kind of *skene* building, which was divided into a series of curtained openings, each representing the house of a different character. This would be called the Terence Stage because it was often used in connection with performances of Terence's plays. This format would quickly be modified by the development of perspective painting. The two men who systemized perspective painting were **Filippo Brunelleschi**, the architect, and **Masaccio**, a painter, around 1425. This was followed by *Della Pittura* by **Leon Battista Alberti** who produced a series of practical directions for making perspective drawings so that other painters could replicate the concept. The first certain example of a play to use perspective scenery is Ariosto's play, *The Casket* which played at Ferrara in 1508.

The book *Architettura* by **Sebastiano Serlio** published in 1545 best sums up 16th-century theatrical production. It is the first Renaissance theatre work on architecture to devote a section specifically to the theatre. It includes illustrations of tragic, comic, and satiric scenes, based on Vitruvius' descriptions. Serlio also tried to recreate the design for an entire auditorium. What he attempted to do was based upon the concept that theatres would be set up in existing buildings, (you don't just build a theatre from the ground up, you construct it in a dining hall); he tried to fit Vitruvius' semicircular auditorium (remember the Roman stage) into a rectangular space, with auditorium-like seating, and an open orchestra space completely devoted to the prince, duke, or lord of the manor and his honored guests. The stage would be raised to adjust to the eye level of the person sitting in the middle of the orchestra space (usually the prince or duke). The view of the prince would be the focal point of the perspective scenery; just looking straight ahead, he would be able to see perfectly everything on the stage.

Behind the acting area, which was a platform at the front part of the stage, there was a very steep rake to help perspective. Everything had to be played downstage. Actors did not walk into the scenery. In actuality, the effect was as if actors were playing in front of a huge perspective painting. This was the kind of theatre production put into practice at the Teatro Olimpico.

Serlio's settings were architectural and not meant to be changed. After his work was published, however, an increased interest in spectacle created a demand for settings that could be changed during performances. One of the first ways to change settings in the Renaissance was the use of *periaktoi*, first used in 1543. It was a man named **Nicola Sabattini**, in his *Manual for Constructing Theatrical Scenes and Machines*, who really offered the best solutions for changing settings. He mentions *periaktoi* but he also introduces other devices for changing angled wings. In this particular period, flat wing had given way to wings at an angle which provided a greater sense of depth. Sabattini suggested that angled wings should be placed one behind the other so that when you wanted to change the set, all you did was take this angled wing and put it in front of the next one, and so on. The first angled wing would function as a kind of false proscenium and every other wing would just keep moving up. Another suggestion for changing the set involved taking canvas paintings that were rolled up on the offstage side of the wings, stretching them across the wings and tying them down. Sabattini also noted that in the back of the set, there would be flat wings, and suggested that flat wings could be changed by putting grooves in the floor and having flat wings (called *shutters*) come from both offstage sides of the stage to meet in the middle. Sabattini also suggested other ways of changing scenery where the wings would be operated like pages in a book.

The real ease in changing scenery came when all angled wings would be replaced with flat wings. It was, in fact, **Guido Ubaldus** in his *Six Books of Perspective* published in 1600 that taught designers how to paint perspective on a flat surface. The man who first applied Ubaldus' theories to theatre was **Giovan Battista Alleotti** in 1606 at Ferrara. By using flat wings with the use of grooves in the floor and tracks in the ceiling, scenery could be changed fairly easily. Until 1650, following classical example, most scenes were exteriors. Borders were often used to mask machinery and the tracks in the ceiling, and painted as clouds or sky. This then divided theatre design into three elements:

1) Side wings;

2) Back shutters which were ultimately the side wings that joined in the middle; and

3) Overhead borders.

The next significant step was the development of the chariot and pole system which was invented by **Giacomo Torelli.** This was first used in Venice at the Teatro Novissimo between 1641 and 1645. All of the flats were on poles that extended through little grooves in the floor to cars or chariots on tracks underneath the stage. All these cars were controlled by a single winch so that all the scenery could be changed simultaneously. By the late 1600s, a box set using three sides and a ceiling was in practice in Italy. In **Fabrizio Carini Motta**'s *Construction of Theatres and Theatrical Machinery*, there is a description of a box set created by the chariot and pole system. The ceiling actually was a painted border that was painted to represent an actual ceiling; the creation of a realistic ceiling like we have in contemporary box sets was something that didn't happen until well into the 19th century.

In *Construction of Theatres and Theatrical Machinery*, Motta also describes theatre lighting equipment of the period which were, generally, candles and oil lamps. The auditorium was lit by chandeliers hung in front of the stage which lit the auditorium and part of the platform stage itself. Footlights were also used to light the downstage acting area creating smoke and haze. This is why actors and actresses could be in their dotage and still playing young characters because with makeup and all the smoke and haze, the audience could hardly tell the difference. What the audience experienced in addition to seeing the actors through a haze was great heat and oil fumes. Lights were mounted on stage and masked by overhead borders or side lamps (there were also reflectors made of tinsel behind the light to give it greater intensity). These lamps were usually mounted on poles or hung on battens, very much the same way we hang lights today. The only difference was, that since these were candles or oil lamps right behind a flat made of muslin and wood, the chance was great that it would catch on fire.

To darken the stage, there were three methods used:

1) Someone blew out the candles (this was a problem however because when you extinguish the lamp, it's rather difficult to light them);

(2) Open cylinders were suspended over the lamps looking a little bit like Campbell soup cans and depending on how far they were away from the light, they would brighten or darken the light;

(3) Lighting trees were designed to revolve, so sometimes the reflector would function as a kind of mask to the light—a kind of early dimmer.

Often special lighting effects were used as well. For example, in 1539 in Florence, a crystal sphere was filled with water and lit from behind with candles. The sphere was suspended on a wire: it rose at the beginning of the play, went to the height, and then set at the end of the play, creating a good sense of the passage of time. Oftentimes containers with tinted liquids were placed in front of the candles to create mood and to change the intensity of the light. What is really significant, too, is when they used the tinted liquids, it cut down on the lighting power, the candle power, so if they wanted to create a particular color, they would have to use more candles which made the risk of fire even greater.

Theorists argued that tragedy should be darker than comedy, and they said that the stage would appear brighter if contrasted with a darkened auditorium (although shutting off all the lights in the auditorium is ultimately a nineteenth century phenomenon. Through the eighteenth century, the people who went to the playhouse were as significant as the play. The people in the audience went to see one another). Theorists also suggested that lighting the stage from one side gives a more pleasing effect than lighting it from the front. They were not only concerned with the concept of lighting from the side to sculpture the actor or the scenery, they were interested in replicating the direction of the sun at various times of the day.

Until about 1637, scenic splendor was a court phenomenon, but in 1637 the Venetian public opera houses opened. This is very significant because scene design, perspective, and lighting techniques were suddenly opened to the public. Soon the theatrical innovations of the Italian Renaissance would be scattered throughout Europe.

There was some very interesting stage machinery developed in this period. There were trap doors. Designers arranged openings in the stage floor so that mountains could rise and sink in the set. For sea scenes, they simulated waves by having two people, one on each side of the stage, rippling a blue cloth. Other methods included moving up and down two-dimensional pieces shaped like waves, or rotating long spherical cylinders, one behind the other. There also were ships, whales, dolphins that were controlled from beneath the stage and even methods of making a whale spout liquid (you put talc, kind of like a talcum powder, and some kind of sparkle in a bag and you puff air through it underneath the whale's spout). They had collapsible walls and buildings. Sabattini suggested that if you want the entire set to collapse, please do it in the last scene of the play, because if not, you will have a hard time reconstructing the set for the next act. Evidently, they broke down pieces of the scenery and they hinged them together with pins. Then they took the pins out and replaced them with string threaded through the hinges, and kept the string taut. When it was time for the building to collapse, they would simply cut the string. The building wouldn't collapse immediately because the traveling of the string would make it collapse in a delayed, realistic manner. To set it up again they would have to rethread everything.

For sound effects they rolled cannon balls or stones through metal troughs to create thunder. To create wind they whirled thin strips of wood through the air. They only used the front curtain at the beginning of the play. It was never used to suggest act divisions.

The oldest surviving Renaissance theatre is the Teatro Olimpico, built by the Olympic Academy of Vicenza between 1580 and 1584. Designed by Andrea Palladio, it was an attempt to reconstruct the Roman theatre inside a pre-existing building. It held thirteen oval tiers of seating around a small orchestra. The stage was 70 feet long and 18 feet deep in front of a decorated façade, in which there were five openings, one on each side of the platform stage and three behind it. For the production of *Oedipus Rex* in 1585, which inaugurated the theatre, perspective scenes were added by **Vincenzo Scamozzi** behind each one of these exits. A drop curtain was used in production to reveal the action.

In 1586 appeared the Teatro de Medici, also called the Uffizi. It was designed by **Bernardo Buontalente** and was said to accommodate between 3,000 and 4,000 spectators. Built in Florence, it had a stage opening 66 feet wide and 46 feet high and was 180 feet deep. The auditorium was raked and was likely the first conscious rake in an auditorium. It was also possibly the first proscenium theatre built during the Renaissance. Built of wood within the Uffizi Palace, it was destroyed during the eighteenth century.

The Teatro Di Sabbionetta was built in 1588 by Vincenzo Scamozzi. Although it was designed as a court theatre, the actual theatre was a separate building created from the ground up next to the palace. Still following the semicircular plan, there was no proscenium arch, but it did have a single opening in the facade which functioned like a proscenium, and angled wings were used for sets. A relatively tiny auditorium, the Teatro Di Sabbionetta could accommodate only about 300 spectators.

The Teatro Farnese at Parma was built in 1618 by Giovanni Battista Aleotti and is the first surviving theatre structure with a proscenium arch. First used in 1628, the theatre could seat 3500 people. In addition to the main proscenium, there were two additional picture frames farther upstage to help with perspective. The auditorium was U-shaped, with a large open orchestra that could be used for dancing, or flooded for water spectacles. Unlike the other theatres of the period, the Farnese placed the royal seat above center rear entrance, rather than on the floor of the orchestra area.

The first record of a public theatre building in Venice appears in 1565. Little importance is attributed to this until 1637 when opera developed in popularity and a public opera house was erected. Because Venice was the only Italian city state ruled by a doge (elected official of the working class) rather than a duke or prince, it was appropriate that its theatres were designed as public buildings rather than as extensions of a palace or other buildings at court. These are some of the characteristics of public theatre buildings:

1) They were designed for all classes of people;

2) There were five balconies, each with 29 boxes. This was the typical set up for contemporary theatres. The first two balconies were for wealthier, noble audiences. The closer to the top, the cheaper the seats. The *parterre*, or pit, was the cheapest area open to anyone (since there were no seats here, it was essentially standing room only);

3) The Venetian opera house incorporated elements seen earlier: a proscenium arch, perspective scenery, seating divided into box, pit, and gallery, and the use of elaborate machinery. Because the theatre was public, allowing admission to anyone, the Venetian public opera house advanced the use of perspective scenery and proscenium arch throughout continental Europe.

Commedia dell'arte

The plays of which we have been speaking up to now were called *Commedia erudita* (or learned plays)—please note that the word, *commedia* means "play" not "comedy." Courts and schools used amateur actors for *Commedia erudita* while professional players, descended from the medieval jongleurs, troubadours, and mimes, were involved with *Commedia dell'arte* (artistic or skillful plays). The *Commedia dell'arte* was an improvisatory theatre, in which actors improvised dialogue and stage-business based on a scenario prepared in advance. Every company was governed (or directed) by an actor-manager and included 7–8 men and 3–4 women. Characters were divided into two groups: the normal characters, who were the young lovers, dressed in the most fashionable clothes of the day, and the *masks*, the various stock character types who wore masks and other identifiable emblems of their characters.

The masks were further divided into two groups. The older men included Pantalone (typically an avaricious father), the Dottore (a doctor of laws, or a medical doctor—usually a quack), and the Capitano (the *miles gloriosus* figure from ancient comedies and farces). The *zanni* (or servant characters) included Harlequin, Colombina, Franceschina, Brighella, Pulcinella, and a long list of comic types. Harlequin's costume began with colored patches sewn on to a doublet and leggings. By the seventeenth century, the patches became blue, red, and green triangles that were connected by yellow braid, and later in the century, the triangles became diamond-shaped.

Harlequin always had a wooden sword or slapstick. A slapstick is two pieces of wood, one hinged to the other so that, when you bring one piece down, air will pull the other up and cause it to make a great, laugh-inducing slap when it falls against the first piece (hence the association of slapstick with comedy). Harlequin was also an acrobat and a dancer, and he became known essentially for physical comedy in the *commedia dell'arte*. Usually Harlequin would make his entrance down (or climbing up) a rope ladder, walking a tightrope, or jumping off the second story of a building—the kind of thing that we associate with swash-buckling in a comic way.

Similar to Harlequin's swash-buckling personality was the Capitano who was not a *zanni* but lived more or less in the world of the Pantalone or the Dottore characters. Remember the *zanni* are always the servant characters. The Capitano had a wooden sword, a long nose, a fierce mustache (and we're talking about one of those that may curl on the end), and a feathered hat. When Spain invaded Italy, the Capitano acquired a Spanish accent and a swagger to make fun of Spain, and the earliest Capitanos had a flesh-colored mask. Because all of these characters, with the exception of the lovers, had masks, they also had a distinguishing gesture or bodily pose. The lovers, however, generally speaking, were more characterized by what they said, in either very florid or very crisp dialogue.

In addition to the comic aspect of the mask, the *zanni* all specialized in what we call *lazzi*, which were set pieces of comic business. Everyone, including Pantalone and Dottore, had a kind of lazzi but it was generally characteristic of the servant characters. Some of them were famous like the fly *lazzo* where Harlequin catches a fly, tears off its wings, and eats the fly. He pantomimes the fly flying around his head, he finally catches it, but the fly attempts to get out of his hand. He holds it tight, pulls off the wing, and finally chews it, causing a kind of comic revulsion at the end. It was very interesting that the rules of the *commedia* emphasized that an actor was not permitted talk while another actor was talking, but that didn't necessarily prevent him/her from upstaging the speaking actor by performing other business.

In an improvised play, it was absolutely necessary that everyone onstage knew when an actor was going to finish speaking. As a result, every actor had a particular gesture to indicate he had come to the end of his improvised dialogue. That way the next actor to speak would not jump in on the dialogue, or walk off the stage before another actor has stopped speaking because psychologically when a character enters or leaves a scene, the audience's focus goes to the new character or the one that is leaving. The entire improvisational aspect kept the actors on their toes and they tried very hard to make sure that no one would step on other people's cues or lines. On the other hand, if a *zanni* had a good piece of business and the audience really enjoyed it, the character could do the same piece of business multiple times in the piece. Harlequin could catch half-dozen flies at various points in the play. Another kind of *lazzi* was what was called the slap *lazzi*. Generally speaking, if someone slaps you in the face, you have a mouth full of water, so that as soon as you're slapped, you spew forth this flood of water on the person who slapped you. There was also the whoopi-cushion *lazzi*. Someone sits down and you hear "Bffff" with the rest of the people on stage smelling and holding their noses. There was nothing subtle about this. Whoopi-cushions were made by taking an animal bladder (or a leather pouch) and inflating it with air. The dentist *lazzi* was also significant because the character of the Dottore acting as a dentist would use blacksmith or carpenter's tools. He would go after the character with a toothache with huge pounding instruments and generally take out every tooth but the aching one. There was a waiter *lazzi* where before meals were cooked, waiters would roll in the mud and then wipe the plates and utensils on their pants which were muddy, getting the plates all muddy and then wipe them with towels that are greasy to clean them up and then put food on top of them.

Perhaps Harlequin's most famous *lazzi* was the suicide *lazzi* where he complains that his beloved Colombina is going to marry a farmer. He attempts to hang himself, but decides that that would be kind of difficult mostly because it would hurt. Then he decides to stab himself but he realizes that he doesn't like the sight of blood. Next, he attempts to strangle himself by holding his nose and putting his hand in front of his mouth so that no air can escape; but, after holding his breath as long as possible, he farts out air and decides that method won't work either. Finally, he tickles himself to death and he dies laughing.

In a book called *The Dialogue of Stage Affairs* written in 1565, the acting style of the *commedia* is described. It suggests that the actors required a certain amount of realism in their performances. In addition, because of the masks and the specific costuming for every character, certain gestures took on specific significance. For example, "clutching" meant terror. Clutching your own clothes or someone else's arm meant you were terrified. If you dance in the midst of the scene, that meant you were extremely happy. Dancing always meant joy. Pulling your cap back on your head would mean despair, and tearing a handkerchief with your teeth meant grief. Finally, the theatre managers, the actor managers who organized the *commedia* troupes, checked audibility, pronunciation, speed, and pitch of the dialogue to resemble familiar talk.

Before the *commedia* companies moved to permanent auditoriums, they carried a permanent stage structure which was housed in a cart with curtained drops, costumes, and props. They were the literal "bus-and-truck" company. The stages were built high so the platform was on the eyelevel of a man standing, and the height of the platform allowed for a storage space beneath the stage which was hidden by curtains. The platform itself was divided into two unequal sections by a drop curtain. There was more space in front of the drop curtain for an acting area than behind it, which was used as a changing space. There were two or three slits cut into the curtain which served for entrances or exits, and often on this drop, there were perspective paintings of streets. There were usually two ladders placed on either side of the platform from the stage to the ground, and if he/she did not have to make an exit, a *commedia* performer would just recline on the ladder when he/she wasn't talking. This also suggests that the *commedia* performers may have gone into the audience for certain effects, very much like the medieval devils would go into the audience and scare them.

There are 700 extant commedia scenarios. Most of them are in Italian. 50 of them have been translated—these are the 50 scenarios printed in 1611 by Flaminio Scala. All of the scenarios are in 3 acts, and 40 of the 50 that he wrote were comedies. Of the remainder, 9 were called fantasies with a great number of nymphs, and one is a tragedy called *The Mad Princess*, of which the following is a summary. The prince of Morocco, in love with the princess of Portugal goes to the court of the king, her father, and after confessing his love for her, elopes with her. Going by sea they pass the Straits of Gibraltar and arrive at the Kingdom of Thessa. Here they stay the night, feeling safe, and are welcomed by the princess of Thessa in the name of the king her father, and invited to enter the city and stay at the palace. Immediately seeing the beauty of the princess of Thessa, the prince of Morocco falls in love with her and, designing to marry her (remember he has just eloped), slips away from the princess of Portugal. He is overtaken by the prince of Portugal, her brother, subsequently killed, and his severed head is presented to the princess by her brother. This is a *commedia dell'arte* scenario. A man's severed head is brought on stage! After lamenting a long time over the head of her lover (an improvised speech very much like Salome with the head of John the Baptist), the princess goes mad and drowns herself in the sea. Since the prince of Morocco was killed by the prince of Portugal, the prince of Portugal is subsequently killed by the king of Morocco, who is killed in turn by his people for murdering the prince. The king of Thessa, gives to his only daughter a gift of a noble youth for a page. The noble youth is so handsome that the king says if he were a woman, he himself would fall in love with him (a little homoeroticism for good measure). However, the princess of Thessa is of such a passionate nature, she falls passionately in love with the page and they begin to make love more and more frequently. The king learns of this, and jealous of his daughter's affection for the boy, he has the page murdered, his heart pulled out from his breast, and sent to the princess. The princess weeps bitterly, puts the heart in a cup of poison and drinks the liquid, whereupon the king of Thessa, in despair, kills himself and the play is over. Also present in the play are Pedrolino, Boratino, and Harlequin who enter as servant characters and do comic business in the middle of the tragedy. This tragic scenario certainly reminds us that Shakespeare has inherited from this tradition the ability to combine real tragedy with comic relief. Just imagine the Harlequin character performing his *lazzi* within this severely tragic action. Severed heads, hearts pulled out and served in cups of poison suggest *Titus Andronicus* or some of the bloodier tragedies of the Jacobean era. All of this action happens in three acts, and there is an indication before the scenario that the play can be done either on land or water. Because the *commedia dell'arte* players travel with a temporary stage, they can set it up next to a manmade lake or a real lake (remember the princess has to drown herself).

At any rate, what is very significant is that the *commedia* scenarios are always based on love intrigue, and rabid passion (even in the comedies when people are in love, they're in love to excess); high and noble sentiments (in other words idealized outlooks); and everyone has the prescribed comic turns, usually in tandem with a Harlequin figure.

It's easy to see as a result of the influence the *commedia dell'arte* had on literature in England and the rest of Europe. There is a *commedia* scenario called *The Tragic Events* which deals with a young man wanting to marry a young lady from a different family and their parents don't want them to get married so they run away and elope. Because their parents discover them, she has to take a potion that makes her appear dead so that she can't marry somebody else (in this case it's the Harlequin character that brings her the potion rather than a priest character). The young man whom she married returns in time to see her wake up, and the two families discovering how far the two children would go to get married, relent and allow them to live happily ever after. Shakespeare's *Romeo and Juliet* was a whole-cloth borrowing from the *commedia dell'arte* scenario *The Tragic Events*.

5. Sexuality in English Renaissance Drama

In 16th century England, the hierarchal society that emerged from the Middle Ages was ruled by men in which children were to be well disciplined and women were expected to be submissive. The phallus was supreme, and ambivalence about the objects of its pleasure was permissible. Sodomy by teachers and those in power was tacitly accepted. Headmasters, who in 1541 and 1594 were found to have sexually enjoyed male pupils, survived with their reputations scarcely tarnished. Throughout the 16th and 17th centuries it was customary at Oxford and Cambridge for a tutor—always a bachelor in his twenties—to share his bedroom with several undergraduates between the ages of 15 and 18. Though satirists like John Marston wrote against the practice, parents either didn't realize or didn't mind the temptations of such sleeping arrangements, since the policy was not changed until the early 18th century.

Confusion and disorder were certainly the catchwords for the playwright Nicholas Udall, who was dismissed as headmaster of Eton School, charged with committing an "unnatural crime" and brought before the Privy Council on 14 March 1641. The criminal report reads:

> Nic. Udall, Schoolmaster of Eton, being sent for as suspect

of a robbery lately committed at Eton by Thomas Cheyney, John Hoorde, Scholars of sad school, and . . . Gregory, servant to the said schoolmaster, and having certain interrogatories ministered unto him, touching the said fact and other felonious trespasses, whereof he was suspected, did confess that he did commit buggery with the said Cheney, sundry times heretofore, and of late the sixth day of this present month in the present yere at London, whereupon he was committed to the Marshalsea

Imprisoned in the Marshalsea since he was found guilty of theft, Udall responded to his crimes by writing a letter of remorse that is somewhat vague about the charges but full of contrition and promises to sin no more. He tries to create the impression that the offense, however serious, is a folly of youth and that he is capable of reformation. The letter which abounds in Latin and Greek phrases certainly achieved the desired effect for it is from this point on that Udall's career as a scholar and playwright really ascends. By 1555, the year before his death, he was appointed headmaster of Westminster School.

The fact that Udall was not condemned for buggery has given scholars a great deal of trouble. Some, like his biographer William Edgerton even suggest that the word buggery was a copyist error in the transcript and should read burglary instead. Rather, Udall's case suggests a paradigm of same-sex love in England in the 16th century. So long as the sin does not touch the political arena [i.e. the practitioner is in favor with the court or is in a neutral position], or the male adult population [who could raise issues at court], it is not regarded as all that reprehensible. On the other hand, Matthew Heaton, a clergyman in East Grinstead, was prosecuted at Sussex in 1580 because he had a same sex relationship with a boy in the parish and James Slater, a barber, was prosecuted in Hertfordshire in 1607 for having a homosexual liaison with his neighbor's son. It seems clear that the social dysfunction of same-sex relationships was more significant to the Elizabethans than the act itself.

Same-sex treatment of servants by their masters was common, and when these relationships were considered scandalous, it was something beyond the simply sex act that outraged society. Francis Bacon, for example, was in the habit of having sexual relations with his male servants. The fact that he was financially overly generous to them was the subject of public concern. Similarly, Mervyn Touchet, the second Earl of Castlehaven, was charged with sodomy in 1631. At his trial, however, the fact that he was a Catholic and persuaded Henry Skipwith, one of his lovers, to impregnate his wife and daughter to gain access to their inheritance merited all the attention.

Perhaps the most specialized form of same-sex relationships existed in connection with the London playhouse. Philip Stubbes in his *Anatamie of Abuses*, published in 1583, condemns the theatre as a nest of debauchery:

> . . .but marke the flocking and running to theatres and curtens, daylie and hourely, night and daye, tyme and tyde, to see playes and enterludes; where such wanton gestures, such bawdie speaches, such laughing and fleering, such kissing and bussing, such clipping and culling, such winkinge and glancinge of wanton eyes, and the like is used as is wonderfull to behold. Than, these goodly pageants being done, every mate sorts to his mate, every one brings another homeward of their way verye freendly, and in their secret conclaves (covertly) they play the Sodomits, or worse. And these be the fruits of playes and enterludes for the most part. [139]

He goes on to condemn certain styles of clothing as "but a visour, or cloke, to hide their sodometrie withall" [29], and tending to make the body "weake, tender, and infirme, not able to abide such sharp conflicts and blustering stormes as many other people" [55].

Edward Guilpin in a work entitled *Skialetheia* describes a sodomite as someone "who is at every play and every night sups with his ingles" and we learn that actors, especially young actors, were referred to as "ingles" since the stage was considered the haven of homosexual behavior. John Florio in his Italian/English dictionary of 1611 gives this definition: "Catamito: one hired to sin against nature, an ingle, a ganymede." Evidently then, actors were not only considered homosexual, but homosexual prostitutes as well. This is not difficult to accept given the status of performer in the Tudor period. A proclamation of 1544 alleged that by attending plays, young men were provoked to the "unjust wasting and consuming of their master's goods, the neglecting and omission of their faithful service and due obedience" and the "loss and hindrance of God's honour and the divine service." A statute of 1572 called all "common players in interludes and minstrels" not patronized by royalty vagabonds, and in 1616 John Downame referred to these masterless vagrants as a "promiscuous generation, who are all of kin, and yet know no kindred, no house or home, no law but their sensual lust."

Even performers under the aegis of noblemen, and therefore not legally vagrants, were not highly regarded. When Stephen Gosson's *School of Abuse* was written in 1579, it came as no surprise that he should suggest that the theatre was little more than an ante-room for the brothel. Even worse, Gosson demonstrated that the theatre "effeminates the mind. Playwrights design effeminate gesture to ravish the sence, and wanton speache to whette desire to inordinate lust." Looking at plays, Gosson believed, made men lose their male identity. As Laura Levine points out, this would only make sense if it implied a homosexual response on the part of the spectator. Her suggestion is reinforced by the fact that, earlier in his book, Gosson associated dramatic poets with hyenas, one of the beasts which symbolized same-sex relationships in the Middle Ages. It seems clear, therefore, that Gosson took the homosexual response for granted.

As the playhouses had a male-dominated hierarchy, like the patriarchal family, its exploitation of same-sex behavior was tacitly accepted even though writers like Anthony Munday inveyed against the training up of boys for the playhouse:

> When I see . . . yong boies, inclining of themselves vnto wickednes, trained vp in filthie speeches, vnnatural and vnseemelie gestures, to be brought vp by these Schoolemasters in bawderie,

and in idleness, I cannot chuse but with teares and griefe of hart lament. O with what delight can the father behold his sonne bereft of shamefastnes, & trained vp to impudencie! How proane are they of themselues, and apt to receiuve instruction of their lewde teachers, which are the Schoolemaisters of sinne in the schoole of abuse! what do they teach them, I praie you, but to foster mischiefe in their youth, that it maie alwaies abide in them, and in their age bring them sooner vnto hel?

As in the case of their response to same-sex activity in the school system, parents either were unaware of the sexual dangers of the playhouse or did not especially concern themselves with them. Evidence indicates that indentured servitude to a theatrical company of adults or children was not only considered desirable by parents but often the parents took pains to seek out an actor or choirmaster to teach their sons the art of performing. Actually, parents were more concerned with the possibility of their sons' being kidnapped by one or another theatrical company when they needed actors than they were about possible same-sex activity.

Each of the boys in an adult company would have been apprenticed to an individual actor from whom he would learn his trade. Sometimes a child actor from one of the schoolboys' companies might transfer into an adult company, but as a youth he would still be under the aegis of an older actor who would provide for his lodging, meals, and instruction in the finer art of playing female characters on stage. As members of an adult troupe, the boys would lead a strange and somewhat precarious existence. They would be trained to dress up daily as fascinating young women and parade before the rowdy populace in the "Suburbs of Sin" where the public playhouses offered plentiful opportunities for the pickpocket and thief.

In many commentaries on the Elizabethan Theatre, scholars suggest that playwrights such as Shakespeare put his heroines in boy's clothes to help his "boy-girls along with their difficult task of impersonation." Baker suggests that far from making this easier for the boys, "such transformation makes their task infinitely more difficult. What it amounts to is asking a boy to impersonate a girl with no artificial aids whatsoever: no skirts to swish, no long hair, no jewelry or accessories, such as fans or handkerchiefs, to flirt with, but merely sheer acting skill."

Jan Kott in *Shakespeare Our Contemporary* argues that Shakespeare was aiming at the triple ambiguity by cross-dressing the boy-girls in his plays. Gaveston's description of a court masque in Marlowe's *Edward II* gives us an insight into the accepted patterns of ambivalence, at least on the aristocratic level:

> Like sylvan nymphs my pages shall be clad
> Sometime, a lovely boy in Diane's shape
> With hair that gilds the water as it glides
> Crownets of pearl about his naked arms
> And in his sportful hands an olive tree
> To hide those parts which men delight to see.
> [I. i. 61-65]

One wonders which parts men delighted in seeing: Diane's or the little pageboy's, coyly cupped in his hand [Baker 88]. In *Twelfth Night*, Shakespeare adds to the ambivalence when Orsino says to Viola, disguised as Cesario:

> Dear lad believe it;
> For they shall yet belie thy happy years,
> That say thou art a man: Diana's lip
> Is not more smooth and rubious; thy small pipe
> Is as the maiden's organ, shrill of sound
> And all is semblative a woman's part.
> [I.iv. 29-34]

Clearly the audience must take this triple ambiguity into consideration when dealing with these plays. Possibly it was the very androgynous nature of the roles that constantly straddled the lines of masculine/feminine behavior that was the source of entertainment. Playwrights certainly used the device over and over again. We must note here the assertion by James Laver in his *Dress: How and Why Fashions in Men's and Women's Clothes Have Changed during the Past Two Hundred Years* that "the ideal of any 'emancipated' age is necessarily a creature half man and half woman" [30-31].

The boy actor had a special affinity with those women who offended Elizabethan and Jacobean society by wearing men's clothes. Condemned by opponents of the stage for dressing as a woman, his disguising that woman as a man made him doubly a monster and exceedingly dangerous. James I, for example, saw women in breeches as a threat to respectable society and instructed the clergy in 1620 to "inveigh vehemently against the insolence of our women, and theyre wearing of brode brimed hats, pointed dublets, theyre hayre cut short or shorne, and some of them stilettos or poniards, and such other trinckets of like moment."

Dramatists took advantage of the dangerous ambivalence to reinforce the feminism of the masculine woman and confuse the all-important distinction between genders. Critics have suggested that they claimed that all clothes are a form of disguise and that theatrical disguise could be a revelation of truth about men and women. Secondly, they suggested that society's modes of identifying sexual behavior required from its members not moral stability but good acting. If femininity and masculinity have any permanent validity, it exists independent of the clothes society ordains for men and women to wear. Thirdly, a woman in disguise—or the masculine woman in breeches—is changed by her male dress only because it allows her to express a part of her nature which society suppresses. Disguise makes a woman not a man but a more developed woman.

The boy actor enabled the dramatist to discover a femininity that transcends the limits of costume and encouraged him to observe the similarities between the sexes; i.e., how boyish behavior is an element of feminine behavior and vice versa. This disarrangement of the accepted gender hierarchy is central to theatrical activity and suggests, in part, why symbols of "unnatural" behavior hound the stage. The Tudor/Elizabethan theatre was essentially an androgynous activity where gender roles were constantly in flux. To the society at large, the playhouse was always controversial. In both the public and private arena, plays acted as forums for political discussions and personal satire. Shapiro suggests that claiming the protection of "saturnalian misrule and juvenile impunity, the children's companies were free to insult their audiences. That same-sex activity might be involved on or off-stage was certainly not the greatest concern of the public, and records show that the crown forbade performances only for matters of religion, politics, or public safety. There are no records whatsoever of a play being cancelled or censored because of same-sex activity.

Today it is generally accepted that the boys assumed flirtatious, feminine attitudes both on stage and off, and were often drawn into same-sex relationships with the older actors. Not unexpectedly, however, many of the child actors married upon reaching adulthood.

Theatrical Transvestism

Not unlike the society of Attic Greece, the Tudor English court had a fascination with boys. Whether it was a fondness for boys' singing voices or a cult fascination in pubescence, boys were a preferred entertainment at court as early as the 14th century when the openly homosexual Edward II ruled. The statutes and curricula of English grammar schools in the 16th century provided for some type of dramatic production by the students in order to acquaint them with Latin dialogue and to train them in correct and elegant diction, poise, appropriate gesture, and graceful movement. Basically, performing plays would assist in teaching "eloquence," the art of effective public speaking. In England, schoolboys not only performed Plautus and Terence, but also neo-classical plays in Latin_ and in the vernacular, such as Nicholas Udall's *Ralph Roister Doister*.

As a result of their academic purpose and the Tudor fascination with boys, children's company plays are full of long passages of lyricism, either in actual songs or flowery language, and heavy doses of transvestitism. The transvestitism did not stop with the practice of boys playing both men's and women's roles but extended to conscious cross-dressing within the dramatic action of the plays themselves. Richard Farrant's *The Wars of Cyprus* [1576-80], which takes place in Assyria, turns on a female character dressing as her page, and the page dressing as his mistress. While in female dress, a prisoner of the Assyrians, Libanio the page is courted by Dinon, the captain guarding him/her:

Dinon: Love—may I call thee love? (Lo, she doth not frown;
  Her looks give warrant for that Epithet)—
  For thee I'll kneel before Antiochus ...
[917–919]

The page appears to waver, affecting girlish coyness before finally capitulating:

Libanio: If I should yield, your honor might suppose
  That dignity and wealth should conquer me;
  Therefore, I blush to say I love my Lord.
[933-935]

The suitor's triumph is short lived for when he falls asleep, lulled by the sweetness of his beloved's voice, the page murders him and soliloquizes in terms that underscore the ambiguous sexuality of his situation:

Sleep Dinon! Then, Libanio, draw thy sword
And manly thrust it in his slumbering heart!
... Now Dinon dies! Alas, I cannot strike!
This habit makes me over pitiful.
Remember that thou art Libanio—
No woman, but a bondman! Strike and fly! [944-957]

Later when the page arrives at the Persian camp, still in woman's clothes, he is taken for a "shameless strumpet and lascivious trull [1052]" yet when he identifies himself is called "precedent of manly fortitude [1128]" though he is still in drag [Shapiro 165]. This gender ambivalence will be a significant factor in the examination of the plays of John Lyly, the vice-master of the Boys of St. Paul's.

John Lyly

John Lyly was likely born between 9 October 1553 and 8 October 1554 since he was 17 when he matriculated at Magdalen College, Oxford on 8 October 1571. At school, he was reputed to be a madcap wit "long since dedicated to a dissolute and desperate licentiousness." Contemporaries refer to his "horning, gaming, fooling and knaving" and there is no reason to suppose that he did not engage in the accepted same-sex activities of typical English schoolboys. In 1574, the year before he took his M.A. at Oxford, he wrote a conventional love letter in Latin to Lord Burleigh, the Lord Treasurer which alludes to some specific favors shown him by the Lord and proceeds to ask for others. Whether the relationship was merely a schoolboy fantasy or had run its course, John Lyly did not get the financial assistance he sought from the Lord Treasurer and he left Oxford for Cambridge where he took an M.A. in 1579. His first literary work, a novel, *Euphues: the Anatomy of Wit* appeared the previous year and was a huge success. The sequel, *Euphues and his England* appeared in 1580. In both books, there is open, passionate homoeroticism in an attempt to recreate, perhaps even to recapture the classic ideal of friendship.

In *The Anatomy of Wit*, Lyly describes the beginning of the friendship between Euphues and Philautus, the development of which constitutes the basic plot of the book. At one point a woman comes between the men but she is quickly dispatched. Women are cursed as being inconstant, and Euphues bemoans the temporary loss of Philautus with whom he is soon reunited.

Continuing the friendship, *Euphues and His England* resembles vaguely the story of Damon and Pythias. Here, Euphues and Philautus travel to England where the latter is overwhelmed by the beauty of English women.

The fairest of these, Camilla, manages to come between the men, but after many unsuccessful attempts to woo and win her, Philautus realizes the injury he has done his friend Euphues. Their eventual reunion, after Philautus swears off Camilla forever, is portrayed as follows: "Many embracings there were, much strange courtesy, many pretty glances; being almost for the time but strangers because of their long absence. But growing to questioning one with another, they fell to the whole discourse of Philautus's love who left out nothing ... And thus, they with long talking waxed weary; where I leave them, not willing to talk any longer but to sleep their fills till morning."

As in Greek novels and legend, Euphues advises Philautus to woo another woman, whom he does and successfully. Euphues then returns home leaving his friend in England. Again, Lyly portrays the departure in a romantic way. What Lyly created was an elegant depiction of male bonding that was socially acceptable purely on the basis of mutual affection rather than mutual interest and, as such, parallels pastoral poetry of the period.

After a successful foray into the realm of literature, Lyly was once again in the service of Lord Burleigh, as a letter written in the summer of 1582 indicates. Later he tried his hand at the theatre and became the vice-master of the choirboys at St. Paul's sometime around 1585. As assistant to Thomas Giles, the choirmaster, Lyly's job was essentially to coach the boys in the acting of plays to be performed before Queen Elizabeth. All of Lyly's plays except for *The Woman in the Moon* were performed by the Children of St. Paul's. Besides writing plays and coaching the boys in acting them, Lyly occasionally took part himself.

Each of Lyly's plays trades in some kind of homoeroticism. In the earliest work, *Campaspe*, the relationship of Alexander the Great and his lover, Hephestion is portrayed. When Alexander falls in love with his Theban slave girl, Campaspe, Hephestion chides him for falling in love with a woman and argues, like Cicero, against romantic love and suggests that Alexander is behaving in an unmanly fashion because of his love for a woman. Seeking support from Diogenes, Alexander asks him what he dislikes chiefly in a woman:

Diogenes: One thing.
Alexander: What?
Diogenes: That she is a woman. [V.iv.]

Such apparent misogyny is reflected in Hephaestion's objections to Alexander's love for Campaspe:

> Campaspe, ah shame, a maid forsooth unknown, unnoble, and who can tell whether immodest, whose eyes are framed by art to enamor and whose heart was made by nature to enchant. Aye, she is beautiful; yea, but not therefore chaste. Aye, but she is comely in all parts of the body; yea, but she may be crooked in some part of the mind. [II.ii.]

When the relationship does not succeed, Alexander returns to Hephestion in defeat saying:

> It were a shame Alexander should desire to command the world, if he could not command himself. I can better bear my hand with my heart, then I could with mine eye. And good Hephestion, when all the world is won, and every country is thine and mine, either find me out another to subdue, or on my word I will fall in love. [V.iv.]

As in Greek romances, a same sex-relationship can exist simultaneously with an opposite sex attraction.

In *Sapho and Phao*, Pandion, a scholar, speaks against female companionship when his companion, Trachinus starts praising the virtues of Sapho:

Trachinus: We will thither strait.
Pandion: I would I might return strait.
Trachinus: Why, there you may live still.

Pandion: But not still.

Trachinus: Howe like you the Ladies, are they not passing faire?

Pandion: Mine eye drinketh neither the color of wine nor women.

Trachinus: Yet I am sure that in judgment you are not so severe, but that you can be content to allow of beauty by day or by night.

Pandio: When I behold beauty before the sun, his beams dim beauty. . . [I.ii]

Two servant characters, critical of the behavior of their masters, make reference to the Greek sexual courtship of beardless youths, and an exchange between Vulcan and Venus introduces the ubiquitous reference to Jupiter and Ganymede [IV.iv] and the play ends with Phao cursing the love of women:

> Phao: I must now fall from love to labor, and endeavor with mine oar to get a fare, not with my pen, to write a fancy. Loves are but smokes, which vanish in the seeing, and yet hurt whiles they are seen. . .Range rather over the world, forswear affections, entreat for death. [V.iii]

The misogynistic message continues in *Endimion*, where the love between the title character and his friend Eumenides is put to the test when Endimion falls in love with Cynthia. Tellus, also in love with Endimion, gets a witch to put a spell on him, and Eumenides discovers how to cure his friend. He is to look into a well and read what he sees written at the bottom. The message is: "Ask one for all, and but one thing at all." Eumenides does not know whether to ask for Endimion, his friend, or Semele, a woman in whom he is interested. Geron, an old man offers him advice:

> Eumenides, release Endimion, for all things (friendship excepted) are subject to fortune: Loue is but an eye-worm, which only tickleth the head's hopes and wishes: friendship the image of eternity. . of all things the most rare. . .

Eumenides decides in favor of his Endimion for: "Mistresses are in every place, and as common as Hares in Atho, Bees in Hybla, fouls in the air: but friends to be found, are like the Phoenix in Arabia, but one, or the Philadelphi in Arays, never above two. I will have Endimion" [III.iv. 111–147]. Once again, we find an idealized friendship between two "gentle" men completely lacking in selfishness taking place in an idealized pastoral locale.

Continuing Lyly's anti-feminine bias, in *Midas*, the page Petulus utters the usual anti-feminine remark to another page, Licio:

> Licio: Thou servest Mellacrites, and I his daughter, which is the better man?
> Petulus: Masculine gender is more worthy then the feminine .... [I.ii. 1-5]

The two go on to create schoolboy sexual innuendo when a woman appears by referring to beastial iconography:

> Petulus: We are no chase (pretty mops,) for Deer we are not, neither red nor fallow, because we are Bachelors and have not *cornu copia*, we wand heads: Hares we cannot be, because they are male one yere, and the next female, we change not our sex: Badgers we are not, for our legs are one as long as another: and who will take us to be Foxes, that stand so near a goose, and bite not? [I. ii. 101–107]

Here the put down of women is accompanied by a corruption of one of the biblical "authorities" on same-sex behavior, the apocryphal Epistle of Barnabas. Eating of the hare was supposed to lead to pederasty and eating of the hyena, which changed its sex every year, led to sexual license. The reference to the badger [or weasel] is evocative of the medieval prohibition against oral sex. The weasel was chosen as icon for this since the female of the species allegedly carried her young in her mouth. The references to fox and goose are fairly obvious animal metaphors of male and female sexuality. Notice, however, that in this case, the speaker wonders who will consider them male since they do not take advantage of the female. Here, once again, we have the anti-feminine stance that pervades Lyly's plays.

Mother Bombie, the most "realistic" of Lyly's comedies, trades on a typically physical relationship between page boys:

Dromio: Hem quam opportune, looke if he drop not ful in my dish.

Risio: Lupus in fabula, Dromio imbrace me, hugge me, kisse my hand, I must make thee fortunate.

Dromio: Risio, honor me, kneele down to mee, kiss my feet, I must make thee blessed. [II.i. 11-15]

This short sequence can be interpreted in a number of ways. On the literal level, it represents two servants attempting to con one another according to the contemporary "gentlemanly" model. It demonstrates evidence of a bedfellow relationship potentially homoerotic. On the other hand, since the characters involved are of the lower classes, it represents the two characters' burlesquing the external manifestations of gentlemen's idealized friendships and ridiculing the sexual potential of such activity. On yet another related level, the boys are satirizing the activities of upward mobility: to be made fortunate, one must kiss and hug; to be beatified, one must kneel and kiss another's feet. What would appear highly honorable and affectionate behavior for the upper classes becomes crass when aped by the lower classes and the mercenary motive which would have been viewed as reprehensible in the activities of a gentleman is, in the behavior of a servant, accepted as funny. Servants are expected to be physical, clever, crass and ridiculous.

The Woman in the Moone which turns on Jupiter's lust for Pandora, portrays Juno chastising her roving, over-sexed husband with a statement implying same-sex lust, and in an attempt to entrap her other suitors, Stesias, another of Pandora's many admirers, dresses up as a woman. The trick results in a kind of unwitting homosexual eros when the unsuspecting suitors try to make love to him:

Melos: And I my love! here she will meet me streight.
See where she comes, hiding her blushing eyes.
Enter STESIAS in womans apparell.
Melos: My love Pandora for whose sake I liue!
  Hide not thy beauty which is Melos sunne.
  Here is none but vs two, lay aside thy vale.
Stesias: Here is Syesias; Melos you are deceaud.
He striketh MELOS.
[IV. i. 260–265]

Earlier in the scene, Stesias in his masculine attire attacks Learchus, yet another suitor to Pandora. That he should follow this by a transvestite attack suggests a double violation of nature: a man dressed as a woman, and a woman physically attacking a man. This unnatural behavior is joined by Melos's homosexual courtship, which, in practical terms was the rule for acting companies before women appeared on stage. Whether the boy in disguise was playing a female character or a male character disguised as a woman, what the audience saw was love-making by individuals of the same sex.

Tranvestitism, or rather sexual-transformation, is significant to both *Loves Metamorphosis* and *The Maydes Metamorphosis*. In the first play, Protea, a farmer's daughter, first escapes indentured servitude by being transformed into the body of a fisherman and then rescues her lover Petulius disguised as the warrior Ulysses. Clearly such gender ambivalence would present no problem to an Elizabethan audience since spectators were accustomed to watching boys parade as girls on stage. In The Maydes Metamorphosis, the shepherdess Eurymine is transformed into a man by Apollo. An astrologer reveals to prince Ascanio (in love with Eurymine, but believing her dead) that the object of his love is a man:

Aramanthus: By proofe of learned principles I finde,
The manner of your love's against all kinde.
And not to feed ye with vncertaine joy,

Whom you affect so much, is but a Boy.
Ascanio: I love a Boy?
Aramanthus: The love that troubles you, is for no maide. [IV. i. 141–147]

Eurymine enters and Ascanio recognizes his beloved even though she is in the form of a boy, and he proceeds to express love to her/him without concern for gender.

Ascanio: ... love me but so
as fair Eurymine lou'd Ascanio.
Eurymine: That loue's denied vnto my present kinde.
Ascanio: I kindly shewes, vnkinde I doo thee finde:
I see thou art as constant as the winde.
Eurymine: Doth kind allow a man to loue a man?
Ascanio: Why art not thou Eurymine?
Eurymine: In name, but not in sexe.
Ascanio: What then?
Eurymine: A man. [V. i. 39–43]

Ultimately, Apollo changes Eurymine back into a woman and the play ends happily. Lyly does make a significant inference in the transformation relationship: it is the person not the gender that one is in love with. It is an outside pressure, either societal, ethno-religious, or simple custom that presents difficulties. Gender ambivalence is central to these early plays written for boys' companies. Not only does it create a convention of boys playing women's roles, but it also indulges the fascination for the androgynous nature of the boy, which was central to Greek culture.

Perhaps the most homoerotic of Lyly's plays is *Gallathea*, taken in part from the fourth book of Ovid's Metamorphoses. The comic matter [again given to servant boy characters] was derived from contemporary almanacs and Lyly's use of alchemical words comes from Reginal Scot's *Discouerie of*

Witchcraft (Bk. xiv. ch.1) published in 1584. The play was performed at court on New Year's Day 1586 or 1587.

Lyly uses fewer emblems of same-sex relationships in this play than any of the others. He does, however, make use of the association between sorcery and homosexuality by introducing the alchemical subplot and the overt use of the word "mystery" in terms of alchemical knowledge as well as the pun on its plural in IV.iv. in the following exchange between Gallathea and Phillida:

Gallathea: I accept that name, for divers before have called me mistress.
Phillida: For what cause?
Gallathea: Nay, there lie the mysteress.

Lyly's contemporaries who understood the punning sense of mystery to represent both prostitution and same sexual intercourse, could certainly have derived several associations from the exchange. Also, the reference to Venus' birth from the sea [V. i.] is a suggestion of her function as homo-platonic icon since she was born of the testes of Uranus after Chronus tossed them into the water. The concept of what is unnatural, in reference to the sacrifice of a virgin to Neptune, is also co-referential to the unnaturalness of the transvestitism in the play, and the unnaturalness of the father to deny his civic duty while he is being natural in his paternal affection. This confutation of what is and what is not natural, at the heart of the play is central to the romantic association between Gallathea and Phillida.

Gallathea is especially plentiful in ambivalent transvestite associations. Both Gallathea and Phillida appear and court one another as boys [II. i; II. iv, v; III. ii; IV. iv; V. iii], Cupid disguises himself as a woman [II. ii], and the Nymphs of Diana crave not to be women [III. i]. That these ambivalences lead to real homoerotic affection is clear from Phillida's monologue at the end of Act Four: "Poor Phillida, what shouldst think of thyself, that lovest one that I fear me is as thyself is; and may it not be that her father practiced the same deceit with her that my father hath with me, and knowing her to be fair, feared she should be unfortunate? If it be so, Phillida, how desperate is thy case; if it be not, how doubtful. For if she be a maiden there is no hope of my love; if a boy, a hazard. I will after him or her, and lead a melancholy life, that look for a miserable death" [IV. iv.]. The problem is developed significantly in the happy denouement when Neptune calls off the sacrificial tradition. Returned to their true form, Gallathea and Phillida are full of concern:

> Gallathea: I had thought the habit agreeable with the sex, and so burned in the fire of mine own fancies.
> Phillida: I had thought that in the attire of a boy, there could not have lodged the body of a virgin, and so was inflamed with a sweet desire, which now I find a sour deceit.
> Diana: Now things falling out as they do, you must leave these fond, fond affections. Nature will have it so; necessity must.
> Gallathea: I will never love any but Phillida. Her love is engraven in my heart with her eyes.
> Phillida: Nor I any but Gallathea, whose faith is imprinted in my thoughts by her words. [V.iii]

The transformation of one of the girls into a boy raises interesting social issues in the play. Tyterus refuses to have Gallathea changed into a boy as it will affect his son's inheritance. Rather, he asks that Phillida be changed into a man since she "loves always to play with men." Venus decides to surprise everyone:

> Venus: Then let us depart. Neither of them shall know whose lot it shall be till they come to the church door. One shall be. Doth it suffice?
> Phillida: And satisfy us both, doth it not, Gallathea?
> Gallathea: Yes, Phillida. [V. iii.]

This ambivalence on the part of each girl renders them both, in a very real way, androgynous. In the play the characters are man/woman in love with man/woman and are symbolically co-referential to the actual androgyny of the boy actors playing women playing boys.

"Kit" Marlowe and the Devil

As the author of the first history play that was indeed a well-crafted tragedy, *Edward II*, Christopher Marlowe had a profound effect on Shakespeare and later dramatists. Not only did Marlowe create the "mighty line" of tragedy in his development of the use of blank verse, he fostered the art of designing tragedies on a grand scale, displaying unity of action, unity of character, and unity of interest. Before his day plays had been pageants or versified tales, arranged in scenes, and enlivened with clowning. To his contemporaries, however, this acknowledged theatrical innovator was also regarded as a homosexual, heretic, and traitor. To many, his assassination at the hands of Ingram Frizer on 29 May 1593, when Marlowe was only 29 years old, was an example of divine justice.

Christopher Marlowe, or Marlin, or Marley, as it variously appears in his school records, was born in Canterbury on 6 February 1564, two months before Shakespeare, to John Marlowe, a shoemaker and his wife Catherine Arthur. In 1578 when he was 14 years old, he entered King's School in Canterbury. The school day began at six a.m. and ended 13 hours later at 7 at night when the day boys went home and the boarders slept in the rooms of one or another of the masters.

The most learned of Marlowe's masters at King's School was John Gresshop, a bachelor, who owned a remarkable library and who, like most schoolmasters, lodged boys at his abode. Though it is difficult to assess the influence that Gresshop might have had over Marlowe, the simple access that the young scholar might have had to the master's books would certainly have inspired the classical bent to his drama and poetry. Following his matriculation at King's School, Marlowe entered Cambridge on scholarship in 1581 with the intention of pursuing Holy Orders. There he resided in a tiny room converted from a store-house with a single roommate whom he referred to as a "sweet chamber fellow."

During this period at Cambridge though separate beds were allowed for scholars above the age of 14, it was the custom for three or more to share a room. The idea of separate beds in such cases is even unclear as the founder of Christ's College said: "Our wish is that the Fellows sleep two and two, but the scholars four and four, and that no one have alone a single chamber for his proper use, unless per-chance it be some Doctor, to whom, on account of the dignity of his degree, we grant the possession of a separate chamber."

At Cambridge, Marlowe came under the influence of Francis Kett, the college steward, who spouted many unorthodox ideas regarding Christianity and who was later burned as a heretic in 1589. Marlowe's subsequent embracing of unorthodox views was not unusual as the university was the hotbed of seditious doctrines, and by 1587 when he matriculated as an MA from Cambridge, he was no longer interested in Holy Orders. In fact, it was rumored that Marlowe converted a fellow student named Thomas Fyneaux to atheism just before he graduated. Evidently Marlowe and Fyneaux would go into the woods at midnight and pray on their knees that the Devil would appear to them. One wonders, given the association of homosexuality and the worship of the devil, how much of this activity was encoded. On the other hand, as same-sex activity was generally tolerated among schoolboys, one wonders how far a-field Marlowe wandered to cause people to gossip about his activities.

The rumors about Marlowe did not cease with the Fyneaux incident. During the period of his aspiring to the master's degree, college records disclose frequent absences. He may have become a confidential agent or messenger working for the government, but rumors indicated that the "atheistic, Catholic, theatre-haunting post-graduate student had slipped overseas." That Marlowe was an atheist or Catholic could not be directly proven but evidence of his interest in the theatre appeared quickly upon graduation when the Lord Admiral's Men produced his *Tamburlaine the Great* in 1587. The following year, a rival playwright, Robert Greene added to the rumor of atheism with an epistle to *Perimedes the Blacke-Smith*: "I could not make my verses yet upon the stage in tragical buskins... daring God out of heaven with that Atheist *Tamburlaine*." He continues to speak of "mad and scoffing poets that have prophetical spirits as bred of Merlin's race." The reference to the magician is an unmistakable pun on Marlowe's name. The pun on Merlin is also fortuitous as Marlowe produced *Doctor Faustus* for the Lord Admiral's Men in the same year.

We know Marlowe was in London as of 1589 because police records indicate his involvement in a brawl. There he enjoyed the acquaintance of Lord Strange, Sir Walter Raleigh, and the Earl of Northumberland and had a more than casual association with Thomas Walsingham, then a bachelor, to whom the publisher Edward Blunt addressed a preface to Marlowe's great poem *Hero and Leander*: "in his lifetime you bestowed many kind favors entertaining the parts of reckoning and worthy which you found in him with good countenance and liberal affection." That Marlowe and Walsingham were for a time inseparable (Marlowe was visiting to keep away from the plague) suggests that they were in fact lovers.

While in London, Marlowe penned *The Jew of Malta* for Lord Strange's Company in 1589 and began expressing his unorthodox beliefs in a number of circles. A government spy, Richard Cholmley, confessed to being converted to atheism by Marlowe saying: "one Marlowe was able to shew more sound reason for atheism than any divine in England is able to give to prove divinity, and that Marlowe told him that he had read the atheist lecture to Sir Walter Raleigh and others." Another government agent, Richard Baines informed against Marlowe accusing him of:

1) Attacks upon the Old Testament, especially in connection with chronology;

2) Jeering at Christ in regard to the Virgin Birth, his divinity, and alleging homosexuality;

3) Criticizing the method of the Christian religion; and

4) Trying to secure converts to atheism.

Some of Marlowe's alleged remarks to Baines might be considered sacrilegious even today:

Moses was but a juggler and one Heriots, being Sir W. Raleigh's man can do more than he.
That the first beginning of religion was only to keep men in awe.
That all they that love not tobacco and boys were fools.
Holy Communion would have been much better being administered in a tobacco pipe.
That all protestants are hypocritical asses.
St. John the Evangelist was bedfellow to Christ and leaned always in his bosom.
The Women of Samaria were whores.
Christ used John the Evangelist as the sinners of Sodoma.

In May 1593, a manuscript alleged to contain heresy was found among Thomas Kyd's papers. Kyd who had been living with Marlowe since 1591 (in rooms, some say were provided by Thomas Walsingham, who was also Kyd's patron). Kyd immediately attacked Marlowe as the author of the heretical manuscript and later wrote two letters condemning him, saying that he was "intemperate and of a cruel heart." Marlowe was accused of "monstrous opinions" and of bringing "soden pryvie iniuries to men" and persuading "men of qualiti to go unto the King of Scots, whether I heare Royden is gon and where . . . he told me when I saw him last he meant to be." Whether the King of Scots was a meeting place for heretics, homosexuals, or roarers is not known. The fact, however, that it was used to indicate the monstrosity of Marlowe's personality, and to vindicate Kyd's innocence, suggests its notoriety.

By the time Kyd had finished his two letters, Marlowe was dead. Robert Greene writing *A Groat's worth of Wit bought with a Million of Repentance* in the fall of 1592 contained a charge of atheism against Christopher Marlowe and the playwright was arrested on 20 May 1593. This would have come as no surprise to him as one of his schoolmates, John Greenwood had been burned for heresy in April and Richard Cholmley, whom Marlowe was supposed to have converted to atheism, was being sought for arrest.

At ten o'clock Wednesday morning, 30 May 1593, Christopher Marlowe, Ingram Frizer, Nicholas Skeres, and Robert Poley had met at Eleanor Bull's tavern. We know little about Skeres, but the three others all had close relations with the Walsinghams, and it is possible that both Marlowe and Frizer were among Thomas Walsingham's lovers. Eleanor Bull's tavern was a noted "half brothel half public house" frequented by "bawdy serving men," "lewd loves," and "harlots." The room in which the men met had a bed, a table, and a bench. After dinner, Marlowe and Frizer evidently got into some dispute over the price of the meal and began to fight. Marlowe pulled Frizer's dagger from its sheath and menaced his opponent, who trying to get the weapon out of Marlowe's hand ended up stabbing Marlowe just above the right eye. The blade went into two inches into Marlowe's head and he died almost immediately. *Edward II* was played by the Earl of Pembroke's Men before 1594 in repertory with *The Taming of the Shrew*, *The True Tragedy of Richard Duke of York*, and *Titus Andronicus*, all plays in which Shakespeare is said to have a hand. Though the great actor Edward Alleyn of the Lord Admiral's Company had played Marlowe's great heroes up to this point, Tamburlaine, Barabas, and Faustus, there is no record of his ever having performed the role of Edward.

Ganymede in Arden

Marlowe's first play, *The Tragedy of Dido, Queen of Carthage*, produced by the Children of Her Majesty's Chapel after his death is essentially a translation of the 4th book of Virgil's *Aeneid* to which Marlowe added a few original scenes that are of influence both to the development of contemporary sexual ambivalence in the theatre generally and to Shakespeare specifically.

Marlowe opens his play with Jupiter "dallying with Idalian Ganymede," petting his cupbearer back into good humor by the praise of a thousand petty things. The god Mercury [Hermes] lies asleep beside them. The tone is one of lush, classical homoerotic fantasy—of the sort that one might find in a painting of Correggio. By 1598 when scholars believe Shakespeare produced *As You Like It*, the playwright's debt to the dead Marlowe was obvious to Elizabethans. Not only does Shakespeare emphasize the Ganymede allusion with Rosalind's disguised name, he apotheosizes the dead Marlowe as the dead shepherd mentioned by Phoebe in III.v.82-83 by quoting a line from Marlowe's own great poem, *Hero and Leander* which had finally been published in 1598:

> Dead shepherd, now I find thy saw of might:
> "Whoever loved that loved not at first sight?"

Shakespeare was born on 23 April 1564 to John Shakespeare and Mary Arden. He received a grammar school education at the King's New School of Stratford-upon-Avon for which he expresses a dislike in his plays. In *Much Ado*, for example, schoolboys are overjoyed with finding birds' nests but not with their lessons. In *2 Henry VI*, Lord Say is condemned to immediate beheading for having committed such enormities as "most traitorously corrupted the youth of the realm in erecting a grammar school." In the second of Jaques' Seven Ages of Man, he depicts:

> the whining school-boy, with his satchel
> And shining morning face, creeping like snail
> Unwillingly to school.

Shakespeare was probably a day student traveling to school at 5:30 a.m. morning to be in his place for prayers at 6 a.m. Lessons continued through the day until six at night with a short recess for breakfast and a lunch break from 11 to 1 o'clock. Students went to school six days a week all year long with short breaks at Christmas, Easter, and other Ecclesiastical holy days. In *Merry Wives of Windsor*, Shakespeare satirizes his Latin schoolmaster Thomas Jenkins in the person of the bumbling parson, Sir Hugh Evans:

Evans: Well, what is your accusative case?

William: Accusativo, hinc.

Evans: I pray you, have your remembrance, child. Accusativo, hung, hang, hog.

Quickly: "Hang-hog" is Latin for bacon, I warrant you.

Evans: Leave your prabbles, woman. What is the focative case, William?

William: O—vocativo, O.

Evans: Remember, William: focative is caret.

Quickly: And that's a good root.

Evans: Woman, forbear.

Mrs. Page: Peace.

Evans: What is your genitive case plural, William?

William: Genitive case?

Evans: Ay.

William: Genitive: horum, harum, horum.

Quickly: Vengeance of Jenny's case; fie on her! Never name her, child, if she be a whore.

Whatever Shakespeare's experience was in grammar school, it was short-lived as he was withdrawn at the age of 15 or thereabouts to assist his father in his leather-working trade. Scholars cite the technical language in reference to hides and animal parts in his plays as evidence of his years working for his father. By the time he was 18 years old, Shakespeare had married Anne Hathaway, some years his senior and several months pregnant. A Church register account (27 November 1582) of another Anne (Whateley) to whom Shakespeare was engaged invites much speculation on what William was doing on his nights off from the tanner's shop.

Six months after Shakespeare was married, his daughter Susanna was born. The twins, Hamnet and Judith were born in 1585. In the years between 1585 and 1592 we hear of Shakespeare robbing deer in Sir Thomas Lacy's park and of several celebrated drinking exploits. Certain scholars suggest that he was employed in the office of some county attorney while others have decided that he acted as a country schoolmaster or tutor in private homes. A more tantalizing suggestion has been advanced that Shakespeare was among the boys who dressed as women for the Whitsuntide plays at Stratford as early as 1580 or thereabouts. Recent records have come to light that indicate that Shakespeare may have been the William Shakeshafte who was among the players of Sir Thomas Hesketh in 1587 or enlisted in the Queen's Men who performed in Stratford in the same year.

The only relationship experienced by Shakespeare that scholars consider potentially homoerotic was the patronage of Henry Wriothesley, third Earl of Southampton, a beautiful, highly educated, young man with golden hair, soft features, and 10 years younger than Shakespeare. *Venus and Adonis* in 1593 and *The Rape of Lucrece* in 1594 were dedicated to the Earl specifically and scholars speculate whether Southampton is the "Fair Youth" urged to marry and propagate in the Sonnets, and there immortalized by the poet who apotheosizes him in extravagant terms of "friendship." A poem printed in 1594 called *Willobie his Avisa, or The True Picture of a Modest Maid, and of a Chaste and Constant Wife* by Shakespeare's acquaintance, Henrie Willobie adds more speculation to the nature of the relationship between Wriosthesley and Shakespeare. In it, Avisa tells how she repels assaults upon her chastity and how after marriage she resists, among the lords who tempted her, a H.W. who has a "familiar friend W.S. who not long before had tried the courtesy of the like passion, and was now newly recovered of the like infection... and in viewing afar off the course of this loving comedy, he determined to see whether it would sort to a happier end for this new actor, than it did for the old player."

Whether Shakespeare's relationship with Southampton actually went as far as same-sex attraction, we do know that Southampton gave Shakespeare £1,000 (possibly to buy a share in the Lord Chamberlain's Company) at a time when the Earl was in financial straits. Clearly, he was impressed with Shakespeare's verse or versatility.

Shakespeare's association with the Lord Chamberlain's (later the King's) Company of actors produced a number of significant roles for transvestite actors. Tradition has given us the names of young actors who likely would have originated one or several of Shakespeare's great women: the first Ophelia is thought to be one Nathaniel Field, the son of a Puritan preacher; the first Desdemona may have been Richard Robinson; Lady Macbeth was originated by Alexander Cooke; Juliet and Cleopatra were probably both introduced by Robert [Bobbie] Gough [Goffe]; and the sexually ambivalent role of Rosalind was probably first played by Willie Ostler. We must remember to take tradition with a grain of salt as it often represents romantic impressions what "should have been" rather than what actually occurred. Tradition also suggests that Shakespeare himself played the Ghost in *Hamlet* and Adam in *As You Like It*.

Boys and Women

Repeatedly we have said that the society was obsessed with finding an ordered function for same-sex relationships, and that playwrights have attempted to provide such an order through the accepted hierarchal order of the theatre. It is appropriate now to examine more closely how such a hierarchy worked through the views of phenomenological critics.

In "Homosexuality in the Renaissance: Behavior, Identity, and Artistic Expression," James M. Saslow suggests that male bisexuality in the 15th and 16th centuries was consistent with the adult man's position at the top of the social system which granted privilege to patriarchy, age, and power. Within this system, boys were considered interchangeable with women because of the still "feminine" physical characteristics of beardless, high-voiced, smooth-skinned adolescents. This situation is compounded by the fact that adult bisexual men who played the active role in homosexual sex did not even consider their behavior a deviation from the adult masculine norm. The male dominated apprentice system by which boys from the ages of twelve or thirteen lived with the master was an acceptable (though covert) system of homosexual love since boys were interchangeable with women.

The theatre clearly replicates this model. Boys, considered female surrogates are easily accepted on stage as women. They are under the tutelage of some master—either choirmaster or adult actor—and are practicing their craft, playing an accepted role in the social system. A similar argument can be advanced for prostitutes or fine artisans. So long as the boys are recipients of sexual advances (in or out of character), they fall within the accepted paradigm of an adult male system of dominance.

At the same time, however, the very role that the boy actor plays, though understood within the hierarchy, violates that very system since the boy is often not only pretending to a role beyond his station (i.e., playing adult men of various social stations, in adult clothing) he is pretending to a role beyond his sex, which is clearly forbidden by the Bible in Deuteronomy 22:5. In *Th' Overthrow of Stage-Playes*, John Rainoldes (himself a transvestite actor at the age of seventeen) argues that the boy transvestite destroyed the fragile moral restraint containing an anarchic male sexuality; that the boy incited his male audience into every kind of sexual excess. In seeing the transvestite boy, the male member of the audience might be moved to lascivious thoughts about women, which he then might transfer to the boy himself. An odd double standard arises here as on the one hand, society can accept the boy as a female surrogate in his own beardless form, but then condemn his acting when, in his beardless form, he puts on a dress. What we discover, then, is that dress was also a significant emblem in the hierarchy and the taking of another's costume was tantamount to a violation of the social order.

According to William Perkins, writing at the end of the 16th century, dress "must be answerable to our estate and dignitie, for distinction of order and degree in the societies of men. This use of attire, stands by the very ordinance of God; who, as he hath not sorted all men to all places, so he will have men to fitte themselves and their attire, to the qualitie of their proper places, to put a difference betweene themselves and others."

In addition to the association between dress and class there was the connection between dress and gender. Philip Stubbes in his *Anatomy of Abuses* insists that "Our apparel was given us as a sign distinctive to discern betwixt sex and sex, and therefore for one to wear the apparel of another sex, is to participate with the same, and to adulterate the verity of his own kind."

The dress controversy came to a head in the theatre which, like the transvestite, was seen both to epitomize and to promote contemporary forces of disruption in and through its involvement with cross-dressing. The transgression of the fixed order of things by willfully confusing the distinction between class, rank, and gender was just one of the "sins" of the theatre. More significant was the belief that the player had no real self apart from that which he was playing. As a result, he was considered a vagrant and rogue, without a fixed abode and identity by which he could be classified in a hierarchal society. Clearly then, the society both embraces and rejects the theatre. How can we account for these opposing views?

In his pioneer analysis, *Renaissance Self-Fashioning*, Stephen Greenblatt argues that Marlowe's heroes remain embedded in what they oppose. "They simply reverse the paradigms and embrace what the society brands as evil, In so doing, they imagine themselves set in diametrical opposition to their society where in fact they have unwittingly accepted its crucial structural elements." Faustus, for example, seals his contract with the Devil by speaking "consummatum est," the words used by Christ as He was dying on the cross.

This is what Jonathan Dollimore, in his study of perversion called *Sexual Dissidence* refers to as a transgressive reinscription: a mode of transgression which seeks not an escape from existing structures but rather a subversive reinscription within them, and in the process their dislocation and displacement. In the case of *Doctor Faustus*, Faustus is actually violating Christianity using the paradigm that is at the essence of Christianity. In the case of *Edward II*, the king is subverting the dominant paradigm of rule by substituting his favorite for his queen and raising a commoner above his nobles. Yet by being acutely aware of such behavior (recalling Gaveston only at the death of his father), he is unconsciously admitting the dominance of the paradigm he is seeking to destroy.

In his [1972] edition of *Cony-Catchers and Bawdy Baskets*, Gamini Salgado described the Elizabethan vagabond as follows:

> Seen through the disapproving eyes of respectable citizens they were nothing but a disorderly and disorganized rabble, dropouts from the social ladder. But seen from within, they appear to be like nothing so much as a mirror-image of the Elizabethan world picture: a little world, tightly organized into its own ranks and with its own rules, as rigid in its own way as the most elaborate protocol at court or ritual in church. [13]

From one view, the rogue/vagabond/actor was among the potentially dangerous dregs of civilization but in no way part of the true social order. From another perspective, however, these characters comprise a mirror-image of that order, not simply an imitation of the dominant paradigm (as Aristotle reminds us regarding tragedy in the *Poetics*), but an inversion of it (as are mirror images always). In this inversion is an interrogation of the order being mimicked. If society is being imitated from below, it is embarrassed by the sub-order. Inversion becomes a kind of transgressive reinscription: the subculture, replicating itself in terms of the dominant society, demystifies that society in its imitation. This produces a knowledge of the dominant paradigm which the dominant society must destroy in order to rule.

The same can be said of the theatre that subverts as it demystifies the paradigm that controls it. The androgynous actor is a replication of some aspect of acknowledged social behavior. We have seen above how the boy was an accepted female surrogate under the emblem of "androgyne." This androgyne, under the aegis of the Feast of Fools, or New Year's Day Celebrations, socially accepted holidays of behavioral inversion, was able to cross-dress with impunity. Once on the stage, however, divested of a specific emblem, the boy-girl challenges society. No contemporary criticism of the transvestite actor condemns him because he makes a poor girl. Rather, he is taken to task because he is too real, too believable; and so, the transvestite actor shares the burden of the transvestite in society in the depiction of roles that either effeminize men or "masculate" women, both of which are transgressive reinscriptions of the social hierarchy. Whether the phenomenon of Elizabethan cross-dressing resulted from the transvestitism of the stage, or developed independently, the social implications of same-sex behavior are inextricably connected with the theatre in the English Renaissance.

Transgressive Reinscriptions

The plays we have seen up to this point involve transgressive reinscriptions of both the macro culture—the real society in which the play is presented—and of the micro culture—the virtual society around which the play is centered. *Gallathea*, for example, involves the reinscription of an unnatural order (the sacrifice of the purest, most beautiful virgin). It confutes that order in transforming the virgins into boys. It mirrors that confutation with the plot of the three lads, each associating with some unnatural situation: Rafe is victim of an alchemist and astrologer, Robin of a fortune teller, and Dick of some unnamed "cozener," and Cupid puts a romantic spell on Diana's three nymphs. The Virgins are deceiving each other, the cozeners are deceiving the lads, and Cupid is deceiving the nymphs. Perhaps central to the idea of transgressive reinscription is the fate of Hebe whose salvation is two edged: the dreaded monster does not come to eat her—but that means essentially that she is not beautiful enough to be chosen.

This micro world turns a mirror to the macro society where a male dominated hierarchy denies women self-autonomy and forces them to take on alternative roles to exist. Yet roles that do not conform to the accepted gender behavior are unacceptable and the woman/boy actors are caught in a catch-22 without the intervention of a *dea ex machina*. This is a clear parallel to Spanish Renaissance drama where the entire destiny of the characters in the play, as well as that of the spectators, is dependent upon the generosity of the reigning monarch. The confusion of sexual identity in romantic involvement, as well as a suggestion of incest, is clearly evocative of the macro society.

In *Edward II*, Marlowe consciously mirrors Gaveston's behavior toward Edward with Mortimer's courtship of Isabella and succeeds in creating a heterosexual reinscription of the same-sex relationship. Like *Gallathea*, the action of the play takes place in a society gone awry. Similarly, Shakespeare's

As You Like It takes place within a transgressive society. Frederick has usurped the kingdom and the principal characters must flee to the forest, the reinscriptive micro society, to save themselves.

Interestingly, it is in the micro society where the homoerotic behavior between Celia and Rosalind, "whose loves/Are dearer than the natural bond of sisters" [I.ii.287-88] matures into the accepted adult behavior of opposite sex marriage. Before the escape into the forest society, Celia describes the relationship with Rosalind:

We still have slept together,
Rose at an instant, learn'd, play'd, eat together,
And wheresoe'er we went, like Juno's swans,
Still we went coupled and inseparable. [I.iii.75ff]

When Rosalind delays her exit to compliment Orlando on his prowess, Celia displays a suggestion of jealousy [I. ii. 245] and this is explained in the following scene when she attempts to reverse her father's banishment of Rosalind because she "cannot live out of her company" [I. iii. 88].

Once in the forest, Rosalind tries to get Celia to play the priest and marry her to Orlando but the girl "cannot say the words" [IV.i.121] and must be prodded three times before she can even give away the "bride." In *Sexual Personae,* Camile Paglia aptly points out that Shakespeare clearly intended this sexual subtext since in the source on which Shakespeare drew [Lodge], it is the Celia character who actually comes up with the idea of the sham wedding ceremony [202]. By the end of the play, the homo-emotional relationship between Celia and Rosalind gives way to a separation and extrication from ambivalent sexual emblems and leads to a double marriage, where the sexual roles are fixed by society.

Hugh Richmond in *Shakespeare's Sexual Comedy* points out Rosalind's "capacity for bisexuality" [137]. She is highly tempted toward her reinscriptive extreme—her male disguise—and in pretending to be a rakish lady-killer, she actually becomes one in her prank with Phoebe. Like the character of

Britomart who loves her nurse in Spenser's epic poem *The Fairy Queen*, Rosalind drifts into an involuntary realm of lesbian courtship. Male disguise elicits wayward impulses from the socially repressed side of both characters' natures. Rosalind, for example, expresses little reticence in jumping into a masculine surrogate:

> Because that I am more than common tall,
> That I did suit me all points like a man?
> A gallant curtle-axe upon my thigh,
> A boar-spear in my hand; and--in my heart
> Lie there what hidden woman's fear there will--
> We'll have a swashing and a martial outside,
> As many other manish cowards have
> To do outface it with their semblances. [I. iii. 117-124]

Rosalind emerges as pan-sexual in the play. In disguise or out, she is potentially homoerotic as is indicated by the scheme below:

Rosalind and Celia: potentially lesbian relationship
Rosalind and Phoebe: transvestite heterosexual potential; unmasked lesbian
Rosalind and Orlando: transvestite homosexual; unmasked heterosexual.

Rosalind is clearly completing the Aristophanic paradigm in Plato's *Symposium* and as such is reinscripting the sexual emblems of the macro culture.

That Shakespeare's androgynous Rosalind is reinscripting the macro society is also clear from her conversation with Orlando when she claims she cured a man of love by pretending to be his beloved thus characterizing boys and girls as emotionally alike:

> At which time would I, being but a moonish youth, grieve,
> be effeminate, changeable, longing and liking, proud, fantastical,
> apish, shallow, inconstant, full of tears, full of smiles; for every
> passion something and for no passion truly anything, as boys and
> women are for the most part cattle of this color. [III. ii. 400-06]

Rosalind's epilogue to the play connects the disguise to the macro world from a metatheatrical point of view:

> If I were a woman I would kiss as many of you as had beards
> that pleased me, complexions that liked me and breaths that I
> defied not; and, I am sure, as many as have good beards or good
> faces or sweet breaths will, for my kind offer, when I make curtsy,
> bid me farewell.

This is clearly a touch of male homosexual coquetry and gives a clear definition to the event the audience has just witnessed: a boy pretending to be a girl [actor/character; Ganymede/Rosalind]. This stepping out of character is, in fact, a reinscription of Jacques's "All the world's a stage" speech in II.vii. in which Jacques defines the world in terms of a theatrical metaphor, identifying everyone according to the role he plays [notice the significant absence of a woman's role in the proceedings with the possible exception of "nurse" which clearly defines woman's function in society].

The character of Jacques is in itself a re-evaluation of melancholy social critics who wrote a plethora of poetic satires late in the age of Elizabeth complaining of society's ills. The name is a corruption of the eponymous character of Sir John Harrington's *Metamorphosis of Ajax* [1596], a scientific treatise on domestic sanitation in the style of Rabelais, where the name Ajax was used for the household offices of British government. Ajax was also considered the classic type of melancholic hero as Harrington in the introduction to his book indicates. After his unsuccessful attack on Ulysses, Ajax "could indure it no longer but became a perfect mal-content, viz. his hat without a band, his hose without garters, his wast without a girdle, his bootes without spurs, his purse without coyne, his heade without wit, and thus swearing he would kill & slay: First he kild all horned beasts."

Harrington suggests yet another association exists between Jacques and Jakes in the person of Lieutenant Iaques Wingfield, who giving his name to his mistress's lady in waiting at court, found himself being represented by her as Mr. Privy Wingfield. Her little knowledge of French did not extend to proper names, Iaques being James in English, and the young woman thought the word was French for bathroom.

Female Cross-Dressing

Though homosexual, King James was not liberal minded. Twice in his reign, he emphasized legislation against sodomy and female transvestitism. The first occurred in July 1610 in a note about amendments to a proposed general pardon, from which he expressly omits sodomy, piracy, and poaching. The legislation against female transvestitism which is implied in a letter from J. Chamberlain to Sir D. Carleton, dated 25 January 1620 also condemns any excess of dress:

> Yesterday the bishop of London called together all his clergie about this towne, and told them he had expresse commandments from the King to will them to inveigh vehemently against the insolencie of our women, and theyre wearing of brode brimed hats, pointed doublets, theyre haire cut short or shorne, and some of them stilettoes or poniards, and such other trinckets of like moment; adding withall that if pulpit admonitions will not reforme them he would proceed by another course; the truth is the world is very much out of order.

Two weeks later, on 12 February, we hear that the condition has reached such proportions that "the players have likewise taken them to taske, and so to the ballades and ballad-singers, so that they can come nowhere but theyre ears tingle; and if all this will not serve, the King threatens to fall upon theyre husbands, parents or frends that have or shold have power over them, and make them pay for it."

James' highly misogynistic reaction was not unusual. Sermons and conduct books of this period constantly chastise the fickleness of fashion and the "vanity of sumptous apparel." Conservative factions tended to link propriety of dress with the coherence of the social fabric. Hence, dressing out of class and certainly dressing out of gender blurred distinctions within a stratified social order. The playwright George Gascoigne is among the first to complain about women cross dressing in a satire called *The Steel Glass* written in 1576:

What be they? women? masking in mens weedes?
With dutchkin dublets, and with Ierkins iaggde?
With high copt hattes, and fethers flaunt a flaunt?
They be so sure even Wo to Men in dede.

Writing later in 1583 Philip Stubbes complains that "these Women may not improperly be called Hermaphroditi, that is, Monsters of bothe kindes, half women, half men." As we move into the seventeenth century, we see a growth in both the volume and hostility of the satire against women, displaying both the misogyny of James' court, the middle-class emphasis on practical issues of a woman's place and the appropriateness of her clothing. Barnaby Rich, for example, in *The Honestie of this Age* complains of the inability to discern class in a class-conscious society: "wee canne hardly knowe ... a Lady from a Landresse." Rich also suggests that women dressing as men mirror the effeminacy of the Jacobean court: "And from whence commeth this wearing and this imbrodering of long lockes, this curiosity that is used amongst men in freziling and curling of their hayre? this gentlewoman-like starcht bands, so be edged, and be laced, fitter for Mayd Marion in a Moris dance, then for him that hath either spirit or courage that should be in a gentleman?"

Louis Wright, writing in *Middle-Class Culture and Elizabethan England*, believes that the hostile response to women in men's clothing was a defensive reaction against an increasingly successful demand for both moral and spiritual equality between the sexes and for greater social freedom for women, that is, from the home, from the double-standard of sexual morality, from wife-beating and forced marriage.

Dekker and Middleton's 1611 play, *The Roaring Girl* is often viewed as the keystone of female transvestite plays. In it, Sebastian, a licentious youth, dotes on a fallen woman, Moll Cutpurse, the transvestite, in order to secure his father's approval for the girl he really loves, Mary Fitzallard. A subplot dealing with shopkeepers and their wives continue the inversion of gender roles: here the wives are the prodigals, abandoning their husbands and households for the excitement of courtly lovers and the husbands act the passive role, usually expected of the profligate's wife. That the husbands and wives end up reunited is significant only for the fact that the wives return to their households of their own accord and not because of social (or moral) pressure. They simply have had enough of the high life and they go back home.

Moll, wearing a short coat with a collar, makes her entrance at a tobacco shop where she smokes a pipe and causes quite a stir:

Goshawk: 'Tis the maddest, fantasticalest girl!—I never knew so much flesh and so much nimbleness put together!

. . . .

Mistress Gallipot: Some will not stick to say she's a man, and some, both man and woman.

Laxton: That were excellent: she might first cuckold the husband and then make him to as much for the wife! [II.i. 204-212]

Later a fellow enters carrying a long sword and Moll berates him for "abusing" her the other night in a tavern. When he denies it, Moll beats him and the fellow runs away. Clearly masculine and feminine roles are confounded here.

When a man tries to treat her like a whore, Moll replies with a kind of female manifesto that sounds modern even in our own day:

> Thou'rt one of those
> That thinks each woman thy fond flexible whore;
> If she but cast a liberal eye upon thee,
> Turn back her head, she's thine; or, amongst company,
> By chance drink first to thee, then she's quite gone,
> There's no means to help her...
> How many of our sex by such as thou
> Have their good thoughts paid with a blasted name
> That never deserved loosely or did trip
> In path of whoredom beyond cup and lip?
> But for the stain of conscience and of soul,
> Better had women fall into the hands
> Of an act silent than a bragging nothing...
> I scorn to prostitute myself to a man,
> I that can prostitute a man to me! [III. i. 72-112]

When, to carry out his scheme, Sebastian dresses his beloved Mary up as a page and kisses her/him, we find even greater gender confusion:

> Moll: How strange this shows, one man to kiss another.
> Sebastian: I'd kiss such men to choose, Moll;
> Methinks a woman's lip tastes well in a doublet.
> Moll: Many an old madam has the better fortune then,
> Whose breaths grew stale before the fashion came:
> If that will help 'em, as you think 'twill do,
> They'll learn in time to pluck on the hose too!
> Sebastian: The older they wax, Moll. Troth, I speak seriously:
> As some have a conceit their drink tastes better
> In an outlandish cup than in our own,

So methinks every kiss she gives me now
In this strange form is worth a pair of two. [IV. i. 45-56]

In the dénouement, sexual inversion is taken to the extreme when Moll (who has appeared throughout dressed as a man) appears in the disguise of a woman to trap Sebastian's father into agreeing to his match with Mary. That accomplished, Moll is asked when she will marry. She replies:

Who, I, my lord? I'll tell you when, i'faith:
When you shall hear
Gallants void from sergeants fear,
Honesty and truth unslandered,
Woman manned but never pandered,
Cheaters booted but not coached,
Vessels older ere they're broached;
If my mind be then not varied,
Next day following, I'll be married. (V. ii. 216-223)

In her cross-dressing, her tobacco smoking, her swordplay, her philosophy, in all of her actions in the play, Moll Cutpurse attempts a transgressive reinscription of a social order. That she mirrors such an order is clear. What is not clear is the extent to which she reinscribes the old society for she appears to maintain an existence outside of that society, claiming independence, but ultimately controlled by its dominant paradigm: the law. Her parting words, "I pursue no pity:/Follow the law" (252-3) suggest only that she maintains the inverted gender model to the end, infinitely more masculine in role than the men in the play—a point emphasized by Sir Alexander's naming Sir Beauteous Ganymede in his closing remarks.

The Theatre of Effeminate Men

A play that acts as a bridge between the concepts of the masculine woman and the effeminate man is Fletcher's *Love's Cure; or, The Martial Maid*, written around 1606 and performed circa 1621. The play concerns one Clara, brought up as a man by her father, and her brother Lucio, brought up as a girl by their mother. As a result of upbringing, Clara prefers to fight along with her father in the wars rather than converse with "Tissue Cavaliers," the likes of her brother. Once the war has ended, the two parents, having lived apart, meet and exchange their children and compete to see who "soonest can/ Turn this man woman, or this woman man." Lucio's training into manhood provides the comic interest in the play while Clara's upheaval is somewhat more serious.

Early in the play she has attached herself to one Vitelli, a soldier whom she admires and rescues from impending death. She betroths herself to him by giving him her sword, saying:

I've kept it long,
And value it, next my Virginity;
But good, return it, for I now remember
I vow'd, who purchas'd it, should have me too. [190]

After eliminating the various obstacles to her affection, among them, Vitelli's attraction to her "manness," Clara finally achieves her biological womanhood through love:

love, true love
Hath made a search within me, and expell'd
All but my natural softness, and made perfect
That which my parents care could not begin. [214]

Lucio's effeminacy, in the comic sphere, actually embodies positive virtues. Unlike his sister, he resists the perpetuation of a family feud and expresses an abhorrence of violence. This so infuriates his father that the latter demands that Lucio prove his masculinity by attacking the very next man he sees, and sexually assaulting the first woman he meets. In this way, Fletcher shows the relation between two of masculinity's basic characteristics, violence and sexual prowess, which he goes on to emphasize by the obsessive association between sword and phallus in the play [II. ii. 86-90; V. iii. 194-196].

The clearest confutation of male sexuality in late Elizabethan society is male transvestitism. Like the woman in man's clothes, the man in drag posed a problem in an emblematic society. Unlike the transvestite actor, he did not have a socially tolerated format within which to effeminize himself and, worse than the transvestite woman, he was lessening his position in the social hierarchy. Post-modern sociologists tend to regard male transvestitism as part of an adult initiation ritual. According to the common belief, the purpose of the practice is to "mobilize a bisexual response as an act of integration in the formation of the new man. This is . . . acted out in certain tribal societies in which both novice and tutor (and/or master of initiation) play maternally supportive and sometimes actively homosexual roles." The Elizabethans clearly did not view the practice in the same way.

Among the earliest Elizabethan documents that discusses male transvestitism is Thomas Middleton's *Micro-Cynicon* published in 1599. The narrator in Middleton's book tells us that his sorry tale began the day that he fell in love with an extraordinarily beautiful woman he saw on the street. That woman turns out to be a man in drag, a "painted puppet" "in a nymphs attire." The narrator, however, is not aware of this at the outset. His love is successful as long as it remains unphysical but the narrator's passion proves too much for him and the ensuing physical attempt reveals his error in judgment:

> Fair words I had, for store of coin I gave,
> But not enjoy'd the fruit I thought to have.
> O, so I was besotted with her words,
> His words, that no part of a she affords!
> For had he been a she, injurious boy,
> I had not been so subject to annoy.
> A plague upon such filthy gullery!
> The world was ne'er so drunk with mockery.
> Rash-headed cavaliers, learn to be wise;

And if you needs will do, do with advice;
Tie not affection to each wanton smile,
Lest doting fancy truet love beguile;
Trust not a painted puppet, as I've done,
Who far more doted than Pygmalion ... [499-500]

While Middleton's poem is largely devoted to the narrator's complaints of how he had been duped, it is a significant aid to the historian in that it does not present the male transvestite as an unusual figure. Rather, the author claims: "The streets are full of juggling parasites / With the true shape of virgins' counterfeits."

The transvestite boy was a favorite Renaissance device in both literature in general and drama in particular. Aretino's *The Stable-Master* [1533], Sir Philip Sidney's *Arcadia* [1578/1590], John Day's *The Isle of Gulls* [1606] and *Humour Our of Breath* [1608], and Ben Jonson's *Epicoene; or, The Silent Woman* [1609] all turn on the device of a boy taken as a girl. In *The Stable-Master*, the transvestite boy is given to an overtly homosexual stable-master in marriage as a practical joke played by the ruling potentate. Much of the play's humor is derived from the stable-master's unwillingness to tie the knot, and his subsequent relief that he has married his own page boy. Other comic relief emerges from ribald innuendo and pointed dirty remarks of the kind for which Aretino was notorious in his *I Sonnetti Lussuriosi*.

The Isle of Gulls takes its plot from Sidney's *Arcadia* where the Duke of Arcadia, having abandoned his court for an island fortress, challenges his daughters' suitors to win them from him by wit. One of the suitors disguises himself as a shepherd/woodman, another as an Amazon princess named Zelmane. The author, John Day's treatment of Zelmane is an extended inversion of the disguised heroine motif found in Elizabethan Romantic Comedies of the 1590s and after (see *Twelfth Night* and *As You Like It*). The obligatory gender confusion is present and expressed in a sentiment from Violetta, Zelman's beloved: "Zelmane's humor would afford project for a pretty Court comedy; my father courts her for a woman, and as I fear she is; my mother dotes upon her for a man, and as I wish he were."

Day also connects the male transvestite and effeminate man with the sycophants at the Court of James I. In the Induction to the play, the First Spectator asks for something "critical" in the hopes of finding some great man's life detailed therein:

Are Lawyers fees, and Citizens wiues laid
open in it: I loue to heare vice anatomized,
& abuse let blood in the maister vaine, is
there any great mans life charactred int? [A2v]

But the Prologue, like the lady who doth protest too much, claims that Dametas, a parasitic courtier, who incidently resembles one of James' favorites, represents not an individual but a type, whose "villany may give the greater luster to the virtuous dispositions of true-born gentility" [A2v].

In *Humour Out of Breath*, Day makes use of a transvestite ploy without the male actually transforming himself. Rather than the beloved dressing as a woman, here the lover, a lustful old man named Hortensio, is blindfolded and makes love to a boy, thinking him a girl:

[Blindman's-bluff is renewed on the lower stage.
Page. Are you in breath, my lord?
Hort. As a brewer's horse, and as long-winded; look to yourself, madame, I come upon you.
Boy. I am ready for you, sir. O for a bulrush to run a tilt at's nose!
Page. A fair miss, i' faith.
. . . .
Hort. Madame?
Boy. Here.
Hort. Where?*[Boy throws him down.*
Help me up, madam.

> Boy. O strange! cannot you get up without help? here's my glove, but come no nearer, as you love me.
> Hort. I do love you, madam.
> Boy. O blind love!
> Hort. True, madam; your beauty has made me blind.
> Page. Indeed, love's sons like spaniels are all born blind.
> ....
> Hort. But will you give me the fingers that hold this glove, madam?
> Boy. And the whole body to pleasure you, my lord; but let me go a little.
> Hort. I will not loose you yet, lady.
> Boy. But you shall, my lord; hist, then keep me still. [IV. iii.]

The boy then proceeds to tie the glove to a post and exits with the page leaving Hortensio romantically pleading his suit until he removes the blindfold to discover that he has been courting a post.

The most misogynistic of the plays mentioned, Ben Jonson's *Epicoene*, acted by the Children of Her Majesty's Revels in 1609 at Whitefriars, presents an anatomy of the process of social change among the upper classes in Jacobean London. Sir Amorous La Foole, for example, is a younger son whose knighthood is an accident rather than a birthright: "I . . . have spent some crowns since I was a page in court, to my Lord Lofty, and after, my lady's gentleman-usher, who got me knighted in Ireland, since it pleased my elder brother to die" [I.i.409-413]. Captain Otter is almost obsessed with impressing his social superiors by speaking Latin (though rather badly, especially when disguised later in the play as a lawyer and priest).

No unmarried, attractive, witty young women exist in the play. In *Epicoene*, the only dramatically interesting women are disloyal wives, who, past their prime, "live from their husbands; and give entertainment to all the wits, and braveries o' the time" [I.i.82-84], and their pretensions to taste and culture outdo those of the male fools. No adulteries take place in the play, however. Rather than satirizing sexual excess, Jonson chooses to portray the commonwealth of women banded into a "collegiate" society, their use of birth control [IV.iii.48-54], their pretensions to wit and taste [II.i.146-81], and the "unnatural" taming of the husband by the wife:

> Haughty: Here's Centaur has immortalized herself, with taming of her wild male.
> Mavis: Aye, she has done the miracle of the kingdom. [IV. iii. 25-27]

Such an inversion of traditional sexual hierarchies is presented to the extreme between Captain and Mrs. Otter. He hates his wife but is financially dependent on her and is thus forced to call her "princess" and obey her irrational whims. When Dauphine indicates the arrival of his wife, Otter says: "Wife! Buzz. Titivilitium. There's no such thing in nature. I confess, gentlemen, I have a cook, a laundress, a house-drudge, that serves my necessary turns, and goes under that title. But he's an ass that will be so uxorious, to tie his affections to one circle... Wives are nasty sluttish animals" [IV. ii.44-49]. And when asked, then, why he married one, the Captain responds: "A pox—I married with six thousand pound, I. I was in love with that. I ha' not kissed my Fury these forty weeks" [IV. ii. 69-70].

Mrs. Otter, on the other hand, continues to command and malign him, perpetually establishing her dominion: "By my integrity, I'll send you over to the bankside, I'll commit you to the Master of the garden, if I hear but a syllable more.... Is this according to the instrument, when I married you? That I would be Princess, and reign in mine own house: and you would be my subject, and obey me?... Who gives you your maintenance, I pray you? Who allows you your horsemeat, and mansmeat?...Who graces you with courtiers or great personages, to speak to you out of their coaches, and come home to your house? Were you ever so much as looked upon by a lord or a lady before I married you...?" [III. i. 24-43].

Jonson not only deflects the institution of marriage in *Epicoene*, he depicts the undoing of it. Similarly, he transforms the traditional use of sexual disguise in romantic comedy where male actors playing female characters who are in turn disguised as males are usually the rule. In romantic comedy the female hero's androgyny represents an ambiguous identification with and experience of male sexuality that is eventually contained through marriage or some retrogression into the original sexual role. But as Epicoene's androgyny is hidden even from the audience, the female disguise creates no sense of sexual ambiguity or dramatic irony.

Heterosexual fulfillment is never reached in *Epicoene*. Rather, heterosexual coupling is viewed with aversion, especially by the men. Truewit has a number of significant tirades against women. He asks Morose: "Alas, sir, do you ever think to find a chaste wife in these times" [II. ii. 28-29]? Then goes on to frighten him, with suggestions of women's characteristics: "If she be fair, young, and vegetous, no sweetmeats ever drew more flies; all the yellow doublets and great roses i' the town will be there. If foul and crooked, she'll be with them, and buy those doublets and roses, sir. If rich, and that you marry her dowry, not her, she'll reign in your house, as imperious as a widow. If noble, all her kindred will be your tyrants. If fruitful, as proud as May, and humorous as April; she must have her doctors, her midwives, her nurses, her longings every hour: though it be for the nearest morsel of man" [II. ii. 57-65].

Truewit reduces feminine pulchritude to a mask: "Is it for us to see their perukes put on, their false teeth, their complexion, their eyebrows, their nails? . . . They must not discover how little serves, with the help of art, to adorn a great deal" [I. i. 104-107]. The art of which Truewit speaks has no noble aesthetic pretensions. Rather, he suggests that women should repair what is naturally ugly about them: "If she have good ears, show 'em; good hair, lay it out; good legs, wear short clothes; a good hand, discover it often; practice any art, to mend breath, cleanse teeth, repair eyebrows, paint, and profess it"[I. i. 95-98].

Truewit's indictment of women is not unwarranted in the play. The Boy describes his gentlewoman's behavior at the beginning of the play: "The gentlewomen play with me, and throw me o' the bed; and carry me in to my lady; and she kisses me with her oiled face; and puts a peruke o' my head; and asks me an' I will wear her gown; and I say, not; and then she hits me a blow o' the ear, and calls me innocent, and lets me go" [I. i. 11-16].

From the Boy's description we also infer a somewhat homoerotic tendency on the part of the women which seems to pervade the play. The beginning of IV. iii. depicts the women maligning men:

Haughty: We wondered why you shrieked so, Mistress Otter.

Mistress Otter: Oh, God, madam, he came down with a huge long naked weapon in both his hands, and looked so dreadfully! Sure, he's beside himself.

Mavis: Why, what made you there, Mistress Otter?

Mistress Otter: Alas, Mistress Mavis, I was chastising my subject and thought nothing of him. [IV. iii. 1-7]

Later in the same scene the women indicate that they are practicing birth control:

Epicoene: And have you those excellent receipts, madam, to keep yourselves from bearing of children?

Haughty: Oh yes, Morose. How should we maintain our youth and beauty else? Many births of a woman make her old, as many crops make the earth barren. [IV. iii. 49-54]

Truewit, in fact, ascribes an ambivalent sexuality to the women early in the play:

> A new foundation, sir, here i' the town, of ladies, that call themselves the Collegiates, an order between courtiers and country-madams, that live from their husbands; and give entertainment to all the Wits and Braveries o' the time, as they call 'em: cry down, or up, what they like or dislike in a brain, or a fashion, with most masculine, or rather hermaphroditical authority: and every day gain to their college some new probationer. [I. i. 65-72]

This gender ambivalence continues in Truewit's advice to Morose: "And then her going in disguise to that conjurer, and this cunning woman: where the first question is, how soon you shall die? Next, if her present servant love her? Next that, if she shall have a new servant? And how many? Which of her family would make the best bawd, male or female?" [II. ii. 108-112].

Truewit reintroduces the theme of the male-bawd in III. v. when teaching Morose how to curse his barber: "If you laid on a curse or two more, I'll assure you he'll bear 'em. As, that he may get the pox with seeking to cure it, sir? Or that while he is curling another man's hair his own may drop off? Or for burning some male-bawd's lock, he may have his brain beat out with the curling iron?" [III. iii. 57-61].

Here, as in the reference to "female courtiers" throughout the play, Jonson is satirizing the practice of transvestitism at the court of James I. One case in particular deserved to be singled out by the playwright. The Prince of Moldavia, Stephano Janiculo, who pretended to be engaged to Lady Arabella Stuart, the king's cousin, escaped a Turkish prison disguised as a woman. This accounts for La Foole's line: "Yes, sir, of Nomentack, when he was here, and of the Prince of Moldavia, and of his mistress, Mistress Epicoene" [V. i. 20-21]. Clerimont who is described early in the play as having a "mistress abroad, and his ingle at home" [I. i. 21-22] and Sir John Daw, a great coward who has pretensions to classical learning appear to discuss distinctions between the sexes, but, in the context of the play, actually add to the ambivalence:

Clerimont: Your verses, good Sir John, and no poems.
Daw: 'Silence in woman, is like speech in man.
Deny't who can.'
. . . .
'Nor is't a tale,
That female vice should be a virtue male,
Or masculine vice, a female virtue be:
You shall it see

Proved with increase,
I know to speak, and she to hold her peace.'

Ultimately, Jonson's device of keeping Epicoene's disguise hidden from Truewit, Clerimont, and the audience, implies that it is impossible to tell the difference between the two sexes and that the solution for reconciling sexuality with city life is neither same-sex or opposite-sex relationships but the absence of all sexual desire. As Truewit expresses by way of epilogue to the play: "Madams, you are mute upon this new metamorphosis! But here stands she, that has vindicated your fames. Take heed of such insectae hereafter. And let it not trouble you that you have discovered any mysteries to this young gentleman. He is almost of years and will make a good visitant within this twelve month" [V. iv. 207-212].

Jacobean Theatre

In the second half of the reign of James I, the emphasis in the drama was taken off wooing with its implications of the more physical aspect of sex and placed on the more spiritual, or idealized plane of masculine friendship,. Rather than being simply overtly homosexual, these plays exhibit a somewhat more homosocial tendency. A brief comparison between two plays that appeared in the same year (1610) will illustrate this point.

John Mason's play, *Mulleasses the Turke*, written for the Children of His Majesty's Revels and probably performed at Whitefriars circa 1610 depicts a clear portrayal of same-sex love in the character of Bordello, "a humorous traveler." In Act One, scene two, Bordello's entrance is greeted with a fanfare:

But who comes heere? oh my spruce he-letcher
That makes his boye saue him the charges of a bawdy house. [C2v]

To prove the veracity of the insinuation, Bordello has the following exchange with his page, Pantofle:

Bord. Pantofle.

Pan. At your pleasure sir?

Bord. Thou hast bene at my pleasure indeed Pantofle, I will retreat into the country, hate this amorous, Court and betake my selfe to obscurity: I tel thee boye I wil returne by this Circyan Isle without transformation since Hebe hath discouered her secrets I will turne Iupiter, hate the whole sexe of women, and onely embrace thee my Ganimede.

Pan. Sfoot sir you are as passionate for the disloyalty of your Sempstresse, as some needy knight would be for the losse of some rich magnificos widdow: doe you not see how the supporters of the Court, the Lady of the labby gape after your good parts like so many grigges after fresh water, and can you withhold the dew of your moyster element?

Bord. I tel thee should the lady Iulia when she was aliue haue profered me her cheeke to kisse, I would not haue bowed to that apinted image for her whole Dukedome: Mercury had no good aspect in the horoscope of my natiuity: women and lotium are recipiocall, their sauour is noysome. [C2v–C3]

In comparison, Nathaniel Field's *Amends for Ladies*, produced by the Children of the Chapel Royal in 1610–11, emphasizes an idealized friendship. When Lady Perfect, Sir John Loveall's wife refers to Subtle as Sir John's acquaintance, her husband replies:

Nay, my virtuous wife,
Had it been but acquaintance, this his absence
Had not appeared so uncouth: but we two
Were school-fellows together, born and nursed,
Brought up, and lived since, like the Gemini:
Had but one suck: the tavern or the ordinary,

Ere I was married, that saw one of us
Without the other, said we walked by halves.

Subtle, in turn replies:

O most sweet friend, the world's so vicious,
That had I with such familiarity
Frequented you, since you were married,
Possessed and used your fortunes as before,
As in like manner you commanded mine,
The depraved thoughts of men would have proclaimed
Some scandalous rumors from this love of ours...

    It is difficult not to see in these words an association with, perhaps even a subtle remonstrance aimed at King James whose affection for Robert Carr deprived his wife, Anne of Austria, his royal attention.
    Sir John is extremely suspicious of his wife's fidelity and asks his friend, Subtle to test her:

Therefore, my dear friend, by this, love's masculine kiss,
By all our mutual engagements passed,
By all the hopes of amity to come,
Be you the settler of my jealous thoughts,
And make me kill my fond suspect of her
By assurance that she is loyal, otherwise
That she is false; and then, as she's past cure,
My soul shall ever after be past care.
That you are fittest for this enterprise,
You must needs understand; since, prove she true
In this your trial, you (my dearest friend),
Whom only rather than the world besides,

I would have satisfied of her virtue, shall see
And best conceal my folly.

Field transforms the convention of friendship from this point by making Subtle a villain who actually wants to seduce Love-all's wife and proves her faithfulness in spite of his efforts to the contrary. Subtle is reformed and Sir John vows to be nevermore jealous and begs his wife's forgiveness which she willing gives him and in an interesting reversal of social behavior, "Here then ends all strife. / Thus, false friends are made true by a true wife" (V. i.).

The touchstone of these homosocial plays with both homosexual and homosocial themes is *The Captain* written in 1613 by Beaumont and Fletcher. The Captain of the title is Jacomo, a woman hater who exhibits overt homosexual tendencies when drunk. The use of drinking as an excuse is significant here as we have encountered no need for an excuse for homosocial behavior before. Act Four scene two presents the following scene between the Host and the Captain:

Host. Shall we bear up still? Captain, how I love thee?
Sweet Captain let me kiss thee, by this Hand
I love thee next to Malmsey in a Morning,
Of all things transitory.
Jac.I love thee too,
As far as I can love a fat Man.
Host.Dost thou, Captain?
Sweetly? and heartily?
Jac. With all mine heart, Boy.
Host. Then welcome Death, come close mine Eyes, sweet Captain
Thou shalt have all.
Jac. What shall your Wife have then?

Before the Host exits, he begs the Captain for kisses. Jacomo in turn asks to hug the tavern boys and indicates that he "could love / Any Man living now, or any Woman, / Or indeed any Creature that loves Sack / Extreamly, monstrously: I am so loving, / Just at this Instant, that I might be brought, / I feel it, with a little Labour, now to / Talk with a Justice of Peace."

In the next scene, Jacomo makes love to Frederick, thinking that he is a woman:

> Jac. Sweet Lady now to you. *[Going to Frederick.*
> Clo. For loves sake kiss him.
> Fred. I shall not keep my Countenance.
> Frank. Try prithee.
> Jac. Pray be not coy sweet Woman, for I'll kiss ye,
> I am blunt,
> But you must pardon me.

The fact that *The Captain* was performed at court by the King's Company, an adult company, is significant. The King would certainly have enjoyed any excuse to see men kiss one another and surely would have appreciated such sentiments as: "the plain truth is, / I love a Soldier, and can lead him on, / And if he fight well, I dare make him drunk; / This is my Virtue, and if this will do, / I'll scramble yet amongst 'em." Perhaps even the incestuous relationship between Lelia and her father in Act Four scene four would have been entertaining to James I:

> Fath. And I do beseech thee
> Leave these unheard-of Lusts, which worse become thee
> Than mocking of thy Father. . . .
> Lel. I purposely cast on you, to discern
> Your carriage in Calamity, and you
> Have undergone 'em with that brave Contempt,
> That I have turn'd the Reverence of a Child
> Into the hot Affection of a Lover. . .
> Fath. Thou art

> Something created to succeed the Devil,
> When he grows weary of his envious course,
> And compassing the World...
> Lel. You are deceiv'd, Sir, 'tis not against Nature
> For us to lie together; if you have
> An Arrow of the same Tree with your Bow,
> Is't more unnatural to shoot it there
> Than in another? 'Tis our general Nature
> To procreate, as Fire's to consume.

King James's wife, Anne of Austria, on the other hand, might have preferred the noble friendship between Julio and Angelo which culminates in Act Three scene four when Julio gives up his pursuit of Lelia because Angelo threatens to leave him:

> Ang. No, I'll kill thee first,
> I love thee so well, that the Worms shall have thee
> Before this Woman, Friend.
> Jul. It was your Counsel,
> Ang. As I was a Knave,
> Not as I lov'd thee.
> Jul. All this is lost upon me, Angelo.
> For I must have her; I will marry ye
> When e'er ye please: pray look better on me.
> Ang. Nay then no more, Friend; farewel, Julio,
> I have so much discretion left me yet
> To know, and tell thee, thou art miserable.
> Jul. Stay, thou art more than she; and now I find it.
> Lel. Is he so?
> . . . .
> Ang. Farewell forever. *[Exit Angelo.*
> Jul. Stay, I am uncharm'd,

Farewel thou cursed House, from this hour be
More hated of me than a Leprosy. *[Exit Julio*

Caroline Drama
The transitional phase of homosocial drama culminated in the Neoplatonism introduced into England by Queen Henrietta Marie, the wife of Charles I. This produced a species of homosocial theatre called **Cavalier Drama** having the following characteristics:

1) Exploitation of platonic love;
2) Nice, artificial code of etiquette;
3) Refined sentiments;
4) Diluted sentiments and emotions;
5) Emphasis on love and honor in an ideal sense;
6) Long, sententious speeches, spinning often cryptic philosophy;
7) Use of rhythmic prose, usually masquerading as blank verse;
8) A marked feminism;
9) A freedom from ribaldry and coarseness;
10) A solemn tone;
11) Usually, the elimination of a comic subplot.

The Cavalier play is a schematic dramatization of the action of Greek romance, peopled by Platonics who deliver themselves of undramatic essays, written in florid cadenced prose, feministic in tendency, grave and refined in tone. The court of Charles was substantially different than that of his father. Mrs. Hutchinson tells us in her *Memoirs of Colonel Hutchinson*: "The face of the court was much changed in the change of the king, for King Charles was temperate, chaste, and serious; so that the fools and bawds, mimics and catamites, of the former court grew out of fashion; and the nobility and courtiers who did not quite abandon their debaucheries, yet so reverenced the king as to retire into corners to practice them." It was not unusual, therefore, for playwrights who held a place at court to know the various homosocial/

sexual scandals and to imply them tactfully in their plays under the guise of exaggerated/obsessive platonic friendships.

Walter Montague [1603–1677] a gentleman in the privy-chamber to the King, on 9 January 1633 produced the first full-fledged courtier's play, *The Shepherd's Paradise*, written for Queen Henrietta's platonic tastes and one of the worst plays in the English language, but epoch-making in its type and in the circumstances of its production. Three times the normal length of a play, it took seven or eight hours to perform, with the Marchioness of Hamilton who played a britches part as the hero, Basilino, lamenting, with cause, that her part alone was the length of an ordinary play.

The paradise of the play's title is a retreat for the lovelorn where the shepherds, who are gentry in masquerade, quite untrammeled by sheep, find a "peaceful receptacle of distressed minds, and a sanctuary against fortune's severest executions." To this sanctuary comes Prince Basilino, alias Moramente, who loves Fidamira. He conquers his love for Fidamira by falling in love with Saphira, alias Bellesa, the chaste and theoretical Queen-elect of the shepherd's paradise. Fidamira retreats there also as does her secret lover Agenor. Everyone takes an assumed name, Fidamira becomes Gamella, Agenor becomes Genorio. This is particularly troublesome as Gamella is later revealed to be neither Gamella or Fidamira but Miranda, Basilino's sister and Genorio turns out to be neither Agenor, the secret suitor, or Genorio but Bellesa's brother Palante. The relationships finally being revealed bring the tangled web of this 170-page play to its happy conclusion.

The characters all talk in paragraphs, commenting on actions and impulses, and analyzing the code of love; and an occasional song offers some lyrical refreshment: "I find a glowing heat that turns red hot / My heart, but yet it doth not flame a jot."

The play introduced *préciosité* to the English stage, made courtier playwrights respectable, and precipitated the Prynne episode which is of historical importance in view of the Puritan reaction to the stage. For years **William Prynne** (1600–1669) had been writing a book that would climax the Puritan attacks upon the stage. The book, shaped like a building block, titled,

Histriomastix, The Players Scourge, or, Actors Tragedy, is among the most obtuse ever written in English or in Latin, and it tells us little about the Elizabethan or Jacobean stage (perhaps with the slight exception that Shakespeare's plays were printed on better paper than were bibles—and henceforth sacrilegious!) The book which drew attention to the moral depravity of women actors would have attracted little attention were it not published in 1632, the day after the queen acted in *The Shepherd's Paradise* at Somerset House.

Prynne claims that the theatre is always a pretext for male homosexuality and lists a long line of precedents for the idea that sodomites are sexually aroused by dressing their boys in women's clothing. This list includes: "Male Priests of Venus" and the sodomites of Florida themselves who have become "very monsters of nature" because of their practice of transvestitism. What is also striking about Prynne's work is the suggestion that is implicit within it that somewhere locked inside man's own body is a woman, waiting for the appropriate attire and the removal of those "virilities" that would allow her to assume her proper shape. Citing Deuteronomy, he suggests that: "If then a woman's putting on or wearing of men's apparell incurres an anathema ... doth not a man's attyring himself in woman's vestments much more demerit?" Clearly Prynne considers male identity per se to be at stake here. Critics suggest that perhaps Prynne was secretly convinced that the "only people with real selves were women."

Following the publication of the book, we hear that Prynne is up before the High Commission Court and Star Chamber; a preliminary hearing is held at once and the author, not yearning for martyrdom, lustily proclaimed that the book had been written before the queen appeared in the play in question [though actually this defense was easily refuted as the queen had appeared as early as 1626 with her ladies in waiting, and in britches parts.] Prynne was eventually judged guilty and ordered to be disbarred, to be expelled from Lincoln's Inn, to forfeit his Oxford degree, to pay £5000 fine, to remain in prison at the King's pleasure, and finally to stand in the stocks while the state executioner branded S.L. [seditious libeler] on his cheeks and cut off his ears!

Lodowick Carlell [1602–1675] had a greater flair for literature than did Montague and, like him, was a gentleman of the privy-chamber to the kingIn 1629 he published *The Deserving Favorite* a play about rival lovers turning on mistaking identity, long-lost brother/sister reunions, exiled fathers, in the person of a mysterious hermit, and a happy ending. Preceding *The Shepherd's Paradise*, it is close to Fletcher's tragicomic mode and virtually free of the 'platonic' philosophizing.

In 1634, he produced *The Spartan Ladies* and in 1636 *Arviragus and Philicia*, Cavalier drama at its best, complete with Montaguean *préciosité*! It was popular enough to be consistently revived through the Restoration. The plot of the play is quite complicated, and a great deal of blood and thunder leads to three weddings that unite Britain, Denmark, and Pictland in beautiful harmony by the end of the play. The play turns on ethical discussions, analyses of witchcraft, tests of love and fidelity, and stage business filled with heroic gallantry. In 1637 came *The Fool would be a Favorite*, the only one of Carlell's plays to turn on a low comic sub-plot, and *Osmond the Great Turk*, the most original of the author's plays, and in 1638, *The Passionate Lovers*, a ten-act romance. *The Fool would be a Favorite* stresses the relationship between Agenor and Philanthus who, in discussing Aurelia, Agenor's sister, says:

'Tis true, shee's full of all that can be excellent
In women, yet so far do I prize you above mine own desires or hopes,
That could your sister recompence me with a love equall to mine,
And yet that love, purchast by you, prove prejudiciall to you
I rather would give o'er the thought of love for ever,
At least in silence rather pine and die.
No, far bee't from my friendship, to build my happiness,
Though ne'er so great, upon your smallest discontent.

When Philanthus unwittingly ends up falling in love with Agenor's beloved, he allows himself to be wounded by Agenor in a duel and falls saying:

> I am remov'd from being a hinderance to
> My friend in his affection. You perceive
> How much he loves you, since it did force him
> To make a sacrifice of me, me, his better halfe.
> Sir, give me your hand; it was my fortune, not my will,
> That crost you in this Ladies love. And, Madam,
> Remember, that my last breath is employ'd,
> To assure you, that I shall never rest
> In peace, if any other shall possesse that place,
> Which you thought me worthy to hold, in your affection,
> Then this Prince, who onely does deserve it.

As Agenor is about to kill himself at Philanthus' tomb, Lucinda, the woman in question, presents herself to Agenor saying that the ghost of Philanthus appeared to her and told her to do so. Suddenly, Philanthus appears in the flesh and explains:

> You being wilfull and enraged, I rather
> Ventured to receive one wound, and so seem slain,
> Than in your death to lose a friend, a Mistresse,
> And my own life too; but life would have bin hatefull
> After your loss, if I could have preserv'd it.

Several critics have remarked that the two plays of Carlell "possess features which were later reproduced in the heroic dramas of the Restoration; the love and friendship theme especially Carlell a forerunner of Roger Boyle, Earl of Orrery, who, after the return of Charles II, laid the foundation of the typical Restoration style."

Sir John Suckling [1609–1642] was rich, generous, a wit, a town rake, and reckless gambler. In 1641 he participated in the royalist plot against parliament which led to his flight to the continent, the rapid dissolution of his health, and ultimate reputed suicide. Suckling's first play, *Aglaura*, was written as a tragedy in 1637 and transformed to a tragicomedy in 1638 so that a reversable fifth act would allow productions of the play either way. The play is laid in a corrupt court where the king lusts after his son's sweetheart and the Queen lusts after her husband's brother. The whole is a nebula of love-affairs and the king is ultimately slain by assassins mistaking him for his son who is killed by his girlfriend mistaking him for the king. The few survivors at the end of the play go off to drown themselves in tears. *Aglaura* resembles Fletcherian tragedy of court intrigue with greater excesses and complications in a more unwholesome atmosphere. The platonic influence is shown in the affectations of the minor characters but touches not the main characters.

Suckling also wrote *The Goblins* [published in 1646] and *Brennoralt, or The Discontented Colonel*, his best play, produced in 1639 by the King's Company. In it, Brennoralt, a large-souled warrior loves Fracelia, daughter of a rebel governor. Fracelia is also loved by the gallant rebel Almerin, who in turn is loved by Iphigene, a woman serving as a man in the royal forces. Almerin slays Fracelia in a fit of jealous rage provoked by Iphigene's politic attentions toward her while still in man's disguise, and Brennoralt kills Iphigene whom he mistakes as the assassin. Having killed the women, the two men fight, with Almerin dying and Brennoralt living on, obviously more tragically discontented than ever!

Of all the cavalier dramatists, Suckling was the one true poet. As a result, of all the cavalier plays, Suckling's had the most successful stage career. All three were produced at Blackfriars before the closing of the theatres and *Aglaura*, if not the others as well, was produced at court. At the Restoration, all three were successfully revived by the King's Men from 1661 through 1668—Samuel Pepys, the famous diarist, saw each of them at least once and *Brennoralt* four times!

William Davenant [1606–1668] was the dramatist who showed most skill in keeping one foot in the public theatre and the other in the royal banqueting halls. During his career as a popular playwright, Davenant was also a soldier, an author of court masques, a writer of complimentary epistles to the nobility, and an intimate companion of the courtiers. His later career demonstrates the phenomenon of a professional playwright who became a royal general and envoy, and was raised to knighthood.

His early plays, *The Cruel Brother* [1627], *Albovine* [1628] and *The Just Italian* [1629] are all reminiscent of the earlier plays of the transitional period. *The Cruel Brother* portrays Lucio as the favourite of the Duke of Siena, once referred to as "molles Senae" by Beccadelli. Foreste, the title character, who addresses him as follows:

> Young Lord, ...
> You are the Dukes Creature! who doates by Art,
> Who in his loue, and kindnesse, Method keepes:
> He holdeth thus his Armes, in fearefull care
> Not to bruse you with his deere embracements.

Similarity, in Act One of *Albovine,* Paradine, the title character's favorite is greeted as follows:

> My Boy, I bring thee home my chiefe Trophy:
> Thou dost delight me more than victory.
> Retire; I am in loue too violent.
> My embraces crush thee, thou art but yet
> Of tender growth—

In *The Playhouse of Pepys*, Montague Summers suggests that the bisexual temperament in rulers is not rare but goes on to question Albovine's simultaneous obsessions with Paradine and the Princess Rhodolinda. He indicates that "there will be a marked predominance in one direction; and if Davenant . . . had in view King James I, who married Anne of Denmark, but was swayed by his favourites, the poet must have known that shortly after her marriage the Queen was 'deprived of the nightly company of her husband,' and consoled herself with many lovers, the earl of Gowrie; one Stuart of the household of the Earl of Murray; Buly, a Dane; and other gallants of the court"[9].

From 1634 on, Davenant's plays alternated between standard popular stage fare and romances which approximated as closely as possible the professional work of the cavalier dramatists. *Love and Honor* [1634], *The Platonic Lovers* [1635], and *The Fair Favorite* [1638] were obviously affected by court interest and looked for their appeal to the gallant sector of the Caroline audience.

In *Love and Honor*, Evandra, doomed captive in Savoy, has three glorious lovers, two men and one woman, each of whom asks nothing better than his life be sacrificed for hers. This play has two obsessive platonic relationships, one male, one female. Alvaro and Prospero, like Damon and Pythias, display intimate friendship and then become rivals in trying to save the other's life. Evandra and Melora engage in a kind of Orestes-Pylades relationship and try to save each other's lives. The Duke, however, rather than being amazed at the loyalty of the women, announces that they both will die.

In *The Platonic Lovers*, Duke Theander and Duke Phylomont are each in love with the other's sister. Meeting after a long absence, Theander says:

Thou breath'st into me, mighty Phylomont,
No other soul but mine. My better thoughts
Are moulded in thy breast, and, could we grow
Together thus, our courteous hearts would not
Be nearer, nor yet more entire.

Whereas Phylomont woos with the traditional objectives, Theander's warmth is all of the spirit; he is content to beget reflections in his mistress's eyes leaving the "coarse and homely drudgeries" of creating children to more common clay. Clearly Theander's solution to the conflict between same-sex, opposite-sex love is to deny sex altogether. Without the physical, a marriage of two minds is acceptable in spite of gender.

In *The Fair Favorite*, Eumena, the platonic mistress and state favorite of a King, is rumored to be unchaste, and becomes the provocation of an odd combat between two devoted friends, her own brother, who believes the rumor, and her new-kindled lover, who does not. As usual, the duel proves fatal only by report, the brother is saved from the scaffold, Eumena weds her champion, and the King forswears platonic dalliance to reciprocate the long-suffering devotion of his faithful queen. In this play more than the others, the author inclines to sacrifice comic subplot in deference to Cavalier practice.

As in the earlier plays, the friends exhibit excessive passion for one another as in an oath-taking scene in Act Two:

> Join now thy noble hand
> To mine, and let us vow a friendship here,
> More lasting than ourselves; for that may live
> With our immortal parts. Danger, henceforth,
> Be it in virtuous glory or in just
> Revenge, we equally will share.

The last professional playwright to write before the Civil War was **Henry Glapthorne** [1610–1643] whose half dozen plays were produced between 1635 and 1640. His *The Tragedy of Albertus Wallenstein* [1635] is an amateurish tragedy of the obituary-chronicle type. *The Hollander* [1636] and *Wit in a Constable* [1639] are comedies of intrigue and *humours*. *The Lady Mother* [1635] brings domestic strife and romantic passions together to form a hybrid tragicomedy. Glapthorne did not hesitate to interrupt realistic intrigue or low farce by sudden explosions of heroic rant, or flowery passages of artificial sentiment. Glapthrone's most interesting plays are *The Ladies Privilege* [1637] and *Argalus and Parthenia* [1638] both Fletcherian romances strongly influenced by the Cavalier mode.

The Ladies Privilege reveals how the lady Chrisea engages the honor of her true lover, Doria, to renounce his suit and force his friend Vitelli to woo in his place. As in the other plays we have examined, Doria and Vitelli are intimately bound, as Doria's declaration suggests:

> The solid earth, or a continued Rocke,
> May by some strange eruptions of the wind,

> Be rent, and so divided: but true friends
> Are adjuncts most inseparable: I have
> Still worne thee here Vitelli, as a Jewell
> Fit for no other Cabinet.

Vitelli, after the proper display of soul-strife, forsakes his own beloved in order to obey the mystifying injunction of his friend. When Doria comes within the shadow of the scaffold as principal in a supposedly fatal duel, Vitelli disguises Sabelli, Doria's page, as a woman to plead the virgin's privilege of rescuing the condemned man by accepting him in marriage. Finally, Chrisea reveals that Doria's supposed victim still lives, that she still loves him, and that her actions throughout have been only a character test of him and his friend. To her surprise, however, Doria had already married the virgin who pleaded for his release. Ultimately, Sabelli reveals his true identity and all lovers are appropriately reunited.

6. Spanish Drama to the 18th Century

From 711, when the Moors first occupied the Iberian Peninsula, through the beginning of the 13th century, Spain was a source of learning, philosophy, and craft. Evidently the Moors were more advanced culturally than the rest of feudal Europe. Around 1200, the Christian kingdoms of Europe united to fight the Moors and, by 1276, had driven them out of all but the southernmost provinces. By 1492, under the rule of Ferdinand of Aragon and Isabella of Castile, the Moors were completely driven out of Spain, Aragon and Castile were united, and Spain became essentially a single nation, on its way to becoming a major power in Europe. By 1550, it was the most powerful country in the world and by 1600, it was already in decline.

As in other European countries during the Middle Ages, drama arose in Spain by way of the liturgy of the Catholic Church. Only a few tropes, some liturgical plays in Latin and one in Spanish exist in support of the thesis that Spanish church drama developed according to the typical European pattern well into the 12th century. Although short liturgical plays in the vernacular appeared in the 15th century, no great Spanish cycles or miracle and mystery plays appear to have been written or performed. However, while dramatic activity in the central kingdom seemed frozen, many liturgical plays called *misteris* appeared in the Catalan-speaking province of Catalonia bordering France.

To celebrate the sacrament of the Holy Eucharist in the 16th century, a genre of play was developed called the *auto sacramental* (sacramental act), a one-act play in verse that presented an allegorical dramatization of ideas related (often more or less) to the Eucharist, using personified abstractions as characters. Autos were performed in the open air between the 16th and 18th centuries and grew to include Biblical stories and various secular events so long as they presented a lesson that enabled the spectator to move from religious doubt to religious belief. As in England, the plays were performed at the Corpus Christi Feast, which began with a parade that included comic masqueraders and *tableaux vivants* on carts (or *carros*) resembling modern floats. Gradually, the *tableaux vivants* became more and more animated until short playlets emerged. Finally, the floats were isolated from the parade and the playlets (still called *autos sacramentales*) began to be performed on the carros in one town plaza after another by professional actors and actresses who were paid by the town. In addition to the financial reward earned by each acting troupe, the city council also awarded a monetary prize for the best auto sacramental. The magnificent costumes and settings used in production were paid for by the city and later used for performances of secular plays. As a result, the production of the *autos sacramentales* greatly assisted the development of secular drama in Spain.

By the end of the 16th century, 3 autos were given each year: after 1592 and until 1647, 4 were performed annually, and after 1647, only two autos were produced in a single year. In addition to the religious plays, actors also performed dances as well as short farcical interludes called *farsas sacramentales*, rough, primitive, rustic comedies designed to entertain the lower classes. When the autos were outlawed in 1765, the reasons given were the predominance of the carnival spirit, the objectionable content of the farces and dances, and the undesirability of having religious plays performed by actors of "questionable morality."

Playwrights

The playwright who did most to advance the auto in its earliest stages was

Diego Sanchez de Badajoz (died before 1550). **Jose de Valdivielso** (1560-1638) and **Lope de Vega** (1562-1635) were the first to recognize the genre's potential and began to adapt secular stories into the structure of the auto while continuing to stress the need for penitence and proper spiritual attitudes. By 1500, a secular drama began to emerge out of the publication of the *Comedy of Calisto and Melibea*, a novel divided into 16 acts with dialogue, published in 1499. Written by **Fernando de Rojas** (c. 1465-c. 1541) the book traded on typical Roman Comedy characters:

> Calisto was a young gentleman of birth and fortune;
> Melibea was a modest and romantic young lady;
> Celestina was a wise, but crafty old bawd;
> Parmeno and Sempronia were braggart servants; and
> Elicia and Areusa were courtesans.

Designed to be read rather than performed, the *Comedy* influenced many later writers of plays and novels because of its depiction of lifelike situations. Though, in the final analysis, the work is more tragic than comic since Calisto falls to his death from a ladder as he departs Melibea's garden, and Melibea commits suicide by flinging herself off a tower. The novel was translated into English in 1530 by John Rastell as the Interlude, *The Four Elements*.

Regarded as the father of Spanish Drama (because his early work predates *Calisto and Melibea*), **Juan del Encina** (1469-1529) began his theatrical career as the author of **eclogues** in the style of Italian pastoral plays. Starting out within a religious context using the historical shepherds of the nativity, he began to experiment with shepherds who were, in reality, courtiers in a rustic setting. Gradually he secularized the drama by changing the focus from Christ to Venus in which romantic love would replace salvation as the primary theme.

Encina's most daring innovations came as a result of a visit to Italy in 1513 when he composed his masterpiece, the *Eclogue of Placida and Vitoriano*, in which a Pyramus-and-Thisbe-like plot resolves in a happy ending due to the intercession of Cupid and Venus. The love of happy endings was characteristic of Encina and his followers who considered it an immutable law of the theatre.

Perhaps the best of Encina's followers was **Gil Vicente** (c. 1465-1539), a Portuguese actor and playwright who wrote for the court of John II of Portugal. In 1523 he produced one of his most important plays, the farce *Ines Pererira*, in which a poor girl who loves and marries a young poet despises an honest, though ordinary, rustic man who loves her. The marriage turns out to be a disaster and, once the poet dies, Ines marries the rustic and cuckolds him with a priest. In spite of the fact that he wrote many Catholic morality plays in the medieval tradition, Vicente was harassed by the Spanish Inquisition because of his criticism of the clergy. In spite of persecution, his work continued to be explorative, continually seeking new possibilities for dramatic expression without bringing any single line of development to perfection. His best play, *Tragicomedia de Don Duardos*, is highly lyrical, evoking the romantic atmosphere of the popular fiction of the period: Prince Edward of England courts the Princess Flerida of Constantinople through the power of love alone. He disguises himself as her gardener. With the advent of spring, Flerida discovers that she is in love with the man who grew for her a perfect rose—a great treasure. Of course, she is not displeased to find out that the object of her affection is in reality a prince!

The first important figure in the professional theatre of Spain is **Lope de Rueda** (c. 1510-c. 1565). We first hear of him in 1542 while he was acting in religious plays in Seville (Miguel de Cervantes noted that Rueda's stage consisted of four or five boards set across a few benches in front of a blanket that served as a backdrop. The four actors wore sheepskins trimmed with gold and leather). By 1551 Rueda was so famous that he was appointed supervisor of the Corpus Christi festivals between 1552 and 1558. Lope was also an important writer of plays for popular audiences. Historians believe that he developed the *entremes* (interlude), a one-act farce written in prose, designed to be performed between the acts of a *comedia* (play). When *entremes* were published, they were called *pasos*. In addition, Rueda composed Spanish pastoral plays based on the Italian model and he was also highly influenced by the traveling *commedia dell'arte* companies he met while touring from town to town as an actor.

In the last half of the 16th century, a kind of Humanistic theatre developed in Seville, producing tragedies and comedies based on classical models. **Juan de la Cueva** (1550-1610), for example, published fourteen tragedies and comedies in 1588. Not only did he write plays based on classical themes, he was also the first to employ plots from Spanish history and traditional ballads in his plays.

Miguel de Cervantes (1547-1616) wrote about 30 plays, though only about 16 still survive. His greatest contribution to Spanish drama was in the further development of the *entremes*, eight of which he published in 1615. He forced into the farcical interlude significant social questions and a kind of satire that reflected his fearless political and social thinking. In *The Wonder Show*, for example, he satirizes the racism prevalent in Spain through an Emperor's-New-Clothes kind of plot: A village is swindled by a confidence-man and his assistants who announce a puppet show that can be seen only by people whose ancestry is "untainted" by Jewish blood. Since the show doesn't exist, no one sees anything but everyone pretends to. When a quartermaster arrives looking for rooms for his soldiers, he innocently admits to seeing nothing and the villagers maliciously turn on him, pelting him with rocks.

Types of Spanish Plays

By the end of the 16th century, several dramatic types had developed:

Comedia was the term used to designate any full-length play in verse, whether it was serious or comic. Typically, in 3 acts, there were two kinds of comedias: *capa y espada* (cape and sword) plays that dealt with soldiers and adventure, and *teatro ruido* (noise) or *cuerpo* (corpse) in which monarchs, noblemen, mythological characters, or Biblical figures are involved in plots set in remote locales or time periods.

Until 1615 every performance began with a *loa* (compliment) or prologue that was either a monologue or brief dramatic sketch which usually included singing and dancing.

Entremes (interlude), short topical sketches, were performed between the acts of the plays. Like the *intermezzi* in the Italian Renaissance, some of these mixed prose dialogue with songs, others were entirely sung. By 1650, the term *sainete* was used to represent these short farces.

Traditional Spanish poetic meters are used with variations within a single *comedia* depending on the dramatic or poetic moods. Prose is reserved for letters and proclamations. The language of the *comedia* tends toward rhetorical embellishment and wordplay. Asides are often used, and two or three shifts of setting may occur within each act.

Several stock characters regularly appear in Spanish theatre: a pair of lovers (the *galan* and his *dama*), a venerable old man, the king (in serious plays), and a *gracioso* (fool), a servant who makes funny remarks and puns but whose main action is to criticize and debunk the action. Developed from the *commedia dell'arte* Harlequin character, the *gracioso* often manipulates the action of the play by devising tricks to bring about a happy ending.

Lope de Vega
Felix Lope de Vega Carpio (1562-1635), Spain's most prolific playwright was a flamboyant lover, a soldier, and a priest. Jesuit-educated, he joined the navy in 1583. When he returned to Madrid after naval service, he fell in love with Elena Osorio, a married woman whose husband eventually had Lope arrested after the affair had been carried on for five years. Instead of serving his time in exile (8 years), Lope eloped with a gentlewoman named Isabel de Urbina and, shortly after they were married, he left to join the Spanish Armada. After the defeat of the Armada by the English fleet in 1588, Lope and his bride set up house in Valencia (to serve out the rest of his exile from Madrid). After Isabel died in 1595, Lope returned to Madrid and began an affair with Michaela de Luzon, the wife of an actor, and the couple set up house in Seville. The affair continued even after Lope married Juana de Guardo, daughter of a

rich butcher. After Juana died in 1613, still *in flagrante* with Michaela, Lope began yet another affair with Jeronima de Burgos, an actress. In 1614, he was ordained a Catholic priest in an attempt to give up his attraction to women but, in 1618, Lope met Marta de Nevares, wife of a businessman, and she became the great love of Vega's life. Unfortunately, in 1620 when her husband died, Lope was unable to marry her because of his vow of celibacy.

By 1609, when he wrote *Arte nuevo de hacer comedias in este tiempo* (*The Art of Writing Plays Today*), Lope de Vega admitted to having produced 483 plays, and it is believed that his total output numbers as many as 1,800 dramatic works. Typically, his plays involve love-and-honor plots that end happily. His characters are representative of every rank of Spanish society, though the female roles and the *graciosos* are typically the best drawn. Lope's dialogue is lively and natural and ranges through a wide variety of verse forms. His most famous plays deal with the effort of the peasantry to right the wrongs inflicted upon them by some perverse member of the nobility. Existing in a kind of pastoral bliss, the peasants' world is shaken when their overlord casts lustful eyes on one or more of the young women of the village. From *Peribanez* (1605–1608) to *Fuenteovejuna* (*Sheepwell*) (1612) to *El mayor alcalde el rey* (*The King the Greatest Alcalde*) (1620–1623), the steps taken by the wronged villagers reveal a progression in Vega's work. A newly-made gentleman, Peribanez kills the overlord who attempted to dishonor him, and wins immunity on the grounds that they are equal in the eyes of the law. The villagers of the Sheepwell all take part in the murder of the villain and refuse to betray the name of the actual killer. Unwilling to condemn the entire community, the king pardons them all. In the last play mentioned, the wronged hero goes to the king and begs for justice. The monarch responds by forcing the hero's fiancée to marry her seducer, a wealthy noble, then has the villain killed. Now a rich widow, the woman is free to marry the man she loves.

In addition to being a prolific playwright, Lope de Vega also wrote about the process of writing. His *Arte nuevo de hacer comedias in este tiempo* (*The Art of Writing Plays Today*) is an important document revealing the aesthetics of dramatic construction in the early 17th century. Lope suggests that plays should be in three acts and that each act should take only 4 sheets of paper. The 1st act is the setup, the 2nd act presents the complication, and the 3rd act depicts the resolution (which should be difficult to guess, in order to sustain surprise and expectancy in the audience). He calls for the integration of serious and comic subject matter, and the relaxation of the neoclassical unities of time and place (though he advocates that the dramatic action should occur in as short a time span as possible). Lope also suggests that the language of the play should accommodate the subject matter and the status of the speaker, and that the subject matter should draw upon Spanish history, legends, and literature, avoiding classical plots and themes. Like Horace, Lope argued that the aim of drama was to entertain, to delight, and to teach; and like the neoclassicists, he noted that tragedy deals with royal and "great" actions, while comedy trades on the actions of the lowly. He advocated one action only without subplots and warned against the plot becoming episodic. Also, like the neoclassical theorists, he advocated verisimilitude, arguing that impossible things should not occur onstage, and that a likeness of truth should be represented. Lope appears to care little about costumes or settings in plays: he suggests that one of Vitruvius's three basic settings would satisfy any plot and that Julius Pollux would be as fine a source for costuming as anything else, since the Spanish tend toward anachronism in their artistic tastes.

De Vega was clearly the most popular writer of cape and sword plays in early 17th century Spain. However, he was surrounded by important playwrights, perhaps the most important of which was **Gabriel Tellez** (1583-1648) whose pen-name was **Tirso de Molina**. A Mercedarian friar, Tirso wrote plays full of strong-minded heroines who were frank and outspoken and who relentlessly pursued the men who promised to marry them. He also created drama that reflects his strong theological interest in the casuistry of free well—in response to John Calvin's doctrine of predestination. *El condenado por desconfiado* (*Damned for Lack of Trust*) (1620), for example, presents a saintly hermit who asks God to reveal his fate in the afterlife. Disguised as an angel, the Devil appears and reports that the hermit's fate would be identical to a certain locale gangster. In despair, the hermit decides to turn to a life of crime so that he might at least enjoy the thrills that lead to his damnation. The gangster, however, is greatly fond of his father who manages to get him to repent before his execution. The gangster ultimately goes to heaven while the hermit, having despaired that God will ever pardon him, goes to hell.

Best known as the author of *El burlador de Sevilla y convivado de piedra* (*The Deceiver of Seville and the Stone Guest*), the first great treatment of the Don Juan Tenorio legend, Tirso wrote three types of plays: comedies, dealing with amorous triangles, jealousy, and unrequited love; historical plays depicting the conflicts between feudal lords and their subjects; and religious dramas, emphasizing the ability of people to choose their acts and, through their choices, control their fate. Tirso was forbidden by the Church to write plays, under threat of excommunication. Like so many of the heroes in his plays, he was banished because of his self-expression, though subsequently pardoned.

Juan Ruiz de Alarcon (1581-1639) was born in Mexico and considered to be a follower of Lope de Vega even though his dramaturgy is quite different. His comedies of manners written between 1617 and 1620 anticipate French classical comedies in their comfortable adjustment to neoclassical rules, their urbane attacks on individuals with a single flaw, and the presence of a valet who directs the plot with a sure hand and clear mind. In many ways, French comedy has its origins in Alarcon's work for it was Pierre Corneille who effectively launched French comedy in 1642 with his translation of Alarcon's *La verdad sospechosa* (*Suspicious Truth*) (1618–1620) called *Le menteur* (*The Liar*). Alarcon's best plays center on court life in Madrid and he sought to make characterization and subtle moral sentiments the basis of dramatic action. Unlike his associates, Alarcon's output was small—only about 30 plays—and neither critics nor the public responded favorably to his work.

If Alarcon anticipates French comedy, **Guillen de Castro** (1569-1631) from Valencia is considered the inspiration for French neoclassical tragedy. His *Las mocedades del Cid* (*The Youthful Exploits of the Cid*) published in 1621 was the source of Pierre Corneille's *Le Cid* in 1636.

Calderon

Perhaps the most significant dramatist to write in Spanish, Pedro Calderon de la Barca y Barreda Gonzalez de Henao Ruis des Blasco y Riano (1600-1681) wrote over 200 *comedias*, 70 one-act *autos sacramentales*, as well as a number of musical plays and libretti. He is said to have written as many masterpieces as Shakespeare and twice as many as Racine or Sophocles. Calderon was the third of five children born to a court official belonging to an old aristocratic Castilian family. In 1613 he wrote his first play, *The Great Bear*, and two years later enrolled in the Jesuit school at Madrid where he studied law and philosophy, contrary to the wishes of his family who wanted him to become a priest. In 1622, Calderon won a poetry prize and was praised publicly by Lope de Vega, after whose death in 1635 he became the director of the court theatre at the palace of Buen Retiro. The following year, two volumes of his plays were published, and in 1637, after his musical *Love the Greatest Enchanter* was produced at court, Calderon became a knight of the Order of Santiago. In 1638, he fought in the battle of Fuenterrabia where the Spanish defeated the French in the Thirty Years War, and he maintained his career as a soldier until 1640, when King Philip IV brought him back to court to write the festival play, *The Battle between Love and Jealousy*. When the play was finished, Calderon returned to the battlefield, where he was wounded in 1642, and honorably discharged from military service.

In 1651 Calderon became a priest and refused to write any more plays because he was not given the chaplaincy in Madrid. Two years later, he became chaplain in Toledo and began directing Corpus Christi plays in Madrid from his post in Toledo. After ten years in Toledo, he returned to his position at court in Madrid in 1663, and became a member of the Brotherhood of San Pedro, a monastic order. The following year, he published a third volume of plays, and eight years later, in 1672, the fourth volume appeared (a fifth volume including a collection of *autos sacramentales* would follow in 1677). On Pentecost Sunday, 25 May 1681, Calderon died in the midst of writing a play. At his request he was buried in an open coffin to illustrate the ephemeral nature of the body, and three thousand people attended his funeral at the Church of the Savior in Madrid.

Caldron's theatrical career began in 1623 with the production of three plays: *Amor, honor y poder* (*Love, Honor, and Power*), *La selva confusa* (*The Tangled Forest*), and *Judas Macabeo* (*Judas Maccabeus*). His drama corresponds very closely to what critic Lionel Abel defines as metatheatre: "pieces of life seen as already theatricalized." The two great themes of metatheatre—the world is a stage, and life is a dream—actually appear as the title of two of his most famous plays, *El gran teatro del mundo* (*The Great Theatre of the World*) (1633) and *La vida es sueno* (*Life is a Dream*) (1635). The first of these (which won the respect of dramatists Lessing, Schlegel, and Shelley in the 19th century) depicts God as playwright calling on various actors from the world, as if life were a theatrical production. Grace of God serves as the prompter for life's drama and, in the end, all the actors exit without role, costume, or props to participate in a great celestial cast party. *Life is a Dream* depicts a Polish king who keeps his son and heir locked up in a tower because a prophecy predicted that the child would be evil. To test the validity of the prophecy, the king has his son drugged and brought to court. When the boy awakes in strange surroundings, he exhibits violent behavior and validates the predictions, so he is locked up again. When a revolution finally liberates the prince (now acclaimed as king), he questions which part of his life was real and what was only a dream.

Calderon's highly organized, deliberately artificial plays reflect a very precise understanding of humans and their place in the world. Drawing close to allegory, even his most secular plays deal with the destiny of humankind: *Life is a Dream* shows the process by which a natural man becomes a moral man; *El principe constante* (*The Constant Prince*) (1629) shows a moral man in the process of becoming a saint; and *El magico prodigioso* (*The Remarkable Magician*) (1637) presents a Faustian character who demonstrates the triumph of free will and faith over the almost unlimited power of the devil. Calderon's lighter plays deal with artificial situations in which young lovers battle against misunderstanding and deception until their true love is rewarded with marriage. As in all of his plays, the world of the senses is unreliable. If these cape and sword comedies do not lead to tragedy or moral transformation, it is because the lovers, still unmarried, are not fully committed to their acts. For Calderon, the world of the unmarried offers a second chance!

Spanish Theatres and Productions

A holdover from medieval times, Spanish city councils supervised the sites and times for performing plays. Gradually, dramatic activity moved into the court as rulers began to enjoy and exploit the pomp and splendor that theatrical productions could offer. Italian Renaissance scenic innovations were introduced at court in 1626 and slowly began to be assimilated into public theatres (though often in a simplified manner), where caros continued to support the scenery typical of the *autos sacramentales* until they were banned in 1765. In the public theatres, three kinds of scenery were used:

1) A facade, serving as the sole background for the action;

2) Curtains, drawn to conceal the facade when the locale was unimportant; and

3) Medieval mansions set up on the main playing area.

After 1650 spectacle increased and painted flats as well as practicable windows and doors began to be set into the facade. Except in rare instances, there was no attempt to use perspective scenery. The stage was typically equipped with several trapdoors and the roof over the stage housed machinery designed to fly the actors (a popular effect in the Spanish theatre).

A growing number of theatrical troupes increased the need for regulation and supervision. In 1603, eight companies held licenses to perform; by 1615 there were twelve companies. Acting companies were formed either on a sharing basis (in which actors all took a share of the proceeds) or on a contract basis (in which actors were hired for one or two-year periods). Most companies toured, but they could only receive a license to perform if a free performance satisfied a city official. Before 1590 playwrights actually toured with the acting companies; after 1590 they simply sold the companies their plays.

According to Augustin de Rojas Villandrando writing in 1603, there were eight kinds of acting companies:

1) *Bululu*: a player who travels alone or on foot. He stands on a trunk and recites a play or *loa* and passes a hat;

2) *Naque*: two men who enact an *entremes* or selections from an *auto*. They wear sheepskin beards, play a drum, and charge a particular fee. Like vagrants, they sleep in their clothes and walk barefoot from town to town;

3) *Gangarilla*: three or four men—one who can play the fool—and a boy who plays the woman's roles. They perform *autos sacramentales*, wear beards and wigs, borrow a woman's skirt and bonnet (which they often neglect to return), play two comic *entremes*, charge each spectator a fee, and accept various foodstuffs as payment. They sleep on the ground and travel constantly, often performing in barnyards;

4) *Cambaleo*: a woman who sings and 5 men who lament, with a repertoire that includes a *comedia*, two *autos*, 3–4 *entremes*. The men carry the woman on their backs (a possible reason for their lamenting) as well as all of the clothes and costumes for the company. They act in farmyards for a loaf of bread, grapes, or cabbage stew, and they ask for donations after the performance. They remain in one place for 4–6 days, hiring a bed for the woman while the men sleep on straw;

5) *Garnacha*: 5–6 men, a woman who plays the 1st lady's roles, and a boy who plays the 2nd woman's roles. They carry a chest containing costumes, beards, and wigs and have a repertoire of 4 *comedias*, 3 *autos*, 3–4 *entremes*. The woman and the chest ride on a donkey while the men and boy walk on foot. They remain in a town for a full week, sleeping 4 in a bed, and give private performances for fried chicken, boiled rabbit, two quarts of wine, and four *reals* in money. For 12 *reals* they can be hired for an entire festival;

6) *Boxiganga*: two women, a boy, 6–7 men (of which there are always a fool, a bully, and a jealous, love-sick character). They travel with 6 *comedias*, 5 *entremes*, 3–4 *autos*, and two chests—one contains the company's baggage, the other has the women's clothes. They hire four pack mules, one for the chests, two for the women, and the last on which the men alternate;

7) *Farandula*: three women, 6–7 men, 8–10 *comedias*, and two chests of luggage. They travel on mules or in *caros*, visit the more important towns, dine separately, wear good clothes, and perform at the Corpus Christi Festivals for 200 ducats;

8) *The Company*: 16 people who act, 30 who eat, and one to take the money at the door! They travel with 50 *comedias* and 300 pieces of luggage on mules, in litters, or in coaches. The Company generally included well-bred actors and respectable women.

When not employed by city councils for religious festivals, professional companies used whatever space was available: courtyards, public squares, and the court of King Philip III (1596-1621) whose queen enjoyed the theatre. Court entertainment peaked in 1626 when Philip IV (1621-1665) installed Italian scenic technology in his court theatre.

In 1579 and 1583 the first permanent theatre buildings were constructed in Madrid. The Corral de la Cruz and he Corral del Principe were based on contemporary courtyard theatres. A raised platform stage stood before a permanent two-level facade. The audience sat on three sides of a stage that was 26–28 feet wide and 23–29 feet deep. Three curtained openings in the lower level of the facade allowed for entrances and exits and led backstage to the *vestuario* (dressing room). The yard (or pit) in front of the stage where spectators stood to watch the play was called the *patio*. In the 17th century, benches were added to the *patio* and called *bancos* (sometimes referred to as *lunetas*). The *gradas*, platformed balconies along the sides of the patio, and the *cazuela* (stewpot)—the women's seating area located opposite the stage over the *alojeria* (tavern) on the far side of the patio—also required benches. Behind and above the *gradas* were *aposentos* (boxes) on the first two floors of the houses surrounding the courtyard, and above the *aposentos* were *desvanes* (attics), where spectators could watch from the tops of buildings. Two galleries above the cazuela housed officials and the clergy who gathered to keep one eye on the play and the other on the female spectators. Several entrances led to the courtyard and at each entrance there were two fee-takers: one for the confraternities (the religious organizations) and the other for the theatre manager. Three-fifths of the proceeds went to the theatre company and the rest went to charity.

The audience enjoyed a rousing time at the public theatre: outside the entrances, ticket scalpers operated; inside, men and women connived to overcome the sexually segregated seating. *Alguaciles* (armed guards) protected the actors and maintained order over the unruly, noisy mob. Vendors sold both fresh and dried fruit, water, sweets, ale, and rolled wafers called *barquillos*. The patio was the location for the most vocal of the spectators, the *mosqueteros* (musketeers) who cheered and booed repeatedly throughout the performance, often starting skirmishes that resulted in injury or death. Respectable women attended plays only if masked, and police, at the door of the cazuela, prevented them from hurling fruit, orange peels, cucumbers, or rattling keys at the actors. A shout of "Viva" typically greeted an especially fine performance.

In contrast, the court audience was much more subdued. Aristocratic audiences enjoyed the fashionable, state-of-the-art Italian scenery at performances that occurred whenever the king wanted them. In 1640 Philip IV had the Coliseo, a permanent theatre, built in El Buen Retiro, his new palace in Madrid. Containing Spain's first proscenium arch and a wing and groove system for changing scenery, the Coliseo was the most modern theatre of its time. Resembling the public *corrales*, it had a *patio*, three levels of *aposentos*, and a *cazuela* over which was located the royal box. The Coliseo was also roofed and occasionally opened its doors to the public.

Public performances were strictly regulated: none during Lent or the summer months; the curtain rose at 2 P.M. in the fall and 4 P.M. in the spring to insure the audience a safe voyage home. Both the court and public theatre audiences witnessed the same formula for theatrical production:

1) Music began the performance with dancing or a song;
2) A *loa* or prologue followed;
3) Another dance preceded the main play;

4) The 3-act *comedia* with *entremes* between each act;
5) A final dance.

Actors remained officially infamous but, in the Spanish "Golden Age" between 1580 and 1680, players enjoyed some degree of toleration and were even occasionally permitted to receive the sacraments. Most women's roles were played by boys until 1587 when female performers were licensed to appear on stage. Women had appeared on the Spanish stage as early as 1550 (there is evidence that Mariana de Rueda, Lope's first wife acted publicly with her husband in the 1550s) but they were more the exception than the rule. Evidently after a very successful tour of the *commedia dell'arte* in 1575, women began to be more easily accepted on stage. The Church's 1596 ban on female performers was never enforced and in 1598 a compromise permitted married women to appear with their husbands. A decree in 1608 stated that only actors were permitted backstage and that priests and nuns were not allowed to go to plays. In 1615, boys were prohibited from playing women, and women were forbidden to cross-dress as men in plays; in addition, the licentious dance, the *zarabanda*, was included in the censorship laws. Finally, in 1631, actors were allowed to form a guild or union, called the Confradia de la Novena, which did much to raise the status of the actor in the community.

The costume practice of the Spanish stage was similar to that in England during the Elizabethan and Jacobean periods. Contemporary clothing was the rule, with historical characters dressed in old-fashioned clothes and Moors distinguished from everybody else! In most cases, costumes were as lavish as money allowed, creating the necessity for government restrictions. In 1534, for example, a decree was issued forbidding extravagant dress onstage. Later, actresses were forbidden to wear extravagant headdresses, low-cut necklines, wide-hoop skirts, and dresses not touching the floor. They were even restricted to one costume per play, unless the script called for more.

Costumes for religious plays were probably more lavish than those for the public theatre and often involved the use of sumptuous materials such as silk and velvet. Minor actors wore less lavish costumes than stars, though some players went to great expense to costume themselves as gorgeously as possible. Costumes were the actor's greatest asset; they could help him/her secure employment and, since they were owned outright, they could be pawned when the actor needed quick cash.

The 1640s showed a decline in theatrical activities at court and in the public theatres. Rebellions in 1640 ushered in a period of uncertainty and following the deaths of the Italian designer Cosme Lotti (with whom Calderon produced elaborate spectacles and musicals at court) in 1643 and the queen in 1644, court theatricals came to a halt. Between 1646 and 1651 public theatres were closed as well. However, in 1651, once Philip IV had remarried and the rebellions that had caused so much unrest had been quelled, the Coliseo at court was reopened to the public, and public theatres were allowed to resume production. After 1670, spectacular productions were produced by Jose Caudi, the first Spanish scene designer of note, though after the death of Calderon in 1681 and Carlos II (Philip's successor) in 1700, theatre in Spain declined significantly.

7. The Theatrical Renaissance in France

The Italian Renaissance found its way into France during the reign of Francis I (1515-1547) when he invited several Italian artists and scholars to his court. This conclave of artists and scholars developed into what is known as the Fontainebleau School. In 1546, Francis commissioned Pierre Lescot to rebuild the Louvre in a Renaissance style and this created the architectural pattern that marked all the great French chateaux of the later 16th century.

Neoclassicism had a great effect on both school and court in France in a typical progression:

1) Study of classical plays;
2) Imitations of classical plays in Latin; and
3) Imitations of classical plays in French.

The Terence Stage, published in the first illustrated edition of Terence's plays in 1493 became the model for staging drama at both schools and court until around 1550. Ten years earlier, in 1540, classical plays and critical works began to be translated into French and by 1550, Sophocles, Euripides, Aristophanes, Seneca, Plautus, Terence, Aristotle, and Horace were all available in French editions. More recent Italian plays and commentaries on Horace and Aristotle were also translated.

Neoclassical influences were accelerated after Henry II, who married Catherine de Medici, came to the throne in 1547. Three years into his reign, the *Pléiade*, a group of seven writers under the leadership of Pierre de Ronsard, formulated a series of rules of grammar and prosody in an attempt to develop the French language as a medium for a literature modeled on classical works. The first vernacular neoclassical plays emerged from the Pléiade in 1552 when **Etienne Jodelle** (1523-1573) produced *Cléopatre captive* (*Cleopatra Enslaved*), the first tragedy and *Eugène*, the first comedy. *Cléopatre*, performed for Henry II with Jodelle enacting the title role, has 1615 lines, few characters, little action, and a chorus. Typical of the Senecan tragic model, *Cléopatre* begins with a speech spoken by Marc Antony's ghost predicting disaster: Cleopatra will die before the day is out. Act five describes her death and the three acts in between prepare Cleopatra to die. Also typical of the Senecan model is the use of dreams, confidants, and sententious monologues. Jodelle's later tragedy, *Dido's Suicide* (written circa 1560) is better written but still evocative of the Senecan formula. *Eugène*, a comedy, predictably makes use of Plautine conventions in dramatizing a farcical situation reminiscent of *Johann Johann*: a dissolute abbot becomes a soldier's rival in love and ends up cuckolding yet another man.

Jodelle's plays were performed in a hall of state though it is unknown whether the Terence Stage or perspective scenery was used. We do know that perspective scenery had been used in France as early as 1548 in a production of *La Calandria*, but though the French knew about Italianate scenery, court entertainment tended toward the use of dispersed decors—medieval-like mansion settings scattered about the hall—rather than in any unified design.

Humanist Tragedy

With the development of neoclassical plays came the codification of neoclassical principles. In 1572 **Jean de la Taille** published a preface to his play *Saul's Madness* in which he advocates the three unities established during the Italian Renaissance; henceforth, all dramatists of the neoclassical school sought to follow these precepts slavishly in their writing.

The best of these tragedians was **Robert Garnier** (1535-1600) who wrote seven tragedies and a tragicomedy between 1568 and 1583. Taking his subject matter from Roman history, Greek legend, and the Bible, Garnier modeled his tragedies after Seneca, depicting rulers crushed by fate who lament their misfortune in an elevated style. More than any other dramatist of his time, Garnier knew how to transform the realization of doom into a poignant and effective piece of theatre. In the hands of Robert Garnier, French Humanist Tragedy had the following characteristics:

1) They were based on the precepts of Horace and the neoclassical rules;
2) They were written in imitation of Seneca and Euripides;
3) There was an obvious neglect of characterization;
4) There was a lack of coherent structure;
5) Plays were filled with rhetorical display;
6) There was much blatant moralizing;
7) Plays were peopled by a multitude of lamenting characters;
8) A chorus provided moral and ethical interludes.

Among Garnier's plays are *Bradamante*, a tragedy about Charlemagne; *Hippolyte*, an adaptation of Euripides' play about Phaedra and Hippolytus, *Marc Antoine*, about Antony and Cleopatra, and *The Jews*, based on II Kings 25:7 and Jeremiah, depicting the story of the sins of Zedekiah and his punishment at the hands of Nebuchadnezzar. Perhaps most typical of Garnier's work is *Antigone* published in 1585. A highly rhetorical play, *Antigone* episodically follows the Senecan formula:

Act 1: Antigone and Oedipus discuss Oedipus' crime and his desire for death.
Act 2: The story of Antigone's brothers, Polynices and Eteocles is related.
Act 3: Antigone speaks to Jocasta about Oedipus.

Act 4: Antigone argues with Creon, her uncle, over the legality of burying her brother.

Act 5: Antigone dies.

Humanist Comedy

The development of Humanist Comedy parallels that of tragedy. In 1567, **Antoine de Baif** translated Plautus's *Miles Gloriosus* and in 1573, he adapted Terence's play *Eunuchus*. Consequently, many humanist critics felt that Humanist Comedy was an amalgam of medieval farce and Latin comedy. Jodelle's *Eugène* and Jacques Peletier's *Art of Poetry* (1555) certainly verified such a view. *Eugène* is in five acts, begins with a prologue, and ends with a command for the audience to applaud, yet its subject matter is straight out of medieval farce. Peletier's treatise suggested that the characters suitable for Roman comedy were the only characters acceptable for classical French comedy.

Italian Renaissance comedy also had an important influence on French Humanist Comedy. In 1545, Jacques Bourgeois translated Ariosto's *The Supposes* while la Taille translated *The Necromancer* in 1573, nearly fifty years after it had been produced in Italy. In 1548 and in 1555 Italian plays were presented at the French court which, for the rest of the century, proved more receptive to comedy (Italian comedy in particular) than to tragedy.

Perhaps even more popular than comedy at court were court festivals. Francis I and Henry II were both especially fond of tournaments (Henry died in 1559 while participating in one of them). After Henry's death, his wife, Catherine de Medici was in a very powerful position and her theatrical tastes ran to "royal entries" and various kinds of festivals that she used to demonstrate France's power to the rest of Europe. A particularly elaborate festival took place in Bayonne in 1565 in which a water pageant was featured. Out of these festivals evolved the *ballet de cour*—the French version of the Italian intermezzo and the English masque—in which dramatic plot, song, dance, and spectacle were united in an "artistic manner." Experiments of this fashion culminated in 1581 with the *Ballet Comique de la Reine*. Based on the myth of Circe, the plot was treated as a moral struggle between virtue and vice with the king portrayed as the hero, delivering his subjects from evil. The ballet was staged in the Salle du Petit Bourbon housed in the palace adjacent to the Louvre. One of the most important court theatres of the 17th century, the Petit Bourbon was 49 feet wide and 177 feet long. Spectators watched from 2 balconies that extended from the side walls while the king and his court watched from a central position on the floor.

Public Theatres

Though court spectacles and neoclassical plays were in high gear, the public theatre was quickly running out of gas. After religious drama was banned in 1548, the Confrèrie de la Passion, organized in 1402 to produce religious drama, was given a monopoly on secular drama. Performing at the Hôtel de Bourgogne (built in 1548), the first permanent theatre to be built in Europe since Rome, the Confrèrie played at regular intervals, but as popularity waned—the company did not perform farce especially well— around 1570 it began to rent the theatre to other acting troupes. There were many acting companies outside of Paris that were formed from defunct religious companies, but few wanted to perform inside the city because of the Confrèrie's monopoly. Whenever any company wanted to produce a play in Paris, it had to pay a fee to the Confrèrie de la Passion.

Theatrical activity both at court and in the public sector came to a halt with the rise of the civil war between the Catholic and Protestant (Huguenot) factions. Unrest came to a head in 1572 when thousands of Protestants were massacred in the St. Bartholomew's Day Massacre, and between 1572 and 1595, it was against the law for French companies to perform plays in Paris. When public theatrical performances resumed, public tastes had changed because, during the years of conflict, *commedia dell'arte* troupes toured Paris (it was not against the law for foreign theatrical companies to perform!) introducing audiences to their particular brand of farce.

Capitalizing on this new development, **Alexandre Hardy** (1572–1632), France's first professional playwright, adapted neoclassical techniques to popular tastes. His plays had five acts, poetic dialogue, ghosts, messengers, and a chorus, but he did not allow rules to interfere with the telling of the story. As a result, he seldom observed the unities of time and place, and he put all important action—even violence—on stage. He imported comic elements into serious plots, carried on dialogue in short speeches rather than in long monologues, and borrowed stories and character details from the Spanish theatre. Hardy began his career as a tragedian but, failing to make a mark, he turned to tragicomedy and pastoral plays. *Mariamne* (1610) is generally considered his masterpiece.

Hardy's early work was done primarily for France's first important theatrical manager, **Valleran Le Comte** (fl. 1592–1613) whose troupe was called Les Comédiens du Roi because it performed for King Henry IV. The title, unfortunately, carried with it no special privileges, but between 1598 and 1612, Valleran's was the most important company in Paris.

The Hôtel de Bourgogne was the usual place for public performances between 1595 and 1625. Around the walls of the auditorium ran two or three galleries, at least one of which had boxes (*loges*). The first floor was the pit (*parterre*) in which there were no permanent seats except for a bench running along the side walls. Behind the *parterre*, facing the stage, was an undivided gallery called *amphithéâtre*. Capacity was about 1600. The stage was raised five or six feet above the *parterre* and, although there was no proscenium arch, the side galleries which extended all the way up to the stage created a kind of frame. The stage occupied the entire width of the building (42– 60 feet) but the visible space was probably only about 25 feet. It is believed that the stage was only about 17–35 feet in depth.

For the troupes that did not perform at the Hôtel de Bourgogne (remember they had to pay a fee to the Confrèrie) the usual location was in a tennis court. During the 17th century, there were between 250 and 1800 tennis courts in Paris and by 1600 these had been standardized to a size of 90 by 30 feet. They had a gallery for spectators along one side or at the end of the room, a large open floor space, and lots of light available from windows just below the roof. To convert a tennis court into a theatre simply required the addition of a platform stage. The Théâtre du Marais, another significant playing space for acting companies had been converted from a tennis court in 1634.

During the early 17th century, performances were given two or three times a week. By 1600, posters were used as advertisements, and announcements of coming attractions were made from the stage. Official regulations required that all performances ended early enough to allow spectators time to get home safely before dark. As a result, starting times tended to vary according to the length of the play (like operas in opera houses today). Because of variable curtain times and the audience's tendency to come early to get a good seat (tickets did not specify seat locations like they do today), each theatre company used a prologist to entertain the audience until the play began. Perhaps the most celebrated actor in this capacity was **Bruscambrille** (fl. 1610–1634). Food, drink, and souvenirs were sold during performances and, with all the movement and jostling around in the standing pit, spectators who always wore their swords or daggers to plays, often ended up fighting.

In the early 17th century, acting companies were bound by two-or-three-year contracts and organized on a sharing plan in which the manager typically received two shares while supernumeraries might get a fraction of a full share. Companies ranged in size from 8 to 12 sharing members, often supplemented by hired men or apprentices. Because of the fondness of Cardinal Richelieu for seeing women on the stage, actresses were included in French companies by 1607. Even though cardinals and other churchmen supported theatrical activity, most actors adopted stage names because of the social and religious stigma attached to the acting profession.

Between 1610 and 1625, the most famous actors were the players of farce which was still the most popular genre in Paris. Like the performers of the *commedia dell'arte*, French farceurs played stock characters with stock costumes and makeup. Often the personal mannerisms or physical characteristics of the actor became associated with the character. Originally members of Valleran's troupe, the actors Turlupin, a rascal servant type, Gaultier-Garguille, a thin, bow-legged contortionist, and Gross-Guillaume, fat and in white-face, were the principal performers of farce at the Hôtel de Bourgogne after 1612.

About 1625 a new troupe appeared at the Bourgogne called the Players of the Prince of Orange. France's first famous tragedian, **Mondory** (1594–1651) and the popular comedian **Jodelet** (1600–1660) belonged to this troupe. After 1634 Mondory associated himself with another group of actors at the Marais. Mondory played heroic figures with tremendous vocal and physical exertion, achieving distinction by introducing the plays of the dramatist Corneille. In fact, during the controversy over *Le Cid* and Corneille's lack of classical unities (see below), critics said that the play achieved popularity only through Mondory's performance. In 1636/37 however, Mondory's strenuous performance technique took its toll: while playing the role of Herod, he was struck by an apoplectic fit and his tongue became paralyzed.

After Mondory's retirement, the Hôtel de Bourgogne acquired the best actors from the Marais Company. These included **Bellerose** (d. 1670) and **Montfleury** (1608-1667) who inaugurated an affected, flamboyant, and bombastic style that became the prevalent mode of acting. It was said of Bellerose that he was an "affected actor who looked where he was putting his hat for fear of spoiling his feathers." Montfleury, a fairly corpulent man, was viciously satirized by Molière in his *Versailles Impromptu* and ordered from the stage because of his artificiality by Cyrano de Bergerac.

Resurgence of Classicism

Henry IV was assassinated in 1610 and was followed by the nine-year-old Louis XIII who ruled until 1643. In the 1620s the real power in France was with Cardinal Richelieu (1586–1642) who concentrated political power in the crown by withdrawing it from nobles and independent Protestant towns. With renewed order in government came a resurgence of interest in Classicism, which developed more or less in three periods:

1) From 1625 to 1653, during which technically proficient and well-educated playwrights began to appear. Audiences began to prefer the new drama to the farces, and professional troupes gained a firm foothold in Paris.

Of the dramatists who appeared, the most notable were Jean de Mairet (1604–1686), Pierre du Ryer (1600–1658), Jean de Rotrou (1609–1650) and **Pierre Corneille** (1606-1684).

2) 1653 to 1664 which heralded a revival of comedy and the development of a new *préciosité* in dramatic literature. Among the major dramatists of this phase were Thomas Corneille and **Philippe Quinault**.

3) The period of High Classicism, 1664–1700, which was dominated by **Racine** (1639–1699) and **Molière** (1622–1673).

First Period—1625 to 1653

From 1628 to 1631 a doctrinal quarrel arose that clearly identified the turning point in the development of the neoclassical spirit in the French theatre. 1628 was considered the high point of "irregular drama": the 5th volume of Hardy's plays appeared that year as well as François Ogier's *Tyr et Sidon*, with a preface calling for the freedom to mix genres, to mix tragic substance with comic details, and demanding the rejection of the authority of the ancients along with their rules and unities.

Two years later, the neoclassical avant-garde asserted itself with **Jean Chapelain** in his *Letter on the 24-hour Rule*, and later in his *Discourse on Representational Poetry*. In the name of faithfulness to life, verisimilitude became the champion of rules, not because of the authority of Aristotle, but because of the good sense and practice of the ancient writers. In 1631 **Jean Mairet** prefaced his pastoral drama, *La Sylvanire* with a manifesto of the new theatre. In the years that followed, even though irregular plays were still being produced, the regular theatre gained considerable ground: respectful of unity of action, unity of time (24–36 hours), and unity of place—within the boundaries of one city, or one forest, though several "rooms" were permitted if they were in a single house or city (the rooms were compartments built side-by-side onstage with curtains that opened and closed revealing them with shifts of the action). Comic elements were significantly reduced and, in most cases, removed altogether from tragedy, and there was a notable search for propriety (*bienséance*): playwrights did their best to avoid too much physical violence and bloodshed onstage.

French neoclassical tragedies came in rapid succession: *Hercule Mourant* (*Dyring Hercules*) (1634) by Jean Routrou; *Sophonisbe* (1634) by Jean Mairet which was considered the first French neoclassical tragedy because of its adherence to all the rules (the lovers are hastened to their deaths within a few hours); *La Mort de César* (*Caesar's Death*) (1635) by Scudery; *Medea* (1635) by Pierre Corneille; and François Tristan L'Hermite's *Mariane* (1636) which was, along with *Sophonisbe*, the most popular tragedy of this period.

Common characteristics of the early tragedies:

1) Three unities;

2) Ancient subject matter;

3) Lamentations by highly sensual characters;

4) Fate symbolized by the "wheel of fortune";

5) A taste for moral aphorisms and memorable phrases;

6) Use of promontory dreams and magic;

7) Philosophical or intellectual debates;

8) Boil down the tragic effects of violence, shock, and surprise into a single psychological crisis.

Pierre Corneille

While tragedy was developing according to the above scheme, comedy began to replace farce as the most popular dramatic form. Pierre Corneille (1606–1684) initiated the form of comedy based on Latin models and the Italian pastoral play. His first play, *Mélite*, was performed in his home town, Rouen, in 1629 by an itinerant acting troupe and produced in Paris the following year. An elegant and witty comedy, *Mélite* was reportedly based on a love-affair Corneille experienced while a law student at the Jesuit School in Rouen. Following the play's reception in Paris, Corneille's career as a playwright began to take off and he followed with a series of comedies and tragicomedies that attracted the attention of Cardinal Richelieu who invited

Corneille to participate in a group called the "Society of Five Authors." This arrangement allowed the cardinal to provide the "inspiration" for plays which the playwrights would then flesh out into five acts. Unfortunately for Corneille, Richelieu expected the playwrights to realize his "inspirations" (which included plot outlines, characterizations, and even phrases of dialogue) exactly, without alteration of any kind. Such a rigid atmosphere was unsuited to Corneille's artistic personality, and even after heated arguments with his patron, he strayed conspicuously from the cardinal's outline in his contribution (Act Three) to *The Comedy of the Tuilleries* in 1635. Even though his artistic independence earned him the enmity of one of the most powerful men in France, Corneille persisted as a playwright, and his next comedy, *The Comic Illusion* (1636) in which a magician evokes visions of distant events in the turbulent life of a young lover, was considered the most striking comic play of the period.

In January 1637 Corneille came to the forefront of tragic playwrights with the production of *Le Cid* at the Marais. Written in response to Mairet's *Sophonisbe* and based on Castro's *The Cid* (1631), *Le Cid* is regarded as the first masterpiece of French neoclassical theatre, even though it does not adhere to all of the so-called neoclassical rules (it is also believed that the production of *Le Cid* was so successful in Paris that it established the practice of audience members sitting on the stage). Typically, audiences loved the play but the critics hated it, and the resultant controversy led Cardinal Richelieu (still harboring a grudge against Corneille's artistic independence) to submit the play to the Académie Française (which had been instituted in 1635 by King Louis XIII) for a decision regarding its artistic merits. In December 1637 the French Academy issued a document in which the play is called "dramatically implausible and morally defective." In calling for verisimilitude, the Academy argued that the theatre should procure reasonable contentment but only on condition that there be no shocking departure from customs, either in the sense of the normal behavior of the characters onstage, or in the sense of morality. This judgment clearly indicated that there were two conflicting concepts of neoclassicism at work in France in the 17th century:

1) A living classicism sought by the public for whom the experience of pleasure and heightened emotions was the goal of theatre, and so only the rules that provided pleasure and emotions were necessary;

2) The classicism of the theoreticians who argued in the name of logic (or Aristotle) that no pleasure outside stringent adherence to the rules could be of good quality.

The consequences of the dispute over *Le Cid* were several:

1) Corneille left the theatre (only to return in 1640!);

2) The spirit of "regular" tragedy and adherence to the rules triumphed;

3) The success of the play, in spite of its departure from the rules, led some playwrights to try their hand at tragicomedy;

4) Certain authors of tragicomedy also respected the neoclassical rules, so the line between tragedy and tragicomedy became blurred.

When Corneille returned to the theatre in 1640, he produced four regular tragedies based on Roman history: *Horace, Cinna, Polyeucte,* and *La mort de Pompée* (*Pompey's Death*). In all of these plays, the heroes and heroines are forced by circumstances and the choice of certain values (family honor, patriotism, religious faith, political duty) to try to outdo one another in generosity and, through greatness of soul, to admire one another in their struggle to the death in order to achieve a higher reconciliation than the revenge or victory they were originally seeking.

In 1644, with the tragedy *Rodogune*, Corneille developed a new conception of characters and their relationships. In this play and those that were to follow until 1652, the generous characters were joined by those who were "monsters," or at least Machiavellian types whose magnanimity is perverted and leads them to commit the foulest of acts. Their behavior is so extreme, so inhuman, that they necessarily provoke the feelings that Corneille considered equal—if not superior—to the Aristotelian concept of pity and fear: admiration.

After the production of *Pertharite*, a huge failure in 1652, Corneille left the theatre once again, this time for seven years during which he labored on a translation of a religious work, *The Imitation of Christ*. Back to the theatre in 1659, Corneille once again was in the ascendant with *Oedipe*, a huge success. By 1674 he had written 11 new plays, one of which, Psyché (1671), was a tragicomedy written in collaboration with Molière and Quinault. However, in 1674, one of Corneille's sons was killed in Louis XIV's War against the European Coalition (1643–1715). The author's grief over that misfortune along with his frustration over the burgeoning popularity of Jean Racine led Corneille away from the theatre forever. From that point until his death in 1684, he spent his time overseeing the publication of his plays and attending meetings of the Académie Française to which he had been elected in 1647.

In the various prefaces to his plays, and in the three *Discourses*, published in 1660 with the complete edition of his works (to 1660), Corneille affirmed his independence within the bounds of the neoclassical formula. For him theatre was a spectacular art that had to astound the spectator. He liked historically true but surprising situations that forced a number of characters into action, and in which, the individual, through his/her heroic and magnanimous decisions, heinous crimes, or renunciations proved his/her powers of transcendence. Faced with a difficult choice, Corneille's heroes always take the most admirable alternative even in crime so that they may shine in their own eyes and in the eyes of others. This is called the "ethics of glory" through which the hero convinces himself and seeks to convince others of his self-possession and superiority. Ordinary morality is replaced by the elucidations of inner conflicts and the explanations of great feats by which a hero contrives to reconcile his will and his passions in order to achieve his goal.

Second Period—1653-1664
The precious or sentimentalized tragedies of the second period were *Romanesque* plays produced by Thomas Corneille (1625-1709), Pierre's brother, and Philippe Quinault (1635-1688). In French neoclassical drama, the term *Romanesque* designates all that is inspired by the romances and novels of Lodovico Ariosto and the French novelists of the 17th century.

These plays have the following typical characteristics:

1) Plots exploiting surprising and extraordinary adventures;
2) Characters with mysterious identities;
3) Exalted and complicated love stories involving perfect lovers and the idealization of love;
4) The awareness of playing a role according to prescribed rules of behavior.

Thomas Corneille began writing for the theatre in 1649 and produced a masterpiece of Romanesque tragedy in 1656 with *Timocrate*, a play based on mistaken identities and the obligations required by a code of love. Thomas respected the neoclassical rules but often adapted them to the popular taste. He was capable of writing in the stark simplicity of neoclassical tragedy but preferred the more complex adventures of the Romanesque style. His most successful plays other than *Timocrate* were typically based on Spanish originals.

Philippe Quinault began his work in the theatre writing comedies based on the Italian *commedia erudita* (e.g., *The Indiscreet Lover*, 1655) and Spanish *comedia* (*The Amorous Ghost*, 1656). The Spanish influence, however, is perhaps best seen in his finest comedy, *The Flirtatious Mother* (1665). After he success of Corneille's *Timocrate* in 1656, Quinault turned to writing Romanesque tragedies as well: *The False Alcibiades* (1658), *The Death of Cyrus* (1658) and *Agrippa* (1662). Sensitive to changes in theatrical tastes, when Racine was in the ascendant, he imitated that playwright's style with *Pausanias* in 1668 and two years later produced *Bellerophon*, a tragedy that anticipated Racine's masterpiece *Phèdre* in 1677.

Beginning in 1672, Quinault wrote a number of opera librettos for Jean Baptiste Lully in which the subject matter of tragedy became a pretext for fantastic musical spectacles instead of conforming to the rules of neoclassical tragedy. Criticized for writing characters with excessive sentimentality, Quinault was popular both with King Louis XIV and the audience, and he was even considered by Voltaire as one of the best poets of the 17th century. Though he lacked originality and tended toward the insipid rather than the truly passionate, he had an excellent sense of theatricality. His most famous librettos are *Alceste* (1674), *Isis* (1677), *Proserpine* (1680), and *Armide* (1688).

Third Period—1664-1700

The acknowledged master of French neoclassical tragedy was **Jean Racine** (1639-1699). Orphaned at the age of four, Racine was raised by his grandmother, Marie des Moulins, who, in 1649, took the boy with her to the Jansenist convent of Port-Royal des Champs close to Paris. Jansenism was a heretical sect within the Catholic Church that denied free will and maintained that all human nature is corrupt. Moreover, the Jansenists argued that Christ died only for a select few and not all humankind. From 1649 to 1653, Racine received a classical—if austere—education at Port-Royal. When he turned 18, he was sent to the College of Harcourt in Paris to study law. It was here that the young student began an association with actors and actresses and decided to try his hand at writing (despite the fact that his Jansenist mentors hated the theatre).

In 1660, Racine wrote two tragedies, one of which was refused by the Marais company, and the other, *Amasie*, was accepted by the Bourgogne troupe but never produced. Disappointed, Racine left Paris to become a priest but, in a short time, he discovered that he wasn't suited to a religious vocation—especially one that required celibacy—and he returned to Paris in 1663, with another tragedy in hand. Soon he had managed to ingratiate himself with Molière, who produced Racine's *Thébaide* in 1664 at the Théâtre du Petit Bourbon. Even though the play was a dismal failure, Molière produced Racine's *Alexandre* in 1665. Even though Molière's production had been a success, Racine was unhappy with the production and gave the play to a rival company at the Bourgogne, a betrayal that created a major scandal in the Parisian theatrical community. To make matters even worse, Racine seduced Molière's leading lady, Thérèse du Parc, and convinced her to go to the rival company along with his play! Needless to say, Molière was deeply offended by Racine's machinations, and the two men became bitter enemies for the rest of their careers.

Between 1667 and 1677, Racine produced a series of seven tragedies that would make him, in the eyes of both critics and audiences, the equal of Corneille as master of the tragic form. *Andromaque*, a Romanesque tragedy written for his mistress in 1667, showed Racine to be inventive and original in his use of love and honor as a motivating force in neoclassical tragedy. In the play, Oreste is in love with Hermione who is in love with Pyrrhus who, in turn, is in love with Andromaque who is faithful to the memory of her dead husband, the Trojan warrior Hector. Since the Greeks insist that Andromaque's son, Astyanax, be sacrificed to them, Pyrrhus presents her with the choice of either marrying him or watching her son killed. Faced with this dilemma, Andromaque decides to marry Pyrrhus and then kill herself. However, Hermione has convinced Oreste to kill Pyrrhus. When the deed is done, Hermione commits suicide out of regret, and Oreste loses his mind.

What Racine managed to do was find the meeting point between the perfect rationalism of form, which had slowly been developing, and the fundamental irrationalism of human nature. With Racine, tension is created by psychology and fate, and the two are always linked: the mechanism of love is irreversible—every cry, very gesture is irretrievable. Thanks to Racine, fate was reintroduced into tragedy in an internal form: love is a curse on the soul that leads infallibly to murder, madness, or suicide. In all of his works the feeling of fate is reinforced by the structure of the plays. The extreme simplicity of the form leaves only one alternative open for the characters to take, without the possibilities and hopes implied by more complex plots. Moreover, Racine begins his plays as close to the dénouement as possible, when the characters are already prisoner of an entire past life of decisions and acts that condemn them to tragedy without the possibility of salvation.

In 1669 and 1673 Racine produced *Britannicus* and *Mithridate*, in the style of Corneille, plays based on a Roman subject centering on a struggle for power. In both works, however, the political and moral tragedy is diverted toward the portrayal of a destructive passion and its inexorable activity.

Although all of Racine's tragedies are based on the concept of destruction through passion, they are eminently varied. *Bérénice* (1670) is a non-bloody three-character play; *Bajazet* (1672) is an Oriental-historical play; *Iphigénie* (1674) is an effort to recreate the noble pathos of Greek tragedy, as is *Phèdre* (1677). Racine wrote only one comedy, a relatively insignificant work called *Les Plaideurs* (*The Litigants*), in 1668, based on *The Wasps* of Aristophanes.

Because of the theatrical backbiting that typically comes with success, and tired of the psycho-sexual intrigue associated with the theatre, Racine retired from the stage in 1677 and experienced a religious conversion. He reassociated himself with the Jansenists, married a pious woman who never saw or read any of his plays, and became the king's historiographer (on the condition that he forsake the theatre completely). Racine briefly associated himself with playwriting in 1689 and 1691 when, at the request of his patroness, Madame de Maintenon (Louis XIV's consort) he produced two biblical plays for her school for girls at St. Cyr, *Esther* and *Athalie*. Except for the publication of his complete works, these would be Racine's last theatrical efforts.

In 1698, the playwright fell out of favor with the king because of his steadfast support of the Jansenists (as a Catholic, Louis wished to limit the power of the Jansenists in France). The following year, Racine died on 21 April from cancer of the liver, ending his life as an austere Christian, interested in nothing but the strict education and moral rectitude of his seven children.

Molière

Comic playwright **Jean Baptiste Poquelin** (1622-1673) was the well-educated son of a prosperous Parisian merchant who, at the age of twenty-one, incorporated with the Béjart family of actors to create a theatre company called the Illustre-Théatre. Because of the infamy associated with actors, Poquelin took the name Molière to spare his family embarrassment. The change of names was fortuitous since the theatre company went bankrupt in two years and Molière found himself in debtors' prison. Upon his release, he left Paris with Madeleine Béjart and other members of the family to join Charles Dufresne's itinerant theatre troupe. For the next thirteen years, Molière toured the French provinces, an absolutely invaluable experience since it allowed him to refine his comic abilities and develop the qualities of a theatre manager. In addition, touring gave Molière the opportunity to write plays that were both inspired by the *commedia dell'arte* troupes he met during his travels, and designed to fit the talents of the various members of his company.

In the fall of 1658, Molière's troupe traveled north to Paris and was granted a performance before Louis XIV, who was so entertained by Molière's farce, *The Doctor in Love*, that he granted the author and his company the use of the Petit-Bourbon in tandem with Fiorilli's *commedia dell'arte* troupe. In 1659, Molière's latest comedy *Les Précieuses Ridicules* (*The Affected Ladies*) triumphed in Paris, though the playwright earned the hostility of the fashionable audience whom he burlesqued in the play. *Sganarelle; or, The Imaginary Cuckold* followed in 1660, and in 1661 appeared *The Impertinents*, one of the king's favorites, *Don Garcia of Navarre*, a rare failure, and *The School for Husbands*, a substantial success at the refurbished Palais Royal, the theatre to which the Molière troupe had moved when the Petit-Bourbon was destroyed in 1661. In 1662, Molière married nineteen-year-old Armande Béjart, Madeleine's sister, and produced *The School for Wives*, causing a scandal throughout Paris, and provoking attacks on the author's ethics, aesthetics, and private life. Undaunted by criticism and energized by scandal, Molière countered with the *Versailles Impromptu* in 1663, and a three-act version of *Tartuffe* in 1664. Denied public performance for *Tartuffe*, Moliere wrote *Don Juan* in 1665, causing yet another scandal with critics calling for the author to be burnt at the stake! The following year produced two of Molière's greatest plays, the five-act comedy *The Misanthrope*, and the three-act farce, *The Doctor in Spite of Himself*. In 1667, a second version of *Tartuffe* was again denied public performance but, finally, in 1669 a five-act version of the play was permitted, beginning on Tuesday, 5 February, and running for forty-four performances, a substantial run in 1669. Following the success of *Tartuffe*, Molière produced *The Magnificent Lovers*, a comedy-ballet based on a scenario suggested by the king and *Le Bourgeois Gentilhomme* (both 1670), a machine-play, *Psyche*, performed at the Tuileries and written in collaboration with Pierre Corneille and Philippe Quinault (1671), and *The Learned Ladies* (1672), after which the king withdrew his support from Molière's troupe. Finally, in 1673, Molière died on 17 February, following the 4th performance of *The Imaginary Invalid*, in which the author played to eponymous role. Since pious Catholics sought to refuse him a Christian burial because of his profession, Molière was interred at night on 21 February to avoid yet another scandal.

As a comic playwright Molière combines the Latin comedy of Plautus and Terence, the high comedy of Corneille, and the farce comedy of the *commedia dell'arte*. Characteristically, his plays are peopled with the following characters:

1) Rich fathers;

2) Amorous sons without money;

3) Knavish servants;

4) Young women in love with anyone other than the choice of their parent or guardian;

5) A feisty young wife married to an older man;

6) Various zanni (grotesquely comic characters).

The Comédie Française

When Molière died in 1673, there were five professional acting companies in Paris: a commedia dell'arte company, an opera company under the direction of Jean Baptiste Lully, and three acting troupes: Molière's at the Palais Royal, and companies at the Bourgogne and Marais theatres. When the opera company took over the Palais Royal in 1673, the king compressed the Molière and Marais troupes into a single company that performed at the Guénégaud Theatre until 1679, when the Bourgogne troupe merged with the Guénégaud troupe to form a single acting company in Paris, the Comédie Française.

When the Comédie Française was formed in 1680 (it gave its first performance on 25 August at the Guénégaud), 21 and a quarter shares were divided among twenty-seven members of the company: 17 actors received full shares, 7 received half shares, and 3 utility players received quarter shares. Since the number of shares in the Comédie Française was fixed by the crown, not all the actors who appeared in a season could be actual sharing members (*sociétaires*) in the company. No new actors could be admitted as shareholders until an actor resigned, retired, or passed away; and when a vacancy came about, the members elected the new shareholder from among the salaried actors (*pensionnaires*) in the company. Once the *pensionnaires* became *sociétaires*, the actors were bound to the company for twenty years and had a voice in all of the workings of the theatre. The actor with the longest seniority always acted as the head or *doyen* of the troupe. After twenty years of services, actors could retire from the Comédie Française with an annual pension.

A Gallery of Actors

Madeleine Béjart (1618-1672) was most successful at performing the feisty maids in Molière's comedies. Armande Béjart (1642-1700), Molière's wife, was a versatile actress who played the heroine in her husband's plays. Mlle. DuParc (1633-1668) was the leading tragic actress at the Bourgogne after 1666 when Racine made her his mistress and lured her away from Molière's company. Mlle. Champmeslé (1642-1698) was a champion of the declamatory style of acting and was considered the fines tragic actress in Paris after 1670. Charles Varlet, known as LaGrange (c.1639-1692) was another versatile actor, playing young lovers and character roles in Molière's plays. He also maintained the company records for the Comédie Française until 1685. Michel Baron (1653-1729), who began his career as a child performer, belonged to the natural school of acting and was considered the leading tragedian of his day.

Actors were required to supply their own costumes for their various roles, except for those playing devils, ghosts, monks, coachmen, or valets, or when a number of identical costumes were needed. Most characters were costumed in contemporary clothes, though exotic characters (classical, Near-Eastern, and Indian roles) were highly elaborate and unlike anything worn in real life. The expensive *habit à la romaine* was the typical costume of classical heroes: Roman armor tunic and boots, with a full-bottomed wig and plumed headdress. Usually, this costume cost the actor the equivalent of one-third his annual income!

Theatrical Production in Paris, 1629-1700

Between 1629 and 1660, there were two major production venues in Paris: the Hôtel de Bourgogne (described above) and Théâtre du Marais. When the Marais was rebuilt in 1644 after a fire consumed the original theatre, it was 115 feet long and 38 feet wide. The side walls of the auditorium had three galleries, the first two divided into boxes, the third a kind of balcony area called the *paradis*. Similarly, at the back of the auditorium two galleries were divided into boxes and the third was called the amphitheatre with bleacher-like accommodations. The stage of the Marais was raked and had a proscenium opening of about 25 feet. There was also a semi-circular *théâtre supérieure*, a raised platform, thirteen feet above the stage floor from which much of the spectacular flying effects took place.

Until the production of *Le Cid*, scenic practices in Parisian theatres were essentially medieval, using mansion settings to represent the various locales required in a particular play (before *Le Cid*, the unity of place regulation was not as rigorously enforced). After 1640 Italianate scenery became inherent to French theatrical production (even though it had been introduced to the French court theatre as early as 1625). Richelieu set the example by having a theatre built inside his palace that would be the first in France with a permanent proscenium arch and a stage designed for the use of flat wings. Called the Palais Cardinal, Richelieu's theatre opened in January 1641 and throughout the year produced plays that demonstrated the possibilities of Italian moveable scenery. In 1642 the cardinal died and the theatre, renamed the Palais Royal, came under the control of the king.

Cardinal Mazarin, Richelieu's successor as Chief Minister to the king, was fond of Italian opera and persuaded the queen to invite the celebrated Italian designer Giacomo Torelli to France. Once in Paris, Torelli converted the Petit Bourbon into an Italian-style theatre and installed the chariot-and-pole system to facilitate changes of scenery. Once work at the Petit Bourbon was completed, Torelli turned his attention to the Palais Royal and in 1646, he installed the chariot-and-pole system in that theatre. Torelli's innovations assisted the development of spectacle theatre in 17th-century Paris, a development that would be continued by Gaspare Vigarani (1586–1663) who was imported from Italy to design a spectacle for the marriage of King Louis XIV to Marie Thérèse of Spain in 1660. Vigarani had a new wing built in the Tuileries and constructed the Salles des Machines, then the largest theatre in Europe, measuring 52 feet wide by 232 feet long, with a stage that was 140 feet deep, with a proscenium opening of 32 feet. The Salle des Machines was opened in 1662 with the production of *Hercules in Love*, in which the entire royal family and their attendants were flown. Even more impressive was the design of Carlo Vigarani (1623–1713)—Gaspare's son who replaced him as court designer in 1663—for the Salle des Ballets at Versailles in 1685. A smaller, more intimate theatre than the Salle des Machines, the Salle des Ballets had the same size of proscenium opening (32 feet) with a stage that was 84 feet deep and an auditorium that was 66 feet long and 40 feet wide.

Carlo Vigarani was succeeded by Jean Bérain *père* (1637–1711) who was entirely French-educated and who was credited with realizing for the first time, the visual style that we now associate with Louis XIV: the use of heavy lines, reverse curves, and encrusted ornamentation. After 1680, Bérain was the main designer for opera and court entertainments until his death when he was succeeded by his son, Jean Bérain *fils* (1678–1726) who continued the family tradition until 1721.

The Comédie Française company performed at the Guénégaud theatre from 1680 to 1689 when it was forced to move because the Sorbonne required the land to build a new college. The Etoile tennis court, in the St. Germain-des-Prés quarter of Paris, remodeled at the cost of 200,000 livres, became new home of the Comédie Française until 1770. The ground floor of the new theatre had a standing pit leading to a bleacher-style amphitheatre raised about six feet from the floor. Along the side walls were two levels of boxes, above which was located an undivided balcony (*paradis*) making the capacity of the theatre about 2,000. Although the stage was 54 feet wide and 41 feet deep, the actual playing space was limited by the presence of spectators on the stage. Benches for seating were also located in the orchestra pit since musicians were not used at the theatre because of licensing conflicts with the Opéra, which had a monopoly on all musical works in Paris. The stage was equipped with machinery for wing-and-shutter scenery, but since set changes were rare in plays performed by the Comédie Française, complicated machinery was unnecessary. The usual set for tragedies was the *palais à volonté*, a neutral royal setting, suggesting a street, a palace, or town square, that could serve any serious play. The *chambre à quatre portes* was the usual setting for comedy, typically depicting the inside rooms of a house. Because the costumes were usually modern dress and the settings were neutral, there was little sense of temporal reality in dramatic production in the 17th century. Instead, there was often much anachronism between the fictive characters, their epochs, and the way they looked to the French audience. Neoclassicism, however, made such incongruities insignificant since it preached that general traits were more important than specific detail.

8. Theatre in England during the Restoration and 18th Century

Between 1642 and 1660, the Puritans took control of the government in England and attempted to suppress the theatre. Between 1642 and 1647, actors complied with the law. Theatres were torn down and costumes were sold off. In 1647, the law expired, and immediately open playing resumed at three theatres: The Fortune, The Cockpit, and the Salisbury Court. Two years later, in 1649, the year the Puritans beheaded King Charles I, a new law was established that prohibited plays, and all theatres were demolished (including the Fortune, the Cockpit, and the Salisbury Court) and costumes were burned. Actors, however continued to perform either at the Red Bull (which was not abolished since it was not always used as a theatre: it was often used for prize-fighting, wrestling matches, and bull baiting) or in private houses. What actors performed during this period were entertainments called *drolls*, which were abbreviated versions of longer plays. During this period two very significant men emerged who would preserve the English theatrical tradition in the face of the Puritan regime: William Davenant and Thomas Killigrew.

William Davenant

William Davenant was born in February 1606. Rumor had it that he was the illegitimate son of Shakespeare (we don't believe it because he started the rumor). He was, however, a page in the house of a Duchess, and he did have patronage from the Earl of Somerset, Robert Carr, who was one of the minions of King James I. William Davenant did have friends in high places. He started his theatrical career by writing tragedies, beginning with *Albovine* in 1629. It is one of the few plays after Marlowe's *Edward II* in which there exists an openly same-sex affair: Albovine is in love with another man, who is in love with a woman, who is in love with Albovine. Davenant produced a number of tragedies, probably the most significant of which is *Love and Honor* produced in 1634, and the prototype of the heroic drama that would flourish in the Restoration. Four years later he produced a play called *The Unfortunate Lovers* which was revived immediately after the Restoration and again prefigured the love and honor motif that would characterize heroic tragedy. In 1639, Davenant received a royal patent from Charles I to erect a theatre. This patent guaranteed him the right to gather together and keep players, musicians, dancers, as well as painted scenery and Italian machinery. This patent is very significant because had the theatre been built, it would have been the first public theatre in England that we know of using Italian scenery. However, because of arguments over the land where the theatre would be located, the plan never came to fruition. The following year he was given the position of Manager of the King's and Queen's Boys (a boys' acting company) at the Phoenix Theatre. The original man in charge, William Beeston, had allowed the company to perform an unlicensed play and the play was considered somewhat dangerous to the crown (it dealt with a royal journey to Scotland and somehow that was very suspicious), so they kicked Beeston out and put Davenant in. He stayed in charge of the Phoenix Theatre until May of 1641 when he had to leave the country because the Puritans were rounding up and jailing all of the King's favorites. When he was on the move, he got together an army to help the King and was knighted as a result. After 1644, he fled to France where Queen Henrietta Marie, Charles

II (the Prince of Wales) and the royal family had escaped to safety. Because Henrietta Marie was the sister of the King of France, she and her family were protected in her brother's kingdom.

By 1646, Davenant had been sent back to England as an emissary, and he became involved in a great deal of political intrigue. During his stay in England, he decided to produce plays at his old manor house, Rutland House. On 23 May 1656, he produced the first of his regular performances under the Commonwealth, called *The First Day's Entertainment at Rutland House*. He called it an "entertainment" so that the laws against plays wouldn't apply, and he wrote anti-Spanish propaganda into the play since Oliver Cromwell, the Puritan leader, hated Spain. The new leader, the Chairman of the Commonwealth, thought that this kind of entertainment would help propagate his own beliefs, so he did not attempt to prevent the performance. This was followed in September of the same year by the first English opera called *The Siege of Rhodes*. It was also among the more complex scenic presentations up to that time and it created a number of very significant innovations in the English theatre:

1) The work was performed in a recitation style, not unusual in opera when characters sing on a particular pitch very quickly. This style became characteristic of early Restoration acting;

2) It is the first mention of a specific actress on the English stage: Mrs. Coleman played the character of Ianthe;

3) A third significant innovation came in the character of Roxolana who would become the prototype of the liberated woman in Restoration comedies. This is the woman character who can hold her own in conversations with the wittiest of men.

The Siege of Rhodes was followed in July 1658 by *A Playhouse to be Let* at the Phoenix Theatre. It should give you an indication of how popular Davenant was during the Commonwealth, when he actually got permission to do a piece in a real theatre not only in a private house. *A Playhouse to be Let* was in five acts: The first act was an introduction thanking the audience for being there, thanking the Cromwells for permission, and reaffirming English antipathy toward Spain (politics, politics). The second act was a translation of Molière's *The Imaginary Cuckold*. The third and fourth acts comprised a short tragedy called *The Cruelty of the Spaniards in Peru*, and in Act five, a burlesque version of Shakespeare's *Antony and Cleopatra* ended the evening. Davenant was producing a five-act play only in structure; he was really presenting three short plays along the lines of the drolls.

In 1659, Davenant and other Royalists were arrested for sedition. Oliver Cromwell was dead by this time and his son, Richard Cromwell, felt the plays were becoming libelous. Theatre began to get a little uncomfortable because it was beginning, once again, to be popular. In this period when people were put under arrest, often they were simply put under house arrest, which meant that they could not leave the city or a part of the city. When certain French figures in the eighteenth century were arrested, they had to pay for their incarceration. They had to pay upkeep for the room in which they were kept. In his prison room in the Bastille, for example, the Marquis de Sade had 80 different changes of clothes, rugs, his entire library, at least one servant. As a result, when we're talking about incarceration during this period, we're really talking about the inability to move freely. We're not necessarily talking about a 5-by-6 cubicle with bars and such. In 1660, the year following his arrest, Davenant closed a lease on a tennis court in Lincoln's Inn Fields, and waited for the King to come home.

Thomas Killigrew

Thomas Killigrew was born in February 1612. He began his theatre career by acting the devil, or a sprite, as a child so he could get in to see plays for nothing. He would stand in the wings and watch the play until his entrance. As a teenager, he served as a page to Charles I. Before 1642, he had written three plays: *The Prisoner, Claracilla, and Love at First* Sight. All of these have love-and-honor plots, a dream setting, and deal with the duality between perfect love and perfect friendship. The three depict the blackest villains and the most gallant heroes (and in some ways anticipate nineteenth-century melodrama). These plays also trade in pirates, storms at sea, disguises, high-blown sentiments, and genuinely happy reunions at the end. His three plays brought him success but not the success he desired, so he tried his hand at comedy and began to pen one of the dirtiest plays ever written, called *The Parson's Wedding*, a production of which had to be put off for about twenty-two years because, as he was completing the play, the King was put into prison and Killigrew had to leave the country. In 1643, Thomas Killigrew sailed with Henrietta Marie to France (note that the two men who originally won a monopoly on producing theatre upon the Restoration were Davenant and Killigrew; one who sailed with the Queen to France as part of her retinue, and the other who fought in an army for the King). Killigrew was literally the playmate of Charles II while in France, and on 23 May 1660, the day Charles sailed back to England, Killigrew was with him on the boat.

While he was in exile, Killigrew completed *The Parson's Wedding* and produced another lascivious comedy called *Tomasso; or, The Wanderer*, a semi-autobiographical adventure comedy about the upper crust in exile. Tomasso goes to Madrid to woo a woman called Ceralina. However, as soon as he gets there, he is enraptured with a Venetian whore named Angelica Bianca, who has a picture hung out in front of her house advertising that whoever wants part of this picture can do so for 1000 lira a week. Tomasso knocks on the door and says, "Can you make it 750?" She says, "No, 1000 is my lowest rate." However, a man named Don Pedro and he get into an altercation over the courtesan and Tomasso kills Don Pedro. The courtesan is so enamored of his prowess at fisticuffs that she says, "I'll give it to you for nothing." However, Don Pedro has friends who are Venetian punks and they plan to kill Tomasso. Unfortunately, they fall upon one of Tomasso's servants, who happens to be wearing his clothes at the time. They attack him instead, and Tomasso goes off to marry the woman he was going to marry in the first place. A subplot traces the adventures of Eduardo who is entrapped by another whore named Lucetta, who turns him out into the street naked and destitute. He falls prey to two rich Jewish women, one of whom is a giant and the other is a pygmy, both seeking cures for their deformities. Eduardo goes to an old rabbi who gives him a potion, but instead of making the two Jewish monsters better, it aggravates their conditions. Eduardo eventually escapes them in time to show up for the wedding between Tomasso and Ceralina. The play presents 40 characters in 73 scenes, and would become the prototype of the adventure comedy of the Restoration.

The Parson's Wedding is significant because when it was finally performed on 6 October 1664, it was acted entirely by women. On the day of his wedding to Mrs. Wanton, a profligate parson is gotten drunk and put to bed with a dirty old hag who is a married woman (on the day he's supposed to be married he's caught with a married woman). A Captain and a Mr. Jolly, disguised as a constable and watchman, arrest him for adultery, taking him before the Magistrate, who is really a character called Mr. Wild in disguise (up to this point, with the exception of the Parson, everyone is in disguise, with women playing men disguised as other characters). In the end, it is discovered that Mrs. Wanton is carrying on with Mr. Wild, the captain and Mr. Jolly reveal their true identities, and the parson, rather than being arrested for his own debauchery, is threatened with blackmail because the woman he's about to marry is being seduced by the person who was originally dressed as the Magistrate.

When Killigrew and Davenant returned to London in May of 1660, there were three companies acting in London: John Rhodes at the Cockpit, Michael Mohun at the Red Bull, and William Beeston who was playing at Salisbury Court. Each of these companies had been licensed at the rate of 4 pounds a week by the Master of the Revels who at the time was Henry Herbert. Davenant and Killigrew combined forces, went to the King and secured a patent for a theatre monopoly in London. Davenant already had an old patent—the patent of 1639 that allowed him to erect a theatre. On 9 July 1660, Charles gave Killigrew a warrant to establish a company of actors and erect a theatre, and on 21 August 1660 both patents were ratified. Davenant and Killigrew were authorized to build two playhouses and place actors under their jurisdiction. In addition, they were also granted censorship of plays. In other words, they were the only people who had to be concerned about what was being performed. This of course angered the Master of the Revels who had been, up to this point, the person who licensed all the plays. The Master of the Revels complained to the King who turned the matter over to his Attorney General.

The patentees began as an amalgamated company, first acting, on 8 October 1660, at the Cockpit where Rhodes and his company had been playing. By the end of the month, the company split. Davenant took the younger actors and went to Salisbury Court where he threw out William Beeston. Killigrew took the older actors and opened on 8 November at the Gibbons Tennis Court which was called the first Theatre Royal. The space was 72 feet long and 42 feet wide, and the first play produced by the newly formed King's Company was *Henry IV, Part I*. On 8 December, they produced *Othello* with the first appearance of an English actress on the professional stage. The prologue to the play says "I come unknown to any of the rest to tell you news. I saw the lady dressed. The woman plays today mistake me not. No man in gown or page in petticoat." Although there was specific reference made of the fact that a real woman was acting in the company, we don't know precisely who she was. Margaret Hughes is the most probable candidate, though a great many actresses of the period claim to be the first.

Later, on 20 December 1661, Killigrew leased land to build a permanent theatre, and the new Theatre Royal, which was the first Drury Lane (there have been five or six Drury Lanes in London because of fires), opened on 8 April 1663. The outside dimensions of the theatre were 112 feet by 58 feet. The internal dimensions were 76 feet by 38 feet. The outside dimensions of this building were substantial but the inside of the actual theatre space was fairly small. Part of the other space was used for storage, offices, etc. The first play produced at the new Theatre Royal was *The Humorous Lieutenant*, and in this play, scenery was used for the first time. Dryden became the playwright in residence of this company, though the audience's favorite shows were *Othello*, *Julius Caesar*, and *Volpone*. Among the chief attractions was an actress called **Nell Gwynne** who was also the King's mistress. There are wonderful portraits of her, usually with one bare breast showing, and there's a famous portrait of her with the King's two bastard children. She was not at all ashamed about being the King's mistress

After the first Theatre Royal opened on 8 April, it played two years until 5 June 1665 when the Lord Chamberlain ordered all theatres closed because of the bubonic plague. Around 100,000 people were killed by this plague. Up to this period, if there were 40 people dead of the plague per week, everything would close. Theatres reopened 18 months later on 29 November 1666 after the great fire of London on 2 September 1666, when the city burned for three days (Historians seem to think that the three sixes in the date had something to do with it). Four-fifths of the city of London within the walls was burnt in the fire. So, we lost 25 percent of the population and 80 percent of the city buildings. Tom Killigrew thought he'd seen the worst of his problems given the plague and fire, during which time he spent a great deal of money to make alterations and refurbish his theatre, adding scenery, and increasing seating capacity while the theatres were closed. All of this came to naught on 25 January 1672 when a fire destroyed half the building and all the scenery and costumes.

If the fire and financial woes (having used a lot of his money to improve the theatre) weren't enough, the Duke's Company (Davenant's Company, so-called for the Duke of York, Charles II's brother who was later to become King James II), opened a new playhouse, the Dorset Garden Theatre on 9 November 1671, with a very popular play called *Sir Martin Mar-All*. This theatre was fairly large—140 feet long by 57 feet wide—lavish, and equipped for the use of spectacular scenery. The King's Company moved into Lincoln's Inn Fields when Davenant's company moved into the Dorset Garden, and by 1674, Killigrew had found the money to build yet a new theatre. This was very plain theatre, with little facility for scenery. Killigrew's troubles continued. He was unable to pay actors, so they began to migrate to Davenant's company. Between 1672 and 1675, there were many complaints about thin audiences at the Theatre Royal. As a result, on 4 May 1682, the King's company merged with the Duke's Company (at the point of the merger, Davenant was dead and his son had taken over. Killigrew died the year after the merger). This joint company opened at the Theatre Royal on 16 November and the big splashy house, the Dorset Garden, was left for opera and spectacle plays. They chose to use the plainer house quite frankly to save on expenses.

George Jolly and "The Nursery"

While all this is happening, an individual named George Jolly presented himself to the King. George Jolly was one of those people in the theatre whom everybody knew and nobody liked because he had a fiery temper and an irascible disposition. We first hear about him in 1648 when he was touring Germany with an English company. For theatre history he's significant because he used Italian scenery and women in his company. In 1655 he gained the patronage of Charles II and in 1660 he was expelled from Germany because of bad behavior. He would go into taverns, pick fights, and make lascivious remarks to women. He was a traditional libertine and masher, and nobody wanted him around. When he returned to England, he applied to Charles for a patent to develop a theatre company. On 24 December 1660, Charles granted the request, even though Charles had already given a theatre monopoly to two other people. Jolly moved into the Cockpit and immediately Killigrew and Davenant went to the King and said, "Excuse us but you gave us a previous patent." To which end Jolly went to the Master of the Revels and asked for a license to tour. This license was given him at the end of 1662, and when he was about to leave, Davenant and Killigrew bought Jolly's patent from him. They said "we'll buy your patent and give you 4 pounds a week rent on your patent while we are in this country." That was fine with Jolly. Then they went to Charles and told him that they bought Jolly's patent outright and that he should issue a new patent in their name. King Charles issued them a new patent ousting Jolly's patent and making everything Jolly would do in the city of London illegal. Davenant and Killigrew didn't tell Jolly about any of this, so when he returned from touring, planning to begin performing in London, Davenant and Killigrew slapped him with an injunction preventing him from playing. Jolly threatened to go to the Privy Council and complain, but the King found a compromise placing Jolly in charge of a recently formed school for acting called "The Nursery," the first of a series of acting schools that would be developed in various countries.

Theatre Audiences

What was the audience like during this period? There were 400,000 people in London and two companies of actors could barely survive. This was in comparison to 1600 when there were only 200,000 people and there were six or seven theatrical troupes. Drama had clearly lost its popular base after the Commonwealth, and the remaining theatre goers constituted a coterie audience. Plays were therefore designed to appeal to certain kinds of people: members of Court, lesser government officials, members of the upper middle class, and law students. Since the Commonwealth was comprised of Puritan supporters, to be a Royalist, one had to abjure everything that was correct to the Puritans. Since the Puritans regarded pleasure as sinful, to be a Royalist mean that pleasure must be regarded as virtuous. If, for example, the Puritans would whip actors, considering them indecent, the King would take an actress as his mistress. Charles was determined to carry pleasure and gallantry even to the church service, where he proclaimed that he only wanted to hear music in church that he could beat time to. As a result, to be debauched was the easiest way for a man or woman to prove that they were in support of the King. If you didn't take a mistress and were actually very religious, your political support from the King was in question. People were sometimes actually pilloried for being good. As far as the King himself, there were various epitaphs written about him. Here's one: "Here lies a great and mighty king whose promise none relies on. He never said a foolish thing and never did a wise one."

The society was one of peer pressure with a real sense of class distinction and a need to fit in. Wit was more significant than goodness or virtue. Style was more important than morality. In fact, during this period, to be vile was in fashion. It was a mark of wit, during a play in the theatre, to make a loudmouthed comment for everyone to hear after an actor delivered a speech. The actors always had to deal with audiences who were talking back to them.

Oftentimes, the play that was occurring in the audience was more interesting than the one on the stage. During performances, prostitutes as well as fruit-vendors would be plying their wares in the audience (rather like a modern sporting event—minus the courtesans, of course).

Charles Sedley was a lord who especially liked the theatre, though his personality, as Samuel Pepys tells us in his celebrated diary, was highly suspect. Because of that he was a firm supporter of Charles. According to Pepys, "In the middle of the day on a balcony he appeared showing his nakedness, acting all the postures of lust and buggery that could be imagined. And abusing of scripture and as it were from thence preaching a mountebank sermon from the pulpit saying there that he hath to sell such a powder that could make all the ladies in town run after him. A thousand people standing beneath the scene and that being done, he took a glass of wine and washed his prick in it and then drank it off. And then took another and drank the King's health." Another of his debauched tales occurs with Sir Charles Sedley and Lord Buckhurst "running up and down all night with their arses bare through the streets and at last fighting and being beat by the watch and clapped up all night. And how the King takes their parts and my lord chief justice kneeling hath laid the constable by the heels to answer it in next sessions." The two naked men who caused the trouble have forced the arresting officer to be jailed and to go to trial. Such is the morality of the period.

Influences on Restoration Drama

The plays of the English Restoration were the result not only of Restoration society but of other factors as well:

1) The historical and social background;
2) The influence of French drama;
3) Renaissance neoclassical theories: specifically, the unities of time, place, and action, and the concept of decorum. Decorum meant that the character must behave as he or she ought according to their position in society. A Lord

in society can be debauched, for example, but a servant can't pinch a lady. Decorum always required that violent acts be kept offstage;

4) Trends in Jacobean and Caroline drama, which of course meant the drama which preceded them; and

5) The vogue for the Spanish romance. The English were no longer denouncing Spain because Charles needed Spain as an ally when he fought the Dutch. England, at peace with Spain and France, now hate the Dutch.

The tragedies of Corneille were admired by the Royalists, and the emphasis that author placed on glory and loyalty to the king was highly respected. In addition, English playwrights became very interested in, and accustomed to the rhymed Alexandrine couplets of French tragedy. To that end, an English tragedy called "heroic," designed specifically to glorify the monarch, was produced, attempting to observe the unities, and to imitate a rhymed Alexandrine couplet with a rhymed pentameter couplet. The first heroic drama was Roger Boyle's *The General*, performed in Dublin in 1662. The form became very popular because the King supported it. As a matter of fact, he even suggested it be created. Moreover, the King gave the players some of his royal robes so they could look heroic and regal in performance. The first heroic play seen in London (in 1664) was *The Indian Queen* by John Dryden and his father-in-law Sir Robert Howard. John Dryden is perhaps the best and most significant of the heroic playwrights.

John Dryden

John Dryden was born in 1631 and died in 1700. His first play, a comedy called *The Wild Gallant*, was a failure so he turned to heroic tragedy. *The Indian Queen*, produced in 1664, centers on the character of Montezuma and his part in the fight between the Incas and the Mexicans. It was so popular a play that it spawned a sequel in 1665 called *The Indian Emperor*. These two plays established the formula for heroic tragedy:

1) Ranting speeches;
2) Rhymed couplets;
3) A militaristic background;
4) Love versus honor themes;
5) Some kind of a happy ending even through there were plenty of deaths;
6) Adherence to the neoclassical unities.

In 1667, Dryden experimented with a mixed genre, heroic tragedy mixed with the comedy of manners in a single play, an example of which was called *Secret Love*. The following year, 1668, he was named Poet Laureate and produced a major critical study called *An Essay of Dramatic Poesy* which is a Ciceronian dialogue among four speakers. The document deals with the distinction between ancient and modern plays, as well as the conflict between French neoclassicism and English neoclassicism. In the essay, Dryden defined a play as a "lively and just representation of human action."

The following years produced two very large-scale heroic plays: *The Conquest of Grenada* in 1670 and *The Conquest of Grenada, Part II* in 1671 (Dryden was extremely fond of sequels). These were not mixed genres, just heroic plays. In 1677 Dryden produced *All for Love* a neoclassical blank verse retelling of Shakespeare's *Antony and Cleopatra*. Here he abandoned the heroic tragedy formula for what he felt would be a pure tragedy in the French style, without the rhyme. Dryden reduced Shakespeare's thirty characters and crowded canvas of scenes and environments to 8 characters and one scene, the last day of Cleopatra's life. In 1678 he produced one of the most licentious of the Restoration comedies of manners, *Mr. Limberham*, and in 1685, he became Roman Catholic. In later life, many of the libertines of Charles' court converted to Catholicism because the Catholic Church tells you that if you repent of your sins and receive absolution, you can go to heaven. Dryden actually turned Catholic to find favor with the new King, James II who was a Roman Catholic. Unfortunately, three years later, with the accession of William and Mary who were Protestants, Dryden became out of favor. His poet laureateship was revoked because he was Catholic and all his property was confiscated, but he continued to write plays until he died in 1700.

Comedies of Intrigue

Spanish plays and romances had a profound influence on English theatre, giving rise to several innovations and character types:

    1) Intrigue comedies with their complicated plotting, of which the most significant example was Aphra Behn's play *The Rover* which is not unlike the play *Tomasso* by Thomas Killigrew;

    2) Fathers who are unusually bombastic and ill-tempered;

    3) Young male leads who are haughty but idealistic;

    4) High-spirited heroines who are virtuous and talkative: they object to prearranged marriages, and talk boldly but never say anything indecent. They engage in a free, open, and possibly equal basis with the men.

All of these ideas coalesced in the first major box office hit of the Restoration, a play called *The Adventures of Five Hours*, written in 1663, by Sir Samuel Tuke. This is a very interesting play because each act has the hero in a different kind of adventure. The play is certainly lively but lacks anything bawdy.

One other aspect must be discussed before we move into Restoration comedy of manners, and that is a new locus of audience participation during performances called the **green room.** During the Restoration, we first hear about the green room, where visitors were welcomed and entertained by actors during the play when they were not on stage. They had a room labeled the green room for several reasons:

    1) Some say it had a green baize carpet and green curtains on the windows;

    2) Others say the word "green room" is a corruption of the idea of "scene room," i.e., backstage;

3) However, when we know that green was the color of prostitution at the time, when prostitutes would always wear a green skirt, it is more likely that the name green room was a pejorative expression for "Where are the patrons going during the play?" They're going to the green room where they can fool around with any of the actors or actresses. This whole practice helped certainly put the reputation of the players and theatres at risk. It also had a significant impact on stage architecture. At the old Drury Lane, to get to the green room, the spectator had to walk across the stage; and, since the King had a terrible habit of wanting to visit Mrs. Nell Gwynne during the play, he would have to walk across the stage to the green room. When Covent Garden was built in the eighteenth century, and later versions of Drury Lane, a way was developed so that the patrons could get to the green room without having to cross the stage. Remember the green room would probably have originally been a meeting place for actors before they walked on stage, but when it became, in the Restoration, a place for the actors to greet spectators, you had to give the spectators another access to it. It really is the origin of our stage entrance/stage door.

Wit Comedy or the Comedy of Manners

The Restoration Comedy of Manners has the following general characteristics:

1) The principal business is the pursuit of women;

2) Wit is the mark of breeding, not morality;

3) Actions are governed by an elaborate code of behavior. There is always satire in these manners plays, usually against going to plays;

4) It satirizes the behavior of audiences, women in masks, old men, young women, country bumpkins versus city wits. Most of these plays deify the city and made buffoons of country gentlemen;

5) As in the morality plays of the Middle Ages, and certainly in Ben Jonson's plays, we find ticket names: Horner and Pinchwife, for example, in *The Country Wife*. Horner has spread it about that he is a eunuch. This will also

give you the sense that anything that was slightly off-color or perverted was always Italian or French;

6) There is typically a normative couple: In *The Country Wife*, for example, the normative couple, Harcourt and Alithea, are the only ones who seem to have normal names;

7) Invariably, there is an older character woman with an obsessive goal, for example, Lady Fidget in *The Country Wife* and Lady Wishfort in *The Way of the World*;

8) The blocking character is usually an older character man with a social flaw, i.e., Pinchwife in *The Country Wife*. Pinchwife's social flaw is an obsession with keeping his wife hidden. If Pinchwife were the older husband saying to all the wits, "Look, but don't touch," things would have been different. He lies instead, and doesn't do it very well;

9) A strong-willed witty woman who holds her own with men, i.e., Marjorie Pinchwife in *The Country Wife*;

10) The fop character: a man who pretends to be witty, thinks he's cleverer than he really is, and who dresses in an effeminate manner, i.e., Sir Foppling Flutter in Etherege's *The Man of Mode*;

11) Plot contrivances such as secret marriages, letters, black boxes, and other devices to resolve the complex plot;

12) Characters are of the upper middle class; no one maintains a 9–5 job. They are upper-middle-class landed gentry;

13) Characters are punished for lack of wit rather than immorality. Their morality was based on Hobbes and Descarte, in addition to a kind of materialism;

14) At the end of the play there is always preparation for some kind of wedding, i.e., Harcourt and Alithea in *The Country Wife*. Alithea makes it very clear to Harcourt that if he wants her, there is only one way he can have her.

The Country Wife was written by William Wycherley who was born in 1641. He converted to Roman Catholicism when he went to France and converted back to the Church of England when he came back to England.

He went to law school, joined the navy, and produced his first play in 1671 called *Love in a Wood*. The play was so successful that he started an affair with King Charles' mistress, the Duchess of Cleveland, which didn't last very long. None of his affairs lasted terribly long. *The Gentleman Dancing Master* appeared in 1672, followed by *The Country Wife* in 1675 and *The Plain Dealer* in 1676. In 1679 he met an old rich dowager, Lady Laetitia Isabella, Countess of Drogheda, and married her for her money. Two years later, she died and a lot of lawsuits followed over who actually had possession her money. The following year, 1682, Wycherley was imprisoned for debt. When James II ascended the throne in 1685, Wycherley saw an opportunity for advancement at court, so he reconverted to Catholicism. As a reward, James gave him a pension for life. Three years later James abdicated, and William and Mary, the new Protestant monarchs, canceled his pension (Mary was James's daughter and William was Charles' nephew: both were very austere Calvinists). Wycherley proceeded to write poems and correspond with the great writers of the day until 1715 when he married another woman substantially younger than himself (he was in his 70s). He got married on 20 December 1715 and, eleven days later, on 31 December 1715 he died.

The Man of Mode

Another of the originators of the Restoration comedy of manners was **George Etherege** (1635-1691) whose first play is a kind of medley of the variety of theatrical forms which existed in the Restoration. It was called *Love in a Tub, or The Comical Revenge* and was produced in 1664. It has four plots, each representative of a different type of Restoration play:

1) Noblemen who fought in the civil war, in the context of a love-and-honor heroic drama;

2) The main plot presents a Restoration man about town courting a widow, both of whom are in the upper middle class. Restoration comedy widows are very important and play a very significant part, because widows are women who have property and have already been deflowered;

3) Gamblers, con men and their victims, presented in the style of an intrigue comedy;

4) The fourth plot traded on a farcical portrayal of the servant characters.

Whether or not Etherege perceived the problems in this breadth of material, he focused on only one group in the next play, written in 1668, and called *She Would If She Could*. This is about a man about-town looking for sexual experiences while pursuing his main goal: marriage to a rich heiress. Eight years later he produced his most significant play *The Man of Mode; or, Sir Fopling Flutter*. In the play he develops the formula for two couples, one of which is normative, the other possessing a young woman who can hold her own in a wit contest with a man, and he establishes the prototype of the fop, with a character named Sir Fopling Flutter.

After the Popish Plot in 1678, comic writers took a more lascivious turn and we come into the high period of sex comedies, the most significant of which was *Mr. Limberham; or, The Kind Keeper* by John Dryden, produced at Dorset Garden in 1678. Critics at the time said that it was "A very good comedy but more indecent than the generality of plays, even at this time." It takes place at Mrs. Saintley's boarding house. Father Aldo is a debauched old gentleman and patron of the women of the town. His son returns from several years abroad under the assumed name of Wouldall. Aldo doesn't recognize him but takes a fancy to him only because Wouldall shares his debauched sensibilities. Once he discovers he's his son, he cannot reveal that he's his father because the son knows too much about him. Wouldall has intrigues with Mrs. Trixie and Mrs. Brainsick. Mrs. Trixie's intrigue is discovered, but that of Mrs. Brainsick is not. Limberham is a dupe to Mrs. Trixie. When he returns in the second act, Mrs. Trixie conceals Wouldall in a chest. In the third act, she and Wouldall are seated on a bed in his room. Mrs. Brainsick is under the bed and Mrs. Saintley is coming in at the door. When she comes in, Mrs. Trixie hides inside the bed. Brainsick then tells Wouldall that she wants to have an affair with him. When the other women reveal themselves, she falls on the bed with the man so that he has a woman on top of him on the bed, a woman in the bed and a woman under the bed. This gets more complicated until Act five when Mr. Brainsick comes and discovers what he thinks is his wife *in flagrante* (though it is really Mrs. Trixie in disguise and his wife is wearing Mrs. Trixie's clothes). He herds Mrs. Trixie in his wife's clothes off to another room, locks the door on his real wife in bed with Mr. Wouldall, and carries a sword, not letting anybody into the room while his wife is cuckolding him. Finally, Mr. Limberham marries Mrs. Trixie and gives her a settlement of 400 pounds a year; Wouldall marries an heiress and he gets 1200 pounds a year, and everyone lives happily ever after.

Burlesque and Farce

In addition to there being a lascivious strain, there was something very cynical and dark in Restoration drama. It is therefore not surprising that two other forms of theatre began to grow during this period: **Burlesque** and **Farce**. Burlesque in the seventeenth century was not the stripper type that we are used to in the USA, but rather a satire of customs, institutions, persons, or literary works. Burlesques always require a known original. The comic effect is produced by a deliberate disproportion between style and sentiment. High burlesque presents the trivial with ironic seriousness, of which the most famous example is probably Alexander Pope's *The Rape of the Lock*, where an entire epic poem is devoted to someone's cutting off a bit of a woman's hair. It would be like writing a five-act play about a hangnail, with complete seriousness. Low burlesque is treating the serious with grotesque levity.

Farce, on the other hand, is low comedy, which means that it is not comedy of wit or repartee, which is considered high comedy. Farce is intended to provoke laughter through gestures, buffoonery, action, or situation. The most significant farceur of this period was a playwright named **Edward Ravenscroft** (1650–1697) who was a prolific adapter of Molière's plays. His most celebrated farce was *The London Cuckolds* produced in 168, and held the stage for 102 years. His most popular in its own day was *Mamamouchi*, based on Molière's *The Cit Turned Gentleman*. Ravenscroft's adaptation was originally produced in 1672 and held the stage for another 150 years. A later farce called

The Anatomist, produced in 1696, is the precursor of many contemporary vaudeville and burlesque doctor routines. In the play an old man is trying to prevent the marriage of a young couple. The young couple has a servant who pretends to be a doctor in order to work everything out for his master. While he is pretending to be a doctor, an old man wanders in on him. The old man is manipulated onto the operating table and the servant takes out hatchet and saws to cut the old man up. The old man, who isn't supposed to be there in the first place, has to pretend to be dead and there follows whole lot of physical business and miscommunication before finally everything is put to rights. By the end of the play, everyone has his turn pretending to be either a dead body or a patient on the operating table. It sounds like a routine contrived for Abbott and Costello, or the Marx Brothers, or the Three Stooges.

Tragic Developments
While this sort of buffoonery was happening, tragedy was undergoing a very important change. Until about 1680, heroic tragedy was the main form of serious drama in the Restoration. After 1680, two playwrights, **Thomas Otway** (1652-1685) and **Nathaniel Lee** (1653-1692) went back to what we call *tragedy of character* which was popular in the Elizabethan period (for example, *Hamlet, Othello, King Lear*, are all character tragedies). They dispensed with the rhymed heroic couplet and began writing tragedies in iambic pentameter without rhyme. The best plays of this period were *Venice Preserved* by Ottway and Nathaniel Lee's *The Rival Queens*, about the two women fighting over Alexander the Great. Both of these plays held the stage for 150 years. The influence of Otway and Lee was short-lived because Otway died in 1684–85 and Lee went crazy in the same year and was put into an insane asylum.

A minor playwright named **John Banks** (flourished from 1677–1696) abandoned the tragic hero in favor of the pathetic heroine. Now plays begin to emphasize the sufferings of a noble woman rather than the heroism of the young hero. In 1682 he wrote *Anna Bullen* about Anne Boleyn, a play in which a weak, vacillating woman is the main character. This became the prototype of what contemporary critics referred to as "she tragedies," and will be very important in the development of the standard heroine of melodrama late in the eighteenth century.

Between 1685 and 1737, there was a gradual change in the demographics of the people who went to the theatre, and in the appreciation of the monarchs for the theatrical entertainment. In 1685 the Catholic James II ascended the throne. Three years later, he was replaced by the Protestant William and Mary, who barely tolerated the theatre. At the same time, a burgeoning middle class was beginning to come to the drama. Plays which were originally written for the court or for the upper-class patrons were now being written for the working class. Our proof is that during the early Restoration, plays began at 4:00 P.M. From 1700–705, playhouses began to push the opening times back to 4:30, then 5:00 and sometimes even 6:30 so they could accommodate people who had to work for a living. Also, in accommodating this burgeoning middle class, there was a change of focus in the style of the drama and in the themes presented:

1) The gallant impoverished soldier becomes a main figure in plays, particularly in the plays by Farquhar;

2) Women and women's rights begin to be discussed in plays. This is an indication that more women were going to the playhouses. In the 1690s women's rights began to be debated, and in 1694, Mary Astell wrote a book called *Reflections on Marriage and a Serious Proposal to the Ladies*. In 1697, Daniel Defoe proposed the foundation of an Academy for Women so that women could actually be educated. This was regarded as highly heretical at the time. In 1702, a woman ascended the throne, Queen Anne, and in 1704 she outlawed wearing masks in public. When women went to the theatre, they went in masks so they would not be seen. She thought that was ridiculous because if you wear a mask, everyone thinks you have something to hide. At the turn of the century, **Susanna Centlivre** (1669-1723) wrote comedies to appeal to the feminist movement.

3) The rise to power of the merchant class caused plays to be written in praise of mercantilism, in tragedy with George Lillo's *The London Merchant*, and in comedy with Steele's *The Conscious Lovers*.

Sentimental Comedy

From 1685 to about 1697, plays, especially comedies, began to follow a new formula dealing with marriage rather than courtship. Most of the manners comedies of this period commenced with the hero and heroine already married, and the play usually dealt with an incompatible couple and what they do to save their marriage or to get out of it. The two most controversial plays of the period were *The Relapse* in 1696 by Sir John Vanbrugh (an architect/playwright) and Vanbrugh's *The Provoked Wife* in 1697. *The Relapse* was a sequel to a Colley Cibber play called *Love's Last Shift* (1696), in which a husband reforms at the end of the play. In *The Relapse* he falls back to womanizing. Because of these two plays, a non-juring clergyman named **Jeremy Collier** (1650–1725) argued that the playhouse had gone far enough and that something had to be done. In 1698, in direct response to Vanbrugh's two plays, Collier wrote a book called *A Short View of the Immorality and Profaneness of the English Stage*. Here are his chapter headings:

Ch. 1—*The Immodesty of the Stage and how it wasn't that way in the Classics*. Aristophanes, Plautus and Terence were never as dirty as we were.

Ch. 2—*The stage is profane*. How is it profane? Actors curse and swear, and they abuse religion.

Ch 3—*The clergy are abused by the stage*. Collier doesn't like the way clergymen are talked about by actors.

Ch. 4—*Immorality is encouraged by the stage*. We make up foppish and smutty characters.

Ch. 5—*A Treatise on Smuttiness*, in which Collier discusses profanity, smut, the disregard of the three unities on stage, and how women are taught to talk *smuttily* on stage. What is significant about this treatise is the philosophy that if you do something on the stage, you do the same thing in real life. Collier's argument was that if we hear women talk smuttily on the stage, we'll think they really are immoral; or by talking smuttily on the stage, they'll become immoral.

After Collier's attack which merited several respondents by the major playwrights of the day, comedy took a very different approach, with a much more conservative attitude and moral outlook. It is important to note, as we transition into sentimental comedy, that the first sentimental comedies actually occurred before Jeremy Collier wrote his piece. Jeremy Collier was not really a voice shouting in the wilderness, but really kind of the tip of the iceberg. There was already a movement in society that was reforming the stage—that was softening the profaneness and leading to a much more moral foundation. The first play recognized as sentimental comedy was Colley Cibber's *Love's Last Shift*. The plot concerns Loveless, a libertine, deserting his wife. Having deserted the wife before the play begins, when he meets her in the play, he doesn't recognize her. She wins him back by becoming his mistress and, when he realizes his mistress is his wife, he returns to the happy state of matrimony. Part of the reason Jeremy Collier resented *The Relapse* so much was because the moral lesson taught in *Love's Last Shift* was completely reversed in Vanbrugh's play.

Later, during the first decade of the eighteenth century, sentimentalism was struggling for expression. In William Popple's *A Cure for Jealousy* in 1701, a wife thinks that her husband is trying to kill her, so she hires somebody to kill the husband before he can get at her. The husband, thinking that his hired killer has succeeded, is brought a mock corpse of his wife. He becomes so fraught with remorse over seeing his dead wife that he vows that, if she were alive, he would never do that again. The wife appears and they live happily ever after, bringing tears and sensitive emotions to early eighteenth-century audiences. In 1704, Cibber produced a play called *The Careless Husband* in which the husband, though he has been cheating, discovers how wonderful his wife is and he begs her forgiveness. The expression of emotion in comedy was becoming more significant than the sexual chase, and feeling was giving way to strong moral reason. By 1722, the transformation was complete, of comedy from the Restoration model to the sentimental model where characters are always taken over by remorse or prevented from evildoing by moral scruples. There are five basic characteristics of sentimental comedy:

1) There is always presence of moral element;

2) There is always a greater emotional than intellectual appeal;

3) Plots and characters are generally artificial, exaggerated, and improbable;

4) There is a firm belief in the perfectibility of human nature;

5) There is an emphasis on tears, pity and virtuous sufferings. Again, much of this will sound like nineteenth-century melodrama.

Sir Richard Steele

The principal exponent of English sentimental comedy was Sir Richard Steele (1672–1729). Like Sheridan and Goldsmith, he was born in Ireland; many of the great English comic writers of the eighteenth century (and beyond) were Irish. He began his literary career as an essayist in newspapers, especially *The Tattler* and *The Spectator*. With the ascension of King George I in 1714, he was appointed Justice of the Peace and made a patentee of Drury Lane theatre. In 1715, he became a member of Parliament as a Whig politician, and previous to this, he wrote a number of plays, the first of which was called *The Funeral* (1701), a satire on the undertaking business and known for its sympathetic treatment of women characters. His next play was *The Lying Lover* in 1703 which was damned for its piety. It featured a famous pathetic repentance scene in which the hero, Young Bookwit, awakens in prison to find he's killed a rival in a drunken duel. Twenty minutes of repentance discourse follows. *The Tender Husband* (1703) provided two prototypes of later eighteenth-century drama: the Tony Lumpkin character of *She Stoops to Conquer* originates in this play as does the Lydia Languish character of *The Rivals*. Both Sheridan and Goldsmith borrowed ideas from a fellow-Irishman. In *The Tender Husband*, the husband tests his wife's fidelity by dressing his mistress up as a man and sending her to court his wife. The last of Steele's plays was *The Conscious Lovers* (1722) a play with a mercantile morality that was as explicit as it was pervasive, and highly influential in the development of tearful comedy in France. Prices were doubled at the theatre for the production of this play because it was given new sets and costumes. It was not common to design brand new scenery or costumes for an individual play. Typically, theatres would just pull from stock.

The Conscious Lovers was produced for the first time on 7 November 1722, a great success at Drury Lane, having a long run of 18 nights. In the seventeenth century, the author's royalties would be all the receipts on the third and sixth nights of the production. By 1690, the authors were given two benefit nights, but later in the eighteenth century, the author's royalties would be the receipts from every three performances. With 18 performances of a play, an author could really clean up. As a patentee, Steele also received income from owning a share in the theatre as well as from royalties. Playwright and actor, Colley Cibber played the servant Tom. It had been Colley Cibber's suggestion that the scenes of Tom and his girlfriend were added to the play, because, when Cibber read the original draft of the play, he suggested that Steele should write some funny lines if he wanted to call the play a comedy. Cibber is said to have adlibbed many of the funny lines of the play, which were then put into the final text. In the comedy, Young Bevil is being forced by his father to marry a wealthy merchant's (Mr. Sealand) daughter, Lucinda, whom his friend Myrtle loves. Bevil is actually in love with Indiana, an orphan, whom he has been supporting financially. He breaks off the engagement with Lucinda, only to offend his friend Myrtle who challenges him to a duel in order to restore Lucinda's wounded honor. In the end, Indiana turns out to be Mr. Sealand's long-lost daughter and the two friends get to marry the women they love. The play abounds in discussions about goodness, honor, feeling, and reason, and reads more like a catechism than a play. It was clearly designed to promote moral goodness among the merchant middle-class.

Pathetic Tragedy

Between 1685 and 1733, serious drama moved in the direction of what we call "Pathetic Tragedy," a tragedy whose focus is on creating pathos and tears. One of the more significant of the tragic or serious playwrights was **Nicholas Rowe** (1678–1718). He was the poet laureate, and the first real editor of Shakespeare. When Heminges and Condell produced the first folio, they really didn't edit the plays, so Nicholas Rowe took it upon himself to edit them, and to provide editorial comment explaining archaic words, and so forth. In his own playwriting Rowe was concerned with female frailty and liked to moralize about it, causing him to employ wild and extravagant climaxes in his plays. He liked to teach morality through shock value. For example, in *The Fair Penitent* (1703), the heroine Calista in the last act is found in her room which is hung with black curtains. She has a skull, a book, and a corpse lying beside her bed. Now, that really sounds like Gothic melodrama.

Also, during this period dramatists were concerned over language and while some tried to revive the high-flown diction of the heroic play to the extent of using rhymed couplets, others sought to write prose tragedies. One of the most famous experiments in tragic prose was *The Famous History of the Rise and Fall of Massaniello* by Thomas Durfey in 1699 in ten acts and divided into two parts. Written entirely in prose, it established the model for future playwrights trying to attempt a serious play in colloquial dialogue.

Domestic Tragedy

George Lillo's *The London Merchant* (1731), the most significant example of prose tragedy in this period, also exemplified the new form of Domestic Tragedy. While other tragedies were based on either mythology or the ruling classes, this was the first of the eighteenth-century tragedies based on the adventures of the common man, and the first domestic tragedy written entirely in prose. *The London Merchant* restored faith in the potential of the domestic tragic form which was developed in the sixteenth century and was particularly influential on German dramatic theory, particularly that of Lessing. A quick perusal of plays like *Miss Sara Sampson* will demonstrate the strong influence of *The London Merchant* on the German theatre.

George Lillo (1693–1739) was the son of a jeweler and was apprenticed to that trade. Not finding his true *métier* in making watches and jewelry, he tried his hand at drama in 1730 with a work called *Sylvia*, a ballad opera. The following year came *The London Merchant, or The History of George Barnwell*. The plot of this play was taken from a ballad printed in 1650 about a murder in Shropshire. In the play, the hero, George Barnwell, is a merchant's apprentice who, led astray by a prostitute, kills his guardian/uncle, and ends up at the gallows, full of repentance. The prostitute who leads him astray, however, is also condemned to death at the end of the play, but she goes to her death insisting on her innocence, and spouting vengeance on her captives. She functions as a foil to set up Barnwell's holy repentance. George Barnwell also has a girlfriend Maria who, of course, preaches to him and convinces him that he's really good inside and just led astray. This is very important because it begins a tradition of tradesman tragedies where there is an emphasis on the merchant class as good and perfectible. Lillo who was essentially a pious playwright looked upon the tragic formula as the opportunity to show and enforce emotionally the consequences of sinfulness.

The London Merchant was produced 21 June 1731 at Drury Lane and played 17 times that summer which is a very good run, and between 1731 and 1739, it was staged 70 times. It established several very important middle-class moral concepts which would resonate through the rest of the eighteenth century:

1) Commercial cleanliness is next to godliness (that means doing business honestly);

2) The importance of trade and commerce was stressed to the point of developing a commercial ethic versus one that is based solely on natural law;

3) It also set up the concept that honest merchant endeavor is capable of infusing love. If one is an honest merchant, love will find the way to solve all problems;

4) The merchant gentleman is equal to any man of quality. Such a concept would lead to the American Revolution in 1776 and the French Revolution in 1789.

The London Merchant was also evocative of two of the main themes of all eighteenth-century serious drama:

1) They are acutely money-minded. Plays exhibit this either in the portrayals of thrifty merchants or wasteful gambling characters, men who like to gamble and waste their money, leaving their wives and children to fend for themselves;

2) They have a preoccupation with preparing for death. Strangely enough, money and death are extremely related, especially in the concern of laying aside a nest egg for one's children.

Pantomime and Ballad Opera

Pantomime began to develop as a kind of entr'acte entertainment between plays on the theatre bill, and as a form it combines elements from the *commedia dell'arte*, farce, topical satire, and stories drawn from classical mythology. Pantomime in England really began around 1702 when a man named **John Weaver** inserted dances into a connected story. However, the most significant name in connection with the development of eighteenth-century pantomime was **John Rich** who eventually became a patentee at Covent Garden, but who in his early years established the accepted pattern of English pantomime: serious scenes based on classical mythology alternating with comic episodes using *commedia* characters. This *commedia* influence suggests why almost all eighteenth-century pantomimes have Harlequin in their title. The comic scenes were not spoken, but the serious portions of the plot had dialogue and songs. English pantomime began as partially sung, partially spoken, and partially mimed. In the original formula, only the comic section that was silent. Everything else had spoken dialogue or music. The main feature of pantomime was spectacle. Under the name **Lun** (Rich's pantomime name)

John Rich developed English pantomime to become the most popular form of entertainment in the early part of the eighteenth century.

Giving pantomime a run for its money was a new kind of burlesque drama called **Ballad Opera**, a genre that hit the ground running with *The Beggar's Opera* by John Gay, produced by John Rich at Lincoln's Inn Fields on 29 January 1728. The popular saying is that *The Beggar's Opera* made John Gay rich and John Rich gay (in its original meaning) because the show ran 63 nights in a row. This was significant because it spawned a spate of imitations, and for the next 30 years ballad operas enjoyed a great popularity. *The Beggar's Opera* satirized the form of Italian opera: instead of using complicated arias it used popular tunes, hence the designation "ballad" opera. It also satirized traditional opera plots: usually about kings, queens, and the upper crust, this was an opera dealing with pickpockets and jailers. Instead of dealing with love versus honor, which always involves a triangle of some sort, this piece dealt with a man named Macheath who promised to marry two women, one of whom was pregnant with his child—certainly an inversion of current middle-class values. *The Beggar's Opera* also began a clear mode of political satire that lampooned Sir Robert Walpole, King George's Prime Minister.

The Licensing Act of 1737

Continuing this formula for political burlesque was **Henry Fielding** who between 1729 and 1737 wrote a number of satirical dramas which he produced at the Little Theatre in the Haymarket (tangential to all of this, when Henry Fielding was the manager of the Little Theatre at the Haymarket in 1736, he began to use footlights in an innovative way—developing the practice that began in the Restoration about 1672 but hadn't been used to as good effect, according to various contemporaneous reports. He also offered two new plays on the same night and abandoned older drama, and was among the first, if not the first, to plant actors in the audience).

One of the reasons that the **Licensing Act** was developed in 1737 was the profound amount of political satire that began to be developed in the plays. In 1729, for example, John Gay wrote *Polly* which has the dubious distinction of being the last play to be banned by the Lord Chamberlain's prerogative—the last play banned before the Licensing Act which set up the kind of censorship that suffocated English drama until 1966. In *Polly*, Walpole was portrayed in blackface to burlesque the infamous Waltham Black Act of 1723, which was a perverse moment of legislation history: every criminal act, even blacking up itself, had become a felony punishable by death, purely at the discretion of the court. John Gay thought that this was pretty ridiculous, so he caricatured Walpole as a character in black face. In 1731, a play called *The Fall of Mortimer* was forbidden on Walpole's behalf. The play wasn't condemned by the Lord Chamberlain, it was condemned by the Prime Minister, because it happened to deal with a historical Prime Minister who made a pact with the devil to accomplish the goals of the country. Moreover, in 1732, a play called *The Restoration of Charles II* was stopped because the title of the play was treasonable. The Hanovers were on the throne of England at the time, not the Stuarts.

In 1733 there was an actors' revolt at Drury Lane led by Theophilus Cibber, the son of Colley Cibber the playwright and actor, because they wanted more money. That's not entirely correct: they really wanted to be paid—the manager hadn't paid them for several weeks at a time. In protest, they began to perform at the Little Theatre at the Haymarket where Henry Fielding had been continuing his series of political satires. In 1736, Fielding wrote *Pasquin*, a double rehearsal play: the first part of the play dealt with rehearsing a comedy, the second half dealt with rehearsing a tragedy. The comedy rehearsed in the play was called *The Election* dealing with corruption in county elections: the practice of putting people who have died on the election lists. The tragedy was *The Life and Death of Common Sense*, in which a character named Ignorance invaded England.

Fielding's *The Historical Register for the Year 1736* opened 21 March of 1736 and asked the audience to "cry at the tragedy and laugh at the comedy being quite contrary to the general practice." What this tells us is that there were a plethora of tearful comedies like *The Conscious Lovers* and tragedies which had become so overblown and ridiculous that people didn't want to go to them. *The Historical Register* held the stage for 35 performances, and managed to satirize every aspect of English society from *castrati* signers in the opera, to politicians taking bribes, to the lack of patriotism in English society. In the play, Walpole was satirized as a cynical fiddler named *Quidam*. This and a work called *The Golden Rump* were what ultimately broke the government's tolerance for political satires on the English stage. *The Golden Rump* was an anonymous farce planned by Giffard's company at Lincoln's Inn Fields. In it, the King was portrayed as a satyr, showing his rump. The queen was dressed as a priestess, injecting him with *aurum potabile*, liquid gold, while Walpole was standing by, in the robes of the chief magician.

Another reason for the Licensing Act was the confusion among Patentees. Remember that Charles II was supposed to have created a monopoly for London theatre given to two people, which meant that there were only two theatres allowed to be patent theatres. In 1682, the companies merged so there was only one company and the Killigrew patent went dormant. Christopher Rich (John's father) had bought the Davenant patent at Drury Lane and his principal actor, Thomas Betterton, purchased a license to perform at Lincoln's Inn Fields (technically speaking Betterton shouldn't have been acting, but he managed to acquire a license from the King because Christopher Rich was a very unpleasant man and Betterton refused to work for him). Betterton's license was then transferred to a variety of people, and Christopher Rich's patent was renewed in 1714 for his son John who was operating under the original Davenant patent at Covent Garden. Gradually new patents began to be developed. For example, Steele bought the original Killigrew patent, and when he was barred from management, a new patent was given to Booth, Wilks and (Theophilus) Cibber, which was subsequently sold to Highmore (the manager who didn't pay his actors) which led to Cibber's defection to the Theatre in the New Haymarket. Cibber continued producing plays because he figured "since I have a patent to perform at one theatre, I can play anywhere I want." This began to get so complicated, particularly since there was another company in Goodman Fields and Giffard had a company in residence at Lincoln's Inns Fields. The government finally stepped in to settle the confusion and created what we call the Licensing Act of 1737.

The law in short had five important parts:

1) It restricted the king's power to grant patents to Westminster and his various residences only (Westminster being the part of the city of London within the walls, within the "liberties." This meant that the King had no jurisdiction beyond the walls of London);

2) It limited theatres to only those having patents. This meant officially that once again there was a two-theatre system; everyone else was closed down. The two theatres that could exist were Drury Lane and Covent Garden. What this means, and this is important, was that only those theatres could produce what they call major and minor drama. The major drama or legitimate plays were five act comedies, five act tragedies. Everything else was minor drama. Any musical comedy, any three act farces were considered minor drama;

3) It authorized the Lord Chamberlain to prohibit any individual performance. What does this mean? We have created a means of censorship (the Master of Revels no longer existed. That position was considerably reduced in 1660 when Charles took away his power to grant patents);

4) It required all new plays, all additions to old plays, all prologues and epilogues to be licensed by the Lord Chamberlain. This meant he had to read everything before it was allowed to be produced;

5) Since the Lord Chamberlain wasn't about to read any plays, he created the Office of the Theatre Examiner whose job was to read and censor plays.

How did people avoid the law? Clearly as soon as the law was passed, managers were creating ways to get around it.

1) At the Haymarket, James Lacy began to produce puppet shows. Since puppet shows were not illegal, Lacy would put on a play between the acts of

a puppet show. The audience was in attendance to see a puppet show, and the play was simply an added attraction;

2) Henry Giffard at Goodman's Fields produced concerts, during the intervals of which he would produce comedies;

3) At the Haymarket, actor-manager Macklin advertised free performances in the concert formula;

4) Mrs. Charke, Colley Cibber's daughter, moved to a boarding house and advertised that for six pence customers would receive a pint of ale. She literally began the first dinner theatre: she would serve a little food and wine and put on a show. Offstage, she had a terrible problem with transvestitism. She spent much of her life dressed as a man, courting rich widows and bilking them of their money;

5) Theophilus Cibber initiated the practice of open rehearsals, during which the audience could come to watch rehearsals of a play. Remember the law only forbade public performances, not rehearsals;

6) Samuel Foote charged customers for a cup of chocolate or tea then gave performances. Later, he developed one of the most original modes of getting around the law. He advertised public auctions of pictures where each picture would have the title of a particular scene of a play. So, if he was doing *The School for Scandal* and the first scene was in Peter Teazle's house, there would be a drawing room portrait and it would be titled, *Sir Peter Teazle's House*. "What am I bid for the picture?" Someone would bid, and after the bidding was closed the bidders would see that scene of the play.

Eventually the law got so complex because of all the creative ways managers managed to get around it, that in 1752, there was an addition to the law, stating that all places of minor entertainment within a 20-mile radius of London were required to secure licenses from local magistrates to produce plays. This meant that the two patent theatres were allowed to perform any kind of drama and the other theatres were only allowed to perform minor drama. This became confusing and 30 years later, in 1788, the law was amended again to allow magistrates outside the 20-mile radius to license theatre for legitimate drama. In addition, Parliament was allowed to authorize theatres royal in various cities throughout England.

Drama after the Licensing Act

Among the most immediate results of the Licensing Act of 1737 was a rebirth of interest in Shakespeare. There were only two legitimate theaters in London, lots of veteran (and unemployed) actors, lots of old plays, and managers who were unwilling to take a chance on new work. Why challenge censorship if they can produce Shakespeare? As a result, Shakespeare got a renaissance in the eighteenth century particularly in the 1740s and 1750s. During this time, a ladies Shakespeare club was created in London, and managers discovered that polished presentations of Shakespearean plays—the most popular by the way were *Richard III*, *Hamlet*, and *Romeo and Juliet*—would be financially viable. Often, rather than doing new plays, the rival patent theatres would perform the same Shakespearean play with their lead actor in the main role. Apparently during the 1746–47 season, *Richard III* became the "test" play with David Garrick at Drury Lane and James Quin at Covent Garden. Quin played it on 20 October and Garrick played it on 31 October, and audiences could go from one theatre to the other to compare performances. Quin is an interesting figure because he was one of the last actors of the "bombastic school" of performance. He believed in the oratorical school of acting, and he is the only actor on record who actually killed a fellow actor for mispronouncing his name on stage. It was in Addison's *Cato*, and a young Welsh actor pronounced it "Keeto," and throughout the play Quin kept correcting him. After the play, the Welsh actor was annoyed because Quin kept correcting him on stage and said, "How dare you do that to me!" Quin defended himself, but the young lad had the audacity to slap him, so Quin took him out to the yard beyond the theatre, and killed him.

New writers during this period began to write minor drama because more of the theatres could produce minor drama than the major drama. As a result, the theatre found itself aping Italian comic opera, French tearful comedy, and German melodrama since translations of other plays were infinitely more acceptable than "original" work. In 1710, authors could sign a copyright with a publisher for fourteen years which was renewable for another fourteen years. The theatres themselves generally bought a play outright giving the author the proceeds of the third performance. If the play was really successful and ran to a sixth performance, the author would get the proceeds of that performance, and the ninth if the play ran that long.

Musical Comedy

The chief exponent of musical theatre during this period was **Isaac Bickerstaffe** (1733–1808), whose chief claim to fame was *The Maid of the Mill* produced 31 January 1765 at Covent Garden, running 29 nights in a row. This was sentimental comedy put to music: Lord Aimsworth loves Patti, the maid of the mill. He wants her physically, but her honor will not allow that. He'd even agree to marry her if she weren't of a different social class. He offers to endow her with 1,000 pounds a year as a dowry if she marries Giles, a tenant farmer who loves her. She'll be on Giles' farm on the Lord's land, and the implication is that if she marries Giles, she'll have a dalliance with the Lord. Patti is torn. She really loves Lord Aimsworth and wants to have a dalliance with him, but can she ignore the security of marriage with a generous dowry? Still, she understands the meaning of his gift, and she doesn't want to be immoral. The musical piece ends with Giles and Lord Aimsworth each giving up his claims on Patti. Giles says, "I desperately want to love you. But I really can't do that because I know Lord Aimsworth wants you, and this is going to be difficult on you." Lord Aimsworth says, "Ah.' I'm going to give up having any carnal affection for you, and I'll give you the 1000 pounds to marry him anyway." To such generosity, Giles replies, "Well if he's going to be so noble, how can I take you away from him." Patti goes from one to the other and finally marries Lord Aimsworth who says, "I'm a lord and you're just a scullery maiden but it's 1765 and a new world."

The overt sentimentality of this work gave way to a number of farces, and one of the greatest farceurs of the period was **Samuel Foote** (1721–1777) who took over the management of the Little Theatre in the Haymarket. Samuel Foote was given a license, actually a patent, to act at the Little Theatre in the Haymarket because the Prince of Wales played a joke on him, resulting in his falling from a horse and causing him to walk with a limp for the rest of his life. Because the crown felt guilty, Foote was given a license in perpetuity to perform at a theatre. As a result, Sam Foote wrote plays emphasizing lameness, i.e., *The Lame Lover,* and *The Devil upon Two Sticks.* In 1773, he wrote a puppet show called *Piety in Pattens* in which he reduced the sentimental vogue to absurdity having Polly, a housemaid, display palpitatingly tender emotions. What we have here is a satire of *The Maid of the Mill* where the heroine's name is Polly instead of Patti. As in the musical comedy, the squire and the young man who are vying for her hand each give her up to the other, but in the satire, Polly decides that she's not going to marry either of them; she calls them jerks and says "if you're going to be so conscious about being noble to one another, why don't the two of you take each other and I'll go out and have a good time."

Later in his career, Foote produced a virulent social satire called *The Trip to Calais* caricaturing the Duchess of Kingston as Lady Kitty Crocodile. The Duchess had the play banned and charged Foote with sodomy. People did not fool around in this period. If they didn't like the play, they'd run you out of town. He was, of course, acquitted, but the trial took so much out of him that he died not long afterwards.

Georgian Tragedy

The weakest form of theatre during this period was tragedy, and since, during this time, playwrights would attempt to "correct" Shakespeare, audiences were being treated to softened versions of Shakespeare's more famous plays. For example, *Romeo and Juliet* was given a happy ending; in *King Lear*, Cordelia lives, and she and Lear go back to France and live happily ever after. All of the bawdiness of Shakespeare was reduced to sentimental morality, and in many of the tragedies happy endings replaced Shakespeare's original versions because that's what audiences really wanted. Romeo and Juliet didn't deserve to die.

Although there were few playwrights who composed tragedies on the cutting edge, there are two Georgian tragedies worth mentioning. The first is by James Thompson and called *Tancred and Sigismunda*. Written in 1745, it held the stage for 125 years and was the most influential tragedy written in the Georgian period. It had the following characteristics:

1) It was highly indebted to Racine, which meant that it adhered to the neoclassical unities of time, place, and action;

2) It used extremely flowery poetic dialogue;

3) It had extremely long speeches;

4) It was filled with emotionally ambiguous conflicts;

5) Philosophically, it ascribed to the principal of (and had a very significant emphasis on) the perfectibility of man.

Tancred and Sigismunda greatly influenced a man named John Home who wrote *Douglas* in 1756, one of the eighteenth century's best blank verse tragedies. It trades in highly romantic settings, sentimental language, and strong patriotic sentiments—Scottish patriotic sentiments, especially. The play continually invokes a mother's feelings for her son, and is about as close to melodrama without going over the edge. Home's best play was arguably *The Siege of Aquileia* in 1760, which dealt with a Roman counsel who must either sacrifice his son or betray his country and personal honor. This was very significant because it allowed for highly complex tragic effects rather than pure pathos and melodrama. Even though it appeared to be a throwback to heroic tragedy with its love versus honor plot, *The Siege of Aquileia* was perhaps the closest thing to true tragedy in the entire period. Ultimately, the Roman consul chooses his own personal honor and his son dies. The consul kills himself as a result.

Genteel Comedy

Around 1776, the time that David Garrick retired from the stage and Richard Brinsley Sheridan bought out his patent to the Drury Lane, a new kind of comedy called "Genteel Comedy" began to flourish. Genteel Comedy has the following characteristics:

1) One or two pairs of lovers;
2) Lovers unable to marry because of certain obstacles, usually complications from parents or guardians;
3) A formula of scheme, complication, counter-scheme—very much like thesis, antithesis, and synthesis;
4) Resolution in chance events or discoveries, sudden revelations delivering the protagonists from their difficulties;
5) Punishing those guilty of villainous behavior.

In Restoration Comedy, people are punished for lack of wit rather than immorality. In genteel comedy, there is an emphasis on the moral nature of society comprised of upper middle-class characters. Some genteel comedies put more emphasis on emotion and feeling than others; some are exceedingly sentimental, and some are "laughing comedies" that are actually funny! All deal with social climbers, popular fads, and marital incompatibility.

The first important writer of this kind of comedy was **Oliver Goldsmith**. He was born in Ireland in 1728 and died in 1774. He was a doctor by profession, but when he settled in London, unable to support himself as a doctor, he wrote for magazines and produced his first play, *The Good-Natured Man*, in 1768 (I should mention that, before he started to write plays, Goldsmith produced at least one famous novel called *The Vicar of Wakefield* in 1766). His comic masterpiece, *She Stoops to Conquer; or, the Mistakes of a Night*, was produced in 1773. A marriage has been arranged between young Marlowe and Kate Hardcastle. Marlowe and his friend Hastings go off to meet the girl and run into Tony Lumpkin, a buffoon character, who talks them into believing that where they're supposed to meet Kate Hardcastle is an inn, not the Hardcastle home. When the men arrive at the house, they treat Mr. Hardcastle as the manager of the inn and not the owner of a mansion, and they think Kate is a maid. Marlowe is unable to speak to women of his own class without stuttering or making an ass out of himself, but he can speak to a woman of a lower class and be perfectly charming. Ultimately, Marlowe and the scullery maid fall in love. All the complications work out very much like the Marivaux play *The Game of Love and Chance* in which the upper-class engaged couple reverse their positions with their butler/maid so the two people who are courting think they're courting the wrong people. Needless to say, everyone matches up at the end with the right person, sending Marlowe and Kate off to the altar. It's a highly sentimental and funny play with terrific wooing scenes.

The School for Scandal

Richard Brinsley Sheridan (1751–1816) was another Irishman rooted in Irish literary and theatrical circles. His father Thomas was an actor, elocutionist, and writer of farces and his mother wrote novels and sentimental comedies. As a matter of fact, the Joseph Surface character in *The School for Scandal* comes from one of his mother's plays. Richard was fond of borrowing themes from his relatives: the relationship between Joseph and Charles Surface in *The School for Scandal* is based on the relationship between him and his brother. Sheridan settled in London in 1773, having married Elizabeth Linley, whose brother and father would provide music for his plays. In 1775 he wrote *The Rivals* first produced at Covent Garden. A failure, it was withdrawn, rewritten in 10 days, and its second opening made Sheridan famous. In this play Sheridan uses twin romantic love plots, and traditional low comedy characters, for example, the braggart (*Miles-Gloriosus* character) named Lucius O'Trigger, and clever servants called Fag and Lucy. At this time, Fag was the name of a young schoolboy. If you were at Oxford or at any one of the grammar schools in England, there were upperclassmen and the underclassmen, or Fags. *The Rivals* also had a blocking father character and an old character woman named Mrs. Malaprop, who always spoke using the wrong kinds of words. She comes from the tradition of the dowager character found in Congreve with Lady Wishfort in *The Way of the World*, or Lady Fidget in Wycherly's *The Country Wife*. The play involved satire on contemporary manners, particularly the sentimental fashion, with lots of double entendre and mistaken identities. *The Rivals* was especially notable because it had a sentimental subplot, unusual because the play was essentially what we would call a "laughing comedy." The focus of the play was not on tears or heartfelt emotion, but laughter. Usually the opposite was the rule: in sentimental comedy, it was usually the laughing characters or low characters that provided comic relief from all the emotion. In Sheridan's play, there was emotional relief from the comedy.

Also produced in 1775 was Sheridan's *St. Patrick's Day*, a two-act farce, and his comic opera, *The Duenna*, a superficial, escapist entertainment dealing with Spanish intrigue that played 75 times in a row, breaking the long-run record for English opera (*The Beggar's Opera* had played only 70 times in a row). *The Duenna*, for which Linley composed the music, became the most popular English opera of the century. In 1776 from the proceeds he earned from *The Duenna*, Sheridan bought out Garrick's share of the Drury Lane patent and, in 1777, he wrote *A Trip to Scarborough*, a revision of Vanbrugh's play *The Relapse* that caused all the trouble in 1698 and caused Collier to write his treatise on the immorality of the stage. In the same year he wrote *The School for Scandal*, often referred to as the last great English comedy of the age. Critics disagree on the sentimental nature of the play. Some say it's a return to the sparkling comedies of the Restoration, others suggest it is much more moral than the plays of the Restoration. The bad people are caught and punished in *The School for Scandal* while Horner gets away with it in *The Country Wife*. What are the sentimental aspects of *The School for Scandal*? Is there anything that plays upon a heartfelt response? The play begins with the Pinchwife/Marjorie problem: an older husband with a younger wife, Lady Teazle, who is tempted into an affair with Joseph Surface. Ultimately, the wife reforms or at least moderates her behavior, and husband and wife come to some kind of an understanding.

The aptly named Joseph Surface and his brother Charles present a satirical look at the eighteenth-century sentimental formula. Joseph falsely speaks all of the great moral pronouncements of sentimentality while Charles lives the life of a rake, though he in fact is more moral because he doesn't lie like

Joseph. What happens to Charles? He is discovered to be moral: the love of a good woman transforms him. Moreover, Charles is willing to sell off all of the family pictures except for the portrait of Sir Oliver, who insists that Charles must be inherently good since he won't sell off his picture. How are Lady Teazle and Joseph caught? In one of the great scenes in theatre—the screen scene. The fact that Sir Peter says kind things about his wife, without knowing that she can hear them, melts Lady Teazle into a confession of her intended affair with Joseph. She is so emotionally affected by Sir Peter's affection for her that she agrees to give up her participation in the ladies' gossip cabal, the school for scandal.

Sheridan followed *The School for Scandal* in 1778 with a satiric farce called *The Camp*, burlesquing the ladies' habit of following around the military, and in 1779, he produced *The Critic*, a rehearsal play that satirized sentimental plays. Sheridan did not like the sentimental form and constantly wrote satires against it, but he used it to great advantage in his own plays. In 1794 he enlarged Drury Lane Theatre and purchased a great amount of scenery. In 1809 he ended his association with Drury Lane when it burned to the ground. It's very interesting because the fire left him with very little except a pile of ashes and the glass of wine he held in his hand—and possibly the greatest exit line in history. Someone said, "Aren't you going to do anything about the fire?" Not missing a beat, Sheridan replied, "Well, cannot a man take a glass of wine by his own fireside?" He died in 1816 from circulatory problems in poverty, beset by creditors. He could not hold onto money. In terms of personality he was moody, often drunk, and indiscrete, but possessing great charm and powers of persuasion.

From a political standpoint, Sheridan was extremely important. During the Regency Crisis between 1788 and 1789, he was advisor to the Prince of Wales (King George III suffered from dimentia and imagined that England was a garden and all his subjects were flowers). The Prince of Wales had to function as Regent and was literally ruling the country with Sheridan one of his principal advisors. He defended those who suffered for supporting the French Revolution and the belief that the French had a right in choosing their own government. He argued in favor of Catholic emancipation and individual rights—even in the eighteenth century, the Catholic religion was still not regarded highly in England.

Actors and Acting

Between 1660 and 1800 actors entered a company on probationary status and learned by observing established performers. There were three training schools: Jolly ran an acting school called "The Nursery," Macklin, and Sheridan also ran acting training schools to help promote their theatres, but none were terribly successful. John Rich trained his actors in pantomime, and after 1750, Garrick taught the young actors at Drury Lane. The beginner actor was called a utility actor. He (or she) played a lot of small roles each season and eventually grew into the type for which he/she was suited, his/her "line of business," a limited range of character types in which the actor would remain for the rest of his/her career. By the end of the eighteenth century, there were four ranks of line of business distinguishable:

1) The first rank—players of leading roles. These were heroes and heroines of tragedy or light comedy;

2) The second rank—players of secondary roles. These were specialists in low comedy;

3) The third rank—players of third line parts. These were walking ladies or walking gentlemen (correlative to the modern "walk-on" roles);

4) The fourth rank—general utility players. These were character parts, including chambermaids, elderly men, and so forth.

Generally, the line of business led to "possession of parts." Once an actor was cast in a role, he (or she) continued to play it as long as he stayed in the company. Therefore, an actor playing Romeo when he enters the company at age 30 is still playing Romeo when he leaves at 65. Lesser actors were employed by the season while leading actors were usually put under contract for a longer period, though never longer usually than five years. Usually an experienced actor was appointed to stage the plays and was given the title, "Acting Manager," when the theatre manager, the man who owned the patent, wasn't able to do that himself (sometimes the theater managers were businessmen rather than theatre professionals). During this period there was no such thing as an actual director. Typically, the first rehearsals of a new play fell to the author who would give line readings and any specific business. Then the acting manager would be in charge of any kind of revival. Essentially what the acting manager did was make sure all the lines could be heard and everybody stayed out of everyone else's way. There was no blocking in the modern sense: actors would stand in a semicircle on stage (or, more correctly, the apron since the scenery was in the stage space). When an actor had an extended monologue, he (or she) would walk to the front of the stage and orate.

Also, until 1762, when Garrick got rid of them, there were audience members on the stage, sometimes as many as 200 of them. There had been legislation in 1704, under Queen Anne that attempted to take the audience off the stage, but they remained there until 1762.

More important than the stage manager, was the prompter. The prompter secured licenses for plays; he copied out the "fair copy" of plays for the Lord Chamberlain; he also copied out actor's parts called "sides." Actors never got a complete script. They only got their own lines and their cues. In addition, the prompter was the one who assessed fines for actors being late for rehearsal, drunk in performance, and other offenses. Actually, failure to learn lines and refusal to play roles were among the greatest offenses in this period. Rehearsals were few, usually held between 10 A.M. and 1 P.M. for about 2 weeks. David Garrick sometimes prolonged them to eight weeks, but that was a rarity. Lines were addressed to the audience as much as to any other actor, and because there were very few pieces of furniture on the stage actors basically just stood around. From eyewitness accounts, it appears that when an actor was not speaking, he/she just hung out on the stage, maybe talked to someone in the audience until he/she had a line. There were a great many documents praising actors when they stayed in character throughout a whole scene.

The style of acting varied from formal (or oratorical) to realistic. Until about 1750 the dominant approach was oratorical, characterized in the work of Betterton, Booth, and James Quin. Macklin and Garrick encouraged a style based upon a direct observation of life, though such a style might not appear realistic to us today. Even the most natural acting of the eighteenth century was not naturalistic by modern standards. Macklin was acting manager at Drury Lane from 1734 to 1743 and Garrick was in charge at Drury Lane from 1747 to 1776. Both of them had a very long time to develop their acting style.

Even after the change to a more realistic approach, certain conventions in acting were maintained:

1) Whenever possible, actors played at the front of the stage. This meant that if an actor was at the far back of the apron, for whatever reason, he would walk down to the front to deliver a line;

2) Actors never turned their backs on the public and were hardly ever seen in profile;

3) Actors exchanged stage positions after every speech. During the Restoration, acting began as oratory: not only did the actor intone a speech (much like recitative in opera), he would come to the front of the stage so that he could be heard. Gradually actors became concerned with talking to one another, but the concept of finding an inner reality or becoming a character was still quite foreign to them;

4) Actors prolonged certain cries and exclamations, what was called "organ point" acting;

5) They frequently plunged themselves to the floor in scenes of great drama;

6) Actors differentiated between high points and lesser passages in a play. They called lesser passages *level speaking*, and the important bits, which they called *points* were sought to be made to the audience throughout. If an actor "made the point," the audience would applaud, and occasionally the actor would do the speech over again. If an actor died well and the audience applauded sufficiently, he might die again;

7) Early in the eighteenth century, actors intoned verse in a play as if it were a kind of chant. This is significant because actors would treat metric

plays very differently than prose plays. Plays in prose would automatically have a much more natural feel than plays written in blank verse or any other kind of meter. However, from 1750 on, actors tried to make verse sound as natural as possible.

A Gallery of Actors

Thomas Betterton (1635-1710) considered the greatest actor in England between Burbage and Garrick, was son of King Charles I's cook. He played 120 roles in his career and was famous for his careful preparation, self-discipline, and majestically restrained (if oratorical) performances. **Elizabeth Barry** (1658-1713), the mistress of the Earl of Rochester, overcame physical handicaps to become the greatest actress of her day. Equally adept in comic and tragic roles, her performances were celebrated for their intensity and emotionalism, and she was often cited as "being the character." **Anne Bracegirdle** (1671-1748) prided herself on virtuous behavior, being highly moral and clean living. She had a considerable reputation as a singer and was particularly adept at breeches parts. In the eighteenth century, **Colley Cibber** (1671-1757) became the archetype for playing fop characters. The butt of much ridicule (for playing effeminate men), he was a noted playwright and theatre manager, and became Poet Laureate in 1730. **Thomas Doggett** (1670-1721) performed the low comic characters with a careful observation of life and specific detail in costuming. **Anne Oldfield** (1683-1730) was the first actress buried in Westminster Abbey, and the great-great-great-aunt of Sir Winston Churchill. **Edward Kynaston** (1640-1706) began his career playing women's parts for which he was celebrated by critics and audiences alike. When women were permitted to act on the stage, Kynaston became a successful leading man. **Mrs. Catherine Corey** was not a very good actress but was significant in terms of developing realism on the stage by making up to look like Lady Harvey, a member of the aristocracy (an attempt to create a resemblance on the stage to someone in real life). The fact that she dressed up to look like Lady Harvey got her arrested. After she was released from jail, she did it again and Lady Harvey's claque pelted her with oranges.

In the later eighteenth century **Charles Macklin** (1699-1797) was the first to introduce true period costume on the English stage. He had an outstanding reputation as an acting teacher (and also for being irascible and difficult as an actor), and was celebrated for his restrained naturalness in performance. **David Garrick** (1717-1779) overcame an unimpressive physical stature to become arguably the greatest English actor of his time. As a theatre manager, he developed several important innovations in production techniques, and his acting was marked by brilliant virtuosity that had a charismatic, almost mystical, effect on the audience. **Spranger Barry** (1717-1777) was the matinee idol of the eighteenth century because of his "plaintive voice" and "melting eyes." **George Anne Bellamy** (1731-1788) was the tabloid goddess of her day, characterized by extravagant love affairs, gambling, and feuds with other actors (most notably with David Garrick). **Dorothy Jordan** (1761-1816) was acclaimed for her delivery of dramatic verse and became the mistress to the Duke of Clarence, bearing him ten children while still maintaining her career.

Theatre Seasons
During the Restoration the theatres were open from October to June, and as the years progressed through to 1800, the theatres began to be open longer, from mid-September, and gradually to seasons which would include the summer. During the Restoration, the typical performance bill included a full-length play with singing and dancing as entr'acte entertainment. Gradually that was extended to include a full-length play, acrobats, trained animals, and other circus-like acts. Around 1700 began the vogue for the afterpiece which was a short pantomime, musical work, or farce. Oftentimes the afterpieces became more popular than the main piece of the evening. In 1702, for example, a play was performed with a vaudeville that included animal imitations, people doing birdcalls and other animal noises, tumbling and acrobatics. The following year, the vaudeville was so popular that a five-act play was shortened to make room for the animal acts. In 1705, two short plays were performed

with scenes from other plays thrown in during the intermissions, followed by rope dancing and acrobatics.

In addition to these complex bills, which begin to suggest that audiences were somewhat restive for legitimate drama and wanted the kind of entertainment that the movie-going public want today, there were a number of theatrical riots in the eighteenth century. At the turn of the eighteenth century, the audience was composed of citizens, apprentices, soldiers, ladies of fashion, and some clergy (the clergy had to go to the theatre so they could complain about it in the pulpit). Often there were specific groups that organized into what we would call a *cabal*, the function of which was to damn a play or support it. One such clique was called the "Mohawks," a group of four young men who liked to catcall at plays. In a magazine around 1750, they're referred to as "the merry young gentlemen who were great improvers of the catcall," who would just go to theatres and kibbutz with the actors. We have records in the 1720s of the freemasons being a very popular audience because they were well-behaved. Gradually into the 1730s and 1740s there grew a kind of political partisanship in the audience, divided among supporters of King George, the Hanover crowd, or those who wanted to maintain an English monarch on the throne. Partisanship was often performer-based as well. In the 1720s there were famous rivalries between female actors and singers, and there are records of riots that occurred when the singers would be performing in the same work—for example, where half the audience would boo, hiss, and catcall while one or the other diva was performing. A third group of partisans were "critics," members of the audience who came precisely to see what was wrong with the play, and who would be extremely vocal during the performance in voicing their opinions to other audience members. As a result, in the 1700s, there were a number of prologues, epilogues, and short inductions before and after plays asking an audience to behave.

Theatre Riots

On 3 February 1721, a drunken earl walked on the stage of Lincoln's Inn Fields to reprimand an actor who got his lines wrong. The audience shouted down the drunken earl who started to pick a fight with members of the audience. Everyone drew their swords and the whole theatre got into a giant duel.

In 1729, a work called *The Village Opera* was hissed off the stage. There was a report of this on 27 February 1729: "No sooner did the actor appear on the stage when his arrival was ushered in with a serenade of catcalls, penny trumpets, clubs, canes, coarse voices, whistling in keys, heels, fists, and volleys of whole oranges." The audience removed candles from their sconces and threw them—some lit, some broken in two—at the actors. In addition, they pulled up the chairs from the balconies and throw them into the audience, making a mess of the theatre, and all because they didn't like the play being performed.

Later, in December 1743 when Garrick and Macklin had seceded from Drury Lane, Garrick had been invited back and he was asked to play one of Macklin's roles. All of Macklin's sympathizers went to Drury Lane. A fight broke out between Garrick and Macklin supporters, and the play had to be halted. In 17 November of 1744, a very famous riot called the O. P. Riot (Old Price Riot) occurred over the practice of raising ticket prices at Drury Lane. On 8 November 1755, a riot stopped the performance of a pantomime called *The Chinese Festival* because the costumes and dances were French, and England was at war with France at the time.

On 25 January 1763, there was another series of riots called the "Fitzgiggo Riots" over half-price tickets. The managers of Drury Lane tried to rescind the usual practice of allowing anyone in at half-price if they were coming in after the intermission. In other words, if you didn't come in at the beginning, you could come in for half-price and just see the afterpiece. Since pantomimes became so popular, people would just be coming in for half-price to see the second half of the snow, so the management decided to charge full price for late entry. The first time this was put into effect, the theatre seats were removed, actors were hit over the head with sconces and furniture, and musicians in the pit ran undercover because of things being thrown and ruining their instruments (we have etchings actually depicting this). On 24 February 1763, the Fitzgiggo Riots extended to Covent Garden. The same individual (a Mr. Fitzpatrick) who started the riot in Drury Lane went to Covent Garden and staged the same disturbance.

On 8 November 1773 a riot ensued over Macklin appearing on the stage. A month before, he had appeared as Macbeth and forgot his lines. He was 73 years old at the time, and when he appeared again on stage on 18 November, the audience pelted him with fruit and booed. Macklin said he'd never appear on stage again and walked off.

Theatre Architecture

Between 1660 and 1700 in London, there were three important theatres: Drury Lane, Lincoln's Inn Fields, and Dorset Garden. These theatres had common features: the auditorium divided into a pit which was raked for sightlines and had backless benches so the audience had the opportunity to sit. The stage was also raked. There were two or three galleries, the first of which was partitioned into boxes (a box was a compartment in which a group of people could sit, separate from everyone else). The front boxes (looking at the stage) were where the royalty watched the plays; the side boxes were where the fashionable people sat; and the stage boxes were where people who wanted to be seen sat. The top gallery was equipped with benches like a modern balcony, and if there was a middle gallery (of three galleries), it was often a combination of the first and third, with some boxes and some backless benches.

The stage floor had a rake from the back of the apron to the back wall of the stage house so that the perspective of the scenery could be better achieved. The apron was flat, though in some theatres there was a slight rake. None of the actors acted upstage of the plaster line because of the perspective scenery. Behind the proscenium, grooves were installed in the stage floor to accommodate wings and shutters. There were also trap doors, flying machinery, and a number of proscenium doors (generally from one to three) which opened on to the apron. Actors most frequently entered through the proscenium doors, though they could make entrances from upstage through the shutters if necessary. In the first Drury Lane, there were six doors, three on each side of the apron. In the second, they were reduced to four, two on each side.

Drury Lane cost £2,400 to build. The pit floor of Drury Lane was steeply raked at about a 19-degree angle for sightlines. The pit benches were covered with green cloth—interesting since green was usually the color associated with whoring during this time. An orchestra pit was in front of—and underneath—the center of the stage. Lighting was supplied by pendant chandeliers hung from the proscenium arch. When Drury Lane opened, there were no footlights, but around the turn of the century, they began to develop as tiny oil lamps and then were transformed into floats—pieces of cork or wick which would float in troughs of oil. Plays were performed in the afternoon and illumination was also created by a kind of domed structure above the audience which let in light. In the early days of both Drury Lane and Covent Garden, the dome structure was open air so it let in light and rain. Changes of lighting were very interesting because they often used moonlight transparencies as in the Renaissance. Dark scenes were created by snuffing out some of the candles.

Covent Garden opened in 1732. It had a smaller stage than Drury Lane but still had seats built on stage for spectators. It did not have any footlights but was illuminated by four hoops of candles forming chandeliers. The chief feature of Covent Garden was that the green room had access from behind the stage, which meant that the king did not have to cross the stage to get to the green room to visit an actor, as he did in Drury Lane. In Drury Lane if the King wanted to go to the green room, he had to walk through the crowd, through a side door, cross the stage and go straight up through the back shutters. Covent Garden took this into consideration when they built the theatre. Apparently, during the Restoration King Charles crossed the stage so often that it became sufficient to reconsider the architecture of the period.

After 1661, scenic units in the English theatre were copies of those used in Italy and France. After 1690, shutters were generally replaced by roll drops. All changes of scenery were made *a vista* since the front curtain was raised at the beginning of the performance and only lowered at the end. This meant that even entr'acte entertainments would be performed in front of the set. After 1750, an act drop was added to come in to hide changes of scenery. Between 1660 and 1800, each theatre accumulated a stock of scenery that was used over and over again. Sets were used interchangeably with a variety of plays since the neoclassical ideal argued that specific time and place were irrelevant to drama: the concern was not for the particular but for the universal.

One of the problems of developing spectacle in the theatre was the fact that the audience was seated on the stage. In 1762 Garrick managed to banish the audience from the stage, and in 1771, he hired a French artist at the Paris Opera, **Philip Jacques (James) De Loutherbourg** (1740-1812), the most important designer on the English stage during the late 18th century. De Loutherbourg continued to paint and design at Drury Lane until 1781 when he resigned because Sheridan proposed to cut his salary. His contributions to theatre design and production techniques are many:

1) He popularized reproductions of real places on the stage. This does not mean he was an antiquarian per se, trying to recapture ancient buildings, but if a particular play took place on the cliffs of Dover, he would try to create the cliffs of Dover;

2) To increase illusion, he broke up stage pictures with ground rows and set pieces. Perfect symmetry doesn't exist in nature;

3) He used miniature figures at the rear of the stage to depict battles, marching armies, sailing vessels. In this he anticipates the great crowd scenes of the late nineteenth and early twentieth centuries;

4) He used sound effects to suggest waves, rain, hail, distant guns. Some critics even suggest that he actually began the profession of the sound designer in the theatre;

5) He also revamped theatre lighting systems by installing overhead battens, using silk screens and gauze curtains to suggest variations in color and to even simulate various weather conditions and times of day.

As an example of the kind of thing De Loutherbourg was doing at Drury

Lane, this is his design for *A Christmas Tale* 1771, a musical play by Charles Dibdin.

Part 2. Scene: *A beautiful landscape.* Trees are practical (meaning people are discovered on limbs of trees). This then develops into Camilla's magnificent garden in which a laurel tree unfolds and shows the words "Valor, Constancy, Honor" discovered in gold.

Part 2. *A cell with prisons around it.* A magician falls asleep, drops his wand, it thunders from above and the prisons break open. All of the locks magically open.

Part 3. *Camilla's magnificent garden in which the flowers change color through the scene.*

Part 4. *A prospect of rocks.* A character sounds the horn, it thunders, the rock splits in half and we discover the castle of Nicromant and a fiery lake with real water around it. It thunders again. A main character plunges into the fiery lake (a stuntman catches fire as he goes into the lake). Then a dance of demons occurs and the demons vanish, a character enters in the costume of a large owl.

Part 5. *A grand apartment in the Seraglio.* The first stage direction is "Eunuchs enter singing." Flames are seen through the seraglio windows. The seraglio breaks to pieces discovering the whole palace in flames. The flames and the rooms of the castle vanish away and discover a fine moonlight scene. Then the stage grows light and the magician descends in a cloud. He waves his wand; the cloud ascends and discovers a fine distant prospect of the sea and the castle at a distance with the sun rising. The cloud ascends then the sun actually rises.

It is this sort of production value in 1771 that is going to lead the English into a desire for realism on the stage—pictorial realism which is first going to exhibit itself in the melodrama, and then in the domestic plays of the next century when all of a sudden, actors were using real cups and real saucers, and eating real food on the stage.

Lighting during the Restoration

Performances were in the afternoon so that windows could provide some illumination. In addition, there was light from the little dome above the theatre, and the chandeliers. By 1744, lights were mounted on vertical ladders behind each wing, and controlled by scene blinds which were shields which could be manipulated to come between the light source and the stage. In the Renaissance the Italians used to hang metal containers (like soup cans) above the light and how close they came to the source would determine how much light the stage would get. The eighteenth-century scene blinds were like the kind of things we use as reflectors. Footlights were mounted on pivots which would allow them to be lowered below stage level for dimming (which also created some problems in a trough full of oil). This was all very dangerous, and scenery, costumes, and theatres often caught fire. Garrick is credited with reforming stage lighting in 1765 but there is disagreement about precisely what he did. It is commonly believed that his chief reform was to remove all visible light sources from the stage, another attempt to go into a more "real" picture, to create the illusion of reality. He is also credited with improving reflectors behind the light to create more candle power. De Loutherbourg made changes using silk filters and silk screens to reflect light, gaining control over color. As a result, he was important in the development of what we now use as gels. De Loutherbourg was also very interested in the direction of sunlight in a scene, and defining the source of light (another attempt to create reality on stage).

Lighting improved after the introduction in 1785 of the Patent Lamp, sometimes called the Argand lamp. This is an oil lamp which allows a better control of the use of oil, using a wick and glass chimney which can control the proportions of oxygen and oil. Effectively, the Argand lamp created a brighter and steadier illumination than other methods of stage lighting. Improvements in lighting encouraged theatres to put more of the action behind the proscenium arch, and gradually in the last quarter of the eighteenth century, the actor began to move from the apron back on to the full stage, amid the scenery.

Costumes

From 1660 to 1800, most actors wore contemporary clothing in performance. As Neoclassicism tended to idealize nature, actors dressed their characters as sumptuously as possible, especially since actors were in charge of their own costumes (there was not a designer to unify everything). However, there were exceptions to the use of contemporary clothes on stage. Classical heroes wore the *habits à la Romaine*, the Roman dress, which was essentially a toga over contemporary clothing so that the actor would dress in his hose and suit and throw a toga over that. Near eastern characters were identified by turbans, baggy trousers, and fur trimmed gowns. Actresses, however, playing classical or near-eastern characters generally added feathered hair pieces or headdresses to contemporary clothing. Certain characters, because of popularity, had specific or conventionalized costumes. Falstaff always wore a ruff and cavalier boots. Richard III was always in pumpkin pants. Henry VIII was always dressed as the famous Holbein portrait. Hamlet was always in black. King Lear wore a white fur piece added to contemporary dress (because of age and the sense of hoarfrost going out into the storm). Macbeth was dressed in a British army uniform.

Concern for greater realism and appropriateness began in 1734 with a Mademoiselle Sallé. She was a French danseuse who introduced costume reform when she performed at Covent Garden in the ballet *Pygmalion*. She dressed with drapery imitating ancient statues—she did not have contemporary clothes on, all she had on was a kind of draped toga. She went against the rule of dressing in contemporary dress with the suggestion of antiquity. In 1741, Charles Macklin clothed Shylock in a black gabardine gown, long trousers, and a red hat. Macklin also removed the red fright wig from Shylock's costume, although he used the red hat to retain the color association. This was considered an innovation because it was the contemporary view of what a Jew looked like. Macklin also attempted to play Macbeth in a kilt and many satirical sketches of the period comment on that experiment.

After 1750, Garrick attempted to costume pre-Commonwealth plays (before 1640) in Elizabethan clothes (if the play was written before 1640, he dressed the characters in pumpkin pants and farthingales). He continued to produce post-Commonwealth plays, however, in contemporary dress.

Initially, there was little information available regarding historical accuracy in costuming. However, in 1757, there appeared in London a book called *Recueil des Habillements* which was a collection of designs, taken from famous paintings, supposed to provide a sense of what clothing looked like in various periods. In 1775 Joseph Strutt wrote *The Dress and Habits of the People of England*, a book that would start a trend (which would develop after 1800) to research what people actually wore and to recreate it on the stage.

9. Scene Designers and Playwrights in Italy during the 18th Century

Scene Designers

Designer and painter, **Giulio Parigi** spent 40 years with the Medici family in Florence. He perfected revolving *periaktoi* for use in rapid scene changes and specialized in landscaped designs, especially landscapes that would change from one locale to another. He was especially interested in transformation scenes and, as a result, he was so successful that he was among the first to have etchings done of his designs. People regarded them as works of art, which is going to be important as we move through the 18th century, that people began to regard theatre design as a significant artistic canvas in the world of visual arts. In 1608, Parigi produced a spectacular finale of an opera which had nine stage machines moving up and down simultaneously changing the set from the pits of hell to the fields of Elysium, all in front of the eyes of the spectator, all moving very slowly to music. He also used lighting to underscore perspective, and brought the setting close to the audience, literally violating the stage space, but making the audience feel that they are part of the event. Rather than giving the illusion that the proscenium is a closed picture frame, he would design columns so that the building would seem to continue to include the audience. Parigi was fond of balance, but it did not necessarily have to be symmetrical balance. He created an asymmetrical set which enlarged the potential of the playing space because he did not always need one wing balanced with another wing. Some of his designs would take very busy foreground space and balance them with perspective pictures at the back so that the sense of space goes off into the distance.

Giovanni Battista Aleotti was the first to employ the flat wing system in 1606. Remember, for perspective in the Renaissance, the first kind of wing system that was popular was the angled wing because it was believed that, if the wing was on an angle, it would be easier to produce a perspective image. Aleotti was among the first to develop a way of painting perspective on a single flat wing at Ferrara in 1606. In addition, he designed the Teatro Farnese in Parma in 1618.

Giulio Troili was the first to deal with flat wings in grooves or runners on the floor and ceiling of the stage. He put borders above each pair of wings to hide the machinery at the top of the stage.

Giacomo Torelli is famous for the synchronization of moving scenery. His chariot and pole system, first used in Venice at the Teatro Novissimo between 1641 and 1645, involved flats attached to poles that extended through little grooves in the floor to cars or chariots on tracks underneath the stage. All these cars were controlled by a single winch so that all the scenery could be changed simultaneously.

Andrea Pozzo was significant in the creation of rounded buildings. This is very important because when we're talking about perspective, everything is at an angle and not circular. Pozzo was the first to create a perspective design which created the illusion of rounded buildings. As a result, his chief designs were of temples and coliseums. He used the fixed groove system and chariot and pole to realize his circular designs, since the chariot and pole system permitted one person to control the entire scene change rather than requiring stagehands to move each set piece.

Ferdinando Galli-Bibiena developed scenes viewed at an angle (the so-called *scena per angelo*), which made the theatrical space appear to be larger because the building or room seems to continue offstage into the wings.

Baldassare Orsini wrote *Le Scene Del Nuovo Teatro Der Verzaro* in 1785. He represents the scenic techniques of the 1770s and 1780s, and he is significant because he presents us with a checklist of stock scenery of the period, where it would have been placed on stage, and how it would have been used. He also provides a detailed description of scene painting involving the selection of colors, the play of light and shadow, and shading particular features in settings. For example, he suggests that exteriors and large interiors, which are generally architectural spaces, consist of yellowish marble and/or gray stone mottled with greens and reds, particularly where the tones enhance the perception of depth. He also suggests that more intimate interiors are in white to imitate plaster, with gold ornamentation. What is obvious from his work is that these scene designs and colors were meant to be illuminated by candle light. In addition, he describes the use or shadow or "chiaroscuro"— the sculpting of a unit. He talks about light and design going to a vanishing point in what he calls the *sfumato effect* which is where colors seem to blend together. I call it the sky-blue pink of a spring evening, where the horizon and sky seem to blend together. For Orsini it was a *sfumato* effect into an area of sky that contained a reddish violet. What we're talking about here is not only a theatrical device but an attempt to recreate what we see in nature.

Filippo Juvara (1678–1736) originally imitated the *scena per angolo* invented by the Bibienas, but beginning in 1708, he departed from the 45-degree angle to set his scenes on semi-circular or octagonal planes. Even more significant than just using the idea of a physical circle, what Juvara sought to do was create a design to allow the eye to go from one point to another on the stage. This was in contrast to Bibiena whose angled sets allowed the eye go offstage. What Juvara wanted to do was create a design so that, wherever the actor would be onstage, the eye could go to that particular point. As a result, there was a circular or fluid movement in his design, and in so doing, he began to develop an aesthetic preference to suggest mood, not only place in his designs. Moreover, in the creation of mood, he preferred light that was diffused rather than strongly focused.

Gian Battista Piranesi (1720–1778), though not primarily a theatrical designer, developed the concept of mood in theatrical design by his production of engravings of Roman ruins and contemporary prisons. What this did was contribute to the interest in ruined antiquity that was beginning to develop in the middle of the eighteenth century. He stimulated this interest in ruined antiquity by making highly realistic etchings of prisons, with the play of light and shadow that created highly emotional dramatic effects.

Playwrights

In the eighteenth century, Aristotle and his three unities, or what they thought were his three unities, were once again the rule. In 1692, the Arcadian Academy was created. This was a social club whose goal was the purification of Italian literature. Here were *their* three rules:

1) Emphasize simplicity—which meant they wanted to emphasize the "simple life," easily apprehended passions, and tender resolutions;

2) They were directing reforms toward purifying an over-blown tragic opera to what would become *opera seria*. By 1700, opera, which had initially been developed as an attempt to recreate Greek theatre, became stuffed with comedy and extraneous vocal flourishes. The Academy wanted to return it to its central focus (of course this took away much of the fun for composers and performers);

3) They employed the elitist theatre of French tragedy as models of simple structure, using Racine as their model;

The first important Italian playwright of the eighteenth century was the Venetian, **Apostolo Zeno** (1668–1750), who was the Caesarian poet (a poet laureate position) from 1718 to 1729. He established the opera seria form, which was very ironic because Zeno hated opera. He knew, however, that he was expected to contribute some kind of formal development to that genre, and now he is known as the revisionist opera librettist. (Obviously, "seria" means serious). Opera seria is a *reformation* of Italian tragic opera, and this is the form that Zeno established:

1) Six, no more than eight characters who are interconnected by love chain. A loves B, but B loves C, but C loves D, but D loves E and E loves A;

2) One main plot, always accompanied by a secondary love plot. In other words, I am the King of Thebes. I want to marry Jeanine, Queen of Syria but she is in love with Jack who is the King of Egypt. That's the main plot. The subplot is Jack has a daughter who wants to marry my son, and in fact did marry my son, but we don't know it yet. Unless Jeanine marries Jack, Jack won't let his daughter marry my son. What turns out is that she isn't his daughter in the first place but is really my daughter, so that the couple secretly married are really brother and sister. At the very end of the opera we discover that my son actually isn't my son but Jeanine's son, so the two of them can stay married, and one of us or all of us kill ourselves;

3) Three, four, or five acts. Italians were never terribly specific;

4) The climax and dénouement usually occur in the form of some triumphal scene. In other words, Jack comes in having conquered the known world, and so we get this big scene where slaves and animals and elephants are brought in so that he can woo Jeanine with great aplomb;

5) Each scene is contrived to end with an exit aria for one of the characters. This means that, no matter what happens in the scene, someone has to sing an aria and get off stage. This creates a rather rigid formula because the audience then begins to know that whoever sings is going to leave. If you sing, you have to leave, unless it's a duet; then only one of you would leave—or both, if it is the end of an act;

6) Characters, with the exceptions of the blocking or villainous characters, are motivated by the highest standards of noble or ethical behavior. Just imagine that the characters in *The Conscious Lovers* are the King and Queen of Syria, so they're all very high-blown and rational;

7) The working out of the plot is focused on the interplay of emotions. This is where we're starting to turn towards the concept of melodrama. Dur-

ing the opera, I tell Jeanine that if she doesn't marry me, I'm going to have her family killed. This is done in two lines. Then we spend the next 25 lines with her saying "Oh woe is me, who should be mistreated thus," and I say, "Oh woe is me, to put her in this position, when if she only loved me as she should." The events are dealt with very quickly and then a great deal of time is spent thinking about the events and making rational and emotional judgments about them. When we come to the nineteenth century, melodrama is precisely the same thing. We put the heroine, Jeanine, into a little room unable to pay the rent. Someone comes on stage (in a black cape) and says "You've got to pay the rent." "No, no! I can't pay the rent." "You must pay the rent." The melodramatic scene is the equivalent of an emotional duet in the opera seria: the event is Jeanine's inability to pay the rent when it is due; the scene plays upon the heightened emotional distress caused by Jeanine's situation.

Zeno's forte was fast dialogue and action. Perhaps two of his most significant works were *Amleto* (*Hamlet*) in 1715, and *La Griselda* in 1721. *Griselda* is the most chauvinistic opera on the boards. It is about a noble young man who falls in love with a peasant girl. He marries her and then subjects her to the harshest tests through four acts to make her prove that she loves him. He forces a friend of his to make love to her so that she has to refuse him; he tortures her; he does all these things and the poor girl stays pure, chaste, and still loves him at the end of the opera. *La Griselda* was set to music by many composers, but is only rarely performed today.

Zeno was followed by **Francesco Scipione**, **Marchese di Maffei** (1675–1755) who attempted to introduce French and Greek classical simplicity into the Italian drama. Scipione was trying to reform the drama in the same way Zeno had reformed the opera—though through the aegis of Aristotle and Racine. In 1710 he and Zeno established a literary journal to refine their ideas and to proselytize. His most significant play is a verse tragedy produced in 1713 called *Merope*—based on Greek mythology, the drama of Euripides, and French neoclassical philosophy. Polifonte kills Cresfonte, the King of Messenia, and two of his sons, to conquer the kingdom. Epitide, the youngest son of Cresfonte and his wife Merope, was saved from the massacre and raised in Ellis under the name of Cleone. After an interval of fourteen years, Cleone returns to Messenia where he is assaulted by a ruffian and ultimately kills him. As a result, Cleone is taken into custody. Merope (who is unaware that she is his mother) thinks that he had in fact killed her son, because it was rumored that the child had been saved and had been raised incognito in the lower class. Merope automatically jumps to the conclusion that the ruffian was her son, not Cleone. She condemns him to death, after which she suddenly realizes that Cleone is actually Epitide her son. Polifonte, who is now running the kingdom, offers to spare him on the condition that Merope will marry him. This is kind of like Claudius and Gertrude in *Hamlet*. Merope vacillates between the love for her son ("I've got to get him out of jail so that he won't be killed.") and her hatred for Polifonte ("How can I marry that villain."). She reluctantly consents to the marriage, and on the day of the wedding, the last scene of the play, as they are about to get married, Epitide grabs an axe and cuts off Polifonte's head (Polifonte's death is a reported death, but the decapitated head is brought on stage in a spectacular finale).

Pietro Metastasio (1698–1782), whose real name was Pietro Antonio Domenico Trapassi, took the name Metastasio because Pietro Trapassi was a priest, and it wasn't quite right for a clergyman to write theatrical material. He wrote operas in three acts and actually his development of the three-act structure was very much along the lines of what we will see Gustav Freytag develop in his "pyramid" play structure. The first act is exposition leading to crisis; the second act is development, leading to a climax; and the last act is the dénouement. Often, he would end the second act in crisis, and begin the third act at the climax—the hero makes a choice and follows through on it. By definition, once the climax has occurred, the destiny of the hero is established.

Metastasio developed his plots with six characters, along the lines of what we think of as a *Well-Made Play*(something that Eugène Scribe will codify in the nineteenth century): A hero and heroine, a foil, loved ones and confidantes. Loved ones are generally parents or relatives. His poetry was flowery, full of metaphor, highly elevated in tone, yet never obscure. He was very pointed in what he wanted to say, just written in an extremely elevated way very much like the poetry of Alfred Lord Tennyson. The series of confrontations, debates, love declarations, and threats which are ultimately the structure of his pieces, all culminate in one grand scene when everything is unraveled—this is called the *scene a faire*, or the obligatory scene in the well-made play. Everything is resolved through:

1) Some revelation [Jeanine is really my long lost sister];
2) A magnanimous act on the part of the tyrant (king or emperor); and/or
3) The triumph of a noble mind.

Metastasio was followed by **Vittorio Alfieri** (1749-1803), a Count, who was much more interested in the overthrow of tyranny than any other theme. He felt that the national spirit of Italy could be revived through drama and lyric poetry and he set out to do just that. You have to remember that during the eighteenth century, Italy was a loose connection of city states, most of which were governed by foreign potentates. They were little territories that some king in Hanover would have a claim to. As a result, the country itself was not at all unified. Alfieri traveled a great deal and absorbed many of the political and cultural philosophies of the countries he visited. In England he espoused the concept of political liberty (when he went to England, England was right in the middle of dealing with the American Revolution); in France, he espoused the literary ideals of neoclassicism. He combined both influences and came out with his first play in 1775 called *Cleopatra*. By 1782 he had completed fourteen plays in an attempt to use verse as a weapon to wage war against tyrants. To do so he chose a harsh, bitter style rather than the highly metaphoric and heroic style of Metastasio. As a rule, his tragedies portray the struggle between the champion of liberty and the tyrant. His heroes were highly moral, honorable, brave, great fighters, and well-respected men. What is unusual about Alfieri's work is that romantic plots have no place in his tragedies. He was among the first to jettison a love interest from an Italian play. He was essentially a political playwright.

Alfieri's masterpiece is *Saul* (1782) considered one of the most powerful dramas in Italian theatre, and regarded by critics as a forerunner of Byron, and the Byronic hero. Saul is a man who is proud, cynical, defiant, miserable in his heart, implacable in revenge, yet capable of deep and strong affection. He was Byron's Childe Harold, the kind of romantic hero we will meet in the nineteenth century. One other contribution made by Alfieri to Italian literature was the *Tramelogedia*. Tramelogedia was Alfieri's attempt to meld tragedy and opera in the same work, and he wrote one experimental play in that direction called *L'abele* in which some sections were sung, and others, spoken. Unfortunately, the attempt was a hopeless failure. About the distinctions between tragedy and opera, Alfieri wrote: "There is too much difference in the effects of the two spectacles [opera and tragedy]. Opera enervates and degrades the soul. Tragedy elevates and strengthens it." The Tramelogedia was, therefore, a necessary and invaluable change "whereby the Italians by turning from their very effeminate opera to virile tragedy will at the same time arouse themselves from their political nullity to the dignity of a true nation."

Goldoni

Carlo Goldoni was born on 25 February 1707 in Venice. In 1725, he wrote his first play, a satire entitled the *Girls of Pavia* which offended a lot of the leading families of Venice. In 1732, he was admitted to the bar, becoming yet another lawyer-playwright, and in the following year, he brilliantly won his first case, but he had to flee Venice because he was financially in debt and didn't want to marry the woman that his parents wanted him to marry. He traveled through Italy, finally arriving in Milan with a musical drama called *Amalasunta* that was never produced. As a result of that misfortune, he traveled more extensively, and in one city he was robbed of all his belongings. He returned to Venice and produced his first successful play, *Belisario*, a tragedy, in 1734. Four years later, he began working for Antonio Sacchi, a famous Truffaldino, writing scenes that the actor could plug into his *commedia dell'arte* scenarios. From this point on, Goldoni started to write scenarios for various *commedia* troupes. In 1744, he settled in Pisa as a lawyer. Right in the midst of his law practice, he was asked by Sacchi to write another *commedia* scenario, and he complied by writing the scenario for *The Servant of Two Masters* (1745), which wasn't completed as a full script for a number of years. In 1749, he produced a play called *A Girl of Honor*, in which common people are given as much importance onstage as the nobility. This began his awakening of social consciousness in his plays. In the 1749/1750 season, he produced *The Gentleman and the Lady*, the first Italian *commedia* performed without masks.

What you can see with Goldoni are two strains of activity: He is writing commedia scenarios but at the same time, he is trying to separate the scenario from the artificiality of the mask; meanwhile, he is trying to be politically correct, involving all social classes equally. This is not unlikely because when you think of *commedia* scenarios—the Harlequin and Columbine—the clever servant characters are every bit as funny as their elders, and really control them. However, with *The Girl of Honor* we see that the social classes can be blended, with the servant character saying, "Don't treat me that way just because I am a servant. I'm a human being too." This is something that was very enlightened at the time, and which we'll see more of as the 18th century progresses. After a flop at the end of the 1749/1750 season, Goldoni promised his public sixteen new comedies within the year and he fulfilled his promise. In 1753 he produced his masterpiece *The Mistress of the Inn*, but found himself in conflict with the actors who did not want to accept his theories. They were not comfortable with performing without masks, and they certainly were not accustomed to a completely written text of a play. In 1762, Goldoni accepted an invitation from the Comédie Italienne in Paris, and spent the rest of his life in France. From the time he had written his masterpiece, he had been in conflict with actors and rival playwrights, among them Carlo Gozzi who began to lampoon Goldoni and criticize him for getting rid of the masks, and altering the tone and structure of the *commedia dell'arte*. Goldoni decided that things were getting too hot for him in Italy, so he went to Paris. It was there, in 1765, where he wrote *The Fan*. Ten years later he became the Italian instructor to Princess Elizabeth, the sister of Louis XVI. This is a very interesting detail, because while Goldoni was teaching the ladies Italian, Beaumarchais was teaching them the harp and guitar. As time passes, Goldoni has health troubles and at the beginning of February 1793, he died poor and blind and was buried in some unmarked grave.

In spite of his many trials and tribulations, Carlo Goldoni produced a dramatic legacy that included: five tragedies, sixteen tragicomedies, 137 comedies, 57 scenarios, 20 intermezzi (short operas), thirteen dramas with music, 55 libretti for opera, three musical farces, and eighteen musical texts for the court theatre in Dresden. What he sought to do was to institutionalize the human (and humane) aspects of the *commedia dell'arte*. What this ultimately entailed was the discarding of fantasy and magic. He also wanted to dispose of improvisation, one of the hardest things to do away with in *commedia dell'arte*, especially for *commedia* actors. He wanted them to perform his texts exactly the way he wrote them (which is difficult with actors to begin with). He also used local dialect and regionalisms (colloquial expressions) to emphasize the reality of his situations. Although the *commedia* always traded on regionalism for the development of their characters, Goldoni not only wanted them to come from particular regions, he wanted them to sound and behave like they did, and to use expressions that would tie them to a particular time and place. Following the European tendency to move toward realism in the second part of the eighteenth century, in his plays, Goldoni would insist on topical references specifically to contemporary events.

Goldoni also wanted to use settings that represented actual places, not simply stylized locales. He tried to imitate the middle-class life of the period and in so doing, he set up an enlightened sense of man's equality. There's still a higher and lower class, clearly. In *The Fan* there are servant characters and upper-class characters, but the way Goldoni portrayed them reaffirmed the concept of "All men are created equal," an idea that would be developed in French theatre, especially in the work of Beaumarchais in the *Figaro* plays. All of Goldoni's work was in contradiction to the *fantesca*, the fantastic aspect of the *commedia*, as well as the aristocratic concept of Italian opera. Not surprisingly, the aristocrats thought that what Goldoni was trying to do was heresy, especially since Goldoni began criticizing social evils and political abuses. In so doing, his chief point of attack was the *cicisbeo* craze. *Cicisbeo* was the word used for a man who would accompany a married woman to public places. Since it was regarded as the worst possible social behavior for a wife to be accompanied by her husband in public, the gallant *cicisbeo* would accompany her. This, of course, led to the implication that the married woman was of ill repute, so Goldoni sought to lampoon that idea in a number of his plays. He also began criticizing the lord's privilege which Beaumarchais would finally succeed in unmasking in the *Figaro* plays. In this period, the lord (or titled landholder) had a privilege over the wives of his vassals, and on the wedding night, he had the right to bed the bride before the husband. Both Goldoni and Beaumarchais argued that such a practice was a terrible abuse of power. Goldoni's chief focus was simply that a man was not good because he was born good, a man was not noble because he was born noble. All men are born equal; let their work and their social skills govern how we view them.

The Fan was written in Paris in 1765. It was one of the first, if not the first play he wrote after writing nothing but *commedia* scenarios for the Comédie Italienne in Paris. It is filled with *commedia* lazzi, routines involving beatings, drawing swords, and sword plays with implements other than real daggers or weapons, such as pestles, spits, and stick of wood. Almost inevitably in a Goldoni play, if a character begins a scene with an implement, something physical, by the end of the scene it will be used as a weapon to hit someone on the head, or the behind. The whole concept of *The Fan* is a basic *commedia* plot: A woman drops her fan, someone picks it up and, before he can give it to her, everyone in the world stops him and gets in his way. The fan passes through virtually every man's hands in the play and finally ends up where it belongs. There is also a wonderful (Harlequin-like) suicide lazzo for Evaristo filled with romantic intrigue (even though all the traditional romantic scenes are kept offstage). Like a typical *commedia* scenario, *The Fan* is more involved with the working out of the confusion than it is with the actualization of what people want. In other words, the characters want to have a wonderful romantic tryst, but all we see is their attempt to get it, and all of the obstacles in the way. When the obstacles are overcome, the play resolves very quickly, in a single speech. Goldoni also refers to Paris a great deal in the play, particularly since the troublemaking fan comes from Paris, and allows him to take wonderful digs at Parisian society which he didn't very much appreciate. Not uncommon in plays of this type, the action takes place in a single day (something we can easily forget with all the action that occurs) causing the comedy to play extremely fast in performance.

Gozzi

One of Goldoni's chief opponents was Carlo Gozzi (1720–1806) who was determined to keep the fantasy and magic, as well as the masks and improvisatory aspects of the *commedia dell'arte*. Gozzi approved of the *commedia*'s disjointed, sometimes illogical plotting, and he wanted the audience to know that they were watching something that was not real. Clearly, by transforming the locale into something that was highly realistic, and by using a colloquial patois for the dialogue, Goldoni wanted the audience to imagine that they were experiencing something familiar, a play that drew upon the realities of their daily lives. Gozzi wanted the audience to appreciate that they were watching a story that extended beyond the limits of their daily lives. Those of you who are interested in Brecht will find some of his alienation techniques in Gozzi (particularly in his attempt at maintaining the fictive and intellectual aspects of the play). Even earlier than Brecht, in the nineteenth century, of all the Italian playwrights, Gozzi had the greatest influence on the Germans. He sought to remove action on stage from a picture of everyday life and transform it into an illusionist diversion for an evening. He claimed that the nonrealistic aspect of the *commedia* was still viable and important. To prove this, he wrote what he called *fiabe* or fables, the first of which was called *The Love of Three Oranges* (1761).

The plot of this piece will clarify the distinction between Goldoni and Gozzi. The King of Clubs is filled with despair because his son, the prince, is melancholy and can only be cured if he is made to laugh. The king instructs his Prime Minister, Leandro, to organize an entertainment to cure the son. Pantalone, one of the king's ministers is worried because he knows that Leandro and his accomplice, Clarissa, are plotting to kill the prince. Thunder and lightning interrupt the action. Cilio (a character who allegedly represents Goldoni in the play), a magician and the king's protector, and a character named Fatamorgana, Leandro's protector, appear and play a hand of cards. Fatamorgana beats Cilio and they disappear. It is soon discovered that if Fatamorgana is present at the entertainment, the prince will die because no one ever laughs in her presence. However, at the party, a jester, named Truffaldino, tries to make the prince laugh but no one does because Fatamorgana is there, disguised, by the way, as an old beggar woman. In a last-ditch effort, Truffaldino knocks Fatamorgana down, and that causes the prince to laugh. The sorceress then revenges herself on the prince by pronouncing that he will set off in search of three oranges with whom he will fall in love.

The prince and Truffaldino are blown away by a pair of bellows worked by the devil and go off to search for three oranges. Cilio, the magician, gives them a magic ribbon to appease the owner of the three oranges who falls asleep so the prince can steal the oranges and escape into the desert. While the prince is sleeping, Truffaldino cuts open two of the oranges and two beautiful princesses step out of them and die of thirst because they find themselves in a desert. The prince awakens, cuts open the third orange, and Ninetta emerges. Before she dies of thirst, one of the spectators in a side box hands the prince a pail of water and the prince pours the water over Ninetta keeping her alive. While the prince runs off to fetch his father, Smeraldina, a black slave, turns the princess into a dove by putting a hairpin through her skull and then takes the place of the princess. The king insists that the prince marry Smeraldina instead of the princess who is now a dove. The scene then changes to the throne room where the dove is seated on the throne. Cilio changes the dove back to Ninetta by removing the hairpin from her head, and general rejoicing follows. Leandro, his accomplice Clarissa, and Smeraldina fall through a trap door as the flames of hell engulf them all, and the prince finally marries Ninetta.

It is easy to see how Gozzi would have a great impact on surrealism and expressionism and all of the "isms" which developed in the twentieth century because this is not real, and yet there are certain realistic aspects about it, especially the way he uses people from the audience participating in the play; and the transformation of one character into another is easy to accomplish (and be believable) with the use of masks.

Gozzi wrote other *fiabe*, of which probably the two most famous are *King Stag* and *Turandot* which was made into an opera by Puccini. Both Goethe and Schiller were highly influenced by Gozzi: Schiller translated all of Gozzi's work into German, and Goethe directed Gozzi's *Turandot* in Weimar in 1804. As mentioned earlier, the most important Italian influence on nineteenth century German literature came from Gozzi's plays and theatricality.

Maintaining the dichotomy of the *commedia dell'arte*, Gozzi always differentiated between the legitimate characters and the masks. He wrote both in prose and verse in his plays, with the prose always restricted to the masks. He was also fond of mixing regionalisms in plays, having certain characters speak in a very heavy dialect, while others speak in perfectly good Italian.

Goldoni and Gozzi engaged in fierce artistic disagreements, and it was Gozzi's dislike of Goldoni's work that drove Goldoni to Paris. Between them there was a lively distrust that was commercially related, because if audiences were going to champion Gozzi, they were certainly not going to support Goldoni. It was more than just a philosophical or aesthetic conflict. It was a battle for artistic survival that each would win in the history books, with Goldoni having a substantial impact on the Realists, and Gozzi heralding Romanticism, Expressionism, Surrealism, and the Theatre of the Absurd.

10. French Theatre in the 18th Century

At the end of the seventeenth century, through the example of Racine, France was committed to Neoclassicism. This meant that there was preference for the ideal rather than the real; the abstract, the general, or universal rather than the concrete; and a precision of form, an almost formulaic structure for plays. The three neoclassical unities—time, place, and action—were slavishly observed as well. In the seventeenth century, French neoclassical critics began to formulate philosophies of the unities to such an obsessive degree that dramatic time in a play could be 36, 24, or 12 hours, or it could be the time of representation (i.e., if the play lasts for five hours, the dramatic action can only take five hours). The unity of place required the dramatic action to occur in only one location. It could be several rooms in a house, or it could be as much of the city as could be seen by the eyes of a single person. As far as the diction of plays, neoclassical playwrights wrote in Alexandrine verse: six feet of iambs, with a break after the third foot, and a regular alternation of masculine and feminine rhyme. Masculine rhyme ends on the syllable or downbeat. Feminine rhyme adds another syllable ending on the upbeat. Neoclassicists limited the subjects of tragedies to the actions of the great, and their aim was to create a general stateliness of incident, thought, and language. The plays were very monotonous because the themes of tragedy were limited to myths and history. Comedy was absolved from these rules because no one took it seriously; it was not a significant genre to the French. As a result, most of the best plays in the eighteenth century were comedies.

In 1680, King Louis XIV had formed a company of players so that he could have control over the drama in France. He gave the company exclusive privilege to perform pieces without music in Paris (this was because he already had an opera company that could perform pieces with music). He put them under the control of the First Gentleman of the Chamber (very much like the Lord Chamberlain in England), and paid them 12,000 livres a year—a fair amount of money at the time. The company was called the Théâtre Française, popularly known as the Comédie Française. The Comédie Française had 27 members who were shareholders. Not all of them had the same number of shares. Some had a full share, others had 1/8 or 1/4 of a share. Promotion depended upon seniority rather than merit. What is significant here is that an actor couldn't get into the Comédie Française until one of the members died or resigned or for some reason was pushed out. The members were called *sociétaires*. Whenever one of them died or left, one of the *pensionnaires*, who were hired actors generally from the regional theatres, would fill the spot. Actors were regarded with great respect because Louis XIV declared publicly that a gentleman did not cease to be one by going on the stage. This certainly raised the public's opinion of actors, but this did not remove the Church's censorship of the plays in any way. The company played at the Salle of the Comédie Française which was located on the Rue des Fossés, and divided into five parts:

1) The orchestra or pit was called the amphitheater;
2) The second level was divided into *loges*, the French word for boxes;
3) The third level was called *loges hautes*;
4) The next level up was termed *loges* of the third level;
5) The top was called the *parterre* (our balcony).

There were backless benches around the side walls of the pit and all the loges had real seats, but most of the spectators stood throughout the performances.

The French theatre was unique in that plays always began after three thumps of a stick. That's to tell the audience to be quiet. Then the curtain (made of green velvet) goes up and the audience sees, within a rail on either side of the proscenium at the Comédie Française, a group of audience members sitting on the stage. The English theatres also had audience members seated on stage during the eighteenth century. What differentiated the French from the English theatre was a rail that separated the audience from the actors in the French theatres. Audience stage-seating seemed to be built into the theatre. Scenery represented some concern for historical accuracy. For example, tragedy was always played in some palace, but the palace was a historical, far-away palace since the plays were about myths and history. Costumes were not concerned with historical accuracy. Like in England, Cleopatra would appear in hoop skirts with a feather in her hair (the feather being the Egyptian detail). The gentlemen would wear togas over their silk stockings and helmets over their periwigs. Performances began at 5:00 or 6:00 in the evening and ended around 8:00 or 9:00; and there was a green room where audience members could be entertained or could entertain the various performers. The Church hated actors, decreeing that no actor should be allowed to marry in church, receive communion, or be buried in consecrated ground. The same priests, however, would give communion and other sacraments to the Italian actors. Catholic performers of another country could receive the sacraments, but not the French!

Minor Theatres in Paris

By 1700 there were only two legitimate troupes of players in Paris: the Opéra which got a patent in 1669 and the Comédie Française. Immediately after the turn of the century, these monopolies began to be challenged. The first of these challenges came from the theatres at the fairs. There were two main fairs in Paris: the Saint Germaine Fair which extended from 3 February through

Easter (which occurred sometime in April), and the Saint Laurent Fair which extended from June to October. As a result, there were eight months where the fairs could provide some kind of theatrical entertainment to the people of Paris in addition (or often, in opposition to) what is scheduled at the patent (or legitimate) theatres. Through the seventeenth century and coming into the eighteenth century, the fairs were accustomed to performing pantomimes, acrobatics, and sometimes little short playlets. However, the Opéra and the Comédie Française ganged up on the fair theatres, claiming a monopoly on singing, dancing, and speaking, and forbade the fairs to use spoken language in their performances. The fair theatres, forbidden to use dialogue, started to write plot scenarios on cue cards and hung the cue cards above their platform stages. Using the cue cards, the audience would sing the lyrics to the melodies of popular songs, generally without accompaniment, little ditties that would get them from one cue card to the next. This was how the fairs managed to cheat the regulation against using spoken dialogue.

Around 1714, the Opéra (having hit hard times financially) managed to convince the crown that it would be a good idea if they would get some kind of revenue from the more popular fair theatres. They were then permitted to charge fair theatres a tithe to allow them to use music, dance, and spectacle. It may sound crazy to us that one theatre could charge another theatre to produce certain works, but the Opéra was granted the right to charge the fair theatres to sing and dance. When this happened, a new musical theatre form called the *opéra comique* began to develop. This is significant because the fairs began to produce little skits with pantomime in them, some social satire, and singing and dancing by the actors, not the audience. Two years later, the *commedia dell'arte* was invited back to Paris by the Duke of Orleans, the brother of Louis XIV, and Prince Regent to Louis' young son, Louis XV. They performed at the Hôtel de Bourgogne and were led by Luigi Riccoboni. Riccoboni realizing that *commedia* scenarios were on the way out, suggested the Italian company offer plays in French and create parodies like at the fair theatres. He gradually added French actors to the Italian troupe and a French playwright named Marivaux started to write for the company.

In 1718, the fair theatres were suppressed because they were too popular. However, around 1720/21 they were permitted to perform again, without music and spectacle. The plays written during this period have little digs at the opera. For example, a character will say, "here we're supposed to sing a song but since the opera won't let us have any musical accompaniment, I'll just recite it for you." Or "Here we're supposed to have a dance and the scene is supposed to change to a palace, but since we can't have a change of scenery, let me describe the change for you." It becomes a kind of cross between pantomime or satire, or what we call in England burlesque. In 1723, the Italian company was legitimized as the "Ordinary Players of the King" which was generally known as the Comédie Itialienne and housed at the Bourgogne. The fair theatres were reopened in 1723 (because the king liked to go to performances) and permitted a limited use of music and spectacle.

The next problem occurred in the 1740s when a musical theatre piece called *Acajou* opened and was so popular that the Opéra suspended the right of the fairs to use music and attempted to control the *opéra comique*. The Opéra was never satisfied with just taking a tithe from the fair theatres because as the musical theatre performances at the fair theatres got more popular, no one would go see musical pieces at the Opéra. As a result, the Opéra petitioned the crown to control the *opéra comique* and managed to get it banned between 1745 and 1751. As soon as the musical theatre productions were banned, English pantomimists came to France to fill the gap left by the dearth of satirical, light comic entertainment. The import from England was important because the ballad opera that had emerged in England during the eighteenth century would now begin to infect the *opéra comique* in France. In 1761 the fairs returned to playing vaudevilles, and the Comédie Itialienne got a monopoly on French comic opera. Throughout the century, the fairs got the short end of the stick, because they were the illegitimate theatres, and of course that made them more popular than the patent houses.

At the end of the 1760s, the fair theatres began playing *drames* and comedies, and relocated out of the fairgrounds to the boulevards of Paris, quickening the development of we call "minor theatrical entertainment" in

France—not unlike what we used to call off-Broadway. In 1784, because the Opéra's finances were still slacking off, it was granted authority over minor companies, a sound business move since audiences were much more interested in the more popular satirical entertainment that the fairs and the Comédie Itialienne produced. In 1791, the National Assembly abolished all monopolies permitting theatres to vie with one another for audiences based entirely on the quality of entertainment. This will all change, of course, when Napoleon comes along at the end of the decade.

Tragedians

Antoine de la Fossé (c.1653–1708) was the son of a goldsmith and a bit of a gold digger himself, with a talent for getting ahead. Regularly hired on by dignitaries as a personal secretary, first by the Ambassador to Florence, La Fossé ultimately became Secretary General to an entire province. He really knew how to maneuver himself into a good position politically, but unfortunately his literary luck was not as good. He produced four tragedies that were very impressive to his academic colleagues who touted him as a second Racine, but audiences didn't feel the same way. To appeal to the tastes of the theatre audiences, he began to produce plays that were horrifying, emphasizing what is savage and ferocious in human nature. With his play *Polixene* (1686), he revived the public taste for tragedy—a hyper-thyroid, science-fiction, action kind of tragedy. *Polixene* was followed by *Manlius Capitolinus* (1698) which played 250 performances, and stayed in the repertory for nearly 100 years. With *Theseus* (1700) he unsuccessfully attempted to write a tragedy with a happy ending and the failure of his last play *Coresus Callirhoe* (1703) turned him away from the theater. Critics generally suggest that La Fossé's one original contribution to the tragic form was his cosmopolitanism. He took mythical tragic themes and transformed them into elements that were recognizable within the city of Paris. His characters ceased to behave like gods and goddesses and acted more like businessmen. He was inspired by English Restoration comedy and paved the way for the tragedy of Voltaire.

François-Joseph de La Grange-Chancel (1677–1758) was a protégé of Racine and his great contribution was a protest against the austere simplicity of classical tragedy. Without violating the unity of action, he produced plays that had enough variety of ingredients to satisfy the lowest class of audience. He was also known for the creation of group of satires called the *Philippiques*. In the Renaissance, Aretino habitually posted little pieces of paper on statues revealing the dirty deeds about certain political figures. The *Philippiques* were virtually the same thing. La Grange-Chancel directed all of his satires against Monsieur, the Duke of Orleans, the homosexual brother of the King, and ultimately, he was thrown in jail for writing them.

Prosper Jolyot, sieur de Crebillon (1674–1762) produced tragedies that were modeled after Seneca, and like those tragedies, his turned on melodrama with an emphasis on horror. According to his preface to *Atreus and Thyestes* (1707), he believed that his function as a playwright was to move the audience to pity through terror. In private life, Crebillon lived in seclusion in a sparsely furnished apartment, befriending birds and animals rather than people, virtually like Euripides who lived in a cave and shouted at the sea.

Comic Playwrights

Comic dramatists are more interesting to discuss because their plays are actually performed today. Very few of the tragedies written between Racine and Voltaire are ever produced, even in France.

Jean François Regnard (1655–1709), born into the French bourgeoisie, led an adventuresome life that provided him with ample material for his plays. In 1678, he was captured by pirates in the Mediterranean and sold as a slave. After two years of slavery in Algiers and Constantinople, he was ransomed by the French government. In 1680, he traveled through Scandinavia and Poland and finally returned to Paris in 1683 to buy himself a treasury post. Regnard was an Epicurean, dedicating his chateau to the god Bacchus, but in 1709 he died of an overdose of horse medicine that he regularly took for indigestion. He wrote a great many farces between 1688 and 1696 for the Italian players and the theaters at the fairs; and from 1694 until his death, his comedies, mostly in verse, were performed at the Comédie Française. He based most of his comedies on the notion of deception to obtain money or manipulate a marriage. He was fond of creating a central character in the style of Molière: a gambler, an absent-minded lover, a laughing misanthrope, an old, amorous invalid, all character types that come right out of Moliere's plays. He produced fast-moving plays with a heavy dose of whimsical theatricality, extravagant disguises, highly cynical comments about society, and portraits of insolent servants who are greedy for money, sex, and drink. Perhaps his most famous play is *The Universal Legatee* sometimes translated as *The Residuary Legatee* which opened on 9 January 1708. A valet acting in the interest of a pair of lovers (doesn't this sound like Molière already) pretends to be an old man on the point of death and dictates a will in the old man's name. The valet promises to give the lovers a fair expanse of property so that they can run off and get married (though ultimately, he gives them only a little bit and keeps most of the territory for himself).

The play was extremely popular because it was based on a true event. About 50 years before the play was written, a very famous case involving the Catholic Church was known in France. An old man on the point of death was going to change his will in favor of giving the Church a certain amount of land. The old man died before he could change his will, but one of the church fathers noticed that one of his parishioners bore a striking resemblance to the old man. The parishioner was persuaded to impersonate the old man and forge a new will. Having a few ideas of his own, the imposter wrote a new will giving the Church a tithe of maybe 50 or 60 *livres* and deeding everything else to himself in his real name. The Church could not do anything about the deception because it would have had to admit the fact that the old man had been dead before the will was written, so the parishioner managed to cheat the Church out of very large benefits. That was the basis of Regnard's play. Needless to say, a lot of people thought that the duplicity on the part of the valet in the play was unfit to be represented on stage, and the reaction to this play was very much the same reaction that Molière experienced with *Tartuffe*, a fact Regnard pointed out when he wrote his next play, *The Critic of the Legatee*, a month later.

At this time, there was also a very famous incident/scandal that caused the resurgence of censorship in France. In 1702, two playwrights, Boindin and Lamotte wrote a one-act comedy ridiculing the wife of the Duke of Orleans. Since the duke was a flagrant homosexual, his wife chose to dress up in male clothes. The play was therefore about a woman in drag, literally dragging along her effeminate husband. The Duchess of Orleans complained bitterly and in 1702 when the play was performed, Louis XIV was still on the throne. He ordered the play to be immediately withdrawn, and in 1704, the government passed a censorship law creating a special government officer, charged with the duty of examining every work designed for the theatre.

The first playwright to fall under the censorship rule was **Florent Carton Dancourt** (1661–1725). Dancourt was born under the worst possible circumstances, especially to be pitted against censorship, since he was born into a family of Calvinists who then converted to Catholicism. When he was about 18 years old, having been educated by Jesuits, he hesitated between entering the priesthood and studying law. So, he eloped with an actor's daughter. Between 1685 and 1718 Dancourt and his wife were actors at the Comédie Française, and from 1718 to 1725 when he died, he devoted himself to translations of the psalms. More than 80 plays are attributed to him, most of which deal with the customs and manners of the day. He wrote about the newest developments in politics or social history, in plays called *The Obliging Notary* (1685), *The Fashionable Knight* (1787), *The Country House*, *The Vine Harvest*, and so forth. However, these were not simply photographic reproductions of what was happening in society. Dancourt saw everything with a very cynical eye, and most of his characters, virtually all of them, are highly corrupt—or if they are not corrupt when the play begins, they are corrupted by other characters during the course of the play. His entire focus as a playwright was to depict corruption in contemporary society, with plays peopled with seducers, social climbers, burgeoning prostitutes, and lower-lives of society who are always self-seeking and unscrupulous.

Alain-René Lesage (1668–1747) was orphaned at the age of fourteen and robbed of his fortune by an unscrupulous uncle. He left school and worked as a tax collector, paid his own way through law school, and produced adaptations of Spanish plays, the most important of which was called *Point of Honor* produced in February of 1702. This is very significant in the history of drama, not because of the play, because the play was a dismal failure. This is the plot: Don Lope, animated simply by a mania for ascertaining the various fights or arguments that might lead to a duel, desires to have them adjusted by a code of laws which he draws up. That's it—boring, even to the French. The play did not receive a second night and as a result the theatre had to produce a second play. *Montezuma* (by Ferrier) based on the history of the Spaniards in Mexico was chosen, but the theatre couldn't use stock scenery for *Montezuma* so it had to commission new scenery for the play. This was the first time in the history of French theatre that a new design was made for a particular play, and the only reason the theatre could justify it was the belief that if a palace was constructed for *Montezuma*, it could later be used for other epic kinds of plays.

In 1707 Lesage finally recovered from the debacle of *Point of Honor* and produced *The Lame Devil*, full of keen satire and polished language. It was a huge success even though its plot was very simple: Asmodius, the devil, flies Don Cliophas to the top of a church tower. Because of services Don Cliophas did for the devil, the devil permits him to see the doings and the thoughts of all the people below him. Here the playwright satirizes society. This was a perfect vehicle for social lampooning, and a great many people were very nervous about what Lesage would reveal about the government. This success was followed by his masterpiece, *Turcaret*, inspired by the famine and trade deficits France endured during the War of the Spanish Succession (1702-1714). Lesage transformed an earlier comedy into one that was an indictment against excesses in the financial and banking professions. He was offered 100,000 francs by various people to suppress the play, and the actors initially refused to rehearse it because they thought the audience would riot at the performance. The actors were finally persuaded to learn the play, and it was produced by royal decree on 14 February 1709. The plot turns on an unscrupulous financier named Turcaret who is courting a baroness who wheedles presents and money out of him. The money and presents she gets from Turcaret she showers on a young chevalier, who, in turn, tricks the baroness with the help of Frontin, his valet and pimp. Turcaret turns out to be married. His wife has come to Paris surreptitiously, disguised as a countess, who is later courted by the chevalier. Suddenly revealing herself to be Turcaret's wife, she exposes Turcaret who has been embezzling from his bank to give money to the baroness, who turns it over to the chevalier, who is subsequently robbed of it by Frontin, his valet. In the end, Turcaret is arrested for dishonesty, and Frontin has amassed a fortune because everybody's money ends up with him. As a result of *Turcaret*, several changes were made in the financial system in France. No longer did a single individual have complete control over all the money in the bank; he/she had to go through various channels to get things done.

Sentimentality

The first writer of note in France who developed sentimentality, was **Pierre Claude Nivelle de La Chaussée** (1692–1754). He recognized the necessity of a dramatic form somewhere between heroic tragedy and comedy, so he wrote a play called *False Anxiety*, produced on 12 October 1733, as an experiment in pathetic comedy which he called *comédie attendrissante* or *comédie larmoyante*. These two words were used to apply to this kind of comedy. "Attendrissante" means tender or sentimental and "larmoyante" means tearful. La Chaussée was trying to create a comedy that could arouse tender emotions. This is very important because up to this point, the comic dramatist was not supposed to write about things that would inspire tender emotions. Instead, he was supposed to write about the low classes, the people who had various foolish foibles. Now he wanted to write about the middle classes, normal people, and what would happen in real life. *False Anxiety* divided Paris playwrights into rival camps: the pro-reform or sentimental, and the anti-sentimental. La Chaussée followed this experiment with a play called *Prejudice in Fashion* in 1735 which strengthened the cause of tender comedy. This play dealt with the prevalent notion among young husbands that it was a sign of weakness if men actually loved their wives. Another very significant play is *The Governess* which was written about ten years later in 1747. Unknown to everyone, the governess is the mother of her charge who, having been brought up from childhood in a convent, is adopted by a baroness. The son of a government official becomes enamored of the girl and wants to marry her, but his father recognizes the governess as someone he reduced to poverty many years before. He restores the governess and her daughter to affluence and, by the way, tells his son that he can't marry the girl because she's really his sister. We're seeing things that seem to anticipate much of nineteenth-century melodrama, and this is going to develop in France into the kind of play that Dumas, *fils*, would write. La Chaussée was influenced mostly by Molière's serious plays like *The Misanthrope*. He developed comedies full of tenderness, morality, and tears designed not only to divert the audience, but to preach good sense and moral codes of behavior. This is very important because it allies itself with the English sentimental comedy which is extremely moral. Remember, there is a moral message in every sentimental play. The sentimental tradition also had the support of Voltaire who thought it was a good idea to preach morality.

Perhaps the most significant of the sentimentalists was a man named **Pierre Carlet de Chamblain de Marivaux** (1688–1763) who was a novelist, essayist, an entrepreneur, and a playwright. His plays were performed at both the Comédie Française and the Comédie Itialienne when they shared the bill with some of the Italian comedies (*commedia dell'arte*) which would have a great influence on his style. Marivaux produced a number of *commedia*-like French comedies characterized by a swift pace, farcical business, and vivaciousness of dialogue. Except for writing one tragedy and a single play in verse, Marivaux wrote comedies in prose in one, three, or five acts. He aimed less at a vividness of characterization than subtle indications of sentiment in epigrammatic prose. As a result, his plays express a delicacy of thought, very clever wit, and have delightful repartee between characters. It's almost as if he's more interested in the style of content than what the characters are actually saying. He subsequently refined *preciosité* (preciousness) in the drama to the extent that now when we hear preciousness in a play, we tend to think of Marivaux, and critics have gone so far as to call some kinds of theatrical preciousness "marivaudage." Marivaudage is the spirit that pervades the comedies of Marivaux. The word is used to define not only his pretty epigrammatic style of writing, but also the nature of his plots. This is typical of a Marivaux plot: pleasant young people fall in love with each other at first sight, but modesty, pride, fear or ignorance keeps them from acknowledging the feelings to themselves, or from declaring it to others. Plot is of less significance here than situation. Marivaux puts his characters into impossible situations and then forces them to make choices designed to give them the opportunity to experience and articulate high-flown emotion and sentiment.

Usually what happens in a Marivaux play is that everyone is in some kind of disguise, and perhaps the best example of this is *The Game of Love and Chance* (1730). This play involves two young lovers who are destined for one another by their families. Not wanting to do this because he has no idea who his fiancée is, the hero and his valet exchange identities. Feeling the same way about marrying an unseen suitor, his fiancée also exchanges places with her servant. As the play progresses, the false servants fall in love with one another, each believing that the other is really a servant. About the third act of the play Marivaux allows the fiancée to discover that the other servant is the master in disguise. She discovers that he's her fiancé, so she starts to flirt shamelessly with him to see how he's going to react. Eventually the whole thing works out, and the servant characters, who are disguised as their upper-class masters, also get involved romantically to balance everything out. Clearly, the discovery of love and its effects becomes the subject of most of Marivaux's plays.

Marivaux and his plays influenced the theatre in the following ways:

1) He has an extreme singularity of ideas, sentiment, and phraseology. What is important about a Marivaux play is that people in real life don't talk this way;

2) He revived *preciosité* (preciousness) and infused it with a metaphysical

subtlety. When you think of Marivaux, think of "pie in the sky." There's always something up here that is not real;

3) Though he borrowed plots liberally from other writers, he set upon them in a very individual way. For example, the idea of servants playing masters and masters playing servants is hardly original, but the idea of having one of them find out about the disguise midway through the play is original;

4) He wrote in a very conceit-laden, elaborate, periphrastic style, trying to create memorable catch-phrases constantly;

5) He was happiest in his portrayal of women. He wrote women characters better than men. He was able to give them a fuller dimension. Voltaire said that the highway of human nature was less familiar to Marivaux than its bypaths. Marivaux was unable to define human psychology on the global level, but he could nitpick a play out of a hangnail. In other words, take the ingredients of a small, ineffectual situation, and Marivaux could create a wonderful soufflé.

Clearly society is changing. Remember with the coming of the eighteenth century, Locke introduced his concept of human nature as a *tabula rasa* (clean slate) and therefore we are not born with all the baggage of our ancestors. That was taken to mean that human nature was therefore perfectible and man by nature was good, not tainted with sin. With that aspect on the one hand, and Rousseau and his cronies on the other, writing about going back to nature, simplicity, and the natural man, audiences were beginning to accept the idea that the lord of the manor was no longer our master, but our equal, and that human activity was the only true measure of nobility. In the beginning of the eighteenth century, John Locke suggested that the way we approach knowledge was through feeling. Because of these notions, plays were beginning to refine the whole idea of sentiment.

The Marquis de Sade
Perhaps the figure who best solidified all these characteristics in a number of unpublished, unperformed plays was the Marquis de Sade (1740–1814)

whose play *The Shyster* embodies every aspect of French comedy written in the eighteenth century. The play was written while Sade was serving time in the Bastille and for a while the manuscript was lost after the Bastille was stormed in 1789. The play was never performed, though it had been submitted to every theatre in Paris. In *The Shyster* the following types of French drama can be found:

1) Satiric comedy: The subject of Sade's satire is the legal system in Paris in the eighteenth century. In this particular play, the magistrate has a position of authority which he clearly does not deserve and he gives legal opinions based on who is going to bribe him best. In turn, he is controlled by his secretary who is very much like Frontin in *Turcaret*. The secretary ultimately gets possession of all of the magistrate's (Philoquet's) money because he has worked out a deal with all of Philoquet's creditors. Philoquet pays the creditors and then the creditors bribe the secretary, giving him the same money, so that he will put in a good word with the magistrate. What is also interesting is that the magistrate is constantly remarking, "They paid me with the customary bribe. And now I'm going to the client who will pay me a little bit more than I'm used to getting to give a good reading of their case." Sade also engages in dramatic satire. A playwright is introduced in the play who has written "every kind of play you can imagine.... tragedies, comedies, melodramas, spectacle plays and they've been performed at every theatre in Paris." That tells us clearly that we are now at a point in French theatre where traditional comedy and tragedy are making room for a number of different kinds of plays.

2) Sentimental Comedy: The fourth act of *The Shyster* is an extended *comédie larmoyante* involving a tearful reunion between father and son. At the dénouement of the play when the villain is exposed, the father says "I will go to him because even though he's bad, he is after all my son. So, I will take care of him anyway." That's very sentimental. You certainly wouldn't expect that kind of forgiveness in a restoration play.

3) Farce: There is the obligatory laughing comedy aspect of transvestitism. Athenais' boyfriend dresses up as a woman so that he can keep an eye on her when she attempts to seduce the magistrate into determining a favorable

judgment of her case. There is also the attendant chauvinism of the period where the boyfriend constantly tells her "You were looking too much at Philoquet. I don't trust you, you're in love with somebody else." As a result, there exists a kind of comedy of manners in the relationship between Athenais and her men friends; sentimental comedy in relationship to the old man and his sons; and, satiric comedy in its approach to the legal system, the drama, and, to some extent, the music of the period.

Voltaire

Let me move on to a more significant figure, François Marie Arouet known popularly as Voltaire (1694–1778). The son of a notary, he studied Greek and Latin, and was the brightest pupil in his school. At the age of twelve he received his first commission to write poetry which he knocked off in a half hour. It drew attention from the king because it was so good. A short time later he churned out a tragedy and produced *An Ode to Ste. Genevieve*. After he graduated from school, he studied law and became a part of the circle of the Abbé Chaulieu, an eighteenth-century Timothy Leary, who taught him refinement, how to drink, how to carouse, and so forth. After he became a lawyer, as an attaché to the French ambassador, Voltaire went to the Low Countries, where he fell in love with a woman named Pimpet. Her mother, who was a celebrated writer of romance novels, didn't think Voltaire had enough money for her daughter, so she broke off the affair. This was a very good thing for Voltaire, because it set him on a career as a writer, inspiring him to produce a tragedy called *Oedipe* (produced 1718) in imitation of the Greek and French classical tragedies.

Voltaire was ridiculed for not using a love subplot in this play and for using long choral passages. This shows the bias of the French classicists at this point. Everything had to do with love (remember that's what Racine did), and playwrights weren't supposed to use choruses. In 1717, while he was writing *Oedipe*, Voltaire was imprisoned in the Bastille (by a political enemy, on a trumped-up charge). He was released in 1718, and arrested again but subsequently released from jail on the condition that he remained in his father's house. House arrest was very important during eighteenth-century France. It was also less expensive, since during this time a person put into jail had to pay for his own upkeep. This also meant he could take all his belongings to jail with him if he could afford it. Once his political troubles were over, François Marie Arouet took the name Voltaire, probably to escape his enemies. He succeeded in getting *Oedipus* produced at the Comédie Française and it was a hit. According to contemporary critics, except for *Le Cid* and *Tartuffe*, no play had created such an impression on French audiences. It was performed 45 times in a row and started Voltaire on his theatre career.

Voltaire followed *Oedipe* with a number of plays, the most significant of which was *Herod and Marianne* in 1724, in which Marianne dies on stage. Not untypically, the audience responded to that event with roars of laughter because it violated the French conception of verisimilitude. Voltaire withdrew the play and completely overhauled the script. He had originally written in the prologue to the play: "[The onstage death] is something I really want to try, this is very important," but as soon as the audience laughed at it, he removed the onstage death scene, revising it completely to create a scene that would be popular with audiences. As a matter of fact, Voltaire's revision ignited a conflict with another playwright who had composed a different Marianne play. That work had failed, and the playwright blamed Voltaire who, he said, had paid a cabal to hiss his rival's play.

This brings up the very important issue of theatre claques. In the early part of the eighteenth century, authors would pay people to go to plays either to hiss the opponent's work or the cheer their own. The playwright who said that Voltaire's claque caused a disruption at his play was proved wrong because people who were in the audience said that the claque that was paid by the rival author to applaud the play, found his play so bad that they gave back the money and started to hiss with rest of the audience. Voltaire's revision of his own play opened later and was much more successful. While all of this is going on, Voltaire got involved in a series of duels with members of Court, and to avoid stiff prison sentences, Voltaire self-exiled himself to England for a number of years. He left on 3 May 1726 and spent the rest of 1726 through

1729 in England, where he was wined and dined by Jonathan Swift, Alexander Pope and John Gay. There he studied Shakespeare, Milton, and William Wycherley. One of his favorite plays was *The Country Wife*, but the playwright and poet he wanted most to meet was William Congreve.

While in England, Voltaire started work on a tragedy dramatizing the semi-mythological story of Lucius Brutus, significant because, for the first time, he wrote the play in English before translating it into French. When he returned to France, he was a changed man philosophically:

1) He now advocated constitutional freedom. He was no longer a supporter of the Royalists;

2) He was a disciple of Newton. This meant that he was less religious, ceasing to believe purely in the Church's attitudes toward physics and the creation of the world, and leaning more toward the scientific approach;

3) He intensified his struggle for liberty of conscience, which meant religious freedom in France. In England he saw 30 religions living together amicably;

4) His study of English dramatists served to enlarge his methods as a playwright. Though he was a neoclassicist, he was no longer doctrinaire about the rules of Neoclassicism. He became less exclusively devoted to antiquity; his subject matter was no longer devoted to only Greek and Roman heroes; he began to produce more action than narrative in a play and use a greater variety of backgrounds—setting plays in more exciting atmospheric locales; he produced a mixture of refined realism with lofty idealism, trying to create a more realistic theatre like that of the English, united with the idealism of the Neoclassical School in France.

The play that expressed Voltaire's new techniques was *Zaire* (1732) set at the time of the crusades in order to contrast European civilization with that of the Near East. In the thirteenth century, after the Saracens achieved control of Palestine, Orismond became the sultan of Jerusalem. Among his Christian slaves were Zaire and Neristan. Neristan was brought up as a knight by St.

Louis, the king of France, but has fallen again into the hands of the Saracens. Since he is a knight, Orismon gives him permission to go off on missions as kind of an emissary slave. Having met with the Christians and secured the release of a number of slaves for a price, Neristan returns to the sultan with the news. Orismon is willing to accept any release of prisoners except Zaire with whom he is madly in love. Zaire, a Christian, is also in love with the Moslem sultan, so much so that she is even willing to give up her Christian faith to marry him. She expresses the highly unusual opinion that religion is more circumstantial than inherent: had Orismon been brought up in France he would have been a Christian, and had she been brought up in a Moslem country, she would have believed in Mohammed. A man named Lucignan appears among a new group of slaves. He sees Neristan and Zaire and claims them as his two lost children. As a result of the Christian family reunion, Zaire finds it difficult to convince her father and brother that she wants to marry the sultan. She meets her brother late at night to try to convince him to leave the seraglio without her. Orismon sees the two of them together and thinks he is witnessing a lover's assignation. The sultan stabs her to death in a fit of anger, and then realizing that Neristan was her brother, stabs himself to death. The play ends with the liberation of the remaining Christian captives. It is clearly a nod by Voltaire to *Othello* since a similar jealous murder and suicide happens in Shakespeare's play. *Zaire* was the popular rage, becoming one of the most popular plays of the period, and solidifying Voltaire in this new style.

In 1743, the performance of Voltaire's play *Merope* was the first time in French theatre history that the audience called for the author. In 1746, Voltaire was elected to the Académie Française and became Louis XV's historiographer. In 1750, because of his subversive ideas, Voltaire moved to Prussia, taking refuge with Frederick the Great. In 1748, during a performance of his *Semiramis*, Voltaire bought out all the "stage seats" and managed to successfully put a stop to the practice of audience members sitting on the stage. This is important because Garrick had to wait until the 1760s to get the audience off the stage in London. In 1753, Voltaire quarreled with Frederick the Great and moved to Switzerland, then as now, a non-partisan country. About 20 years later, in 1778, he returned to Paris with great ovation by the people. They paraded him into the city, gave him parties, floats, wined him and dined him until he died of over-excitement and fatigue. These are Voltaire's important theatrical innovations:

1) He introduced scenes drawn from natural history and exoticism. Not only does he introduce them on the stage in the scenery and costumes, he introduces them into the plots of tragedy;

2) He also tried to include mob scenes and ghosts in tragedy;

3) He wrote philosophical tragedies whose object was to illustrate the effects of ideological prejudice. Voltaire substituted ideological principles for tragic fate. In Voltaire's world, Oedipus would not marry his mother and kill his father because he was fated to do so, but because of an ideological prejudice—the way he thought made him do that;

4) He supported the actor Lekain (who was his favorite actor, and who originated many of his tragic heroes) in his attempt to create a more realistic acting style in acting and costuming. It was Lekain who introduced Chinese detail in Voltaire's *The Chinese Orphan*;

5) Voltaire also supported the actress Adrienne Lecouvreur who had a simple delivery which suggested a natural rather than an oratorical acting style. Lecouvreur was a very important case: she had a very small vocal instrument; she didn't have a very loud voice and she mumbled a lot. Necessity being the mother of invention, she parlayed that into a very natural acting style that everyone found exceptionally realistic. Voltaire supported her aggressively when the Church would not allow her to be buried in Christian ground, writing many polemical essays against the Church and advocating Christian burial for actors (about 30 years after she was originally entombed a group of actors exhumed her body and buried her in holy ground).

Beaumarchais

The immensely popular playwright Beaumarchais was born Pierre Augustin Caron (1732–1799). Apprenticed to his father's watch-making business,

Caron's first wife was his mistress who divorced her husband to marry him. As a matter of fact, when he became a playwright, he took her name "Beaumarchais" so that the watch-making firm of Caron could be free of the scandal and intrigue often associated with the theatre. He taught harp playing to the King's daughters which aroused the jealousy of all the other courtiers (he, and the Italian playwright Goldoni, were the chief instructors to the King's children), and one of his first adventures was following the man who jilted his sister to Spain, where he tried to convince him to do the honorable thing by her, at the point of a sword of course. As a result, the erstwhile groom tried to get Beaumarchais convicted on a trumped-up charge. Beaumarchais succeeded in beating that rap and getting the guy ousted from his political position in Spain. Beaumarchais was from the start a fighter, a trait that was clearly in evidence both in his playwriting and his political work. His sojourn in Spain was especially important because it inspired him to write plays: he went to the Spanish theatre, hated it and said, "If these people can write plays, I can too." As a result, he produced his first play *Eugénie* in 1767. It was in the style that Diderot was developing called *drame bourgeois*. This was a serious and sentimental play in prose based on the philosophy that man was essentially good but misled by social prejudices. The *drame bourgeois* was directed towards, and thematically concerned, the middle class, emphasizing a moral lesson which was applicable to the daily life of the middle-class spectator. This was extremely sentimental, with an appeal to the heart rather than the head, and a heavy reliance on middle-class occupations and settings. Gradually, this type of play would become the substitute for tragedy in French theatre. Tragedy would deal with the upper crust, but playwrights could deal with the middle class in situations of tragic significance.

Eugénie was not a success in performance, but Beaumarchais was undeterred. On 13 January 1770 he produced *The Two Friends*, a five-act *drame* in which two friends, one of whom is a tax collector, find apartments in the same house. The other expresses a real need for money and the tax collector lends him money from taxes he's collected to help him pay off his debts (believing, of course, that he'll get the money back before he actually has to put the tax money into the general till). He doesn't get the money back and has to confess that he stole the tax money to give to his friend, who instead of defending the act, turns indignant toward the thief, saying, "How dare you? How dare you steal on my behalf! I would have rather died in the street than to have you dirty yourself with this money." Fortunately, the tax collector's boss had a bit more sensitivity than the friend and said, "I understand how you took pity on him and I'll take pity on you. Just don't let it happen again." The drama played ten performances and expired. Beaumarchais determined that if he wanted to be a successful playwright, he should try writing comedy rather than the serious genre. The first comedy that he attempted was called *The Barber of Seville*.

The Barber of Seville was first written as a comic opera for the Italian players but was rejected for one very obvious reason: the head of the Italian Comedians was an ax-barber and he didn't like the way the barber was portrayed in the play. While Beaumarchais was writing the play, he was thrown into jail on another trumped-up charge. He was accused of poisoning his second wife and was put in jail, ready to be guillotined if found guilty at his trial, when he discovered that the wife of the prosecutor took a bribe. At his trial, Beaumarchais defended himself and broke down the prosecutor's wife on the witness stand. Suddenly Beaumarchais the wife-murderer was lifted on the shoulders of the population and marched through Paris as a great hero. Two years later in 1775, he produced *The Barber of Seville*, the comedy he had worked on in jail. The opening of the play was not a success, so Beaumarchais withdrew it from performance, rewrote it, and, as they say, the rest was history. *The Barber of Seville* became one of the great comedies of French literature. It deals with Figaro, the barber, who is aiding and abetting Count Almaviva's pretensions to the favor of the Countess Rosina who is under the protection of a lord who wants to marry her. The plot was straight out of the *commedia dell'arte*, but since the author was writing for the Comédie Italienne, that did not seem inappropriate. A more important play would appear when he wrote the sequel, *The Marriage of Firago*.

After *The Barber of Seville* had opened a second time and was finally successful, Beaumarchais went to London to do some business for the King on

8 April 1775. He was supposed to meet with the Chevalier d'Eon, a double agent working for France and England simultaneously. What made matters especially interesting for d'Eon was that until the day he died no one knew if he was male or female because he always walked around in dresses. In English society, he was the Countess d'Eon and everyone thought he was a lady (even though in France, he had been the Captain of his military battalion). For the King of France, Beaumarchais had to secure the transfer of some secret document that d'Eon was holding for ransom. Sent to negotiate this deal, Beaumarchais met the Chevalier in drag, courted her, and ultimately succeeded in negotiating the deal. The Chevalier, by the way, returning to France was not allowed to wear his military uniform so he spent the rest of his life in skirts.

The year after Beaumarchais dealt with the Chevalier d'Eon, he started shipping arms to the American colonists: this was in 1776. While he was a gunrunner to the Americans, he started writing a five-act comedy called *The Marriage of Figaro*. Before the play was completed, in 1779, Beaumarchais urged the writers who were creating plays for the Comédie Française to strike because they were not being paid enough money. Consequently, all the writers struck and they ultimately got an increase in royalties for their plays. In 1780, he submitted *The Marriage of Figaro* to the Comédie Française, beginning a five-year journey to get the play performed. In 1781, it was officially accepted for performance, but in 1782, Louis XVI read the play and said "I can't let you do this. This man mocks everything that must be respected in the government." The following year, Louis reluctantly agreed to allow the play to be done privately at Versailles. The performance was rehearsed for 30 days, but ten minutes before the curtain rose, a minister came from the King stopping the performance. Later, in September 1782, the King did allow a performance of the play at a residence outside of Paris, and historians record that Beaumarchais had to break all the windows of the theatre so the audience would not suffocate. Finally, in 1784 a group of censors met to help Beaumarchais revise the play for a performance at the Comédie Française on 27 April 1784, at a new theatre called the Odéon. The play was advertised to begin at 6:00 P.M. At 10:00 A.M. 5,000 people crowded the theatre to get in. By the time the curtain rose, every seat in the auditorium was taken. The play was an unprecedented triumph. The audience applauded nearly every line and the performance took five-and-a-half hours. It was such a success that it continued to play for 68 performances in a row. Beaumarchais had fought for newly negotiated contracts with authors and with *The Marriage of Figaro*, his efforts certainly paid off. The play earned 350,000 livres in box office receipts and 40,000 livres in royalties for the author. For the first time in French history a play made the author rich.

The Marriage of Figaro was considered a step toward the French Revolution. Danton said, "Figaro killed the aristocracy." Napoleon said, "If I had been King, a man such as he would have been locked up. There would have been an outcry but what a service it would have rendered to society. *The Marriage of Figaro* is already the revolution in action." Beyond its revolutionary leanings, the play involved all aspects of French drama. Social Satire: It satirized the lord's privilege—the entire play turned on Figaro's concern about Almaviva bedding his wife Susanne. It satirized the class system. It satirized English behavior in Figaro's celebrated monologue: "When I go to England, I'll have to say 'goddamn you' all the time." It also satirized treatment of women and can be regarded as an early French feminist play. Interestingly, the only thing cut from the original text of the play when it opened in Paris was the feminist sequence. There was one very long scene after the trial when Marceline was revealed to be Figaro's mother, where she said: "I had to give you up because women were not allowed to do such things. If only women could have their own autonomy and take jobs, we would not be reduced to this kind of behavior." The sequence was cut from the original performance. We know this because of a pirated English translation made originally by Thomas Holcroft who went to see the first performance of *Figaro*, subsequently saw it eleven times in the theatre, and copied the text by memory. Holcroft's version has everything in the play except for the long passage on feminism. Even some modern translations of the play still omit that passage.

Figaro also participated in the comedy of intrigue: there was a lot of disguising in the play, and the character of Cherubino, played by a woman (though, hardly unusual for a woman to play a youth in the theatre) was a less than subtle nod to the Chevalier d'Eon. Moreover, *Figaro* explored a turn of pure vaudeville with the comic characters, Bridlegoose and Barthelot. The play was also in many ways biographical: Figaro was Beaumarchais—we hear about his going to London, his attempts at being a playwright, his writing a drama that wasn't successful. Finally, Marceline, Figaro's mother, provided *The Marriage of Figaro* with a large dose of sentimentality. Long-lost children and mothers are the standard for sentimental plots.

Beaumarchais followed this huge success with an opera called *Tarare* in 1787, with a score by Mozart's rival, Antonio Salieri. *Tarare* was interesting because it advocated divorce, the freeing of slaves, and the marriage of Catholic priests. Despite its revolutionary ideas, it managed to hold the stage for 33 performances. By 1789, Beaumarchais, now a major success, aroused the suspicion of the revolutionaries who thought him too sympathetic to the old regime. He was imprisoned several times and finally forced to leave France until 1796. He wrote one final play, *The Guilty Mother*, in 1792, which completed the *Figaro* story. In *The Guilty Mother*, Count and Countess Almaviva have been reduced to Mr. and Mrs. Almaviva. The action takes place after the French Revolution and no titles exist in France. There are two young people in the Almaviva household: Almaviva's illegitimate daughter, and a young man who is the "natural" or illegitimate son of Rosina and Cherubino. While Almaviva was away in the New World, Cherubino and Rosina had an affair. When Rosina discovered she was pregnant, she wrote to Cherubino at the front lines saying that they could not see one another anymore. Cherubino replied with a letter saying, "All I can do is die for my country." He went off and got himself killed, and Rosina kept the letter in the bottom of a jewel box.

Enter a villain who wants to marry Almaviva's illegitimate daughter and take all the wealth of the family. He spies Rosina looking at the letter and he tells Almaviva about it. When Almaviva confronts her with the letter, Rosina is prostrate on her knees. The ghost of Cherubino appears to her with his bloody heart in his hand, and Rosina reveals everything to Almaviva. Finally, the villain is unmasked and everything goes back to normal.

This was the beginning of high melodrama in France: people down on their knees, appearances of ghosts, highly emotional settings, and fainting spells. There was a nice twist at the end of the play: because Figaro managed to unmask the villain, Almavia offers to reward him. To the count's proposal, Figaro replies: "No. If it please you, shall I spoil by a vile salary the good service I have rendered? My reward shall be to die among you." In other words, Figaro says, "Don't pay me for doing a good deed." This really begins to suggest the kind of sensitive, sentimental moralizing that would characterize the melodramas of the nineteenth century.

French Critical Thought

Throughout the eighteenth century, there continued the quarrel between the Ancients and the Moderns in France that had begun in the seventeenth century. The quarrel was quite simply, who wrote better literature, the Greeks or the French? In 1711, Mme. Dacier published her version of *The Iliad* saying that no new version could do justice to the original poetry. This was followed in 1713 by a version by De La Motte with "offending passages" omitted. He liked the Greek but removed the passages that offended the French. What he suggested was that French literature was capable of surpassing the Ancients and that there was nothing that the Greeks had written that couldn't be improved upon by good French scholarship. Two years later in 1715, the Abbé Terrasson argued that literary principles like those of science should be constantly re-examined. We should constantly look at things to see if we would not change our opinions. De La Motte also opened another can of worms when he maintained that poetry could say nothing that could not be said better in prose. Finally, the Abbé Dubos developed a theory suggesting that arts depend on insight, feeling, and intuition, as opposed to the sciences which come from deductive reasoning. Dubos stressed the importance of cultural background, climate, and geography in terms of appreciating the arts. In other words, he said (and he was among the first to suggest this), that if you come from a particular locale, you may have a preference for a particular kind of artwork that differs from someone in another climate. The French thought that everyone from every part of the world would view things the same way they do. Dubos argued on behalf of a relativity of tastes.

In 1738, another important development occurred when the Abbé Prevost analyzed several of Shakespeare's plays in a French literary journal. This presented challenges to the classical tragedy of France because Shakespeare's plays, of course, did not adhere to the three unities. Voltaire ultimately spoke in favor of Shakespeare and said that, though he was a genius full of forceful ideas, he was without good taste and not well schooled in the rules. Discussion of Shakespeare waged hotly in France through the rest of the century and Voltaire began to attack his dangerous influences on French dramatists. For example, he said that Shakespeare's obscenities, his monstrous irregularities, his mixed genres were all shocking, and that the triumph of Shakespeare would ultimately threaten the very existence of French classical tragedy. We will discover the truth of Voltaire's prediction in the nineteenth century when English theatre companies touring with Shakespearean plays in Paris were instrumental in the creation of a French romantic tragedy.

Perhaps the most significant theatrical form to emerge from the argument about the neoclassical unities was Denis Diderot's (1713–1784) *Drame Bourgeois*. Diderot is probably most known for the *Encyclopedia* he wrote in 1751, but he started his creative life as the writer of "adult novels." I have found two semi-pornographic novels by Diderot, one of which, called *The Indiscrete Jewels*, tells the tale of a magic ring that, in addition to making its owner (Sultan Mangogul of Congo) invisible, when pointed at the genitals (the "indiscrete jewels") of a woman, it allows the wearer to learn about the sexual background of the woman and hear her unspoken thoughts.

More important, however, was Diderot's development of the *drame bourgeois* in which he stressed more naturalness in acting and dialogue. He also suggested that the device of a confidante should give way to a more convincing technique of exposition, where the character is actually placed in dramatic situations from which information can be forthcoming. This is a real advance in playwriting. He also suggested that stage settings might be evocative of real places, quickening the movement towards realistic detail on the French stage.

Typical of sentimental plays, the new drama was supposed to preach a moral that would have special resonance among the middle classes.

In connection with this new realism, Diderot developed the concept of the **Fourth Wall**, forcing actors to perform as if there was no audience present (we erroneously tend to think that the Fourth Wall was a concept developed at the Moscow Art Theatre). Diderot also created living statues called *tableaux vivants* at the end of emotional scenes to leave the audience with some kind of shocking effect. This device would be used to great effect in nineteenth-century melodramas.

In 1694, all actors were condemned by the Church. They were excommunicated, heavily penalized financially and not allowed to be buried in hallowed ground. In 1701, the Lieutenant of the Paris police was given complete control over the drama, and everything that was performed had to be approved by him. It is significant that in 1701, however, the law though on the books was hardly ever observed, and the Superintendent of Police did not tend to censor plays. In 1704, however, formal censorship did begin, and in 1709, ecclesiastical essays appeared, telling us that tragedy must serve a moral purpose. In 1713 Jeremy Collier's book *A Short View of the Immorality and Profaneness of the English Stage* was translated into French by Courbeville who emphasized that the ever-present love interest in French plays should be expunged. Love, he argued, has a tendency to make people lascivious. However, he did point out that having translated Jeremy Collier's work, he discovered that French theatre is a lot cleaner than English theatre. Two years later, in 1715, the theatre was defended on the principle that people can be made better through attending plays. One priest even came to the conclusion that people are easily more reformed by going to the theatre than by listening to sermons because sermons put people to sleep and the theatre at least keeps them interested.

About 1715 the long pent-up desire for free speech in Paris began to explode and found its chief expression in Voltaire's *Oedipe* which appeared in 1718. In that play he openly assaulted the Church, calling priests parasites on the credulousness of their parishioners. The attack on the Church was extremely popular; it played 45 times, and sent more people to church and to the play than anything else because of the great controversy. People would go to the pulpit to hear what the priest would say about Voltaire, and then go to the play and hear what Voltaire said about the priest. The controversy succeeded in creating a time of great discussion that was all out in the open. The debate over religion began to extend over politics as well. Plays started to express the idea that all rulers are responsible to the people for their deeds. In other words, the King cannot behave autonomously. This is something that was revolutionary because it questioned the divine right of kings. Heated discussions of rights and duties from both the religious and political point of view were voiced, and gradually the plays of the period reflected an optimism suggesting that perfection could be obtained through reason. This became a problem, however, because plays at the time were condemned for the fact that they promoted emotion. Critics argued that, if we're going to be perfected through rational thought, then anything which stimulates our senses may not be good because it gets in the way of rational behavior. There appeared a great number of essays talking about how the theatre creates emotion from two different perspectives: one group would argue that theatre is bad because it creates emotion getting in the way of rational thought, and another group complained that the theatre was bad because the emotions exhibited on stage were actually putting thoughts in the minds of the audience, creating "false emotions." In 1719, a priest named Jean Baptiste Dubos connected the two objections and turned them into a positive force. He said that the chief merit of plays was their ability to excite in us real passions that are vicarious. In other words, we can feel the passion of lust, we can feel the passion of anxiety, of hatred, of murder without actually having to experience them. Therefore, we are discouraged from being lustful or murderous because we feel what it is like, so the plays are actually making us moral. He also argued that plays are in fact a release of pent up desires which is something that Freud would talk about 150 years later. In 1726, another priest stressed the social aspect of the theatre and argued that the theatre should be geared toward the improvement of public morals. Plays should only be done if they reflect the politically correct morality of the time.

In 1729 the stage was in good graces because, in honor of the Dauphin's birthday, the Comédie Française received a gift of 10,000 francs in addition to the 12,000 that it normally got for that year. That certainly indicated the King's support of the theatre. This did not mean, however, that an actor could be buried in hallowed ground even though the king was in favor of the theatre. Here was the problem: actors were supported in Paris by the King, the Pope, the bishops and by the public. The only people who did not like the acting profession were the parish priests, and they were ultimately the people who would confer the sacraments. There are even records of parish priests actually defying papal legislation. These priests are Frenchman and since the Pope was still Italian, it didn't much matter what he said. As a result, actors determined that when they retired, they would become devout churchgoers so that they would go to heaven. Others wore sackcloth and ashes and walked on their knees to a cathedral where they would officially repent being an actor.

I have found that nearly half the tracts, essays written against the theatre, were written a year or so following the refusal of a theatre to perform a play by the priest who wrote the tract. The religious persecution by the parish priests was very politically motivated. In 1735, the Pope issued a brief ordering that actors be given communion. It also noted that the profession of actor is not in itself a sin: "It is not itself a sin provided [actors] employ their talents honestly, avoiding forbidden words and actions and do not perform at times which are not permissible." In 1756, another priest argued against the portrayal of love scenes in the theatre. For some strange reason French critics thought that romantic scenes were too racy for an audience to to tolerate, and they thought the emotions of the audience would become so heated that, after the play, they would go off to rape and ravage throughout the countryside. The same priest, however, saw nothing wrong with reading plays in the privacy of your own room. It will be a long time before critics against the theatre would accept the fact that if we see an action acted out, we are not somehow transformed by it, and that an actor performing a certain kind of scene or character, is not actually transformed into that kind of person. This was part of the *transubstantiation* theory. Remember that the Church believed that the host which the priest uses at mass is transformed into the body of Christ. Churchmen could therefore easily transfer the notion of transubstantiation to the acting profession.

In 1786, a ritual was established in Paris. A ritual is like the Book of Common Prayer, explaining how priests should behave, how parishioners should behave. The ritual of 1786 said that all French persons connected with the stage must be ejected from communion service. It wasn't that they were simply not given communion, they must be forcibly removed from the church. However, in 1789, the year of the French Revolution, all actors were permitted the rights and privileges of citizenship, but the public still regarded them as outcasts because in the parishes, they would still be looked upon as "the actors." Napoleon feared all expressions of individual opinion. He hated the idea that a play could have an opinion other than his own, and he placed heavy restrictions on the theatre during his administration. In 1816 with the Restoration of the Bourbon Monarchy, actors were divested of all their civil rights. We began in 1694 with actors being condemned without any civil rights, and by 1816, the actors are exactly where they were over 100 years before.

11. German Theatre in the 18th Century

Coming into the eighteenth century, German theatre had three forms: school, public, and court theatre. In the seventeenth century, German schools, both Protestant and Catholic, presented plays, some in Latin, some in German. The height of educational drama came with the Jesuit-run schools. Like in all the countries we've talked about, plays started first in Latin, but then move into the vernacular, adding low comedy to keep the masses interested, as well as music and spectacle. The highest point of educational drama was a play called *Pietas Victrix* in 1659. *Pietas Victrix* dramatized Constantine's victory over the pagan emperor with a great deal of spectacle along with the Hapsburg emblem floating over the stage, indicating that the Austrian Empire owed its life to Constantine. In other words, the play was about Constantine's victory over paganism and the rise of the Holy Roman Empire of which the Austrian Empire was a part—religion and politics successfully blended together. Interest in Jesuit theatre waned in the eighteenth century and Catholic religious plays were finally suppressed in 1773.

Public Theatre

While schools were performing plays, there was a very active public theater essentially devoted to touring acting troupes. Before 1650, English troupes toured Germany, and since they were performing in English, they had to adapt their plays to suit the German audience. To do this effectively: they simplified plots; they also added low comedy; they added pantomime with music and dance; and, they began to develop stock clowns, among which two names are very important—Stockfish and Pickled Herring. Finally, they began to add German phrases and sometimes entire scenes in German. By 1626, troupes started to include German actors and by 1680, all English actors had been phased out, replaced by German players. It's easy to see why they would be replaced. If you're going to appeal to a popular audience that isn't terribly educated, you're going to have to speak to them in a language they can understand

The first German troupe of note was Paulsen's troupe (1650–1687). When companies toured, they set up in town squares, inns, and tennis courts; and to attract an audience, the plays had to change daily. One company, Velten's Company (1640–1695), had about 85 or 90 plays in its repertoire—certainly a fair number. By the end of the seventeenth century, the theatrical program of the touring companies included a main play, which was called either *Hauptaktion* ("chief play" or "high action") or *Haupt-und-staatsaktion* ("chief and state play"). The names are virtually synonymous, and both of them could be either comic or serious. This was usually followed by a *nachspiel* which was an afterpiece, usually a farce. No matter how serious the play, the clown was usually the central figure. This has a direct parallel to the *commedia dell'arte* in the Harlequin character. By 1707, all of the clowns coalesced into a single figure called Hanswurst, and Hanswurst was given its chief traits by an actor named **Joseph Stranitzky** (1676–1726). Stranitzky's Hanswurst was a jolly, beer-drinking, peasant type with a Bavarian accent. He had a green pointed hat, a red jacket, and long yellow trousers. Stranitzky virtually created the public theatre in Vienna because he was the mainstay of the first public theatre built there in 1708.

Dramatic conditions were bad. First of all, due to Stranitzky, there was a strong tradition of improvisation in the theatre. Actors were unrehearsed and oftentimes uneducated. A lot of actors in the German theatre couldn't even read the scripts they were performing. If they were going to improvise, it didn't really matter. We have the same sort of thing in the *commedia dell'arte* where many of the actors were also illiterate: all the actor/manager had to do was tell them what the scene was about and they could play it. A second problematic factor was the dramatic repertory, which was designed for an unsophisticated audience. If the audience was going to hoot and holler, actors were going to mug, and that's exactly what happened with a lot of German actors. In addition to actors not wanting to rehearse, there was actually little time to prepare a play, and no space given to rehearsals. The actors would simply rehearse the play on the cart on their way to a new location. In performance, actors would have a prompter on the side feeding them lines, but generally they would just improvise dialogue. As a result, aristocrats stayed away from this kind of theatre and churchmen damned it from the pulpit.

Court Theatre
The Court Theatre, on the other hand, employed professional theatrical touring companies starting around 1650, but monarchs and their followers seemed much more inclined toward the opera and ballet. About 1665, an elaborate court theatre was built in Vienna for opera, and that city would become the center for opera in the German states until 1740. By the end of the seventeenth century, every court had an opera company and Italian scenery (this is all that perspective technique we were talking about in Italy as well as the machinery to change scenery). For the prosperous middle class, as well as the court, opera and ballet were the preferred entertainment. They might actually go to the theater, but the rich spent all their money on other higher-class entertainments.

Early German Playwrights
The first of the significant German playwrights in this period was **Andreas Gryphius** (1616-1664) who was influenced by Shakespeare, Seneca and the *commedia dell'arte*. His chief theme in writing was that all earthly existence is transitory. Everything passes. He praised the joys of Christianity and em-

phasized that worldly vanity leads to nothing. His first major play was *Charles Stuart; or, Majesty Murdered*, written in 1649 the same year that King Charles I of England was beheaded. Ultimately the play is an essay between rival camps, those who believed that one shouldn't kill a King, and the others who insisted that he was an inept ruler and had to be eliminated. Eventually the play comes to the conclusion that a crime against the crown is a crime against God. Gryphius was a little more successful when he wrote comedy and, in his play *The Beloved Dornrose* (1660) he began to develop a kind of realism in the German theatre by introducing dialect comedy. *The Absurda Comica; or, Master Peter Squenz* (1658) was his version of the mechanical scenes in *A Midsummer Night's Dream*. It was a slapstick farce, employing play on words, mistaken identity, and a burlesque of high style.

Gryphius made five lasting contributions to German theatre:

1) He firmly established a five-act structure;
2) He used a chorus, especially to moralize;
3) He developed the use of dialect as a major language in a play;
4) He enjoyed the depiction of torture and murder on stage;
5) He produced the first German bourgeois tragedy with *Cardenio and Celinde* in 1647. Another of his comedies, *Horribilicribrifax* (1663) is a farcical satire dealing with seven interrelated pairs of lovers. It's amazing how many triangles can be created out of seven pairs of lovers and how everyone gets in everybody else's way. It's a very funny play, not unlike some of the Restoration Manners comedies.

The next is **Christian Weise** (1642–1708), a forerunner of Lessing who wrote in clear prose, attempted realistic details, and stressed the power of the intellect. His intention was to create plays of and for the middle class. He was the first of the German writers to portray the middle classes as they really were as opposed to some idealized view of the peasantry. A typical play is *The Alliance of Love* composed in 1703. In it two older people want to marry two younger people. The four of them all get together and the older people see how well the younger people get along and decide that it's really silly for them to marry those younger people. Instead the older pair get married, freeing the younger couple to fall in love. Other German plays, those by Gryphius for example, tried to create a moral by producing black and white characters. Weise sought to create a moral lesson through the presentation of more rounded characterizations showing people as they really are. Perhaps the most interesting of his plays to a modern audience all would be *The Comedy of Nasty Catherine* (his realistic adaptation of Shakespeare's *The Taming of the Shrew*).

German Theatrical Reform

Reformation has always had a great association with the German states, in religion, politics, and drama. The significant theatrical reformer in the eighteenth century was a man named **Johann Christoph Gottsched** (1700-1766) whose play *The Dying Cato* (1732) attempted to instill French neoclassical principles into the German drama. When he was twenty years old, Gottsched was living in a city named Leipzig which was the intellectual capital of Germany. He was attracted to the theatre because in it he saw a means of reaching the illiterate masses. He sought connections with theatrical companies so that he would be able to persuade the theatre-going public to increase its knowledge, to raise its taste, and to refine its intellectual level. In 1727, he met the Neubers, Carolina and Johann who were touring in a company called the Royal Polish and Electoral Saxon Court Comedians, which the couple had formed in 1727. They agreed to work with Gottsched in reforming the theatre. In the years that followed, between 1727 and 1739, we find the first alliance between a literary figure and a professional acting company in Germany. This is very important because it was the first time a German theatre company was actually concerned with literary significance.

This is what Gottsched did:

1) He determined that a completely new repertory was needed for the German theatre. He wanted to get rid of the *Haupt-und-staatsaktion* plays, improvisation, all satiric afterpieces, and especially the clown, Hanswurst. He

was trying to refine the literary merit of plays and make them infinitely more serious;

2) To accomplish his goals, Gottsched and his associates set out to write new plays, which they did essentially by translating or imitating French neo-classical plays. This, to them—as to everyone else in Europe—was the ideal form of drama. The most famous of these plays was Gottsched's own *The Dying Cato* which is very interesting because it is a German imitation of a French imitation of an English imitation of Racine.

Carolina Neuber, on the other hand, sought to raise the level of production:

1) She demanded careful rehearsals of plays, no improvisation;

2) She assigned additional duties to actors, i.e., painting scenery, sewing costumes, doing publicity;

3) She also policed her performers' personal lives. She gave them curfews. She refused to allow gentlemen actors into lady actor's rooms. This was designed to combat the moral prejudice against actors. She believed that if her actors could start behaving themselves according to conservative morality, people would take them more seriously and treat them better. Needless to say, her actors did not take to her efforts very kindly at first.

Now, this may come as a surprise to you, but Gottsched and Neuber were unable to drum up an audience that appreciated the new theatre. Spectators found it boring without the traditional comedy and improvisations, and in order to survive, the reformers were forced to compromise. By 1735, Hanswurst still found a home in over half of the afterpieces. In 1737, Carolina Neuber wrote a little play banishing Hanswurst from the stage, but the following year Hanswurst reappeared in a new costume and under a new name. In 1739, Neuber broke off her association with Gottsched deciding she couldn't afford to lose any more money trying to reform the theatre, and in 1740 she went to Russia to tour. Six months after she arrived, the Empress of Russia died and all the theatres in Russia were closed. As a result, in 1741 she returned to Leipzig to find Gottsched and some of her actors who didn't go to Russia with her, performing at her theatre. In retaliation, she took a theatre virtually across the street and began to satirize Gottsched, producing plays about an idiot reformer/scholar and destroyed Gottsched's leadership over the German theatre. After she succeeded in doing that, she traveled around Europe touring until she died in 1760.

The most significant result of Gottsched's and Neuber's reforms was that, by the 1740s, regular drama (imitations of French classical plays and English comedies) was being performed throughout Germany, and Neuber's production techniques were adopted by other German theatre troupes. In Gottsched's orbit were a number of playwrights who had a more or less significant impact on the future of German theatre. The first is **Luise Adelgunde Viktoria Gottsched** (1713–1762), the reformer's wife, who wrote better plays than he did. She wrote the German equivalent of French tearful comedies and perhaps her most significant work in that genre was *Pietism in Whalebone Skirts*. She wrote to evoke heavy sentiment and placed a great emphasis on rational behavior, high moral issues, and laughter through tears. Hers were plays in which the audience could feel for the characters and yet still be able to chuckle at their ridiculousness. **Johann Elias Schlegel** (1719–1749), perhaps the best of Gottsched's followers was a playwright deeply committed to the Enlightenment. His plays emphasized mind over matter, and high principals over emotion. But like so many other scholars, playwrights, and philosophers of the Enlightenment, he believed that the way to get to rational behavior was through the senses. As a result, emotion could lead to mental decisions. Schlegel copied a great deal from Racine, and his plays based on classical models, *Brother and Sister in Tauris* (based on *Iphigenia In Tauris)* or *The Trojan Women* are enlightened with characters who criticize the wisdom and justice of the gods in terms of modern philosophy. His more adventurous plays came in the form of histories and comedies, especially his *comédie larmoyante*, *The Triumph of Good Women* (1747), but perhaps his greatest impact on the history of German theatre though comes in his appreciation of Shakespeare.

He wrote many critical essays about Shakespeare, suggesting that, at times, Shakespeare was even truer to Aristotle than the French were.

The most popular of the Gottsched group was **Christian Furchtegott Gellert** (1715–1769) who wrote comedies intended to enlighten by smiling at folly and weeping at both rewarded and unrewarded virtue. He did not like satire in his plays and substituted instead kindly sentiment, and humane citizenship. He was dedicated to the ideals of the bourgeois enlightenment (middle class rational behavior), and his literary hero was the English novelist Samuel Richardson. Many of his characterizations and situations exposed behavior patterns of middle-class life at the time. Interestingly, though he did not like satire, two of his plays, *The Prayeress* and *The Lottery Ticket* were both incisive indictments of moral abuses of the period. Unfortunately looking back at a lot of these plays which were serious indictments of a particular social issue, we tend to look upon them satirically when the author, at the time, may have looked upon them very seriously. **Johann Christian Kruger** (fl. 1750–1780) was one of the earliest resident dramatists working for a theatrical company in Germany. Kruger's model was Marivaux, the French playwright who was more interested in the way people said things than the substance of what they said. His comedies were extremely literate, pastel, light, full of froth, and it is perhaps this kind of flimsy, insignificant work that best prepares us for Gotthold Ephraim Lessing, the serious playwright who sought to fight against it.

Gotthold Ephraim Lessing
Gotthold Ephraim Lessing (1729–1781) began his career (between 1746 and 1748) as a theology student in Leipzig. He encountered the Neuber troupe, the Royal Polish and Electoral Saxon Comedians, and started to do translations for them. Like so many other playwrights who were studying to be lawyers or priests, the attraction towards the theatre was too much for him, so he left school to become a theatre professional. In 1748, Carolina Neuber produced his first play, *The Young Scholar*, an original play, not a translation. He finally got a Master's Degree from the university in 1752 and three years

later, he wrote *Miss Sara Sampson*, his domestic drama, and started work on a Faust play anticipating Goethe. In 1756, the year after *Miss Sara Sampson* was produced, the Seven Years War broke about and he became a military secretary. His experiences as a military secretary were then put to use in 1767 when he wrote *Minna Von Barnhelm; or, The Soldier's Fortune*. Following the war, he spent two years as drama critic at the Hamburg National Theatre, for which he wrote "The Hamburg Dramaturgy." In 1772, he wrote *Emelia Galotti* and started to tour Europe, especially Italy (not with a theatre company, he was a traveling companion to a prince). In 1776, he married Eva Koenig who died two years later, and in 1779, he wrote *Nathan the Wise* his masterpiece. Lessing died in 1781.

Lessing's plays were the acknowledged culmination of German drama of the Enlightenment. His early models were Plautus and Molière, but later he took on more serious intellectual and psychological ideas and he began to argue for the tolerance of different views and beliefs. He was not afraid to bring spirits or ghosts on stage (even though Neoclassicism looked down on such things) because he felt that if the spirits were effectively presented (as for example in Shakespeare), the audience would willingly suspend disbelief. For Lessing, feelings were the essential ingredient of high drama, and the two most significant feelings that he thought could move in an audience were fear and compassion (sounds strangely like Aristotle's pity and fear). He insisted that Aristotle's *phobos* was not *terreur* (terror) as the French classicists thought, but a deep human fear in an audience experiencing the destiny of the characters on stage—an empathetic response. This is coming into a kind of burgeoning realism because, up until this point, audiences were constantly reminded that they were watching a play. Lessing also suggested that mere declarations of fear or portrayals of terrible events on the stage did not necessarily produce catharsis; nor did an audience identify with all black and white characters. They cannot be all good or all evil. He insisted that characters need to be rounded and developed; and if they are, the audience will be deeply affected by their struggles, both in comedy and tragedy.

To prove his point of view, Lessing (who disliked Corneille and made fun of Gottsched) produced four significant plays, starting with *Miss Sara Sampson*, which was first performed in Frankfurt in July of 1755. It is a long-winded domestic tragedy, a prose portrayal of a fair middle-class maiden done to death by a wastrel lover, his jealous mistress, and a foolish father. The play was fashioned from all of the material that was present in eighteenth-century bourgeois tragedies in England. It is virtually a replication of Lillo's play *George Barnwell*. However, Lessing brought enough human passion into the play to produce the feelings of destiny and pity, and elicit buckets of tears from the audience. He was seeking to affect the spectators by the dénouement of the play, with poison, imminent suicide, the kidnapping of a child and threats to kill her—domestic melodrama to the highest (even though this prefigures domestic melodrama by almost 50 years). For an audience that was used to characters being high-minded, speaking about nobility, virtue, and honor, this was something that was highly emotional; and of course, Sara's dying scene in which she asks forgiveness of everyone, particularly her long-suffering father, evoked the highest of bourgeois values. The father's choice to take on young Arabella (the child of his daughter's lover) as his own daughter's legacy is also quite sympathetic, and the villainess, the blocking character, does not as in melodramas of the later period seem just purely black and white. She does have a cause for revenge: she was abandoned by Sara's lover. Similarly, Sara did disobey her father to run off with the man, so she is not entirely good. Lessing composed the play as an experimental expression of his own dramatic philosophies.

Perhaps a more successful play, *Minna Von Barnhelm*, was a prose comedy produced on 30 September 1767 at Hamburg. Critics called it Lessing's most German play since it deals with opposite sides of the Seven Years War. A Prussian major, by the name of Von Telheim is in love with his Saxon sweetheart named Minna. Because after the war, Von Telheim has been reduced to poverty, he cannot justify his wanting to marry her. Minna borrows money to give him so that he will think himself worthy of her; but by the end of the play, a trumped-up charge that had reduced him of his money is reversed, and Von Telheim finally feels worthy of Minna's love. *Minna Von Barnhelm* is high comedy par excellence complete with an abrupt financial *deus ex machina* occuring a page before the curtain. It is sparkling, it is witty, and, in its own way, it is great fun.

Emelia Galotti (1772), on the other hand, is a prose tragedy set in Italy to disguise its association with German politics at the time. Marinelli, a prince and shallow man of the world, abducts Emelia from her fiancé and hides her away. About to be raped by the villain, Emelia asks for death rather than dishonor. She's unable to kill herself because she's too weak, so she begs her father (who managed to find her) to kill her. Her father is determined to save her from shame and stabs her with a knife belonging to the prince's previous mistress who, jealous of Marinelli's attentions to Emelia, tried to convince the father to kill the prince. The father, however, having to decide between killing his daughter and killing his prince, decides to kill his daughter because he can't bring himself to kill the prince who would dishonor her. Instead of fighting a social order that permits such things, an individual would rather kill his own flesh and blood. The play was an indictment against German politics and not terribly popular, especially during Hitler's regime in Germany.

Even less popular during the Nazi years was Lessing's last play, *Nathan the Wise* (1779), written in iambic verse and considered the first true "classical" German drama. Invariably whenever you hear the words "classical drama," poetry should immediately come to mind. *Nathan the Wise* is based on one of the Crusade stories in the *Decameron* by Boccaccio: the parable of the rings revealing that the three chief religions of the world are of divine origins. In the play, Lessing presents a sultan, an adopted daughter of a Jew, and a Christian knight who discover by the end that they all belong to the same family. The reason they were brought up in different faiths was purely environmental, a concept that was very important during the Enlightenment, when a variety of religions were permitted to exist at the same time. Thematically very much like Voltaire's *Zaire*, Lessing's play is united by a character named Nathan who was modeled after Moses Mendelssohn, Felix and Fanny Mendelssohn's father who was the prototype of the enlightened Jewish philosopher. The text is highly poetic, written in iambic pentameter, and the verse was so effective that it became the model for all German classic drama. *Nathan the Wise* has great battle scenes (taking place during the Crusades) and is filled with emotion, exoticism, and provides an excellent segue into the next strain of German theatre: the *sturm und drang*.

Sturm und Drang
The *Sturm und Drang* (Storm and Stress) developed out of the emotional elements of Lessing's plays, and were a hyper-thyroid reaction to Lessing's classicism. Another reaction to Lessing's work came about in plays that exhibited a high degree of sentimentality. Both *sturm und drang* and sentimentalism were more theatrical, more visceral, and more intensely Shakespearean than anything in Lessing. The Sentimentalists emphasized pictoralization and astonishment (i.e., long narratives painting pictures to astonish the audiences). The two most significant playwrights of this school were **Frederick Klopstock** (1724-1803) and **Christoph Wieland** (1733-1813). Klopstock added a kind of religious fervor and patriotism to sentimental plays, and Wieland was significant because he wrote prose translations of 22 of Shakespeare's plays which led to yet another Shakespeare cult in Germany between 1762 and 1766. In fact, it was the combination of Lessing's emotional classicism and the new Shakespeare cult that gave rise to the *sturm und drang*.

From the sociopolitical point of view of the second half of the eighteenth century, there were a number of political and social rumblings that needed to find some kind of expression in the drama. Between 1760 and 1785 such expression appeared in the *sturm und drang*. The storm and stress plays emphasized emotion, imagination, exclamation, and suspense. These were stressed in bombastic, wildly exaggerated language— "Ha! Ho! What!" and various other bombastic exclamations in addition to colorful and exotic language and explosive ideas. The plays employed a multitude of scenes, dialect, pantomime, and folk songs. They concentrated on the problems of the middle and lower classes and expressed a significant disdain for organized religion. For the storm and stress dramatist, the poet was the reincarnation of God. The movement demanded freedom of expression in order to glorify nature and individual genius. Tragedy and comedy were blended into a single genre. The Neoclassical Unities were set aside. Time could span several years and one play was usually set in several different cities. Essentially *sturm und drang* was a free form, irrational, hyper-thyroid entertainment, and the distinguishing mood of these plays was a pervasive cynicism. Characters denounced the evils of society but were incapable of escaping them. A happy ending was granted only to those individuals who accepted their social circumstances.

What is significant about the storm and stress playwrights is that, even as they demand social reform, they doubt the success of any solution. Hence there is always a pessimistic/cynical tone in these plays, and this is going to have a great influence on Büchner, Hauptmann, Weidekind, and Brecht.

Sturm und Drang Playwrights

The first dramatist of note in the *strum und drang* tradition was **Michael Reinhold Lenz** (1751–1792). Lenz considered Shakespeare an equal to God, and he felt that any genius who could shed his critical inhibitions and give his imagination free reign could accomplish as much as God/Shakespeare. He attempted to emulate Goethe (whom he considered a genius), but such attempts made him socially unacceptable. Everywhere he went he dressed like Goethe, acted like Goethe, even tried to talk like Goethe. He was also fond of experiencing ecstatic trances and airing his frustrations in public. He might see something that he found beautiful and suddenly deliver a twenty-minute lecture about the ecstasies of a tree or a plant. This ultimately led him to insanity at the age of 40.

Lenz created two very original and unconventional social comedies of the *sturm und drang* tradition: *The Family Tutor* and *The Soldiers*. *The Soldiers* is a tragicomedy about the "little man" who becomes a soldier to avenge the seduction of his fiancée by a playboy officer. This begins the tradition, which will become really important in German Expressionism, of the little man becoming a titan or being driven to attempting an activity that is beyond him. The plays have lots of action, lots of scene changes, very strong language—lots of "Ha! Ho!"—and various expletives. They have exciting characters who are particularly modern in their compassion, and the plays themselves seem to express great sensitivity to human suffering.

Perhaps the most notable of the crew for historical purposes is the man who gave the movement its name, **Friedrich Maximillian Klinger** (1752-1831). He became a *sturm and drang* dramatist through his association with his neighbor in Frankfurt, Goethe. Klinger wrote plays that are referred to as glorified orgies of passion. His first produced experiment in the drama was *The Twins*. An earlier play, *Otto*, was a kind of *Hamlet* exercise that he wrote upon seeing one of Goethe's *sturm und drang* plays, but *The Twins* won the Schröder contest for playwriting in 1775 and is significant because it is based on the Cain and Abel plot and ends in total slaughter. What is beginning to develop in the *sturm und drang* tradition is the raising of characters to archetypes and when a playwright is dealing with Cain and Abel, he is certainly dealing with archetypes. In 1776, Klinger was appointed resident dramatist for one of the acting troupes and wrote the play *Sturm und Drang* for them, from which we get the title of the movement. *Sturm und Drang* resolves all of the prevalent European social malaise in an action-packed love story (borrowed heavily from *Romeo and Juliet*) that occurs in revolutionary America. For the Germans of the eighteenth century, America was exotic. What better kind of situation could foment high passion and hyper-thyroid action! To fill out the play he borrowed entire scenes from Shakespeare, and added a number of comic characters dealing with the seduction of women. On the one hand, the play is about a comic seduction. On the other, there is the family rivalry from *Romeo and Juliet*, both aided and abetted by the revolutionary environment in which all this activity occurs. At the end of the play everything works out perfectly well; lovers are all appropriately paired up, and long-lost sons and fathers are reunited (but not without exploring the gamut of passion first). Whether it is logical or has little bearing on the action, the enabling of explosive emotions is the principal business of the play.

In 1780, Klinger moved into the realm of comedy and started to write plays based on classical themes. He wrote a comedy based on *Medea*, still in the *sturm und drang* style, and in 1791, he produced a titanic novel called

Faust's Life, Deeds, and Descent into Hell. It is very interesting how, during this period, the myth of Faust becomes a primary focus for German writers. They are fascinated by this Titan literally waging war against both God and the devil. They seemed to be obsessed with the passions of a single man struggling against the universe.

Another of the principal *sturm und drang* playwrights was Heinrich Leopold Wagner (1747-1779) who wrote a number of Shakespeare clones, one of which was *Macbeth*. More significant was a six-act bourgeois tragedy called *The Murderess of Her Child* (1776), a play about an unwed mother who murders her child. Parts of this play Goethe felt were stolen from his *Faust*, but Goethe's play hadn't been written when this play appeared. In rebuttal, Goethe argued that he had been planning *Faust* as early as 1770. When Wagner's play appeared in 1776, Goethe claimed "they took some of my ideas."

Goethe

The most significant playwright of the entire *sturm and drang* tradition was **Johann Wolfgang von Goethe** (1749-1832), the acknowledged master of *sturm und drang* and the leader (with Schiller) of German classicism. Goethe was born to a merchant family in Frankfurt and introduced to theatre by a French officer during the French occupation of Frankfurt. He was highly influenced by *Punch and Judy* shows, studied in Leipzig, and wrote rococo plays in verse. Rococo plays are highly ornate, ornamented, very light, frothy dramatic works. Perhaps the most significant of these was *The Lover's Wayward Humor*. This play established one of Goethe's themes that would extend throughout his career: feminine wiles and wisdom cure masculine ills. Goethe, like so many other playwrights, took a law degree in 1771 and, the following year, he served as a clerk in a law firm about which he wrote an extremely popular novel called *The Sorrows of Young Werther* (1774). After 1774, he returned to Frankfurt to develop a law practice and his home soon became a meeting place for the young artistic rebels of the storm and stress movement. It was a "Memorial on Shakespeare's Birthday" that Goethe wrote in 1771, while he was still in school, that became the manifesto for the *Sturm und Drang*.

Goethe's own storm and stress oeuvre began with a play called *Goetz Von Berlichingen*, a sprawling historical action fest with 56 scenes in five acts and about 102 characters. Written in Frankfurt in 1773, it was based on an historical character, a German knight who was an idealistic robber-baron, described in the play as a "titan of justice." The word "titan" is going to be very important in all of these plays—a titan of justice, a Robin Hood, a "righter of wrongs" who is ultimately destroyed by his own trusting goodness. This is another important theme for Goethe: the creative idealist versus his own conscience in a world full of selfish and destructive villains. So many of these plays deal with the attempt to do the right thing, but in a world full of destructive villainy, how can a man know what the right thing is to do? The play is clearly a conscious imitation of Shakespeare with changes of scenery galore. There are some scenes in the play which are no more than three or four lines long before the scene changes to a new locale.

While working on *Goetz*, Goethe discovered the dramatic possibilities of schizophrenia and started to sketch the prison scene of the child murderess Marguerite as the foundation for his monumental drama, *Faust*. Writing *Faust* Goethe began to develop a verse form that he found in Hans Sachs, a medieval dramatist, called *knittelvers*. *Knittelvers* is a four-beat rhymed pattern that will become the verse structure for *Faust*. Goethe would end up writing *Faust* in prose, *knittelvers*, and occasionally free verse, a substantial innovation since up to this point, tragedy was generally composed in one kind of verse or prose. And at the same time, he began to compose two other titanic plays, *Egmont* and *Prometheus* at this point.

Weimar Classicism

Late in 1774, Goethe's career reached a turning point when he accepted an invitation from Carl August, the Duke of Saxe Weimar to become a court minister. Goethe went there at the end of 1774 and remained there for the rest of his life. He was in charge of court theatrical activities, the administration of finances, mining, and the military establishment of the duchy. While he was there, he also carried on extensive research in botany and anatomy which would become very significant to his development as a director, in his attempts to have actors use more natural or realistic mannerisms in their performances. His association with the Weimar court also led Goethe to impose classical restraints upon his life and work. To wit, he wrote a number of new classical tragedies in an attempt to observe some of the neoclassical unities. The most interesting of these plays is probably *Stella* (1776), about Fernando, a Don-Juan type, who leaves his wife and child to live with Stella, and at the end of the play he leaves Stella to go back to his wife and child, leaving both of the women unhappy. In the first version of *Stella*, the play ended with a *menage á trios*, uniting the two women and Fernando. In the revised version of the play, the Don-Juan character kills himself.

There is an emphasis on mood and character analysis rather than action, and a change is beginning to show in Goethe's focus from one of hyperthyroid action to one of character development and investigation. Perhaps the best example of the change lies in Goethe's last *sturm und drang* play, *Egmont* which was composed in two different versions. In the first version of the play, *Egmont* was essentially a social revolutionary drama full of bombast and energy. When it was revised in 1788, the focus was on the central character, a Titan of idealism, a noble criminal, too gracious to survive in a world controlled by ruthless realists. This idealistic tone in Goethe's work will ultimately give form to what is usually known as **Weimar Classicism**. The emphasis on the ideal rather than on the real points toward the emerging classical bent in Goethe and this tendency is going to be fueled by his partner in Classicism, **Johann Christian Friedrich von Schiller** (1759–1805), the critic who gave *Egmont* a good review.

Schiller, who also happened to live in Weimar, was a moralist. He felt that freedom of conscience was a product of conflict, and believed deeply that true freedom (remember we are in a time with revolutions—the French Revolution would happen very shortly) could conquer destiny but could not conquer God. Schiller's theatrical background came from theatre operas, and he wrote a play while he was in school called *The Robbers*. He wrote it secretly and smuggled it out so it could be performed. And the story goes that he had to miss a couple of days of school to see the first performance of the play on 13 January 1782. Eventually, when he was 23 years old, Schiller decided to give up college to become a professional dramatist. In *The Robbers*, Franz von Moor, a rebellious titan of vengeful immorality, steals his brother's birthright and his fiancée. Carl Von Moor, the brother, is a rebellious titan of justice and freedom. So, you get a rebellious titan of immorality in conflict with a rebellious titan of justice and freedom. What does the rebellious titan of justice and freedom do? He forms a band of robbers comprised of victims of social injustice (like Robin Hood). His rebellious brother commits suicide, and Carl, realizing at the end of the play that such robbing antisocial behavior doesn't do any good, gives himself up to the authorities. The play was a huge success, and convinced by theatre managers and publishers to continue writing, Schiller started to crank out a number of plays.

In 1784 he began to question the function of a merely therapeutic catharsis in plays; instead, he wanted to develop a kind of intellectual and moral edification from drama. He sought to have drama achieve a quiet grandeur and noble simplicity and thus provide leadership in showing the way to a life of brotherhood, beauty, and dignity (this is not unlike the French revolution—liberty, fraternity, and equality) and this will become the central idea of Weimar Classicism. In an attempt to provide an exemplum of the new style, Schiller produced *Don Carlos, Infante of Spain* (1787) (later made into a rather good opera by Verdi). In 1788, Schiller even moved further in the direction of Classicism with his translations of *Ihpigenia in Aulis* and *The Phoenician Women*. He also produced an important trilogy called *Wallenstein* (completed in 1799), Aristotelian in structure and Shakespearean in verse. He tried to incorporate what he considered the unities and wrote in Shakespearean blank verse. It achieved nobility and grandeur but left a great deal to desire in simplicity. He also wrote a *Macbeth* in 1800 and *Mary Stuart* (1800) which was his most performed classical play. His last completed play was *William Tell* (1804) which was actually based on the life of an historical republican leader. This play was structured in the form of a classical idyll, called a *schauspiel*. *Schauspiels* were kind of patriotic plays (though literally it meant a serious festive play with a happy ending). Schiller's play uses blank verse, songs, and a panoramic background—the Alps. It glorifies the family, home, community, and the Fatherland. *William Tell* is perhaps the best example of Schiller's wanting to preach or use the drama to teach utilitarian conservative values.

While Schiller was writing his plays, Goethe continued to write in a more classical format. One of the results of his experimentation was *Ihpigenia in Tauris* (1779), not to be confused with Schiller's *Ihpigenia in Aulis*. Perhaps the most extreme of Goethe's classical plays, however, comes with his super drama, *Faust*. Part one was published in 1808 and part two appeared in 1832. It is a very long play, and typically called a tragedy because Marguerite dies and Faust ultimately meets his end. Yet there is a happy ending to the piece because Goethe felt that every man who could be redeemed is redeemed, and therefore redemption being happy, we should look upon the play as a comedy. The play turns on a bargain made by Faust with the Devil. The prologue of Part One depicts God allowing the Devil to make a bargain with Faust—the Devil could not strike a bargain a human unless God permitted it. Faust commits to the following bargain: if Mephistopheles can grant him one moment of complete contentment, a moment that he might wish would last for eternity, he will give his soul over to the Devil.

In Part One, Mephistopheles rejuvenates Faust and presents him with the world of desire and passion. Faust falls in love with, and seduces young Marguerite. She bears him a child, panics, drowns it, and is thrown into jail as a murderess. At the end of Part One, Faust tries to rescue Marguerite from prison. She says, "No, I should be condemned because I committed a crime." Refusing to flee, Marguerite puts her trust in God, and her soul is taken up to heaven on angel's wings.

Having failed to discover a moment so wonderful that he wished it would last forever in Part One, in Part Two Faust enters the world of history, politics and culture (highly consistent with the idealism of the German Weimar classicists). He tastes every form of intellectual and worldly power but is unable to grasp his moment of joy until he turns again into an old man and begins to take interest in a reclamation project. All of a sudden, a project that brings

Faust no personal gain but does good for hundreds of people, gives him the pleasure that he wishes would continue for a lifetime. The Devil shouts, "Ah ha! He found something. I have his soul." Unfortunately, as Mephistopheles is about to take Faust to hell, a choir of angels is heard singing, "He who exerts himself in constant striving, him we can save." Because Faust was constantly striving to find this one moment, he, by a technicality, doesn't deserve to go to Hell. God says all bets are off, and Faust's soul is taken up to heaven. Ultimately, the moral of the play is that Mephistopheles has lost the wager, not with Faust but with God. The play is really the epitome of Weimar idealism because it once again points out, as Schiller would have us believe, that freedom of conscience can allow man any autonomy except over God. God's law of the universe is inviolate.

Goethe's Theatre Reforms

When Goethe went to Weimar, he found a second-rate acting troupe full of actors who mugged and improvised. In a short time, he transformed it into a true ensemble. To do this he set out a series of rules that covered linguistics, enunciation, principles of movement, and so forth. These rules were aimed at achieving grace, dignity, and ease in performance. For example: Rule #38—The actor must constantly remember that he is on the stage for the sake of the audience. Rule #466—To acquire an easier and more suitable movement of the feet, one must never rehearse in boots. Rule #71—The actor should also make no movement in rehearsal which is unsuitable to the role. Rule #72—He who places his hand in his bosom in rehearsing tragic roles, runs the risk in the actual performance of fumbling for an opening in his armor. Rule #74—The actor should show no pocket handkerchiefs on the stage, even less should he blow his nose, still less spit.

In his reforms, Goethe became an absolute dictator. He began each new production with a series of reading rehearsals where he would correct errors in line readings, pronunciation, and interpretation. To help in blocking, he divided the stage into squares (this is the man who gave us down right, down left) and consulted painters about set composition and blocking so that when he did stage a play, there would be an appropriate balance to his pictures. He was so concerned with rhythm and cadence of a play that often he beat time with a stick during rehearsals. Rather than seeking to create the illusion of reality, Goethe attempted to attune the spectator to an ideal beauty. He was not trying to be naturalistic or natural; Goethe tried to attune the spectator to an ideal beauty through a harmonious and graceful picture in combination with intelligent line readings.

Goethe sat in his box at the theatre and treated the audience as autocratically as he did the actors. If the audience did not applaud when they should, he would stop the play and reprimand the audience. He forbade the audience to express any reaction in the play by anything other than applause or silence. He commanded them: if you don't like it, quiet. If you like it, applaud. If anyone dared to hiss or boo, he would have them forcibly removed from the theatre. In a very real way Goethe is the first theatre director in a modern sense. As finance minister, he was in charge of the duchy's money, so he had the political clout to wield this kind of power.

Satellite Classical Playwrights

There were many playwrights who were tangential to Goethe and Schiller in their appreciation of Classicism. Some of the more important of these are Christian Felix Weisse, August Wilhelm Iffland, and August von Kotzebue who would become the most influential of the German playwrights in English and French melodrama. **Christian Felix Weisse** (1726-1804) was a friend and disciple of Lessing who produced comedies. This is important because Classicism typically relegated comedies to a lower stratum than tragedy. Perhaps the most significant of his works was a blockbuster adaptation of an English musical theatre piece called *The Devil to Pay*, which would be instrumental in popularizing the *singspiel* and propelling the music theatre tradition in Germany. Weisse's tragedies, on the other hand, were generally unsuccessful. The only one of note was *Jean Calais* which was modeled on *Goetz Von Berlichingen*. His comedies were essentially adaptations of what was currently in vogue in France and, to some extent, in England. As a result, they were highly sentimental and moral plays.

Weisse was bettered by **August Wilhelm Iffland** (1759-1814) who succeeded in creating overly sentimental and highly moralizing melodramas. Iffland created characters with which the middle-class audience could easily identify, following the tradition in both England and France where the merchant character was raised to a very significant place in plays. Comedies no longer dealt with the lower classes of society, and tragedies or serious plays no longer dealt with kings. Plays were concerned with the merchant middle class. Iffland's major vehicle was the family play in which virtue is always rewarded and vice is always punished, and rather than providing the audience with raucous laughter or the cathartic release of tragedy, he usually bathed his plays in buckets of tears. In other words, he was immediately appealing to the emotions and wanted tears as the ideal reaction to his plays. Typical among his titles were *Crime for Glory*, *The Hunter*, *The Gambler*. These titles are significant because he was writing about contemporary social abuses and how they should be rectified.

The most successful of all the sentimental German playwrights, still writing in a kind of tangential classical idealistic form was **August Von Kotzebue** (1761-1819), a prolific writer of sentimental comedies and perhaps the most popular playwright of his day in Germany. He wrote over 200 plays over a not especially long lifetime. All of his plays were tremendous successes in Germany, and translations generally were produced in other countries simultaneously with the original German productions. Of the 4000 productions played at Weimar, over 600 were plays written by Kotzebue, whose work was not only popular in the theater, but also as private reading in the home. People would buy Kotzebue's comedies and read them as moral lessons to their children. Although he wrote some tragedies and dabbled in political plays, his idiom was sentimental comedy and the subject of his plays tended toward the exotic. One wonderful play that was translated into English called *The Stranger* deals with a husband, shipwrecked on a deserted island, who marries the princess, the daughter of the chieftain of the island. His long-suffering wife takes a boat and finds him after about fifteen years, and the whole body of the play is about what the man is going to do. He's in love with the native woman who is bearing him children. He is in love with his wife who has considered him long-lost or dead. How does it finally resolve? Of course, the long-suffering wife is willing to give him up because of this wonderful native girl who has taken care of him. The native girl is willing to give him up because of his wife, and the play ends in a "menage á trois" in which the husband keeps both of them. The wife does not go back to England (in the translation), but decides to stay on the island where such things as "menages á trois" are possible.

Because the central focus of Kotzebue's plays was the exciting of strong emotions (remember that was the same thing that Lessing wanted to do), he did little to advance theatrical history as far as the Germans were concerned. However, since his plays dispensed with using the stage as a pulpit (he did not preach; clearly a play like the one just described could not be considered preaching), and capitalized on middle class expectations and attitudes, they were great escapist entertainment—like the penny novels that would be popular in England in the eighteenth and nineteenth centuries. Kotzebue would be a kind of comic book dramatist for our age, providing an escape from a humdrum existence. His best-known plays were *Misanthropy and Repentance*, *Father and Son*, and a play called *German Small-Town Folk*. What attests to the popularity of Kotzebue's work is the fact that the play *Father and Son* remained in the German repertory until 1951. That's 150 years. In spite of his great popularity, Kotzebue was assassinated on 18 March 1819 by a theology student who insisted that Kotzebue was an enemy of the German people. The playwright had been the director of the German Theatre in St. Petersburg, Russia, but when he returned to Germany, people thought he was a Russian spy. Unfortunately, Kotzebue's work is hardly taken seriously today. We tend to read it and laugh because of its highly melodramatic aspects. However, we can appreciate that it was Kotzebue who truly gave a shot in the arm to the melodramatic genre and propelled it in both England and France. His plays were so popular that there were imitators and translators by the score.

12. Theatre in Russia through the 18th Century

Theatre in Russia developed from three principle impulses: 1) Popular ritual, 2) Church drama, and 3) Court theatre. This should sound very familiar since it follows the pattern of theatrical development in Western Europe in the Middle Ages: medieval rituals, church drama, and the kind of interludes that would be found at court.

Ritual

In Russia popular ritual took the form of sowing and harvesting rites performed generally by young girls (a possible origin of the ethnic stereotype of the hefty Russian woman plowing the fields). One of the girls is elected harvest queen and the others become part of her court; suddenly we have a "Harvest Queen Festival." The 25th of March produced a ritual called "The Conjuring of Spring" during which girls imitated birdcalls and sang to one another. Ritual games accompanied various events in family life, especially weddings. In the wedding ritual, the bride is the chief character and a short play accompanies the wedding ceremony in which the bride seeks refuge from the character of the husband. The husband is portrayed as the villain, ripping the bride from the bosom of her family and must be finally tamed by the end of the ritual. Christmas rituals involved townsfolk masquerading as bears, goats, foxes, and gypsies. These impersonators, who are not unlike the kind of people one would meet at *Mardi Gras* in various costumes, began to improvise short scenes among themselves. In addition, the *skomorokh*, who were professional storytellers or wandering buffoons, went from house to house begging for food and lodging, paying for their keep with a story and the dissemination of the local news. These Russian troubadours and news readers came to Russia from Istanbul during the late middle ages. Among other things, they introduced puppet shows into Russia. Interestingly, as a side note, in 1589 an imperial document set up a hierarchy of buffoons. Apparently the *skomorokh* were considered dangerous buffoons because going house to house they were known to ravage and pillage as they went. It appears that traveling actors never had a very good reputation.

Religious Drama

At the same time religious drama was developing. The first records we have of this appear around 1548 about a fiery furnace show, *Meshach, Shadrach, and Abendigo*, performed on the Saturday before Christmas. What's interesting about this is that the lay people who participated in the religious drama had to cleanse themselves of the sin of acting by jumping into the frozen river. However, after they had cleansed themselves and performed in the play, they could wear their costumes out on the street for the whole week of Christmas. If an actor had a funny costume, he could wear it in public. Apparently, the members of the congregation loved to do that sort of thing. Special Christmas shows were later developed dealing with the nativity, shepherds, and wise men, and begin to establish a series of specialty characters. The shows always had Herod and the devil, of course, but they begin to add more specifically Russian types: the soldier character, the old peasant woman, and the Cossack. This was an attempt to take people from contemporary life and integrate them into the liturgical drama. The soldier was essentially a young hero, the Cossack was probably a retired soldier at home, scruffy and out of work. The

Cossacks were very much like the Hessians who fought in the American Revolution. They were military people but generally were regarded by the Russians with some kind of disdain. They weren't accepted as part of Russian society.

Via Poland, Catholic morality plays were imported into the Kiev Academy. At this point, the Kiev Academy was kind of a theological school. The plays were not only produced privately within the college, but publicly as well during summer months when students needed money (a kind of Russian sixteenth-century summer stock). The most noteworthy aspect about the school plays was the notion of presenting a humorous scene after each act of a serious play. These comic interludes would become the bridge between a drama comprising myth and liturgy and a drama built from observing life.

Court Theatre

Court theatre generally developed by way of travelers and diplomats coming to and from the Russian countries. Avráamy was a bishop who traveled to France between 1437 and 1439, and there he saw a play called *The Annunciation*. That is the first record we have of a Russian visiting a foreign country and seeing a play. From that time on, the news spread, and by 1660, Czar Alexei called for foreign actors to come and perform in Moscow. Alexei wanted to have his own court theatre comprised of foreign actors because there were no actors per se in Russia at the time. What the czar managed to get was a trombone player, an actress, and an out of work dancer. Those were the only people he could talk into coming to Russia to perform, and so he decided that a theatrical troupe had to be developed indigenously in Moscow. This would actually be possible because there was a ghetto within Moscow called the German village consisting of foreigners, mostly from Germany, and many of these people were amateur actors who went to Moscow to make a better living for themselves. Out of this village came a priest, **Johann Gottfried Gregori**, who was commissioned by the Czar to develop theatrical productions in Russia. In 1672, Gregori staged a comedy using the biblical Book of Esther as a plot, with 69 children of government officials as the cast.

Called *Artaxerxes*, the play written in German and Slavic, was rehearsed for 3 months, and musicians from the local church formed the orchestra.

Gregori's work exhibited the great influence of the English comedians who emigrated from England to Holland in the sixteenth century and developed a jester called Pickled Herring (as opposed to Hanswurst, the clown created in Germany). It was Pickled Herring that became the quintessential clown and the comic figure of Gregori's comedy and later plays in Russia (perhaps because Pickled Herring wasn't as fat or beer-drinking as Hanswurst). *Artaxerxes* was performed in the comedy chamber of the palace in Moscow, a room that was 70 feet square and 40 feet high. The stage was raised above the floor about 4 or 5 feet, and a curtain was used as well as perspective Italianate scenery. Some records say nine, others say it took eleven hours to perform, and every eyewitness account emphasizes the fact that the czar stayed awake through the entire performance and didn't get up once.

In 1673, as a result of the success of this work, the first dramatic school was established in Russia with the children of 26 families enrolled. However, in 1676, the Czar died and that put an end to theatrical activities at Court. In fact, the comedy chamber was dismantled and thrown out into the snow.

The first playwright in Moscow was a man named Simeon Polotski. He was the tutor to the Czar's children and was required to write plays. One of his finest plays was called *About Nebuchadnezzar, the Golden Calf, and the Three Children Who Did Not Burn in the Furnace*. The next significant playwright was St. Dimitri of Rostov who not only imitated foreign plays, but also integrated characteristically Russian phrases, characters, and identifiable locales. He would take a medley of Russian expressions and throw them into a play; it was not necessary that they actually fit the dramatic situation. Russian theatre acquired at this time a characteristic that has survived through the nineteenth century. The theatre was financed out of the Czar's treasury. Therefore, all those who worked in the theatre were government employees; and since they were considered government employees, theatre practitioners had to conform to the wishes of the Czar.

Peter the Great who ruled from 1682 to 1725 tried to Europeanize Russia as quickly as possible, and he saw in the drama an efficient medium to achieve this goal. He Imported from Germany an acting company headed by Johann Kunst, and in 1702, to reach a larger audience, he moved the theatre from the imperial palace to Moscow's red square. Peter wanted to use the theatre to project political ideas. This not only gave Russian audiences an opportunity to see some of the latest Western plays (remember that a German company of actors is performing), but it also enabled Kunst and his successors, to train native Russians in Western acting and playwriting styles. Importantly, in 1705, to encourage more people to attend the theatre, Peter decreed that plays should be performed both in Russian and German, and guaranteed safe passage to audiences who might be downtown at the play after dark. Peter's decree actually did little to solve the problem of poor attendance, for most audiences did not speak German, and Russian actors were terrible. So, in 1706 Peter closed the theatre in Moscow and, in 1709, he built an imperial theatre in St. Petersburg, his new choice for the capital city.

While Peter was having a difficult time establishing a popular theatre, his court ministers were developing amateur productions in their own private homes. This, of course, was an attempt to court favor with the Czar who liked the theatre. In the private theatres, the performers were typically serfs who, by the way, were beaten if they didn't do their roles correctly. As a result, during Peter's reign there were three different species of theatrical activity: popular theatre, court theatre, and school theatre.

The Czar's idea of theatre as a political weapon was clarified when he produced a play on 18 May 1724 in Moscow entitled, *The Russian Glory, the Work of the Sovereign Emperor of All Russians Peter the Great Who Bestowed Benefactions Upon Russia and Who Created Out of Ignominy Russian Glory and the Solemn All Russian Triumph of the Coronation of the Most Supreme Empress Catherine Represented in Person at the Moscow Hospital.* Yes, that's just the title of the play. To sustain this kind of political polemic, Peter ordered that actors perform plays no longer than three acts. He believed than an audience (at least a Russian audience) could not be engaged for more than three or four hours at a time, and he clearly understood that an audience that goes to sleep during the political message does not really comprehend it. He also forbade love plots, again believing that the emotional appeal of plays gets in the way of the audience's comprehension. What he was asking for was the kind of alienation device that Brecht would develop in the twentieth century. In addition, he demanded that plays be neither too funny nor too sad. Clearly what he wanted were pleasant short plays without a romantic interest. Another significant play of this period was called *The Play about Esther*, the plot of which involved a king abandoning a wicked wife and choosing a foreigner to replace her. He finally marries the foreigner because of her great moral qualities. This play was significant because Peter was trying to divest himself of his present wife. Hoping to marry a foreigner, the Czar used this play to argue the biblical precedents for his action. When Peter the Great died in 1725, the theatre was once again deprived of government support.

Under Peter II the court theatre did not develop significantly, but with the ascent of the Czarina, Anna Ivanovna, in 1730, there was a revival of theatrical life in court. In honor of the coronation, the King of Poland sent a *commedia dell'arte* troupe, and in 1734, a space was set aside specifically for theatrical presentation in the winter palace where, in 1735, an Italian opera company came to perform. In the same year an Italian ballet company appeared and in 1738, a French ballet master was brought in. Not to appear terribly biased, in the same year, Anna invited Carolina Neuber's company, a German troupe, to perform in the capital. Unfortunately, Anna died in the middle of the Neuber's tour and the German claque at court was no longer in favor. The acting company was replaced by a French troupe and gradually a repertoire of plays by Racine, Corneille, and Molière began to develop.

Under the reign of the Czarina Elizabeth, the necessity of creating a Russian national theatre became profoundly clear. As a result, the Czarina sought to replace all the foreign actors who were performing in Russia with indigenous actors. She found her professional actors in a place called Yaroslavl where the Volkov brothers (Fyodor, Gavrilo, and Grigory) were directing plays. The most significant of the Volkovs was Fyodor Grigoryevich who is considered the father of professional theatre in Russia. This is particularly astounding because the Volkovs had gone to St. Petersburg, witnessed a play and an opera, went back stage to see the scenery and said, "Oh, we can do that." They returned home and, without any training or previous experience, hired some seminarians as performers and crew, and started to put on plays. On 21 December 1750, Elizabeth issued a decree granting permission to perform plays in private homes, and on 18 March 1752, the Yaroslavl troupe performed a play for the Czarina. She was so pleased by the performance that she encouraged the company to give public performances of the play. On 30 August 1756, Elizabeth issued a decree assuring the status of actors in Russia and laid the foundation for the imperial theatre. She named the playwright Sumarokov as the director of the imperial theatre, which was built on Vasilevsky Island, and appointed Fyodor Volkov as the leading actor in the company.

While this was being done, the aristocracy continued performing plays on their estates (something Chekhov would dramatize in *The Seagull*) with companies of serfs. The fetish for dramatic entertainment grew to such an extent among all classes of people, that a play was written called *A Queer Gathering* which depicted a lower-class Muscovite dedicating all of his time (and money) to staging private theatricals. As far as the State Theatre was concerned, however, actors were recruited from several sources:

1) Pupils of the drama school; every time there was a new theatre at court, the drama school would be reactivated;

2) Persons who had acted on other stages, people who had performed in private theatricals at home or court;

3) Dancers from the burgeoning ballet company; typically, women actors began their career as ballet performers and then moved into acting roles.

Actors in Russia were permitted to marry only with their supervisor's authorization. Failure to do so resulted in arrest and incarceration. Salaries were fixed by the government and the principal actors were paid four times the amount of the rest of the actors (not unlike the star system in Western

Europe). Actors were also given housing by the state and, as a result of the theatre Regulation Act of 1789, four benefit performances yearly were granted to the company (benefit performances are those productions the proceeds of which go to the actors or the playwright). Theatre management proscribed that state-owned costumes should be worn by actors playing character parts only. Actors playing leading roles or romantic roles would wear their own clothing. Regulations in the actor's contract warned, "A stage costume shall not be soiled or spoiled through neglect under threat of penalty of its repair at the expense of the actor responsible." Actors were engaged for a specific category only, very much like in England where they played a line of business. The category and the roles were specified by contract and the actor had to submit to the assignment of roles. If the actor refused to play a role, he was punished by a fine.

Moving back a bit, in 1779, a new school of training was established by the legendary and notorious Catherine the Great. In the same year that she established a new school for training actors, she established the Bolshoi Theatre (Bolshoi means "big" or "grand"). Catherine's new school for the training of actors was designed for fifteen boys and fifteen girls, and most of these pupils were children of theatrical parents. The school assumed the obligation of clothing and feeding the students as well as teaching and housing them. They did not do a particularly good job because I have found letters written from the school children to the Czarina and Czar saying, "Please can we have a meal." If the students received one meal a day, they considered themselves fortunate. In addition, the dwellings in which they were housed were very cold. Some of these abuses were subsequently addressed in another decree (1783), designed to define the school's function and improve conditions for the students. Finally, a decree in 1794 codified the kind of curriculum students should be studying: music, dancing, and language. Students were trained in physical movement, in having a mellifluous and supple voice, and an ability to handle language—a system of training Stanislavski would build upon at the Moscow Art Theatre at the end of the nineteenth century. In 1800, another decree limited the number of pupils to 50 of both sexes. Clearly a theatrical education was very popular.

Selecting the repertoire of plays for the Russian National Theatre (the imperial theatre that was founded on Vasilevsky Island) was extremely complicated. Plays were examined by a special censor, not unlike the English theatre examiner who cut out the offending passages. Then they were sent to the supervisor of the Russian company who was in charge of staging them, and then finally from the director they went to the Czar. *The Dramatic Lexicon* in 1787 gave a comprehensive list of plays that were produced at the Russian National Theatre: of the foreign plays produced, it is particularly interesting that *Richard III* and *Julius Caesar* were both quite popular in Russia.

Eighteenth-Century Playwrights

There were several indigenous Russian playwrights operating in the 18th century. The most significant was **Alexander Sumarokov** (1717–1777) who tried to bring the best works of French classical theatre to Russia. Although he used subjects from Russian history (as opposed to Western mythology or the Bible), he obeyed the Neoclassical unities, divided his tragedies into five acts, wrote in a lofty heroic tone, and did not employ comic interludes (this mirrors Neoclassicism in every country we have examined thus far). He is regarded as the playwright who infused structure into Russian drama. Concerned with social welfare and politics, he also created heroes who preached the ideals of civic virtue and called for monarchs to base their laws on truth rather than on despotic whim. Like Racine, he focused the dramatic interest on the heroine, and in the Russian theatre, he was the first to champion a woman's right to an independent emotional life. In other words, his women did not have to rely on their association with men to achieve a self-identity. For a great many plays, the only female characters are so and so's daughter, so and so's wife, so and so's betrothed. Sumarokov argued against such stereotypes: "Why should the emotional of life of a woman be purely dependent on a connection with a male," and in so doing, he became the first to distinguish the moral aspect of love from the sensual one. Sumarokov's most significant plays are *Khorev*

(1747), his first tragedy, produced by students at the Noble College of Land Cadets in St. Petersburg, and *Hamlet* (1748), based on French adaptations of Shakespeare's play.

Along with the neoclassical tendencies of the nobility during the second half of the eighteenth century, a new tendency arose in playwriting reflecting the taste of the middle class. This is exactly like what was happening in France and England, and gradually tearful comedy found its way into Russia, principally from France. In the 1760s, Russian translations of *The Natural Son* by Denis Diderot and *The London Merchant* by George Lillo were extremely popular, and Russian playwrights tried to move into that direction. The most important of the sentimental dramatists were Lukin and Peter Alekseyevich Plavilshchikov. Lukin wrote didactic and sentimental plays in an attempt to create a national theatre in which all of Russian life would be reflected. He was actually opposed to everything that was not Russian, which meant that he had a problem with the unities because he considered the neoclassical unities French. He had a problem with the five-act division because that wasn't indigenously Russian. He wanted a more or less free-form, idiomatic Russian drama. He was eventually persuaded that, since Sumarokov who was Russian codified the plays into five acts, he might go along with the formula if he wanted to be produced. Plavilshchikov also believed that priority should be given to everything Russian, and he sought to portray the middle classes in their natural environment. Lukin tended to idealize the middle class in his attempt to make everything Russian. He wanted to show everything in a good light. Plavilshchikov wanted to show the middle-class as it really existed, to which end, he wrote several important plays. *The Store Clerk* is perhaps his most characteristic work. A virtuous clerk overcomes a variety of obstacles and ends up marrying the boss's daughter. To us, it sounds like a hackneyed plot. For the Russians, this was extremely realistic and sentimental. Another play called *The Wretched and Solitary One* dealt with a homeless farmhand and was peopled with a variety of Russian peasant types.

The period did, however, produce one magnificent playwright, **Denis Fonvizin** (1745-1792), arguably the first truly indigenous Russian writer.

Born and educated in Moscow he was influenced by Diderot, Rousseau, and Voltaire. When Catherine the Great ascended the throne in 1762, he obtained a position as translator in the foreign affairs office. She took one look at him and, in 1764, she transferred him to the imperial cabinet. While he was working for Catherine, he wrote a number of fables satirizing the government, but since he wrote in the style of Voltaire and his kind of political idealism, Catherine who professed to admire Voltaire, did not incarcerate Fonvizin. She knew he was talking about her behind her back, but she was a cool-headed monarch and would not do anything to abrogate his freedom of speech (there is also the implication that she and Fonvizin had more than a professional relationship). Fonvizin's views on the abuses of serfdom during Catherine's regime appeared in his first play *The Brigadier* (1769) demonstrating the ignorance, brutality and primitive ways of the gentry.

Serfdom was a kind of indentured servitude where the peasant class worked for the overlord. It was not unlike serfdom in the middle ages where the lord might offer you protection, a bit of money, and the land you would harvest. As a serf you had no legal rights and were under the control of your master; and if the master wanted the wife of a serf, the master had every right to bed her before her husband. *The Brigadier* deals with a matchmaking in which everybody wants to marry everybody else, except the perspective bride and groom. The wedding guests are happily coupled up, but the bride and groom can't stand one another. It pointedly addresses the effete French fashions that have come into Russia, only to effeminize Russian men. It talks about the good old boys of Russian society who deny anything new because change gets in the way of solid Russian ideals. In addition, it satirizes the stupidity of the Russian middle class—the landowners, or so-called "new nobility." The play was extremely popular and, because it was so well written, the people who were the object of Fonvizin's attacks didn't really realize it.

As time progressed, Fonvizin began to describe Catherine's regime as one in which every citizen must be either a victim or an oppressor. When the Czarina got wind of that, she fired him. Undaunted, the author retired to devote himself to polemical and satirical writings, of which *A Comprehensive*

Grammar for the Courtier (1785), a long text about flattery and sycophancy, is a good example.

Fonvizin's most important and influential play was *The Minor*, a five-act comedy written in 1781 and considered the first truly seminal Russian play by the likes of Nicolai Gogol and Anton Chekhov. Produced in 1782, *The Minor* exhibits a rather stereotypical plot: Sofya, an orphaned ward turns out to be an heiress, and the greedy landowners who have given her a place to live, want to marry her off, first to the landowner's brother whose only interest in life is the raising of pigs, and then to their spoiled moronic son, Mitrofan. Mitrofan's adoring mother is Mrs. Protakov, a kind of "Wicked Witch of the West," who becomes the target of the author's satire on the matriarchy of Russian society. She beats her husband, whips her servants, and dotes on a good-for-nothing son. Ultimately, the play ends happily with Sofya marrying the man she loves—a noble Russian soldier. This gives us an indication of how highly regarded the soldier class was in Russian society. If you wanted to be honest and noble, you would fight for your country.

The Minor accomplished a great deal in terms of satire and the development of sentimentality:

1) It satirized the Czarina's court. It displayed the selfishness of the upper class, and the circuitous route of getting to court: a person has to flatter a variety of people and grease the palms of others;

2) It emphasized the noble soldier motif;

3) It ridiculed the landowner class, the upper middle class;

4) It was highly anti-intellectual. Prostakov wants her son to learn everything he has to know to be a good citizen. When one of the tutors comes to teach him geography, she says, "Why should a young man clutter his mind with such things as geography when a person in his position can just hail a cab and give the coachman the address where he wants to be driven?" At another point she says, "I want you to teach him all there is to know in world history. You've got the weekend";

5) It supported the servant class. As in every Molière play, the servants are the good guys;

6) It abounded in sentimental recognition scenes and advocated sentimental morality: honesty, obedience, respect, virtue, and the natural goodness of the common man (very much like what was going on in England and France at the same time);

7) It employed *commedia* lazzi. In the eighteenth century one could not escape the *commedia dell'arte* anywhere in Europe;

8) It employed dialect humor;

9) It exhorted a great ruler—a ruler who can see through the flattery and all the dishonesty at court. What was the author doing? He was doing exactly what Molière did at the end of his plays by having the King (or his minister) come in and say, "You all can't solve the problem. I'll solve it for you." Only a great ruler was able see through the hearts of everyone.

The Minor is a very interesting piece because the fourth act is literally a treatise on morality. You could do the play without the fourth act and very little would be missing. Although Fonvizin creates three-dimensional characters in the body of the play, his polemical purpose in writing the play is never absent. In addition, the play is a satire on prearranged marriages, and, not unlike England and France during the period, love gives way to concerns about money because the essential interests of the middle class are money and upward mobility. Many critics have suggested that *The Minor* is the prototype of Russian realistic theatre. Whether or not it actually deserves such a claim, it is a play that had a great impact on nineteenth-century Russian playwrights and one that still might engender laughter in production, even today.

13. Romantic Drama throughout Europe in the 19th Century

At the end of the eighteenth century, France was in a great flux politically. After the Revolution that decapitated the King, the First Republic was followed by an Empire which was followed by a return to a monarchy which was followed by a Second Republic then a Second Empire until finally the Third Republic ended the nineteenth century. The political musical chairs had a profound effect on the drama. Whoever happened to be on the throne, whether in a republic or a monarchy or an empire, the theatre somehow had to please the tastes of the various monarchs. As a result, drama followed several interesting paths during the period:

1) Neoclassicism, for those who enjoyed old-fashioned, conservative plays;

2) Romanticism, for those who sought innovation, and freedom of expression and emotion;

3) Realism, which occurred at the end of the century, for those who felt the drama should depict ordinary people doing ordinary things.

Napoleon favored classical drama and, between 1800 and 1830, Neoclassicism vied with melodrama, a form which would grow up in the minor theatres as the prominent theatrical form. After 1830, Romanticism became the primary form. During this period, French theatre, not unlike the English theatre, was divided into major and minor houses. Between 1800 and 1807, Napoleon had established a system of theatres similar to that in the eighteenth century with a few large subsidized houses. These were the major theatres and their names were: the Odéon, the Comédie Française, the Opéra, and the Opéra Comique. The Opéra was just for serious operatic fare; the Comédie Française was for regular (typically five-act) tragedy and comedy; the Opéra Comique was for the vaudevilles and the lighter musical comedy work; and the Odéon was the only other theatre where serious plays were allowed to be performed. These were the major houses, and they were dominated by Neoclassicism in philosophy, repertoire, and style of production. Napoleon also established minor houses for more popular entertainment, and they were rigidly restricted in what they could offer (very much like what was happening in England). On 16 November of 1799, Napoleon banned all propaganda plays and, in 1800, he guaranteed the Comédie Française possession of their building, although they still had to pay rent. In 1801, state funds were allocated for pensions and insurance for actors and in 1803, rules were established for debuts, retirements, and pensions, as well as the selection of new plays and profit sharing between performers. In 1804, the Comédie Française was rechristened the Theatre de l'Empereur (Theatre of the Emperor), and very significantly in the history of acting, in 1805, actors' names were announced on playbills, in an attempt to stimulate business. Up to that point in France, actors' names were not given on the playbill, just the name of the play, the author, the set and costume designers, and anyone else who contributed to the physical production.

In 1807, Napoleon closed the minor theatres because they were becoming too popular, and because the plays they presented were more than slightly problematic. These were theatres where satire would abound. Although the minor theatres were closed, four were left open: the Ambigue Comique, the Gaité, the Vaudeville, and the Variétés. These were probably the only theatres that were not producing any controversial material at the time and were therefore considered safe. These particular houses flourished with melodrama, farces, and pantomimes; and the Vaudeville and Variétés were especially popular for presenting peasant plays and musical entertainments.

Dramatists were encouraged by Napoleon to use classical themes and produce imitations of Racine and Molière, to which end, he established dramatic contests (Best New Comedy, The Best New Tragedy). Unfortunately, the plays that were produced were arid imitations of the classics that no one wanted to see, but the Emperor was very pleased. In 1814, the Allies seeking to restore the French monarchy entered Paris (Napoleon was not terribly popular with everyone), and a great number of Royalist plays began to appear on every stage. The following year, the Superintendent of Spectacles, a post that was established during the Revolution, became a Royal Commissioner. A very important play appeared in 1817 entitled *Germanicus*. The play itself was inoffensive, but unfortunately the playwright was a good friend of Napoleon in exile. The playwright's friends went to the theatre wearing Napoleonic colors, but an actress wore the Bourbon or royalist colors in the play. As a result, the audience quickly became divided into rival political camps, and a major riot ensued. The opening night caused so much turmoil that the play itself was forbidden to be performed again, and sticks and canes were banned in all theatres.

In 1824, when Charles X came into power, freedom of the press was restored in France, but censorship of the theatre was maintained vigorously. New authors were few and hired claques dominated audiences. Feuds between members of the Comédie Française became debilitating to the company, and in the middle of a great feud between two titanic actors over the lead in a play in 1823, Baron Isidore Taylor, a military hero and archeologist, was hired to take charge of the Comédie Française. Taylor's theatrical experience had been relegated to minor boulevard entertainment, and he approached the problem of poor attendance at the major theatre by trying to inject it with what was working in the minor theatres—spectacle. In the production of a play called *Léonidas*, he established a kind of middle ground between the spectacular melodramas of minor entertainment and the neoclassical tragedy of the major houses. *Léonidas*, produced in 1823/24, had a classical subject and a classical form, but it violated unity of place. In addition, it was romantic and emotional enough to appeal to those people who were tired of the old tradition. Trading on the 1821 Greek revolt against the Turks (the one that Lord Byron was fighting in) the production of *Léonidas* used scenery that exhibited a concern for local color and historical accuracy. Up to that point, local color and historical accuracy had really been the province of the minor houses because they were the ones doing the satires, spectacles, and peasant plays. The designs were created by a man named **Pierre-Luc-Charles Ciceri**. (1782-1868) who began to design for the boulevard theatres in about 1820, and excelled in romantic designs depicting exotic foreign cities, ruined castles, desolate mountain passes, and the like. When he produced that kind of gothic-romantic scenery for the Comédie Française, Ciceri began a kind of changeover of the neoclassical play into what would become romantic drama ten years later.

Melodrama and Vaudeville

While the major theatres were becoming more spectacular and exotic, the minor houses were flourishing with a new theatrical genre called *melodrama*. Melodrama was first used as a term in 1766 by Jean Jacques Rousseau as a synonym of "opera" and, in a looser sense, a play where music interrupts the dialogue. By the end of the eighteenth century, melodrama as we know it did not come out of any musical form, but out of the dialogue pantomimes of the 1780s and 1790s. The dialogue pantomime was a way of skirting the rules of what may or may not be played at a minor theatre. Regular plays in three or five acts were forbidden, but pantomime-like acrobatics were allowed. Therefore, if a minor theatre wanted to produce a French tragedy it had to produce the play only in pantomime, like a ballet with musical accompaniment. That kind of thing which involved spectacle, musical underscore, and exotic settings gave way to what we now call melodrama. After 1791, when the dialogue pantomimes were no longer needed to skirt the rules, the visual aspect of these productions, the scenery as well as pantomime was so well established that neither audiences nor actors would tolerate a shift to a more literary form of drama. So that even when theaters were allowed to perform complete plays, the audience wanted the pantomimic melodrama. Many of the plot situations and basic characterizations of melodrama were already well established by the 1790s, such as the persecuted heroine, the evil guardian, and the noble rescuer. The German *sturm und drang* movement contributed an interest in rebels and outcasts, and the English Gothic revival provided exciting effects, such as the apparition of ghosts, suits of armor that come alive, and so forth. Musical numbers, such as songs and ballets were added as additional decorative elements in the late 1790s as well.

By 1799, audiences were turning away from gothic horror and exotic fancy to adaptations of sentimental bourgeois dramas, especially the plays by Kotzebue. The first and most successful dramatist to combine the new interest in sentimentality with the old melodramatic form was **Gilbert de Pixérécourt** (1773-1844) in a melodrama called *Coelina, Child of Mystery*. *A Tale of Mystery* by Thomas Holcroft is an exact English translation of this play, and the first play in English which is called a melodrama. The *Child of Mystery* involves Coelina driven from her home on the day of her marriage to the son of her guardian because a jealous suitor calls her illegitimate. She flees in shame (and in disguise), but the villain is revealed to have been duplicitous and is captured after a spectacular battle involving a group of archers against a mountain panorama. At the end of the play, Coelina is united with her fiancé and begs forgiveness for the villain of the piece. The play was performed 387 times in a row in Paris (at a time when 75 performances was regarded as a huge hit), and it played over a thousand times in the provinces. *Coelina* racked up about 1476 performances within the lifetime of the author and helped Pixérécourt establish the traditional hero, heroine, and tyrant as archetypes of melodrama. In addition, he added sufficient sentimentality to make the hero and heroine the models of goodness and middle-class behavior, and for comic relief, he added a fourth character called the *niais*. This is the archetype of the simpleton character, the village idiot who is always allied with the hero. In *The Drunkard*, an American melodrama, the *niais* is the character who has no sense but ends up being the hero of the piece, almost unwittingly. He is not stupid—he is simply too innocent to have any sense of the world—rather like Gilligan of the *Gilligan's Island* television series.

The similarity of the *niais* to Gothic romances which were pervasive in English literature, did not present anything new in France, but the fact that Pixérécourt was mixing genres in French theatre, in other words, melding a serious formula with a comic device was something that was extremely unusual and was very *avant-garde* at the time. Pixérécourt was never subtle. All actions in his plays were violent, simple, direct, and frequently underscored by a variety of musical styles. If you look at a Pixérécourt script you will see the indications, "sad music," "noble music," "music of torture." There's even a cue for "music of a distressed mind." Clearly, he is attempting to develop a kind of drama that will appeal not only to the intellect but very much to the emotions.

Among Pixérécourt's most popular plays is *The Dog of Montargis*, produced in 1814. A blind boy is falsely condemned for murder but he's saved from the scaffold by a dog that recognizes the murderer and barks at him. How many times have we seen this plot on television in *Lassie* or *Rin Tin Tin* or *Benji*? Pixérécourt was also very interested in historical subjects. He produced a melodrama called *Christopher Columbus* in 1815 based on the writings of Columbus's son. However, Pixérécourt's concern for historical accuracy didn't prevent him from taking artistic license to create spectacular effects. Instead, he would write an essay in the program providing the exact history of the event so that he did not feel morally or ethically unjustified about changing it when it appeared on stage. He would argue, "This is what it really was. Now I'm going to give you my interpretation of it." He seldom took more than 20 days to write a play, more often he took about a week, and he spent more of his time developing the scenic effects for the individual productions rather than the plotting of the play. In *Tekeli*, for example, he insisted on a realistic river for the second act because someone had to float down the river on a pile of logs. *Christopher Columbus* required a two-story ship with complete rigging and only eight theaters in France were equipped to produce the play. In *The Daughter of Exile* in 1819, Pixérécourt required a flood scene with the heroine floating offstage on a plank, and *The Head of Death* in 1827 featured an eruption of Mount Vesuvius with a lava flow on stage. Characters were literally engulfed in the molten lava.

Pixérécourt's major rivals in melodrama were Caigniez and Ducange, and both of them were extremely influenced by the work of Pixérécourt. They differed from him as they were much more interested in the domestic problems of the little man rather than the large-scale spectacles that Pixérécourt preferred. For example, Victor Ducange's most famous work was *Thirty Years; or, The Life of a Gambler*, and Louis Caigniez's most famous play was *The Illustrious Blind Man*, again dealing with the little man in a domestic situation.

The only challenge to the melodrama of this period came from another form of theatre called *vaudeville*. In 1792, two men, Piis and Barre, produced a new theatre called the Vaudeville to present a form of light comedy, thoroughly decorated in song. Until Napoleon, this light vaudeville entertainment had been based on social issues and political concerns, but by 1804, the genre turned to literary satire or broad depictions of the lower classes. The person who brought vaudeville to the forefront of French theatre was **Eugène Scribe** (1791-1861) who we will come to again when we deal with the Well-Made Play. Scribe became interested in the theatre while studying law and first found success with a play produced in 1812 called *The Inn*. Encouraged by the success of this play, he experimented with melodrama and comic opera, both of which attempts were terrible disasters. However, in 1814, he produced a vaudeville called *A Night with the National Guard*. Published in 1815, it became the first in a series of triumphs. Scribe revolutionized the vaudeville by breaking away from traditional subjects and stock characters to present a sketch of real contemporary life. And he produced these sketches of real life in brilliantly articulated plots, witty dialogue, and well-constructed verse. He took a popular form and gave it literary merit, bringing together vaudeville and traditional comedy. In 1819 he stopped writing vaudevilles and started to develop what we call the Well-Made Play (discussed below). The genre, however, continued to attract audiences with staged anecdotes, and sentimental pieces all closely related to real life.

Spectacle Houses

There was great potential for the minor theatres to make money with vaudevilles, melodramas, and other kinds of musical entertainments, so the minor theatres that were ultimately closed by Napoleon tried to resist his rulings. Two of the theatres that challenged the 1807 closing of minor theatres were in fact allowed to stay open. One was the Cirque Olympique and the other was the Porte-Saint-Martin. Laurent Franconi, who directed the Cirque Olympique, argued that Napoleon's ruling against the minor theatres only applied to *theatres* and since his room was a circus involving animal acts as well as actors, it could not possibly apply to him. As a result, Franconi created elaborate pantomimes and spectacles which had literary as well as dramatic merit. As a matter of fact, Alexander Dumas *père* wrote *Caligula* for the Cirque Olympique where Caligula's horse had the leading role. Dialogue began to creep in at the Cirque Olympique about 1815, and after the restoration of the monarchy in 1815, minor theatres were allowed to reopen. What's important here is that again when the audience came to the Cirque Olympique, even though they were allowed to see plays, they wanted to see the animal acts. They wanted to see historical pageants. They wanted to see the kinds of things they were used to. As a result, an amorphous kind of theatre would begin to develop in which spectacular elements might be woven into a classical tragedy (we will find the same thing in England when theatre managers would interpolate real animals into productions of Shakespeare's plays).

The Porte-Saint-Martin was the only theatre in Paris that actively decided to resist Napoleon's law. While the Cirque Olympique felt it had a loophole in the law, the Porte-Saint-Martin actually argued against it. It had been given the first rights to melodrama in Paris and felt that, having managed to sustain a large audience, it deserved to remain open. After two years of petitioning the government, in 1809 the theatre was allowed to reopen, presenting acrobatics, historical tableaux, military displays, and prologues. Needless to say, gradually the Porte-Saint-Martin began to interpret these elements more broadly and real plays began being added to the repertoire. As a result, the theatre was closed again in 1811. It was reopened yet again in 1815 and became noted for spectacular productions, under the directorship of J. T. Merle and scenery by Ciceri (the Porte-Saint-Martin was where Ciceri first started to develop his romantic scenery). One of the more significant plays produced at this theatre was a piece in 1826 that Merle adapted from Mary Shelley's *Frankenstein* called *The Monster and the Magician*. In this play, the monster swallowed ships whole, set fire to villages, let loose tempests, floods, and lightening. Later in an adaptation of Goethe's *Faust*, the stage of the Porte-Saint-Martin was divided in half to depict hell and paradise, one on top of the other.

After 1800, many theatres devoted to light entertainments sprang up in Paris designed to produce spectacle rather than actual plays. In 1804, the Théâtre Pittoresque was opened by Louis-Jacques Daguerre to present sunrise gardens, pictures of streets and famous buildings, but no plays. In 1822, the Diorama opened and attracted audiences with a huge painting, about 65 feet long and 42 feet high, lit from various angles to create a variety of effects. The chief draw was a piece called "Midnight Mass at St. Etienne," created by screens, shutters, and transparent cloths (scrims). As it was lit from the front or the back, you could see drawings on the scrim and the screens. People were depicted going into the church before the service and leaving the building once mass was done.

The most important of the spectacle theatres was the Panorama Dramatique. This house was significant to the theatre because it was allowed to produce dramas, comedies, and vaudevilles as long as there were never more than two speaking actors on the stage at one time. This is very much like Charles Ludlam's *Mystery of Irma Vep* where two characters play all the roles, constantly going in and out of various disguises. Other non-speaking actors were allowed on stage at the Panorama Dramatique, very much like in the Greek formula, but the two-actor rule was strictly adhered to in dialogue scenes. The principal writer for this theatre was Isadore Taylor who subsequently became the director for the Comédie Française. In the years between 1815 and 1830, the minor houses produced 369 new comedies, 200 new melodramas, 200 new comic operas, and 1300 new vaudevilles. During the same period, only 72 new classical tragedies were performed in the major houses. What does that tell us about audience preferences? They wanted the spectacle and melodrama available at the minor theatres.

Romanticism in France

The major source of Romanticism in France was **Jean Jacques Rousseau** (1712–1778). He emphasized the primacy of emotions, what is natural in life, and a zest for political upheaval (violation of rules). However, the greatest shot in the arm that romanticism would get socially and culturally was the French Revolution because it ruptured all of the old forms of government, and the cultural and philosophical models that attended an aristocratic formula. The new bourgeoisie evoked by the French Revolution was much more in tune with Romanticism than the more formal Neoclassicism of the monarchy. So, what is Romanticism?

1) First thing you should note about Romanticism as a movement is that it has a major contempt for rules;

2) A great emphasis is placed on the imagination. For the romantic author, the art of creation is every bit as important as the work itself;

3) It also deals with a harmony with nature. We have a reemphasis on what is "natural" in life;

4) The examination of nature gives us a revelation of truth;

5) The concerns of Romanticism are with the mystical and the spiritual, the sublime and the grotesque.

French Romanticism was given a major impetus in the 1820s at the Porte-Saint-Martin theatre when, in 1822, J. T. Merle organized a guest appearance of an all English troupe. England was still widely hated in France, just as France was hated in England, and the French audiences regarded the troupe as inflammatory. The English company performed *Othello* and very little of the play could be heard because the audience was shouting all the way through it. Some of spectators even said, "Down with Shakespeare, he's a flunky of Wellington" which is rather humorous given Wellington's defeat of Napoleon. The English also produced *The School for Scandal* but it fared no better, even though the author was Irish

Fortunately, in 1827, the Paris public was ready to see English performers. There had been a smoothing out of relations between the two countries and there were a variety of newspaper articles that made Shakespeare a more interesting figure to the French. Emile Laurent managed to convince the Odéon Theatre and later the Théâtre Italienne, to produce a tour of a company put together of English actors from Covent Garden, Drury Lane, and the Haymarket Theatre. On September 11, 1927, the amalgamated company produced Shakespeare's *Hamlet*, with Charles Kemble in the title role. The following week Charles Kemble played Romeo in *Romeo and Juliet* and the title role in *Othello*. Remember J. T. Merle attempted an *Othello* in 1822; that's what got the ball rolling. The French people didn't much care for the play then, but in 1827 it became an immediate hit. French audiences adored Kemble for two reasons: he was one of the best-known names in the English theatre and his leading lady was Constance Harriet Smithson. Not only was she a great actress (she played Ophelia to Kemble's Hamlet), but she was also a great beauty. Hector Berlioz wrote his *Symphony Fantastique* for her and, in 1833, married her, causing her to leave the stage.

In 1828, William Macready, the English actor, arrived and presented *Macbeth*. He was followed by Edmund Kean who played Richard III, Shylock, and King Lear. The newspaper that reviewed these performances said, "Never has the French seen such violence, such mad scenes, such stage fighting, such unleashing of emotions." Please remember that up to this point,

French theatre acting was essentially "stand down center and orate." Occasionally if a character did something with a realistic detail, the audience created a riot. Suddenly, Paris audiences could see the English style of performance with real sword play and actors who were hurling themselves to the ground in order to create an emotional response in the spectators. Before the English season was finished, English mannerisms could be detected in some of the young actors of the minor theatres. This is important because the actors of the major theatres were the last to absorb the innovations. In the charged atmosphere of the English performances, Victor Hugo created a play called *Cromwell* and wrote a preface which embodied his ideas of dramatic reform. What he sought to do was to unify the grotesque and the sublime aspects of human nature and put them together in the same play. This would have been a violation to the classicists because it was against the rules to meld tragedy and comedy together. The grotesque is clearly the subject of comedy because it is "less than we are." While Hugo was doing this, Alexander Dumas *père* began a romantic drama, *Christine*. It would not be long for the new trend to affect the major theatres. And between 1828 and 1837, romantic plays were actually performed at the Comédie Française.

The first significant work of the new trend at the Comédie Française was a play called *Henri III* by Alexander Dumas, *père*. It was written in 1828 and produced on 11 February 1829. It was his fourth play, a sprawling historical pageant conspicuously plagiarized from Sir Walter Scott and Schiller. Classicists became irate. In the second act, an actor fires at another with a pea shooter. In the third act, a character crushes his wife's hand with an iron gauntlet on stage. Such stage violence was anathema to the classicists. Despite a petition circulated by the major classical dramatists to have this play stopped, the play ran 38 performances and a vogue for romantic drama had begun. In 1829, Alfred Davini's play *The Moor of Venice*, his version of *Othello*, made concessions to classicism with simple settings and furnishings, but it was romantic enough to engender protests during every one of its thirteen performances. Its most unusual characteristic was that it used words that had not been used previously in French classical tragedy. For example, it used the word "handkerchief," not a word that was used in French classical tragedy because it was something used to blow your nose. It was something that was grotesque to the French. Davini used the word and the audience rioted. Some people applauded; others demanded the play be stopped because of that word. Davini also created a realistic drunken scene for Cassio with Cassio falling over, slurring his words. Moreover, the French audience was offended that the poetry (remember tragedies were *always* written in verse) wasn't spoken in clear articulate fashion.

Dumas, *père*

Alexander Dumas *père* (1802–1870) was a grandson of a Haitian woman. He fathered Dumas *fils* during a slight affair with a seamstress whom, when she was pregnant, he speedily abandoned (Dumas *fils* would write a lot of plays about bastard children being left by their parents). *Christine* was his first serious play written in response to the performances of the English troupe in 1827, and it was subsequently performed in 1830. *Henri III* was the most significant of his early plays because it was the first tragedy at the Comédie Française to have a romantic element in it. *Henri III* uses a very important aspect of local color: the play takes place in 1578 and Dumas asks for historically accurate costumes and period allusions. Why is this so unusual? The classicists argued for universality, morality, and generality. Now the romantics were saying, "Let's get as specific as possible." Dumas *père* was the initiator of romantic historical drama and also the inventor of the modern drama of passion. In *Antony* written in 1831, he composed "a drama in modern dress." The play is about a Byronic hero who, being a bastard without his biological father or mother, decides that since he has to live on the outskirts of society, why must he pay attention to society's rules? The classicists would write that character off immediately as a villain, or argue that he is doomed. Not so in this play. Antony manages through the entire play to skirt the social requirements of proper behavior: he has affairs; he murders people; though, he finally gets caught in the end because of a situation from which he cannot escape. But the whole sense of the play is not "this kind of behavior will doom you," something you'd expect from classicism. *Antony* exhibits blind passion, adultery, violent death (all on stage), and it is regarded by some critics as the first example of a modern adultery play, complete with the smashing of windows, breaking of doors, and murders. After 1832, Dumas would suffer a loss of literary stature and have a great deal of trouble getting plays produced. As a result, he turned to writing novels in 1839 with *The Three Musketeers* and *The Count of Monte Cristo*.

Victor Hugo
On the other hand, Victor Marie Hugo (1802–1885), who now is best known as the author of *Les Misérables*, was the acknowledged leader of French Romanticism. His professional life falls into five distinct periods:

1) 1819–1827, an early experimental period with Classicism;
2) 1827–1843, the period of greatest contribution to the drama;
3) 1843–1851, the Political period;
4) 1851–1870, the period of the great novels; and
5) 1870–1885, the retirement when he became the grand old man of Parisian letters, venerated, and idealized.

Hugo had his creative roots in Neoclassicism with which he experimented in the first period. However, his classical verse gradually gave way to a warm, personal, exotic mode of poetry. He was less interested in the structure of the language than in the imagination and the putting of odd words together—to put something which would be grotesque together with something which is quite beautiful. In *Hernani*, for example, when the protagonists are dying, Dona Sol remarks about the grotesqueness of the poison killing her, the kind of thing that the classicists would never talk about. The second period began with the publication of *Cromwell*, the preface of which championed a free, outspoken style of dramatic poetry that would embrace both tragedy and comedy, the sublime and the grotesque. Hugo sought to reproduce a Shakespearean drama for the French. He also sought to eliminate the traditional caesura in the French dramatic line. French tragedy was always written in Alexandrine verse, six feet of iambic hexameter. In speaking the poetry, actors always took a pause at the end and in the middle of the line. Hugo felt that such conventions were unrealistic, and wanted to encourage the smoother, subtler, more natural rhythms of language.

Hernani opened on 25 February 1830 at the Comédie Française. Hugo's claque was admitted to the theatre at 2:00 p.m. in an attempt to tire them out before the curtain went up at 7:00. After the opening line of the play (which did not observe the traditional pauses in verse structure), the audience rioted and stopped the performance for a half hour. Then, when another character began speaking in the middle of a line, interrupting the sequence of the verse, this was just as reprehensible to the audience. Later in the play, Hernani actually delivered a line upstage with his back to the audience who responded with hoots and boos and the play had to halt yet again. By trying to recreate the movement of the English stage using curves and diagonals, rather than the back and forth downstage movement of French classical tragedy, and by actually having characters disregard the audience, a practice that is going to become prevalent at the end of the nineteenth century in realism and naturalism, Victor Hugo initiated the romantic tradition of stage production. From this point on, the war waged between the old guard and the new.

What was unusual about *Hernani*? First of all, there was violence on stage. Secondly, the play violated every neoclassical rule of decorum. For example, in neoclassical plays, a king would not hide in a closet. In *Hernani*, he does! In addition, the play employed specific costuming and time periods. For example, one stage direction read: "She ushers him in. He drops his cloak and reveals a rich dress of silk and velvet in the Castilian style of 1519." There existed onstage violence throughout and there were also several references to the grotesque. Late in the play, the heroine Dona Sol remarked, "Oh, my Don Juan, this drug is potent. In the heart it wakes a hydra with a thousand tearing teeth devouring it. I knew not that such pangs could be." To the French that would be terribly grotesque and apparently Victor Hugo directed the actress to say it with an unnatural voice as if she was possessed by great pain. What about the settings? Was there unity of place? Each act had a different setting. What about unity of time? All that actually happened in the play was virtually impossible within 24 hours. Characters were neither all good nor all bad but something in between, another very significant influence from Shakespeare. And to be sure, the play wallowed in great emotionalism, hence the suggestion of melodrama for a contemporary audience. However, what appears to be melodramatic to us was viewed as tragic in the early nineteenth century. Like Shakespeare, Hugo tried to commingle that which was tragic and comic in human experience. As a result, many critics have said that Hugo's most distinguishing trait as a playwright was his conception of life as a series of paradoxes and antithesis. To emphasize this, he made extensive use of disguise. Virtually everyone in the play appeared in disguise at one point or another. Although his characters did seem somewhat larger than life, they were certainly more "realistic" to the nineteenth century than the highly rational archetypes of neoclassical tragedy.

While the war between romantics and neoclassicists was raging at the Comédie Française, a new political revolution was taking place in 1830: King Charles X abdicated and Louis Phillippe took over. Theatrical censorship was abandoned, but by 1831, a law had to be passed to protect living persons from being portrayed on stage. In 1835, there was an abortive attempt at assassinating the King, and even stricter restrictions were placed on the theatre with the election of a board of censors. After *Hernani*, Hugo produced a number of plays: *The King Amuses Himself* which became the Verdi opera, *Rigoletto*, and three very mediocre prose plays written for his mistress—*Lucrecia Borgia*, *Marie Tudor*, and *Angelo, Ruler of Padua*. By 1837, Romanticism as a dramatic movement in France was already on the decline. And in 1838, Victor Hugo took a lease on the Salle Ventadour to try to recapture the impetus of Romanticism. He renamed it the Theatre of the Renaissance and its opening production was his play *Ruy Blas*. The financial backer of the theatre felt that Romanticism had run its course and did not want to continue producing romantic plays there. Therefore, whenever *Ruy Blas* was presented, the heating didn't work, the orchestra played out of tune, the claque hissed. After the theatre's major actor left, the Theater of the Renaissance only produced musical comedies.

Hugo's *Ruy Blas* deals with a commoner who, disguised as a nobleman, takes the Queen as a lover. The villain of the piece, a Marquis attempts to capitalize on the situation, blackmailing the Queen in order to keep the affair silent. To save the Queen embarrassment, Ruy Blas kills the Marquis and takes poison himself. The idea of a commoner killing a Marquis was highly unrealistic to the French classicists, as was a character taking poison on stage. And a Queen actually being in love with a commoner was viewed as a significant breach of decorum and taste. The poetry was called ranting, and one critic concluded "romantic drama is nothing but melodrama ennobled by verse."

Victor Hugo left the theatre and between 1843 and 1851 wrote a number of political tracts. During this period, Louis Napoleon set himself up as the President of the Second Republic. But Victor Hugo, seeing that Louis Napoleon had pretensions to even greater glory, decided to go into exile in 1851. From 1851 to 1870, during the Second Empire in France, he was an exile in the Channel Islands where he composed *Les Misérables*. With the coming of the Third Republic in 1870, Hugo returned to France as the intellectual leader of the age. He appraised himself as a genius whose function was to inspire mankind to liberate itself from the tyranny of society. To that end he wrote *Torquemada* a play about the Spanish Inquisition

Between 1830 and 1850 in Paris, the major houses opened at 7:00 at night but the boulevard or minor theatre programs usually started earlier at 5:15 or 5:30 because a police decree in 1834 ruled that all theatres be closed by 11:00. The audience had become inundated with spectacle, and every theatre was equipped with a well-organized claque. These were a group of people hired to praise or damn a play. The claque had a leader who would attend rehearsals so that he could schedule the applause at the appropriate parts during the play. He would sit among the claque in the pit and organize the rabble rousers, very much like the warm-up announcer (or the applause sign) in television shows. Theatre performance had developed into a highly melodramatic, organic response between stage and audience.

Between 1830 and 1850, the Cirque Olympique was the major theatre devoted to spectacle because it was the only house in Paris that could comfortably present a Napoleonic battle complete with horses. Even though the Cirque Olympique had a permanent company of 100 actors and 30 horses, the scenery was still the major concern. Technical and production elements at the theatre were handled by two of Ciceri's best students, Philastre and Cambon, a machinist whose name was Sacre, and a lighting designer named Desmarais. At this theatre a play was produced in 1832 called *The Republic, the Empire, and the 100 Days* for which 40 separate sets were designed. Another play in 1834 called *Za Ze Zi Zo Zu* featured an infernal ballet in an enchanted palace, and an underwater spectacle. In 1837, the play *Austerlitz* included a panorama which showed the entire city of Paris. When night fell over the city, lights appeared in the windows of various houses. Finally, in 1839, came *The Pills of the Devil* which had a train that rolled onstage and exploded. There is little wonder that the journals of this period talked about the scenery more than the literary merit of these plays, and how, at the end of a performance, the audience would shout out "Machinist!" rather than "Author," or "Actor." They wanted to see who developed the fascinating machinery. The machinist was really the special effects designer of his day, and he became, in the mid-nineteenth century, the great artist of the theatre, in place of the author or actor.

What does this say about the dramatic literature of the Romantic Movement? It begins to disintegrate. Romanticism was virtually coming to a dead halt and returning to spectacle and melodrama. Romanticism only began around 1830 and by 1850, it was dead and gone. Shortly after 1850, even the minor houses began reassessing the commercial problems of producing romantic plays, instead of doing musical theatre pieces or purely spectacular kinds of shows. Ultimately, what we have at the end of this period is a turn toward a more realistic approach to the art of theatre, obvious through the increased use of "realistic" spectacle. What we will find when we return to France is a kind of domestic play which stresses regular structure, simple and natural situations, and an unaffected tone in a kind of dramatic writing called

"The School of Good Sense." Like everything else, once spectacular theatre reached its height, the pendulum began to swing in the other direction. Realism would emerge, reproducing domestic situations rather than spectacular visuals.

Romanticism in Germany

As a conscious movement, romanticism in Germany dates from 1798, the year when Goethe and Schiller started to work together in Weimar and when a literary journal called *Das Anthenaeum* was published. This magazine set out the basic principles of German romanticism:

1) Truth is defined in terms of the infinity of existence rather than in observable norms. What this meant, behind all earthly phenomenon there lies a higher truth, because all that exists was created by an absolute being. There is a strong sense of deism in German romanticism;

2) Since all creation has a common origin, a careful observation of any part may give insight into the whole. What this is going to signify is our tendency to look at a tree and see it as a symbol for society. Looking at the organic principle of a tree can give us the concept of the organism of the body. The less spoiled a thing is, the less it deviates from its natural state. Therefore, the more likely it is to embody some fundamental truth. This is going to give rise to the German affection for the primitive, the noble savage. Many of these characteristics are going to be generally true for romanticism throughout Europe;

3) Human existence is formed of dualities, for example, the traditional ones—body/soul, physical/spiritual, and so on. Because of duality, humanity is divided against himself. Human beings live in a physical universe but the soul seeks to transcend it. Art is important because it is a way that man may free himself momentarily from everyday existence. For the Germans, art was the ability to coalesce the physical and the spiritual;

4) To appreciate the unity behind the apparent diversity of existence requires an exceptional imagination, and the only place such an imagination is

found is in the genius/artist or the philosopher. This is a development of the *sturm und drang* philosophy that the artist or playwright is God;

5) Happiness and truth are to be found in a spiritual realm. They are impossible to achieve in life. This concept will help to explain why most of the German romantic playwrights died between 24 and 35 years of age (and often by suicide);

6) The spirit is eternal and infinite. Man's mind is limited and can never encompass truth in totality.

The members of the German Romantic Movement that were concerned with drama were **August Wilhelm Schlegel** (1767-1845) and **Ludwig Tieck** (1773-1853). Schlegel was an important theorist who had a great appreciation for Shakespeare, and translated seventeen of his plays. As a critic, he paid little attention to dramatic form, but felt that the dramatist should emphasize tragic and comic moods as opposed to dramatic structure. He believed that mood, emotion, and character were the main ingredients of drama. For Schlegel, plot was simply a contrived device to keep a play moving. These ideas will be very influential to playwriting of the 19th century.

Tieck, on the other hand, had great interest in Elizabethan drama and the *fiabe* of Carlo Gozzi. He wrote several (what he called) fantastic comedies that satirized eighteenth-century rationalism and theatre practices. In his play *Bluebeard the Knight*, for example, he deals with the real and the imaginary, the long ago and far away as well as the contemporary, farce, horror, pathos, and spectacle. The characterizations are willfully contradictory and erratic. On page one a character is motivated by a particular desire to do something. On page 2 he changes objectives, and goes about doing something completely opposed to everything he said on page one. The play ridicules its own plot, criticizes its author, and ultimately leaves the audience in total confusion. It should come as no surprise that *Bluebeard the Knight* prefigures the surrealistic movement by about 50 or 60 years. A somewhat less problematic play was *Puss in Boots* (1797) which ridiculed contemporary plays and their audiences, and experimented in different genres. Like a play by Shakespeare, a good part of the text is in prose and some of it is poetry. Also, like in Shakespeare, one actor speaking prose will speak to another who replies in poetry. This is very unusual in the German drama at the time. *Zerbino,* a sequel to *Puss in Boots,* followed in 1799. Zerbino, the son and heir of Puss, goes on a pilgrimage in search of good taste. In the process, Zerbino tries to destroy his own play, forcing it to run backwards, until critics, editors, and audience members appear on stage to set things in order. With this and other plays, Tieck is trying to disrupt the concept of "them and us," players in opposition to audience. In the play, both groups are part of the same kind of happening, an experience that prefigures the environmental theatre of the twentieth century.

Perhaps the finest dramatist of German romantic playwrights was **Heinrich von Kleist** (1777–1811). He was not really connected with the Romantic Movement as much as he shared its prejudices against reason and standardized attitudes. His life is perhaps the saddest of any of the playwrights under discussion. He committed suicide in 1811 never having seen any of his plays produced. Not a one. He was never encouraged and completely unknown until Tieck published his work in 1821, ten years after he died. By 1900 he was the most famous of the German playwrights.

Kleist was obsessed with the illusory nature of the world which, he felt, was almost malevolently determined to thwart the expectations of human reasoning. His first play was *The Family Schroffenstein* (1803) where two branches of a princely house destroy each other in mutual suspicion. It's a very simple plot: A law determines that if either line of this family lacks a direct male heir, its possessions will go to the other. Obviously, they gradually kill each other off. *Robert Guiskard*, a tragedy he began in 1803, was burned before he completed it because he was in the midst of one of his characteristic bouts with despair. He was manic depressive and would burn a play if he was having trouble with a line. Next came six very significant plays, the first of which was *The Broken Jug* (1806). Adam, a judge in a small Dutch village, attempts to seduce Eve, a village girl, but is interrupted during the rape by her fiancé, Ruprick. To prevent the act, Ruprick claws the judge on his face and punches him, but does not recognize him. Eve keeps quiet because she's afraid that if Ruprick makes an issue about this, the judge will have him sent away. Ruprick, however, demands that she take the case to court and Eve capitulates. They come into the courtroom and the judge who is trying the case is the judge with the clawed face.

Kleist's next plays were *Amphitryon* (1807), and *Penthesilea* (1808), his most internal play dealing with the love/hate relationship between an Amazon Queen (Penthesilea) and Achilles, filled with cruelty, passion, and irrational behavior. *Katherine Von Heilbronn* (1808) trades on the clichés of standard German romantic drama: a tempest at night, a besieged castle, duels, and clearly defined forces of good and evil (with good being suitably rewarded). Unable to get a play produced earlier, Kleist tried to do something more traditional, writing *Katherine Von Heilbronn* in an attempt to appeal to popular taste. Finally, in 1810, he produced his masterpiece, *Prince Friedrich Von Homburg*, where once again, the hero's fate is in the hands of an external force that seems to thwart all reasonable expectations. Playing into the mysticism of the Romantic Movement, the play turns on sleepwalking and dreams. That's the whole problem with Friedrich. Because he's in love, his comrades play a joke on him, connected to a recurring dream. When his dream appears to come true (as a result of the practical joke), he doesn't hear the orders given him by his commander. He disobeys the orders, and even though his disobedience causes the army to win the war, he is thrown into jail. Gradually as the play progresses, Friedrich admits his wrongdoing, and by the end of the play, he doesn't know if he's alive or dreaming when the Elector pardons him. None of his actions are really indigenous to his own volition. Having made the mistake early on in the play, he ends up at the mercy of exterior forces: for example, the woman he loves tries to plead on his behalf, the Elector tries to lighten his sentence. This begins a kind of tradition which we'll find in the English Romantics involving the Byronic hero who is moody, dreamlike, and acted upon, rather than entirely active. We will find the same sort of thing in the plays of Georg Büchner.

When Napoleon overran Germany and Austria in 1805, an increasingly nationalistic tone began to take shape which was eventually going to lead to a united Germany. When Napoleon was defeated in 1815, repressive political regimes were installed in the German states so they would never be overrun again. Strong censorship discouraged innovations, and the dramatic repertory became inundated with classical plays and harmless new plays. The few significant new writers who appeared were associated with a group called **Young Germany** which emerged in the 1820s out of disillusionment with Romanticism and its philosophies. Young Germany functioned as a transition between romanticism and realism and produced two playwrights who were very important but completely unknown in their own day. The first is **Christian Dietrich Grabbe** (1801–1836) who died at the age of 35, and as a playwright created demonic visions of life, producing a grotesque world suggestive of Shakespeare's *Titus Andronicus*. Among his more famous plays is *Cinderella*, a very dark iteration of the fairy tale, and *Napoleon, or the Hundred Days* which required all of Europe as a stage, and an army of actors. There are about 97 named characters in the play, which is a Brecht-like historical saga. During his career as a playwright, he was the pride of his hometown, Detmold where his play *Don Juan* was performed at the court theatre. Unfortunately, he was only the pride of Detmold and was unable to successfully produce his plays anywhere else, and in 1836, he died of discouragement.

More important to our drama, but who wrote fewer plays, was **Georg Büchner** (1813-1837), the forerunner of Naturalism. He died at the age of 24. He wrote three plays, the first of which was *Danton's Death*, perhaps the best first play in dramatic literature. This play presents again a central figure of a hero who is acted upon by exterior forces. In the play, Danton speaks the philosophy of Büchner: "I feel as though I have been crushed beneath the fatalism of history. I find in human nature a terrifying sameness. In the human condition an inexorable force granted to all and to none. The individual is no more than foam on the wave, greatness mere chance." This is a rather pessimistic view of the inability of an individual man to change history—to amount to anything. Clearly this was Danton's problem in the play. Having helped realize the French revolution, then what? We've revolted, then what? Danton realizes that the only thing he could do, having set a revolution in motion is to become a victim of it. That's the sort of philosophical issue with which these German romantics are dealing. Büchner's second play *Leonce and Lena* was a romantic comedy dealing with a kind of Pierot and Columbine relationship—Leonce and Lena—who are trying to escape everyday existence to live a life of voluptuous languor. Dramatically they were hoping to be able to avoid a preordained marriage by the exertion of their free will. Of course, they lost out in the end.

Büchner's most famous play is *Woyzeck*, written in 1836. It is one of the first plays to treat a lower-class protagonist sympathetically in any language. It depicts the gradual degradation of a man trapped in his heredity and environment. This play would be very significant to the German Naturalists about 50 years later, foreshadowing Naturalism in its subject matter and Expressionism in its structural devices and dialogue. The play is written in very short scenes which do not necessarily have a causal relationship to one another. Büchner died of typhoid fever in 1837 and his fiancée, feeling that some of his plays were too ribald to be preserved, burned them. As a result, all we have of his output are the three plays mentioned above. We know that he wrote a play called *Pietro Aretino* about the Renaissance playwright and author, but it was destroyed by the fiancée because of its profanity.

The German playwright most honored in his lifetime was **Friedrich Hebbel** (1813-1863). Hebbel first accepted Romanticism but, unhappy with its philosophy, he found consolation in his version of the Hegelian dialectic. Hebbel came to view society as a reflection of an absolute spirit which lies behind human existence and works out its own perfection through humanity. He believed in a kind of organic flow of history—history happens no matter what we do. In Hebbel's view, human problems arise because values tend to harden into conventional patterns rather than remaining flexible to meet changing situations. Hebbel viewed history as a series of conflicts, and his plays reflect a preoccupation with moral evolution. This is where Hegel comes in: there is always a thesis (the old guard), an antithesis (the new guard), and a synthesis (Hegel developed the philosophy that all life is the operation of one idea counterpoised by another, and their conflict leads to a synthesis of ideas). Hebbel's plays generally represent the old and new order in which the old has the power of established authority so that the young (or new) order is usually destroyed. However, in its destruction, it foreshadows the death of the old order. Perhaps his most famous play is *Mary Magdalena* (1844). It draws its characters from ordinary life in prose dialogue and ends with the suicide of the heroine because of society's narrow mindedness. Mary Magdalene is representative of the new order and society is the old order. The moment when she kills herself becomes the synthesis between old and new points of view, forcing society to deal with the repercussions of the suicide.

Austrian Playwrights

During this period, Austria also produced a number of notable playwrights. **Franz Grillparzer** (1791-1872) is among the most important. He tended to depression and self-doubt mostly because his mother and one of his three brothers killed themselves in their home. His plays dwell on hubris and vanity and are linked to a profound pessimism about the human condition. He is skeptical about the value of ambition in the individual and the notion that mankind can progress. He philosophically prefigures the Theatre of the Absurd in its sense of the futility of existence, and he's highly pessimistic about our ability to improve ourselves and our situations, or to accomplish anything. Grillparzer's plays essentially deal with characters whose higher ideals come to nothing. Among his notable plays are *The Golden Fleece*, a classical trilogy dealing with Medea and Jason, *Waves of the Sea and Love* (1829), dramatizing the myth of Hero and Leander, and *Woe to Him Who Lies!* (1832).

Somewhat more positive a playwright was **Johann Nepomuk Nestroy** (1801-1862) who wrote dialect farces, the most famous of which is *He Wants to Have A Fling* (1842), significant because it is the basis of Thornton Wilder's play *The Matchmaker*, and thus the precursor of the mega-hit musical, *Hello, Dolly!* His *On the Ground Floor and the First Story* (1835) is very important because of its innovation in terms of scene design: it uses a split-level playing area. The play is also important because it prefigures an *Upstairs/Downstairs* kind of plot. Upstairs is the upper-class family and downstairs are the servants. We find parallel situations in both planes of existence. Another innovative design was necessitated by *The House of Temperaments*, a later play about 4 families, each ruled by a father with a different personality and how different personalities affect the people in their household. *The House of Temperaments* depicts four individual apartments simultaneously on stage. Scenes of family life come together, but there isn't a single protagonist in the whole play.

Ludwig Anzengruber (1839-1889) is very important because he turned the peasant play into a serious picture of real life. All of a sudden, we see real peasants on stage as opposed to idealized, musical comedy peasants. While *The Cross Singers* (1872) was a variation of Aristophanes's *Lysistrata*, Anzengruber found his niche when naturalism called attention to his depiction of characters rooted in their particular environments. Anzengruber is very heavily devoted to environmental determinism—how the environment has an impact on the development of a personality. That will be very significant to the naturalists.

Nineteenth-Century Production Techniques

In Germany, theatrical productions in the nineteenth century begin to use much more historical accuracy, both in settings and in costumes. However, during the first half of the century, to about 1850, only five periods of costumes were sufficient for all historical eras: classical, medieval, sixteenth century, seventeenth century, mid-eighteenth century. All classical costuming from pre-history to medieval period was costumed in the same way. Then all medieval characters were dressed in the same way. They were dealing with fairly large parameters for historical accuracy. More detailed treatments came after 1850 because of the publication of a very important book called *The History of Costume* by Jacob Weiss, published between 1856 and 1872. After 1874, there would be much more specificity in scenery and costumes because of the Meinengen players.

Scenic development began with **Karl Friedrich Schinkel** (1781-1841). He stimulated accuracy in scenery, and he was the best-known architect/scenery designer of his day. He opened a Diorama in Berlin in 1827 patterned on Daguerre's Panorama in France. This was important because it influenced scenery by encouraging the use of still panoramas and moving dioramas at the back of the stage. That would be extremely effective for theatre where instead of having a circular diorama, a long painting that could be rolled up on one end and drawn across the back of the stage could allow an actor to stand in one place and pretend that he is traveling because the set was actually traveling for him. By 1850, several theatre companies became noted for their innovative staging. **Franz Dingelstedt** won acclaim for his Shakespeare productions in Munich; he was the first producer to do the history plays as a cycle. **Friedrich Hasse** won his reputation for a historically accurate production of *Hamlet*. Both of these individuals derived much of their inspiration from the pioneer work of Charles Kean.

Most sets were made of wings and drops, but the box set began to be used with frequency by the mid-century. Not everyone was satisfied with the prevailing theatrical conditions, especially in the climate of the burgeoning realism and historical accuracy. The most important of the innovators seeking higher standards in the theatre were Tieck and Immerman. By 1820, Ludwig Tieck was considered Germany's top authority in the theatre, but his ideas were considered highly impractical. He advocated psychologically realistic acting on a platform stage. He attempted after 1837 to reconstruct the Elizabethan Fortune Theatre based on existing documentation. This is the first attempt of this kind, but it was never completed. Tieck was also the first modern critic to advocate a return to the open stage. He believed that true illusion stems from acting and is destroyed by pictorial realism. He also believed in the supervision of all theatrical elements by a single autocratic director (this is another element developing during this period: the concept of the strong, individual director controlling all elements of production). In 1841, Tieck staged a production of *Antigone* at the Court Theatre in Potsdam. This was an innovation because the Greeks were virtually unknown in Germany. In 1843, he produced a very influential production of *A Midsummer Night's Dream* in which he adapted Elizabethan acting styles and scenic conventions to the proscenium stage. It is also the production for which Felix Mendelssohn wrote the now-famous incidental music. Tieck's work was made possible because William IV of Prussia liked his work and ordered all personnel to follow his orders. Not untypically, after William IV died, all the old theatrical practices were resumed.

Karl Immerman (1796-1840), on the other hand, was a novelist (critics suggest that he created the contemporary novel in German), who tried to consolidate the ideas of Goethe and Tieck. Immerman believed that the salvation of the theatre depended on drama of high quality rather than in technical excellence or spectacle. At the State Theatre of Dusseldorf, he tried to put his ideas into practice, producing Shakespeare, Goethe, Schiller, and Lessing. He asked real painters to design the settings; he staged carefully posed tableaux, to achieve a kind of high quality of pictorial composition, and often these tableaux were based on famous paintings. He also did a great deal of research as a director and he inspired his actors to do similar research on their various roles. As a result, each play was carefully prepared even though it received only ten rehearsals. In all, he produced and directed 355 plays. The public was indifferent to his attempts and, since he was not subsidized, his experiments failed miserably. He is most noted for a private production of *Twelfth Night*, produced the year he died. An architect named Wiegman designed a fixed facade and forestage with entrances at each end and an inner stage at the rear. Historically this was the first important attempt to return to the stage like the one for which Shakespeare wrote. This is the first time we actually saw a production the way Shakespeare may have seen it.

Romanticism in England

Between 1790 and 1843, the population in England doubled, and a large portion of the increased population belonged to the working class who now began to attend theatres. The expanding demand for theatrical entertainment caused several things to happen:

1) The patent theatres were enlarged. Covent Garden was enlarged to 3,000 people. Drury Lane was enlarged to hold 3,600. What does this sug-

gest to you in terms of development of dramatic literature and acting style? It has to be much larger because an actor who could just speak in a normal tone in a small house now has to fill a room that will fit 3,600 people. And certainly, the need for spectacle will increase as well;

2) Minor theatres were opened. Remember in 1752, the law allowed minor theatres to be opened under a license. After 1804, the Earl of Dartmouth became Lord Chamberlain and he interpreted the Licensing Act as authorizing minor theatres in London as long as they did not infringe upon the patent houses. Consequently, he issued permits for several different theatres, and by 1843 there were 21 companies in London;

3) The repertory was significantly affected by this increased audience. Remember regular drama could only be done at the patent theatres, Covent Garden, Drury Lane, and later the Haymarket; but any theatre could do "minor" incidental entertainment such as farces, and musical theatre. To keep audiences interested, the patent theatres began to play more farces and other minor drama. The evening bill began to be extended to at least 5 or 6 hours to include something for everyone. As the repertory changed in the patent houses, many of the usual patrons turned to opera where they felt they could get high-brow entertainment; and the popular audience that was left cared little for poetic drama. By 1843, Shakespeare was driven from the English stage.

The minor theatres, remember there are 18 of them now, still could only perform minor entertainment. They sought to find loopholes in the Licensing Act so that they could compete with the major theatres. To which end, they fostered two theatrical forms: *burletta* and melodrama. The burletta was a short play, usually in 3 acts or less, in rhymed couplets burlesquing a classical original (very much like a droll). Gradually, however, the burletta became so convoluted in its original intent as a satire, that the Lord Chamberlain accepted any play as a burletta if it was written in no more than three acts and had at least five songs in each act. This meant that theatres could do a burletta of *Hamlet* by reducing it in three acts and adding five musical numbers to every act.

Melodrama permitted similar loopholes and soon became the most popular genre on the English stage. Until about 1840, melodrama appealed mostly to the unsophisticated theatre goers. However, with the work of Edward Bulwer-Lytton (1803-1873) and John Westland Marston (1819-1890), a species of melodrama called "gentlemanly melodrama" began to develop. This type of melodrama would attract the more discriminating audience because it involved situations in which the upper classes were interested. Essentially, gentlemanly melodrama turns on the lower or middle classes trying to improve their lot in society, or the people who are on the top trying to stay there. Therefore, the principal motivation of characters is the raising and maintaining of money, and the plot invariably turns on the revelation of some past secret. Bulwer-Lytton's most significant play was *The Lady of Lyons* (1838). In it, a snobbish woman of the country-club set is married off to the gardener's son who is disguised as the Prince of Como. In the past, this woman had been so snobby that she turned away all of her suitors. As a result, one of her admirers said, "I'm going to pay her back. I'm going to convince the gardener's son to play some dignitary and have him court her and see if she'll agree to marry him purely out of snobbery." The gardener's son marries the Lady of Lyons, then tells her who he really is and renounces the marriage (there are a lot of reasons why he has to marry her and is unable to tell her about his true identity beforehand since the villain is virtually blackmailing him into carrying out the whole masquerade). However, after he renounces her, he says, "All right, I'm not worthy of you but I will come back to claim you after I have made myself worthy of you." Typical of gentlemanly melodrama, he goes off, fights in a war, becomes a hero, and returns a rich man having made money in the war. The woman's father is now destitute and is going to have to sell off his land. The young man buys the land in disguise, and when the father hands over the deed to the property, he takes off the disguise and says, "My beloved, receive back your land." He hands the deed to the daughter who gives it to her father and they run into each other's arms. It's like a gothic novel, except that it specifically deals with money and the upper class, trying to survive in high society. That was really what the upper class was interested in going to see. The lower classes lived under the delusion of upward mobility, that someone within the body of this play could actually become a war hero, a millionaire, and return to claim his love. This had a huge appeal for all members of the audience.

John Westland Marston, on the other hand, established the gentlemanly species of melodrama with two plays *The Patrician's Daughter* and *Anne Blake* both of which treated contemporary subjects in poetic dialogue. He tried to raise to Shakespearean heights the dramatic problems of the upper classes. Also, during this period, audiences continued their demand for spectacle. Whether the play was Shakespeare, a ballet, an extravaganza, a pantomime, it didn't matter. As a result, two main developments occurred in stagecraft:

1) There was a modification of the fixed flat and groove system in favor of a more varied system of sets which allowed free plantation scenery—like what we do now, literally taking a piece of scenery and bracing it or screwing it into the stage floor;

2) All components of the stage picture were locked within a single neutral framework. This was the development of what we call the picture frame—that gilded frame around and above and sometimes even below the proscenium. What did this do? It separated the visual from the audience and got rid of the apron stage and the proscenium doors. This development was prompted by two things: 1) the desire for greater artistic consistency in set and costumes; and 2) the inspiration of archeology and the urge to wrap the stage and the players in something that was historically authentic. To accomplish this, it was necessary to separate the elements of the play from the audience so that the audience could maintain a perspective. The curtain went up and suddenly, they were in a different world; if the actor came out of the picture frame, or the audience could see one another over stage boxes, it violated the sense of being in the world of the play.

14. The Development of Realism in the 19th Century

While gentlemanly melodrama was in development in England, between 1850 and 1870, the French were experiencing a Second Empire with Napoleon III, in which two complementary genres were blossoming. The first involved the glittering fantasies of operetta, especially in the hands of Offenbach, that poked fun at a pompous court and the military ambitions of the Emperor. The more dangerous the subject of their criticism, the more these operettas used Greek myths to veil the criticism of the court: what they did essentially was take Greek classical heroes and convert them into buffoon characters suspiciously similar to contemporary Parisians. On the other side of the coin were the realistic dramas in the hands of Augier and Dumas, *fils*, which had the clearest reflections of the concerns of the newly affluent French middle class. These were the dramas in France that were aligned with the gentlemanly melodrama of England, in the way that playwrights dealt with subject matter pertinent to the upper classes, and would be called "problem" or "thesis" plays. The main themes of this kind of drama were:

1) Tension between new money and old social positions;
2) Financial speculation (playing the market);
3) The threat posed to family life by illicit liaisons; and
4) The courtesans of high society.

The basic moral position of this kind of drama was founded on an enlightened mercantilism. Money rules these plays—and the family was sacrosanct, inviolable. Rich was good. Rich and married with children was better! One of the most significant issues in the plays of the Second Empire was how a person acquires money. Does the woman who earned the money have to acquire it as a courtesan? If she has acquired it as a courtesan did she have the right to marry into high society? If so, did she have to keep it hidden? If she did want to marry into high society and the parents refused to allow her to marry the gentleman of high society, do they buy her off? In this kind of play, it was perfectly ethical (or at least, justifiable) for them to offer her 40,000 francs to call off the wedding. They believed that keeping the family name pure was worth the expenditure. A dollar value was attached to purity and the sanctity of the family name—both important issues in the late eighteenth and nineteenth centuries.

The Well-Made Play

The new drama worked its way slowly into the Comédie Française, but the minor houses, particularly the Gymnase and the Vaudeville, were the major homes of social drama until the 1860s. The Comédie Française was essentially the home of Scribe and the Well-Made Play.

The Well-Made Play which was developed by Eugène Scribe after he stopped writing vaudevilles had a series of structural devices designed to translate the excesses of French melodrama into some kind of realistic plotting. What he did was create another formula which was, in many ways, as awkward as melodrama because of its stringent rules. Every Well-Made Play had the following characteristics:

1) A plot based on a withheld secret;

2) Initial exposition that summarizes the story up to the raising of the curtain. This would invariably involve a character called a confidante. Additional dramatic devices included: precisely timed entrances and exits, letters that miscarry, mistaken identities, quid pros quos, two or more characters misinterpret a situation and become hopelessly entangled in misinformation;

3) A series of ups and downs in the battle of wits between two adversaries;

4) A reversal in the action followed by the *scène à faire*, or **obligatory scene**. This usually represented the highest and lowest points of the hero's fortunes. If the play is going to turn out badly for the hero, the obligatory scene depicts the hero saying: "Aha! I have won," and then some other character (usually the antagonist) enters and says "Wait a minute, this letter has just come into my possession that proves that, on the 18th of October 1786, you did this." The hero replies, "Oh my God, I didn't think anybody knew about that," and suddenly, he/she acknowledges defeat. Similarly, the hero could lament, "Oh no, I have lost," when someone enters and says, "No, I have a letter here showing that the villain has proven his villainy, and now you win." So, the *scène à faire* was the scene that needed to occur, where there was an ultimate change of fortune;

5) A logical, credible denouement;

6) Every act was a microcosmic repetition of the overall structural pattern of the play. Every act had its own rising and falling action and *scène à faire*. This was, of course, designed to create suspense and interest in the audience.

In the Well-Made Play, Scribe also identified the solid values, tastes, and ideals of the French middle class; and, although many of the realistic dramatists were critical of Scribe, they owed a great deal to his structure and to his emphasis on middle-class values—the values that other social dramatists would build on. Scribe also helped bring about a number of reforms in theatrical production:

1) He emphasized the possibilities of collaboration between the author and the producer of the play;

2) In musical theatre—in the operas and musical comedies of Paris—he brought the chorus downstage to be an active participant in the drama. For example, in *Robert the Devil* he introduces a chorus of defrocked nuns;

3) He also sought ways to integrate the newest technical developments into his plays and operas. In 1849, for example, he put a skating ballet into a work called *Le Prophete* because roller-skating had become the rage in Paris;

4) He was also fond of shock value: in a piece called *The Huguenots*, he inserted a titillating bathing scene, in which the women would appear "nude" to the audience;

5) Perhaps his most significant innovation was the development—if not the invention—of the *tableau curtain*. Remember Diderot posed actors at the end of acts in *tableaux vivants*. What Scribe did was climax an act with an unexpected twist of the plot or grand culmination of the action, and then pose the actors. What would develop was a *pose plastique* full of virtual action, interrupted by the curtain falling on the act. This device was called the TORNADO CURTAIN in England and would have a great effect on melodrama, and on the more realistic social dramas of the later nineteenth century.

Next to Scribe, the most prolific writer of the Well-Made Play was **Victorien Sardou** (1831-1908). Sardou used to build his plays backwards from the climactic scene. He would decide on the grand scene of this play and then determine now he would get there. Often, he would read the first act of a play by Scribe and then invent the rest to create his own original play. He preferred to build plots out of some trivial or insignificant fact that became tremendously important as the play progressed. Perhaps the best example of that occurred in *Madame Sans-Gêne* (1893), in which a spirited washer woman becomes the Duchess of Danzig. When various members of the aristocracy attempt to oust her from Napoleon's court, she calmly produces Napoleon's unpaid wash bill. Not wanting to be known as an emperor who does not pay his bills, Napoleon keeps her secret and she is allowed to remain the Duchess of Danzig. Unfortunately, Sardou tended to be more exploitive than sincere in the issues he raised, and George Bernard Shaw called his type of bourgeois drama, "sardoudledum."

In reaction to Sardou and the Well-Made Play, **François Ponsard** (1814-1867), a vigorous opponent of romanticism, developed what he called "the school of common sense." His playwriting style, with its emphasis on common sense served as a transition between the Well-Made Play of Scribe and the romantic tradition to the new generation of social dramatists. The only playwright of note to come out of this school was **Emile Augier** (1820-1889), who championed the virtues and ideals of the middle class—chiefly the home and the family. His best plays involved weak individuals who succumbed to the temptations of material prosperity—characters who could not handle money, who could not handle upward social mobility. Augier also wrote about virtuous people who embodied the traits and values which he felt would unity French society. The most outstanding characteristics of his work were an unswerving balance and perspective, a broad outlook, and clear-headed good sense. After taking a degree in law, he began to write plays, of which his first success was *Hemlock*, a two-act verse comedy about a repentant debauchee. The next several plays that he wrote were in verse and significant because they preached a very strong moral. *The Adventuress*, for example, tells us how an adventuress can destroy a family; *Gabrielle* on the other hand demonstrates how a family is strengthened when a wife remains faithful. Interestingly, in contrast to the romantic plays, *Gabrielle* takes a serious attitude toward marital fidelity. *Olympe's Marriage*, in fact, was written in reply to Dumas's successful play *Camille*, and depicts a scheming courtesan who marries into an aristocratic family to enhance her social position. In this particular plot, her father-in-law tries to buy her off to get her to disavow the marriage. She refuses, and in the last act, she is shot dead on stage.

One of Augier's stronger themes was the power of money to corrupt, though Augier would present various perspectives on this issue. In one of his most interesting plays, *Mr. Poirier's Son-In-Law*, a wealthy businessman marries his pure daughter to a prodigal marquis in order to buy a title. This is a terribly mercenary deal. The marquis, who is poor but landed, wants the money from this rich businessman. The rich businessman wants to ennoble his family name by having "Lord" or "Marquis" or "Earl" in front of it. The young girl ultimately reforms the prodigal, and the marriage is a happy one. However, in *A Fine Marriage*, marrying for money is presented as completely undesirable.

Unlike Dumas who was considered a pioneer dramatist, Augier was considered a defender and preserver of middle-class ideals. He was a writer who was completely in the middle of the road, choosing not speak about the high or low points of society. However, Augier did provide insight into many of the social and moral evils of the empire, essentially stemming from the phenomenal economic prosperity of the period. Worldly possessions and money invariably caused the downfall of his characters.

Alexandre Dumas, *fils*

The great reformer, as I have suggested, was Alexandre Dumas, *fils* (1824–1895), critically acclaimed as the person who "created" French realistic social drama on 2 February 1852 with his very first play *La Dame aux Camélias* (AKA *Camille*). He was the illegitimate son of Dumas, *père*, and his only claim to fame before 1852 was a standard volume of verse called *Sins of My Youth* and a short lyric drama, a curtain raiser written in 1848. *Camille* had been accepted at the Vaudeville Theatre in 1850, but it was forbidden by the censors until 1852 when a change of administration permitted the play to be performed. On opening night, it was a success from the first act on. Actors and audiences were caught in the rising tide of emotion; women and men wept profusely at the play—all of the contemporary accounts wrote about the number of tears shed at performances. People would sit in their seats after the play and weep. No one yet had dealt with contemporary society in so daring a way on the stage. No one had more successfully captured the details of contemporary life. What is *Camille* about? Marguerite, a prostitute/courtesan, falls in love with Armand. She pawns her possessions to rent a country house for Armand and herself. Armand's father begs her to break off the affair to save the family name. She complies reluctantly and writes Armand that she no longer loves him and goes off with a former lover. She ends up doing this because his father says, "If you really love him, set him free." Armand, ignorant of the truth, wins money from her previous lover and hurls it at her in disgust. However, in the last act Marguerite is dying of tuberculosis and Armand discovers the truth. He goes to her and begs forgiveness which she gives him on her deathbed and she dies in his arms happy that at least he knows that she really loved him.

The audience was beside itself. This was truly a situation that would inspire tears: the whore with the heart of gold who was less interested in money than in true love; the whore who understood the constraints of society which demanded that she give up Armand. The innovation here was a new kind of morality. Idealism was gone, replaced by law or society. Critics suggest that in the play, morality is a law or cause of the same order as electricity or gravity. The laws of the play, the laws of society, are as natural as nature and people cannot escape them. In the play there was no more a right to happiness. Instead, there exists a fatality of conditions and circumstances: the beginnings of environmental determinism.

To French audiences, Dumas's fifteen major plays were referred to as "thesis plays," a welcome relief from both the romantic drama and the Well-Made Play of Scribe. However, to make these plays palatable to an audience, Dumas used many of the devices of the Well-Made Play, and sought to combine moral elements with entertainment value. Most of Dumas's plays deal with marriage and the evils of money (money is the paramount theme of these plays), adultery, prostitution, and illegitimacy. In the seven years that followed *Camille*, Dumas had five plays produced. *The Demi-Monde*, a play even more realistic than *Camille*, since the courtesans are not portrayed sympathetically, was produced in 1855. Interestingly, Dumas coined the word "demi-monde" for the underworld or half world that characterizes the society of the courtesans. *The Demi-Monde* was followed by *The Natural Son* in 1858 in which the subject of illegitimacy was introduced. In the play, the natural son is spurned by his father. Later in the play the son becomes famous. The father needs his help but the son refuses to recognize the father.

Dumas followed these with a number of plays that deal with adultery and symbolism. Perhaps the most significant play on adultery was *Princess George* (1872) in which a melodramatic heroine forgives everything when her unfaithful husband comes home. What is interesting about this play is that the husband does not come back to his wife out of any sense of ethics or morality. He comes back because he discovered that the husband of the woman he's been fooling around with, killed her last two lovers. Since he wants to live, he decides to give up his lover. This is very different from the kind of morality one might find in Augier, where the husband would behave with some strong sense of morality. Dumas is saying, "Why do people really do what they do? Because it hurts or because it doesn't? Not because of ethics or morality."

The following year, *Claude's Wife* (1873) presented in a highly symbolic manner a debauched heroine who seduces one of her husband's students. Her husband is a scientist. She persuades the student to steal the plans for a secret rocket, a super weapon, so that she can give them to her real lover. This married woman seduces a student and makes love with a double agent. In the last scene of the play, after she has made love to the student, he gives her the plans. She's about to throw them through an open window to her lover who is waiting in the street. Her husband comes in, catches her and says, "Don't do that or I'll kill you." She says, "You're not man enough to kill me. I have you wrapped around my little finger. You we're never anything to me." He pulls out a gun, shoots her dead, and she falls out the window.

Dumas was elected to the Académie Française in 1874 and did not produce an important play until 1885 when he composed *Denise*, a fascinating play demonstrating the importance for girls who are engaged not to keep secrets from their fiancés. A girl betrayed in love vows never again to reveal her reason. It seems that the boy she was about to marry abused her and molested other women. She vowed never to reveal the truth about him out of fear for her life. However, when the man in question is about to marry yet another woman, she tells his fiancée the truth about him.

In addition, Dumas produced a number of other symbolic plays, one of which was *The Foreigner* (1876), which is important for us because it sparked a feud between two of the leading ladies of the day, Sarah Bernhardt and Sophie Croizette.

Dumas's main contribution to the technique of the thesis play was the use of a character device called *raissoneur*, the spokesperson for the author. The *raissoneur* really is the person who speaks the moral issue of the play, the person who is most logical. Although this character is interactive with other characters in the play, his chief function seems to be the clear expression of the author's point of view.

By the 1880s, a phenomenon began to take shape in France that would affect drama for all time to come: the long run. By 1880, no play was considered a success unless it played 100 performances, and many even got up to 300. What does this do? It begins to undermine the repertory system. Actors are hired for a single show rather than for an entire season, and fewer plays would be needed to fill out a season. This led to the creation of matinee performances, a phenomenon that started on a regular basis in France in 1875. Throughout the last half of the nineteenth century, two demands were evident in theatrical production: increased realism and theatrical virtuosity. The increased realism became the province of a strong theatrical director, and virtuosity became the province of the actor.

Actors and Directors

Adolph Montigny (1805–1880) was the first to treat directing as an art in France. In 1853 he achieved fame by placing a table and chairs downstage center and forcing the actors to sit at the table and talk to one another during the scene. This was innovative because the actors were used to talking to the audience directly and not to one another. Montigny also furnished sets with real room furniture, putting props all over the stage to motivate actors to cross from one part of the room to another. This of course would have a profound influence on the development of realism in settings and in costuming. Another important innovator during this period was **François Delsarte**

(1811-1871). Delsarte was apprenticed to a porcelain painter and applied to the Conservatoire in 1825, but could not finish his studies because he lost his voice due to faulty training. He could speak but not project; his voice as an actor was ruined. He renounced the stage forever and began to formulate his own method of actor training which became quite popular and boasted a number of famous actors and actresses: among whom, the celebrated actress, Rachel. His ideas had a curious vogue in the United States during the last half of the nineteenth century, although to the modern eye, the Delsarte Technique was very external and melodramatic: "show and tell" acting at its worst.

Delsarte was attempting to apply scientific principles to the study of acting and was thus concerned with the outward manifestations of human emotions. He said that it did not matter if the actor was "feeling" the part if the audience did not perceive an emotion. So, in order to study internal emotions, Delsarte divided human behavior into physical, mental, and emotional spheres. Then he related all of these to every action, thought, and emotion that a person might experience, and he began to codify a system of exterior manifestations of this idea in a series of pithy statements:

> "The artist should have three objects: to move, to interest, to persuade. He interests by language; he moves by thought; he moves, interests and persuades by gesture" (evidently, for Delsarte the exterior gesture was the combination of all these potentials).
>
> "Routine is the most formidable thing I know."
>
> "Nothing is more deplorable than a gesture without a motive. Perhaps the best gesture is that which is least apparent."
>
> "Any interrogation made with crossed arms must partake of the character of a threat."
>
> "The mouth is a vital thermometer, the nose a moral thermometer" (perhaps the sneer of the nose gives a sense of ethics or morality to an issue).
>
> "If you cannot conquer your defect, make it beloved" (if you have a terrible habit, work with it so it becomes a part of the entire character).

The Development of Realism in the 19th Century

Into this climate of experimentation and regulation came the actors of the period. The most important actors of romantic tragedy were Mlle. Mars, Regnier, and **Rachel**. I think Rachel's statement sums up the ethos of the entire body of romantic actors: "In studying for the stage, take my word for it, declamation and gesture are of little avail. You have to think and weep." And ultimately what is she talking about? You have to be able to feel it and you have to understand what you're saying. Of course, the greatest of all French actresses of this period, especially to American audiences, was **Sarah Bernhardt** (1845–1923). In 1869, she was introduced in a play called *The Wayfarer* (*Le Passant*) by Francois Coppée. She had made an undistinguished debut at the Comédie Française in 1862 and was fired. She tried to debut with another play, *The Game of Love and Chance*, but this was not terribly successful. However, by 1868, she proved that she could successfully quiet down a student demonstration, and theatre managers realized that she had finally come to the fore as an actress, and Bernhardt was given her first major role (This is significant because in *The Wayfarer,* she played a britches role, and male roles were going to be very important for the rest of her career. Britches roles were very popular in the nineteenth century because they allowed the audience to see the line of a woman's body: to be able to see the line of the body that is not covered by hoop skirts and petticoats, but to see the real leg and perhaps even see some calf, or bare arm or the elbow, was highly alluring.).

However, as soon as she began to be successful, the Franco-Prussian War was declared and her career was put on hold. Nevertheless, when Emile Perrin took charge of the management of the Comédie Française in 1871, one of the first things he did was hire Sarah Bernhardt and Jean Mounet-Sully. Sarah made her debut playing Chimène opposite Mounet-Sully playing Rodrigue in Corneille's *Le Cid*. She received a review that most actresses just dream of. The gist of it was that she was "statuesque," and that she had a very beautiful and subtle mouth which, when she formed words, was very seductive to the listener. The review concluded, "Make no mistake, the engagement of Mademoiselle Sarah Bermhardt at the Comédie Française is serious and violently revolutionary. It is poetry entering the house of dramatic art. It is a wolf in the fold."

Sarah Bernhardt's career fell into three periods: six years at the Odéon theatre, from 1866-1872; eight years at the Comédie Française, from 1872-1880; and a long career touring and managing her own theatres, from 1880-1923. Having the temperament of a star, no theatre could tolerate her for a long time, and her longest career was under her own management in Paris and tours of Europe, the United States, South America, and Australia.

The major concern of the Comédie Française during the 1870s was a rivalry between Sarah Bernhardt and Sophie Croizette, and the fact that Sophie was accepted as a member of the Comédie as societaire in 1874 before Bernhardt created particular bitterness. Tempers flared up in a production of *The Sphinx* in 1874. *The Sphinx* is about the agony and death of an unfaithful wife. To create the role, Croizette consulted toxicologists inquiring about interesting symptoms that accompany death, and she exhibited spasms and agonies, according to the reviews, never before seen on the French stage (this is in front of a theatre audience used to actors walking down front and orating). The review reported that Croizette turned a pale shade of green as she was dying; that "her eyes rolled in their sockets, her hands and legs trembled convulsively, and her head was shaking in the convulsions of lockjaw." To the French, this was extremely exciting (the year before, the actor Mounet-Sully created a sensation in Paris because he smoked a cigarette in the middle of a play. For a nineteenth-century audience, an actor actually doing what he was pretending to do was a great shot in the arm of illusion). Bernhardt hired a claque to boo Sophie as she was dying, and this just inflamed the rivalry even more.

The rivalry continued in 1876 when Bernhardt and Croizette appeared in *The Foreigner* by Dumas, *fils*, both together in the same play. During rehearsals, the Duchess who was played by Bernhardt, appeared to have all the best lines and the best scenes. As a result, Croizette wanted to exchange roles in the middle of the rehearsal period. Bernhardt agreed, "Fine, you can take the role of the Duchess, I'll take the role of the American." When the play opened, she upstaged the Duchess in every scene and all the reviewers wrote about the American. Bernhardt also began a tradition which a great many stars have followed since. In a play called *Rome Conquered*, also in 1876, Bernhardt requested to play a minor role, that of a blind grandmother. She made such a sensation playing a small role that it began her career playing character parts (something that stars have done since then, appearing in a cameo role in a play, earning a great deal of focus just by appearing onstage for eight minutes or less).

Throughout all of this, relations between Bernhardt and the Comédie-Française manager Perrin were deteriorating. He found her feuds unproductive and her quirks really problematic. She liked to do odd things. She slept in a coffin. In the 1878 exposition, she risked her life in a balloon-ascension. Her household pets were a wolf, a half a dozen chameleons, and a cheetah which she kept on a leash and walked through the streets of Paris. When she didn't like someone or the way someone delivered a line, especially a fellow actor, she'd have the actor horsewhipped. However, the biggest problem for Perrin occurred when, in 1879, Bernhardt tried to force her way onto a Comédie-Française tour to London. When the theatre refused to take her on the tour, Bernhardt wrote an open letter to the newspaper offering her resignation to the company. Matters came to a head when Bernhardt didn't want to play a role in a play by Augier. When she was forced to play the role, she walked out on stage and mumbled her lines, making it very clear that she hated the role. She got a horrible review, was fired from the Comédie-Française, and left on a tour of America.

When she returned to Paris in 1893, she became the directress of the Renaissance Theatre (the theatre that Victor Hugo was running during the time of romantic drama). She managed that theatre until 1898, when she decided it was bringing her bad luck, and took a lease on the Théâtre de Nation which she renamed the Théâtre Sarah Bernhardt. She presented not only herself in various roles but also presented the Italian actress Eleanora Duse there. She played the title role in *Hamlet* in 1899, and though she continued to triumph on stage, she experienced many traumas in her personal life. In 1915, her leg became gangrenous due to an infection and had to be amputated, causing her to appear onstage with an artificial leg. Ultimately, she died of exhaustion in 1923, collapsing during a dress rehearsal of a play.

Actor-Managers in England

In England, the end of the eighteenth century gave rise to a series of great actor managers who flourished in the nineteenth century. The first of note was **John Philip Kemble** (1757-1823) who managed both Drury Lane and Covent Garden. He excelled in heavy dramatic roles such as Brutus, Hamlet, Coriolanus and was unrivalled in declamation but was not always able to express strong or subtle emotions. Critics suggest that he acted in the artificial statuesque style then in fashion. "Larger than life." At Drury Lane he made important theatre reforms in costume, scenery, and theatrical management. He paid great attention to historical detail in his designs and generally tried to dress his characters appropriately according to period (though critics found his dressing Hamlet in black with an elephant—in miniature, of course—suspended on a blue ribbon around his neck somewhat eccentric). He is probably best remembered for introducing live animals on stage in his Shakespearean productions (one of several managers of the nineteenth century to use furry creatures on stage). He also is noted for bringing aquatic effects to the stage and for attempting to introduce greater discipline and precision in the conduct of performances and rehearsals. Because he insisted that actors be prompt for rehearsals, he had a reputation for being difficult. Among his characteristics as a theatre manager are the following:

1) He objected to the neglect of smaller parts, and secondary players were required to perform the parts as rehearsed (as opposed to the tendency in a long run or a tour for smaller parts especially to be "improved");

2) Blocking and all physical actions were carefully planned;

3) He handled crowd scenes expertly. He could paint a good stage picture and paved the way for the mobs of Charles Kean and the Saxe-Meiningen Company;

4) He required his set designer, William Capon, to make detailed studies of past styles of architecture, and then to combine them to create some sense of period.

After he had a dispute with Sheridan at Drury Lane, he moved on to Covent Garden where he attempted to raise ticket prices in 1809. This led to another Old Price riot that suspended performances for nearly three months. His sister, Sarah Kemble (Mrs. Siddons), was also extremely significant as an actress. According to historians, Mrs. Siddons was not given to dependence on inspiration but achieved results through careful study of every role she took. She was very meticulous in her preparation. Of her process in approaching a role, she noted: "When a part is first put before me for studying, I look it over in a general way to see if it is in nature. And if it is, I'm sure it can be played." She was trying to adapt something natural in her performances, working from within outward. Her biographers suggest that, in rehearsing a part, she first yielded to the "spontaneous flashes of her sensibility," very much along the lines of sensory recall. Then she became the person represented; and then from becoming, internally, the person, she developed the "external indications peculiar and personal." And unlike Garrick who, when he came offstage would joke with the stage hands completely out of character, Mrs. Siddons stayed in character throughout the entire play.

Reactions to the Kemble style of management prompted the following developments between 1814 and 1843: the Passionate intensity of Edmund Kean; the trend toward greater familiarity (i.e., realism) with William Charles Macready; and the drawing room manner of Mme. Vestris at the Olympic Theatre.

Edmund Kean (1789-1833) who debuted at Drury Lane as Shylock, was small and unimpressive in stature. With large, dark, and singularly expressive eyes, and flexible limbs, Kean was nothing if not passionate. He developed an ability to perform subsiding emotions, to connect feelings from one moment to another (as opposed to the "jump-cut" kind of emotional acting prevalent in the period). Critics claim that he also treated death scenes in a more realistic way. We are told that when he died on stage, the passion of the soul leaving the body was a great moment in the theatre. Rather than feeling pain of death, the audience would experience the sense of the soul transcending—complete with bulging eyes. Kean, however, was not a naturalist in the modern sense. He said that he never felt a part unless he was acting with a pretty woman. And like actors who were more "outside in" in their approach, he never made a move or gesture on stage that he had not rehearsed beforehand. He did not rely on instinct or an internal feeling to propel him. In parts that suited him, he gave the impression of being the role, but he always needed a big scene to show off his energy and passion. Representative roles include: Richard III, Iago, Shylock, Macbeth. A Drury Lane playbill for 8 June 1815 suggests the breadth of Kean's repertoire: Friday night—Hamlet; Tuesday—Othello; Wednesday—Zanga (in *The Revenge*); Friday—Iago; Saturday——Shylock; Monday—Richard II; Tuesday—Leon (in *To Rule A Wife and Have a Wife*).

Kean came to the United States to perform twice. The second time he came because he had been brought to trial for seducing yet another actress and had to flee from England. His final performance was in 1833 playing Othello to his son, Charles Kean's Iago. He retired in March and died two months later. In addition to his innovations as an actor, Charles Kean was important to theatre history in the development of representational realism.

William Charles Macready (1793-1873) who was acting manager of Covent Garden and Drury Lane, also was devoted to long study and detailed rehearsals; he truly anticipated the natural method of acting developed by Stanislavski. In 1837, as the manager of Covent Garden, he was the first to impose a principle of unity on the theater. He suggested that the actors, the designers, everyone involved in a production were guided by the central concepts of the playwright. For Macready, the playwright was the chief force of the theatre and the actor and the director were charged with realizing the playwright's vision. He did much in promoting historical research for designs and the manners of his characters, and his two tenures of management marked a deliberate attempt to bring the fashionable, the educated, and the respectable back to the legitimate theatre. This, of course, would give a good

The Development of Realism in the 19th Century

shot in the arm to gentlemanly melodrama. The upper classes now wanted to come to the theatre instead of just going to see operas. In 1842, as manager of Drury Lane, he refused admittance to prostitutes, the first time that prostitutes were barred from the theatre.

In rehearsal, Macready blocked actors, told them where to move. He considered blocking as part of the theatrical event. He was concerned that the physical association of performers would be reflective of what they were doing or what they were saying. He also asked actors to act during rehearsals, not save it for opening night. Macready insisted, "I want to see what this play is going to be like before the audience does." As a result, the idea of the director as the surrogate eye of the audience was beginning to develop. Macready was still acting in the plays he was mounting, so he was not a director in the modern sense who could step off the stage, but we are moving in the direction of the single-focused director. Macready also developed some very interesting innovations with an artist named Clarkston Stanfield who was a designer skilled in panorama. With Stanfield, Macready made use of moving dioramas in his Shakespearean productions. For example, in *Henry V* the moving diorama created the illusion that the actors were actually going from England to France. Unfortunately, Macready created such gorgeous scenic effects, that the audience began to want the effects without the plays.

Spectacle drama became the ruling taste of the Victorian public. However, we should not forget the interior scene. Not all plays take place outside. Did the taste for spectacular drama help or hinder the interior scene? It certainly helped it because the audience desirous of exterior spectacle now wanted an interior scene that looked real—with real furniture, realistic props and costumes. Developments in this area appeared with Lucy Elizabeth Bartolozzi—better known as **Mme. Vestris** (1797-1856)—and her husband **Charles Mathews the Younger** (1803-1878). Mme Vestris made her reputation as a singer and dancer, playing britches parts, and Charles Mathews was a light comedian. They managed the Olympic Theatre from 1831 to 1838, and in 1832 began to use a box set. We don't know if Mme. Vestris used a ceiling cloth to enclose the roof but we do know she used a full box set with real-life furnishings. The stage was divided into six traps so most of the furniture could be pre-set and changes of scene could be realized as efficiently and effectively as extravagant exterior spectacles. Mme. Vestris also preferred to use real life costumes, not exaggerated or theatrical clothes. In addition, like Macready, she paid close attention to the integrated whole of a production. Although she was concerned less with authenticity than Macready—she wasn't slavish to historical accuracy—she was concerned with a consistent style in design.

In addition to making inroads in acting and scene design, Mme. Vestris and Mathews were influential in bringing an Irish-born playwright, **Dion Boucicault** (1820-1890) to London. Boucicault achieved his first success with a play produced by Mme Vestris called *London Assurance*. Having written this play, a comedy, he turned his attention to the school of French melodrama and proceeded to go work for Charles Kean at the Princess Theatre where he produced two French adaptations, *The Corsican Brothers* in 1852 and *Louis XI* in 1855. *The Corsican Brothers* brought to the stage a new kind of trap called "the Corsican trap." The melodrama dealt with twin brothers played by a single actor: one brother is in a scene and the other brother has to appear to him. The brother who has been talking goes to a desk to write a letter and exits to mail it. When he returns looking out a window (facing away from the audience), it is the double dressed like him. The brother who has just left has gone down a trap into the cellar. He is now standing on the Corsican trap that is going to come out of the floor at a .45-degree angle, and move up along the set.

In addition to writing blood and thunder melodrama, Dion Boucicault also wrote a. series of native Irish melodramas, *The Colleen Bawn* (1860), *Arrah-Na-Pogue* (1864) and *The Shaughraun* (1874). His growing interest in America led him to settle there and to capture the American theatre scene in several plays which are essentially American in theme and tone: *The Octoroon* (1861), *The Poor of New York* (1864), *Rip Van Winkle* (1865). Boucicault wasn't interested in contemporary issues but he was interested in scientific progress, not because of the good it could do for mankind but because of the good it could do for his plays. For example, the denouement of *The Octoroon* was brought about through a new invention called a camera. The villain's evil-doing was exposed because someone took a snapshot of him. In *The Long Strike* (1866) a key witness to a lawsuit was on board a ship and was contacted through the newly developed telegraph to return to shore to give testimony at a trial.

Boucicault created what we call the "sensation scene." Every one of his plays has one. Sensation scenes were designed to produce a novel and spectacular effect. In *The Colleen Bawn*, for example, he depicted an attempted drowning (requiring practical water of some sort); in *The Octoroon*, there was an exploding steamboat; in *The Poor of New York*, a house burned to the ground on stage; *Arrah-Na-Pogue* required the hero to ascend a prison tower built of bricks (so he had to take ropes and climb up the side of the set, about three stories high); and in a play called *Formosa* there was an actual a boat race on stage. What is important about Boucicault's sensation scenes is that they were woven into the fabric of the play; they didn't exist only for entertainment value. They always emerged as a pivot of the story, and quite often they were connected to the *scène à faire*, or the obligatory scene.

Another playwright along this line is **Tom Taylor** (1817-1880) who was at the Lyceum from 1845-1847 and functioned as the house playwright for both the Olympic and the Haymarket theatres. He followed the example of Scribe and the Well-Made Play and was particularly fond of historical plays with invented history (for example, he might write a play about Henry VIII and his six wives. The only resemblance to actual history was the fact that Henry VIII and the six wives had their real names. The rest of the incidents would be his own invention). Taylor's debt to Scribe is clearest in a play called *Plot and Passion*, a preposterous story of spy and counter-spy in the age of Napoleon. It has all of Scribe's theatrical devices such as sliding panels, secret documents, and hiding places.

Taylor's most popular and I think greatest achievement was a play called *The Ticket-Of-Leave Man* (1863), which told the story of an innocent man convicted of passing counterfeit checks. Once his innocence is proven, he's let out of jail only to be hounded by the real criminal who thinks he knows more than he does. The play was very original in two aspects: it introduced the stage detective, a character named Hawkshaw; and it was scrupulously detailed in the description of settings, and in the speech of street characters.

During this period, comedy on the Victorian stage was waning considerably. With theatres seating 3500 spectators, drawing-room comedy dealing with four or five characters was fated to look even smaller than it was. Audiences wanted something somewhat larger, and so the tradition of comedy was replaced by two other forms: burlesque and fairy extravaganza. Burlesque was a dramatic representation aiming at exciting laughter by the comical treatment of a serious subject or the caricature of the spirit of a serious work. The fairy extravaganza, on the other hand, was a whimsical treatment of a myth or fairy tale with special emphasis on dance or spectacle. There were formal considerations as well: burlesques were rhymed and in iambic pentameter.

James Robinson Planché (1796-1880) became a professional playwright following the success of his first play *Amoroso, King of Little Britain*, produced at Drury Lane on 21 April 1818. In the same year he wrote a speaking pantomime called *Rudolph the Wolf* and proceeded to turn out melodramas and *burlettas* over the next several years. The burletta is a species of burlesque which generally is in three acts and has five songs per act. The burletta was one of the theatrical forms that people used to get around the Licensing Act, since virtually any five-act play could be compressed into a burletta. Planché's first significant success appeared in 1820 with *The Vampire*, which would have a great influence on stagecraft in England because of the Vampire Traps. Planché's melodrama introduced two significant escapes: falling through the floor (the actor just stood onstage and all of a sudden he was gone, with the cape of the vampire all that remained on the floor), and escaping through scenery (in which the flat would be cut in the middle and hinged like doors—actors would pass through and the flat would snap back making it appear that they had disappeared through the wall). From 1822 until 1828, Planché joined Charles Kemble as a stock author at Covent Garden, where he fostered an interest in antiquarianism which inspired Kemble to produce the first antiquarian production of a Shakespearean play— *King John* in 1823. This was the first time that Shakespeare was produced with costumes and scenery that really looked like they would have during the era of King John. From this point on, we will find many of the other theatres becoming antiquarian in their productions.

In 1830, Planché was instrumental in gaining recognition by music publishers of librettists' copyrights in operas. This was the first time that the librettist got any kind of recognition for his/her work. In 1831 he began his collaboration with Mme. Vestris at the Olympic Theatre with a piece called *The Olympic Revels*. In 183,4 he published his *History of British Costume to the Close of the 18th century*, and in 1836, he began a series of fairy extravaganzas at the Olympic Theatre with *Riquet with the Tuft*. From 1837 to 1839, he was the stock author at the Olympic; from 1839 to 1842, he returned, as stock author, to Covent Garden; and, in 1847, he moved on to the Lyceum Theatre.

When Planché turned his attention to the burlesque formula, he sought to refine both the style and the staging of the form. Before Planché, classical burlesques, the debunking of classical myths and plays, were literally free-for-alls. They were poorly written and poorly produced, generally used as afterpieces or curtain raisers, something to keep the audience quiet. Planché argued that this could be a formula which would also please a gentlemanly audience; he sought to develop the style and staging by making the burlesque more literate, hence, the use of punning as a principle source of laughter. After the classical burlesques, he turned to the French fairy tales of Perrault, producing *Riquet with the Tuft* in 1836, *Puss in Boots* in 1837 and *Bluebeard* in 1839. When Mme. Vestris moved from the Olympic Theatre to Covent Garden (which had a stage five or six times the size of the Olympic stage), the fairy extravaganza became what we now think of as a spectacle play. Planché used many of the same burlesque devices in his extravaganzas: puns, rhymes, and songs.

In 1843, the Theatre Regulation Act abolished the monopolies of the patent theatres. Now, if a theatre had a license and the plays were allowed by the Lord Chancellor, it could produce anything it wanted. There was little change in the bills of the minor theatres after 1843. Remember these were the theatres that couldn't do legitimate comedy and tragedy. After the Theatre Regulation Act, they didn't change what they were producing because the kinds of entertainment offered by them—melodrama and burlesque—were what the audiences wanted. Of the minor theatres, two were especially important: Sadler's Wells under the management of Samuel Phelps, and the Princess Theatre under the direction of Charles Kean.

Samuel Phelps at Sadler's Wells

Between 1844 and 1862, Samuel Phelps (1804-1878) managed the Sadler's Wells Theatre, where he produced chiefly a classical repertory, including all of Shakespeare's plays except *Henry VI*, *Troilus and Cressida*, *Titus Andronicus* and *The Two Noble Kinsmen*. Phelps made Sadler's Wells, an out-of-the-way house, the home of poetic drama in London. His most famous production was *A Midsummer Night's Dream* using a moving diorama to shift from one part of the forest to another, and placing the action behind a green gauze scrim to create an atmosphere of mist. However, to acquiesce to the tastes of the audience, every classical play was followed by an operetta, farce, or a pantomime. To combat rude behavior in the theatre, Phelps ousted children in arms and beer sellers. He also forcibly removed any person speaking foul language while in the precinct of the theatre (this also meant there would be no foul language in his plays), using as precedent an act of Parliament which forbade foul language in a public place. Phelps enforced good audience behavior to such an extent that he would stop a play to have an offender removed. The curtain always rose at 5:45 during the summer as opposed to the customary 6:30 because the bills at Sadler's Wells would be rather long, often extending from 5:45 to about 11:00 P.M.

To ensure a standard of acting Phelps enforced discipline by posting 29 rules for actors, among which:

1) Contracts were terminable at a month's notice on either side;

2) Illness was notifiable in writing. After a month it led to the cancellation of the engagement;

3) No one was allowed in the front of the theatre without permission. Actors were not permitted go into the lobby.

Actors' transgressions were similarly codified by Phelps. Here are fees for various faults:

1) You will pay a month's salary or be dismissed for performing elsewhere without written permission;
2) You will forfeit a week's salary for refusing to appear, or causing the cutting of a scene by missing an entrance;
3) A half a week's salary for defacing notices, be carelessly or wrongly dressed, or being obviously drunk on stage;
4) Seven shillings for being absent from a whole rehearsal, or not being word-perfect at dress rehearsal;
5) Six shillings for not entering or exiting according to rehearsals; or not returning the prompt or harpsichord book;
6) One shilling for appearing or exiting when you were not required to do so;
7) If the prompter does not report the offence, he is liable for the fine.

Phelps was also as strict with audiences: No free seats except to the press; no child under three would be admitted; all children in the pit had to pay full price.

In addition to *A Midsummer Night's Dream*, another of Phelps's remarkable production was *Pericles, Prince of Tyre*, produced on 14 October 1854, the first time Shakespeare's play was performed in nearly 200 years. The panoramic voyage to the temple of Diana was the hit of the play: moving scenery behind, floating scenery in front, treadmills to create the impression of actors on barges going through water. Two years later, an 18-year old named Henry Irving was in the audience. Amazed and impressed by this kind of theatrical spectacle, he took note of it and later used it in his own work. Roughly during his tenure at the Sadler's Wells, Samuel Phelps produced 3000 nights of theatre, 2,000 of which were productions of plays by Shakespeare.

Charles Kean at the Princess

At the Princess Theatre, Charles Kean (1811-1868) was regarded as the director who perfected pictorial realism. Most of his realistic theories were developed during his third American tour between 1845 and 1847 when he produced *King John* and *Richard III*, productions that started him thinking in terms of historical or pictorial realism. When he became manager of the Princess Theatre (a tenure lasting from 1850 to 1859) he implemented a number of the ideas which were developed during the American tour:

1) He rearranged the evening bill. Performances would begin with a curtain raiser, a short play to offset latecomers to the theatre;

2) He eliminated incidental entertainments between acts;

3) He also developed the trend toward gentlemanly melodrama. Part of this was helped by the fact that he was appointed Master of the Revels by Queen Victoria in 1849;

4) He also established the long run as a policy with his production of *Henry VIII* in 1855;

5) He developed antiquarianism that was begun in 1823 by Planché and Charles Kemble, in the use of historically accurate costumes. His two most significant productions involving historically accurate costumes were *Macbeth* and *King John*;

6) He replaced descriptive passages in Shakespeare with spectacle. Rather than hearing someone talking about Cleopatra barging down the Nile, he depicted it. When a messenger entered, saying that Cordelia landed with the army of France, instead of that speech, Kean added a scene depicting Cordelia sailing back from France (part of the reason Kean got rid of the entr'acte entertainment was that he was increasing the running time of each play);

7) He established the director as the primary artist in the theatre. He hired no stars. He wasn't interested in the star system. Like Macready, he was

very concerned with the care and coordination of the entire production. Kean had tremendous influence on the next most significant figure in the development of realism, a playwright director whose name is **Thomas William Robertson** (1829-1871). Gradually we are getting away from the practice of the actor-director. After Robertson started writing plays, he didn't perform anymore. He would only write them and direct them. After Tom Robertson will develop the convention of the director who neither writes nor performs but stands in front of the stage to block and direct the actors, but we're not there yet.

Thomas William Robertson at the Prince of Wales
Robertson's philosophy was that "drama should represent, if not an exact transcription of men's daily lives, then at least the impression of events and behavior consistent with normal experience." With Thomas Robertson the seeds of realism were planted deep in the English theatre. He was an actor at Sadler's Wells; a prompter at the Lyceum Theatre; he served as a drama critic; and finally, when he joined the Bancrofts at the Prince of Wales Theatre (1865-1879), he inaugurated a new era in the English Theatre. Essentially Robertson created a drama which had all of the trappings of melodrama, but he took that formula and created a drama which was evocative of both the philosophy and the technical resources of the age. His plays, therefore, dealt with significant social issues, as a quick glance at his titles might suggest: *Society, Caste, Home, Progress, Work, War, School.* Unlike Shaw and Ibsen, Robertson was less interesting in developing new ideas than in reinforcing the prevalent philosophy of his own day, occasionally making the gentlemen who come to the theatre feel good about themselves.

It was in the handling of technical resources, however, that Tom Robertson really made a name for himself as a stage director. For example, he required real doorknobs, and practical cups and saucers so that people could really drink out of them. It may sound foolish to us, but that was *avant garde* then. The fact that Tom Robertson would write scenes about people sitting around a table sipping real cups of tea gave him the title "cup and saucer dramatist," and critics used to call his plays "cup and saucer comedy." He was also fond of using atmospheric devices to create mood and tension in plays. For example, in *Ours* in the third act, autumn leaves fall from the trees throughout the act. In *Society*, he calls for the effect of the setting sun seen in the windows of houses. Gradually he began to develop a kind of realistic business that would embody not only the mood but a major action of the play. For example, in *School* (1869) he used moonlight to develop a relationship involving a lord who is in love with a lower-class woman. Walking in the moonlight, the lord says, "What long shadows the moonlight flings. See, there I am." Bella, the woman replies, "But so tall—so high." And he says, "And there are you," to which Bella replies, "But not so tall as you are." Robertson's stage direction reads, "The moonlight throws long shadows from right to left," and Bella remarks while her shadow unites with that of the lord on the ground before them, "And now we are joined together." Until Robertson, no one had conceived of using something that was a technical effect as a metaphor for the action of the play.

Robertson's play *Caste* is perhaps the most significant drama we have encountered in England up to this point, mostly because it was the beginning of English theatrical realism. It was presented at the Prince of Wales Theatre on Saturday 6 April 1867. It employed all of the traditional characters from the melodrama and the comedies of the previous age: A good girl heroine; a secondary character who is honest but low class; a drunken father; an eccentric old lady; the honest lower-class hero. What did Robertson do in this play to make it more realistic? The drunken father did not reform at the end of the play. The light comedian in plays was always portrayed as a blond and the leading man was always supposed to have dark hair. When *Caste* was produced, Squire Bancroft played the comic in a dark wig, and the leading man was given a blond wig, literally reversing the character types. Why? Because in real life, a hero might have any color of hair, and so could the comic sidekick. To an audience, such reversal of expectations ruptured one of stereotypes of theatrical production in England.

Robertson created many innovations at the Prince of Wales Theatre through the management of the Bancrofts, Marie Wilton and Squire Bancroft:

1) The development of the long run, mostly by plays of Robertson: *Society*—150 performances; *Ours*—150; *Caste*—156; *School*—381; even today, 381 performances constitute a decent run for a straight play;

2) The theatre began to sign actors to a run of the play contract—the first time in theatrical history;

3) The benefit performance was eliminated, and to offset the loss of revenue for the actors, they raised salaries. The Bancrofts paid as much as ten times what the other theatres paid actors, so the performers did not complain about losing the benefit;

4) They also developed the idea of touring with complete cast, sets, and properties, beginning with *Caste* in 1867. After the show closed at the Prince of Wales Theatre, it was taken on tour;

5) They eliminated the afterpiece and the curtain raiser that Charles Kean had added and established the single-play bill;

6) They also helped establish the practice of matinee performances during a production of *Diplomacy* in 1878 (matinees in England had begun in the late 1850s but they became expected with the Bancrofts. It would be Gilbert and Sullivan with comic opera in the 1880s that would firmly solidify the matinee convention in England);

7) They firmly anchored acting behind the proscenium arch. With the production of *Caste*, the "fourth wall" was always respected at the Prince of Wales Theatre;

8) And when the Bancrofts moved to the Haymarket theatre in the 1880s, they eliminated the apron stage entirely, and extended the proscenium across the bottom of the stage to form a picture frame;

9) They also established the orchestra as the favored seating area. They put in chairs, what we call "stalls," and because there were separate seats and not only benches in the orchestra, they started to number the seats so that spectators could make advance reservations for performances. We tend to

forget the fact that with the exception of the boxes, most of the open seating area was benches. So that if the theatre could seat 3500 people, they'd sell 3500 tickets and people would storm in to get the best seat. When the long run becomes the rule, seat reservations become a necessity.

Spectacular Devices

The return of polite society to the playhouse (which had begun with Macready, and was encouraged by Robertson and the Bancrofts, and developed to a great extent by the Gilbert and Sullivan operas which extended from 1871 to 1896) was essentially bolstered by the work of **Henry Irving** (1838-1905). Henry Irving inherited a whole series of theatrical effects which were prevalent during the late 1800s:

1) DeLoutherbourg's *eidophusikon* which was developed in 1781. This was a combination of lighting, sound, scene painting, transparencies, and cutouts to create a realistic kind of scene. This of course is going to have a great impact in the area of free plantation scenery where there is a backdrop, a scrim in front of that, and scenic elements which are anchored at various areas in front of the stage. The way the scrim is lit will allow the audience either to see in front of it or behind it;

2) The panorama and stereoscope: the stereoscope, which developed in England in 1832, was a device where one could see two photographs viewed side by side, like an old view-master, creating the illusion of a 3-dimensional perspective;

3) The diorama which was developed in England in 1823; and

4) The cosmorama which was a cross between the diorama (where the audience would see a great spectacle in front of them) and a peep show. They'd look into a small box to see large spectacles.

Another aspect of theatrical spectacle which became very important in the nineteenth century was stage lighting. One of the earliest developments that we have was inspired by authoress **Joanna Baillie**, who, as early as 1812, called for a removal of footlights and suggested overhead lamps with reflectors. She also suggested that battens should be built out from the top of the proscenium beyond the stage so that lights could be hung at a good angle. In addition, she also urged the replacement of oil and candle lighting by gas light. Gas was first used in the London theatre in Covent Garden in 1815, and the Olympic was the first to light its house with gas. In 1817, the Lyceum used gas light over the entire stage and by September 1817, Covent Garden and Drury Lane were completely gas lit. In 1822, the Olympic theatre regressed back to candle light because of the problems with gas light: the smell and the possibility for explosions. In 1828, Covent Garden had an explosion of some of the gas functions, and returned to oil and candles for a while. In 1834, scrim lighting was beginning to be used at the Olympic Theatre, and sometime between 1826 and 1837 limelight made its way onto the stage. The use of limelight was perfected by Charles Kean although it was used experimentally by Macready. Historians suggest that Kean introduced focused limelight in 1855 in his production of *King Henry VIII*. There are two kinds of limelight: open limelight for a general wash, and a lime spotlight for concentrated beams. A piece of lime is put into the gas jet and creates a bright light; with a reflector behind it, it shoots a better beam of light than any of the gas fixtures. It was also discovered that limelight responded better to gels and to colors than the previous gas light.

Footlights also began to be improved. In 1861 what we call a new style of footlights was installed at the Paris opera with reflectors. They were designed so that the footlights would not take up much space on the apron. Up to that point, for footlights to show enough light, the whole apparatus had to be so open that it would impair the view of the audience. With better reflectors to enable the footlights to throw more light, the apparatus could be sunk lower on the apron, substantially improving sightlines. In 1863 this style of footlights was used at the Lyceum with an added mechanism for changing color.

Henry Irving

Director and manager of the Lyceum Theatre from 1878, Henry Irving wasn't as slavish to historical accuracy as Charles Keen, nor was he quite as lavish as another theatre director, Herbert Beerbohm Tree. His outstanding achievement lies in a unity of style in production and the creation of the director-actor as the primary agent in the theatre. He managed to create harmoniously conceived productions brought about by a disciplined company. To achieve this artistic unity, he evolved technical advances:

1) To focus attention on the action of the play he insisted on the regular lowering of the auditorium lights—he is the first in England to demand that the house be darkened—and he increased the illusion of the play by equipping the stage with a black false proscenium to mask the wings;

2) He handled limelight more subtly and elaborately than his predecessors. He began to explore the uses of color, and he used transparent colored lacquers on the glasses of the limelight boxes. He later transferred coloration to the electrical lamps themselves. In addition, he broke up the rows of footlights into different colored groups that were individually controlled. With greater control of color and intensity, Irving was able to light different parts of the stage space selectively and this was important because now one could stage the action in one particular playing area and darken the rest of the space;

3) He put all the controls of lighting into the prompter's hands. Suddenly, the prompter began to function like a modern stage manager;

4) He used free plantation scenery, ground rows, and other scenic elements that could be placed at various positions and anchored to the stage floor;

5) He was the first producer to use the front curtain to mask changes of scenery. While other producers had used a show curtain, or *a vista* scene changes in front of the audience, Irving argued that if the audience saw the scene change, there would be a break in the illusion;

6) He tried to make an art of theatre lighting, using black masking to hide spill. To maintain the dramatic illusion, he would also use teasers to hide any lights that would be above;

7) He also became a leading figure in the public life. This is important because he did so to raise public opinion of the theatre and actors. When he was offered knighthood in 1883, he declined it, but he did accept the honor in 1895.

In addition, many of Irving's production techniques were not only innovative but ingenious. In his production of Boucicault's *The Corsican Brothers*, he used real men and women at the front of the stage to form crowds. As the crowd would extend to the back of the stage, he used children dressed exactly like the men and women to enforce the perspective. At the back of the crowd, he painted people on the backdrop to enforce the illusion of a stage filled with people. To create snowfall on the stage, he used coarse salt that was dropped on to the stage from above by stagehands using sifters. In addition, Irving positioned men in the wings with great sacks of salt. So not only were there people on the top with sifters, but you had stagehands on the side going "Whoosh! Whoosh! Whoosh!" with the snow. As actors were coming onstage, they'd get a burst of snow in their faces, and since it was coarse salt, it would stay in the actor's hair and hold onto his costume; and, if he should get it in his mouth, it would dissolve like snow. It was a very realistic effect.

Irving's chief concern as an actor was with strong passions achieved by means of bold effects. These effects were always artistically conceived and painstakingly executed. He was one of those actors who would pace through every movement in a play. Nothing was left to chance. He was terribly awkward, tall, slender, and he had an extremely limited voice. The roles which suited him best were those of high melodrama and his most famous role was Mathias in *The Bells*. Just before the end of the piece the protagonist has a vision that he's on trial for committing murder (when in fact what he did was allow someone to die when he could have prevented it). Stage direction: *Mathias staggers and falls on his knees. The crowd make a movement of terror. The death bell tolls. Lights lower gradually. The curtain at back of gauze descends disclosing the scene as at commencement. Lights up. Music. Bells heard ringing.*

The crowd calls, "Burgermaster, burgermaster." He does not answer. *Several violent blows are struck upon the door which falls into the room from its hinges. Crash. Enter Christian hurriedly. He runs to the alcove. Music heard. Mathias looks at the alcove. Mathias appears from the alcove. He is dressed in the same clothes as when he retired as the commencement of the scene. His face is haggard and ghastly pale. He comes out, his eyes fixed, his arms extended as he rushes forward with uncertain steps. Children are in back. It looks like there's a large group of people here.* MATHIAS: "The rope, the rope. Cut the rope." *There is a rope that is pealing the bells. Mathias now has a vision that someone has a rope around his neck and is going to strangle him. The hand clutches the throat as if to remove something that strangles him.* "Take the rope from my neck. Take the rope from my neck." *He looks pitifully around as if to recognize those about him and his falls on his breast. Katherine kneeling places her hand on Mathias's heart.* "Dead." *The bells cease. Annette bursts into tears. The women in the crowd wail. The men remove their hats and bend their heads upon their breasts. Tableau. Curtain.*

Ellen Terry

Henry Irving's leading lady was one of the most beloved actresses of any generation, the talented and charismatic Ellen Terry (1847-1928). She debuted as a child actress in *The Winter's Tale* under Charles Kean in 1856. In 1864, she left the stage to get married to a painter named Watts who left her within ten months because his rich patroness said his wife must go. She returned to the stage in 1867 with Henry Irving, playing Katherine to his Petruchio in *The Taming of the Shrew*. In 1868, she left the stage for six years to live with Edward Godwin who fathered her children, Editha and Edward Gordon Craig. In 1874, she left Godwin, and producer Charles Reed talked her into returning to the stage. In 1875, she played Portia in *The Merchant of Venice*, one of her best roles. And in 1877, she finally got a divorce from Watts and married an actor named Charles Kelly, after which she joined Henry Irving at the Lyceum Theatre where she was Irving's only major leading lady between 1878 and 1902. Typical of the kind of things being done in the English theatre, she played Ophelia in 1878 to Irving's Hamlet; Portia in

1879; Desdemona in 1881; Juliet and Beatrice in 1882; Lady Macbeth in 1888; and Cordelia in 1892.

Throughout his career, George Bernard Shaw tried to get Ellen Terry away from Henry Irving because Shaw believed that Irving was not making the best use of her talents. He thought that Irving's melodramatic style was holding her back. Yet Terry without Irving didn't flourish too terribly well. In the 1890s she began a paper courtship with Shaw, and in 1902, after Henry Irving's retirement from the stage, she appeared with Herbert Beerbohm Tree in *The Merry Wives of Windsor*. Finally, in 1905, she appeared Lady Cecily Waynflete in *Captain Brassbound's Conversion* written for her by Shaw. In 1906 she celebrated her golden jubilee (50 years on the stage), and in 1907, she married a thirty-year-old American actor named James Careu. They soon parted.

Shaw saw Ellen Terry as the shining example of the modern intelligent actress capable of natural and intellectual performance, and since Shaw was promoting a more natural school of playwriting and acting, she was the embodiment of his theatrical beliefs. Throughout the 1890s he constantly urged her to leave Henry Irving so that she could dedicate herself to the modern drama as exemplified by Ibsen and Shaw. She had an instinctual genius, and great beauty, charm and an immediate command of sentiment. She last appeared on the stage in 1925 when she was made a Grand Dame of the British Empire.

15. Realism and Naturalism

The 19th-century trend toward realism was hastened through the innovations of Richard Wagner, primarily a composer of operas, and the Duke of Saxe-Meiningen, a director.

Richard Wagner
While actually rejecting the contemporary trend toward realism—as in plays trading on day-to-day society—Richard Wagner (1813-1883) did share the realists' belief in total illusion on stage, and their concern for the depiction of social problems. He believed in a symbiosis between art and society and argued that true art could thrive only in a free society—but until society is truly free, art could have a liberating effect, freeing the spectator, if only momentarily, from oppression and exploitation. In his essay, "Art and Revolution," Wagner called for an "artwork of the future," free of capitalist speculation and profit-making, that would restore the integrity of classical Greek tragedy by uniting all the arts (i.e., music, painting, and drama) under the aegis of theatre. In later essays, "The Artwork of the Future" and "Opera and Drama," he called for a *Gesamtkunstwerk* (*Total Work of Art*) combining music, poetry, and dance on an equal basis along with architecture, sculpture, and painting. Because all of these elements needed a strong director to maintain a unified production,

Wagner's concept of *Gesamtkunstwerk* aided in the advancement of the art of directing in the theatre.

Wagner also influenced theatre architecture. To house his idealized music-dramas, he set out to create a new opera house in Bayreuth, Germany. Begun in 1872 and finally opened four years later, Wagner's *Festspielhaus* inspired many reforms in theatrical design:

1) It abandoned the box, pit, and gallery format. The main part of the auditorium had thirty stepped rows of seats;

2) There were no side boxes or center aisles. Each row led to its own side exit;

3) At the back of the auditorium was a single large box with a small balcony above it;

4) To provide excellent sightlines, the auditorium was shaped like a fan measuring 50 feet at the proscenium and 115 feet across the back of the house;

5) Since all seats were considered equally good, a uniform admission price was charged;

6) The orchestra pit was hidden from view, most of it extended beneath the stage floor;

7) The auditorium lights were dimmed during the performance;

8) The stage was framed with a double proscenium.

The stage itself was rather conservative: there was a slight rake and scenery was changed using the chariot-and-pole method. The principal innovation in terms of scenery came from a system of steam vents to create realistic effects of fog and mist, and a steam curtain that was used to mask set changes. Although the stage was 80 feet deep and 93 feet wide with 100 feet of overhead space and 32 feet of basement space, the actual proscenium opening was 40 feet wide.

Wagner's theories would spawn later non-illusionistic approaches to the theatre, but his own productions aimed at complete illusion:

1) He forbade musicians to tune in the pit;

2) He did not permit applause during the performance, or curtain calls at the end;

3) He demanded precise historical accuracy in sets and costumes;

4) He employed moving panoramas to suggests moving from one place to another (Wagner's emphasis on realistic detail was such that in the production of his opera *Siegfried*, he used a dragon with realistic scales and moveable eyes and mouth).

For Richard Wagner, the ideal production was to be achieved through total illusion.

The Duke of Saxe-Meiningen

While Wagner's opera house was being built in Bayreuth, the company directed by Georg II, Duke of Saxe-Meiningen (1826-1914) was becoming known for its realistic productions. In his youth, Georg II was an avid theatre goer: he witnessed Tieck's productions in Berlin, Charles Kean's Shakespearean productions in London, and the great ensemble performances at the Comédie Française. On 16 January 1853 Georg saw Ira Aldridge perform Othello, Macbeth, and Mungo (from Isaac Bickerstaff and Charles Dibdin's *The Padlock*) at the court of King Frederich Wilhelm IV. So impressed was the Duke with Aldridge's performance that he invited him to play Shylock, Macbeth, and Mungo in Meiningen in 1858.

Upon succeeding to the throne in 1866 after his father's abdication (over hostility toward Prussia which was at war with Austria), Georg took a personal interest in the affairs of the court theatre and began to alter its repertory. In managing the troupe, he relied heavily on Friedrich von Bodenstedt (1819-1892) until 1871, and then Ludwig Chronegk (1837-1891) who had been employed as a comic actor with the company in 1866. Chronegk was a chronic worker who conceived and arranged the tours that would make the Meiningen Company famous. Ellen Franz (1839-1923), an actress and the duke's 3rd wife (his first wife Charlotte died in 1855, and his second wife Feo died in 1872) was another major influence on the company. After 1873 when she married the Duke, Ellen suggested plays for the repertory, adapted the texts for production, and supervised stage speech,.

Between 1866 and 1874, the company played only in Meiningen. In 1874, it performed in Berlin and took the audience by surprise. The response to the players was so great that the company went on tour between 1874 and 1890, playing 38 cities in 9 countries (Russia, Sweden, Austria, Denmark, Belgium, the Netherlands, and England), and giving 2600 performances of 41 plays. When it stopped touring in 1890, the Meiningen Company was the most respected acting company in the world.

The Duke sought to create the illusion of reality with accurate spectacle and lifelike acting. His repertory, composed of Shakespeare, Schiller, Grillparzer, and 19th-century Romantic playwrights, was not particularly innovative: he was less concerned with doing unusual plays than he was in producing first-class drama. He did, however, experiment with "realistic" drama of the new school—he produced Ibsen's *Ghosts*, for example—but most of the repertory consisted of poetic and Romantic plays.

The Meiningen Company emphasized pictorial realism in which it excelled all previous standards because of its greater accuracy. The Duke divided each century into thirds and further distinguished national differences within the various time periods. Accuracy was further insured by the Duke's refusal to allow actors to tamper with their costumes, and he insisted on authentic materials in place of less expensive fabrics. Along these lines, he introduced genuine chain-mail armor, swords, and other practical accoutrements into productions; this demand for authentic materials led to the creation of supply houses that manufactured the props, costumes, and furniture which the Duke had designed for stage use (not only did the Duke direct productions, he designed them as well).

Strong colors were employed in scenery, reversing the tradition of having actors perform in front of pastel sets; as a result, the scenery for Meiningen productions was often criticized as being "garish." The Duke also did away with "sky borders" (the conventional masking for overhead battens) and, instead, used foliage, beams, banners, and other more realistic devices as overhead masking. He avoided symmetrical balance in his designs and insisted on proportion, using painted and 3-dimensional elements convincingly. He also considered the stage floor as part of the design and broke it up with fallen trees, rocks, steps, and platforms (recalling De Loutherbourg's work with Garrick in England).

The company's ace was its ensemble acting. The Duke held complete control over the actors who, for financial reasons, were either beginners or older actors without outstanding success. Even though guest actors occasionally appeared with the troupe, there was a no-star policy clearly evidenced by Saxe-Meiningen's requirement that all actors not cast as leads must appear as supernumeraries in productions. This made possible the crowd scenes for which the Meiningen Company was famous. Even when the number of available bodies might be limited, Georg managed to create the illusion of large masses of people through the following devices:

1) He created sets that forced the actors into the wings, suggesting great numbers of people offstage;

2 He staged crowd scenes using diagonal and contrasting movement patterns to create confusion and agitation;

3) Each member of the mob was given individual characteristics and specific lines, then the whole group was carefully coordinated.

The Duke of Saxe-Meiningen could count on long rehearsal periods. At the time, Meiningen had a population of 8,000 and the theatre was open only twice a week for six months of the year. Each play was rehearsed from the beginning with full sets, furniture, and props. Costumes, though not always available at the beginning, were used for some time prior to the opening of the play. Actors were required to "act" from the first day rather than merely walking through their parts, as had been the case in other theatres. Rehearsals were generally held at night after the Duke's state duties were discharged and often lasted five or six hours. There was no fixed number of rehearsals: actors continued to rehearse a play until it was ready to be shown to the public.

The Duke's notable innovations, or departures from traditional production techniques included:

1) The discontinuation of the popular (and melodramatic) practice of *tableau vivant* at the end of acts;

2) The abolishment of orchestral accompaniment to songs in plays and orchestral interludes between the acts;

3) Actors were encouraged to turn their backs to the audience when speaking to other actors on stage so that actors could actually look at one another;

4) The use of straight lines or semicircles in blocking was discontinued;

5) The employment of a quick curtain, to heighten the dramatic moment of a scene.

In the area of illumination, gas lighting, colored, if necessary, by silk screens, served for general illumination of the Duke's productions. However, Georg was fascinated by unusual and striking effects which he achieved by departing from the usual lighting positions at the front and sides of the stage, and by adding electric spotlights for special effects (i.e., the appearance of Caesar's ghost in *Julius Caesar*).

The impact of the Meiningen Company arose from the complete illusion achieved in every aspect of the production. It stood at the beginning of the movement toward unified production in which every element was selected because of its contribution to the total effect. The actor has given way to the director as the dominant artist in the theatre, and Saxe-Meiningen, as an autocratic director interested in creating the illusion of reality, would have a profound influence on the development of the modern theatre.

Realism

Like Romanticism, Realism is subject to a great many interpretations:

1) It may suggest the literal reproduction of every-day life, a trend already in progress by reformers such as Montigny but carried much farther by André Antoine;

2) It may refer to the use of contemporary, as opposed to classical or mythological, subjects. Since Scribe and Augier had already mined the moneyed classes in the Well-Made Play, the contemporary subjects that interested the later realists were the lower classes;

3) Realism can also involve a concern with historical accuracy (a trait it shares with Romanticism), in an attempt either to recreate the historical period in which a play is set (like the productions of Pixérécourt and Sardou), or to recreate the conditions of the original production of the play (like Tieck and Immerman's attempts to recreate the Elizabethan playhouse).

The development of theatrical realism occurred simultaneously with a period of scientific and sociological growth that both nurtured and necessitated the theatrical movement. In 1848, the year of workers' revolutions in Paris, Milan, Rome, Berlin, Vienna, and Prague, Marx's *Communist Manifesto* was translated and distributed to working classes around the world. In the same year, the first woman's rights convention was held at Seneca Falls, New York, the 1st Public Health Act was established in Great Britain, and the California gold rush was under way. In 1849, Amelia Bloomer reformed women's wear in the United States; the following year the College of Science and Technology was established in London, and the 2nd law of thermodynamics was formulated. In 1851, Singer developed the sewing machine, and Lord Kelvin developed the laws of conservation and dissipation of energy; in 1852 Herbert Spencer wrote "The Development Hypothesis," in which the word "evolution" was voiced for the very first time. The following year saw the creation of the first railroad through the Alps, the development of anesthesia in Great Britain, and the compulsory use of the smallpox vaccination. It was in the wake of such innovations that theatrical realism blossomed.

Bjornstjerne Bjornson

Bjornstjerne Bjornson (1832-1910) was a poet, dramatist, novelist, and theatre director who made a greater impression in his native Norway, Scandinavia, and Europe during his lifetime than Ibsen. His mission as an artist was to educate and stimulate a patriotic feeling on behalf of the emerging Norwegian nation. From 1857 to 1859, Bjornson was director of the Norwegian Theatre in Bergen, a post he inherited from Ibsen, and he first came to prominence as the writer of stories from peasant life (i.e., *Arne* in 1859, *A Happy Boy* in 1860) that broke with Romanticism providing a less idyllic view of peasant life than what was then in vogue. These stories were composed in a vigorous style demonstrating the influence of Scandinavian sagas and folk-tales, which Bjornson utilized to help him express the true national spirit of Norway.

In 1865, 14 years before Ibsen's *A Doll's House*, Bjornson created the first domestic problem play with the one-act *The Newly Married Couple*. Between 1865 and 1867 he was director of the Christiania Theatre in Oslo where he fought hard to establish a national dramatic trend: Norwegian plays with Norwegian actors. In 1875, anticipating Ibsen's *Pillars of the Community* by two years, he produced *A Bankruptcy* and *The Editor*, realistic plays urging greater honesty in the business world and in the press.

Starting in the 1880s, Bjornson's literary output had a more precise didactic aim: *A Gauntlet* (1883) attacked the sexual mores of the day and called for the same purity in men before marriage that was typically demanded of women; and *Beyond our Power* (1883), a play equal to the best of Ibsen's works, attacked all striving and aspiration which ran counter to our limited human nature. In *Beyond our Power*, faith-healer Adolph Sang has been unable to heal his wife Clara because she does not share his faith in miracles. When a landslide miraculously spares the church from destruction, Sang decides to pray publicly for his wife's cure. To protect her husband's reputation, Clara gets up from her sickbed and walks to the church—an apparent miracle. At the church, however, she collapses and dies, and Sang realizes the selfishness of his desire to cure his wife publicly. The guilt is too much for him to bear and he collapses by her side.

Bjornson is not remembered today because his plays are so much a part of the time and place in which he wrote that they do not transcend national and temporal boundaries. The universality that made Ibsen great is almost completely lacking in Bjornson's work.

Henrik Ibsen

Henrik Johan Ibsen (1828-1906), perhaps Norway's most famous playwright, began his professional life as a druggist's apprentice. His first play, *Cataline* (1848) was an unproduced academic exercise, an attempt to recreate classical tragedy. Two years later, *The Warrior's Barrow*, a one-act play evocative of the Danish plays of Adam Oehlenschläger, was Ibsen's first produced work. Though the play was not a success, Ibsen's work showed sufficient promise for Ole Bull to hire him to work at the newly organized National Theatre in Bergen, Norway. There Ibsen began to write plays based on Norwegian myths (like Wagner, Ibsen was interested in mining the potential of national mythologies), and he directed several well-made plays by Scribe whom he learned to respect through the teachings of Johann Luise Heiberg. In 1852, the National Theatre sent its staff on a tour of theatres in Denmark and Germany, and it was during this tour that Ibsen witnessed four comedies by Ludwig Holberg, an 18th-century Norwegian playwright highly influenced by Molière. From Holberg, Ibsen acknowledged that he learned the art of keeping the action of a play moving forward. Also, at this time, Ibsen discovered Herman Hettner's book, *The Modern Drama*, which stressed psychological conflict as the basis of drama. This influenced him in the creation of characters that were neither wholly good nor evil but a true-to-life mixture of both qualities.

Returning to Bergen, Ibsen produced *Lady Inger of Ostrat* (1855) and *The Feast at Solhaug* (1856), his first real theatrical success. He was director of the Norske Theatre from 1857 to 1862 where he failed in his attempts to create an indigenous Norwegian theatre art. In 1858, he married Suzannah Thornsen which brought him stability in his home life and the ability, with her dowry, to sit at home and write. After four years of marriage he produced a play in verse, aptly called *Love's Comedy*, Ibsen's first attempt at contemporary social criticism. His realistic reflections on marriage, suggesting a thin line between the comic and tragic in a marital situation, awakened public indignation. Critics said that he should not air his dirty linen in public (there will be a similar reaction to Strindberg when he wrote a number of his earlier realistic or naturalistic plays). Ibsen followed his domestic verse play with *The Pretenders*, a successful history play, which dealt with national responsibility. From 1864, the year he wrote *The Pretenders*, until 1891 he lived abroad, mostly in Italy and Germany. This was significant because it made his work cosmopolitan and gave it the kind of universality that Bjornson's work did not have.

Ultimately Norway's failure to support Denmark's war with Germany during this period gave rise to two verse plays: *Brand* and *Peer Gynt* which deal essentially with inflexible idealism and wayward irresponsibility. It is interesting that the hero in *Brand* is consumed in an avalanche, and at the end of Ibsen's last play *When We Dead Awaken*, the hero is also killed in an avalanche. It is almost as if he comes full circle as a playwright. Ibsen seems to be reflecting on an essential theme of Greek tragedy: the individual man who is trying to function on the level of the gods and cannot succeed. In 1869, he produced *The League of Youth* which was followed by the "problem plays," notably: *Pillars of Society*, *A Doll's House*, and *Ghosts*. With *Pillars of Society* Ibsen began to write his version of the problem play, a play using the Well-Made Play formula, dealing with social or ethical issues (similar to the thesis plays of Dumas, *fils*, in France, though Ibsen managed to create a more realistic portrayal of society's problems). In 1879, appeared *A Doll's House* which was extremely significant because Nora slammed the door and walked out on her husband and children at the end of the play. This was highly unusual for the audience who wondered how a playwright could end a play so inconclusively. The play suggested the existence of a world where a woman could exist without a man, and reminded us that plays do not have to be tied up in nice little neat packages.

Three years later, Ibsen produced *Ghosts* (in which a person inherits syphilis from his father) and creates a play about internal hysteria, continuing a line of investigation into the minds of his characters. Interestingly, *Ghosts* was first produced in Chicago in 1882 by a Dano-Norwegian acting company on an American tour. In 1883, he produced *An Enemy of the People*, which explored man's role in society, and introduced a kind of folk symbolism which would be reflected in the plays from then on: *The Wild Duck, Rosmersholm, The Lady from the Sea, The Master Builder*, and most importantly *Hedda Gabler*. Critics suggest that Ibsen managed to raise symbolism to the level of a character in a play. In *Hedda Gabler*, burning Luvborg's book is burning a baby. There are clear dramatic connections that align those symbols. In *Rosmersholm*, there is the symbol of the water wheel which characterizes the family and the kind of lifestyle in which they are engaged. In *The Master Builder*, there exists a great phallic symbol of a tower being constructed. Solness, the master builder, is convinced into climbing up to the tower to crown it with a wreath. In this act exist symbols of a wedding and sexual intercourse and, after he succeeds in crowning the tower, the master builder dies.

Ibsen's major theme is a search for self in a context of conflicting social demands. The search, of course, is generally marked by failure and self-inflicted death. This does not necessarily mean the character must die physically because that is not the only way a person can inflict death upon himself.

Few dramatists have been as influential as Ibsen on the development of realism in the theatre:

1) He is the father of the modern problem play;

2) He teaches us how to endow people, events, and things with a symbolic value. Before Ibsen, little pieces of business would not be so specifically detailed in a play script. There might be an explanation of the locale, or a suggestion of some kind of scenic effect. Ibsen, however, is very specific about what every character does even when he or she is not speaking. For example, in *The Master Builder* while his secretary is working Solness enters the room. As soon as she sees him, she lifts the eyeshade from her eyes because it casts a strange green shadow across her face. Ibsen specifies that she removes this costume piece. She doesn't want to look ugly for the master builder. We find

out that she's in love with him. In addition, the boss enters the room speaking in a whisper, "Is anyone here?" Why would a boss whisper? Ibsen provides very specific details that connect to the characters and the action of the play;

3) He structures his plays around the climax so that they move almost like a snowball running down the hill to the big scene (the "obligatory scene of the well-made play). Every one of Ibsen's plays, at least the mature plays, are structured so that the audience will anxiously anticipate the obligatory scene;

4) He improved the techniques of dramatic exposition. Unlike playwrights up to this point who would generally provide all the background information at the very beginning of the play, Ibsen spreads it out through the entire play, waiting to reveal the last part of the puzzle at the climactic scene. In a way, this is not unusual: in the Well-Made-Play there is always a character with a secret. Ibsen, however, would always build the play in such a way that the secret is something the audience would have known all along if they'd heard the exposition correctly. It's easy to decipher but it always comes out as a surprise (even if only to the characters onstage). Typically, with Ibsen, it is a misinterpretation of the events by a character on stage that causes the dramatic problem and, as a result, he transforms the Well-Made Play into a compact vehicle for theatrical realism. An excellent example is found in *The Master Builder* with Solness thinking that his wife will never forgive him for the fire that burned their home and caused the deaths of their two children. His wife, on the other hand, is less concerned with her two children (who she believes are living in heaven) than the loss of her family home and her childhood dolls. Because of this misapprehension, the two of them miscommunicate throughout the play, and the audience perceives the reality of the situation through the way Ibsen manipulates the exposition.

Naturalism

The most significant of the early recipients of Ibsen's influence was **Emile Zola** (1840-1902), a novelist who felt that the theatre was dying of inanity and believed that the only way to save it was to infuse it with a scientific and experimental spirit. What this meant was that the theatre should pay greater attention to detail, especially that of everyday life, and be concerned with the effects of milieu on character. Also, it should develop an interest in the pathological and treat everything with a kind of disinterested, almost ironic point of view. The first attempt at applying this experiment which Zola called "naturalism," was *Thérèse Raquin*, produced in 1873 at the Renaissance Theatre. This was a dramatization of his novel which was published in 1867. The play was hissed and emphatically condemned. Critics said: "These brutal incongruities I found displeasing enough in the novel are insupportable on the stage." In *Thérèse Raquin* Zola argues that one cannot escape one's past and that one's character is one's fate. In the play, a sensual woman plots with her lover to drown her sickly husband. A year later the lovers marry but their passion has turned to guilt, fear, and hatred. The dead man's mother, discovering the truth, is stricken with paralysis and cannot speak. She gloats and watches the couple first try to kill each other out of guilt and finally commit suicide. At the moment the lovers die, the mother-in-law begins speaking again, her debility is removed.

The double suicide and the mother's recovery of speech at the final curtain are highly melodramatic, but the characters are examined with naturalistic detail. With this experiment, Zola argued that the stage must become a laboratory where human behavior can be clinically dissected and examined to prove an irrefutable law of nature: that human actions, desires, and goals are determined not by free will but by social forces beyond the control of any individual. To achieve the concept of laboratory theatre, every play must offer a slice of life, "tranche de vie," and not be governed by artistic structures, such as the formula of the Well-Made Play. Zola also sought to reveal the impact of heredity and the lower-middle-class environment on its victims, to which end he portrayed characters in all their sordid and unsavory situations. What does this suggest about naturalism? It suggests that naturalism is dirty; it stinks, it is drab, it is unhappy; it presents a group of people who are manipulated by society and by situations over which they have no control.

Zola's second play was *The Rabourdin Heirs* (1874) which was called "dull, repulsive and immoral" by the critics. As a result, Zola took a job as a theatre critic and, in 1877, he produced a novel called *The Tavern* which was extremely popular. When he wanted to present it on the stage, he asked another playwright to adapt it, just in case the audience would not appreciate his own work. While waiting for *The Tavern* to be produced, Zola produced one last play called *Rosebud*, a domestic farce. The riots in the theatre were so bad that the actors could not even finish the play. The audience began to hoot and catcall to such a degree that the curtain came down and never rose again.

Zola then turned to examine the claims of religious and social organizations, and wrote books that debunked various charities, arguing that religious societies designed to help the poor do not give the money to the poor. In 1903, he produced a very important book called *Truth* which dealt with the Dreyfus case. There was a court martial at the end of the 1890s that dealt with a Captain Dreyfus and his alleged misconduct with a superior officer—an issue that was trumped up allegedly because of Dreyfus' Judaism. Since it was an anti-Semitic situation, Zola jumped on the bandwagon and attacked the attacker with his famous newspaper article, "I accuse!"

To stay out of prison, by the way, during the Dreyfus case, Zola went to England from 1898-1899, where he met his English publisher who was put in prison for publishing his works.

Henri Becque

One of the chief apostles of Zola was Henri Becque (1837-1899) who both inherited Zola's point of view and also some of his problems. After *Thérèse Raquin* appeared in Paris, censorship was reintroduced in France, and Henri Becque became the first major victim of this situation. He attended school in Paris and became a secretary in the household of a French diplomat. Becque started his theatrical career by writing opera librettos but, deciding that he didn't like playing politics with theatre managers who kept giving him the run around, he decided to become a theatre critic. He directed his own first serious play *Michael Pauper* in 1870, a failure which he produced at his own expense, after a major disagreement with the theatre that promised to do it. Another attempt called *The Elopement* the following year failed as well. This forced Becque to take a job as a stockbroker, during the performance of which, he discovered the avarice and corruption in the financial world.

In 1877, Becque composed his most famous play *The Vultures* which was finally performed in 1882 at the Comédie Française, after it had been refused by seven other theatres. It was considered by critics the prototype of the French naturalistic play even though it came after the production of *Thérèse Raquin*. Like Zola's play, it portrayed an unpleasant slice of life, but rather than presenting it with a dispassionate, scientific point of view, Becque created real flesh-and-blood characters, causing critics to suggest that the play was more filled with life than anything Zola wrote. The premiere occurred on 14 September 1882 and sparked a violent clash between the conservatives and the new avant-garde, very much the way the classicists and the romantics battled it out after the premiere of Hugo's *Hernani*. In the play, a happy family prepares for the marriage of their youngest daughter to a neighbor's son. The gaiety is shattered because at the end of the first act, we learn that the girl's father has been killed in an accident. The dead man's aged business partner (who is a lecher and the shrewdest vulture of them all) and the family lawyer, another vulture, move in to despoil the grief-stricken family's wealth. Because the daughter now lacks a dowry, the neighbor's mother uses the fact that the daughter and her son slept together before their marriage as an excuse to call off the wedding. The poor girl, without a husband and discredited in society, goes insane, and the play ends with another daughter, the maid of honor, agreeing to marry the business partner to avoid his robbing the family of all of its property. *The Vultures* is really a dark, vile play depicting the hypocrisy of lawyers and how business interests reduce women to virtual prostitution. At the end, as he's about to marry the young girl, the business partner remarks: "Don't worry honey. I'll keep you away from all those vultures who are trying to get at this household." Predictably, he is the one who is destroying the household most!

The Vultures was a very important play and sped Becque on his way to fame in the last quarter of the nineteenth century with other plays, notably

The Parisian Woman, the prototype of the *comédie rosse* or "cynical comedy" in which conventional morality is reversed. In *The Parisian Woman*, for example, a wife named Clotilda is having an affair with a lover and her husband accepts the lover into his own household. In order to help her husband acquire an important government post, the wife takes another lover, causing the first lover to become terribly annoyed and jealous. The husband is neither jealous nor annoyed, but the lover claims that it is it neither the Christian, nor noble thing to do (a point of view that makes him appear ridiculous in the play). Ultimately, the new lover spurns the wife, and the old lover leaves her as well. The woman is left with her husband who remains perfectly complacent and she, once again, takes to the streets in search of adventure.

Despite Becque's success, the difficulty he had in getting plays produced, guaranteed that few contemporary playwrights would follow in his footsteps. Slowly, however, Parisian theatres began to evolve less difficult procedures to nurture new talent:

1) Ferdinand Louveaus created a dramatic society called *The Intimate Art Circle* which produced unknown work by established writers;

2) Ballande formed the *Society to Patronize Unknown Dramatic Authors* which supported matinee performances by unproduced playwrights;

3) Tallien (an actor manager) introduced what he called "Unpublished Matinees" in 1879. These served to introduce the work of new playwrights, using actors from the professional theatres. The performances were not necessarily open to the public. Rather they were like a club to which the audience purchased a membership.

The Independent Theatre Movement

These presentations serve as a prelude to the most important figure in the development of experimental theatre in the nineteenth century: **André Antoine** (1858-1943). Antoine, who functioned as a very significant entrepreneur of theatrical activity, worked as a clerk at the gas company. His theatrical experience was limited to appearing as a supernumerary with Parisian professional companies, and guest spots with amateur groups. When he set out to produce a program of new plays, his amateur group, the Cercle Gaulois, refused to cooperate, so he set off on his own. He adopted the name Théâtre Libre, "the independent theatre" for his company, and produced his first bill on 29 March 1887, a resounding success. The following month, in April 1887, he produced his second series of plays, and inspired by an article in the *Wagner Review*, he darkened his auditorium for the first time. This marks the first time we have a Paris house darkened during a play. By the end of the year, Antoine was famous. He gave up his clerkship in the gas company, and he devoted himself to the theatre until 1914.

Organized as a subscription theatre, the Théâtre Libre was open only to members and, therefore, exempt from censorship. Many of the best plays available to Antoine were those that had been refused licenses by the ordinary playhouses, and most of these were naturalistic. Much of the notoriety of this theatre came from the *comédies rosses*, the cynical comedies inspired by Becque, and in 1888, he began to produce one foreign work each year. Characteristically, Antoine would schedule two or three bills a year and perform two or three shorter plays in repertory per bill. When the Théâtre Libre began to explore longer plays like *Ghosts* and *The Wild Duck*, the bill would be reduced to only one play. In addition to being a showcase for new and unusual theatre pieces, the Théâtre Libre experimented with a variety of new production techniques:

1) After 1888, when he saw the Meiningen Players and Henry Irving's company, Antoine sought to reproduce the environment in every detail in his plays (we are now approaching photographic realism in France). For example, in *The Butchers* (1888), he hung real carcasses of beef on the stage so that the audience could both see and smell the environment;

2) After the production of *Sister Philomene* in 1888, the concept of the 4th wall would be observed consistently;

3) When he designed settings, Antoine arranged rooms as they might be in real life and then only after rehearsing the play for some time, he decided

which wall should be removed for the audience to peer through. Now what is that going to do to the actor? He's going to act naturally and pay little or no attention to the audience. If Antoine decided that the audience was going to be the back wall of the room, then the actor was going to play with his back to the audience providing a sense of "a slice of life" rather than a theatrical performance. Often furniture was placed along the curtain line (downstage, facing upstage) and actors were directed to behave as if there was no audience;

4) Through his belief in the importance of the environment, Antoine helped establish the principle that each play requires its own setting;

5) Antoine's actors were amateurs whom he coached in the techniques of ensemble acting. He discouraged conventionalized movement and declamatory speech, and instead sought natural behavior. Why was it important that Antoine's actors be amateur? Professional actors would have fought his attempts to alter their performance styles.

Antoine's successes, however, began to work against him because as soon as new playwrights who were introduced at his theatre became successful, they went to the more established theatres who could pay better. Antoine's high standards also proved to be very costly and kept him constantly in debt. Perhaps his most expensive production was *The Weavers* in the 1892-93 season. It was extremely impressive because of its realistic detail, but it cost him so much money that he considered closing the theatre.

In 1895, the Théâtre Libre folded completely, after presenting 62 bills which comprised 184 plays. But Antoine didn't stay away from the theatre long. In 1897, he opened a theatre called the Théâtre Antoine which was run as a professional theatre with traditional bills, and in 1906, he was appointed the director of the Odéon theatre. Realism still dominated his work and his most famous productions of the era were French classical dramas in which he tried to recreate the theatrical conventions of the 17th century. This provides us with yet another view of realism. Realism not only involves a reproduction of real places on stage; it also involves a realistic reproduction of a historical performance technique. In other words, realism could be performing a play the way it was done in the 17th century complete with an artificial acting style, putting chandeliers on the stage, putting audience on the stage, and so forth. Other aspects of realism involved realistic detail in historic costuming, in set design, and a realistic portrayal of actual life on the stage. By the time he retired in 1914, Antoine presented 364 works at the Odéon and was, perhaps, the most influential of the theatre figures of his generation.

Eugène Brieux

Of all the playwrights to graduate from Antoine's theatre, the most naturalistic and most significant was Eugène Brieux (1858-1932) who came originally from the Théâtre Libre and then moved with Antoine to the Théâtre Antoine. He was most concerned with social and moral problems that needed reform, and he is among the first playwrights to deal with a sympathetic concern for the upbringing of children, particularly when the children's lives are affected by parental separation, divorce, or death of one of the parents. In his plays, Brieux attacks the causes of marital incompatibility, the problems of money related to love, and the concept of the conventional dowry marriage.

His work is divided into three periods. The first, extending from 1879 to 1896, is a series of critical satires and political plays. The first important play of this period is *Artists' Households*, a satire of the symbolist movement, produced in 1890 at the Théâtre Libre. As soon as realism took hold in the theatre, a group of poets started to write anti-realistic theatre in a format called Symbolism, producing plays in which action was like sleepwalking with characters talking in monotonous tones. *Artists' Households* was a satire of this kind of play. *Blanchette*, another significant play which criticizes government handling of higher education, was produced in 1892 at the Théâtre Libre, and *The Escape*, staged at the Comédie Française in 1896, attacks pseudo-science and the kinds of doctors known as "faith-healers."

The second period (1897-1903) produced plays focusing on the family and social reform. The most significant of these is *Mr. Dupont's Three Daughters* (1897) which indicts the dowry marriage as cold-blooded and argues that, because of dowries, women are often trapped in completely unpleasant relationships that lead them to marital unhappiness and sometimes even to prostitution. In his play *The Divorce* in 1898, we witness the first attack on divorce in the drama and the resultant suffering inflicted upon the children. *Damaged Goods*, written in 1901 but censored until 1905, talks openly about venereal disease, and *Maternity* (1903) deals with abortion and birth control.

The last plays (1904-1932) are philosophical treatises, the best of which is *The Dizzy Ones* (1906) which presents an unromantic picture of free love. Perhaps the most significant for our own age is *Woman on Her Own* (1913), which exposes the prejudices against women making an independent living, and argues that women should be allowed to work. With compassion, Brieux breathed life into convincing lower-class characters, and created believable human situations that depict injustice and degradation. He judged life from a humane perspective of sentiment tempered by common sense.

On the other side of the coin, is a playwright named **Georges Courteline** (1858–1929) who was the leading comic playwright for the Théâtre Libre. His plays are generally realistic farces that portray the tyranny of law and bureaucracy. His most famous play is *Article 330* which presents a character who out-argues lawyers and judges on legal technicalities. In the play—and here is a good example of a realistic farcical idea— the protagonist is indicted for mooning 1000 spectators. It is a realistic situation that goes beyond the pale, and the man who is indicted proves legally, acting as his own lawyer, that he did not do it, though in fact he did. While he is acquitted of that charge, another charge is trumped up and he is fined and imprisoned. By pleading his own case he gets away with the crime, but because of the way he pled the case, the judge cites him in contempt, so he ends up in jail anyway. What does that tell us about the society? Society must somehow punish this individual because man can never "get away with it" entirely.

A figure who is somewhat off of the beaten track of the new realists is **Edmond Rostand** (1868-1918) whose claim to fame is the reawakening of the romantic spirit during the height of realism. Thirty years earlier, Rostand would have been old hat and not popular, but the fact that he was old fashioned during a period of Realism, gave him an edge. He was born in

Marseilles of wealthy, cultured parents who sent him to school to study law and literature. His first successful play was *The Romantics* in 1894, produced at the Comédie Française and is still being performed today as *The Fantasticks* (the longest running off-Broadway musical). This was followed by *The Faraway Princess* and *The Woman of Samaria*, both written for Sarah Bernhardt, and finally his masterpiece, *Cyrano de Bergerac*. *Cyrano* depicts a heroic spirit in the face of disillusioning reality. The man with the big nose and romantic spirit cannot succeed with women because of his appearance. However, when he has a handsome surrogate, his words can provide a soul to the handsome character's beautiful, but shallow body. What happens at the end of the play? Roxana does discover the fact that Cyrano loved her and he can die with a kind of heroic realization that his love was not given in vain. Ultimately in this period of naturalistic detail, this is highly romantic and highly idealized, and provides a wonderful counterpoint to plays that were not idealized slices of life at all but depictions of life in all of its ugliness.

In 1910 Rostand produced a most interesting play called *Chantecleer* in which he began moving in the direction of the symbolists with a play that has actors costumed as barnyard animals. Unfortunately, the play was not successful: the rooster costume got all the reviews. Rostand is indebted to Victor Hugo for his verse, but his characters seem to be indebted to the burgeoning style of realism because they are much more three-dimensional than anything Hugo wrote. Rostand's plays abound in virtuosity, and he was able to create poetic dialogue filled with lyricism and heavy doses of idealism. His best play, *Cyrano* works every bit as well today as it did in its own day.

German Realism

While Naturalism was developing in France, a similar pattern was in evidence in Germany. Theatrical reform appeared in 1880 with the Deutsches Theater, opened in Berlin by Adolf L'Arronge (1838–1908) and Ludwig Barnay (1842–1924). This was important because a repertory of plays was produced in the style of the Meiningen Players (which meant excessive realistic detail).

This raised the level of production in Berlin, but ignored all new playwrights except those in the tradition of Schiller.

At the same time a group called Youngest Germany (in the early part of the nineteenth century when Büchner was writing there was a group called Young Germany, and its reactionary spin-off was called Younger Germany) which was advocating a new art based on objective observations of reality. This sounds like Realism/Naturalism. In addition to Youngest Germany, there existed a parallel group called *Durch* (which means "through") which goes even farther than Zola in its demands for naturalistic drama. *Durch* is the movement which one can say is responsible for plays in which characters actually urinate on stage, and other kinds of naturalistic behavior. Both groups found inspiration in Ibsen's plays, sixteen of which had been translated by 1890.

The new spirit found its focus in the formation of an independent theatre called the **Freie Bühne** (1889) in Berlin. This was a democratic organization with officers and a governing council under the guidance of a theatre critic named Otto Brahm (1856–1912). This theatre gave performances on Sunday afternoon using professional actors from other theatres (Sunday was the dark day for German theatres). Characteristically, the Freie Bühne performed plays that were forbidden by the German censors. The opening production was *Ghosts*, and this was followed by plays by Hauptmann, Zola, and Becque. After the 1890-91 season, regular performances were discontinued, though an occasional performance was given when a play was forbidden a license. If someone, for example, discovered that a major theatre wouldn't give a license to a particular play, the Freie Bühne would read it, and if they thought it should be done, they would get it performed or at least read on Sunday afternoon. They could do this because they were an independent subscription-based theatre club. Censorship, by the way, was instated in Germany after 1815 when the government began to finance the theatre and put court officials in charge of organizations. This meant essentially that, in subsidizing theatres, the government had people on the board of every major theatre to read plays to determine if they were politically correct. The Freie Bühne ended forever in 1894 when Brahm was named director of the Deutsches

Theater. From that point on, Brahm took his philosophies over to the more established theatre.

Gerhart Hauptmann (1862-1946) was the only important German dramatist to come out of the Freie Bühne. His reputation was established by the play *Before Sunrise*, and *The Weavers* (1892), which is considered the first socialist play in Germany, was the most noteworthy of his early works. Like Ibsen, Haupmann would write plays in a variety of styles, sometimes in highly naturalistic or realistic terms, other times in a highly symbolic vein; but all of his plays, in which his protagonists are in situations beyond their control, demonstrate compassion for human suffering. Haupmann's plays are highly evocative of the philosophy of environmental determinism.

Hauptmann was also extremely important as a theatre producer and director. In his personal life, he was also one of the major figures of the "Lolita" syndrome. After divorcing his first wife, he married an actress 12 years younger than he, and in life, he had an affair with a 17-year old. In 1912 he won the Nobel Prize, and his fame was unequaled until the Nazis rose to power. From a production standpoint, he was a good director of his own plays, paying great attention to meticulous detail when the play was realistic, making the plays appropriately vague if they were symbolic, and pacing a farce like any comedian. Soon we will talk about Max Reinhardt as an eclectic director able to realize on stage each play according to its own style. Hauptmann actually evokes him in that practice.

Perhaps the most interesting of his plays, *The Rats*, was produced in 1911. In poverty-stricken Berlin, Mrs. John buys her servant's new born child as a substitute for her own baby who died. When the maid wants her own baby back, Mrs. John has the maid murdered. Rather than face a trial, she commits suicide (now the child becomes a ward of the state). What is interesting is that the entire play is told from the perspective of a theology student renting an upstairs room from the woman. There's a third person observer of the play who, curiously, does nothing to change the situation. The play makes incisive statements about society, social pressure, and how there are certain kinds of environmental determinants that render human beings incapable of getting involved, even when they know that crimes are being committed.

Inspired by the Freie Bühne was a new group called the **Freie Volksbühne** which was organized in 1890 by a socialist group interested in raising cultural standards of the working classes. The Freje Volksbühne produced plays on Sunday matinees with a subscription audience. The subscription grew from 600 in 1890, its first year of operation, to 12,000 in 1908. In 1892, there was a new group called the Neue Freie Volksbühne that offered a similar program. By 1905, this group was providing subscribers with a variety of productions at several different theatres. Before WWI, the two groups joined and counted 50,000 members between them.

Austrian Realism

The most important of the Austrian dramatists to follow in the pattern of Hauptmann and the realists was **Arthur Schnitzler** (1862-1931), the first practitioner of stream of consciousness in the drama. The play in which this was first developed was *Anatol* in 1893. Stream of consciousness is kind of a continual thought process in literature, almost like a dream state. Schnitzler was fond of creating short scenes in plays, each of which seems not necessarily causally connected with the other, and yet taken as a whole, the disparate scenes create an entire situation or idea. Hence, the stream of consciousness. A play called *La Ronde* in 1900 is perhaps the most famous example of this technique. *La Ronde* is a series of short scenes involving ten characters in a kind of daisy-chain-like situation. Character A and B are undergoing sexual intercourse. Then B and C, C and D, D and E, E and F, so that's there's always a similar person in each segment, until the last scene, when H finally gets together with A, connecting the pattern to its beginning.

Critics have suggested that, being a friend and admirer of Freud, Schnitzler believed in the centrality of sexual behavior, but he was equally convinced that love cannot be built on pure ego gratification. As a result, his plays are reflections of the fall of Imperial Vienna typified by decadence and hedonism. His plays disclose an atmosphere of sultry decline verging on disease. His chief themes are the omnipresence of an angel of death in society, and frenetic sex used as an escape from a crumbling society.

Among the more interesting of his plays is *The Green Cockatoo* (1899), in which Schnitzler combines reality and illusion, treading the fine line between Realism and Surrealism. The play begins with a group of people who are playing a game of pretense and, by the end of the evening, everyone is slaughtered by the other. The whole thing is kind of like a child, not knowing that he can kill, playing with a loaded revolver. When the gun goes off and kills someone, the child does not understand why he is being punished for something that is only 'make believe." In his plays Schnitzler is trying to deal with the ramifications of reality through people who don't even believe that what they are doing is real.

Realism in Russia

The celebrated Russian contribution to the Independent Theatre Movement, the Moscow Art Theatre, was the result of a collaboration between a playwright **Vladimir Nemirovich-Danchenko** (1858–1943) and an actor–theoretician **Konstantin Stanislavski** (1853–1938). At the moment the Moscow Art Theatre was formed, Danchenko was the more famous and successful. He was highly influenced by the Meiningen Company and by 1891, he sought changes in Russian theatrical practices. He wanted to codify rehearsal techniques. He wanted dress rehearsals for plays in costume and on scenery. This was not common practice in Russia. Actors would get together, read the play a few times, and invite an audience. Danchenko wanted colorful and theatrically relevant settings; he was tired of the dark and pastel grayish sets that characterized Russian productions.

Stanislavski, on the other hand, was an actor who had spent his inheritance creating a group called The Society of Art and Literature in Moscow. This Society was kind of civic center where there would be music, dance, and theatrical activity. Unfortunately, by 1894–1895, the Society had failed to find an audience, so Stanislavski reorganized the venture and began his quest for truth and honesty in acting. He also suggested that he wanted to get rid of the star system which had cost him a great deal of money at the original Society of Art and Literature.

In the same season, Danchenko secured the first dress rehearsal in Russian theatre history for a play called *Gold*. The following year, Danchenko wrote a play called *The Price of Life* which was awarded Best Play of the Season. This is an interesting play since it contains a suicide at the beginning of the play (rather than at the end)! The action of the play concerns the result of a suicide as opposed to suicide being the culmination or end of the play.

In 1897, Stanislavski met Danchenko at the Slavic Bazaar Restaurant, and after eighteen hours of discussion, they came up with the idea for the Moscow Art Theatre. They produced their first play in the summer of 1898, *Tsar Fyodor* by Alexis Tolstoy. Later in December they produced Chekhov's *The Seagull* with Meyerhold in the role of the young author. In 1902, after five years of renting auditoriums, the Moscow Art Theatre built its own theatre, due to the financial assistance of Savva Morogov, a rich merchant. The new theatre had a revolving stage, many of the newer theatrical effects, and a stage house capable of flying scenery. Also, in 1902 the Moscow Art Theatre increased its acting company from 39 members to 100, and began to stage three to five new plays a year, in addition to maintaining a successful repertory.

Between 1911 and 1912, Stanislavski founded the First Studio to train students, and between *My Life in Art* which was published in 1924 and *Creating a Role* which was published in 1961, Stanislavski developed his principles which we now call the Stanislavski System. A great many of our misconceptions about the Stanislavski System go back to the fact that the English translator eliminated a great many passages and mistranslated others. There is currently a joint collaboration between Russia and the United States to retranslate Stanislavski's books so that we might finally grasp exactly what he had to say.

Here are the principles of Stanislavski's system (popularized by the Actors' Studio as the "Method"):

1) Train an actor's body and voice to meet all demands;

2) School the actor in stage technique to enable him/her to project characterization without seeming contrived to an audience. That means the actor had to know style, how a character would look or walk in a particular era. This also means an actor has to be able to project honest emotion;

3) Actors should be skilled observers of reality on which to base their characterizations. Reality is basis of role;

4) Actors should seek inner justification for everything done on stage (the concept of "motivation");

4a) Actors must learn to depend on the magic "If": If I were that character, what would I do?

4b) Actors should learn to develop an emotional memory (though Stanislavski would downplay the concept of emotional recall in his later work in favor of the "What if?");

5) Actors must make a thorough analysis of the script and work within the given circumstances (this is to counter the terrible habit of Russian actors: improvisation). To that end, actors must define character motivation in each scene, in the entire play, and in relationship to other roles. This has been translated variously as the actor must find a primary objective or through line;

6) Actors must focus attention on the action as it unfolds *moment by moment* creating the illusion of what Stanislavski calls the "illusion of the first time." He suggests that creating this moment-to-moment presentation enables the actor to subordinate his ego to the artistic demand of the production. If it's happening the first time, the actor will be less concerned with "How do I look?" and more concerned with playing the event;

7) Actors must continually strive to attain perfect understanding and proficiency in their craft. This means that actors never stop studying. In America, the Stanislavski System or "Method" has become so internalized, recreating the initial emotion, that we tend to forget that Stanislavski's primary focus was on training the actor's body and voice to be able to physicalize what was inside. His "Method of Physical Action" demonstrates that Stanislavski was very clearly involved with the outward manifestation of internal feelings.

Anton Chekhov

The most important playwright produced by the Moscow Art Theatre was Anton Chekhov (1860-1904). Born into a family of serfs (his father was the proprietor of a store), Chekhov went to Moscow to study medicine. Even though he eventually became a doctor, Chekhov was inclined toward literary pursuits, both as the author of a large number of short stories and later as a playwright. His first play was *Platonov* (1881), also called *Don Juan in the Russian Manner, a County Scandal*. Four years later in 1885 *On the Highway and Other Plays* was published, and *Ivanov*, his first study of Russian inertia and despair, appeared in 1887. After a number of short plays were produced, *The Seagull* was performed disastrously at the Aleksandrinsky Theatre in 1896 and believed to be unproduceable until it was revitalized by Stanislavski at the Moscow Art Theatre in 1898. This was followed by the three great plays: *Uncle Vanya*, *The Three Sisters*, and *The Cherry Orchard*.

Chekhov's major theme is the entrapment of sensitive intelligent people in ineffectual lives. In Chekhov's plays, plot lines are indistinct, characters speak in arias rather than traditional conversation. In many of his plays a character will speak in long passages, and then the character to whom that character was speaking will say, "Excuse me, did you say something?" People do not communicate with one another. Chekhov insisted that rather than an outward show, the whole meaning of drama is *inside* a person. To that end, he chose to write what he called "comedies" of modern life. The chief influence on these comedies was Gogol since generally in Chekhov's plays there is an abundance of farcical elements. Invariably there are character exaggerations: a next-door neighbor who has some sort of physical malady. Either his face is pockmarked or he will talk incessantly without making any sense. Chekhov also makes use of type characters, especially the old husband with the young wife. That goes straight back to Menander, but in a more modern sense at least to Molière. He also portrays characters who have only a single focus in their lives, who cannot see the world collapsing around them. People talk incessantly about doing something they never do, and yet they are unable to see the rut that they are in. Chekhov also thrives on the stereotype of A loving B, but B loves C, and C loves D, who actually loves A. Nobody loves the person they ought to love: everyone is mismatched. What does that tell us about society? There's something vastly wrong here. In addition, characters treat every event in the play as if it were life and death, until a real life or death situation occurs, of which they are blissfully unaware. Chekhov's view of life is distinctly pessimistic.

Like Ibsen, Chekhov uses symbols and sound effects very much like characters in a play. Where Ibsen uses a wild duck, as a symbol, Chekhov uses a seagull. Unlike Ibsen, however, Chekhov integrates music in his plays to create mood and rhythm. Critics note that Chekhov's lasting influence on playwriting in the twentieth century, and on theatre history in general, lies in his focusing the action of his plays on the internal lives of his characters rather than on the depiction of external events.

Maxim Gorki
Another playwright who was significant during this period who employed a slightly different formula was Maxim Gorki (1868-1936) who worked at every occupation imaginable before becoming a playwright. He was a bootmaker's apprentice, a domestic servant, a dishwasher on steamboats. He knew police stations and flop houses from the inside, and he was great friends with derelicts. His best-known play is *The Lower Depths* (1902) which reflects his personal experience of living in squalor and longing for a better life. Gorky was influenced by Tolstoy's pessimistic philosophy concerning Russian middle-class society, the political views of Lenin, and the new playwriting style of Chekhov. *The Lower Depths* turns on a group of derelicts who live in a dark, wet flophouse run by a brute named Kostilyev, whose wife is in love with one of the flophouse dwellers, a thief. She wants him to kill her husband (an influence from Tolstoy) so that they can have an open affair. He does ultimately kill the husband, but to save the wife's younger sister who is raped and battered by the husband. Other derelicts include a former-actor, now alcoholic, an unemployed locksmith and his dying wife, a prostitute, and an old bum who invents reasons for others to hope for something better. In the end, the

locksmith's wife dies, the actor hangs himself, and the bum leaves for other flophouses in search of a new religion. Nobody is any better off. It was an extremely popular play in the heyday of Naturalism when the drama sought to attain a realistic portrayal of the lower-classes.

Note that, as in Chekhov, we are less concerned with plot and more with the depiction of characters and how these characters feel about a situation. After the Soviet takeover in Russia, Gorky's popularity continued because his work was viewed as an exposé of Czarist evils. He was viewed as the founding father of Soviet literature and credited with establishing the literary theory of Socialist Realism. This is important because, for the rest of the twentieth century, Russian playwrights who write in a symbolist or surrealist fashion will be slapped on the wrist or even killed. The line that they have to tow is Socialist Realism. Gorki's attitude, however, toward Communism was ambiguous; he fought to save other writers whose work did not conform to the party line, and often argued against Lenin's politics. Even though he was censorious of various political regimes, Gorki was embraced by the Communists as one of the few significant writers who was actually "of the people." In 1934 he became the first president of the Soviet Writers Union, but in 1935 he began to speak out about the abuses of Stalin's regime. Suddenly, 1936 he died mysteriously of a cold, though most historians believe that he was assassinated because of his repeated attacks against Stalin.

Realism and Naturalism in England
Between 1893 and World War I, while Naturalism was developing in Russia, fashionable society was returning to English theatre. This produced a number of long-lasting effects on play-production in England:

1) A later curtain hour: plays began at 7:30 or 8.00. This was accompanied by a reduction in the length of the performance. If the curtain rose at a later hour, the length of the bill must be abbreviated;

2) The disappearance of the half-price ticket which used to be a big draw for the lower middle classes. Higher prices meant that only the fashionable classes would come to the theatre;

3) Orchestra seats invaded the pit. The old division of private and public boxes gave way to open balconies called the dress circle, the upper circle, and the balcony;

4) The introduction (on a permanent basis) of matinee performances;

5) The development of the practice of bookable seats. Because of the growth of the long run, spectators could book seats in advance; as a result, every seat in the auditorium was given a number. These innovations did not happen instantaneously, but by the 1890s they were the rule.

Among the actor managers of note in this period, **Herbert Beerbohm Tree** (1853-1917) was established at the Haymarket Theatre in 1887. Famous for elaborate productions of Shakespeare, he founded a school for actors which became the Royal Academy of Dramatic Art (RADA). These are Tree's theatrical contributions to production:

1) He used live animals in his productions of Shakespeare—that is one of the things he is most noted for: bringing livestock on to the Shakespearean stage. He used rabbits in *A Midsummer Night's Dream* and horses in *Richard II*;

2) He was fond of cutting and rearranging Shakespeare's texts to fit his production concept;

3) He substituted spectacle for all of Shakespeare's descriptive passages, a practice he borrowed from Charles Kean;

4) Realism in sets and costumes was based on paintings and descriptive writings of the period in question;

5) He extended the time devoted to rehearsals; two months was a typical rehearsal period;

6) He was lavish in costumes and properties. For example, in Tree's production of *Henry VIII* (1910) 172 performers wore 380 costumes. In the banquet scene alone, 235 props—much of it, real food—were used;

7) Having constructed an apron over the pit, Tree reestablished the apron stage as a primary acting area (after years of theatres placing the action behind a "picture frame");

8) He is one of the first to emphasize realism in facial hair. For example, when he produced *Henry VIII*, he had the actor plying Henry dye his beard red so it would look exactly as it did in the Holbein portrait. Tree was adamant about creating pictorial realism;

9) Offstage noises (i.e., sound effects) were cued by lights beneath the stage (under the stage is where the supernumeraries usually made such noises). This is beginning the convention of using cue lights controlled by the stage manager;

10) House lights were up to 3/4 during the play. Unlike Irving, who liked to dim the houselights completely, Tree kept the house up. He brought the lights down but did not have the theatre completely in the dark. He liked the interplay between actor and audience. While he was emphasizing a sense of reality in production techniques, he did like the actor to be able to see the audience;

11) Curtain calls were taken after each act as in opera, and the actors bowed in character. In a very famous production of *Henry VI*, when he was playing Cardinal Woolsey, Tree took his curtain call eating an orange because apparently Woolsey loved oranges. He would take his bow, throw a piece of orange in his mouth, smile, and take another bow with the orange. That curtain call made the headlines in the newspapers;

12) He established the most lavish processionals in theatre history. For example, in the coronation scene of *Henry VIII* there were 122 people on stage;

13) To create the illusion of even greater crowds, Tree used dummies intermingled with the live actors. The dummies had full facial features, true wigs, and were costumed just like everyone e1se. The actors would bring them

on stage and converse with them to create the illusion that they were real people;

14) He developed pantomime business to further illustrate Shakespeare's narrative passages;

15) He developed a training style for actors which, though essentially realistic, was large, imposing, theatrical, and pictorial;

16) He developed pace to set roles apart from one another. In other words, he would direct one actor at particular rhythm or tempo and direct another actor to work at a different rhythm as part of their characterizations.

Tree was only bested by Max Reinhardt in terms of creating large stage spectacles. We will discuss Reinhardt in the next lecture, but I'll give you some numbers now for comparison. In 1911, Reinhardt produced a play called *The Miracle* for which he transformed the huge Olympia Hall in London into the interior of a Gothic cathedral. The production had a cast of 2,000, a choir of 500, an orchestra of 250, and a ballet company of 175 making the total, 2,925. It was an enormous pageant.

During this particular period English playwrights began to experience an increase in status, particularly after the legislation of the International copyright Act in 1887. Before that time, piracy was rife among English authors (if there was no copyright on a play, someone could just steal a dozen pages from it and throw them into another play). Another important development, the American Copyright Act, was established in 1890.

Society Drama

Society drama began to develop in the 1890s, building plays around a handful of themes that were easily recognizable to the humblest patron, but which were directly related to the wealthy society people who theatre managers wanted to lure back to the theatre. Essentially these plays traded on the efforts of the lower classes to penetrate the magic circle of London society, and the efforts of those once admitted into society to remain there. This would produce a whole body of plays having at their center a woman with a past.

Because of this, they turn on Scribe's Well-Made-Play formula because of its emphasis on a well-kept secret which is finally revealed in the *scène à faire* (the obligatory scene). The revelation of the fatal secret always ultimately sends the offending characters to their death, to prison, to the colonies, or to church (they get married). The term "problem play" which we spoke of in connection with Ibsen is oftentimes connected with what we call society drama. When Shaw writes it, it will be called "blue book" drama.

One of the first exponents of society drama was **Oscar Wilde**. Oscar Wilde (1854-1900), whose comedies were performed successfully at the St. James Theatre, produced plays in a structure modeled on French melodrama to which he added novelty, glamour, and sparkling dialogue full of epigrammatic wit. Most of his plays, in typical society-drama fashion, revolved around a secret. *Lady Windemere's Fan* tells the secret of a heroine's mother who deserted her husband and child twenty years earlier. *The Importance of Being Earnest* exposes the shameful secret of Mr. Worthing's origin in a handbag. More significant in the development of society drama is **Sir Arthur Wing Pinero** (1855-1934) who, with *The Second Mrs. Tanqueray*, produced society drama that was serious and evocative of realistic social mores. *The Second Mrs. Tanqueray* employs the convention of the woman with a past: Paula, the heroine, is struggling to fit into the upper levels of society (remember that was one of the themes of society drama: those once admitted into society want to remain there). The play also makes use of the Well-Made Play and French melodramatic techniques because it relies very heavily on coincidence. Pinero also turned to fantasy and created plays that dealt with the social role of the theatre (for example, *Trelawney of the Wells*, a backstage play about an actress appearing at Sadler's Wells Theatre).

In the 1870s and 1880s, the growing popularity of the matinee performance was fostered by the demand of a small but very influential section of the public for plays outside the established repertoire. By 1890, this demand crystallized into a movement to familiarize the English audience with the plays of Henrik Ibsen. The first complete English translation of Ibsen's plays appeared under the editorship of **William Archer** in 1889-1890. Archer considered himself a missionary to bring to the English theatre as much new and realistic theatre as possible. In his attempt to reform the theater he produced a book called *English Dramatists of Today* (1882), and he was very significant in introducing **George Bernard Shaw** (1856-1950) to Ibsen. In 1890 Shaw combined his loyalty to Archer and Ibsen with political and social enthusiasm by delivering to the Fabian Society a series of lectures about Ibsen that was published as *The Quintessence of Ibsenism* (one of those books that every graduate student in theatre finds himself having to deal with).

While Shaw was going in the direction of social realism, in 1891, the Independent Theatre was founded mostly through the efforts of a critic named J[acob] T[homas] Grein (1862–1935), and modeled on the Théâtre Libre in France and the Freie Bühne in Germany. The Independent Theatre offered performances on Sundays for a subscription audience of plays that normally would not be done in the public theatres. The manifesto of this theatre was "to give special performances of plays which have literary and artistic merit rather than commercial value." Its first production was *Ghosts*, on 13 March 1891, which received the most interesting review of any play that season. Clement Scott referred to *Ghosts* as "an open drain, a loathsome sore unbandaged, a dirty act done publicly" (a review like that today would sell out a play for at least a dozen years). Such a challenge to a man of Shaw's personality was irresistible. Shaw thought, "if *Ghosts* is going to get such a terrible review, I've got to produce something along those lines." And he did. He had an unfinished script of a play that he had begun in 1885 called *Widowers Houses*, and he managed to get it produced by the Independent Theatre on 9 December 1892. Although Show's play received only slightly better reviews than *Ghosts*, Shaw's career as a playwright was off and running from this point on, in spite of the fact that it took him many years to be produced in the traditional houses (*Pygmalion* was really the play through which Shaw made his mark as a "traditional" playwright).

Shaw took Ibsen's problem play and the social drama that was being developed by Pinero and Wilde and transformed those formulas into what he called "blue book drama," a propagandist play, a play with a purpose. Shaw defined the purpose of "blue boo drama" as "playing off your laughter at the scandal of the exposure against your shudder at its blackness." The audience laughs because something is going to be exposed and yet it is offended at the enormity of what is being exposed. There's always some central moral, financial, ethical, or social issue at the core of every play by Shaw, and as if the message were not absolutely clear in the play, Shaw would write a lengthy preface or epilogue to drive the point home.

Before taking the post of drama critic for *The Saturday Review* between 1895 and 1898 (Shaw's reviews were collated into a book called *Our Theatre in the 90s*), Shaw began to use models of the commercial theatre to write a play about a woman with a past, *Mrs. Warren's Profession*, in which Mrs. Warren had been the proprietor of many houses of prostitution. However, he adjusted that formula to include a woman with a future—Mrs. Warren's daughter Vivie. It is one of the few plays coming out of the 1890s in England that expresses the possibility of a woman capable of making a living on her own.

Shaw's ultimate recognition as a playwright emerged at the hands of John Vedrenne and Harley Granville Barker, the managers of the Court Theatre. Under the Vedrenne-Barker management, the Court Theatre was designed to play little known works on matinees while another more familiar or commercially viable play performed at night. They had a very interesting system: if the play they were doing at matinees engendered enough interest, they would then mount it at night and do another on the matinees (like the present system of doing a play in workshop, and then, if the workshop is successful, the play is mounted fully). The Court Theatre was known essentially for ensemble acting (no stars) and for producing each play in the style that suited it. They would do a realistic play realistically and a melodrama, melodramatically. This had become the typical style at the turn of the century—eclecticism rather than Realism or Romanticism. Vedrenne and Barker also emphasized simplicity in acting and design. They didn't have a large production budget; therefore, less was more. Whatever the style of play being produced, the emphasis was on subtlety rather than elaborateness.

The greatest of the Vedrenne-Barker management's achievements at the

Court Theatre was probably making known Shaw's plays in performance to an influential, if restricted, audience. When King Edward VII ordered a command performance of Shaw's play, *John Bull's Other Island* in March of 1905, audiences suddenly took note. Vedrenne and Barker moved to the Savoy Theatre in 1907, but it was Herbert Beerbohm Tree's production of *Pygmalion* in 1914 that ultimately made Shaw popular with the general public.

Within a few months after Vedrenne and Barker left the Court Theatre in 1907, a repertory theatre was opened in Manchester under the direction of. A[nnie] E[lizabeth] F[redericka] Horniman (1860–1937) who was also very important in the establishment of the Abbey Theatre in Dublin. Horniman called her repertory theatre the Manchester Gaiety. This was followed by the establishment of repertory theatres devoted to the presentation of *plays of intellectual as well as theatrical worth* in a variety of cities in England. Called an "Independent Theatre Movement," playhouses, "independent" of the commercial theatre, were interested in producing "artistic works" that did not necessarily have to make money. This repertory movement fostered the avant-garde in the pre-war theatres of England.

While this artistic work was being done, on the other side of the coin, the commercial theatre was thriving with productions of melodrama and musical comedy. Although melodrama maintained its existence into the 1890s, the Adelphi Theatre, which was the house of melodrama, forsook that form after an actor named William Terriss was stabbed to death at the stage door in 1897 by another actor, Richard Arthur Prince, who believed himself slighted by Terriss. Quickly, musical comedy took up the slack and became the most popular commercial form of theatre before World War I. The first step in the development of musical comedy in England occurred when a man named John Hollingshead opened the Gaiety Theatre in 1868. Over the next twenty years, the Gaiety was the home of English burlesque. This does not mean Minsky's (stripper) burlesque. This means satirical burlesque written in rhymed doggerel verse spoofing a known original.

When George Edwardes became manager of the Gaiety, he made it his mission to woo the fashionable society to the theatre. To that end he developed a romantic side of the Gaiety's entertainment by producing a series of musicals that glorified the English girl. These generally had to do with a waif—a working girl—who somehow finds herself, in the second act, at some costume ball and, in the third act, in some exotic locale. A list of the titles suggests the kind of musicals Edwardes produced: *The Shop Girl, My Girl, The Circus Girl, The Runaway Girl, The Quaker Girl*. Each of these had a fine feminine chorus with enough changes of costume to make them very interesting, and usually at least one opportunity for the girls to wear pants so that the audience could examine the shape of their body. One of the important treats, by the way, in burlesque was the existence of what was called "the principle boy." The principle boy (the leading young man) in a burlesque was always played by a girl. This was a very popular convention with audiences for it allowed an actress to wear pants. The stronger appetites for which burlesque was developed—those who really liked low-class comedy and farce then moved to what we call the English Music Hall. As a result, the formula which was originally English burlesque—low comedy with a kind of spoof of a literary original—transformed into two sub-genres: Music Hall and English Musical Comedy.

16. Nineteenth and Twentieth Century Reactions to Theatrical Realism

While the problem play was developing in England, France was beginning to react to Realism. The action of the play had been moved behind the proscenium. Now we are on the way to moving the action back in front of the proscenium. The most significant protest against Naturalism and Realism came from the **Symbolists** who issued their first manifesto in 1886. Symbolism was inspired by Edgar Allen Poe's alliterative, assonantal poetry, the English romantic poets, Ibsen's symbolic plays, Wagner's aesthetic theories, and Dostoyevsky's novels. It believed that subjectivity, spirituality, and mysterious internal forces present a higher form of truth than that which can be derived from the observance of external reality. What is subjective, what is inside an individual is more real than what can be viewed objectively or externally. The symbolists said that this deeper significance is incapable of being represented, but can only be evoked through symbols, moods, legends, and myths.

In 1890, **Paul Fort** (1872–1960) established the Théâtre d'Art where he used non-realistic scenery and amateur actors to produce plays (based on the Bible or the *Iliad*) that would provide audiences with a subjective interpretation of those works. In 1892, that theatre was absorbed into the Théâtre de l'Oeuvre (the Theatre of Work) headed by **Aurelien-Marie Lugné-Poë** (1869–1940), and between 1893 and 1897, the Théâtre de l'Oeuvre produced plays with scenery reduced to lines and color painted on backdrops—very cartoon-like. The first production was *Pelléas and Mélisande* by Maurice Maeterlinck (1862–1949). Using no props or furniture, the stage was lit from overhead, lighting not the faces of the actors but their heads. Most of the action was in semi-darkness. A gauze curtain hung between the audience and the actors suggesting mist. The backdrops were painted grey to suggest an air of mystery. Any kind of bright color or line was painted over in grey so that no discernible color or line would appear in the settings. Draperies of an indefinite period created vaguely medieval costumes. Actors spoke in staccato chants and, according to some critics, behaved like sleepwalkers with stylized gestures. Part of the symbolist technique of acting required the actor to speak in a monotone, and to try to make no sense of the line, so that equal worth is given to every word. In this way, the audience could interpret the dialogue personally, independent of the performance. If the actors give weight to particular words, they no longer permit the audience to be subjective because they are layering the text with their own interpretation.

The best of the symbolist repertoire was created by **Maurice Maeterlinck** who felt that the most dramatic moments in a play are the silent ones because during those silent moments, the mystery of existence, which is obscured during real-life activity, makes itself felt. Another significant author at this time was **Stephan Mallarmé** (1842–1898), a schoolteacher by day and a chronic insomniac by night. He attempted to construct a revolution in poetic language by creating meaning through organization, sound, and contrast of words, not through sense. In other words, the sound of the words suggests the meaning as opposed to the context of the words. Every Tuesday evening, people would gather at Mallarmé's home for poetry readings. He only permitted people to speak when the room was filled with cigar smoke so that individual faces were indecipherable. He also emphasized simultaneous poetry readings in which several poems were read concurrently in order to obfuscate the literal meanings of words, and to focus instead on tone and ambiance in language.

The greatest figure to emerge from the authors of this period was **Alfred Jarry** (8 September 1873–1 November 1907), a slight-statured alcoholic, who always traveled by bicycle, carrying a revolver that was always loaded. He had a racking cough and grating voice most of his life, which wasn't very long to begin with, and yet was extremely charming. He produced a mockery of one of his schoolteachers in 1888 called *The Polacks*. Eight years later, the play would become *Ubu Roi* and take Paris by storm.

Once he started writing for a living, Jarry contributed to a variety of magazines, some of which were quite unusual. He was an illustrator for a magazine that turned on religious iconography. He also wrote for magazines that dealt with Elizabethan English theatre and science. Obviously, his interests went in a variety of directions. In 1894, when he was called for military service, he swallowed acid to get out of it. Although unsuccessful in his first attempt, he finally did get out of military service because of his gallstones. In 1895, Jarry decided to abandon life to the hallucinatory world of the dream; thus, began his strong use of alcohol, which he called "holy water." When his addiction to alcohol was concretized, he began a quest for an artistic goal. In 1896, he published six different fragments of the *Ubu* texts, all based on his schoolboy writings. In 1897, he exhausted his inheritance and moved into a dingy room on the third and a half floor of an apartment building where everything was about at least a foot to two feet lower than a normal room. On the staircase to get to the apartment there were hand prints in blood, and in his apartment, he had a huge whale phallus on the mantle. Once a woman went to see him at his apartment and looked at it and said, "Is it yours, Mr. Jarry." He replied, "Yes;" and she said, "Oh! It's an enlargement." Without missing a beat, Jarry quipped, "No Madame, a reduction."

In 1898, he produced *Faustroll*, a pseudoscientific novel in which he began to explore the scientific philosophy of *pataphysics*. Pataphysics is the science of imaginary ideas. You've heard of the mathematics of imaginary numbers which deals with concepts not concrete amounts. Pataphysics is exactly that kind of intellectual exercise. What is strange is that some of Jarry's pataphysical ideas about splitting the atom and space exploration have been proven in the twentieth century by scientists. For Jarry, these were not concrete concepts, but the science of "What if?" There is still in France a College of Pataphysics, and it is a kind of "think tank." In 1900, Jarry began writing for a Paris magazine called *La Revue Blanche*. After about three years, the magazine folded, he stopped getting his checks, his health began to fail, and he spent all of his money buying ether to get high. By 1905, he was going without regular meals and without heat in his apartment. In 1907 after his friends hadn't seen him for five or six months, they went to pay him a visit and found him paralyzed. He died of acute meningeal tuberculosis on the 1st of November.

As an artist Jarry combined science, symbolism, humor, and the occult, and he aimed at copying Rabelais in his usage of perverse dirty language: *Ubu Roi (King Ubu)* is the first play in French to open with the word "shit." The first word spoken really isn't "shit" because it's "merdre." "Merde" is the French term for shit so, with an extra "r," it isn't exactly the word. It's also very difficult to translate. If you say "shrit!" it doesn't have quite the same impact. Jarry was fascinated with Elizabethan drama and marionette theatre, and like the symbolists, he liked conventionalized gestures and schematic sets. He went a little farther than they did because he also called for masks in performance, and he advocated the use of indicative signs in his sets. If the scenery was a sketch of a house, he would have a sign over it saying "house" with an arrow pointing to the building.

Ubu Roi (King Ubu) was first performed on 11 December 1896. Directed by Lugné-Poë at the Théâtre de l'Oeuvre, it had a magnificently turbulent premier, creating perhaps the greatest riot in French theatre history. Originally based on one of Jarry's professors, *Ubu Roi* is also his version of Shakespeare's *Macbeth*. Father Ubu, nagged by a shrewish wife, kills the King of Poland and subsequently kills all the noblemen in the country with his *disembraining* machine. Ubu commits massacres for the sake of a sausage and an umbrella, both of which are major phallic symbols. Jarry also uses the sausage and umbrella as symbols of gluttony and the bourgeois lifestyle (the "businessman with the umbrella" kind of thing). Here again, symbols have a major focusin the play. Ubu becomes an evil force in the universe, killing people for what is called their "phynances" before he is ultimately defeated in the end. A very interesting thing about this character is that his colloquial epithet is not "By Christ" or "By God," but "by my green candle," another phallic symbol. In the Elizabethan period, the green disease was a venereal disease. Green was also the symbol of whoredom—prostitutes would wear green clothes to announce their trade. Scholars believe that "by my green candle" is a reference to a venereal condition on Father Ubu's penis.

For Jarry, it was very important that, in performance, the play maintained a supernatural atmosphere, affected mannerisms of speech, mechanical gestures, and the use of masks. All of these were highly antirealistic devices that influenced a mode of theatricality called *Surrealism* ("beyond realism"). This movement aimed to destroy the notion of literal categories and genres, replacing them with a non-slavish adherence to life. Surrealists tend to say that there is no such thing as pure comedy or pure tragedy. It's all mixed up. An idea or image becomes more important than objective reality. Remember *Ubu Roi* premiered in 1896. This was well before the surrealistic movement was firmly in place. The first piece of work, by the way, that is tagged as surrealist is a play by André Bréton called *The Magnetic Fields* (1919), a juxtaposition of two soliloquies, one which triggers the other. *A* says something which causes *B* to say something which causes *A* to speak again. The actors are not actually talking to one another.

The year after the premiere of *Ubu Roi*, Lugné-Poë broke with the symbolists arguing that, "Their plays are too immature (I tend to think that dealing with Alfred Jarry was too much for him). And that being tied to only one style of production was too limiting." And, because of the influence of Ibsen, he began to move into a more realistic format. However, even though he stopped being a surrealist or non-realist, through the articles written about his early work, Lugné-Poë influenced nearly every other departure from realism between 1893 and 1915.

While Lugné-Poë was producing in the '90s, modern non-illusionistic theatrical design was also being developed by two very important figures: a Swiss named **Adolphe Appia** (1862-1928) and an Englishman named **Edward Gordon Craig** (1872-1966). Their work was very similar though they developed their theories independently of one another. Appia concluded that stage presentation involved three conflicting visual elements: perpendicular scenery, a horizontal floor, and a three-dimensional actor who would travel on the one and stand in front or behind the other. What he sought to do was replace the two-dimensional set with three-dimensional units: steps, ramps, or platforms that would enhance the actor's movement and also blend the upright scenery with a horizontal floor, attempting to create a completely three-dimensional environment on the stage. What he did to blend movement with design was emphasize the role of light which fused all the visual elements into a unified whole. Like a musician, he sought to orchestrate and manipulate light to create moods, color, and emotions so that plays no longer needed to stop for scene changes. The actor moved from one part of the stage to another: he went from light to light, so that directors could begin thinking in terms of continual motion rather than the stop and start of scene changes.

Appia's greatest influence on other designers arose from his theoretical books, among which are *The Staging of Wagner's Musical Dramas* (1895), *Music and Stage Setting* (1899), and *The Work of Living Art* (1921). Appia was of course most interested in designing scenery for Wagner's operas because there he could associate his own theories of light and color with Wagner's theories of music and color and discover ways of blending both ideas. Essentially, on an Appia set, you see steps, platforms, occasionally some kind of construct that would suggest a large vertical unit, but essentially when you look at it, you are not saying, "This is a house. This is a room," but "This is a space." What Appia accomplished was the artistic design of a three-dimensional space in which the actor was prominent.

Edward Gordon Craig, on the other hand, was the son of Ellen Terry and Edward Godwin. He began his theatrical career as an actor in Henry Irving's company, and started designing at the Imperial Theatre in Russia in 1903. He produced his theoretical book, *The Art of the Theatre*, in 1905 which established his reputation as a theatre technician and practitioner. His designs for the Moscow Art Theatre in 1911 created controversy because Craig believed that the actor and text were material to be molded by the master artist who was the director. Craig felt that the actor was too proud and that the writer moralized too much, and several times he argued that the theatre would be better off without both. In their place he suggested the "Übermarionette," a giant marionette or puppet that could be controlled in every motion or activity. What he sought therefore was an actor who functioned as the puppet of the director. He opposed realism, sought the elimination of unessential details, and employed simple nonrepresentational forms to capture the feeling or essence of a play. Whereas Appia was more concerned with a kind of continuum of visual design, connecting the horizontal and vertical into the creation of space, Craig seemed to be more concerned with the creation of what could be called *Gestalt* design. If he were designing Ibsen's *The Master Builder* he might simply design a large tower that could be lit from various sides to suggest different locales. Or if it were a play about a king, there might be a dais for a throne and nothing else because that image is the embodiment or essential element of the play. Regardless of all that he said about playwrights or actors, Craig was adamant about getting to the essence or feeling of the play in his designs, and that has had a major impact on the way designers design now.

While Appia and Craig were developing their theories, **Max Reinhardt**, born Max Goldman (1873-1943), was developing as an actor (and later as a director) at the Freie Bühne in Berlin. In 1902, he opened the Kleines Theater (also in Berlin) and produced his first hit, Oscar Wilde's *Salome*. In an attempt to break down the separation between stage and audience, and to rescue the actors from behind the proscenium, he took plays out of the theatre and produced them in places that were not traditionally used for theatrical performances (anticipating Antonin Artaud who will do the same thing in France). In 1903, Reinhardt opened his own Neues Theater, and in 1905, he won acclaim for his production of Shakespeare's *A Midsummer Night's Dream* (designed by Ernst Stern) because of its color and theatricality. As a director, Reinhardt was especially significant because of his eclecticism: he rejected the idea that there is only one way to do a play and argued that modern plays demand a more realistic style of performance than classical plays. But while he maintained a realistic style of acting and production, he wanted to avoid the drab exactness of Naturalism. What he wanted was reality and theatricality. For the classics, however, he wanted lively and supple speaking rather than slow and ponderous delivery that the traditionalists had customarily used in classical plays. He also forced his actors think about their characters from fresh perspectives rather than assuming ready-made characterizations, a very important innovation. It was the traditional view that when an actor played a particular role, he would rely on the way that role had been played for the last 100 years. When he did Hamlet, he did it in black. He's going to brood; he's going to do all the things that Hamlet has always done. Reinhardt said, "All right. But why don't you try something different? Look at the role from a different perspective." Thus, Reinhardt was extremely important for encouraging the actor's creativity in finding new ways to perform a role.

In 1906, he bought the Deutsches Theater, rebuilt it and began a theatre school. Interestingly, there was a tavern in the same block, so he bought the tavern and converted it into a small black box theatre for chamber plays. He really began the LORT practice of having the big room for large, commercially viable plays, and the small room for the experimental work. In 1907, his Deutsches Theater Company toured Europe and the United States, creating a significant effect on audiences and performers throughout the world, and in 1910, he produced Sophocles' *Oedipus Rex* in a circus arena in Vienna. In 1911, for the monumental drama, *The Miracle*, he transformed the Olympia Exhibition building in London into a cathedral. In this particular space, the audience became part of the congregation of the play. What is also very interesting, and rather unusual, Reinhardt, a master of spectacle, was also versatile enough to direct subtle and intimate plays in small spaces. Reinhardt was interested in very specific detail in addition to the huge canvas. Until WWI his personality directed the German stage, and nearly all the young directors or actors, who would make a name for themselves through the war years and after, were trained by him or worked in one of his theatres or schools. In 1913-1914, he brought about a Shakespearean revival, mounting ten plays with few or no settings and in 1920, when he gave up the position of artistic director of the Deutsches Theater, he created the Salzburg festival and retired to his castle in Austria. In 1933, when the Nazis assumed power, Reinhardt came to the United States, leaving his theatrical empire to the German people. In 1934-35 he made the very famous Hollywood film of *A Midsummer Night's Dream* with Mickey Rooney as Puck, and he finally settled in the United States in 1938 when he opened a theatrical workshop in Hollywood. He staged *Everyman* in modern dress and planned, though never completed, an all-black production of the same play. In 1943 he died in New York City having lost his ability to speak.

Expressionism

After WWI, two of Reinhardt's former company members, the expressionist **Leopold Jessner** (1878-1945), and the epic theatrical wizard **Erwin Piscator** (1893-1966), became leading directors of the German stage. The productions of these two men used actors on a bare, darkened stage. The actors were picked out by shafts of light against a black background and scenery was limited to one or two small pieces which were symbolic rather than realistic. Leopold Jessner, who was the director of the Berlin State Theatre, was especially noted for an imaginary use of flights of steps and platforms. A famous Jessner set would be one large flight of steps (often called *Jessnertreppe*) extending from the apron up to the back of the stage. Piscator, on the other hand, who worked with the Proletarian Theatre, tried to create a kind of working-class or Socialist drama, and would have a significant influence on, and association with Bertolt Brecht. In 1927, Piscator founded the Piscator Theater and began to produce early versions of epic theatre (a Socialist drama closely associated with Brecht). In 1933, he left Germany and six years later moved to the United States where he taught at the New School for Social Research in New York City.

While the German Expressionist School of drama developed from the stylized staging of people like Jessner and Piscator, two of the most significant Expressionistic dramatists were Georg Kaiser (1878-1945) and Ernst Toller (1893-1939). In Expressionistic drama, characters become symbols instead of people and their names express their roles in society: The Salvation Army Girl, The Bank Teller, the Lady, the Lady's Son. Dialogue is stripped of everything but key words and phrases, and technical devices are used openly onstage emphasizing theatricality over reality. The actor functions as a ritualized, almost priestly figure, celebrating the concept of the super-individual (anticipating the master race philosophy that's brewing)—the superman, though later on, Marxist economic theory begins to replace the idea of the super-individual. Inevitably, since all the people who secularized the German theatre were involved with politics, German Expressionistic drama was very politically oriented.

In the 1920s when steel, timber and other building materials became plentiful, Piscator directed a series of productions using elaborate and expensive machinery. The front of the stage was constructed as a conveyor belt. In the center there was a cantilever bridge that moved up and down. Lantern slides and motion pictures were projected on the back wall. All of this constituted a constructivist scene design. Why was it called constructivist? Because we are concerned with the construction of a scene, not simply the finished product. The interest is in how the thing is made (or constructed). Piscator also used slogans above the proscenium arch that provided information about what was happening—like the titles in silent films. In addition, gigantic shadows of pulsating machines were thrown onto gauzes reminding audiences of the machine age, the working man, and the evils of Capitalism.

Critics consider **Georg Kaiser** the classicist of German Expressionist drama. He was influenced by Plato, Shakespeare, Goethe, and Ibsen, but his chief influence came from Nietzsche because of the "superman" concept of a higher order of man capable of redeeming, what Kaiser called "the fragmented man of modern technological society," the man who can overcome the machine. To that end he developed the concept or notion of "the new man," and his aim in writing plays was to depict the extraordinary, intellectual, moral, and spiritual efforts of the new man, and to record his arrival at the state of perfection. Like all classicists, he was an idealist.

Generally speaking, Expressionistic drama is an intensely subjective expression of the writer's deepest feelings. Often, it is described as "drama of the soul." It rebels against the structure of society, and emphasizes language at the expense of plot and psychologically-drawn characters. We're much less interested in watching a three-dimensional portrayal of the protagonist in an expressionistic play, than we are in understanding the inner substance of his feelings, or his perception of what is happening to him.

Linguistically, German expressionistic drama was heavily influenced by a poet named August Stramm. He was significant because he experimented with language, cutting it to the bone, and forcing monosyllabic words to act as the barometer for feeling and emotion. This resulted in what we call the expressionistic *schrei* or scream. Unlike a Shavian character, for example, who will have a great deal of dialogue or a long monologue to express a feeling or idea, the expressionist character doesn't speak a lot of words; he often utters monosyllables in very simple grammatical constructions, while the play is centered around his/her expression of grief or anxiety (the *schrei* or scream). Many expressionist plays have a scene in which children assert their individuality by upbraiding their parents, often doing them violence sometimes to the extremes of rape or murder. Part of what the expressionists were reacting against was the patriarchal family system which, in itself, tended to smother the development of youthful individuality. This was not a satirical device because Expressionistic plays were hardly ever funny. Instead, it was a literal an indictment against the system.

We were talking about Georg Kaiser and his notion of the new man. Kaiser's plays are idea plays, the most famous of which is *From Morn to Midnight* which premiered on 28 April 1917 in Munich. It was a very inauspicious year to premier this play because it was the year of the October revolution in Russia, the year Germany bombed London, the year Lenin was appointed Chief Commissar, and the year the United States declared war on Hungary and

Austria. Three years later, in 1920, the play was made into a film which began to experiment with new cinemagraphic techniques such as the "dissolve," and film historians say the film version of *From Morn to Midnight* marks the first time we see what we now think of as modern film techniques. In the same year, *From Morn to Midnight* was produced in London on the experimental stage of the London Stage Society, an important production because it was part of the Independent Theatre Movement (the theatre movement that strove to develop the noncommercial kind of play). Interestingly, in England the play was reviewed as a "regrettable breach of taste." In 1922, however, it was produced in New York by the Theatre Guild and was so highly regarded that it marked the beginning of Expressionistic drama in the United States.

From Morn to Midnight is among the earliest examples of what is called *station drama* and consists of two parts and seven stations. The plot is simple, episodic, and the stations are loosely linked, not developing from one another in a necessarily causal way, but producing their effect via montage. The characters in the play are types and have only generic names: Cashier, Bank Teller, Salvation Army Girl. In part one, station 1: The Cashier at a bank, excited by a lady dressed in silk and furs, steals 60,000 marks from his bank to impress the lady. Station 2: He goes to the lady's hotel, hoping she might be a lady of easy virtue. The Lady is both surprised and shocked by the theft, and the Cashier discovers that she has a son. He leaves dejectedly and becomes depressed by the futility of his actions. Station 3: In a snowfield, the Cashier meets the image of death—a skeleton—and he investigates the meaning of life (here is where Woody Allen and Ingmar Bergman start to rely on the German Expressionists). He has a dialogue with death and, typical of Kaiser's heroes, the Cashier is a gambler. If life doesn't meet up to his expectations, he decides to escape into death. Part II begins with Station 4: The Cashier returns to his home earlier than usual. In a kind of satire on the lifestyle of the bourgeoisie, his family is so disconcerted by his unexpected arrival from work that his mother has a heart attack and dies. In terms of the bourgeois pattern, the husband works from 9 to 5. If he comes home earlier than that, the whole household is turned upside down. Station 5: The Cashier tries to manipulate the crowd in a sports palace by offering large sums of money as prizes. Whoever wins will get a certain amount of money. Suddenly the crowd is more interested in his offer of money than in watching the event. Unfortunately, the Cashier discovers that, as soon as the Emperor walks into the room, the crowd immediately loses interest in the money. The Cashier leaves the sports palace disgusted. Station 6: The Cashier attempts to have romantic adventures with a group of female masks in a nightclub. This scene is designed to demonstrate his lack of education, and the anti-intellectual stance in expressionistic plays. Finally, Station 7: The Cashier is led to a Salvation-Army hall, under false pretenses, by a Salvation-Army girl who turns him into the police for the reward money. The Cashier returns to the snowfield where he sees the skeleton again. He decides to accept death, and in the last moments of the play, the Cashier dies, outstretched on a Salvation Army cross. The tone of the play expresses man's disillusionment and loss of values in the world. It also expresses the journey of the individual to try to achieve a higher reality. This is the greater self, the perfect man; and, typical of most expressionist plays, the only way that man can achieve a higher reality is through his own failure to achieve it in life. His only choice for salvation is to pursue death.

Like Kaiser, **Ernst Toller** was rooted in German Classicism and Romanticism. Unlike Kaiser who actually escaped from Nazi Germany and continued to write in Switzerland and other European countries, Toller left Germany in 1933 and moved to New York City. In 1939, he was discovered in his hotel room with a bullet in his head. He committed suicide having become as disillusioned by the American system as he was by Nazism. His plays are somewhat more strongly ethical and idealistic than Kaiser's. For example, *Man and the Masses* (1918) portrays a revolutionary in personal conflict, trying to reconcile bloodshed with the ideal of universal peace. In 1927, he wrote *Hurrah, We're Alive!*—possibly his most interesting play, because the end of the play comes to the conclusion that human differences are impossible to resolve, and that Western society requires a binary premise. In other words, if there is a thesis, our society demands an antithesis. If there isn't an antithesis forthcoming, people will create one in their own minds. Freud tends to talk about the individual who always seeks to put problems in his own way—being one's worst enemy. This play assigns Freud's analysis to the political arena.

Another voice in the world of Expressionistic drama belongs to **Johann August Strindberg** (1849-1912), a Swedish playwright whose work falls into three specific periods:

1) Naturalism, in which he wrote the first naturalistic play in Scandinavia—*Miss Julie*;

2) Inferno, between 1894 and 1896, when Strindberg lived in Paris, where he experimented as a chemist, drug addict, painter, and photographer.

3) Expressionism, which extended from 1898 to1909. With his expressionist plays, most significantly *The Dream Play* and *Ghost Sonata*, Strindberg frees the stage from the bonds of time and place. In *The Dream Play*, for example, like in a dream world, a variety of events happen on stage that are not causally related, and which are not even organized by traditional time or space. In *From Morn to Midnight*, the exploits of the Cashier all happen in the same general locale, and they are all situations in which he would have involved himself. In *The Dream Play*, the various events come out of nowhere because they are part of the subconscious mind (just as we can dream of being in a field, and then the next moment find ourselves in the third act of *Othello*, and then later find ourselves submersed in a pool of pink whipped cream). In *The Ghost Sonata* Strindberg introduced the grotesque into drama with a kind of musical formula. Grotesque characters seem to pop in and out thematically rather than dramatically. There appears to be no causal reason for their entrances, they just seem to come in—like motifs that appear and disappear in a piece of music. The characters are used symbolically or *motifically* rather than dramatically in any traditional way.

Strindberg was also highly influenced by mysticism, and he had a strong identification with Beethoven. Antonin Artaud saw *The Ghost Sonata* as the precursor of the Theatre of Cruelty, and other critics suggest that it anticipates the Theatre of the Absurd. Critics also suggest that Strindberg might be the father of Theatrical Expressionism through his use of the unconscious and dream state in plays, and everyone seems to agree that Strindberg's chief contribution to drama is the freeing of the stage from causality, or traditional causality—the restrictions of time and place.

Married and divorced three times, Strindberg seemed to be an inveterate misogynist, yet kept getting married. He was constantly trying to find himself in a variety of means of expression. Not only was he a playwright, he was also a short story writer, a poet, and an artist. There is a fascinating painting of his called *The Red Room* which looks like one of the circles of hell, and it's certainly not surprising why the great eccentric, Antonin Artaud, would look to the Swedish eccentric August Strindberg as a model for much of his work.

Before we talk about Artaud, however, we have to go back to France and talk about **Jacques Copeau** (1879-1949) who developed a theatre troupe called the Vieux Colombier in 1913. Like Reinhardt, Copeau sought to break down the barrier between actor and the audience. He had an unframed stage without wings and no line of demarcation between stage and auditorium. Sets were used sparingly, and atmosphere was created for each play almost entirely with lighting. Before he opened the Vieux Colombier, Copeau created a School of Young Actors and took his actors/pupils to a country home where they improvised scenes and practiced group acting exercises (well in anticipation of Jerzy Grotowski who did virtually the same thing with his actors—taking them into the field to do improvs and exercises). Copeau's actors also learned from Montmartre performers, experts in the improvised comedies that were still popular at the French cabarets and fairs. In addition to their training in movement, in improvisation, and in comedy, Copeau's actors also were also educated in classical acting techniques. Copeau developed many of his ideas about theatrical movement from Emile Jacques Dalcroze (1865–1950), who had developed the system of *eurythmics* in which certain sounds create movement in the body, and one begins to associate a particular sound with a particular movement. *Eurythmics* was a device to get into sense recall and produce an externalization of internal emotions.

In 1917 Copeau took the Vieux Colombier troupe to New York City where it performed extensively to excellent reviews, and in 1924, he moved the School of Young Actors to Burgundy where they studied, worked in the fields, and experienced local wine festivals. In 1926 the company changed its title to *Les Copiaux*, taking Copeau 's name and Michel St. Denis began to write for them. By 1930, Michel St. Denis took over the company and renamed it the Company of Fifteen. Even though he was no longer in charge of the Vieux Colombier, Copeau influenced French theatre production for the rest of the century, especially in the use of extensive expressive gesture and mime. His employment of mime in production was further strengthened and extended through the work of Louis Jouvet and Charles Dullin, and among Copeau's greatest contributions was the idea of a permanent architectural stage for modern productions, i.e. a unit set. For acting he combined the Stanislavski method of inner truth with the search for theatrical form.

Dada and Surrealism

While Copeau was rehearsing his troupe of actors, a Romanian poet named Sami Rosenstock who changed his name to **Tristan Tzara** (1896-1963) began to develop a form of art called *Dada*. The movement began on 8 February 1916 at 6:00 p.m. at the Café Terrasse in Zurich where, in his spare time, Tzara played chess with Lenin. The name was chosen because it means everything and nothing: Father, "Yes, yes" in Russian, and Hobbyhorse. That's why the word was chosen. It had so many meanings, it didn't mean anything. On 30 March 1916 at the Cabaret Voltaire in Zurich, the first manifestation of Dada occurred. Dadaists recited poems simultaneously preventing the audience from understanding a single word, and thus did away with the notion of rational comprehension. In the same year Tzara wrote his first dramatic work called *THE FIRST CELESTIAL ADVENTURE OF MISTER ANTIPYRINE*, and on 14 July 1916, *MISTER ANTIPYRINE'S MANIFESTO* was read by Tzara. This was the first of Dada's manifestos (as opposed to the first of the manifestations of Dada!) and it espoused incoherent spontaneity in literature. It championed an unleashing of unconscious contents, a creative process devoid of logic.

The second Dada manifesto occurred on 23 March 1918 and launched an attack on outworn notions concerning a work of art. Tzara felt that "schools of art," for the codification of form, betray life experience and that an individual vision, born out of one's own imagination, should replace any model or set of rules. He did not believe in progress and was convinced that hope of any kind was devoid of meaning. For Tzara, hope was artificial, superfluous, and illusory. He believed in spontaneous incoherence and the dislocation of language, and he preferred to express his ideas through scandalous demonstrations. As an example of this, we are now going to write a Dada poem. Give me a word, any word.

UmEvaporate
ShooRules
BowOink
There's our poem: "Um Evaporate Shoo Rules Bow Oink."
Or,
"Um shoo bow evaporate rules oink."
Or
"Bow oink rules shoo um evaporate."

Does that not have a contextual meaning? Could you not develop it in any way you like? Dadaists liked to take words they cut out of newspapers, put them into bags, shake them up, pull them out word by word, and paste them into poetry. The tendency towards photographic realism must have been so strong in trying to reproduce real things, that artists were desperate to do something different. In addition, realism was consciously associated with the bourgeois political and social issues that developed into World War I. Dada was a conscious and nihilistic reaction to the art form that was advocated by a society that plunged all of Europe into mass destruction. The immediate impact of Dada lasted for only a short time, but its influence on Surrealism and the Theatre of the Absurd, and even on MTV videos, is felt to the present day. Every time we encounter, in an Ionesco or Beckett play, characters who seem to speak gibberish, we're going directly back to Tristan Tzara and his Dadaist poems.

Eyewitness accounts indicate that Dadaists would physically attack their audience as part of the performance, in what they called "scandalous demonstrations." Dadaists were very fond of using Gallagher-like tendencies: throwing water or oil into the audience. Sometimes a Dada manifesto would be involved in something like the following scenario: I come in with a knife covered with blood and look as if I'm going to attack someone in the audience. I don't really attack the person, but the rest of the audience starts to scream and tries to prevent me from doing any harm. Then a group of my associates comes out and laughs at everyone in the audience for thinking that something violent was going to happen. Not only does the audience have the experience of being frightened and concerned, it experiences being ridiculed for thinking that something would have happened. In that way, not only do I physically attack the audience, I mentally attack it as well. This is not far removed from the kind of thing that Artaud wanted, and it's not unlike the methods that were used by Richard Schechner and various theatrical groups in the United States to shock an audience into experiencing something immediate and visceral in the theatre. Dadaism was trying to arouse an audience out of its accustomed lethargy, to give it what it does not expect. And by giving it what it does not expect, it forces the audience to arrive at an honest reappraisal of what it has just seen. Seeing a realistic play, what does the audience expect: real life on stage. Dada is saying, "Don't do that. Treat every moment as unexpected."

Another manifesto was read on 5 February 1919 at the Grande Palais des Champs Elysées in Paris. At this performance, Tzara called the audience idiots. At another manifesto on 23 January 1920, Tzara read a newspaper to the audience amidst catcalls and threats. This was one of the greatest manifestos because the audience went to the performance expecting Tzara to call them idiots and to do strange things, when all he did was stand on the stage and reads to them from a newspaper. The audience shouted "Get him off," and spectators started to run onstage to attack him. Theatre for Tzara was designed to provoke, to shock, and to move people out of their characteristic indolence. To that end, he wrote *The Gas Heart* which was performed in Paris on 10 June 1921. In the play, all the characters are organs of the face: Ear, Mouth, Eye, Neck, Nose and Eyebrow. The *dramatis personae* allowed Tzara to create new spatial concepts in the theatre, very much like the Cubists were doing in painting and sculpture. Ear, Mouth, Eye, and Neck all live in spatial relationship to one another, like they do on the face. The author also introduced a new sense of time because he felt that clock time or linear time kills beauty, and he tried to create what he called "mythical time," in which everything can exist simultaneously. When you really think about it, time is only a convention because in our minds everything exists simultaneously. If you call upon a memory in your mind, a memory that happened 20 years ago is not in a different time in your mind than a memory of something that happened yesterday. You can remember them simultaneously. As a result, Tzara argued that chronological time is purely a convention that destroyed art.

The plot (such as it is) of *The Gas Heart* is virtually incomprehensible. Critics, however, have constructed a narrative based on their personal interpretations of Tzara's text. Basically, Mouth and Eye are a couple. The French word for "eye" is masculine and the French word for "mouth" is feminine so, in a very traditional way, a masculine eye can be in love with a feminine mouth. Ear explains to Eye the ramifications of love, including the possibility that Mouth may be unresponsive to Eye's love. Eye pursues a character named Clytemnestra in an attempt to make Mouth jealous. Mouth, annoyed by Eye's passionate outburst, leaves the stage, and Nose, Eyebrow, and Eye express their frustrations at an industrialized society. That's the end of the first act. In act two we discover that Clytemnestra is a horse and Mouth must be a horse as well. In fact, Mouth and Clytemnestra are the same being. Romantic dialogue is expressed in terms of a racing form. Mouth announces she has won lots of money at the races and mentions that a young man followed her on the street on a bicycle (a subtle reference to Jarry). Eye was trying to make Mouth jealous, now Mouth is trying the same tactic with Eye. It works. Eye gets jealous and criticizes Mouth's insensitivity. She exits and Eyebrow screams, "Fire! Fire!" implying that Eye's passion can no longer be contained. End of Act II. At the beginning of act three, Mouth's decision to marry Eye is represented by the symbol of a sewing machine. Nose and Neck attack her for yielding to the illusory condition of marital bliss. Eye declares once again his passion for Mouth who is also Clytemnestra. Ear discovers that his horse won. Mouth enters on all fours only to find Eye on all fours and the cast tells the audience to go home to bed.

Surrealism

The Surrealist Movement was inspired by Jarry and **Guillaume Apollinaire** (1880–1918), whose play *The Breasts of Tieresias* was subtitled a "surrealistic drama." Apollinaire's play is about a woman named Theresa who loses her breasts. They fly into the air as colored balloons, and she transforms into the Greek prophet Tieresias. Her husband meanwhile intends to repopulate France, and through a pure act of will, he gives birth to 40,049 children while being observed by a mute, unemotional citizen of Zanzibar. That's the play and these are the characteristics of surrealism:

1) The cult of the dream;

2) The representation of the absurd or illogical. If it doesn't seem to make sense, it is appropriate to Surrealism;

3) The erotic;

4) The expression of psychic experience through automatic writing in which a person, in a trance-like state, makes no conscious effort in putting words down on paper. Sometimes automatic writing will make grammatical sense, sometimes it will not. The surrealists liked having the flexibility of making syntactical sense in the dialogue as well as absolute gibberish. This is going to have a very great influence on the Absurdists;

5) Free association;

6) Explosive metaphors. The explosive metaphor is a symbol or idea which is so strong it forces you to rethink a particular idea. For example, if

someone would say "I love you as much as a trough full of pig dung, the idea is so incongruous that we are forced to think about it;

7) The plays are designed to evoke a direct and convulsive reaction.

The spokesman for this particular formula was **André Breton** (1896-1966) who issued the first manifesto of Surrealism in1924. He said that "Surrealism is pure psychic automatism by which is intended to express verbally or otherwise the real process of thought." The surrealists were trying to free humans from the strictures of real life in which they had lost faith. Living in a post-war society where all the traditional values seem to have been exploded (and exploited), they were trying to find other values in which to believe. The subconscious mind or dreamlike state represented for them the basis for artistic truth. The man who made most effective use of surrealistic techniques in drama was **Jean Cocteau** (1892-1963) who was also one of the first twentieth-century writers to restore Greek tragedy to modern audiences. He did this by writing his own versions of *Antigone* and *Orpheus*. He also wrote a number of surrealistic plays that seem to have no basis in logic. For example, in *The Wedding on the Eiffel Tower* (1921) there is a dissociation of both time and space. The only speaking characters are two phonographs, and the rest of the characters (including an ostrich and a lion) emerge from a huge camera when a picture is taken. His pantomime called *Ox on the Roof* (1920) is set in a speak-easy in America during Prohibition. Cocteau's genius lies in making the dream and the absurd tangible and alive, allowing the absurdities of surrealism to become available to a contemporary audience. As a result, he was accused of commercializing surrealistic techniques and subsequently shunned by the surrealists. Cocteau's theatre essentially lacks the rebellious spirit of the surrealistic movement, though he uses all of its techniques.

Theatre of Cruelty

In the mold of Surrealism, but going one step farther, was an actor-theorist named **Antonin Artaud** (1896-1948). Artaud dreamed of establishing a new kind of theatre, not as an artistic spectacle but as a communion between art and spectator. He sought to create a new intermingling ritual between the actor and the audience. He called it a *Theatre of Magic*, a mass participation in which an entire culture could find its vitality and truest expression. This clearly suggested that everyone was becoming dissatisfied with realistic and traditional theatrical experiences. After WWI, Realism did not seem to be the appropriate expression of the political and/or social experiences in Europe. While the surrealists would go in the direction of the hallucination and dream, Artaud's interests led him into creating a ritualized "Total Theatre," that he would call the Theatre of Cruelty. In 1913, Artaud was put in a mental hospital. After his release, he had several more attacks of mental disorder (in 1916 and 1918), and in 1940, he was put in a mental institution for a period of eight years. In 1926 (after spending two years with the Surrealist Movement), Artaud created the Théâtre Alfred Jarry, which led to his immediate disassociation with the surrealists who not only attacked him in the press, but also disrupted his productions. Believing that the theatre experience should be like "a police raid on a brothel," Artaud produced two seasons of productions at the Théâtre Alfred Jarry before closing in 1928. In 1932 and 1933, after being influenced by the performances of Balinese dancers, he created the manifestos of the Theatre of Cruelty, a surreal theatre based on ritual and fantasy that would launch an attack on the audience's subconscious in an attempt to release deep-rooted fears and anxieties that are normally suppressed.

The fact that playwrights and theorists have become so interested in dreams and the subconscious is in no little part due to Freud who had been publishing his work since 1895. Until Freud, there was never a clearly defined sense of the subconscious. Now that a sense of the subconscious was available to playwrights and theatre theorists, they began to question the various layers of human behavior and forced people to view themselves and their private natures without the shield of civilization. Like so many others, Artaud believed that civilization hides man's truest feelings. In order to shock the audience into releasing its deepest instincts and feelings, the extremes of human nature were graphically portrayed on stage. Ultimately, this meant that Artaud's theatre turned on madness and/or perversion. For Artaud, the style of physical production was more important than the text performed so often he would take an existing play and adapt it to his needs. He also employed a number of unlikely places in which to perform. He might stage a play in an airplane hangar or on a busy street corner. He wanted to force the audience to be in a situation where it would have a first-hand experience of what was going on in the drama. Artaud wanted to see stage gesture elevated to the rank of exorcism. He wanted the actor to be able to exorcise the evil spirit from the general consciousness of the audience, and he maintained that art goes far beyond human understanding in its attempt to reach a metaphysical truth. In other words, we are only able to reach truth metaphysically through this kind of ritual, not through our conscious minds.

One of his most significant productions was *The Cenci* (1935) adapted from the play by Percy Bysshe Shelley. In his production at the Theatre Folies-Wagram, Artaud initiated the fundamental notion of "theatre in the round" by bringing the spectators and actors in very close contact, virtually having the audience surrounding the action, and then having the action surround the audience. As a result, the audience actually felt that it was in the middle of everything. Artaud created frenzy by such devices as whirling stage sets, strident and dissonant sound effects, and grating lighting effects. Artaud was particularly fond of bathing the actors in very bright white light that would cause glare and make the audience have to squint to see. He also wanted the actors to have to shout at the audience, like the kind of thing that Richard Schechner and his satellites were doing in the 1960s. Artaud's influence is apparent in the work of many important twentieth-century directors: Jean Louis Barrault, Jean Vilar, Roger Blin, and Peter Brook.

The major playwright of the movement of the Theatre of Cruelty was **Jean Genet** (1910–1986), a social outcast who turned erotic and obscene subject matter into a poetic vision of the universe. Most of his critics suggest that he uses obscenity to suggest the way the world is. Genet spent his early life in reform school, and described the degradation of his incarceration in his first novel, *The Miracle of the Rose*. His autobiography *The Thief's Journal* gives an account of his life as a tramp, pickpocket, male prostitute, aesthete, existentialist, and pioneer of the Theatre of the Absurd. Perhaps the most important aspect of Jean Genet's philosophy is that man's essence is all in his externals (i.e. I have stolen an apple. You say I am a thief. It may be the only time I have stolen anything, but every time you see me, I am a thief. Therefore, I might as well become a thief since that's what you made me). Genet maintained that whenever anyone is introduced to another, an identity is created based on observable facts: A is introduced to B. B establishes in his mind what A is, whether or not that is the essential truth of A. Therefore, what does it matter what A has inside, since it will never be appreciated by B anyway.

Genet's first forays into drama, *The Maids*, and *Deathwatch* are compact, neoclassical dramas in one act. They also demonstrate the strong influence of Jean-Paul Sartre, the seminal philosopher of existentialism. In *The Maids*, two maids feel the need to assert themselves because they feel their status as human beings has been reduced by serving their mistress. When the mistress is away, one of the maids always plays at being the mistress and in their fantasy world, they formulate a plot to kill her. When the mistress leaves to pick her lover up after his release from prison, the maids once again decide to play their game of maid and the mistress, and the maid actually kills the maid who is enacting the role of the mistress. The philosophy here is: If you're playing the role of the mistress, you *are* the mistress.

Genet's *The Balcony* (1956) trades more than any other play on a confusion of roles: what a person is and why he/she belongs in a particular role. A number of men from a variety of professions go to the "Balcony," a brothel, to enjoy sex according to the specific fictive roles each plays. When a political revolution occurs, the men who are playing the role of Bishop, Magistrate, or General in the brothel are required to play those roles outside the Balcony because the real Bishop, Magistrate, and General have been killed. Genet keeps raising the issue of "What is real? Is the interior or exterior real?" If you see a person dressed in ecclesiastical roles and people call that person a Bishop, how do you know that the person is only playing a role? And if the person plays the role well, why should he/she not be the real thing. Genet suggests that the role defines essence: a person is what he does. Genet was a rebel and anarchist. He rejected all forms of social discipline and political commitment. He created large-scale shocking dramas designed to explode political, racial, and religious prejudices. He wanted to make the audience come face to face with their own values and to realize how stupid they all are. With both Artaud and Genet, the journey into man's interior self was realized through the erotic and the obscene.

Similar to Genet but somewhat more gothic in his sensibilities was a playwright named **Michel de Ghelderode** (1898-1962), a Belgian dramatist and eccentric whose plays resonate with madness, violence, demonism, and satirical pornography. During World War II he became recognized as one of the masters of the avant-garde since he was among the first to exploit Artaud's ideas of "Total Theatre" in which every sort of appeal is made to the eye, to the ear, to the emotions in order to stir the intellect. In production, he sought to use visible stage craft, stream of conscious dialogue, and character transformations in full view of the audience. A character would become another personality in the middle of a scene, for example, to show that traditional views of characterization are impossible.

Epic Theatre

However, the playwright who, perhaps, most significantly appealed to the intellect during this period was the Marxist playwright **Bertolt Brecht** (1898-1956), who was noted for what was called the *verfremdungseffekt* which is often translated as the "alienation effect" but really means "making strange effect." However, you choose to translate it in English, *verfremdungseffekt* is a production (and writing) technique that attempts to estrange the spectator, to make him view that which is ordinary in a different way. This does not mean that Brecht did not want to involve the audience in the action of a play. It does however mean that he sought to make the spectator think. To this end he developed certain theatrical tendencies and techniques so that everything in his plays could be viewed critically and with intellectual curiosity. To achieve this effect Brecht used episodic plots, songs, narration, visual aids—such as legends or titles (signs that would tell you what's going to happen in the scene), masks, and chorus. Why would a playwright want to tell an audience at the beginning of the scene the outcome of that scene: "This is the scene where Grusha meets the man and kills him." Because the audience knows what the outcome will be, it is less concerned with what happens than with how it happens. Brecht felt that since the spectator has to step away from a picture to appreciate it (typically, when looking at a piece of art you step away from it to get a sense of the entire picture, then you look closely at it to study the brush strokes), the same kind of distancing must happen in the theatre.

To create distance between spectator and play, Brecht employed the following devices:

1) He had actors adopt the third person when talking, so that audiences do not entirely lose themselves in the characterization, but realize that this is an actor playing a character;

2) Often, actors will adopt the past tense, giving a sense of narration; and

3) Brecht would have stage directions and comments spoken in the middle of a play. This technique is employed in his play *Man Equals Man* (1925) in which the play stops at dead center, an actor comes forward, and says "And now a word from our author, Mr. Bertolt Brecht." Brecht then provides a kind of public-service announcement, "This is the play I wanted to write and it has Marxist philosophy, and so forth," and when he is through proselytizing, the actor concludes, "Now back to the play." It's like a commercial. Actually, it's like what George Bernard Shaw does in his prefaces at the *beginning* of his published plays. Brecht inserts his ideas in the *middle* of his. What does this technique do to the audience? It takes them out of the action of the play, and makes them rethink it.

Other of Brecht's theatrical innovations include:

1) The use of bright light on actors to create a starker look;

2) The use of costumes not perceived as costumes but as clothes which

have been worn before. These are not theatrical creations; they just come off the backs of the actors as they come in from the street;

3) A scene design that generally begins with a bare stage and uses only what is necessary to perform the play. Often there is a dichotomy between what is setting and what is costume. In *Galileo*, for example, the Pope's great robe turns out to be the window curtains;

4) The actor often demonstrates both himself and the character in performance. By not completely identifying himself with the character, the actor makes the audience take a step away from the characterization to enable it to see the character from the outside. It is almost as if the actor is giving a lecture, and the character is purely an illustration of an idea;

5) Music is used as a comment on the play, often in direct contrast to the mood or moment of the text. When Brecht uses music in a play, often the most romantic scenes are underscored with the most dissonant music. In *The Rise and Fall of the City of Mahogany*, for example, Brecht has composer Kurt Weill underscore a scene between a whore and her client with very romantic, very lush music and the language being spoken is "Should I pay you now or later?" "Do you want me with or without my panties?" "No, don't put your hand there it hurts." "You're squeezing me too tight." And through this, the music is extremely lush and romantic. One of the most beautiful tunes in the entire piece accompanies the words, "If somebody's going to get the shit knocked out of them, it's going to be you and not me" and "I'll kill the son of a bitch."

6) To attempt to instruct the audience, Brecht created a form of epic theatre where the action will move in spurts not necessarily causally, and where the audience will see visible stage machinery. The audience may be attacked by the actor, and dialogue may be contradicted by stage activity. Through all of these techniques, Brecht expected the audience to gather evidence objectively and perceive the moral issues involved in the play. Why is the word "epic" singled out to describe this kind of theatre? From epic poetry, Brecht derived a sense of episodes that are simply connected by "And then I did" rather than necessary causality. For the word epic, think episodic, not vast.

In Brecht's world, evil is most often the active force and goodness is passive. This is perhaps a very significant detail: two of the chief influences on Brecht were Charlie Chaplin and American gangster movies.

Futurism

The technology of the twentieth century and love for speed were both reflected in an artistic movement called **Futurism** that was developed by a man named **Philippo Tomasso Marinetti** (1876-1944). The movement was inspired by Henri Bergson's concept of the *élan vital*, was fascinated with automobiles and airplanes, and ultimately became a celebration of man the machine. The most important plays of the futurists were *sintesi* (syntheses), brief plays which sought to synthesize facts in the least number of words. Traditional standards of verisimilitude and photographic realism were attacked, and the *sintesi* emphasized simultaneity and a more direct, non-contemplative involvement of the spectator with the play. In other words, where Brecht wanted the spectator to be intellectually involved to make an objective judgment about the play, the Futurists did not want intellectual involvement. They wanted the spectator simply to feel—to experience a mood or expression of delight or revulsion in relation to their plays.

The *sintesi* were developed in a manifesto called *The Futurist Synthetic Theatre* on 11 January 1915, in which they developed the idea of a paradox between simultaneity and nihilism which would have a great influence on Luigi Pirandello. Nihilism is the philosophy that nothing happens, nothing matters, nothing is important. It's a terrific paradox because simultaneity suggests that everything is happening at the same time. What's important also in the *sintesi* is that they attack consistent, well-developed characters and suggest, rather, that the actors should play themselves. This is also going to have an influence on Pirandello in terms of his delineation between the actor playing the role and the role itself (an issue not unknown to the French theatre with Artaud and especially with Genet). *The Theatre of Surprise* manifesto on 9 October 1921 was written in response to the lack of recognition for the futuristic movement. Here improvisation becomes an important tool. An emphasis is placed on physical madness and a deep involvement with direct sensory experience. The pugnacious audience/actor relationship is maintained, with actors who end up laughing at the audience for just sitting there when nothing happens on stage.

The Theatre of the Absurd

As a theatrical movement, the Theatre of the Absurd was spawned by the *Ubu* plays, while the term itself was coined by a man named Martin Esslin who argued that "Theatre of the Absurd" was just a title that his publisher forced him into using for his book. He never had any intention of developing a theatre movement under that banner. However inadvertently, Esslin did provide a theoretical platform for the non-realistic, post-WWII genre, suggesting that the plays offer a vision of humanity that is struggling vainly and absurdly to control its fate in a world that seemed bent on its destruction. There are certain recurring themes: futility, hopelessness, and the inability of humans to communicate. In absurd plays, texts are much more important than they are in the Theatre of Cruelty but many of them seek to convey the total inadequacy of words as a means of communication. Hence, we get a lot of gibberish, a great many pauses and repetition in these plays, to such a degree that words cease to convey any kind of meaning.

Very important to the absurd playwright is the concept of Existentialism, of which one of the principal advocates was **Jean-Paul Sartre** (1905–1980). Existentialism is a doctrine which emphasizes each man's responsibility for making his own nature: being is defined by choices and actions freely made, not necessarily governed by traditional morality, nationality, or peer pressure. The existentialists also tend to talk about the futility of human life, using the *Myth of Sisyphus* as a paradigm (the Greek myth of the individual who is rolling a ball up a hill and just as he's about to *get* the ball over the hill, the ball drops down and he has to start all over again. He continues trying to get the ball up to the top of the hill because every time he does, he gets a little closer, so he clings to the hope that tomorrow it will work). The absurd playwrights tend to argue that human nature has this constant sense of hope, of trying to reach perfection. Yet, on consideration, what does all of this mean, because no matter what we do, we are going to be interrupted by death.

Absurd playwrights seek to express the senselessness of the human condition by abandoning rational devices. Hence logical continuity in the drama is replaced by episodic structure, and sometimes even a circular structure in plays, where the action ends where it began. The antecedents of Absurdism are: the *commedia dell'arte*, Surrealism, the circus, the music hall, and film. Often in the absurdist plays there is no plot or story in the traditional sense, and no real characters in conflict. Often in these plays there is much physical activity that leads nowhere, presenting the theme that no matter how busy you are, nothing actually happens in life. By and large, the absurdist play presents no coherent, recognized version of truth. The idea that there is a single truth in life is questioned. Rather, what we get is an individual's perception of the ultimate realities, and since no two individuals have exactly the same perception of truth, therein lies the conflict of the absurdist theatre. The most significant playwrights of the Theatre of the Absurd are Samuel Beckett, Eugene Ionesco, and Harold Pinter.

Conditional Theatre
While futurism and surrealism were beginning to develop in Europe, Russia was also experiencing a reaction to realism. In 1905 Stanislavski created a small studio theatre for experimentation with reactions to realism, and appointed **Vsevolod Meyerhold** (1874-1940?) as the director. Formerly a member of the Moscow Art Theatre, Meyerhold left in 1902 when he became a convert to the symbolist movement. As a result of his experimental tendencies, Stanislavski thought that he might be an appropriate person to head the experimental studio. After several months of rehearsal, Meyerhold staged two productions, both of which Stanislavski detested greatly, and the studio was closed. In these productions, Meyerhold began to develop his idea of what he called "Conditional theatre," with the following techniques:

1) *Biomechanics*: An acting system that trained the actor to become as efficient as a machine in order to respond instantaneously to the director's need. This meant that the actor had to train his body, had to be able to move as well as a dancer, had have immediate reflexes, and absolute control over the physical mechanism—both his body and voice;

2) *Theatricalism*, which for Meyerhold was the elimination of stage conventions such as the fourth wall, and the ultimate rejection of the traditional approach to the theatre as illusion. Now we are back to the concept of a theatrical event (Remember, we started with the audience knowing they're watching a play, then we gradually moved to the audience demanding realistic illusion. Now we're back to the audience knowing that it is in a theatre, watching a play);

3) *Constructivism*. If you're going to develop the idea that the audience is watching a play, one of the most effective ways to do that is to use abstract, three-dimensional settings consisting of ramps, wheels, rolling discs and platforms. So now we no longer have representational settings. Rather we have the audience look at things that are constructed—stage scenery made of building blocks.

Meyerhold also embraced the conventions of the oriental theatre and mysticism. Stanislavski hated the work because he felt that the actor was being used as a puppet, and he believed that the actor's slavish obedience to a dictatorial director was not the way to go. However, seeing actors in that kind of relationship did have an important effect on him, and Stanislavski determined that the actor should be his collaborator, not his subordinate. In addition, he began to do further research into the inner realism of an actor developing his craft.

Meyerhold continued to work in a variety of theatres. His most important production was probably Fernand Crommelynck's *The Magnificent Cuckold* which was performed in 1922. Since the play takes place in a windmill, the scenery designed for the production by Lyubov Popova makes use of circles, ramps, and slides, and the whole thing looks like a big toy machine. Although significant innovations, Meyerhold's concepts of constructivism and bio-mechanics became politically unsound for him because they demonstrated that he was not embracing Socialist Realism, the brand of theatrical activity mandated by the Communist government. As a result, in 1938 he was arrested and imprisoned, and in the same year, a few weeks later, his wife was found brutally murdered in their home. Nothing was heard of Meyerhold until 1958 when his death was announced by the *Soviet Encyclopedia* as occurring in 1942. When a later edition changed the date to 1940, it seemed clear that Meyerhold was yet another martyr to the new Soviet regime. Among his major experiments was the use of *commedia* methods in production. He also explored the merging of *commedia dell'arte* farce with the grotesque (something the Renaissance scenarios had already done). With *commedia* masks there exists already the potential for the grotesque because of the self-conscious caricatures of noses and faces. Meyerhold enjoyed exaggerating the grotesque aspects of theatre and juxtaposing them with slapstick routines, creating very interesting images theatrically.

Under Meyerhold's direction a number of other young directors and symbolists fought against psychological and realistic theatre in a very impressive piece called *The Love of Three Oranges* (1917) after Gozzi's farce. One of the most significant of the young directors who was influenced by Meyerhold was **Yevgeny Vakhtangov** (1883-1922), whose most famous production was probably *Turandot* (1922) which combined *commedia dell'arte* and futuristic theatre performances. One of the most significant aspects of this production is that he had the actors put on the *commedia* costumes right in front of the audience to suggest complete improvisation. Opposed to Stanislavski's method, Vakhtangov wanted outer technique rather than inner realism, and to achieve his greatest effects, he worked with a company of Jewish actors called the Habimah Players. They were better than amateur, but not quite professional actors, and he was able to instruct them in outer improvisational technique His masterpiece with the Habimah players was *The Dybbuk* (1922).

Another director who was reacting to realism was **Nikolai Okhlopkov** (1900-1966). Though he was originally the director of realistic theatre in

Moscow, he was highly influenced by Meyerhold and experimented with anti-realistic ideas such as eliminating the platform stage, and removing the distinction between audience and actor. He wanted the audience to get involved in production, so he developed the idea of arena staging, and even experimented with having actors around the audience. Critics agree that he produced the first true environmental theatre in the 20th century. Okhlopkov also tried to involve the audience through various emotional devices which include striking sound effects. He experimented a great deal with theatrical montage techniques and was one of the first to put various sounds in different parts of the theatre: for example, a shotgun might explode behind the audience to make them feel part of the event. The most famous of Okhlopkov's post-war productions was *Hamlet* in 1954, in which the entire set was divided into little compartments to suggest that Hamlet was trying to escape from a prison-like world.

The Bauhaus

While the rest of Europe was reacting to realistic techniques in the theatre, in Germany, a man named **Walter Gropius** (1883-1969) created the Bauhaus at Weimar in 1919. This was an attempt to unite architecture, painting and sculpture into a communal expression, an important experiment because it developed the concept of the master artwork which could be a total design for living. Gropius tried to eliminate the elitist status of art, connecting it functionally and aesthetically to real life. Between 1923 and 1929, Oscar Schlemmer directed plays at the Bauhaus and sought to unify three dimensional actors with abstract stage space (remember Appia and Craig). His way of doing it was by transforming actors into ambulant architecture. In other words, the actor was now a moving piece of the scenery. He mathematically controlled actors' movements (four steps to the right, eleven steps down) and dressed them in padded costumes that completely obliterated the performer's real physique (not unlike the costumes of the ancient Greek and Roman theatre). In 1927, for the director Erwin Piscator, Gropius developed a formula for a |

"total theatre" that could be transformed into arena, thrust, or proscenium. Because of the outbreak of WWII, the theatre was never built.

Much along these lines are the innovations of **Josef Svoboda** (1920-2002) in Czechoslovakia. His technical achievements include: the *polyekran*, the *laterna magika*, and, the *diapolyekran*. The *polyekran* is a simultaneous and synchronous projection of slides and film on several static screens during which the images on the individual screens are in dramatic interplay with one another in the creation of a total organic composition. The *laterna magika* is a hybrid medium combining film and slides with live actors. The play of actors does not exist without the film nor can the film exist without the actors. The film is not purely just a background. There is a fusion of actors and projection, and the same actors appear on screen and on stage, and interact with one another. An actor comes from a far distance on projection and walks closer and closer and opens a door and appears on stage. The *diapolyekran* is a multi-screen, multi-projection system tighter and shallower than the *polyekran*. In this case, the projection screens form a wall composed of 112 cubes. Each cube has two 35 mm slide projectors mounted at the rear; and each cube is capable of sliding backward or forward about a foot. Each of the slide projectors flash about 5 images per second, if they need to, using about 30,000 slides. What happens, of course, is that you get a sense of 3 dimensions, even though the *diapolyekran* does not use live performers.

Other significant techniques used by Svoboda include: the low voltage unit, in which each lighting instrument has its own transformer, which makes for a smaller filament. As a result, the beam of light is more intense—whiter and more controllable. Svoboda took these individual units of light and combined them with aerosol spray to create walls of light; mirrors—particularly reflective surfaces bonded to flexible material that could be remotely controlled to change the shape of the mirrors. That would then distort the shape of the reflection; and, laser beams and holograms—projections without projection screens or projections on air.

Svoboda also created a number of series of designs using a variety of styles:

1) Theatre of light, in which light creates the space and atmosphere of a play;

2) Projections and color in space, in which he would use a variety of surface forms to suggest locales and moods;

3) Projection and synthesis, in which he would combine screens for projection and acting surfaces, so that the entire set could either be used for projections and/or actors;

4) Kinetics, lighting and mirrors;

5) A curtain of life—teasers and drops to suggest various locations;

6) Collage, to combine real, everyday technical elements to reveal the influence of contemporary technical civilization on our thinking;

7) Theatre within a theatre technique, in which he would extend the architecture of the auditorium onto the set to be the background of the play.

Poor Theatre

In Poland, the son of a painter and sculptor, **Jerzy Grotowski** (1933-1999) was influenced by Stanislavski and Meyerhold. In 1959, after witnessing the Berliner Ensemble's production of Brecht's play, *Mother Courage*, Grotowski established the Polish Laboratory Theatre. He sought to develop a "poor theatre," a theatre which was devoid of razzmatazz and glamour. He wanted to eliminate all technical elements except those which were indispensable—the actor and the audience, and would rearrange spaces to meet the needs of each production. Actors used simple costumes, little makeup and minimal props and created their own music with drums, voices, or natural instruments. Like Artaud, Grotowski believed that theatre was a ritual in which both actor and audience participate. Unlike Artaud, however, who wanted the audience to participate actively in the theatrical ritual, Grotowski permitted the audience participate passively, and to remain the spectator of the ritual in his productions.

Index

Absurda Comica, The, 334
Académie Française, 213, 215, 317, 408
Acajou, 303
Accius, Lucius, 32, 41
Acharnians, The, 5, 22
Adventures of Five Hours, The, 240
Aeschylus, 8–11, 13, 14, 15, 23, 32, 41, 48, 104
Afer, Publius Terentius, *see* Terence
Afranius, 46
Aglaura, 178–179
Agonosthesia, 8
Alarcon, Juan Ruiz de, 193
Aleotti, Giovanni Battista, 111, 284
Alfieri, Vittorio, 290–291
Alione, Giovanni, 95
Alliance of Love, The, 334–335
Ambigue Comique (Theatre), 371
Aminta, 100
Anatol, 458
Anatomist, The, 246
Anatomy of Abuses, 147
Andromaque, 218
Andronicus, Livius, 29, 31
Anger, 26
Antigone (Cocteau), 493

Antigone (Garnier), 205–206
Antigone (Sophocles), 11, 395
Antoine, André, 441, 450–453
Antony, 381–382
Antony and Cleopatra, 205, 230, 239
Anzengruber, Ludwig, 394
Appia, Adolphe, 478–479, 505
Arbitrators, 27
Archer, William, 468–469
Architettura, 106
Aretino, Pietro, 93–95, 161, 305, 392
Arion, 2
Ariosto, Lodovico, 91–92, 106, 206
Aristophanes, 5, 21–23, 203, 219, 248, 394
Aristotle, 13, 17–19, 78, 98, 101, 102, 103, 104, 106, 149, 203, 211, 214, 286, 288, 338, 339
Ars Poetica, 47, 101
Artaud, Antonin, 479, 486, 487, 490, 493–495, 497, 500, 507
Artaxerxes, 358
Arte Poetica, 101–102, 105
Article 330, 454
Artists of Dionysus, 25
Arouet, François Marie, *see* Voltaire
Arviragus and Philicia, 177
As You Like It, 143, 146, 151, 161
Athenaeus of Naucratis, 48
Atreus and Thyestes, 305
Augier, Emile, 401, 405–406, 408, 413, 441
Austerlitz, 386
Auto sacramental, 186, 194, 196, 197

Bacchae, 14
Badajoz, Diego Sanchez de, 187
Balbulus, Notker, 53
Bale, John, 80–81
Baillie, Joanna, 428–429
Balcony, The, 496
Ballad Opera, 253, 254, 255, 303
Ballet Comique de la Reine, 206
Bancroft, Squire, 425, 426, 427, 428
Banks, John, 246
Barber of Seville, The, 320
Barker, Harley Granville, 470–471
Baron, Michel, 222
Barry, Elizabeth, 271
Barry, Spranger, 272
Basochiens, 72–73

Bauhaus, The, 505
Bawd, The, 91–92
Beaumarchais, 293, 294, 318–323
Becque, Henri, 448–449, 451, 456
Beggar's Opera, The, 255, 266
Behn, Aphra, 240
Béjart, Armande, 220, 222
Béjart, Madeleine, 219, 220, 222
Bellamy, George Anne, 272
Bells, The, 431–432
Beolco, Angelo, 95
Beeston, William, 228, 232, 233
Bérain, Jean, *fils,* 224
Bérain, Jean, *père,* 224
Berliner Ensemble, 507
Bernhardt, Sarah, 409, 411–413, 455
Betterton, Thomas, 257, 269, 271
Beyond our Power, 442
Bibiena, Ferdinando Galli, 285
Bickerstaffe, Isaac, 261
Biomechanics, 503
Birds, The, 23, 102
Bjornson, Bjornstjerne, 442–443, 444
Bluebeard the Knight, 388
"Blue Book" Drama, 468
Boccaccio, 91, 341
Boucicault, Dion, 418–419, 431
Boy and the Blind Man, The, 71–72
Bracegirdle, Anne, 271
Brahm, Otto, 456–457
Breasts of Tieresias, The, 492
Brecht, Bertolt, x, 295, 343, 360, 391, 481, 497–500, 507
Brennoralt, 179
Breton, André, 477
Bridegroom, The, 56–57
Brieux, Eugène, 453–454
Brigadier, The, 365
Broken Jug, The, 389–390
Brothers, The, 35
Bruno, Giordano, 97
Büchner, Georg, 343, 390, 391–392, 456
Bulwer-Lytton, Edward, 398
Buontalente, Bernardo, 111
Burlesque, 28, 220, 230, 245, 246, 255, 256, 303, 334, 420, 421, 422, 471, 472
Burletta, 397, 420

Cain and Abel, 65
Calandria, La, 92, 204
Calderon, 194–195, 196, 201,
Calf Hatching, The, 85
Caligula, 376
Calmo, Andrea, 95
Camille, see *Dame aux Camélias, La*
Campaspe, 129–130
Candle Maker, The, 97
Captain, The, 171–172
Carlell, Lodowick, 177–178
Careless Husband, The, 249
Casket, The, 91, 106
Caste, 425, 426, 427
Castelvetro, Lodovico, 98, 104–105
Castle of Perseverance, 66, 67–68
Castro, Guillen de, 193, 213
Cato, 260
Cavalier Drama, 174, 177
Cenci, The, 495
Centlivre, Susanna, 247
Cervantes, Miguel de, 188, 189
Chambre à quatre portes, 225
Charke, Mrs. Charlotte, 259
Chekhov, Anton, x, 361, 366, 460, 462–463, 464
Choerilus, 4–5
Christmas Tale, A, 278
Christopher Columbus, 374, 375
Chronegk, Ludwig, 437
Cibber, Colley, 248, 249, 251, 256, 259, 271
Cibber, Theophilus, 256, 257, 259
Ciceri, Pierre-Luc-Charles, 372, 377, 386
Cid, Le, 193, 210, 213, 214, 223, 315, 411
Cinthio, Giovanni Battista, 98, 102
Cirque Olympique (Theatre), 376, 386
City Dionysia, 4, 6, 7, 8, 9, 11, 21, 23, 24, 26, 36
Claude's Wife, 408
Cléopatre captive, 204
Clouds, 22, 23
Cockpit (Theatre), 227, 232, 233, 235
Cocteau, Jean, 493
Coelina, Child of Mystery, 373
Coliseo, 199, 201
Collier, Jeremy, 248–249, 266, 326
Comédie Française, 221–222, 224, 225, 300–301, 302, 306, 307, 310, 315, 321, 328, 370, 371, 372, 378, 380, 381, 383, 384, 402, 411, 412, 413, 437, 449, 453, 455
Comédie rosse, 450

Comédie larmoyante, 309, 313, 337
Comedy of Calisto and Melibea, 187
Comedy of Manners, 239, 240, 241, 243, 314
Commedia dell'arte, 28, 84, 96, 112, 116, 117, 118, 189, 190, 200, 207, 220, 221, 302, 333, 360, 367, 504
Commedia erudita, 112, 216
Conditional Theatre, 502–503
Confrèrie de la passion, 72, 207
Conquest of Grenada, The, 239
Conscious Lovers, The, 248, 251, 256, 287
Construction of Theatres and Theatrical Machinery, 108–109
Constructivism, 503, 504
Copeau, Jacques, 487–488
Copiaux, Les, 488
Corey, Mrs. Catherine, 271
Corneille, Pierre, 193, 210, 211, 212–215, 218, 221, 238, 339, 360
Corneille, Thomas, 211, 215–216
Corpus Christi Feast, 59–60, 186, 188, 194, 198
Corpus Christi Guild, 61
Corral de la Cruz, 198
Corral del Principe, 198
Corsican Brothers, The, 418, 431
Country Wife, The, 241, 242, 243, 265, 266, 316
Courteline, Georges, 454
Court Theatre (Vedrenne-Barker), 470–471
Covent Garden, 241, 254, 257, 258, 260, 261, 265, 274, 275, 276, 280, 379, 396, 397, 414, 415, 416, 420, 421, 429
Craig, Edward Gordon, 432, 478–479, 505
Cratinus, 21
Crebillon, Prosper Jolyot, sieur de, 305
Creed Play, 61, 67
Croizette, Sophie, 409, 412
Cromwell, 380, 382
Cure for Jealousy, A, 249
Cycle Plays, 58, 59–62, 64, 65, 66, 80, 83
Cyclops, 3
Cyrano de Bergerac, 455

Dada (Dadaism), 488–490
Daguerre, Louis-Jacques, 377, 395
Dalcroze, Emile Jacques, 487
Damaged Goods, 454
Dame aux Camélias, La (AKA *Camille*), 405, 406–407
Danchenko, 459, 460
Dante, 90
Dancourt, Florent Carton, 370
Danton's Death, 391–392

Davenant, William, 179–180, 227–230, 231, 232–233, 234, 235, 257
Decameron, 91, 341
Deceived Ones, The, 95–96
Delsarte, François, 409–410
Demi-Monde, The, 407
Deutsches Theater, 455, 480, 481
Devil to Pay, The, 351
Diapolyekran, 506
Diderot, Denis, 319, 325–326, 364
Dingelstedt, Franz, 395
Dionysus, 1–2, 3, 4, 6, 7, 8, 9, 15, 20, 24, 25, 44
Diorama, 377, 394, 395, 417, 422, 428,
Discourse on Comedy and Tragedy, 102
Doctor Faustus, 140, 148
Doggett, Thomas, 271
Doll's House, A, 442, 444
Domestic Tragedy, 252, 340
Dorset Garden Theatre, 234, 235, 244, 275
Douglas, 263
Drame (Bourgeois), 303, 319, 325,
Dream Play, The, 486
Dress and Habits of the People of England, The, 281
Drolls, 227, 230
Drury Lane, *see* Theatre Royal (Drury Lane)
Dryden, John, 233, 238–239, 244
Duenna, The, 266
Dulcitius, 55
Dumas, Alexandre, *fils*, 310, 381, 401, 406–409, 412, 444
Dumas, Alexandre, *père*, 376, 380, 381–382, 406
DuParc, Mlle., 222
Durch, 456
Dying Cato, The, 335, 336

Eccyclema, 15, 49
Edward II, 124, 138, 142, 148, 150, 228
Edwardes, George, 471–472
Egmont, 346, 347
El condenado por desconfiado, 192–193
El mayor alcalde el rey, 191
Emelia Galotti, 339, 341
Encina, Juan del, 187–188
Endimion, 131–132
Enfants des Maintenants, Les, 73–74
Enfants-sans-souci, 72–73
Ennius, Quintus, 32, 41
Entremes, 188–189, 190, 197, 200
Epicoene, 161, 163–168

Epicharmus of Syracus, 20
Epic theatre, 481, 497, 499
Essay of Dramatic Poesy, An, 239
Ethelwold, 54–55
Etherege, George, 242, 243–244
Eugène, 204, 206
Eugénie, 319
Eunuch, The (AKA *Eunuch*us) (Terence), 35, 206
Eunuchus (Menander), 35
Euripides, 3, 8, 11, 12–14, 17, 19, 23, 31, 32, 41, 98, 203, 205, 288, 305
Eurythmics, 487
Everyman, 67, 70–71, 481
Expressionism, 297, 343, 392, 481, 486, 487

Fabula Atellana, 30
Fabula Crepidata, 32, 40
Fabula Palliata, 31, 40
Fabula Praetexta, 31, 42
Fabula Riciniata, 40
Fabula Saltica(e), 40, 44
Fabula Togata, 31, 46
Fair Penitent, The, 252
Fair theatres, 302–303
Faithful Shepherd, The, 100–101
Fan, The, 293–295
Farce, 20, 21, 24, 30, 40, 45, 46, 52, 71–72, 74, 84, 90, 182, 188, 206, 207, 209, 210, 212, 220, 221, 245, 254, 257, 266, 267, 272, 313, 332, 334, 388, 422, 448, 457, 472, 504
Fastnachtsspiel, 84–85
Father and Son, 353
Faust, 55, 339, 345, 346, 349–350, 377
Fescennine Verses, 29
Fiabe, 295, 297, 388
Fielding, Henry, 255–256
Fonvizin, Denis, 364–365, 366, 367
Fool would be a Favorite, The, 177
Foote, Samuel, 259, 261–262
Foreigner, The, 409, 412
Fort, Paul, 473–474
Fortune (Theatre), 227, 395
Four Elements, The, 78, 187
Four Ps, 82
Fourth Wall, 326, 427, 503
Franconi, Laurent, 376
Franz, Ellen, 437–438
Freie Bühne, 456, 457, 458, 469, 479
Freie Volksbühne, 458

Frogs, 23
From Morn to Midnight, 483–485, 486
Fuenteovejuna, 191
Futurism, 500–501, 502

Gaiety Theatre, 471
Gaité (Theatre), 371
Gallathea, 135–137, 150
Gallicanus, 56
Game of Love and Chance, The, 265, 311, 411
Garnier, Robert, 205
Garrick, David, 260, 263, 268, 269, 270, 271, 272, 274, 277, 279, 280, 317, 415, 439
Gas Heart, The, 491–492
Gauntlet, A, 442
Gay, John, 255–256, 316
Gellert, Christian Furchtegott, 338
Genet, Jean, 495–497, 500
Gentlemanly melodrama, 398, 401, 417, 424
Germanicus, 371
Gesamtkunstwerk, 435–436
Ghelderode, Michel de, 497
Ghosts, 438, 444, 445, 451, 456, 469
Ghost Sonata, 486
Giotto, 90
Girl from Samos, The, 26–27
Girl with Her Hair Cut Short, The, 26
Glapthorne, Henry, 182–183
Goethe, Johann Wolfgang Von, 55, 297, 339, 343, 344, 345–347, 349–351, 387, 396, 482
Goetz Von Berlichingen, 346, 351
Golden Rump, The, 257
Goldoni, Carlo, 291–295, 296, 297, 319
Goldsmith, Oliver, 250, 264–265
Gorki, Maxim, 463–464
Gottsched, Luise Adelgunde Viktoria, 337
Gottsched, Johann Christoph, 335–337, 338, 340
Governess, The, 310
Gozzi, Carlo, 292, 295–297, 388, 504
Grabbe, Christian Dietrich, 391
Great Theatre of the World, The, 195
Green Cockatoo, The, 459
Green room, 240–241, 276, 301
Gregori, Johann Gottfried, 357, 358
Grein, J.T., 469
Grillparzer, Franz, 393, 438
Gropius, Walter, 505–506
Grotowski, Jerzy, 487, 507

Grouch, 26
Gryphius, Andreas, 333–334, 335
Guarini, Giambattista, 100
Guénégaud (Theatre), 221, 224
Guilty Mother, The, 323
Gwynne, Nell, 233, 241
Gymnase (Theatre), 402

Habits à la Romaine, 280
"Hamburg Dramaturgy, The," 339
Hanswurst, 332, 335, 336, 358
Hardy, Alexandre, 207–208, 211
Hasse, Friedrich, 395
Hauptmann, Gerhart, 343, 456, 457, 458
Hebbel, Friedrich, 392–393
Hedda Gabler, 445
Henri III, 380, 381
Henry IV, Part I, 233
Hernani, 382, 383–384, 449
Herod and Marianne, 315
Heroic tragedy, 228, 238, 239, 246, 263, 309
Herondas, 27
Heywood, John, 81–82
Hickscorner, 79
Higden, Ranulph, 60
Hilarius, 56
Hilarotragoediai, 28
Hippolyte (Garnier), 205
Hippolytus (Euripides), 14
Hippolytus (Seneca), 41
Historical Register for the Year 1736, The, 256
Histriomastix, 176
Home, John, 263
Horace, 47–48, 49, 91, 101, 102, 103, 192, 203, 205
Horribilicribrifax, 334
Hôtel de Bourgogne, 207, 208, 210, 223, 302
Hot Iron, The, 85
House of Temperaments, The, 394
House on Fire, 46
Hrosvitha, 55–56, 58
Hugo, Victor, 380, 382–385, 413, 449, 455

Ibsen, Henrik, 425, 433, 438, 442, 443–446, 456, 457, 463, 468, 469, 473, 477, 479, 482
Iffland, August Wilhelm, 351, 352
Immerman, Karl, 395, 396, 441
Independent Theatre Movement, 450–451, 456, 459, 469, 471, 484

Indian Emperor, The, 238
Indian Queen, The, 238
Interlude, 67, 71, 75–76, 77–80, 81–84, 90, 187, 188, 189, 190, 205, 355, 357, 363
International Copyright Act, 467
Irving, Henry, 423, 428, 429–433, 451, 466, 478

Jarry, Alfred, 475–477, 491, 492, 494
Jessner, Leopold, 481–482
Jessnertreppe, 481
Jew of Malta, The, 140
Jodelle, Etienne, 204, 206
John Bull's Other Island, 471
Jolly, George, 235–236, 268
Jonson, Ben, 161, 163, 164, 167, 168, 241
Jordan, Dorothy, 272
Julius Caesar, 233, 363, 440
Juvara, Filippo, 285–286

Kabeiroi, 10
Kaiser, Georg, 482–483, 484, 485
Katablemata, 15
Kean, Charles, 395, 414, 416, 418, 422, 424–425, 427, 429, 432, 437, 465
Kean, Edmund, 379, 415–416
Kemble, Charles, 379, 420, 424
Kemble, John Philip, 414–415
Kemble, Sarah (Mrs. Siddons), 415
Killigrew, Thomas, 227, 230–235, 240, 257
King Henry VIII, 429
King John (Bale), 81
King John (Shakespeare), 420, 424
King Torrismondo, 99
Kleist, Heinrich von, 389–390
Klinger, Friedrich Maximillian, 344–345
Klopstock, Frederick, 342
Knights, 22
Komos, 3, 19, 20, 21
Kotzebue, August Von, 351, 352–353, 373
Kruger, Johann Christian, 338
Kynaston, Edward, 271

La Chaussée, Pierre Claude Nivelle de, 309–310
Ladies Privilege, The, 182–183
Lady of Lyons, The, 398
La Fossé, Antoine de, 304
La Grange-Chancel, François-Joseph de, 305
Lame Devil, The, 308
Las mocedades del Cid, 193

Laterna magika, 506
Lazzi, 113–115, 117, 294, 367
Le Comte, Valleran, 208
Lecouvreur, Adrienne, 318
Lee, Nathaniel, 246
Lenaea, 6, 8, 23, 26
Lenz, Michael Reinhold, 343–344
Leonce and Lena, 392
Léonidas, 372
Lesage, Alain-René, 308–309
Lessing, Gotthold Ephraim, 195, 252, 334, 338–342, 351, 353, 396
Licensing Act of 1737, 255–256, 257, 258, 260, 397, 420
Life is a Dream, 195
Lillo, George, 248, 252, 253, 340, 364
London Merchant, The, 248, 252–254, 364
Lope de Rueda, 188–189
Lope de Vega, Felix, 187, 190–192, 193, 194
Lotti, Cosme, 201
Loutherbourg, Philip Jacques De, 277–278, 279, 428
Love in a Tub, 243–244
Love of Three Oranges, The, 295–296, 504
Love's Cure, 158–159
Love's Last Shift, 248, 249
Lower Depths, The, 463–464
Lucian of Samosata, 48
Ludi Romani, 29, 31, 35, 36, 37
Lugné-Poë, Aurelien-Marie, 474, 476, 477, 478
Lukin, 364
Lun, *see* Rich, John
Lusty Juventus, 80
Lying Lover, The, 250
Lyly, John, 128–130, 132, 133, 135, 136
Lysistrata, 23, 394

Macaris and Canace, 43
Macbeth, 345, 348, 379, 424, 476
Machiavelli, Niccolo, 92, 214
Macklin, Charles, 259, 268, 269, 270, 272, 274, 275, 280
Macready, William Charles, 415, 416–418, 424, 428, 429
Madame Sans-Gêne, 404–405
Mad Princess, The, 116–117
Maeterlinck, Maurice, 474
Magnificence, 80
Magnificent Cuckold, The, 503–504
Maid of the Mill, The, 261, 262
Maids, The, 496
Mairet, Jean, 211, 212, 213

Mallarmé, Stephan, 474–475
Mandrake Root, The, 92–93
Mankind, 67, 69
Man of Mode, The, 242, 243–244
Manual for Constructing Theatrical Scenes and Machines, 107
Marescalco, The, see *Stable Master, The*
Marinetti, Philippo Tomasso, 500
Marivaux, Pierre Carlet de Chamblain de, 265, 302, 310–312, 338
Marivaudage, 311
Marlowe, Christopher, 124, 138–143, 148, 150, 228, 264, 265
Marriage of Figaro, The, 321–322, 323
Marriage of Wit and Wisdom, The, 78–79
Marston, John, 119
Marston, John Westland, 398, 399
Mary Magdalena, 393
Master Builder, The, 445, 446, 479
Master Pierre Pathelin, 74–75
Mathews, Charles, the Younger, 417, 418
Mechane, 16
Medea (Corneille), 212
Medea (Euripides), 14, 32
Medea (Klinger), 344
Medea (Seneca), 41
Mélite, 212
Melodrama, 14, 231, 247, 250, 252, 260, 263, 278, 287, 288, 305, 310, 313, 324, 326, 340, 351, 352, 370, 371, 372, 373, 374, 375, 376, 377, 378, 384, 385, 386, 397, 398, 399, 401, 402, 404, 417, 418, 420, 422, 424, 425, 426, 431, 468, 470, 471,
Menander, 25–27, 32, 33, 34, 35, 66, 462
Merchant of Venice, The, 432
Merle, J.T., 377, 379
Merope (Scipione), 288–289
Merope (Voltaire), 317
Merry Play, A, 82–83, 85
Metastasio, 289–290
Meyerhold, Vsevolod, 502–504, 505, 507
Midas, 132
"Midnight Mass at St. Etienne," 377
Midsummer Night's Dream, A, 45, 334, 395, 422, 423, 465, 479, 481
Miles Gloriosus (Plautus), 33, 34, 206, 265
"Miles gloriosus" (character type), 20, 30, 113, 265
Minna Von Barnhelm, 339, 340–341
Minor, The, 366–367
Miracle, The, 467, 480
Miracle of Theophile, The, 58–59
Misanthrope, The, 220, 310
Miss Julie, 486
Miss Sara Sampson, 253, 339, 340

Mr. Limberham, 239, 244–245
Mr. Poirier's Son-In-Law, 405–406
Mistress of the Inn, The, 292
Mohun, Michael, 232
Molière, x, 72, 210, 211, 215, 217, 219–221, 222, 230, 245, 306, 310, 339, 360, 367, 371, 443, 462
Mondory, 210
Montague, Walter, 175, 177
Montigny, Adolph, 409, 441
Moor of Venice, The, 380
Morality Plays, 58, 67–71, 75, 78, 83, 88, 90, 188, 241, 357
Moscow Art Theatre, 326, 362, 459–460, 462, 479, 502
Mother Bombie, 133
Mother Courage, 507
Mother-in-Law, The, 35, 36
Motta, Fabrizio Carini, 108
Mounet-Sully, Jean, 411, 412
Musical Comedy, 258, 261–262, 370, 394, 471, 472
Myrmidons, 10

Nathan the Wise, 339, 341–342
Naturalism, 383, 391, 392, 394, 435, 446–447, 455, 456, 464, 473, 480, 486
Nature, 78
Nausikaa, 11–12
Nemirovich-Danchenko, *see* Danchenko
Neoclassicism, 203, 213, 225, 239, 280, 290, 299, 316, 339, 363, 369, 370, 378, 382,
Nero, 42, 43, 44, 46
Nestroy, Johann Nepomuk, 393
Neuber, Carolina, 336, 337, 338, 360,
Newly Married Couple, The, 442
Niais, 374
Night with the National Guard, A, 375

Obligatory scene, 290, 403, 419, 446, 468
Octavia, 41–42
Odéon (Theatre), 321, 370, 379, 412, 452, 453
Oedipe (Corneille), 215
Oedipe (Voltaire), 314–315, 326
Oedipus at Colonus, 11, 41
Oedipus Rex, 9, 11, 41, 111, 480
Okhlopkov, Nikolai, 504–505
Oldfield, Anne, 271
On the Ground Floor and the First Story, 393–394
Opéra comique, 302, 303
Opéra Comique (Theatre), 370
Opera seria, 286–287, 288
Orbecche, 98

Oresteia, 9
Orpheus (Cocteau), 493
Orpheus (Pastoral Play), 99
Orsini, Baldassare, 285
Othello, 233, 246, 317, 379, 380, 486
Ottway, Thomas, 246

Pacuvius, Marcus, 32
Palais à volonté, 225
Palais Royal (Theatre), 220, 221, 223, 224
Palladio, Andrea, 111
Pantomime, 40, 44, 45, 47, 254–255, 268, 272, 274, 302, 303, 332, 342, 371, 372–373, 376, 399, 420, 422, 467, 493
Paphnutius, 56
Parabasis, 20, 23
Parigi, Giulio, 283–284
Parisian Woman, The, 450
Parson's Wedding, The, 231–232
Pastoral plays, 99–100, 187, 189, 208
Pasquinate, 93
Pataphysics, 475–476
Pater Noster Guild, 60–61
Pathetic Tragedy, 252
Peace, 23
Pelléas and Mélisande, 474
Pepys, Samuel, 179, 237
Periaktoi, 15, 49, 107, 283
Peribanez, 191
Pericles, Prince of Tyre, 423
Persians, The, 9
Petrarch, 90–91
Phelps, Samuel, 422–424
Philoctetes, 11
Phormio, 35
Phrynicus, 5
Phylakes, 28, 30
Pietas Victrix, 331
Pills of the Devil, The, 386
Pinakes, 15, 16
Pinero, Sir Arthur Wing, 468, 469
Piranesi, Gian Battista, 286
Piscator, Erwin, 481–482, 505
Pixérécourt, Gilbert de, 373–375, 441
Plain Dealer, The, 243
Planché, James Robinson, 420–421, 424
Plato, 13, 17, 152, 482
Plautus, Titus Maccius, 32–34, 36, 66, 92, 126, 203, 221, 248, 339

Plavilshchikov, Peter Alekseyevich, 364
Play about Esther, The, 360
Playhouse to be Let, A, 229–230
Play of Adam, The, 58
Play of the Canopy, The, 59
Play of St. Nicholas, 58
Play of William Tell, The, 84
Plutus, God of Wealth, 23
Poetica (Castelvetro), 104
Poetica (Daniello), 101–102
Poetica (Denores), 105
Poetics, 17–19, 101, 102, 103, 106, 149
Point of Honor, 308
Pollux, 49–50, 192
Polyekran, 506
Ponsard, François, 405
Poor Theatre, 507
Porte-Saint-Martin (Theatre), 376–377, 379
Pozzo, Andrea, 284
Pregnant Farmer, The, 85
Pride of Life, The, 67
Prince Friedrich Von Homburg, 390
Prince of Wales (Theatre), 425–427
Princess George, 408
Princess (Theatre), 418, 422, 424
Problem play, 442, 444, 445, 468, 469, 473
Prynne, William, 175–176
Pseudolus, 33, 34
Puss in Boots (Planché), 421
Puss in Boots (Tieck), 388–389
Pygmalion (Ballet), 280
Pygmalion (Shaw), 469, 471

Quem Queritis, 53, 58
Quin, James, 260, 269
Quinault, Philippe, 211, 215, 216–217, 221

Rachel, 410, 411
Racine, Jean, 194, 211, 215, 216, 217–219, 222, 263, 286, 288, 299, 304, 305, 314, 336, 337, 360, 363, 371
Raissoneur, 409
Ralph Roister Doister, 126
Rats, The, 457–458
Ravenscroft, Edward, 245–246
Realism, 14, 16, 64, 115, 271, 278, 280, 293, 316, 326, 334, 339, 370, 383, 387, 391, 395, 401–433, 435, 438, 440–441, 445, 446, 451, 452, 453, 454, 455–467, 469, 470, 473, 477, 479, 489, 494, 500, 502, 503, 504

Recueil des Habillements, 281
Red Bull (Theatre), 227, 232
Regnard, Jean François, 305–307
Reinhardt, Max, 457, 467, 479–481, 487
Relapse, The, 248, 249, 266
Rhinthon of Tarentum, 28
Rhodes, John, 232
Richard III, 260, 363, 424
Rich, Christopher, 257
Rich, John, 254, 255, 257, 268,
Ritual, 2, 3, 4, 42, 86, 149, 160, 329, 355–356, 494, 495, 507
Rivals, The, 250, 265–266
Roaring Girl, The, 156–157
Robbers, The, 347–348
Robertson, Thomas William, 425–427, 428
Rodogune, 214
Rojas, Fernando de, 187
Romanesque play, 215–216
Romanticism, 297, 369, 370, 378–379, 382, 384, 386, 387, 391, 392, 396, 405, 440, 441, 442, 470, 485
Romeo and Juliet, 55, 118, 260, 262, 344, 379
Ronde, La, 458
Rostand, Edmond, 454–455
Rover, The, 240
Rowe, Nicholas, 252
Royal Academy of Dramatic Art, 465
Ruy Blas, 384–385

Sabattini, Nicola, 107, 110
Sachs, Hans, 85, 346
Sade, Marquis de, 230, 312–313
Salisbury Court (Theatre), 227, 232, 233
Sallé, Mademoiselle, 280
Salle des Machines, 224
Sapho and Phao, 130–131
Sapientia, 56
Sardou, Victorien, 404–405, 441
Saul, 291
Saxe-Meiningen, Duke Georg II of, 414, 435, 437–440
Scala, Flaminio, 116
Scaliger, Julius Caesar, 98, 103–104
Scamozzi, Vincenzo, 111
Scène à faire, see Obligatory scene,
Schiller, John Christian Friedrich Von, 297, 345, 347–349, 350, 351, 380, 387, 396, 438, 456
Schinkel, Karl Friedrich, 394–395
Schlegel, August Wilhelm, 388

Schlegel, Johann Elias, 195, 337–338
Schnitzler, Arthur, 458–459
School, 426, 427
School for Scandal, The, 259, 265, 266–267, 379
School for Wives, The, 220
Scipione, Francesco, Marchese di Maffei, 288–289
Scribe, Eugène, 289, 375–376, 402–404, 405, 407, 419, 441, 443
Second Shepherd's Play, 65
Secrets, 63
Sedley, Charles, 237
Self-Tormentor, The, 35
Semiramis, 317
Seneca, Lucius Annaeus, 32, 40–43, 91, 98, 203, 205, 305, 333
"Sensation scene," 419
Sentimental comedy, 248–250, 261, 266, 310, 313, 314, 352
Serlio, Sebastiano, 106–107
Servant of Two Masters, The, 292
Seven Against Thebes, 9
Seven Books of the Poetics, 103
Shakespeare, William, x, 95, 117, 123, 124, 138, 142–146, 151, 194, 228, 252, 260, 262, 316, 325, 333, 337, 338, 339, 342, 343, 344, 345, 346, 379, 384, 388, 389, 395, 396, 397, 399, 421, 424, 438, 465, 482
Shaw, George Bernard, 405, 425, 433, 468, 469–471, 498
Shepherd's Paradise, The, 175, 176, 177
Sheridan, Richard Brinsley, 250, 263, 265–268, 277, 415
She Stoops to Conquer, 250, 264–265
She Would If She Could, 244
Short View of the Immorality and Profaneness of the English Stage, A, 248–249, 326
Shyster, The, 313–314
Siddons, Sarah, *see* Kemble, Sarah (Mrs. Siddons)
Siege of Rhodes, The, 229
Skene, 15–16, 106
Skomorokh, 356
Small Theatre at Pompeii, 39
Socialist Realism, 464, 504
Society drama, 467–468
Sofonisba, 97–98
Soldiers, The, 343
Sophocles, x, 3, 8, 9, 10–12, 13, 14, 15, 17, 19, 31, 32, 41, 48, 194, 203, 480
Sophonisbe (Mairet), 212, 213
Stable Master, The, 93, 95, 161
Stanislavski, Konstantin, 362, 416, 459–461, 462, 488, 502, 503, 504, 507
Statius, Caecilius, 32, 34, 44
Steele, Sir Richard, 250–251, 257
Stella, 347
Stranitzky, Joseph, 332
Strindberg, Johann August, 444, 486–487

Strutt, Joseph, 281
Sturm und Drang (Klinger), 344
Sturm und drang (movement), 342–345, 347, 373, 388
Suckling, Sir John, 178–179
Sumarokov, Alexander, 361, 363–364
Suppliants, The, 9
Surrealism, 297, 459, 477, 488, 489, 492–493, 502
Svoboda, Josef, 506–507
Symbolism, 408, 445, 453, 473, 476

Tableau curtain, 404
Tamburlaine the Great, 139–140, 142
Taming of the Shrew, The, 142, 335, 432
Tancred and Sigismunda, 263
Tarare, 323
Tartuffe, 220, 306, 315
Tasso, Torquato, 98–99, 100, 105
Taylor, Baron Isidore, 371–372, 378
Taylor, Tom, 419–420
Teatro de Medici (Uffizi), 111
Teatro Di Sabbionetta, 111
Teatro Farnese, 111, 284
Teatro Olimpico, 107, 111
Telephus, 14
Tellez, Gabriel *see* Tirso de Molina
Tender Husband, The, 250–251
Terence, 32, 34–36, 38, 55, 66, 106, 126, 203, 206. 221, 248
"Terence Stage," 106, 203, 204
Terry, Ellen, 432–433, 478
Théâtre Alfred Jarry, 494
Théâtre Antoine, 452, 453
Théâtre d'Art, 473
Théâtre de l'Oeuvre, 474
Théâtre du Marais, 209, 210, 213, 217, 221, 223
Théâtre Libre, 451, 452, 453, 454, 469
Theatre of Cruelty, 486, 493–495, 501
Theatre of the Absurd, 297, 393, 486, 489, 496, 501, 502
Théâtre Pittoresque, 377
Theatre Regulation Act (1789), 362
Theatre Regulation Act (1843), 421, 422
Theatre Royal (Drury Lane), 233, 241, 250, 251, 253, 256, 257, 258, 260, 263, 266, 267, 268, 270, 274, 275, 276–277, 379, 396, 397, 414, 415, 416, 417, 420, 429
Theophrastus, 25
Thérèse Raquin, 447, 448, 449
"Thesis" play, *see* Problem play
Thespis, 4, 5, 8, 48
Thompson, James, 263

Three Laws, The, 80, 81
Thyestes (Ennius), 41
Thyestes (Rufus), 41
Thyestes (Seneca), 41–42
Ticket-Of-Leave Man, The, 419–420
Tieck, Ludwig, 388–389, 395, 396, 437, 441
Timocrate, 216
Tirso de Molina, 192–193
Titus Andronicus, 99, 117, 142, 391, 422
Toller, Ernst, 482, 485
Tomasso; or, The Wanderer, 231–232, 240
Torelli, Giacomo, 108, 223–224, 284
Trade guilds, 60
Tragedy of Dido, Queen of Carthage, The, 142–143
Tragic Events, The, 117–118
Tragicomedia de Don Duardos, 188
Tramelogedia, 291
Treatise on Roman Architecture, 106
Tree, Herbert Beerbohm, x, 430, 433, 465–467
Triptolemus, 11
Trissino, Giangiorgio, 97–98
Troili, Giulio, 284
Tuotillo, 53
Turcaret, 308–309, 313
Twelfth Night, 96, 124, 161, 396
Two Friends, The, 319–320
Tzara, Tristan, 488–491

Ubu Roi, 475, 476, 477, 501
Udall, Nicholas, 119–120, 126
Universal Legatee, The, 306

Vakhtangov, Yevgeny, 504
Valdivielso, Jose de, 187
Vanbrugh, Sir John, 248, 249, 266
Variétés (Theatre), 371
Vaudeville, 246, 272, 303, 323, 370, 372, 375, 376, 377, 378, 402
Vaudeville (Theatre), 371, 402, 406
Vedrenne, John, 470–471
Venexiana, The, 96
Verfremdungseffekt, 497–498
Vestris, Mme. Lucy Elizabeth (Bartolozzi), 415, 417–418, 421
Vicente, Gil, 188
Vieux Colombier, 487–488
Vigarani, Carlo, 224
Vigarani, Gaspare, 224
Vitruvius, 49, 106

Volkov, Fyodor, 360–361
Volpone, 66, 233
Voltaire, 217, 304, 305, 310, 312, 314–318, 325, 327, 365, 488
Vultures, The, 449

Wagner, Heinrich Leopold, 345
Wagner, Richard, 435–437, 443, 473, 478,
Wandering Scholar from Paradise, The, 85
Way of the World, The, 242, 265
Weaver, John, 254
Weavers, The, 452, 457
Wedding on the Eiffel Tower, The, 493
Weimar Classicism, 346–347, 348
Weise, Christian, 334–335
Weisse, Christian Felix, 351–352
Well-Made Play, The, 289, 375, 376, 402–403, 404, 405, 407, 419, 441, 443, 444, 446, 447, 468
Wieland, Christoph, 342
Wilton, Marie, 427
Wilde, Oscar, 468, 469, 479
Wild Gallant, The, 238
William Tell, 348–349,
Wisdom, 67, 68–69
Wit Comedy, *see* Comedy of Manners
Woman in the Moone, The, 133–134
Woman of Andros, The, 34–35
Woman on Her Own, 454
Women at the Thesmophoria, 23
Women in Assembly, 21, 23
Wonder Show, The, 189
World and the Child, The, 79
Woyzeck, 392
Wycherley, William, 242–243, 316

Youngest Germany, 456
Young Germany, 391, 456

Zaire, 316–317, 341
Za Ze Zi Zo Zu, 386
Zeno, 25
Zeno, Apostolo, 286–288
Zerbino, 389

Zola, Emile, 446–448, 449, 456

www.ingramcontent.com/pod-product-compliance
Lightning Source LLC
Chambersburg PA
CBHW051106230426
43667CB00014B/2461